DOMESTIC VIOLENCE

How will Your Church Respond to the Crisis?

Mable C. Dunbar, Ph.D., LPC & Colin A. Dunbar, D.Min

No More Excuses: Domestic Violence
How will Your Church Respond to the Crisis?

Copyright © 2009, 2nd printing, 2014
Mable C. Dunbar, Ph.D, LPC & Colin A. Dunbar, D.Min.

Available from:
Advent*Source*
5120 Prescott Avenue
Lincoln, NE 68506
402.486.8800
www.adventsource.org

Authors: Mable C. Dunbar, Ph.D., LPC & Colin A. Dunbar, D.Min.

Managing Editor: Brad Forbes

Editor: Barbara Hernandez, Ph.D

Copy Editors:
Trudi-Ann Holmes-Caines, Ph.D and Jeannie McCarter, Ph.D, LPC

Cover, page design and layout: Ornan Anthony

Printed in the United States of America

ISBN 978-1-57756-609-0

About The Authors

Mable C. Dunbar, Ph.D., L.P.C.

Mable Dunbar has a Ph.D. in family mediation and is a licensed professional counselor, certified cognitive behavioral therapist, and Certified Domestic Violence counselor, level IV. She is founder, president and CEO of Women's Healing and Empowerment Network, a non-profit organization that addresses the issues of domestic violence and sexual abuse from a Christian perspective. Dunbar is an author, educator, motivational speaker and a member of the executive committee of the Upper Columbia Conference of Seventh-day Adventists.

Colin A. Dunbar, M.Div., D.Min

Colin Dunbar has served the church for over 30 years as a pastor, evangelist, church builder, publishing and ministerial director. He has been an adjunct professor at Andrews University Theological Seminary and is a certified grief recovery counselor.

Table of Contents

————◆◆◆————

Dedication

◆

Dedicated to
Dr. Douglas and Carole Kilcher
for making a great impact on our lives,
for their dedication to providing hope and
healing to hurting families
and for giving us the opportunity to educate
seminarians and their wives
on marriage and family issues.

———◈◉◈———

"Every human being, created in the image of God, is
endowed with a power akin to that of the Creator—
individuality, power to think and to do."

Ellen G. White, *Education*, p. 17

Special Thanks

To the late Dr. Jere Patzer, president of North Pacific Union and Sue Patzer, Elder Max Torkelsen, president of North Pacific Union and Linnea Torkelsen, Vivian Mcgee, Linda Schultz, Bob Folkenberg, Jr., President of Upper Columbia Conference, Wayne Hicks, Gerald Haeger, and Richard Parker of Upper Columbia Conference for their support.

To the men and women who shared their stories with us and gave us permission to share them with you. Their names and other identifying characteristics have been changed to protect their privacy.

To the seminarians who allowed us to be a part of their lives. Thank you for staying in contact with us over the years and affirming our ministry to hurting families. You are very special to us because we can identify with your challenges as well as your victories.

To the perpetrators and victims, church members, and community members who attend our workshops and seminars and encourage us to continue in spite of many challenges and obstacles.

To VersaCare and others who support Women's Healing and Empowerment Network (formerly Polly's Place Network) through your prayers, financial support and encouragement.

To Dusty Chenowith, Cheryl Wallace, and Dianne Dempsey, who have been faithful and loyal through many difficult circumstances and never wavered in their commitment to our ministry. Even though they had limited financial means they gave the widow's mite to keep the network operational when no other funds were available.

To Dr. Jeffrey Evans and his wife Pauline for their support and commitment to healing families.

To Dr. Barbara Hernandez who edited the manuscript and helped prepare it for publication. She has been a tremendous asset in supporting abuse prevention initiatives in various ways.

To our mothers, Irene and Ellen, who rose above their challenges and abusive experiences to be courageous, empowered, and dynamic Christian women of faith.

To our children, Elrene, Elizabeth and Colin II, we feel blessed that God has given us the opportunity to be your parents. Thank you for helping us in our journey of healing and growth.

To you, dear reader, for purchasing and reading this resource.

—※◎※—

"Blessed be God, even the Father of our Lord Jesus Christ, the Father of mercies, and the God of all comfort; Who comforteth us in all our tribulation, that we may be able to comfort them which are in any trouble, by the comfort wherewith ourselves are comforted."
2 Corinthians 1: 3-4.

Introduction

*"What is it that the Lord requires of us?
It is to be just, to show mercy and
to walk humbly before our God."*

Micah 6:8 (The Clear Word)

---

*It was about 3 o'clock in the morning. There was a frantic knock
on the door. We jumped out of bed to see who was at the door. One
of our church members stood outside on our front porch, crying
and bleeding. As we ushered her into our living room, she reported
that her husband had beaten her and threatened to kill her. We
sat down, speechless, hardly believing what we were hearing. We
helped the best way we could. We took her children to school; we
provided meals, and gave emotional support. But it took her years
to leave the abusive relationship because she believed it was her
Christian duty to stay.*

---

*For almost an hour we gave a presentation on domestic violence
and abuse to a group of about 75 participants. Then we decided
that it was time for a break. We noticed that one of the young men
stared at us in a way that we could not interpret. Was he angry at
what we were saying? Or did he agree? As soon as the break was
announced he approached us. He said, "I have been listening to you*

and I am very angry with what I am hearing. I have never been able to tell my story before, but now that you are talking about this topic, I praise God that I can be free of the burden of secrecy. You see when I was 14 years old I was raped by the head deacon at my church. He was my uncle. I felt that no one would believe me if I told because he threatened that if I ever let anyone know what happened, I would burn in hell forever and ever. Thank you for discussing this topic. People like me in hiding need to hear more presentations like this."

The enemy targets Christian families every day. His goal is to deface and destroy those created in the image of God. When family members are assaulted in their own homes through means of physical, mental, spiritual, sexual, verbal, and emotional abuse, we can know the enemy has been involved. Unfortunately, the Christian community has been slow to denounce domestic abuse as sin. In some situations, religious ideas have even prevented victims and perpetrators from receiving encouragement and help to correct the course of their relationships and end abuse. Regrettably, the religious community has not taken a clear stand against interpersonal violence and has instead offered mixed or even erroneous messages, bolstered by the use of Scripture texts out of context to condone or ignore abusive relationships and systems. Bewilderment, confusion, and hopelessness have been the fruit of such counsel.

The purpose of this manual is fourfold:

1. To describe and discuss the social dynamics and foundational elements that perpetuate domestic violence and abuse in Christian homes and religious institutions.
2. To explore the interpretation of texts used out of context to justify abuse.

3.   To provide information for training leaders and laymembers to effectively respond to both victims and perpetrators.

4.   To provide lists of resources designed to help the religious community address and minimize domestic violence and abuse in homes, churches, schools, and communities.

God created us in His image, male and female, with the plan that we would reflect His image in our homes and in His church. Ideally, when a man and woman unite, their union is based on mutual admiration, respect, support, and love for each other. Such a union creates the greatest joy we can know on Earth. However, the potential for abuse is present when a union is founded on attributes other than these. Marital partners are responsible for recognizing and acknowledging personal actions that contribute to abusive patterns. When partners take responsibility for their abusive behaviors, the incidence of abuse diminishes. God has given us knowledge, understanding, and power to order our lives in ways that free us from abuse-related entanglements.

God wants families on earth to reflect His family in heaven. Therefore, it seems only natural for Christian leaders and others to encourage marital partners to stay together when abuse is occurring in the relationship. However, this advice is an affront to God and is directly opposed to His desire for His children to live in peace. *"Finally brethren, farewell. Be perfect, be of good comfort, be of one mind, live in peace; and the God of love and peace shall be with you"* (2 Corinthians 13:11).

If you are currently suffering abuse, it is essential that you comprehend the truth about your value in God's eyes. Wrap yourself in God's comforting words of life, courage, and hope, and take strength in Scriptural counsel and admonition that forbids any form of abuse or violence. Apply His gracious truths to your circumstances, especially as you work through religious beliefs that may contribute to your victimization. We pray that you will understand clearly and without any doubt that God is always there to protect and guide you. He has promised:

1. *He is always there. "I will never leave thee nor forsake thee"* (Hebrews 13:5b).

2. *Nothing can separate you from His love. "For I am persuaded, that neither death, nor life, nor angels, nor principalities, nor powers, nor things present, nor things to come, nor height, nor depth, nor any other creature, shall be able to separate us from the love of God, which is in Christ Jesus our Lord"* (Romans 8: 38, 39).

3. *He came to give everyone abundant life. "I am come that they (man, woman, children) might have life, and have it more abundantly"* (John 10:10b).

4. *His thought for you is peace. "For I know the thoughts I think toward you, saith the Lord, thoughts of peace and not of evil..."* (Jeremiah 29:11a).

Part 1

Social Dynamics
&
Foundational Elements
that Perpetuate
Domestic Violence
in Christian Homes

Chapter 1

—◉◉◉—

"My God, my God,
why hast Thou forsaken me?
Why art Thou so far from helping me,
and from the words of my roaring?
O My God, I cry in the daytime,
but Thou hearest not...
Deliver my soul from the sword...
Save me from the lion's mouth...
my darling from the power of the dog....

Psalm 22:1-2, 20-21

—◈◈◈—

DOMESTIC VIOLENCE:

DO CHRISTIANS EXPERIENCE IT?

We were Christians. As long as I could remember my mother was
verbally abusive to my father then got physical towards him. Even-
tually she started beating me and my sister. My father did nothing
to protect us. Many times she would leave us in the middle of the
night when he was at work. We would call him and he would send
someone to stay with us. We were too small to understand that she
was a drug user and sleeping with other men. She left my father
many times but he would always take her back. She finally left for

good and has never changed. I wish that my father had spent more time protecting us from our mother, rather than worrying about his image in the church. I want no part of being a Christian if you need to be a doormat in order to be one. — Richard

Since the earliest moments of Earth's history, Satan has exercised power and control over the citizenry of this planet. Through subtle manipulation, he lured Eve into believing that she could have power and control over her life, even suggesting that if she ate of the forbidden fruit she would be as a god. *"For God doth know that in the day ye eat thereof, then your eyes shall be opened, and ye shall be as gods, knowing good and evil"* (Genesis 3:5). Eve took that first fateful bite, and then gave some to her husband. Adam remembered God's warning against eating from the tree of the knowledge of good and evil, but chose to disobey. When God asked for an account of what had happened neither elected to take responsibility for their actions.

"And the Lord God called unto Adam, and said unto him, where art thou? And he said, I heard thy voice in the garden, and I was afraid, because I was naked; and I hid myself. And He said, who told thee that thou wast naked? Hast thou eaten of the tree, whereof I commanded thee that thou shouldest not eat?" (Genesis 3:9-11).

Ashamed of their nakedness, Adam and Eve hid from God. In Genesis 2 and 3, we observe sin's insidious influence. When God asked Adam if he had eaten from the forbidden tree, he blamed Eve. In so doing, he failed to assume responsibility for his own disobedience. *"And the man said, the woman whom thou gavest to be with me, she gave me of the tree, and I did eat"* (Genesis 3:12). When God asked for a report of her activities, Eve, in turn, shifted responsibility. *"And the woman said, the serpent beguiled me, and I did eat"* (Genesis 3:13). Using the tactics of blame and shame, Satan intended to deface the image of God in mankind. He employs the same strategies today to erase the impress of God in our hearts and homes.

In many Christian faith communities, the Bible has been used to condone "abusive Christian relationships." Texts quoted out of context have been used to justify abuse or influence victims to stay in very dangerous situations. Here are a few examples:

1. "For the husband is head of the wife" Ephesians 5:23.
2. "What God has joined together, let no man put asunder" Matthew 19:6, Mark 10:9.
3. "Turn the other cheek" Matthew 5:39b.
4. "Do good to them that hate you. Pray for them that despitefully use you" Matthew 5:44.
5. "Let your women learn to keep silence in the churches" 1 Corinthians 14:34a.
6. "Therefore as the church is subject unto Christ, so let the wives be to their own husbands in EVERYTHING" Ephesians 5:24.
7. "Likewise, ye wives, be in subjection to your own husbands" 1 Peter 3:1a.
8. "Forgive and you shall be forgiven" Luke 6:37b.
9. "The wife see that she reverence her husband" Ephesians 5:33b.
10. "Wives, submit yourselves unto your own husbands." Ephesians 5:22a.
11. "The wife hath not power of her own body, but the husband" 1 Corinthians 7:4a.
12. "Forgive...but until seventy times seven" Matthew 18:22.
13. "Blessed are ye when men shall revile you and persecute you... Rejoice and be exceedingly glad for great is your reward in heaven" Matthew 5:11-12.

14. "Let the woman learn in silence with all subjection"
     1 Timothy 2:11.
15. "...And thy desire shall to thy husband, and he shall
     rule over thee" Genesis 3:16b.

These texts neither advocate nor condone abuse, but abusers
commonly reference them as justification for their actions. It
is not unusual for God-fearing victims to read these texts and
conclude that their abuser is correct; that they have no choice
but to suffer in silence. So they live out their lives in pain and
blind compliance. Sadly, the Christian community also conveys
messages, such as the following, to influence a victim's belief
system.

The Message	Victim's Belief System
1. "Marriage is a private affair."	"Whatever happens in my marriage, no matter how life-threatening, don't tell!"
2. "A woman should obey her husband."	"I need to submit regardless of my thoughts or feelings."
3. "Women are emotional and tend to exaggerate."	"Men are logical and more accurate in their perceptions."
4. "There are traditional male and females roles."	"I must stay in my place."
5. "Keep the family together at all costs."	"It is my duty to keep my family together even if it costs me my life."
6. "Do not air your dirty laundry."	"I should only talk about the good and positive aspects of my spouse even if he/she is abusive."
7. "Every child needs a father."	"I must provide my child with a father/mother even if he/she is abusive."
8. "You need a man."	"I am not capable or competent without a man. He gives me value and identity."
9. "She needs to be taught a lesson to keep her in line."	"I should not act or speak independently or I will be punished."
10. "Women are the weaker vessel."	"I am weak; he is strong and in control."
11. "As long as he is providing for you, you should stick it out. There are plenty of women who wish they were in your shoes."	"I must be thankful that I have a man who takes care of my material needs, other women want what I have. I have a nice home, car, and clothes. How he treats me or makes me feel is irrelevant."
12. "You can't make it on your own."	"I am powerless, without hope, without skills, without talents. I cannot accomplish anything without a man's help."
13. "What did you do to make him act that way."	"My behavior is directly related to how he treats me. If I am good and do what he says, I can control his violent eruptions."
14. "Pray about it, God will give you the strength to endure."	"If I cannot endure the abuse God has not heard my prayers. I am not a good enough Christian."
15. "If you change, he'll change."	"I am responsible for his behavior."
16. 'If you leave, what will people think of the church?"	"I must present a good image so that people will not think badly of the church.

Messages of this nature have influenced countless abused women to wrongly accept sole responsibility for their marriages, believing that they will incur God's wrath if they break the marriage covenant.

We do not subscribe to the idea that all abuse is inflicted by men. However statistics do indicate that more violent victimizations are committed by men against women than the reverse. In fact, according to Tjaden & Thoennes (2005), *"In the United States every year, about 1.5 million women and more than 800,000 men are raped or physically assaulted by an intimate partner. This translates into about 47 intimate partner violence assaults per 1,000 women and 32 assaults per 1,000 men."*

(The terms abuser, batterer and perpetrator, will be used interchangeably in this manual to indicate an abuser. The terms *battered, abused* and *victim* will be used to indicate the person who is victimized by the abuser. However ANYONE can be abusive or abused.)

The real issue is not which gender or group is more abusive. The real issue is that **Satan wants to keep us blaming and shaming each other to prevent us from uniting and becoming wise to his wiles, for he is the one who is the true enemy of our souls.** *"For we wrestle not against flesh and blood, but against principalities, against powers, against the rulers of the darkness of this world, against spiritual wickedness in high places"* (Ephesians 6:12).

Satan manipulates, orchestrates, and directs interpersonal abuse of every variety to maintain power and control over God's creatures. He turns woman against man, children against parents, poor against rich, strong against weak, young against old, educated against illiterate, religious against secular, state against church, teacher against student, employer against employee, brother against sister, pastor against member, black against white, husband against wife, vegetarian against non-vegetarian, conservative against liberal, majority against minority and on and on…

Do we contribute to the preservation of domestic violence in our homes, schools, and churches? Yes! How?

- When we turn a deaf ear to the cries of people who are hurting as a result of domestic violence, we are condoning it.

- When we put our heads in the sand and pretend that it does not exist in "my church or home," we are perpetuating its continuance.

- When we do not assume personal responsibility for unresolved anger (stemming from our own personal pain), we perpetuate domestic violence.

- When we refuse to seek professional help (despite evidence that we are projecting our anger on others), we contribute to domestic violence.

- When older women stay in abusive relationships, they set an example for the younger women, who then suppose that enduring the abuse (for the sake of the children, marriage, or church) is acceptable or even honorable.

- When older men show little or no respect for women making derogatory remarks about their roles, bodies, or skills, younger men are encouraged to disrespect and disregard women.

- When women disparage and belittle men, saying "They can't help it, they're men!" Comments of this nature diminish positive regard and advance an attitude of disrespect for men by women.

- When parents victimize each other and model unhealthy behaviors in the home, they contribute to the inter-generational cycle of abuse.

- When parents fail to create safe environments in which their children can grow and thrive, they contribute to a social climate of fear.

- When pastors use forms of abuse to maintain power and control in the church, they create a confusing and oppressive worship community.

- When church leaders fail to establish and enforce policies to protect victims and vulnerable individuals from victimization and predatory tactics, they empower molesters and predators to continue their deviant behaviors in the church as well as the community.

- When church administrators and leaders fail to hold an abuser accountable for his or her actions by permitting them to be transferred from one district to another without requiring professional intervention, they perpetuate the spread of abuse.

• When church administrators and leaders fail to provide opportunities for educational programs and services to address this issue, they perpetuate abusive systems of worship and church government.

• When teachers and educators treat students with disrespect and openly devalue their thoughts and expressions, students remember a controlling and abusive system of education.

• When church leaders and members do not financially (or otherwise) support programs, services, or facilities that provide safety, healing, and resources for victims and abusers, they contribute to the prevalence of domestic violence.

• When we ostracize, criticize, condemn, and demoralize victims because they leave an abusive relationship, or divorce because of domestic violence, we are inadvertently pressuring them to either stay in, or return to, an unsafe environment.

Do Seventh-day Adventist Christians really abuse one another?
To answer this question, the family ministry committee of the Southeastern California Conference together with the Center for Health Research at Loma Linda University teamed up to

survey church members regarding the prevalence of domestic abuse in our congregations. This study of 500 Southern California SDAs revealed that 56% either witnessed or experienced physical abuse in their families of origin. Thirty (30%) percent were physically abused at home before they turned 18 years of age and 16% experienced incest. Forty-three (43%) percent reported that they had experienced verbal or emotional abuse (Kasischke & Johnson, 1994).

Drumm et al. (2006) studied abuse in the lives of 1,431 Seventh-day Adventists and discovered that 65% had been subjected to controlling and demeaning behavior, twenty-nine percent (29%) had been sexually victimized, and 10% had endured severe physical abuse. Forty-six (46%) percent of these church members experienced minor violence by their spouse, such as being grabbed, shoved, threatened, or having cherished possessions destroyed. Perhaps you read these statistics and think, "29% and 10% aren't really that high. We must be doing pretty well!" However, if these statistics hold across our collective membership, potentially over four million people have been sexually victimized and approximately one and a half million have experienced severe physical abuse. A sobering six and a half million couples in our church may also have experienced what is regarded as minor abuse: threats, pinching, shoving, and the like.

It is also of interest to learn that the broad category *"controlling and demeaning behavior"* included injustices such as being left out of major family decisions, being isolated from others, having whereabouts and activities monitored, being accused of having an affair, and being forced to listen to a spouse express contempt for one's gender (Drumm et. al., 2006). You might agree that it would be difficult to live with emotional insult and injury of this nature.

What did the victims do to try to cope with their abuse? Ninety-eight percent (98%) prayed, and 80% tried to reason with their abusers. Only 42% sought out a mental health professional or 27% a support group. 11% called a hotline, and 9% went to a shelter. Sadly, 23% considered suicide. 19% used alcohol for its numbing effect, and 19% used prescription or street drugs to try to cope with the abuse. Thirteen percent (13%) found a way to secretly take revenge, and 15% struck back violently (Drumm et al., 2006).

According to these findings, it is clear that Seventh-day Adventist Christians do experience domestic violence and child abuse. Why do so few seek help? Why do so many consider ending their lives? Why are our brothers and sisters attempting to cope with abuse by turning to mood-altering drugs and alcohol? Does the average abused Adventist have hope of finding a new life, free of abuse?

The church as a whole is responsible for addressing these serious questions. We hope that through study of this information, you will gain a clearer understanding of what domestic violence is and its impact on individuals, couples, families, and the church; and that you will discover ways to help victims of violence among us who are suffering and afraid. It is God's will that His children live free of abuse. On the pages that follow, we hope you will learn more about His will for each of our lives.

References

Drumm, R., McBride, D., Hopkins, G., Thayer, J., Popesa, M., & Wrenn, J. (2006). "Intimate partner violence in a conservative Christian denomination: Prevalence and types." *Social Work & Christianity* 33(3), 233-251.

Kasischke, F. & Johnson, A. [with the family ministry committee of the Southeastern California Conference: Cathcart, C., Curtis, K., Jones, R., Mazat, A. Tomlin, R., Versteeg, D., and Wilson, H.] (1994). Adventists & family crises: Getting the facts. *Adventist Review*, August 18 edition.

Tjaden, P. and Thoennes, N. (2005) *Findings from the National Violence Against Women Survey*, Washington, D.C: Department of Justice US; Publication No. NCJ 181867.

Chapter 2

"Hear my cry, O God; attend unto my prayer.
From the end of the earth will I cry unto Thee,
when my heart is overwhelmed:
lead me to the rock that is higher than I."
Psalm 61:1-2.

THE DYNAMICS OF DOMESTIC VIOLENCE
(Myths, Realities, and Statistical Information)

Patricia was sexually abused by her pastor when she was 19 years old. She told no one, but decided to leave the church. She is now 48 years old, has been married for 18 years and has two boys. Recently she was rebaptized. Her former pastor approached her and asked her to go out with him. She refused and threatened to tell the conference administration if he continued to harass her. He told her that if she ever mentioned what happened between them he would deny it, that her marriage would be jeopardized, and he would make sure that she was disfellowshipped from the church. She kept silent for many years until she went to a church and heard a presentation on domestic violence.

Carol is 55 years old and has lived in an abusive relationship with her husband for over 20 years. She worked in a Christian school and told the administrator about her problem. He informed her that he was aware of her husband's abusive nature. However, he felt that she should stay in the marriage because her husband needed her. When she told this to me (Mable) she had a broken arm and swollen lips, as a result of her husband's abuse. She said that she did not want to embarrass the church by leaving her husband. She was afraid to tell her local pastor because he was her husband's friend. Since her husband was head deacon in the church, she did not think that any of the members would believe her story. Even though I encouraged to leave the abusive relationship for a time to get a reprieve from the abuse, she stayed.

What Is Domestic Violence/Abuse?

What does it mean to be in a domestically-violent relationship? Domestic violence is a pattern of assaultive and coercive behaviors that adults or adolescents use to gain power and control over an intimate partner and others. The Michigan Coalition against Domestic Violence (1995) provides this helpful definition in *Domestic Violence: An Informational Guide:*

> *"In its broadest sense, domestic violence is the abuse of another individual in the same family or household, including child abuse, sibling abuse and elder abuse. Domestic violence also includes abuse of another individual in a dating or sexually intimate relationship."*

If someone were to suggest that you were being abused though no one was hitting you, would you believe them? Is it possible for abuse to be expressed in words and deeds alone, apart from physical violence? The answers to these questions are often unclear to people in abusive relationships. Let's clarify what we mean when we talk about abuse. Abuse is commonplace in modern times, taking a variety of forms. Physical abuse includes but is not limited to slapping, beating, kicking, burning, choking, pinching, and pushing. Sexual abuse is also a broad umbrella term encompassing any unwanted, coerced, or forced sexual activity with another person. Emotional abuse always accompanies physical and sexual abuse. Likewise, emotional abuse is always a feature in verbal abuse, including name calling, threatening, and making belittling, degrading, sarcastic, and demoralizing statements. Emotional abuse is present when the abuser uses ignoring behavior, withholds affection, or refuses to recognize his or her partner in public or private settings. It is emotional abuse when an abuser pretends to punch the victim only to stop his swing just short of actual contact; or when the abuser threatens harm to children or other family members if the victim is noncompliant.

When an individual chooses to mistreat or degrade another, he or she is demonstrating a profound lack of appreciation for the inherent value of humankind. Abusers are less interested in respectful human interaction, and more interested in control. They use an arsenal of dominance behaviors including harassment, coercion, humiliation, deception, threats, and force to maneuver their victims into compliance. Domestic violence frequently presents as an amalgamation of physical force strategies calculated to cause physical, sexual, psychological, social, spiritual, economic, mental, and emotional harm. These abusive tactics - some physically injurious and some not, some criminal and some not – are carried out in multiple, sometimes daily episodes by adults or adolescents against family members, or against current or former dating partners.

Abuse occurs in the home in the form of battery, spousal rape, or incest; and in the workplace, most commonly in the form of sexual harassment and stalking. It is present across the lifespan, from child abuse to elder abuse, and is a serious social and cultural problem, i.e., hate crimes. Abuse affects every life it touches: victims, perpetrators, immediate and extended family members, even friends or confidants seeking ways to help. Social activists who devote their lives to the promotion of social change do so because they are keenly aware of the systemic injustice that marks our lives on every level. Abuse is socially-entrenched because it is allowed, ignored, concealed, justified, and protected.

Who Gets Abused?
How do perpetrators select their victims? Counselors have offered insight into the thinking of convicted rapists based on information shared in therapy sessions. One rapist reported that he would go to a supermarket and intentionally run his grocery cart into a woman's cart. If the woman looked startled and apologized, as though she had done something wrong, she would become his target. If she looked perturbed or waited for him to apologize, he would determine that she would not be a good choice because she was the type of woman who would fight back. Other rapists report asking test questions of a potential target, i.e., "Do you know where the nearest hospital is?" or "Do you have the time?" As she responds, he assesses the relative strength or weakness of her demeanor. These chilling scenarios illustrate how stranger assailants evaluate a potential victim's vulnerability and accessibility.

Abusers who target a family member also take into account whether or not that person will divulge the abuse to others, fight back, speak out, or otherwise hold them accountable. Abusers are characteristically very charming and attentive to their victims, particularly in the early stages of a relationship. To the public, an abuser can appear to be warm, loving, and compassionate. This is the primary reason why victims are often not believed. "Dr Jekyll/Mr. Hyde" is an apt profile of the abuser. Victims report that their abusers are often selective about the location in the home where abuse takes place, preferring rooms such as the kitchen (where knives are easily accessible) or a bedroom (where the victim is most isolated and vulnerable).

In this manual the terms *domestic violence* (DV) and *intimate partner violence* (IPV) (describing a broader population), are used interchangeably. The following statistics paint a very sobering picture.

How common is intimate partner violence?
According to Heise, Ellsberg & Gottemoeller (1999), between 2 to 6 million women are assaulted by an intimate partner each year and one quarter of all women will be abused in their lifetime. Worldwide, at least one woman in every three has been beaten, coerced into sex, or otherwise abused. Most often the abuser is a member of her own family (Massey, 1999). The FBI Uniform Crime Reports (1991) showed that one in every three adult women experiences at least one physical assault by a partner during adulthood. This means that every 15 seconds a woman is beaten by her husband or boyfriend (FBI, 1991). Women with disabilities are abused much more frequently than able-bodied women because they are unable to resist, and may be unable to access help when needed. Disabled women may also be more dependent on their abuser. According to Price (1991), eighty-five percent (85%) of all women with disabilities have been victims of domestic violence. Is there one widely-held belief that encourages this evil? Yes, indeed. Even

today as many as one in four men and one in six women believe that under certain conditions it is appropriate for a husband to hit his wife (Gelles & Cornell, 1990).

How old are people who get abused?
The National Family Violence Survey results showed that all forms of marital violence occur most frequently among those in the under-30 age category (Gelles, Lackner & Wolfner, 1994; Strauss, 1980). The rate of marital violence among those younger than 30 years of age is more than double the rate for the 31-50 age group (Steffensmeier, Allan, Harer, & Streifel, 1989). Fagan, Stewart, and Stewart (1983) found that the mean age for women who turned to agencies or shelters for help is 30 or younger. This is not to suggest that abuse rates subside when couples reach middle age or become senior citizens. In fact, the elderly are often too embarrassed to report spousal abuse, and fear having to leave their home for a nursing home. This matter of keeping private matters private is particularly perilous since elderly victims typically do not seek help (Block & Sinnott, 1979).

What are the Racial and Socio-Economic Characteristics of Victims? A 1989-1990 study commissioned by the Texas Department of Human Services in conjunction with Midwestern State University examined the racial and socioeconomic status of abused women. Of the 6,000 women they surveyed over a six month period, more than 50% of those abused by their spouses reported family incomes that placed them in the middle class range. Racially, 70% were Caucasian, 10.4% were African American, and 9.5% were Hispanic. The women reported that more than 18% of the abusers had a bachelor's degree or higher education (Moewe, 1992). Domestic violence is a feature in every population category.

Results of the National Woman Abuse Prevention Project (1989) showed intimate partner violence occurring in all racial, economic, and religious groups. They noted, for example, that police responded to as many domestic disturbance calls in a mostly White, upper-class Washington D.C. suburb of Montgomery County, Maryland as were received during the same time period in Harlem, New York City (NWAPP, 1989). It is true, however, that battered women who have fewer financial resources are more likely to seek help from shelters and hospital emergency rooms. This is one reason why lower-income women tend to be over-represented in official statistics.

What are the Consequences of Domestic Abuse?
In 1989, Surgeon General Everett Koop warned that violence was the number one public health risk for adult women in the United States. Surgeon General Antonio Novello (1992) agreed, stating that "violence remains the leading cause of injuries to U.S. women ages 15 to 44." Unfortunately, violence continues to be one of the leading causes of injuries to women, more common than automobile accidents, muggings, and cancer deaths combined (102nd Congress, 1992). Battered women receive medical treatment for injuries related to domestic violence more frequently *after* they have separated from their abuser than they do while they are living together. In fact, three-quarters of the emergency-room visits by battered women take place *after* separation (Stark & Flitcraft, 1988). In addition, roughly 75% of domestic violence calls to the police are from women needing help *after* separation from batterers (Langen & Innes, 1986). Bernard, Vera, Vera & Newman (1982) found that half of the homicides of female spouses and partners were committed after separation from their male batterers. *The period just following separation is the most dangerous time for women attempting to escape abusive partners.*

A significant percentage of hospitalized patients are victims of domestic violence. Domestic violence patients are treated for a variety of injuries: 33% are treated for face and neck injuries from punching, slapping, or choking. Other physical locations of injuries include arms (16.2%), head (14.4%) back and buttocks (12%), and legs (5.4%). Genitals are targeted in 3.6% of the victims. Breast injuries account for 10% and abdomen injuries 5.4% (National Woman Abuse Prevention Project, 1989). Abusers beat and injure every part of the victim's body. Strauss & Gelles (1989) found that women who endure severe beatings spend twice as many days in bed as other women. They experience twice as many headaches and report having bad health three times more often. They suffer depression four times more often than non-abused women and are five-and-a-half times more likely to attempt suicide. Abused women are also more liable to take time off work, particularly if they are severely assaulted, in part, to hide their bruises from coworkers (Strauss & Gelles, 1989).

Several studies have shown that the incidence of domestic violence tends to remain stable over time (Wooldrege, 2007; Catalano, 2005). Essentially, domestic violence continues uninterrupted because we, as a society, allow it. It is intimidating to attempt an intervention when an angry abuser is harming someone. We fear for our own safety. Police officers report that domestic disturbances calls are among the most dangerous (Thomas, 2009). Police understand that they could potentially be threatened with the same weapons the perpetrator was using on the victim if he is still angry and desperate enough.

Domestic violence is an ongoing problem due to widespread misinformation, unfounded beliefs, failure of both the religious and secular community to appropriately address this issue, and the unwillingness of both civic and church leaders to set and enforce higher standards of conduct on all levels.

The Cycle of Domestic Abuse (See Figure 1, p. 37)
After listening to hundreds of victims of domestic violence describe similar patterns in their abusive relationships, Lenore Walker (1979; 2009) and other researchers began to see a reliable and repetitive progression. They sought to create a model that could adequately illustrate and explain the dynamics of abuse in intimate relationships and families. They recognized that though interpersonal violence follows a fairly predictable and cyclical pattern, there is no clear starting or ending point. Bearing in mind the fluid nature of this cycle, we will begin describing an arbitrary stage in the cycle, phase 1. The three distinct phases of the cycle of abuse are outlined as follows:

Phase 1: Tension Building Phase
During this phase the family experiences elevated levels of tension. Tension may arise in concurrence with such day-to-day challenges as insufficient finances, health problems, issues with children, or external difficulties such as unemployment, conflicts with the law, or problems with in-laws, etc. Verbal abuse and minor battering incidents often occur during this phase of the cycle. The victim attempts to prevent the abuser from escalating to more dangerous aggression by becoming compliant and obeying his wishes. She believes that she is able to stop the abuse by doing what she believes will appease him. She experiences a simmering frustration, but denies her own anger and rationalizes the situation by making excuses for the abuser's irritability (Walker, 1979; 2009).

The victim further seeks to control events and other people in the environment around the abuser, attempting to suppress or redirect any potential provocation. Though she may be able to delay the violence, she is unable to prevent it. If the abuser has no constructive outlet or coping mechanism in place to manage his escalating anger, the tension inevitably erupts into an acute battering incident. The victim functions under tremendous strain during this phase, preoccupied with how and when the abuser will attack. It is not uncommon during the tension-building phase for victims to seek medical attention for complaints that accompany severe stress such as heart palpitations, digestive problems, high blood pressure, stiff neck, insomnia, and nervousness. The woman feels as though she is walking on eggshells as she attempts to restrain the abuser from terrorizing the whole family with his violence, chaos, and destructive acts. She feels propelled toward the inevitable. And as her feelings of fear and dread escalate, the victim tends to withdraw and become more distant. The abuser's jealousies intensify in response to the distance. Ultimately, the victim may provoke an impending attack because she cannot bear the tension, or because the date for a special occasion (a family reunion, graduation, wedding, etc.) is fast approaching, and she is eager for the tension to end so that everyone can relax and enjoy the time together (Walker, 1979; 2009).

Phase 2: Acute Battering Incident
Toward the close of the tension building phase there comes a point at which the victim can no longer control stressors in the environment. At this point, both abuser and victim are aware of the inevitability of the assault, and resulting release of tension. The abuse may seem to erupt spontaneously without any visible precipitating event. Many abusers are consumed with

feelings of unreasonable jealousy. If an abuser fears his partner is interested in someone else, he may become particularly enraged. His attacks are of a serious nature. Reasoning with him or trying to silence him only aggravates his rage. There are times when he continues the assault even after he sees that his victim is gravely injured. The abuser sometimes accepts the fact that his rage is out of control. He tries to justify his abusive behavior, however, and during the actual battery may experience confusion. In exceptional cases, the abuser may have some degree of difficulty with memory retrieval following an abusive incident. According to Porter, Birt, Yuille & Herve (2001), "red-out" is a term often used to describe amnesia as a consequence of strong emotions (e.g., rage). "Apparently, an individual can get so angry with his/her intimate partner that s/he can severely beat or kill that partner and then not remember doing so: that is, they can experience a red out resulting in circumscribed amnesia" (Porter, et al., 2001). The memory of crimes committed in a state of altered consciousness, such as extreme rage, anger, or psychosis, can be encoded and stored in an unusual context so that memory retrieval is hampered.

Usually the victim is in such a state of shock and emotional paralysis that she does not immediately seek help. However, at the conclusion of this phase the victim generally does reach out for help from family, friends, her pastor, or the police. It is during this phase that death can occur. After the attack, if there is no intervention, the cycle moves into phase three. The second phase is of a shorter duration (typically two to forty-eight hours) than the first or third phases and tends to occur in private (Walker, 1979; 2009).

THIS IS TIME FOR INTERVENTION!

Phase 3: Honeymoon/Respite Phase

The tension built in phase one and released in phase two dissipates following the battery. Both victim and perpetrator welcome this period of calm. He exhibits charming, loving, kind, and contrite behaviors. He believes he will never have to hurt his victim again because "he has taught her a lesson." During phase 3, the abuser begs for forgiveness, demonstrates genuine regret, and effectively persuades the victim and others that he has changed. He is very convincing, and all involved want to believe him. If the victim leaves, he becomes active and urgent in his attempts to contact her and reconcile. He makes promises and often enlists friends, relatives, even pastors, to pressure her. Naïve to his manipulation, this well-intentioned group campaigns to break her resolve by playing to her sense of guilt until she becomes vulnerable. Frequently, the victim will give in to a false sense of hope because she wants to believe that the changes she sees are "real," and that her abuser has truly become a "new" person. The abuser often buys expensive gifts in an effort to persuade her to return. Eventually the over-spending can become a factor in tension-building, particularly if financial concerns are an issue. If she returns too soon, he will forget his promises and begin abusing her again as old patterns resume. If the victim and abuser stay together through this phase, their bonding and passion for each other can become very intense, further cementing the relationship. But when this phase has ended, the couple will once again move into a tension-building phase and repeat the cycle (Walker, 1979; 2009).

It is important to note that as the cycle repeats, changes occur in the timing and nature of the phases. As the frequency and intensity of the violence escalates, both abuser and victim find their trust, hope, and self-worth diminished. As the victim becomes more familiar with the cycle, she finds herself unable to trust the abuser's apologies and promises. Her hopes for authentic change die, and despair replaces hope. Over time, the abuser, too, comes to recognize that his contrition is meaningless; his promises, empty. This is the point at which he stops the pretense and the cycle loses phase 3, leaving the couple alternating between tension-building and battery (Walker, 1979; 2009).

Prevention is the ideal, of course, but even early intervention is safer than no intervention. Before embarking on a committed, lifelong relationship, prospective partners should, with the aid of a trained counselor, explore character and personality qualities that could potentially predispose them to patterns of abuse. *Couple counseling or marriage counseling is not advised when abuse is occurring in the relationship.* The victim will be unlikely to disclose information about the violence for fear of reprisal. If she does risk revealing the abuse while the abuser is present, she will likely face his retaliation and revenge following the session.

Children of Domestic Violence
Early in life children observe the relational interplay between their parents and/or between caregivers and other adults. Children raised under the specter of domestic violence are likely to internalize messages that lead to dysfunctional thinking and behaving as they mature and form intimate relationships. Children who observe one parent beating, berating, or harassing the other grow to believe they are powerless to stop the abuse. The abused parent feels this way as well. Women who experience chronic abuse often exhibit a hopeless resignation known as *Learned Helplessness* (Seligman, 1975; Walker, 2009). Not

believing they can escape their abuser, end the abuse, or even fight back, they become emotionally paralyzed and incapable of acting in their own behalf. Jaffe & Sudermann (1995), suggest that there may be a correlation between childhood observation of abuse and adult incidence of victimization and perpetration. Experts in abuse studies warn that children who witness the abuse of a parent are more likely to start fights with others their age, have more health problems, and experience depression and anxiety (Jaffe & Sudermann, 1995).

Wolfe, Reitzel, Wekerle & Gough (1995) note that suicide, prostitution, substance abuse, and sexual crimes are more common in abused children. And *Fact Sheets* from The National Organization for Men against Sexism (1993) caution that teenage boys who witness an abusive family member using force, blame, and aggression tend to behave the same way, while girls are more likely to become clingy, helpless, and withdrawn. In fact, many abused and battered women were raised in homes where abuse was present. Women who observed their fathers (or other adult) beating or abusing their mothers never developed protective behaviors and many behaved as though being abused was a normal way of life (Brown, 1993). A study of children in abusive home environments found that over 68% of abused married women had mothers who had experienced similar types of abuse (Rosenbaum & O'Leary, 1981). Knapp (1992) found that boys from abusive home environments tended more toward violent acting out and run-ins with the legal system. In fact, abused children are arrested by the police four times more often than non-abused children (Gelles & Strauss, 1988).

Sadly, we see abusive and violent behaviors in many children attending our schools and churches. If we want our children to experience fulfilling, productive, and abuse-free lives we must become positive role models for them. Ellen White understood this in 1902 when she wrote,

> *"A parent gives way to temper before the child and then wonders why the child is so difficult to control. But what could he expect? Children are quick to imitate, and the child is but putting into practice the lessons taught him by his parents in their outbursts of anger..."* Ellen G. White, *Review and Herald*, July 6, 1902.

Children observe how we treat ourselves and others at home, church, and school. They listen to what we say, how we say it, and how we express our thoughts about others. Our children need to be educated regarding issues that can potentially result in adverse life circumstances. We teach them about observing the Ten Commandments, keeping the Sabbath day holy, not getting divorced or committing adultery, respecting others' property, not swearing, and keeping civil laws. As a part of these important discussions we may also talk to them about rape, HIV, drugs, alcohol, smoking, sex, sexuality, homosexuality, and abortion. But beyond discussions of moral laws and personal decision-making, we further need to equip our children with an understanding of God's claim on our identity and individuality. Discussions about maintaining our identity and individuality may provide our children with a protective barrier against compromise with the dynamics of power and control. Our children should be encouraged to talk about what it means to responsibly exercise personal power.

God has given each of us, including our children, individual rights – the right to be, the right to individuality, the right to think, feel, and act. *"Every human being created in the image of God is endowed with a power akin to that of the creator – individuality, power to think and to do"* (Ellen G. White, *Education*, p. 17). Even though domestic violence is learned behavior, it can be unlearned by "the renewal of your mind, that you may prove what is the will of God, what is good and acceptable and perfect." (Romans 12:2 *Revised Standard Version*).

Myths About Domestic Violence
Social and cultural myths are preserved because, frankly, it is difficult for us to imagine that violence of this nature can occur in the lives of our family members, friends, neighbors, and church members. The following is a list of common societal myths addressing the dynamics of violence in families (adapted from the National Coalition against Domestic Violence).

1. *Men are more aggressive by nature and are therefore unable to control violent impulses.* If this were true, men who abuse their wives at home would also be abusive across the board – toward people on the street, coworkers, and other church members, both male and female. In reality, most men and women maintain relationships with others outside the family without the use of violence.

2. *If women didn't use words to abuse men, men wouldn't abuse them.* A number of studies show that, as a rule, women tend to have superior verbal ability compared to men. This can be frustrating for a man who is less capable of responding quickly to his wife's comments. In 1999, John Gottman, a

University of Washington researcher, wrote
that men typically become more anxious
than women during conflict. The anxiety
may actually feed the man's frustration and
irritability during arguments. However,
women typically employ a variety of strategies
to keep their husbands calm during conflict to
avoid a violent incident (Gottman, 1999).
In fact, the abuse generally occurs before an
argument ever arises.

3.   *Domestic violence is a private family issue.*
An angry abuser can be intimidating,
however, most family members and friends
will try to help if asked for assistance. This
is why the abuser works to isolate the victim
from family and friends. Violence in the home
is a criminal offense in a number of countries.
The fact that domestic violence occurs behind
closed doors only means that it is concealed
criminal activity.

4.   *Drugs and alcohol cause family violence.* Problem
drinking in men increases the chance   of
partner abuse eightfold. It also doubles the risk
that abusive husbands will kill or attempt to kill
their wives (Behrman, 1999). Even moderate
levels of alcohol consumption serve   to
reduce the natural inhibitions of the abuser
and contribute to aggressiveness. Some drugs
such as PCP (angel dust), speed, and metham-
phetamines, cause agitation, paranoia, rage,

and unpredictable behavior. Approximately 46 percent of men who commit acts of intimate partner violence also have substance abuse problems (Black, 1981). Not all men who are dependent on alcohol or drugs become violent. In the same way, not all violent men abuse alcohol or drugs. Even among men who abuse drugs and batter their partners, a third of the violence happens when they are sober. In fact, patterns of domestic violence remain stable whether or not the abuser is using drugs or alcohol (U.S. Department of Justice, 2001).

5. *Victims are to blame for inciting the abuser to batter them.* A common myth holds that women who provoke their husbands deserve to be abused. This is not true. No one deserves to be abused, beaten, or berated, no matter how poor their judgment, or desperate their circumstances. Abusers assault their victims because they can get away with it.

6. *Victims like to be beaten.* This myth arises in response to the question, "why do women keep going back to their abuser?" A woman doesn't go back to her abuser because she likes being hurt. She may return because she loves her husband. She may return because she may not have the financial resources to live independently. She may return because she feels guilty about forsaking her husband, believing that her own actions prompted her husband to become violent and abusive.

7. *Men are always the abusers and women are always the victims.* In reality, women's violence towards men is also a serious social problem (Loseke, Gelles & Cavanaugh, 1994). Crime studies consistently indicate that men are substantially more likely than women to use violence against their intimate partners, whereas family studies research shows that while men are more likely to inflict injury – when all acts of physical aggression are considered in total, women are equally as violent as men (Dutton, 2007). Men may be abused by a wife, girlfriend, or gay partner. Women may also be abused by a lesbian partner. Many abused men don't report the abuse because they are ashamed that they could not prevent it or protect themselves. Woman-to-man or man-to-man abuse frequently goes underreported because of the resulting shame.

8. *People who abuse others are seriously mentally ill.* A very small percentage of domestic abusive incidents are perpetrated by individuals who have been diagnosed with a major mental illness. In fact, most batterers test "normal" on psychological tests, while their victims are sometimes misdiagnosed with mental illness. Many psychological tests fail to distinguish a psychological reaction to domestic abuse from mental illness (National Council of Juvenile and Family Court Judges, 2006). Similarly, an insignificant proportion

of domestic abusers would be considered
incompetent to stand trial. Consider Virginia's
state department of policy and legal affairs
criteria for incompetency: "No person can be
tried or sentenced for a crime if – because of
a mental disease or defect – he cannot under
stand the nature of the proceedings against
him or assist his lawyer in preparing his
defense" (Honberg, n.d.). A close examination
of the abuser's methods, i.e., premeditation,
and victim restraint, etc., commonly shows
an intelligent, artful, but malevolent intent.
Abusers with severe mental illnesses are more
likely to exhibit violence across the board, and
less likely to either premeditate or calculate
abusive patterns that often go undetected, i.e.,
injury to parts of the body covered by clothing
or hair.

9. *Abusive men do not abuse pregnant women.*
Sadly, domestic violence is too often a
complicating factor in pregnancy. In fact,
between four and nine women in every 100
are abused during their pregnancies and/or
after the birth (Taft, 2002). Lewis & Drife
(2005) found that 30% of the time, domestic
violence begins during pregnancy. Abuse often
escalates during pregnancy as the woman's
attention shifts from her abuser to the new life
growing inside her. According to Mezey
(1997), domestic violence has been identified
as a prime cause of miscarriage or stillbirth.

The abuser is more likely than ever to take advantage of the woman's dependence and limited mobility during these months, and actually intensify the abuse.

10. *Abuse stops once an abuser marries the victim.* Of course not! The abuse typically increases because the abuser is now more likely to assume that the victim is his property and that she has no recourse but to stay with him.

11. *Christian beliefs prevent them from abusing others.* There's good news and not-so-good news about this myth. The good news is that religious involvement does seem to have a limited protective effect. Research by Ellison, Trinitapoli, Anderson & Johnson (2007) found that regular attendance of religious services was related to fewer acts of violence, less social isolation and more social support, and a reduced likelihood of alcohol or substance abuse – decreasing the risk of psychological problems. These researchers suggested that "Religion may encourage values of altruism and self-sacrifice, encouraging individuals to defer immediate personal gratification and self-interest in favor of promoting the well-being of family members…" (Ellison, 2007). The not-so good news is that religious experiences are interpreted, applied, or misapplied according to the belief system and worldview of the

individual interacting with them. For some, religion is definitely not a deterrent to family violence, including spousal, child, and sexual abuse. In fact, according to Dr. Nancy Nason-Clark (2006), "there is just as much abuse in Christian homes as in non-Christian homes." Many abusers have found ways to play church," and continue their hidden agenda, seemingly unaffected by the atmosphere of worship and Bible teaching. Prayer and church affiliation can provide strength and comfort but it does not stop an abuser from believing he is powerful enough to control the life of another person if that is his goal.

12. *Abusers are unsuccessful people.* Violent abusers represent every occupation, income level, race, religion, and educational group. Severe abuse can be perpetuated by professionals (doctors, lawyers, professors, police officers, pastors, etc.) who stand to lose a great deal if their violent behavior is made public.

13. *Police can protect victims of abuse.* Police routinely respond to domestic abuse calls. An officer can remove the abuser and assist the victim in accessing a restraining order. But many abusers violate restraining orders, stalk their victims, and harass them at work. In some situations, even after repeated arrests, a resentful abuser will openly defy legal mandates.

14. *If you have been abused you will always fall into abusive relationships.* This is decidedly not true! People become victims as they learn over time how to capitulate to their abusers. This is a learned behavior which can be unlearned.

15. *Abusers will always be abusers.* Just as victims learn how to maintain a defenseless demeanor, abusers learn early on how to be inappropriate, malicious, and cruel. This is learned behavior that can be unlearned with professional intervention.

16. *Abusers are not nice people.* Many abusers are actually quite charming and pleasant to people outside of the family. They often have a "Jekyll and Hyde" personality that allows them to abuse their victim(s) inside the family, and simultaneously show respect and good humor to folks outside the family. People outside of the family who have seen only his good side are often unable to envision him as a violent abuser.

17. *Victims are poor, uneducated people with few opportunities.* Victims without resources find it almost impossible to leave because they have no way to support themselves or their children. These are the women most likely to access community resources. Battered women who are highly educated and successful often keep the abuse hidden because of embarrassment, and often do not seek help.

18. *Abusers always abuse their children.* According to Bowker, Arbitell & McFerron (1988), 70% of batterers also abuse their children. Even if the children are not physically abused, simply witnessing the abuse of one parent by another is considered child abuse and certainly leaves an enduring wound.

The list that follows summarizes the nature of domestic violence:

1. *It is a learned behavior:* Children who witness domestic violence are affected by it. Some learn to be aggressive; others learn to be passive and succumb to abuse.

2. *It is selective.* Abusers select their targets, usually those in their household, or those over whom they believe they can exercise control.

3. *It is permissible.* Domestic violence continues because its impact is minimized by myths, and religious and social beliefs.

4. *It occurs in a cycle.*

As we learn about the pain and consequences of domestic violence, how important that we make every effort to create family environments that are peaceful, loving, and free of abuse. God never intended for us to abuse our family members or anyone else, and does not expect us to tolerate abuse that damages us or our children. *"For I know the plans I have for you, declares the LORD, plans to prosper you and not to harm you, plans to give you hope and a future."* Jeremiah 29:11, NIV.

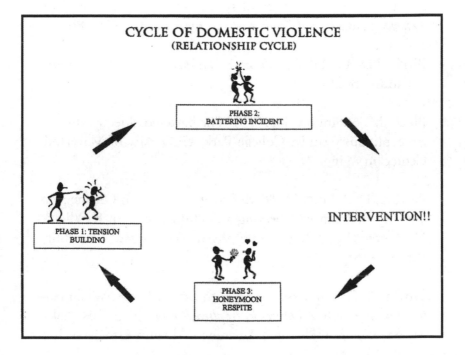

Figure 1

References

Behrman, R. (Ed.) (1999, Winter). Domestic violence and children. *The Future of Children*, 9(3). The David and Lucile Packard Foundation. Available online at http://www.futureofchildren.org

Bernard, G., Vera, H., Vera, M., & Newman, G. (1982). Till death do us part: A study of spouse murder. *Bulletin of the American Academy of Psychiatry and the Law*, 10, 271-280.

Black, C. (1981). *It will never happen to me.* New York: Ballantine Books.

Block, M. & Sinnott, J. (1979). The battered elder syndrome: An exploratory study. College Park, University of Maryland, Center on Aging.

Bowker, L., Arbitel, M. & McFerron, R. (1988). On the relationship between wife beating and child abuse. In K. Yllo & M. Bograd (Eds.), *Feminist perspectives on wife abuse.* Newbury Park, CA: Sage.

Brown, A. (1993). Assault and homicide at home: When battered women kill. *Advances in Applied Psychology*, 3. Eds., Saks, M., Saxe, L., & Hillsdale, J. Lawrence Erlbaum Associates, Inc.

Catalano, S. (2005). Intimate partner violence in the United States. *U.S. Department of Justice, Bureau of Justice Statistics*.

Dutton, D. (2007). Female intimate partner violence and developmental trajectories of abusive females. *International Journal of Men's Health*. University of British Columbia: Men's Studies Press, 54-70.

Ellison, C., Trinitapoli, J., Anderson, K., & Johnson, B. (2007). Race/ethnicity, religious involvement, and domestic violence. *Violence Against Women*, 13(11), 1094-1112.

Fagan, J., Stewart, D., & Stewart, K. (1983). *Situational correlates of domestic and extra-domestic violence.* Newburg Park, CA: Sage.

FBI Uniform Crime Reports (1991).

Gelles, R. & Cornell, C. (1990). *Intimate violence in families.* Newbury Park, CA: Sage Publications, 21.

Gelles, R. J., Lackner, R., and Wolfner, G. D. (1994). *Risk-Markers of Men Who Batter.* Paper prepared for the Family Division, State of Connecticut Judicial Branch.

Gelles, R. & Strauss, M. (1988). *Intimate violence: The causes and consequences of abuse in the American Family.* New York: Simon & Schuster.

Gottman, J. (1999). *Seven principles for making marriage work.* New York: Three Rivers Press.

Heise, L., Ellsberg, M., and Gottemoeller, M. (1999). *Ending violence against women.* Baltimore, MD: Johns Hopkins University School of Public Health, Population Information Program, Population Reports, Series L, No. 11.

Honberg, R. (n.d.). A guide to mental illness and the criminal justice system: A systems guide for families and consumers. *National Alliance on Mental Illness.*

Jaffe, P. & Sudermann, M. (1995). Child witness of women abuse: Research and community responses. *Understanding partner violence: Prevalence, causes, consequences, and solutions.* Eds. Stith, S. & Straus, M. Minneapolis, MN: National Council on Family Relations.

Knapp C. (1992). A plague of murders: Open season on women. *The Boston Phoenix.*

Koop, E. (1989). U.S. Surgeon General warning. *Los Angeles Times, January 4,* Column 5, 17.

Langen P. & Innes, C. (1986). Preventing domestic violence against women. *Bureau of Justice Statistics Special Reports.* Washington, DC. Department of Justice.

Loseke, D., Gelles, R., & Cavanaugh M. (Eds.), (1994). Current controversies on family violence (2nd edition, 55-77). Newberry Park: Sage Publications.

Lewis, G & Drife, J. (2005). Why mothers die 2000-2002: Report on confidential enquiries into maternal deaths in the United Kingdom (CEHACH).

Massey, J. (1999). Domestic violence in neurologic practice. *Archives in Neurology,* 56, 659-660.

Mezey, G. (1997). "Domestic violence in pregnancy" in Bewley, S., Friend, J. & Mezey, G. (1997, eds.). *Violence against women.* Royal College of Obstetricians and Gynaecologists.

Michigan Coalition against Domestic Violence. (1995). Domestic violence: An informational guide.

Moewe, M. (1992). The hidden violence: For richer and for poorer. *Fortworth Star-Telegram*.

Nason-Clark, Nancy (2008) When Terror Strikes the Christian Home. In Kroeger, Catherine Clark, Nason-Clark, Nancy and Barbara Fisher-Townsend (eds.) *Beyond Abuse in the Christian Home: Raising Voices for Change*. Eugene, Oregon: Wipf and Stock, pp. 167-183.

National Coalition against Domestic Violence: *Common societal myths regarding the dynamics of domestic violence in families*. Available online at http://www.ncadv.org.

National Council of Juvenile and Family Court Judges (2006). The role of psychological testing: Navigating custody and visitation evaluations in cases with domestic violence, a judge's guide. Reno, NV: University of Nevada. June issue, 20-21.

National organization for men against sexism (1993). *Fact sheet on children of men who batter*. Louisville, CO: NOMAS. Available online at http://www.nomas.org.

National woman abuse prevention project (1989). Answers to some commonly asked questions about domestic violence. *Domestic violence fact sheets*.

National woman abuse prevention project (1989). Understanding domestic violence. *Domestic violence fact sheets*. Available online at http://www.samhsa.org.

Novello, A. (1992). From the Surgeon General, U.S. public health service, *Journal of the American Medical Association*, 236(23), 3132.

102nd Congress, 2nd session. (1992). Violence against women: A week in the life of America: a majority staff report/prepared for the use of the Committee on the Judiciary, United States Senate.

Porter, S., Birt, A., Yuille, J. & Herve, H. (2001). Memory for murder: A psychological perspective on dissociative amnesia in legal contexts. *International Journal of Law and Psychiatry*, 24, 23-42.

Price, R. (1991). *Love and violence: Victims and perpetrators.* Conference lecture: New York City Coalition for Women's Mental Health.

Rosenbaum, A. & O'Leary, K. (1981). Children: The unintended victims of marital violence. *American Journal of Orthopsychiatry*, 51(4), 694-695

Seligman, M. (1975). *Helplessness: On depression, development and death.* San Francisco: W. H. Freeman.

Stark, E. and Flitcraft, A. (1988). Women and children at risk: A feminist perspective on child abuse. *International Journal of Health Services*, 18(1), 97-118.

Steffensmeier, D., Allan, E., Harer, M., & Streifel, C. (1989). Age and the distribution of crime. *American Journal of Sociology*, 94:803-831.

Strauss, M. (1980). A sociological perspective on the causes of family violence. In M.R. Green (Ed.), *Violence and the Family*, 7-31. Boulder Co: Westview.

Strauss, M. & Gelles, R. (1989). *Physical violence in American families: Risk factors and adaptations to violence in 8,145 families*. Edison, NJ: Transaction Publishers.

Taft, A. (2002). Violence against women in pregnancy and after childbirth: Current knowledge and issues in healthcare responses. *Australian Domestic and Family Violence Clearinghouse Issues*, Paper 6.

Thomas, L. (2009). Domestic disturbances pose risks. *Pittsburgh Post-Gazette*. Available online at http://www. huffingtonpost.com/2009/04/04/police-several-pa-officer _n_183130.html.

U.S. Department of Justice, Office of Justice Programs. (2001). *Stalking and domestic violence: Report to Congress*. Washington, DC. Available online at http://-/www.ojp.usdoj.gov/ovc/ assist/nvaa2002/chapter22sup.html.

U.S. Department of Justice, Office of Justice Programs. (2001). *Intimate partner violence in the U.S.*: http://www.ojp. usdoj.gov/bjs/intimate/victims.htm.

Walker, L. (1979). *The battered woman*. New York: Harper & Row.

Walker, L. (2009). *The battered woman Syndrome, 3rd edition, (Focus on Women)*. NY: Springer Publishing Company.

Wolfe, D., Reitzel, C., Wekerle, C., & Gough, R. (1995). Strategies to address violence in the lives of high risk youth. *Ending the cycle of violence: Community responses to children and battered women*, Eds. Peled, E., Gaffe, P. & Edleson, J. New York: Sage Publications.

Wooldredge, J. (2007). Convicting and incarcerating felony offenders of intimate assault and the odds of new assault charges. *Journal of Criminal Justice*, 35(4), 379-389.

Chapter 3

*"..It was not an enemy that reproached me; then I could
have borne it: neither was it he that hated me
that did magnify himself against me;
then I would have hid myself from him:
But it was thou, a man mine equal, my guide,
and mine acquaintance."*
Psalm 55: 12-13.

BEHAVIORAL CHARACTERISTICS OF ABUSERS AND VICTIMS

Where do abusers come from? Does violent behavior lie dormant until abusers connect with someone they feel they can overpower and victimize? Are they abusive to everyone or just a few people? These are questions we ask when we hear about terrible injuries and shocking deaths caused by batterers. Let's look a bit closer at the profile of abusers to see what we can learn about them.

THE ABUSER

There are a number of signs that could indicate an abusive personality. (For clarity and the purposes of this chapter, the male pronouns he, him, and his are used to specify an abuser and she or her to designate a victim. But bear in mind that ANYONE can be an abuser or a victim.)

Quick Involvement
An abusive individual sometimes seeks commitment from a partner within a few weeks or days of meeting. He comes on strong and gives the impression that she is the only one who can help him; that he needs her; and that without her he is nothing. Because of her need to be needed and her desire to take care of someone, she finds his overtures appealing and makes the commitment, even against her better judgment and counsel from others. She may have experienced abuse in her past and now feels valued because here at last is someone who seems to really love her and wants to be with her. *His intent is to get her in his grasp before she is able to really get to know him.*

Isolation
As the relationship progresses he occupies much of her time. He tells her that he wants to spend every spare moment with her; that he can't stop thinking about her and misses her when they're apart. He convinces her that she does not need the company of other people because his love is enough. Slowly her supportive network shrinks for he is always there, dominating her time, energy, and activities. She is captivated by his lavish gifts and royal attention and begins to feel like a queen. Very soon she loses regular contact with her relatives and friends and becomes emotionally dependent on him. He tells her that he is the only one she needs in her life and that other people do not understand how much she means to him. She believes him because her own feelings of self-worth are at stake. She is not allowed to notice or speak to other males. Eventually he puts an end to her going out alone or with friends. *His intent is to keep others from warning her against a relationship with him.*

Manipulation and Control

At the beginning of the relationship, the abuser shows signs of control and possessiveness. Initially she interprets this as "jealousy" because he loves her so much. As the relationship deepens, she tries to make him feel secure by assuring him that he is the only man in her life. He begins to control where she goes, what she does, who she sees, what she wears, her make-up, hair style, friends, and so on. He sometimes gets angry if she is late for an appointment with him. He accuses her of flirting, being unfaithful, or having affairs. He begins to make it difficult for her to continue regular activities such as going to work, school, church, social events, etc. He drops by her place of work unexpectedly or calls her frequently to make sure that she is where she said she would be. He devalues her point of view. His opinions, attitudes, beliefs, and value system must always prevail. *His intent is to control and manipulate her thinking, opinions, time, and space so that her worldview will be the same as his.*

Manipulation and Control of Others

He is charming and attempts to convince everyone outside the family that he is good to her. To most observers, he appears to be the ideal husband, father, or partner. In many situations, the victim is seen as the problem in the relationship and the abuser gains sympathy because of the "kind of woman" she is. The abuser deceives and manipulates unsuspecting onlookers into believing that he is the one who has been victimized. (The question then becomes – if she is that "kind of woman" why does he stay in the relationship)? *His intent is to convince others that she is unstable or crazy so that the focus is on her inadequacies rather than on his abuse.*

Unrealistic Expectations

He wants her to take care of all his needs. He rationalizes that if she truly loves him, she'll be able to anticipate his needs and fulfill them. She should always be willing to do what is right for him. He makes her feel guilty if his life does not go the way he thinks it should and blames her whenever something goes wrong. He expects her to sacrifice everything so that his dreams can come true. He establishes rules and regulations, but changes them to suit his mood, yet expects her to abide by them at all times. *His intent is to demean her and make her feel incompetent and inefficient.*

Moody

The abuser's moodiness causes the victim to be confused much of the time. There are periods when he is very loving and compassionate. But at other times he is hateful, revengeful, and hyper-critical. Abusers often have wildly fluctuating moods, reminiscent of a Dr. Jekyll/Mr. Hyde personality. Some excuse the abuser's mood swings as mental illness. But, while it is apparent that the abuser does indeed have emotional problems, more often than not, he does not fit the criteria for mental illness because he is able to control his environment and prevent others from seeing his abusive nature. Furthermore, the victim frequently fears his bad mood so she tries to prevent him from feeling irritable. *His intent is to keep her close to him by giving what she most desires, his love and attention, when he decides she is worthy of it.*

Blaming and Shaming

He blames her and everyone else for his problems, if he admits he has them. When confronted about this behavior, he becomes angry and retaliates by lashing out at her and others.

He feels justified in his retaliation because his feelings were hurt. If he makes a mistake, he twists reality in order to place the blame on her or someone else. He also blames her for his feelings because if she had only "done it right" or "said it right," his weakness would not have been exposed. He shames her into believing that she is the cause of his mistakes and that she does not know how to treat a man. *His intent is to make her and others responsible for his behavior. Then, if he is abusive, the fault lies with them.*

Sexually Abusive

The abuser will force himself on his victim and try to get his sexual needs met at any cost. He shows little or no concern for her satisfaction and may even resort to raping her. He demands sex when she is tired or sick. He encourages her to watch objectionable movies against her will to "get her in the mood." He even forces her to engage in sexual activities that she finds uncomfortable or disgusting. *His intent is to make her fearful and to let her know that she is his property.*

Rigid Role Expectations

Abusers commonly harbor negative feelings against the female gender, as evidenced in the harsh and degrading language they use when referring to women. In the mind of the abuser, all women are, or should be, dependent, submissive, and compliant, while men are, or should be, tough, dominant, the boss, and the decision-maker. Women should be homemakers; men should be breadwinners. *His intent is to keep her stuck in one role without options or opportunities.*

Low Self-Worth

He has a poor self-image and feels intimidated if his partner proves in any way to be more competent or qualified than him. When he feels his "superiority" is threatened he resorts to put downs, name calling, and other forms of abuse. Because he feels inferior to others, he aims to place himself above them, which he believes will increase his feelings of self-worth and personal value. *His intent is to put others down so that he will feel better about himself.*

Home Life/History of Abuse

He likely has experienced violence or witnessed abusive situations as a child. He learned that he can get what he wants if he uses control tactics or violence. He may have witnessed his father abusing his mother, or he may have been abused by a parent, sibling, or other relative. If he was never held accountable for his own abusive behavior, he is likely to reoffend. If his behavior is not challenged, he believes it is normal. *His intent is to continue a way of life that appears normal and gives him desired results because he is fearful that if he changes he will lose power and control.*

Cruelty and Destruction of Property

He tends to be very cruel to animals, punishes them brutally, and exhibits insensitivity to their pain and suffering. This cruelty can also be demonstrated when he rigidly expects others to be capable of doing things beyond their ability. For example, he might whip a one year old child for wetting his diaper. He will destroy property belonging to the victim and then become irritated with her sentimentalism. *His intent is to get rid of anything that will take away attention from his authority.*

Hypersensitivity

He is easily insulted and believes that everyone is "out to get him." The slightest setback is seen as a personal attack. He rants and raves about the injustice of life events, day-to-day mishaps that are really just a part of living, such as having to work over time, getting a traffic ticket, or having to repeat a task. *His intent is to be seen as perfect, or having it all together in order to hide the lack of control he feels over his own life and emotions.*

Intimidation
He displays behaviors that can lead to physical violence such as hitting walls, throwing objects, and name calling. A victim tells the story of how her abuser intimidated her and their children so that they would obey him. She reports that he never hit her, but somehow discovered that she was planning to leave him. One day he called her and their three children and asked them to stand in front of him. Then he took her pet dog, broke its neck and told her that if she ever left him that's what he would do to her and the children. She was so frightened by his behavior that it took years for her to finally escape. *His intent is to prevent himself from ever losing.*

Displaced Aggression
Consciously or unconsciously he finds fault with something unrelated to his present problems. Rather than face his own needs and issues, he distracts himself by focusing on side issues, i.e., something that may have happened at work. He may ruminate about what his boss said, build resentment, and rather than confront his boss, turn on his partner. *His intent is to take his anger out on those within his control, rather than risk punishment from those he believes has control over him.*

It is important to remember that women are also abusive in about a quarter of cases reported to law enforcement (Loseke,

Gelles & Cavanaugh, 1994). "Seventy-three percent of family violence victims were female and 76 percent of persons who committed family violence were male. Simple assault was the most frequent type of family violence" (Durose, et al., 2005). Women who abuse often manifest the same behaviors as male abusers, while male victims may exhibit characteristics similar to a female victim. Anyone can be an abuser or a victim!

THE VICTIM

In this section, we will examine predictable characteristics of a victimized person. Though previous abuse and low self-esteem may be risk factors for becoming a victim, anyone can fall prey to abuse. Embarrassment, shock, or fear for children's wellbeing may keep the victim locked in a relationship with an abuser. Women who expect God to miraculously deliver them from such relationships without taking decided steps to help themselves can be at high risk for remaining in an increasingly dangerous relationship. Let's look at some of the likely attributes of an abused woman.

Quick Involvement
She has probably been hurt in former relationships, or does not feel that she is good enough to be loved for who she is. She has a low opinion of herself. She finds it difficult to protect herself and feels that if a man is intent on pursuing her and intense in his attention, she should give in to his demands because he might be her last or only chance for an intimate relationship or marriage.

Isolated

She feels alone and misunderstood in her predicament. She tends to isolate herself from friends out of fear of angering her partner. She feels uneasy around other people, especially authority figures and individuals with strong, assertive personalities. Even though she isolates herself, she is fearful of rejection and abandonment.

Judges self harshly

She perpetuates negative messages heard from her parents (or significant others) and judges herself and others harshly based on those messages without first investigating their veracity or usefulness. Because she is often isolated from friends and family who could otherwise affirm her value, she hears only negative feedback from her abuser. Under this controlled negative focus, the victim experiences a sense of hopeless inadequacy in nearly every corner of her life.

Seeks approval, affirmation, recognition and acceptance

Because she is desperate for love, acceptance, affirmation, and approval, she'll do almost anything to be liked. Never wanting to hurt others, she remains loyal to undeserving people, even in the face of accumulated evidence. She often attracts emotionally unavailable people with addictive personalities.

Blaming

She lives life as a victim, blaming others for her circumstances, and is attracted to folks who are controlling, who like to "take charge" and "be in charge." She often confuses love with pity and associates with people she can care for, or rescue. Because of her intense desire to be needed, she misinterprets her abuser's dependency as love.

Super-responsible or super-irresponsible behavior
She takes responsibility for solving others' problems, or alternatively, expects others to be responsible for solving hers. This comes as no surprise since her abuser tells her that the abuse is her fault. She may wait for someone (including God) to save her from her abusive relationship. This enables her to avoid being responsible for her own life and choices.

Co-dependent
She has difficulty with intimacy, security, trust, and commitment in her relationships, and because her abuser has forced her to focus on his needs, wishes, and requirements, she loses sight of who she is as an individual. Lacking clearly defined personal limits and boundaries, she becomes enmeshed in her partner's needs and erratic emotions to the point of adopting his reality, and justifying his abusive nature.

Controlling
An abused individual has a strong need to be in control. The abuser keeps her focused on trivial demands such as timing of the meals, the type of clothes she wears, or the rules of the house. She hopes that if she carefully controls these things, he will not abuse her. When her abuser lashes out at her and criticizes her efforts to comply with his rules, she experiences feelings of shame and frustration and becomes more determined than ever to control her surroundings. She overreacts to changes, especially those things over which she has no control.

Dependent
She has learned to be dependent and terrified of abandonment, so she stays in harmful relationships or situations. Her fears and dependency stop her from ending unfulfilling relationships, and prevent her from entering into fulfilling ones. Because she

feels unlovable it is difficult or impossible for her to believe that anyone can really love her for who she is. She therefore does everything she can to please others in the hopes of being good enough to merit "love" from them. She has difficulty defining a healthy relationship, and doesn't allow herself to dream of a relationship in which her needs would be considered or met.

Denies Feelings

The victim denies, minimizes, or represses feelings that accompany memories of her traumatic childhood or her present painful relationship. Her limited ability to identify and express feelings exacts a toll on her life in ways she may not be aware. She has a difficult time maintaining intimate relationships. She often describes herself as feeling numb.

Helplessness and Hopelessness

Denial, isolation, control, shame, and unfounded guilt feelings can be legacies from the victim's family of origin or other abusive relationships, resulting in feelings of hopelessness and helplessness. She perceives herself through these defeating ways for she has learned that nothing she does will make a difference. She does not expect that she can do anything right, a belief reinforced by her abuser. She does not trust her ability to govern her own life or address external threats.

Impulsive

An abused woman may make an impulsive decision (or take a decided stand) without weighing her options, or giving serious consideration to possible consequences. Because she has limited experience following her own volition, she may make rapid and unwise choices when faced with an opportunity. As a result, she may feel confused, hurt, and full of self-hatred.

Serious and burdened

She finds it difficult to have fun especially if she had an un-healthy childhood. Because she is daily required to account for her whereabouts, decisions, and behaviors, dark feelings of dread, apprehension, and despair weigh heavily on her heart. Constant criticism and disappointed hopes for a happy relationship drain the prospect of joy from her life.

Prone to perfectionism

She sets unrealistically high and generally unattainable standards for herself that leave her angry and self-critical when she falls short. She covers her disappointment by becoming controlling, manipulative, bitter, and angry.

Lack of Self Care

Some abused women tend to display behaviors that present health risks, including substance abuse, alcoholism, suicidal attempts, cutting, eating disorders, and sexual promiscuity. I have found that the more severe the abuse the battered woman experiences, the greater her tendency to become involved in high risk behaviors. She feels guilty when she nurtures herself, or acts in her own best interests. She gives in to others' needs and opinions instead of taking care of herself.

This is quite a list of character qualities, isn't it? Abuse victims are forced to adapt to the hard reality of the violence, but these character adaptations don't happen overnight. It is a gradual transformation – like drops of water that ultimately erode the stone. Stealthily and insidiously these distortions take root in the belief systems, behaviors, and emotions of victims. In the next section, we will examine just how abuse develops over time and how the victim responds to it.

STAGES OF ABUSE
(Clinical Observation)

In the last half of the 20ᵗʰ century, the domestic abuse movement grew out of grassroots recognition that violence is not just another marital problem. Before behavioral scientist became interested in the study of domestic violence, in crisis centers nationwide, there had emerged a collective sense of anecdotal *knowing* based on thousands of interviews with batterd women describing the downward course of their thoughts, emotions, and forced accommodations to violence. The *Stages of Abuse* is such a composite depiction.

Stage One
When a victim experiences abuse for the first time, she is usually shocked and surprised. She wonders if she misperceived something or if she may have taken something the wrong way. A victim may feel responsible for misunderstanding what her abuser wanted her to do that warranted a beating. She may feel embarrassed to find herself married to someone who would harm her. How will she tell her family? What will she say to her friends? What will people think if they learn of the abuse? She tries to make sense of this initial abusive episode by taking into account her abuser's feelings of inadequacy, weariness, or distress about work. She convinces herself that he will not hurt her again and to ensure that he won't, she becomes all the more loving and considerate of his needs. She feels that if she changes aspects of herself, he will not abuse her again. Her reasoning and efforts are logical: giving him the benefit of the doubt, taking personal responsibility, and renewing her emphasis on kindness, love, and generous impulses. In marriages unmarked by domestic violence, such attempts would likely

result in feelings of deeper appreciation and connection, and may even inspire reciprocity – but this is not the case in relationships operating under the influence of abuse.

Stage Two

The second time a woman is abused she experiences fear in the core of her being. She recognizes that she cannot trust the man she married, and that she is not safe. Though she tends to downplay the gravity of her situation, she often tells someone about the abuse. Still making excuses for her abuser, she begins to move into the victim role, particularly if there is no help available, or if she doesn't know where to turn. The abused woman begins to suppress her outrage at the man who has betrayed her trust, and whose abusive actions mock her devotion to him. Instead she feels shame and guilt for failing to create a healthy relationship.

Stage Three

After years of intimidation, threats, abuse, and injury, the victim resigns herself to a life of hopelessness and helplessness. The abuser has successfully isolated her, and she feels alone in her painful existence. It is not surprising that so many abused women consider suicide. She may experience side effects of chronic stress and trauma such as depression, physical ailments, nightmares, panic, or a wide range of emotions. She is isolated from people who could help her see the impossibility of her situation, and who could provide the very feedback that might otherwise bolster her resolve to leave. Drained, despairing, and distressed, she goes through life like a robot, unable to escape the violence and fear of death that characterizes her life until death finally and mercifully comes.

An abusive relationship is a slippery slope. Many good-hearted, gentle-natured individuals marry abusers, completely clueless about what lies ahead. When the victim sees the futility of her attempts to stop the abuse or appease the abuser, she experiences confusion and an abject sense of failure. Her abuser will be quick to reinforce this idea. Counselors tell us that it is an uphill struggle for a battered wife to embrace the possibility of hope for a happy life. Some women endure abuse for years, helplessly watching their children's desperate, acting out behaviors. In some situations, though, it is the very heart-wrenching reality of her children's suffering and distress that finally prompts a woman to leave an abusive situation. The following list outlines parallel characteristics of an abuser and a victim in relationship.

SOME BEHAVIORAL CHARACTERISTICS
OF COUPLES IN ABUSIVE RELATIONSHIPS

Abuser	Both	Victim
Emotionally dependent, psychologically dependent	Codependent	Emotionally dependent, economically dependent
Verbally explosive	Poor communication skills	Suppressed anger
Aggressive, needing control	Unable to control the cycle of violence. They learn to expect and tolerate it.	Passive, but can exhibit periods of aggressiveness and/or craziness
Learned violence response	Either witnessed or experienced abuse in childhood.	Learned helplessness response
Demands quick commitment, traditionalist, makes all the decisions.	Seeking to be loved, seeking someone to love, or someone to care for	Short courtship, can be pregnant when married or seeking father for children
Jealous, possessive, and compulsive	Learns to manipulate situations to present normalcy in the relationship.	Accommodating and compliant to the point of adopting the abuser's reality.
Rationalizes that women are weaker and need to be controlled or put in their place.	Rationalizes that the relationship will get better with time.	Rationalizes that she can control his anger and becomes an accomplice in the abuse cycle.
Does not know how to express feelings appropriately. Has little sense of guilt and remorse.	Cannot express true feelings.	Feels unique, misunderstood, isolated, helpless, and hopeless.
Unrealistic expectations of partner	Looking for someone to fulfill needs	Idealistic expectations of partner
No personal boundaries – drawn to someone who appears weak and easy to control.	Unable to assess danger in the relationship.	No personal boundaries – will give in to anyone who appears to be powerful.
Accuses partner of "affairs"	Poor sexual image	Always defending self against accusations
Homicidal	Resigned that death can occur at anytime in the relationship.	Suicidal and suffers from psychosomatic illnesses.
Dr. Jekyll/Mr. Hyde personality	Personality adapts in order to hide abuse in the relationship.	Meek, mild or aggressive, bold, manipulative, cold and controlling

Figure 2

SOME CHARACTERISTICS OF
EMOTIONALLY HEALTHY PEOPLE

1. They are able to set boundaries so that their personal relationships are satisfying and lasting.

2. They are tolerant of self and others.

3. They give and receive love.

4. They make good use of their natural abilities and acknowledge their limitations.

5. They have a good sense of humor and can laugh at themselves.

6. They are tolerant of themselves and others.

7. They are open to new ideas, new experiences, and new possibilities.

8. They address problems and find solutions when they arise.

9. They shape their environment rather than allowing their environment to shape them.

10. They set realistic goals while planning for the future.

11. They take responsibility for their behaviors, and do not makes excuses for their mistakes.

12. They are not afraid to try new experiences.

13. They seek to have control over themselves rather than seeking to control others.

14. They do the best they can and gain satisfaction from their accomplishments.

15. They seek help if they have a need.

16. They consider the interests of others.

17. They are able to compromise, negotiate, and give others freedom to make their own choices.

18. They care for themselves and others.

19. They are able to share their feelings, wants, and appreciation of others.

20. They communicate clearly and directly.

21. They are non-violent and peace-seeking.

22. They expect to like and trust others and take it for granted that others will like and trust them.

23. Their cycle of life is that of relative comfort and contentment.

24. They encourage balance and mutuality in relationships.

25. Their priority is to develop self as a healthy, spiritual, functional, moral, and ethical human being.

References

Durose, M., Wolf, C., Langan, P., Motivans, M., Rantala, R. & Schmitt, E. (2005). "Family Violence Statistics" (NCJ-207846). Bureau of Justice Statistics. Following publication, the document can be accessed at: www.ojp.usdoj.gov/bjs/abstract/fvs.htm.

Loseke, D., Gelles, R., & Cavanaugh M. (Eds.), (1994). Current controversies on family violence (2nd edition, 55-77). Newbury Park: Sage Publications.

◆

Chapter 4

"In the past two decades, there has been growing
recognition of the prevalence of domestic violence in our
society. Moreover, it has become apparent
that some individuals are at greater risk for
victimization than others. Domestic violence has adverse
effects on individuals, families, and society in general."
Joseph S. Volpe, Ph.D.

EFFECTS AND FORMS OF ABUSE

No one involved escapes the devastation of domestic violence and abuse. **No one wins when it is allowed to continue!** As we discussed in Chapter 2, both victims and their children sustain emotional injury from living with abuse. Victims experience isolation, low self esteem, anger suppression, depression, and anxiety. Feeling helpless and hopeless, they begin to doubt the existence of healthy relationships, and come to fear healthy intimacy. Under the tyranny of abuse, many stay dependent and insecure. Abused individuals may adopt a martyr-like attitude, and believe that they are suffering for Christ's sake. They may attempt to numb the emotional hurt with drugs, alcohol, or other high risk behaviors. Physical changes directly attributable to the abuse may result in permanent disability, illness, or chronic pain problems. Physical injuries may contribute to lost work time, decreased productivity, or inability to access helpful resources. Physical injuries may also prohibit victims from seeking employment. Domestic abuse can plunge families into economic distress, making survival challenging. Each of these considerations magnifies the complexity of abuse. These interrelated factors undermine a victim's attempts to either endure or recover.

Effects on Children

Children who witness the abuse of a parent or who are themselves personally abused, are at an increased risk of post-traumatic stress disorder (PTSD), and ultimately reenacting the family trauma in adulthood by becoming abusers or victims in turn. We have a tendency to understand and gravitate toward that which is familiar (root word, *family*). PTSD is a diagnosis given to individuals who have suffered a type of stressor outside the usual range of human experience, i.e., death of a parent or sibling, repeated physical or sexual abuse, torture, concentration camp experience, floods, earthquakes, military combat and the like (American Psychiatric Association: DSM-IV, 1994). Our youth with PTSD feel out of control, and often experience intrusive thoughts, the flooding of emotions, flashbacks, and nightmares. The anxiety that accompanies violence displaces a child's natural ability to steady himself and concentrate; it steals his contentment, and his overall sense of being centered or settled. Generally children have few resources for coping with stress, so when they discover they're unable to challenge the abuse on equal terms, they either try to escape, or they simply freeze (while waiting for the abuse to stop) – and then blame themselves, later, for "going along with the abuse." Because they are in survival mode, and because they actively try to diminish their moment-by-moment awareness of the abuse, they often show lapses in social, academic, or emotional development. In concurrence with such problems as truancy, low self esteem, anger and acting out, or pseudo maturity, children and teens from abusive home environments often display high levels of anxiety and feelings of hopelessness. They may become abusive to others, or may feel so responsible for helping and protecting an abused parent that they actually become *parentified* and begin performing the functions of an adult in the household. This role-reversal can lead them to draw conclusions such as these: life is difficult, home is unsafe, and relationships are dangerous. Children of various ages may believe that they caused the abuse. The ensuing guilt combined with their inability to stop it often leads to depression (APA: DSM-IV, 1994).

Social and Legal Effects
Abusers who are not confronted with their actions learn that they can get away with using power and control to get what they want. This leads to more violence and increased involvement with law enforcement. On some level, the abuser may begin to lose self-respect, and become depressed, anxious, hopeless, vigilant, and sometimes suicidal. It has been said that homicide and suicide are two separate but similar ways to express aggression. Abusers may kill themselves or their victims, particularly if they threaten to do so. The violent behavior worsens over time. Few people confront abusers, and even fewer church members take steps to hold them accountable for their actions. Most of us are afraid of abusers, never really comprehending their feelings of inadequacy and acute levels of despair.

When our legal and law enforcement systems fail to adequately address domestic abuse, the incidence of violence increases, resulting in higher federal, state, county, and local costs for law enforcement, medical, counseling, and incarceration services.

Insurance premiums soar as the overall quality of life in communities is compromised. Social values such as family cohesion and community pride are weakened as the intergenerational cycle of abuse breaks down family relationships. As violence becomes more commonplace, society becomes increasingly apathetic towards abuse. Apathy means giving in to prevailing norms, and, in this case, resorting to stereotypical beliefs about violence, the inequality of men and women, and the use of power in society.

Effects on the Church

Our church families are also negatively affected by abuse. It is common for abuse survivors to doubt God's understanding and care. When Bible texts are misinterpreted or misrepresented, parishioners can form an erroneous view of God, concluding that He is harsh, tyrannical, and exacting. Misleading or incorrect ideas about headship, submission, rules, and roles are perpetuated. Unity (the brotherhood and sisterhood within the church), is threatened as believers lose faith in a church leadership that fails to discern, protect, or advocate for the hurting.

A common belief in society, and particularly in our churches, is that all marriage problems have two sides; that there is no innocent or non-abusing party. So the victim is seen as exaggerating and attempting to destroy the reputation of "such a nice guy." The victim sees her abuser's efforts at building support among friends and family as a double-edged sword. She's aware that, on one hand, he is less likely to act out violently in obvious ways (because he's actively courting the opinion of others), but he's also more likely to expand his power base (and, so doing, isolate her further from support).

Abuse can divide congregations as church members take sides. Typically, some church members will feel the abuser should be held accountable, whereas others naively support the abuser, refusing to suppose such a pleasant and polite individual capable of abuse. If the church does not take decided action, a variety of regrettable consequences can follow. Biblical instruction and church doctrines may be called into question as congregants go on the attack. Some members may become angry with a church that seems more concerned about rules, traditions, and the status quo than the safety of victims, and a vision of healthy relationships. Others may express rage toward ones who "rock the boat." They angrily dismiss warnings about ignoring patterns of abuse, and permitting abusers to hold positions of power in the church.

Church members may learn that honesty is not welcome at church and resolve to hide their thoughts, feelings, and experiences of abuse. Victims (and those who love them) are wounded anew the moment they recognize that it is not safe to mention abuse in church. The church's priorities and values are tested at the point of action, or inaction. What do we value more – personal pride, money, institutional structure, unity, image, or an individual's soul? (See Figure 3).

Causes, Effects, and Impact of Domestic Violence on Families, Churches and Society in General

On Women	On Children
-Isolation from others	-Isolation from others
-Depression, helplessness, hopelessness	-Depression, helplessness, hopelessness
-Increased alcohol and drug use (dependence)	-Low self-esteem
-Illness	-Illness
-Suppression of anger	-Increased fear / anger
-Lost work time, decreased productivity	-Truancy
-Pain and injuries	-Increased risk of abuse, injuries, and death
-Permanent physical damage	-Repetition of abusive behavior
-Poor communication skills	-Poor communication skills
-Dissociative states	-Confusion with identity / role
-Death	-Death
-Suicide	-Suicide
-Fear of abandonment	-Fear of abandonment
-Anxiety and panic attacks	-Excessive attention seeking
-Dehydration	-Bed-wetting, night terrors
-Manipulation, dependency, and mood swings	-Manipulation, dependency, and mood swings
-Eating disorders	-Passivity with peers or bullying
-Emotional "over-reactions" to stimuli	-Difficulty in trusting others, especially adults
-General emotional numbing	-Somatic complaints, headaches, and stomach aches.
-Somatization disorders	-Nervousness, anxious, short attention span
-Poor adherence to medical recommendations	-Tiredness and lethargy
-Poverty	-Poor personal hygiene
-Sleep Disorders	-High risk play
-Repeated self-injury	-Self abuse
-Sexual dysfunction	-Developmental delays
-Self-neglect	-Post-traumatic Stress Disorder (PTSD)
-Strained family relationships	
-An inability to adequately respond to the needs of their children	

Figure 3

On Men	On Society
-Reinforced belief that power and control are legitimately achieved by means of violence and manipulation -Increase in violent behavior -Risk of homicide -Increased involvement with law enforcement -Increased emotional problems -Decreased self-esteem and self-respect -Feelings of inadequacy	-Increase in criminal activity -Increase in legal, police, medical, and counseling costs -Cost of incarceration -Lost work time -Increased insurance costs -Perpetuation of myths of inequality of women and men -Perpetuation of intergenerational cycle of abuse -Decrease in general quality of life -Breakdown of the family structure

The umbrella of behaviors that comprise domestic violence is most frequently observed in patterns of coercion and control. The following list of abusive behaviors, (some criminal, some not), illustrates the range of behaviors that an abuser may use against a victim. Remember that statistics show a greater percentage of abusers are male (Loseke, Gelles & Cavanaugh, (1994). That is why, in this text, we use male pronouns in reference to the abuser and female pronouns in reference to the victim. But to reiterate: **anyone can be an abuser or a victim!** If you are a victim of violence, take a moment to check how many of these abuses you have survived. If you are an abuser, check how many of these abuses you have perpetrated. If you are a pastor, church leader, church member, or service provider, check how many of these abuses have been reported to you as you work with either a victim or perpetrator.

Physical Abuse

_____Slapping	_____Burning with acid
_____Smacking	_____Setting her on fire
_____Smacking in the face	_____Scalding
_____Pushing	_____Shaking
_____Shoving	_____Suffocating
_____Pushing down stairs	_____Choking
_____Punching	_____Throwing her
_____Kicking	_____Throwing objects at her
_____Hitting	_____Attacking with a weapon
_____Hitting with objects	_____Stabbing
_____Holding her against her will	_____Stripping her clothing off
_____Holding her down	_____Forcing her to hurt herself
_____Banging her head against the floor	_____Forcing her to drink alcohol
_____Banging her head against the wall	_____Forcing her to take drugs
_____Bruising	_____Withholding medication
_____Giving her a black eye	_____Withholding care from the disabled
_____Biting	_____Holding her head underwater
_____Breaking bones	_____Drowning
_____Burning	_____Attempted murder
_____Burning with cigarettes	_____Murder

"All acts of injustice that tend to shorten life–the spirit of hatred and revenge, or the indulgence of any passion that leads to injurious acts toward others or causes us even to wish them harm...are, to a greater or less degree, violations of the sixth commandment" (Ellen G. White, *Patriarchs and Prophets*, p. 308).

*"A **disposition to cause pain** whether to our fellow human beings or brute creature is Satanic... A record goes up to heaven, and a day is coming when judgment will be pronounced against those who abuse God's creatures"* (Ellen G. White, *Patriarchs and Prophets*, p. 443).

"If the will of God is fulfilled, the husband and wife will respect each other and cultivate love and confidence. Anything that would mar the peace and unity of the family should be firmly repressed, and kindness and love should be cherished" (Ellen G. White, *Signs of the Times*, Nov. 14, 1892).

"Without employing any compulsion, without using any violence, He (Christ) blends the will of the human subject to the will of God. This is the science of all true science, for by it change is wrought in the mind and character – the change that must be wrought in the life of everyone who passes through the gates of the city of God" (Ellen G. White, *My Life Today*, p. 340).

Sexual Abuse

_____Rape
_____Forced oral or anal sex
_____Having affairs to humiliate her
_____Having sex while she is sleeping
_____Insisting on having sex anytime/anywhere
_____Refusing to have sex
_____Having sex with others in front of her
_____Denying her sexuality
_____Denying her sex
_____Expecting her to have sex after physical abuse
_____Using objects during intercourse against her will

_____Forcing pornographic involvement
_____Forcing sadomasochistic activity
_____Forcing her to perform sexual acts in front of children or other people
_____Forcing her to perform sexual acts with animals
_____Refusing access to contraception
_____Forcing abortion
_____Assaulting her when pregnant
_____Refusing to practice safe sex
_____Sexually abusing her children
_____Sexual name calling
_____Forcing sexual acts she does not like

"If the wife feels that in order to please her husband, she must come down to his standard, when animal passion is the principal basis of his love and controls his actions, she displeases God... If she feels that she must submit to his animal passions without a word of remonstrance, she does not understand her duty to him or to her God" (Ellen G. White, *Testimonies for the Church*, Vol. 2 p. 477).

"Sexual excess will effectually destroy a love for devotional exercises, will take from the brain the substance needed to nourish the system, and will most effectively exhaust the vitality. No woman should aid her husband in this work of self-destruction. She will not do it if she is enlightened and has true love for him" (Ellen G. White, *Testimonies for the Church*, Vol. 2, p. 477).

Intimidation	
____Making partner afraid by looks, actions, gestures	____Telling her how he would like to hurt her
____Breaking objects	____Locking her out of the home, bedroom, etc.
____Breaking or destroying her valued possessions	____Keeping her locked in a cupboard, under stairs, or in a confined space
____Driving dangerously	
____Driving a car at her or her children	____Taking away her possessions, or clothes
____Being violent to others to teach her a lesson	____Taking away her green card or driver's license
____Hurting children	____Scaring others so that they do not intervene to help
____Relating stories about how he hurt others	____Getting family and friends to intimidate her
____Having the gas or electrcity turned off during the winter months.	
____Keeping her locked in a room	

"How Satan exults when he is enabled to set the soul into a white heat of anger! A glance, a gesture, an intonation, may be seized upon and used, as the arrow of Satan, to wound and poison the heart that is open to receive it. If the Spirit of Christ possesses us wholly, and we have been transformed by His grace, there will be no disposition to speak evil, or to bear reports freighted with falsehood" (Ellen G. White, *Signs of the Times*, Sept. 21, 1888).

"Above all, let there be no shadow of hate or ill will, no bitterness or sourness of expression" (Ellen G. White, *Testimonies for the Church*, Vol. 2, p. 52).

Threats

_____Saying "Next time it will be you!"	_____Threats to kill her
_____Sending threatening letters	_____Threats to take her children away
_____Threatening her by phone	_____Threats to harm or kill another loved one
_____Not letting her use phone	
_____Cutting off the phone	_____Threats to harm or kill pets
_____Mocking or humiliating her, alone or in front of others	_____Threats to self harm or commit suicide
_____Abusing her in front of others	_____Threats to have her deported
_____Threats of physical violence	_____Threats to report her to the authorities
_____Threats of future physical violence	_____Threats to destroy her possessions
_____Threats of sexual violence	
_____Threats of future sexual violence	_____Threats to burn down her home
_____Threats with weapons or objects	_____Setting fire to her home
_____Threats to expose things she is ashamed of to others	_____Threats to exclude her from her family or community
_____Preventing her from keeping appointments	_____Threats to make her lose her job

"You think yourself sufficient to be head in your family and feel that your head is sufficient to move every member, as a machine is moved in the hands of the workmen. You dictate and assume authority. This displeases Heaven and grieves your pitying angels" (Ellen G. White, *Testimonies for the Church*, Vol. 2, p. 253).

"Unless men and women have learned of Christ, His meekness and lowliness, they will reveal the impulsive, unreasonable spirit so often revealed by children. The strong, undisciplined will seek to rule. Such ones need to study the words of Paul: 'When I was a child I spake as a child, I understood as a child, I thought as a child: but when I became a man, I put away childish things'" (Ellen G. White, *Adventist Home*, p 118).

Isolation

_____Restricting her movements
_____Preventing her from keeping appointments
_____Timing her movements
_____Following her everywhere
_____Making decisions for her
_____Making her work long hours
_____Preventing her from working
_____Keeping her from friends and family
_____Making her family and friends too scared to contact her
_____Turning her family and friends against her
_____Telling her no one else cares about her
_____Taking away her documents and passport
_____Preventing her from learning local language
_____Having others believe him over her despite evidence to the contrary

_____Making her tell lies for him
_____Preventing her escape
_____Allowing her no privacy
_____Destroying her letters
_____Watching her at home or work
_____Being jealous of her
_____Sending her unwanted gifts
_____Being obsessive and possessive
_____Getting information about her from her children
_____Having her children taken away from her
_____Using child contact to harass her
_____Harassing her after separation
_____Turning her children against her
_____Telling her children things she doesn't want them to know
_____Manipulating her children
_____Telling her children lies about her

"Neither the husband nor the wife should attempt to exercise over the other an arbitrary control. Do not try to compel each other to yield to your wishes. You can not do this and retain each other's love. Be kind, patient, and forbearing, considerate and courteous. By the grace of God you can succeed in making each other happy, as in your marriage vow you promised to do" (Ellen G. White, *Review and Herald*, December 10, 1908).

Emotional/Psychological Abuse

_____Only letting her use the bath room or toilet at certain times of day

_____Ignoring her, refusing to talk to her, repeatedly interrogating her

_____Forcing her to take abuse from others

_____Making her afraid to go to sleep

_____Making her afraid to wake up

_____Preventing her from eating

_____Making her eat inedible food or disgusting things

_____Making her lick dinner plates clean

_____Making her redo tasks after finding fault with what she has done

_____Finding endless trivial tasks for her to do

_____Telling her there is no escape

_____Forcing her to be friends with people she does not like

_____Making her do things she doesn't want to do to prove her love

_____Continually breaking promises

_____Keeping her constantly on edge

_____Telling her that her reactions are irrational

_____Withdrawing affection

_____Using racism against her

_____Preventing her from sleeping.

_____Making her sleep on the floor

_____Enforcing a routine

_____Making her polish the soles of his shoes

_____Making her put things back in an exact order

"Instead of respecting the feelings of your wife and kindly avoiding, as a gentleman would, those subjects upon which you know you differ, you have been forwarded to dwell upon objectionable points, and have manifested a persistency in expressing your views regard-

less of any around you. You have felt that others had no right to see matters differently from yourself. These fruits do not grow upon the Christian tree" (Ellen G. White, *Testimonies for the Church*, Vol. 2, p. 418).

"The husband and father who is morose, selfish, and overbearing is not only unhappy himself, but he casts gloom upon all the inmates of his home. He will reap the result in seeing his wife dispirited, sickly, and his children marred with his own unlovely temper" (Ellen G. White, *Ministry of Healing*, p. 374-375).

"The giving way to violent emotions endangers life. Many die under a burst of rage and passion" (Ellen G. White, *Mind, Character, and Personality*, Volume 2, p. 519).

Emotional Abuse

_____Preventing her from getting or keeping a job

_____Destroying her work

_____Refusing her money

_____Demanding receipts for all spending

_____Keeping her misinformed about her entitlements

_____Forcing her to commit acts of fraud

_____Making her give him her money

_____Not letting her be part owner of home, car, or other large items

_____Preventing her from learning how to balance checkbook

_____Preventing her from studying

_____Taking her money

_____Refusing her economic independence

_____Making her ask or beg for money

_____Incurring debts in her name

_____Not providing modern conveniences to help lighten housework

_____Not having her name on bank accounts

_____Preventing her from writing checks

_____Ruining her credit score

"Give your wife a share of the money that you receive. Let her have this as her own, and let her use it as she desires. She should have been allowed to use the means that she earned as she in her judgment deemed best. If she had a certain sum to use as her own, without being criticized, a great weight would have been lifted from her mind" (Ellen G. White, *Letter 157*, 1903).

"...I tried to show him that it was necessary for the health as well as the morals of his children that he should make home pleasant and provide conveniences to lighten the labor of his wife" (Ellen G. White, *Adventist Home*, p. 378).

"You must help each other. Do not look upon it as a virtue to hold fast the purse strings, refusing to give your wife money" (Ellen G. White, *Adventist Home*, p. 378).

"Women should be trained to some business whereby they can gain a livelihood if necessary" (Ellen G. White, *Adventist Home*, p. 91).

Verbal Abuse

_____Shouting at her
_____Insulting her
_____Telling her what to wear
_____Criticizing her abilities
_____Criticizing her work or housekeeping
_____Telling her she is crazy
_____Telling her she is stupid
_____Telling her she is a slut
_____Telling her she is worthless
_____Telling her she is a bad mother
_____Telling her no one would believe her
_____Making her accept that his behavior is normal

_____Screaming at her
_____Undermining her
_____Criticizing her appearance
_____Criticizing her sexual performance
_____Criticizing her in front of others
_____Telling her she is ugly
_____Telling her she is a disgrace
_____Telling her she is useless
_____Telling her she is a failure
_____Telling her nobody else would want her
_____Telling her that his behavior is normal
_____Telling her he only abuses her because he loves her

"When one once gives place to an angry spirit, he is just as much intoxicated as the man who has put the glass to his lips. Christ treats anger as murder…Passionate words are a savor of death unto death. He who utters them is not cooperating with God to save his fellow men. In heaven this wicked railing is placed in the same list as common swearing. While hatred is cherished in the soul there is not one iota of the love of God there" (Ellen G. White, *Our High Calling*, p. 235).

"Burning words of passion should never be spoken, for in the sight of God and holy angels they are as a species of swearing" (Ellen G. White, *The Youth's Instructor*, Sept. 20, 1894).

"Be kind in speech and gentle in action, giving up your own wishes. Watch well your words, for they have a powerful influence for good or ill. Allow no sharpness to come into your voices. Bring into your united life the fragrance of Christlikeness" (Ellen G. White, *Testimonies for the Church*, Vol. 7, p. 47).

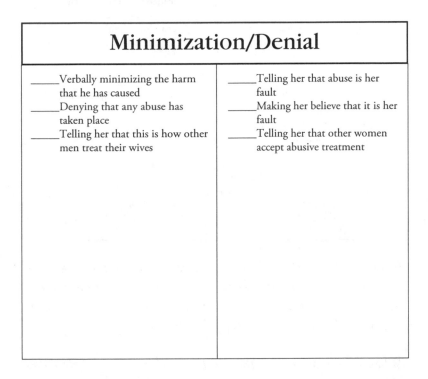

Minimization/Denial

_____Verbally minimizing the harm that he has caused

_____Denying that any abuse has taken place

_____Telling her that this is how other men treat their wives

_____Telling her that abuse is her fault

_____Making her believe that it is her fault

_____Telling her that other women accept abusive treatment

"Let no one feel, even though he may theoretically be established in the present truth, that he makes no mistakes. But if mistakes are made, let there be a readiness to correct them. And let us avoid everything that is likely to create dissention and strife, for there is a heaven before us, and among its inhabitants there will be no strife" (Ellen G. White, *Counsels on Health*, p. 244).

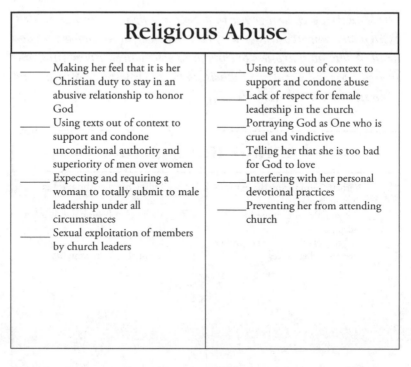

Religious Abuse

____ Making her feel that it is her Christian duty to stay in an abusive relationship to honor God

____ Using texts out of context to support and condone unconditional authority and superiority of men over women

____ Expecting and requiring a woman to totally submit to male leadership under all circumstances

____ Sexual exploitation of members by church leaders

____ Using texts out of context to support and condone abuse

____ Lack of respect for female leadership in the church

____ Portraying God as One who is cruel and vindictive

____ Telling her that she is too bad for God to love

____ Interfering with her personal devotional practices

____ Preventing her from attending church

"It is no evidence of manliness in the husband for him to dwell constantly upon his position as head of the family. It does not increase respect for him to hear him quoting Scripture to sustain his claims to authority" (Ellen G. White, *Adventist Home*, p. 215).

"When husbands require the complete subjection of their wives, declaring that women have no voice or will in the family, but must render entire submission, they place their wives in a position contrary to the Scripture. In interpreting the Scripture in this way, they do violence to the design of the marriage institution. This interpretation is made simply that they may exercise arbitrary rules, which is not their prerogative" (Ellen G. White, *Adventist Home*, p. 116).

"If he is a coarse, rough, boisterous, egotistical, harsh, and over-bearing man, let him never utter the word that the husband is the head of the wife, and that she must submit to him in everything; for he is not the Lord, he is not the husband in the true significance of the term..." (Ellen G. White, *Adventist Home*, p. 117).

"The Lord has constituted the husband the head of the wife to be her protector; he is the house-band of the family, binding the members together, even as Christ is the head of the church and the Savior of the mystical body. Let every husband who claims to love God carefully study the requirements of God in his position. Christ's authority is exercised in wisdom, in all kindness and gentleness; so let the husband exercise his power and imitate the great Head of the church" (Ellen G. White, *Adventist Home*, p. 215).

"We must have the Spirit of God, or we can never have harmony in the home. The wife, if she has the Spirit of Christ, will be careful of her words; she will control her spirit, she will be submissive, and yet will not feel that she is a bondslave, but a companion to her husband. If the husband is a servant of God, he will not lord it over his wife; he will not be arbitrary and exacting. We cannot cherish home affection with too much care; for the home, if the Spirit of the Lord dwells there, is a type of heaven" (Ellen G. White, *Adventist Home*, p. 118).

We are responsible to God for the quality of our relationships. By careful examination of our interpersonal interactions, and by comparing our own behaviors with the loving kindness of Jesus, we can evaluate whether we are creating home environments that are peaceful, inviting, and safe. As we ask for His guidance, God will supernaturally empower us to accurately represent the character of Jesus to our children, family members, friends, neighbors, and community.

POWER AND CONTROL WHEEL
(Used by permission)

Figure 4

References

Domestic Abuse Intervention Project (n.d.). *Power and Control Wheel.* Duluth, MN: 206 West Fourth Street, (208) 722-4134.

Loseke, D., Gelles, R., & Cavanaugh M. (Eds.), (1994). Current controversies on family violence (2nd edition, 55-77). Newbery Park: Sage Publications.

◆

"I believe that there is a devil, and here's Satan's agenda.
First, he doesn't want anyone having kids.
Secondly, if they do conceive, he wants them killed.
If they're not killed through abortion,
he wants them neglected or abused
physically, emotionally, sexually...
One way or another, the legions of hell want to destroy children
because children become the future adults and leaders.
If they can warp or wound a child,
he or she becomes a warped or wounded adult
who passes on this affliction to the next generation".
-Terry Randall in TIME Magazine, October 21, 1991.

DOMESTIC VIOLENCE: WHY IT CONTINUES

Tina reported that she grew up in a well-ordered, strict Christian home. Her father was very disappointed that she, his oldest child, was not a boy. He required her to do heavy chores on the farm. When Tina was 18 she was raped by the Youth Leader in her church who came from a similar home environment. She became pregnant. Furious, her father kicked and verbally abused her, and encouraged her siblings to do likewise. Once he pinched her ear-lobes with a pair of pliers because she did not hear him calling her. Her mother tried to shield Tina from the abuse, but was herself abused. Tina is now a grown woman with children. She does not understand how her father, a Christian, and a church leader could

*have abused her. Although she attends church, the memories of her
father overshadow any concept of a loving God.*

———⚬❦⚬———

*Charles came for counseling because his marriage was falling apart.
He is the father of 5 beautiful daughters, but life was getting to
be very difficult for him. He told his counselor that his mother, a
"Christian" forced him to watch her have sex with her boyfriends
when he was five to ten years old. Even though he felt uncomfortable
with her behavior, he thought that it was normal. As he got older
he realized that what his mother did was sexually abusive. Now as
a husband and father he is having difficulty relating to his wife and
daughters. He realizes that the anger he is taking out on his family is
directly related to the anger he still has towards his mother.*

These are sad but common stories for those of us who work
with abuse survivors. The question burns in our minds, "Why
doesn't she (or he) leave the abuser?" Leaving may not be as
easy as it may first appear. A client who had been viciously
abused, bruised, and beaten for over 15 years once asked me,
"Where were the people who were supposed to come forward
and help me? Why didn't anyone ask how they could help? I
had no money. My husband told me that he'd kill me, and
everyone knew it. But no one did anything. They just told me
that they were praying for me." Why does abuse continue and
why don't more people step forward to end it? The segments
that follow offer some rationale for why individuals and institutions do not take swifter action to end abuse.

Because We Disregard its Source
We are supporting and perpetuating Satan's agenda when we
try to determine which spouse or partner is to blame for the
abuse and which is being victimized; when we allow ourselves

to focus on any part of the issue other than the act or source of violence. We are being diverted if we believe that domestic violence is just about angry women or power-hungry men. Domestic violence is qualitatively different from "family feuds" or "family problems." Domestic violence is a societal problem, a sin problem. It is the presence of evil manifesting in thoughts, feelings, and practices. Alsdurf & Alsdurf (1998) summed up the problem of spouse abuse in this way: *"Before Satan can be defeated, he must be identified. And, once identified, he must be fought on spiritual ground. The problem of wife abuse (husband abuse) is not one of feminism, secular humanism, or a lack of headship in the home. It is the problem of evil – unseen and unopposed."*

Family violence cuts across all racial, socio-economic, educational, cultural, and religious lines. It occurs in middle-class and upper-class homes, as well as the working-class and poor. Christian homes are not exempt. Adventist homes are not exempt!

"The reign of violence within many homes is evidence most basically of Satan's kingdom at work destroying order, love, and happiness in human relationships. And until we enter the arena of domestic violence willing to battle evil, our efforts to see violence stopped and families transformed will be ineffective at best. We cannot dismiss evil as some vague spiritual force that presides outside of human behavior. Evil is rooted in a superhuman personality: Satan. And when people are violent, hostile, argumentative, deceiving, accumulating, as it were, a treasure of evil goods within the economy of Satan, they gradually permit Satan to restructure their character and own them. Whether using psychological or theological language, the truth remains that acts of evil are acts of sin. They are assaults on God's moral laws. They separate the evildoer from God and from fellow human beings" (Alsdurf & Alsdurf, 1998).

Because of Our Incorrect View

There are many false ideas that contribute to the existence and prevalence of domestic violence in Christian homes:

1. *Parenting.* Victims are often told that it is their Christian duty to provide a good home for their children. So they stay in abusive relationships concerned that if they leave, they will not be able to adequately provide shelter, food, and other necessities for their children. But experience has shown that many children raised in abusive homes learn to keep secrets. They learn to wear masks. They learn to hide their feelings. Such children tend to grow up frustrated, disillusioned, and full of anger towards God and the church. If there is no intervention along the way, they grow into adulthood primed and liable to perpetuate the cycle of violence.

"I wish my mother had left my father when I was 5 years old. She stayed thinking that she was doing the best for us children and honoring God. I ended up marrying a man just like my father. I am afraid to leave him because my church family thinks he is wonderful. They would never believe it if I told them that he is abusive. So I keep the secret, just like my mother did. I love my mother, but she should have left my father." (Pam)

2. *Victim blaming.* Some victims blame themselves for the abuse. They believe that they did something terribly wrong for which they deserve to be punished. Their abusers and others try to convince them that if they would just change their behavior, the abuse would stop. This is rarely, if ever, the case. Changing a victim's behavior will not necessarily influence the abuser's behavior. When we counsel abused women, men, or children, it is imperative that we describe and emphasize positive and

correct views of marriage and intimate relationships. The natural outgrowth of a truly Christian marriage or relationship involves both mutual respect and mutual giving that recognizes the full equality of both individuals.

"I came from a dysfunctional home. I was excited because James wanted to marry me. I was determined to be a good wife. When the abuse started I thought that if I would only be a better wife, he would change. My pastor told me that I should be more submissive and he would change. I thought that his anger was because I was not good enough. It took me years to realize that I could not change him and that the abuse was not my fault." (Diana)

———❧———

"I hear often that men are more abusive. Well, I don't believe that when it comes to verbal abuse. My wife would yell and scream at me all the time. I could not understand why she was so angry, especially after our first child was born. She finally admitted that she was sexually abused by a neighbor when she was 12 years old. We went to see the pastor. He told me that I should try and be more loving and kind to my wife. I should give her the opportunity to vent her anger and this would help bring the demons out of her. I did everything he told me, but my efforts were in vain. The ending to this story is a happy one for I realized that I was not responsible for healing my wife, she was. We eventually went to a Christian counselor, and we stayed happily married." (Phil)

3. *Male privilege.* – Historically, the man has assumed the role of "breadwinner," "king of the castle," and "head of the home." Some abusers derive prestige, power, and status from ordering their homes according to their will. Ben Kinchlow (1986) made the following comment on the Christian television program, The 700 Club: "In every place where you find a woman in

charge, you find a weak man. Men were designed to be the head of the family. If you are reading this... and the husband is not head of the family, without even talking to you, I can guarantee that you have financial problems, marital problems, and perhaps emotional problems with your children." This viewpoint is decidedly discriminatory toward women, particularly single mothers, and these comments are not supported by research.

4. *Submission.* There appears to be a dehumanization standard operational in cultures worldwide when women are viewed as objects created to be dominated or controlled. *"Throughout history man, through pride, ignorance, or moral perversion, has treated woman as being greatly inferior"* (Lockyer, 1977). Bible texts have been misused as women have been required to *"learn in silence with all subjection"* (2 Timothy 2:11), not only socially, but also in the church (1 Cor. 14:34). They have been told to "reverence" their husbands (Eph. 5:33).

5. *Cultural influences.* Traditional gender roles and stereotypes contribute to domestic violence, according to sociologist Sara Teiran, *"The rules for gender roles, natural as they may seem, were not given by God, there is nothing wrong in following them when so doing fulfills each partner's goals and aspirations. But when either partner feels oppressed or stifled, a reexamination is in order"* (Teiran, 1992).

6. *God's Requirements.* Some Christians elect to stay in abusive relationships fearing that they will incur the wrath of God if they "break" the marriage covenant by leaving. They don't want to be "lost." Although they may be in danger of losing their lives, they feel they must be prepared to die at the hands

of an abusive spouse, and hope that their sacrifice will be "acceptable unto God."

The ideology that a woman's lot is to bear her cross by suffering at the hands of an abusive husband is not a new concept. Many victims believe that a traumatic, apprehensive life is the price they must pay for having made a hasty decision to marry, having sexual relations before marriage, or for some other secret sin. Others believe that the purpose of a woman's life is to make her husband perfect through her suffering. Reformer John Calvin gave voice to these views when he wrote to a woman parishioner who had appealed for help because her husband beat her:

"We have a special sympathy for poor women who are evilly and roughly treated by their husbands, because of the roughness and cruelty of the tyranny and captivity which is their lot. We do not find ourselves permitted by the Word of God, however, to advise a woman to leave her husband, except by force of necessity, and we do not understand this force to be operative when a husband behaves roughly and uses threats to his wife, nor even when he beats her, but only when there is imminent peril to her life, whether from persecution by the husband or by his conspiring...We exhort her to bear with patience the cross which God has seen fit to place upon her, and meanwhile not to deviate from the duty which she has taken before God to please her husband, but to be faithful whatever happens..." (Hughes Translation, 59).

7. A Distorted Image of God. Other victims see in God a stern judge who seeks retribution for sins, or a controlling Father who hurts them, withholds protection, and expects total obedience in all circumstances. Their theology is incorrect and their ideas, faulty – particularly in reference to the character of God as a kind, gracious, and nurturing father.

Even though she grew up in a Christian home, Barb, now 60 years old, remembers the terror she felt whenever her father would open her bedroom door to "kiss her goodnight." As she tells her story she begins to tremble. Her hands shake and she twists and turns the pen in her hand. She reported how much she loved her father when she was five years old, but could not understand why he would hurt her. Many years later as an adult she was always searching for love but could never find it. She decided to give up on life. If it was not for her children she would have committed suicide. Through the prayers of faithful friends, and with the help of her church family she has come to know Jesus as her Elder Brother and Faithful Friend. She is unable to call Him Father for her vision of a loving Heavenly Father is blurred by memories of an abusive father. She is determined, however, to help her two boys find safety and healing in the knowledge that there is a Father who will protect and provide for them. She volunteers at a Community Services Center because she feels that many women who access those services have had to do so because of abuse. She believes that the center can play a very important role in helping abused families find resources, support, and friendships.

8. *Interpretation of Scripture.* We sometimes misinterpret and misapply Scripture texts with abused women. We emphasize that "what therefore God hath joined together let no man put asunder" (Matthew 19:6). We encourage them to pray about their circumstances. We remind them that God hates divorce and that He will change their abuser or give them the strength to endure the suffering if they pray hard enough. But the victim reasons, "If I pray long and hard and the abuse continues, does this mean that God is not hearing my prayers? Is something wrong with me because I can't endure? Am I not a good enough Christian?" (See chapter 7 and 8 for appropriate interpretations of texts used in relation to domestic violence).

Because Abusers Can Abuse

The impact of abuse allows abusers to maintain power and control in a relationship. They continue to be abusive because no one confronts their sin, or calls it by its right names, i.e., "violent" or "criminal." Since they are not held accountable for their abuse, when questions do arise, they make excuses, and shift the blame:

"If only she would…..I wouldn't have to….."

"I needed to let her know who's in charge."

"She's a pathological liar."

We open the door for abusers to justify and continue the abuse when we sympathize with them.

Because of Lack of Resources

Historically, victim assistance resources have been scarce, but that is gradually improving. If service providers do not fully understand the dynamics of domestic violence, they can very easily be manipulated by the abuser to revictimize the victim. Victims are revictimized when service providers, health care professionals, or members of the legal or law enforcement community express disbelief in her testimony, or when they blame her for provoking a violent episode. The victim is being further revictimized when she is made to take responsibility for the health of the relationship and is encouraged to engage in couple counseling, which could expose her to more violence. It is therefore imperative that only properly trained service providers occupy these critical positions of trust.

Because of Cultural Beliefs

In some cultures (including certain areas in North America), there is a subtle dehumanization of women. Some men view females as objects created for their pleasure. We hear terms such as "arm candy" and "trophy wife." In these cultures and cultural enclaves, churches and other institutions are reluctant to view or condemn as criminal physical violence towards women and children.

Because Women Stay in Abusive Relationships

The question arises again and again, "Why do women stay in abusive relationships?" First, women are trying to avoid more extreme violence. A battered woman is justifiably concerned that the act of leaving will trigger more severe violence. In an earlier chapter, we reviewed research showing that the most dangerous time for a battered woman is when she tries to leave, and immediately after she has left. It is during this time of transition that women are in the greatest danger of being stalked, harassed, or harmed. The batterer may threaten to kill her children, her family, or himself. He may vow to follow her wherever she goes and kill her when she least expects it. A battered woman seldom doubts that the abuser is able to carry out his threats.

An abused woman is embarrassed and ashamed to leave. She is pressured by society – and often the church – to keep the family together regardless of the cost. She is hesitant to confide in anyone for fear of being chastised for "airing dirty linen," or for tarnishing her family's reputation. Though abused and humiliated, she may genuinely love her abuser. Women are socialized to believe that they are responsible for their husbands' emotional needs. As the battered woman observes her husband, raging and abusive, she recognizes a serious dilemma and resolves to regain his trust and help him work through the problems that trigger his behavior. She determines to stay, hoping that in a magical moment she will find the key to his transformation.

Traumatic memory loss is the reduced ability to remember abusive incidents. Traumatic memory loss is a primary reason why the victim needs a supportive network of friends and family – people who are not suffering memory loss, and who can remind her of what her abuser has done in the past, help her hold on to her sense of what's real, and what's right and wrong. Traumatic memory loss (either organic – from injury, or functional – from the impossibility of her circumstances) is a significant consideration in why battered women do not leave the abuser, and why they go back.

Christian victims fear that if they leave, they will be doing "something wrong," and in so doing, sin against God. Men who are abused may bear the additional burden of not living up to their role as spiritual leader or priest of the family. An abused woman may fear that if she were to leave, she would no longer be in a position to influence her abuser for Christ; that she would have to abandon hope that her Christian example might have a grace-inspiring, ennobling, or refining effect, or at the very least, soften his heart. The decision to leave an abusive relationship means sacrificing home, material possessions, financial security, and hope for the marriage. It means giving up the known for the unknown. An abused man might worry about how his wife and children will fare without the benefit of his income.

The victim finds herself between a rock and a hard place. On one hand, she wants to give her children the gift of their father in the context of an intact family. On the other hand, if she stays, she knows that her children will be emotionally damaged (at a minimum) and their future sorely compromised. The concept of *staying regardless* is reinforced in the ideology of some communities who believe that it is better for children to live with both parents (even if abuse is occurring) rather than live with the non-abusing parent. However, in a previous chapter, we reviewed the effects of domestic abuse on children, and this option does not provide a secure foundation for their development or success in future relationships.

Victims are sometimes criticized for "destroying" rather than protecting the reputation of the church, which is an issue "good Christians" are concerned about. "What kind of a witness does it give to the community for our families to be splitting up?" we sometimes hear from the pulpit. A victim is sometimes threatened or made to feel uncomfortable or unwelcome if she maintains membership in the church, particularly when the members do not know the whole story. A married couple tends to have a higher social status in the church (and sometimes in the community) than a single woman who has been divorced, separated, or is unmarried with children. It is just one of the many paradoxes of abuse that victims lose standing in the church as they are gaining freedom from their abuser.

Recall that those outside the family often see the abuser as an endearing, charming, and genuine guy, and because he appears so calm, sincere, and emotionally stable, the victim's testimony is frequently viewed as emotional, crazy, disoriented, or way too extreme. As an outcome, she receives limited emotional support or understanding. As good people turn away from her, she is flooded with feelings of despair, hopelessness, and self-doubt. Sadly, because victims are often isolated, they are not aware of helpful resources. The victim is keenly aware of these social barriers and concludes that she has no option other than to stay, fully aware that the abuse will escalate once she dares to seek help.

Living with an abuser is exhausting and anxiety-producing. But leaving carries its own set of uncertainties and fears. How will the victim survive financially? Will she have community support, or will she need to start life over with a whole new set of friends, new job, and new neighborhood? It is often the fear of the unknown and a victim's concern for the stability and well-being of her children that prevents her from leaving. A loving, supportive church family can truly be a blessing to victims who have to make this heart wrenching decision.

References

Alsdurf, J. & Alsdurf, P. (1998). *Battered into submission: The tragedy of wife abuse in the Christian home.* Eugene, OR: Wipf and Stock Publishers, 62.

Calvin's Work, Hughes translation, column 59.

Kinchlow, B. (1986). Straight Talk from Ben Kinchlow, Family Life Today, March Issue, 21.

Lockyer, H. (1977). *All the Women of the Bible.* Grand Rapids, MI: Zondervan.

Tieran, S. (1992). *Adventist Review,* April 2 Edition, 27.

Chapter 6

*"To him that knoweth to do good,
and doeth it not,
to him it is sin."*

James 4:17

WHAT YOU CAN DO TO END
DOMESTIC VIOLENCE AND ABUSE

Now that we have examined the face and character of domestic violence, the theoretical models, research, and relational dynamics, how can we apply this understanding on a practical level? The following paragraphs equip you with starting ideas for the design of a domestic abuse program at your church, and thoughts on how you might take a stand in your community to address this issue.

Gather Information About Domestic Violence and Abuse
Reach out to your community by contacting programs and centers that serve domestic abuse victims and their children. Continue your education in the area of domestic violence. There is always more to learn and understand. Read books, watch video tapes, and attend community awareness programs. Proactively assist in the work and services that provide safety, advocacy, support, and other critically important resources for victims as well as abusers. There will likely be times when your

own feelings about the violence may make it difficult for you to maintain involvement. When that happens, contact your local domestic violence hotline or crisis center and talk to their staff about your concerns. Domestic violence advocates can be an excellent source of support for you, a victim, or a perpetrator of domestic violence.

Give Her Information About Community Agencies

It is important for the victim to know that there are people who care about her circumstances, and who are standing ready to help her. Encourage her to seek assistance from programs and agencies already in place whose workers are trained and fully prepared to help her stay safe once she's made the decision to leave. Reassure her by offering to accompany her to her first appointment. Some victims are apprehensive about accessing community services but will do so with the loving, caring support of a friend. Tell her that you're there for her when she needs you. Provide transportation, child care, and financial assistance as feasible.

Support a Community Response

Rev. Marie M. Fortune, an ordained minister in the United Church of Christ, and Director of the Center for Prevention of Sexual and Domestic Violence writes, *"The crisis of family violence affects people physically, psychologically, and spiritually. Each of these dimensions must be addressed, both for victims and for those in the family who abuse them. Approached from either a secular or religious perspective alone, certain needs and issues tend to be disregarded. This reflects a serious lack of understanding of the nature of family violence and its impact on people's lives. Treatment of families experiencing violence and abuse requires integrating the needs of the whole person. Thus, the importance of developing a shared understanding and cooperation between secular and religious helpers to deal with family violence cannot be emphasized too strongly"* (Fortune, 2001).

Develop and Support A Church Response
In a crisis people tend to turn to those they believe can help them. Many opt to speak with their pastor. The choice of a pastor (or other church contact) to turn the victim away unaided will land a devastating blow to her heart, and her hopes for safety, healing, repentance, and restoration. The following suggestions provide a guide for those wanting to help in domestic abuse circumstances. It is in the best interest of everyone involved for local law enforcement and legal services to be consulted for assistance in obtaining protective or restraining orders and other related resources. We are responsible to obey the laws of the land in regards to protecting, reporting, and assisting victims and abusers.

Provide help for the Victim
1. We should never look the other way when we are aware of abuse occurring in the church. In so doing, we create a climate for justification of abuse. It is imperative that we take allegations seriously, and decisive action, immediately. The responsibility of church leaders and members is to provide safety first and ask questions later. Helping the victim find a safe place to stay is priority.

2. Give her the opportunity to talk with you independent of the abuser. If the abuser pursues her and/or refuses to allow her to speak with you alone, do not hesitate to call the police immediately. It is tempting to pass the responsibility to a marriage counselor, but marriage

(or couple) counseling cannot stop abuse. In marriage counseling, the "client" is the relationship, and the focus is on the dynamic interplay of a relational system in which each party has at least some influence and decision-making power. Marriage counseling assumes a level of flexibility and openness in the system. Domestic violence is qualitatively different. Domestic violence is not about relationship; it's about the arbitrary exercise of power and control.

3.   Advise her from the start that you will notify the proper authorities if you learn that she is suicidal, threatening harm to another, or you believe her life is in danger.

4.   Listen as she recounts the events that led her to this moment, and communicate emotional support without touching her, especially if you are male. If at all possible, arrange for a female third party to be present as you talk with the victim.

5.   If you are not trained in the area of domestic violence, refer her to someone who can be a healing resource. If you are not aware of any Christian helpers or programs, it is definitely better to refer her to a secular program than to encourage her to return to her abuser.

6.   Share Scriptures that affirm her. Do not misquote texts to imply that the responsibility for "fixing" the marriage, "providing her children with a father," or "converting" her abuser rests in her lap. Do not revictimize her by suggesting that she must have done something "to make him act that way" or to "push his buttons."

7.   Refrain from cliché statements, i.e., "Just pray about it," "God will give you the strength to endure," or "God will make a way of escape for you." She could interpret statements such as these to mean that you are encouraging her to go back and take the abuse. The fact that she escaped the abusive relationship proves her strength through God's great provision and protection, not her weakness.

8.   Examine your own beliefs before giving advice. Ask yourself the following questions:

- What is my history or experience with violence in my own family of origin?

- What are my thoughts regarding female roles, submission, and headship?

- What is my perception of domestic violence and abuse?

- How do I understand the Biblical interpretation of marriage, separation, and divorce?

- What are our moral imperatives regarding victim safety, and the provision of a stable, emotionally-healthy home environment?

9.   Help her find support as well as appropriate help for her children if she decides to stay with the abuser. Encourage her to develop a protection plan for herself and her family. Help her think through the steps she should take if/when her abuser becomes abusive again. Help her make a list of people she can call in the event

of an emergency. Suggest that she hide a suitcase of clothing, personal items, money, social security cards, the children's birth certificates, school records, and other important documents such as marriage certificate, tax records, Medicaid cards, pay stubs, credit card records, etc. This emergency suitcase should be hidden at a remote location with someone she trusts will not be deceived or manipulated by the abuser. Most victims are very aware that if they were to try to hide a suitcase (or anything else) at home, the abuser would definitely find it. She does not live with the illusion that she has any privacy or autonomy.

10.   She should be encouraged to make an extra set of keys, or leave keys, important papers and extra clothing with a friend or a trustworthy family member. She should identify transportation options should she need to escape quickly. She should create a signal with someone to let them know that "it's time," or "call the police." For example, one victim asked her neighbor to immediately contact the police if she turned her front porch light off and on three times.

11.   Offer her options in her search for safety, healing, and recovery. Options should include her continued education in areas of personal growth such as self-esteem, assertiveness, conflict resolution, family of origin issues, etc. Unless you are a trained therapist, do not try to perform domestic abuse counseling with a victim. You can explain to the victim that these issues are important to address with a therapist or counselor and that you are willing to be supportive by attending at least one counseling session with her, if needed.

12.   Assure her that she has shown strength and courage by coming to you for help and that you will be confidential nd prudent in helping her as appropriate. Secure her permission before you ask others for help. If you are male, be careful to arrange that you are not the only person assisting her. If she refuses to permit others to become involved, be very specific in letting her know how you can or cannot help.

13.   If she decides to return to the abuser, share with her your concerns for her safety and well being. Never condemn her for her decision. The victim can more accurately assess lethality than you. If you sense that she is making the decision to return without a careful evaluation of the evidence, gently remind her. If, after compassionately reviewing the facts, she still decides to return, let her know that you respect her decision and that you will offer whatever assistance you can if she needs you in the future.

14.   Help her to develop a safety plan for the future in the event she decides to leave and live apart from her abuser. Encourage her to file court papers for a personal protection order (PPO) or restraining order. Once the abuser is made aware of his legal constraints, advise her to document each time he violates the order, and to immediately call the police. She should alter her daily routines, change phone numbers, set house alarms, and rearrange furniture to block entrance or walkways, if necessary. (The sound of someone tripping over rearranged furniture could buy time to call 911 in the event of a nighttime break-in). She should ask neighbors

to call the police if they hear unusual noises in her home. She can ask a friend or family member to stay with her. Most significantly, she needs to keep contact with the outside world including neighbors, church members, family, and friends. Help her understand that she should leave when the abuser is not at home, and that she should not give any forewarning regarding her intention to leave!

15. If you are a service provider be sure to keep a record of your contacts with the victim (See Incident Report form in Appendix A).

16. Remember, if you are unsure about what to do refer, refer, refer!

Provide help for the Abuser

1. When a crisis occurs in your church, be honest. Secrecy only strengthens the hand of the perpetrator. If there is knowledge of family violence, credence should not be given to individuals who exhibit violent behaviors, present themselves as victims, and are skillful at soliciting sympathies from the church.

2. Speak directly and clearly to abusers and let them know that you do not approve of their abusive behavior. Body language, nodding or agreeing, and helping batterers to deny their abusive behavior is dangerous.

3. Our primary obligation is the safety and welfare of the victim, regardless of the position of the abuser.

4.   Hold the abuser accountable for his actions. Refer to programs designed to assist perpetrators. Do not enable him in:
   - *Minimizing his behavior:* "I only gave her a love tap" (You see her swollen eye or split lip.)
   - *Lying about his behavior:* "I have never abused my wife" (You visited her in the hospital a few months ago after he attacked her.)
   - *Rationalizing his behavior,* "I was stressed out."
   - *Allowing Blame - Shifting to wife, children, job:* "She pushed my buttons."
   - *Provide legal support:* by appearing in court as a character witness for him.

5.   If he is a church officer, suspend all leadership activities until he deals with his abusive behavior – threats, blame-shifting, and manipulation.

6.   It is not wise to perpetuate stereotypical beliefs. Anyone can be abusive or abused. If he is abusive, he must be held accountable, regardless of his strengths in other areas.

7.   Support him in accessing help and offer necessary services.

8.   Acknowledge your limits. Soberly assess your preparedness to intervene in domestic violence issues. If you are not trained, refer the abuser to someone who can be a healing resource.

9.   Give him hope to believe that he is not locked into his abusive behaviors. He can change if he wants to.

Show your support by praying for him, and attending counseling or group meetings with him, if appropriate.

10. Help him develop a safety plan that will deter or prevent further abuse. The safety plan should include the following:

- Taking a time out (leaving the situation when he recognizes he is becoming angry, and learning to effectively de-escalate his feelings.)
- Calling someone to whom he can be accountable.
- Attending a batterer's treatment group
- Attending other classes that focus on family of origin issues, stress management, self-esteem, anger management, conflict resolution, and gender role issues.

11. Keep records/documentation of your interactions. (See Incident Report Form in Appendix A)

12. Do not attempt to provide counseling or other services which lie beyond your own competency or training.

13. Remember, if you are unsure about what to do refer, refer, refer!

General Assistance:
1. Follow state reporting laws related to child abuse, elder abuse, and domestic violence.

2. Think carefully about priorities – the saving of souls and safety of people are ministry activities that rank above preserving the church's image.

3.   Provide continuing domestic violence education in your church and community. Break the code of silence and raise awareness through the use of brochures, articles, bulletin inserts, videos, sermons, and educational programs for the church and community.

4.   Become aware of community resources and the best ways to expedite access. Create a resource and referral list for the church, pastor(s), and staff.

5.   Address the long-term impact of abuse on victims, children, and perpetrators in reference to religious beliefs and teachings.

6.   Reexamine teachings that predispose Adventist Christians to abuse and violence.

7.   Instead of relocating a conference-employed family mired in domestic violence, facilitate professional involvement for every member of the family. Without intervention, the problem will simply be transferred to a new location.

8.   Support initiatives to supply resources for victims and children. For example, establish an assistance fund that can be used at the discretion of the church for this purpose. Some initiatives include:
  o   Individual and group counseling
  o   Emergency housing
  o   Emergency transportation
  o   Food
  o   Clothing

      o Legal advocacy
      o Residence at a Seventh-day Adventist or other Christian shelter

9.   Organize conferences, workshops, and seminars to provide ongoing education and support for church leaders.

10.   Develop a church protocol and/or policy to protect victims as well as perpetrators.

ABUSE IS LEARNED BEHAVIOR.
WITHOUT INTERVENTION,
THERE IS *USUALLY* A NEXT TIME.

References

Domestic Abuse Intervention Project (n.d.). *Power and Control Wheel.* Duluth, MN: 206 West Fourth Street, (208) 722-4134.

Fortune, M. (2001). *A commentary on religious issues in family violence.* Seattle, WA: Center for the Prevention of Sexual and Domestic Violence.

DOMESTIC VIOLENCE EQUALITY WHEEL
(Used by permission)

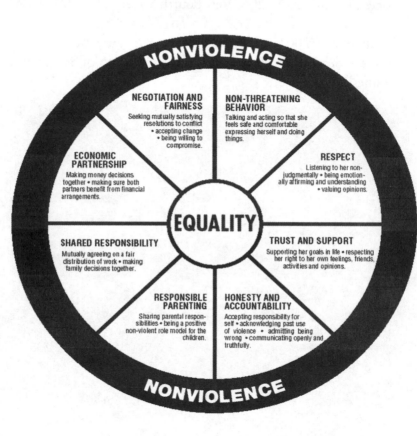

DOMESTIC ABUSE INTERVENTION PROJECT
202 East Superior Street
Duluth, Minnesota 55802
218-722-2781

Figure 5

Part 2

Texts and their Contexts:
Abuse and the Scriptures

◆

Chapter 7

*"People generally have enough common sense to
determine what is right
and wrong, and so do you.
You know what behavior heaven approves
and what behavior it doesn't approve"*
Matthew 18:18 (The Clear Word).

"A man without self control is like a city without protection"
Proverbs 25:28 (The Clear Word).

ABUSE AND THE SCRIPTURES
Physical Abuse

Many of us have heard messages about who we are (not good
enough), where we came from (product of evolution), what
we should think and believe (what people in authority tell us)
and what we should do (put self aside and always seek to please
others). These messages help determine our self concept and
the position we take in relationships. For instance, if I don't
feel that I am good enough, I might believe that everyone else is
better than I am. So I live my life trying to measure up to their
expectations or change my identity to be someone I am not.

If I believe that I am not created in the image of God and of inestimable worth to Him, that I am not a prince or princess, I might not value who I am and may allow people to treat me in any way. If I believe that people in authority always have the right answers and their opinions are better than mine, I might not think of myself as being intelligent and allow their thoughts and concepts to condition my opinions to the point that I merely reflect their thoughts and beliefs. If I believe that my purpose on earth is to please others and take care of them, then I might not take care of myself and never explore, or accomplish anything that is new, different, or creative.

As we have discussed in the first section of this manual, there are times when ministers, church leaders, and members quote texts that can inadvertently lead to, purposely condone and/or perpetuate a course of conduct in relationships that robs individuals of their uniqueness, spontaneity, creativity, and individuality. This course leads to abusive and controlling behaviors in relationships. We will now examine some of the Biblical passages that have been used to support various relational styles that we believe fall short of the ideal that was envisioned in Eden.

Before we start, let me ask you a question… Have you heard of the saying, "You see what you look for?" This phrase applies in many areas including interpretation of scripture. There are individuals who can "read into," "twist" or even "enlarge" on what a Biblical writer originally intended in order to justify their perspectives on behaviors that sanction their agenda for power and control over others.

We would like to challenge you to journey with us as we endeavor to discover additional insight into some Bible passages that have been misused and misinterpreted to justify various types of abuse. We must approach the Bible from the viewpoint of finding what God is trying to say instead of what we are trying to prove. We also need to approach it as a learner asking, "Lord, what are you saying to me in this text or passage?" In contrast, some individuals have searched the Bible with this approach: "Let me see what text I can find to prove my point." When we study the Bible we need to approach it with open sincere minds; we need to be prepared to let the Bible and its authors talk to us. As we do so, here are some simple guidelines that we would like for you to take into consideration:

1. Accept the Bible just as it reads, with the exception of times when a figure of speech is being used by the author. When the authors wrote their messages, they wrote so that the intended readers would understand. As with us, they too used figures of speech to convey thoughts and feelings beyond the actual words. It is by observation and comparison that these grammatical tools are recognized.

2. Explain the thought or passage according to its obvious meaning. Based on the preceding thought, we, the readers, should be careful to convey the thought expressed in the passage based on its logical meaning. In other words, use common sense.

3. Consider the immediate and enlarged context of the passage. In order to correctly interpret the text under consideration, we must not only look at the immediate thought, we need to look at how what is being said fits into the larger context.

4. Consider the nature, personality, historical setting, and the purpose for which the author was writing. Think about the specific audience for which the passages were written. Were their customs and beliefs similar to ours? Did their context support the same interpretation of the author's words as our context does today?

Using these important rules, we will now examine some texts that are often quoted by abusers to support or justify their controlling and abusive behaviors, particularly in reference to physical abuse.

As we examine each text we will explore the following questions:
1. What is the speaker talking about?
2. What is the speaker saying about the topic?
3. What does the text/passage mean?
4. How does 'what is said or meant' relate to the experience of abuse and domestic violence?

Genesis 3:16

*"Unto the woman He said, I will greatly multiply thy sorrow and thy conception; in sorrow thou shalt bring forth children; and thy desire shall be to thy husband, and **he shall rule over thee**."*

What is the speaker talking about?

To ascertain the true meaning of this passage, we must apply the principles of interpretation, that is, to accept Biblical passages just as they read. So what is being talked about in Genesis 3:16? The immediate context is chapter 3:14-19. The enlarged context is chapter 3:1-21. Therefore, the immediate subject is the punishment of the serpent and Eve. Taking the Bible literally, with the exception of the figure of speech that is being used, we see in Genesis 3:15 that God is speaking to the serpent saying that He will put variance between the serpent (the devil) and the woman (Eve). This variance or disagreement will extend to the seed or followers/children of the devil (John 8:44; Acts 13:10) and the seed or followers of the woman/Eve, the church (Jer.6:2). "It," the seed of the woman, (here in the singular, therefore an individual member of the church, i.e. Christ), shall bruise/crush Satan's head, not the heads of the followers of Satan.

What does the speaker say about the topic?
The woman's conception and delivery of children would be a very sorrowful experience. Though experiencing the pains of conception and childbirth, the woman would still feel an intense desire (Heb.- t@shuwqah/tesh-oo-kaw: stretching[1] out after; a longing) for her husband. Having impaired her heaven born status of being a "helpmeet" and having an intense desire for her husband, she will now be ruled [Heb. mashal, maw-shal[2] , a primitive root; to rule: (have, make to have dominion, governor, reign, bear, have ruling, have power over) by her husband.

---

[1] Strong, James. *Strong's Exhaustive Concordance of the Bible*. Nashville, TN: Crusade Bible Publishers, 1980, p., 126.

[2] Ibid, page 74.

What does the text mean?

Based on the larger context of Adam and Eve's sin, God would instill within the minds of Satan's and Eve's heritage a variance that will not permit them to live in harmony. One of her seed, Christ, the Messiah, will crush the serpent's (Satan's) head and the serpent shall bruise the heel of Christ, the Messiah. For the immediate text under consideration, Eve and all women shall:

a. Have sorrowful experiences associated with both conception and child delivery,

b. Have a longing after or desire for their husbands,

c. Their husbands shall rule (have power over them) because of their longing/desire after them (husbands)

How does what is said relate to the experience of abuse or domestic violence? It is important to note that the statement, "He shall rule over thee" is predictive in nature in that it will happen as a result of the woman's desire or longing for her husband. This was not a statement that it was God's will for the husband to become ruler, or that the status of ruler was arbitrarily conferred as a result of sin. Therefore a woman's husband will end up governing her because she will have an intense desire for him as seen in her strong tendency to please and care for him. As with the pronouncement relating to the serpent, so too with Eve and all wives, it is predictive. (See Gen. 4:7, 24:2, and 37:8 for examples of how the concept of 'rulership' is viewed). In all cases, the rulership or lordship was not arbitrary. It was a rulership within parameters of stewardship and respect of the person, their property, and individual rights. This type of rulership is reflected in the life, ministry, and Lordship of Christ over the church (Col. 3:18-19; Eph. 5:25-30).

The wife's individual rights and individual stewardship to God takes precedence over her subjugation to others. Beyond this, in Christianity, women are viewed as being on the same plane as men with regards to the blessings of the gospel (Gal. 3:28) and are joint heirs to the kingdom (James 2:5; and Titus 3:7). The rulership of man is conditioned by his relationship to and expression of Christ. His governorship is occasioned by the wife's desire after him and is in accordance with the God ordained prerogative granted to each wife at creation. When God created the first couple, He made both of them "in His image" (Gen. 1:27), blessed both of them with power akin to Himself (Gen. 1:28), and invested them jointly with the responsibility "to be fruitful, multiply, replenish, and have dominion over the earth" (Gen. 1:26-28). From the beginning, both the husband and the wife were on equal ground, bequeathed with skills, powers, and responsibilities as stewards and managers.

Matthew 5:11, 12
"Blessed are ye, when men shall revile you, and persecute you, and shall say all manner of evil...rejoice, and be exceeding glad: for great is your reward in heaven: for so persecuted they the prophets which were before you."

What is the speaker talking about?
The enlarged context is the Sermon on the Mount of Matthew 5:1-7:27 where Jesus shares with His disciples what the character and life of the 'citizens of His Kingdom' are to be. The immediate context is the Beatitudes (Blessings or 'happy' sayings) of Matt. 5:3-12. In verses 11 and 12, Jesus is specifically talking about the blessings of being reviled and persecuted.

What did He say about the subject of being reviled and persecuted? Citizens of His Kingdom, male and female, are blessed when men do three things:

A. Revile them,
B. Persecute them,
C. Say all types of evil[3] things against them falsely for Christ's sake.

What does the speaker say about the topic?
Citizens of the kingdom are blessed when they are persecuted. These Christians should respond by rejoicing and being very happy. This response is warranted based on the fact that (1) they will be rewarded in heaven, and (2) the occurrence identifies them with the prophets who suffered persecution like them, and is in line with the nature of the conflict with evil.

Two verbs are crucial here: Gr. 'oneidizo' translated 'revile' means to defame, that is to rail at, chide, taunt, suffer reproach, upbraid. The evident confrontation is verbal, not physical, in nature. Gr. 'dioko' translated 'persecute' means 'to pursue" (literally or figuratively), by implication to persecute. The tenor of this verb is one that implies and emphasizes some type of movement that the Believer is 'being pursued' as opposed to the idea of one 'living with' another.

---

[3] Gk. 'poneros,' hurtful, i.e. evil (properly, in effect or influence). In the spirit of the kingdom this would include anything vicious, malicious, grievous, harmful, lewd, and wicked.

What does the text mean?
Citizens of the Kingdom are blessed when they experience negative verbal comments and accusations and are further pursued with the intent of doing harm as was experienced by the prophets.

How does what is said relate to the experience of abuse or domestic violence? Jesus, in outlining the principles of His kingdom and addressing all who intend on being a part of that kingdom, informs them that they are 'blessed' when they are hurt by what is wrongly said about them. This is true also when they are wrongly represented and pursued by those who are not part of His Kingdom. More than this, the three actions (revile, persecute, and say evil) are occasioned by the modifier 'for my sake.' Therefore the reason for the three actions is rooted in the believer's association with the speaker, Jesus, and not with the person to whom the believer is married.

Of note also is the fact that the nature and manner of persecution is likened to that which the prophets experienced. One needs only to look at the life experiences of the prophets to see that the passage under consideration does not address itself to domestic abuse occasioned by filial relationships or interactions.

Matthew 5:24
"Leave there thy gift before the altar, and go thy way; first be reconciled to thy brother, and then come and offer thy gift."

What is the speaker talking about?

Matthew is stating here that the subjects of God's kingdom were told that they should not kill and if a person did, they would be in danger of the judgment. For the subjects of His Kingdom, being angry[4] with a brother[5] is incorporated in the spirit of killing. Saying derogative things[6] that influence an individual's self-worth places the speaker in danger of hell fire. In the light of this, if one comes to worship and remembers that a brother has anything against the bearer of the gift, he should leave his gift that he brought as an act of worship at the altar, go find his brother and endeavor to be reconciled to him, and then come and worship, presenting his gift.

What does the speaker say about the topic:

A. For the subjects of His Kingdom, being 'angry' with a 'brother' is incorporated in the spirit of killing.

B. Saying 'derogatory things' that influence an individual's self-worth place the speaker in danger of hell fire.

C. In the light of the above, if one comes to worship and remembers that a brother has anything against the bearer of the gift, he should leave his gift that he brought as an act of worship at the altar.

D. Go find his brother and endeavor to be reconciled to him and then come and worship, presenting his gift.

---

[4] Gk. 'orgizo,' to provoke or enrage, i.e. (passively) become exasperated: be angry (wroth); from a root that suggests violent passion.

[5] Gr. 'adelphos.' meaning a brother (literally or figuratively) near or remote: brother.

[6] Gr. 'rhak-ah' of Chaldee origin; carrying the sentiment of 'O empty one,' i.e. thou worthless (as a term of utter vilification): Raca; and 'thou fool' Gk. 'mo-ros' dull or stupid (as if shut up), i.e. heedless, (morally) blockhead, (apparently) absurd: (moron).

What does it mean?

The entire inference of verses 22-24 is couched in the context of "thou shall not kill." Only the Owner, Creator God—not the spouse—has the right to take life. A married couple is entrusted to each other under God, but the Creator maintains the sovereign rite of 'ownership' and 'life.' A Believer should not be angry with any other subject of the Kingdom, nor should he verbalize anything that is derogatory or infers anything less in worth than what the Creator establishes. If he does, he is answerable to God (represented by 'the judgment, the council, fire of hell' vs. 22.), and reveals the moral corruption of his heart.

How does what is said relate to the experience of abuse or domestic violence? Jesus encourages us to remember that true worship of God can be experienced only as we have a reconciliatory disposition. Verse 23 makes it clear that the innocent need to take action as well as the offending party (vs. 25-26). Properly understood, Jesus is addressing the act and spirit of 'killing.' He is not talking about intimate relationships. There is nothing in these verses to suggest that an innocent spouse is expected to go back into an abusive relationship, a relationship characterized by cycles of tension, explosion, and respite. True reconciliation is evidenced by a changed heart and is lived out in the life for all to see. At the least, this reconciliation in Matthew 5:23-26 is not a change on the part of one party induced by an action on the part of another, but rather an exchange in cases of **mutual** hostility yielding to **mutual** concession. Can this be said of most domestic violence or abuse cases?

1 Timothy 2:12
"For I suffer not a woman to teach,
nor to usurp authority over the man,
but to be in silence."[7]

1. What is the speaker talking about?

Paul begins I Timothy, chapter 2 by encouraging Timothy to pray for everyone, and in particular for those in authority. The reason for which is seen in verse 2: "That **we may lead** a quiet and peaceable life in all holiness and honesty." Verse 3 gives the support for the believer's aspiration to 'lead a...life,' and verses 4-6 substantiate the rationality in the light of God's overall will.

In verses 7 and 8 Paul affirms his call to ministry and on that basis appeals to men to pray everywhere. Then from verses 9-15 he appeals to women to do their part in "leading a quiet and peaceable life" (i.e. how to dress and behave). Specifically as it relates to vs. 12, Paul is talking about 'leading a quiet and peaceable life' as evidenced in the life of the church.

What does the speaker say about the topic?

Paul desires women not to teach in the church. He also desires that women not exercise authority over a man and that they keep silent in the church. Based on our understanding of what this is saying, it would seem that it is God's will for women to occupy a lower or inferior position in life. But is this so? The sincere inquirer must ask these relevant questions:

---

[7] It is of the gravest importance to utilize the interpretive principle: Consider the nature, personality, and the time of the person and the purpose for which he/she was writing.

1.   Was Paul expressing a principle or law that was the universal will of God?
2.   Why did Paul give this advice?

Once again we must let the Bible interpret itself. Notice the tone of the passage. Paul begins chapter 2:1 with the words, "I exhort." This word translated 'exhort' conveys the idea of encourage'[8] as in advise. Then in verse 8, he says "I will"[9] suggesting the idea of 'I am minded...' Further the construction of the word is the 'reflexive middle indicative' portraying the result of the action being realized by the participation of the speaker. In other words, it was Paul's will or desire. If there is any realization of 'praying everywhere' it is because of Paul's 'mindedness,' not God's will.

As Paul shifts his council to the women in verse 9, there is the same tone of "it's my will." This is conveyed by his use of the phrase, "in like manner."[10] Under the same conditions and in the same way, he now advises the women. This is further supported by his choice of "let the women"[11] and "but I suffer not"[12] in verses 11 and 12 respectively. Evidently in Paul's thinking it was not wise to "turn a corner" by deviating from a norm that was practiced at the time.

---

[8] Gr. 'Parakaleo,' to call near, i.e. invite, invoke (by imploration) beseech, call for, be of good comfort, desire, (give) exhort(-ation), entreat, pray.

[9] Gr. 'Boulomai,' pronounced: 'boo'-lom-ahee,' be willing, be disposed, minded.

[10] Gr. 'Hosautos,' pronounced, 'ho-sow'-toce' meaning 'in the same way,' or 'likewise, after the same (in like) manner.'

[11] 3rd person singular present imperative. This is an action that is being encouraged to continue, i.e. 'let her continue to learn in silence.' It was something that was in practice before.

[12] This carries the idea of Paul saying, 'I am not going to turn this corner.' Gr. 'epitrepo', pronounced, ep-ee-trep'-o, to turn over (transfer), i.e. allow: give leave (liberty, license), let, permit, suffer.

How do we know that the tone of Paul's advice is not a Biblical injunction to be upheld throughout Christendom? We know it is not a divine command because there is no passage in the entire Old Testament that tells us that women have to "learn in silence" or that it is not right for a "woman to teach, or usurp authority over a man." If that were the case, why is there no additional evidence in other Pauline Epistles or New Testament writings? Of particular interest is the fact that the word 'woman' here refers to a 'wife.'[13] It was not a custom for 'wives' to....etc.

This is further supported by the counter play between the words 'woman' and 'man'[14] in verse 12. Woman being understood to imply a 'wife' is set against 'man as in 'husband.' This too alludes to the advice in verses 9-15 being given in the context of a husband-wife relationship and in particularly, vs. 11 where a wife is encouraged to learn in silence or stillness[15] while assuming an appropriate role: one of subordination, or subjection.

---

[13] Gr. 'goo-nay' a woman; specially, a wife: wife, woman.

[14] A man (properly as an individual male): fellow, husband (Matt. 1:16, 19; Mark 10:12), man, sir as compared to the Greek 'anthropos' man-faced, i.e. a human being: male or female.

[15] stillness, i.e. desistance from bustle or language: quietness, silence. This word is used in Acts 22:2 and 2 Th. 3:12. In both instances, it does not imply silence as in no verbalized communication. It is believed to be from a feminine form: properly, keeping one's seat (sedentary), i.e. (by implication) still (undisturbed, undisturbing): peaceable, quiet. It was lawful for men in public assemblies to ask questions, or even interrupt the speaker when there was any matter in his speech which they did not understand; but this liberty was not granted to women.

[16] Eve's sin is called a 'transgression' which basically means 'to go contrary to,' i.e. violate a command. Said of Adam also in Rom 5:14.

We are now compelled to look at the phrase in vs. 12 'usurp authority over a man.' Notice that this phrase is a part of Paul's 'It is my desire, wish, will' statements, indicating that it is advisory in nature. 'Usurp' comes from the Greek word ' auyentew' pronounced 'ow-then-the'-o' and carries with it the thought of 'a worker acting on oneself' (i.e. figuratively dominate: usurp authority over). It suggests that a wife should not work on her own, or independent of the man or husband. Paul then proceeds to give plausible reasons for this advice: The man was made before the woman. Adam was not deceived 'but the woman being deceived was in transgression.'

What does it mean?

Once again, the interpreter must ask if the first reason is verified in the writings of other authors, or was Paul suggesting something else besides the actual words used? Nowhere do we find in the Bible that women are to be ruled by men because she was brought into existence after him. We do find in the Hebrew mind, 'the right of the first born' but it cuts across gender or sex. Logic suggests that just as the Bible links sin's reign on earth to Adam, so too, if there is any 'penalty' for sin, it should rest on the individual who consciously chose to violate the Divine precepts.[16]

It would seem that the Genesis pronouncement of "Eve's desire being towards her husband" (Gen. 3:16) as a safety catch to her 'transgression' or 'going aside' (vs. 14) was what Paul is alluding to here. This would coincide with the Divine mind in making a help meet for the man.

She was taken from his side, a physiological message, indicating that in the Creator's mind the woman was not to rule over the man or the man over the woman. God's intent was that the first couple, in recognizing their stewardship, should maintain a mutual relationship of respect, support, and love expressed in the uniqueness of each of their personalities and gifts.

This leads us to ask if Paul was trying to give some credence to an established Roman norm regarding relationships between men and women.[17] It would seem so.

Therefore what Paul was saying is that it is expedient for the new Christian community to observe the established protocol as it relates to male-female communication as a means of achieving the goal mentioned in verse 2: "That we may lead a quiet and peaceable life in all holiness and honesty." This is further supported by the SDA Bible Commentary when it says, "Because of the general lack of private and public rights then accorded women, Paul felt it to be expedient to give this counsel to the church. Any severe breach of accepted social custom brings reproach upon the church. Christians should avoid even the appearance of evil (1 Thess. 5:22)."

---

[17] A woman should attempt nothing, either in public or private, that belongs to a man as his peculiar function. This was prohibited by the Roman laws: In multis juris nostril articulis deterior est condition foeminarum quam masculorum,; 1.9, PAP. LIB. 31, QUAEST. Foeminoe ab omnibus officiis civilibus vel publicis remotae sunt; et ideo nec judicis esse possunt, nec magistratum gerere, nec postulare, nec pro alio invenire, nec procurators existere; 1.2, de Reg. Juris. ULP. LIB. i. AD SAB.-Vid. POTH. Pand. Justin., vol. i. p. 13.

How does what is said relate to the experience of abuse or domestic violence? Individuals who are bent on making the Bible say what it is not saying or who are determined to control the opposite sex use this passage to support their need for power and control. Was this advice to be understood and practiced unequivocally? It would seem not. This would contradict the Biblical position of female leadership as supported by both the Old Testament (Joel 2:28-32) and the New Testament (1 Corinthians 12: 4-11). No. To the contrary, the Bible empowers women to use their gifts consistent with the need of the church, the community, and in other areas orchestrated by God.

Paul is simply appealing to the believers to make the best of social norms expressed in prevailing societal demands for the purpose of the corporate witness of the church. His witness involves the unity of believers and the task of missions and should supersede evolving social climate. Conclusively, the setting is clear. This was advice to be practiced in a worship setting and merely encouraged what was considered appropriate behavior at the time.

I Peter 4:12, 13

"Beloved, think it not strange concerning the fiery trial which is to try you, as though some strange thing happened unto you: But rejoice, inasmuch as ye are partakers of Christ's sufferings, that, when his glory shall be revealed, ye may be glad also with exceeding joy."

What is the speaker talking about?
The heart of this Pastoral Epistle is Peter's loving concern about the Believers' awareness of the troublesome times in which they were living in the light of the perils of persecution. The passage

under consideration (4:12, 13) is nested in Peter's appeal to exercise Christlike control (4:1-6), soberness and charitable living (4:7-11) in the face of imminent 'fiery trial;' en route to being true and steadfast while being persecuted (4:12-19).

What does the author say about the topic?

We should not think it strange[18] when we experience fiery[19] trials that are sent to try us. To the contrary, we should be happy because when we are tried by fiery trials, we are partakers of Christ's suffering. This will enable us to have a joyous experience when Christ's glory shall be revealed.

What does the text mean?

In the cosmic conflict between good and evil, Christ and Satan, believers should expect to experience burning trials. They need to have a mindset that recognizes this imminent conflict, view the experience as a precious opportunity to participate in their Master's suffering, and look forward to joy unspeakable when Christ is glorified. God permits Satan to try the faithful believers' characters. Further, the sufferings that we go through in this life are not sent by God. He permits them and will override them if it is in accordance with His will, therefore making them the means of developing character in His children (See Job 42:5; Psalm 38:3; Psalm 39:9). Christians can rejoice because they know that they will not be called upon to endure more than Christ suffered (Heb. 2:18; 4:15, 16).

How does what is said or meant relate to the experience of abuse or domestic violence? These passages do not suggest that God supports women being subjected to physical abuse in any way as an acceptable matrimonial lifestyle.

---

[18] Literally, "do not continue to be astounded."

Under the new covenant banner, and in the light of the universal priesthood of all believers, all human entities are equal in Christ. Properly understood, the context of each passage makes this perfectly clear. The expressions and responsibilities of each gender may differ, but all are under solemn obligation to maintain a stewardship relationship with their Maker. Prudence, in the light of persecution and culture, may influence the expressions of this relationship, but the principles must never be violated.

The stewardship concept compels believers to view their bodies as the property of God (1 Cor. 6:13, 19-20). He/she is responsible to the Creator for the maintenance and use of the body to the glory of God. Not only is there 'possession' but there is also a 'residing or indwelling' of the body by the Holy Spirit. The Divine record plainly states that our bodies are the temple of the Holy Spirit (1 Cor. 3:16-17). A proper understanding of individual stewardship dictates that we are not to defile[20] our bodies[21] or permit them to be defiled.[22] When a woman permits anyone to abuse God's body temple, she is falling short of her sacred trust as a steward.

---

[19] Gr. 'Purosis' meaning 'a burning or scorching.' Increasing Jewish and Roman harassment was only a prelude to Nero's fierce persecutions. *Strong's Exhaustive Concordance of the Bible*, p. 63

[20] *Strong's Exhaustive Concordance of the Bible*, p. 75 on 'defile' says its from Gr. 'fyeirw' pronounced 'fthi'-ro' probably strengthened from phthio (to pine or waste); properly, to shrivel or wither, i.e. to spoil (by any process) or (generally) to ruin (especially figuratively, by moral influences, to deprave): corrupt (self), defile, destroy.

[21] Nichol, Francis D. *The Seventh-day Adventist Bible Commentary*, Vol. 6 Washington, D.C.: Review and Herald Publishing Association, 1978. Commenting on 1 Cor. 6:19 states: Because they are the members of Christ (v. 15) and temples of the Holy Spirit, which is given to us by God (see John 14:16, 17), every sin that is committed against our bodies is a sin against our Maker and against the Holy Spirit.

Who has the final authority? Is a woman answerable to her husband or to her Creator? To put it bluntly, the Christian woman should not encourage or permit any one to punch, push, shove, hit, choke, pull hair, pinch, kick, grab, beat, throw down, scratch, or otherwise wound her.

Power, control, and unquestioned authority: these are the issues. In the beginning, authority (the right to be and act) was equally delegated to Adam and Eve. Power and control was also imparted to the pair in harmony with their respective endowments and proportionate to their growth or development. Absolute authority, control, and ownership are always retained by God.

Beyond this, the believer's obligation and duty to his/her Maker takes precedence over any human commitment. Wedding vows, pledges, and promises involving blind unconditional commitment to a human being must give way to the higher call of God.

---

[22] The above writer commenting on 1 Cor. 6:20 "glorify God in your body" says this: "Because men have been redeemed from eternal death, it is their duty to do all in their power to keep their bodies in the best condition, so that they may best glorify God by serving Him acceptably (see CH 40, 41, 73, 74). An understanding of physiology, anatomy, and the laws of health is necessary if the body is to be taken care of intelligently (see CH 38; FE 321; COL 348).

The Christian is to do all he/she can to remain true to the wedding vows and to maintain peace in the home[23], but never to give up his/her right 'to be and to act.' The power and control elements in a relationship are rooted in Adam and Eve's attempt to blame and not take responsibility for their sinful actions.

Could it be that those who propose any other standard than mutuality are dwelling in the arena of blaming and irresponsibility? Christ desires us to operate in the same redemptive status here on this earth where there should be no power and control issues of male or female; where together they are looking forward to being joint heirs and citizens of His coming kingdom. May God help us to keep our bodies as near as possible to the perfection of Eden before the Fall, and recognize His glory and power through male and female.

---

[23] Commenting on *'As much as lieth in you'* in Rom 12:18, *The Seventh-day Adventist Bible Commentary* Vol. 6 says: "as to that which proceeds from you," meaning, "so far as it depends on you." ... So far as the Christian is concerned, he is to do everything he can to maintain peace. But there are times when fidelity to principle may necessitate his incurring the antagonism of others. Therefore Paul adds the qualification, "if it be possible." The record of Paul's own life, which was one of almost constant conflict, shows that it is not always possible to be at peace. In a world whose prince is Satan, soldiers of Christ must not expect that all will be peace. Nevertheless, the Christian must see to it that whenever the peace is broken, it is not his fault.

Additional Comments by Ellen G. White

"Both husband and wife should be willing to yield his or her way or opinion. There is no possibility of happiness while they both persist in doing as they please". (*Manuscript 3*, 1911).

"The Lord Jesus has not been correctly represented in His relation to the church by many husbands in their relation to their wives, for they do not keep the way of the Lord. They declare that their wives must be subject to them in everything. But it was not the design of God that the husband should have control, as head of the house, when he himself does not submit to Christ. He must be under the rule of Christ that he may represent the relation of Christ to the church. If he is a coarse, rough, boisterous, egotistical, harsh, and overbearing man, let him never utter the word that the husband is the head of the wife, and that she must submit to him in everything; for he is not the Lord, he is not the husband in the true significance of the term. . . ." (*Adventist Home* p. 117).

"Those who at any supposed provocation feel at liberty to indulge anger or resentment are opening the heart to Satan. Bitterness and animosity must be banished from the soul if we would be in harmony with heaven". (*Desire of Ages*, p. 30).

"He who will abuse animals because he has them in his power, is both a coward and a tyrant... Many do not realize that their cruelty will ever be known, because the poor dumb animals cannot reveal it. But could the eyes of these men be opened, as were those of Balaam, they would see an angel of God standing as a witness to testify against them in the courts above. A record goes up to heaven, and a day is coming when judgment will be pronounced against those who abuse God's creatures". (*Patriarchs and Prophets*, p. 443).

"Be kind in speech and gentle in action, giving up your own wishes. Watch well your words, for they have a powerful influence for good or ill. Allow no sharpness to come into your voices. Bring into your united life the fragrance of Christlikeness" (*Testimonies for the Church*, Vol. 7. p. 47).

"Cultivate a kind, conciliatory spirit and let no feeling of retaliation come into your minds and hearts" (*Testimonies for the Church*, Vol. 5, p. 331).

"Practical home life is the great test of character. By his tender thoughtfulness in the home, by the exercise of patience, kindness, and love, a man determines his character (Letter 17, 1895).

"The Lord has constituted the husband the head of the wife to be her protector, he is the house-band of the family, binding the members together, even as Christ is the head of the church and the Savior of the mystical body. Let every husband who claims to love God, carefully study the requirements of God in his position. Christ's authority is exercised in wisdom, in all kindness and gentleness, so let the husband exercise his power and imitate the great Head of the church" (*Adventist Home*, p. 215).

"Actual wrong should be made to appear just as sinful as it is, and a firm, decided course should be pursued to prevent its recurrence...." (*Child Guidance*, p. 279).

◆

Chapter 8

*What? Know ye not that your body is the temple of the
Holy Ghost which is in you,
which ye have of God, and ye are not your own?
For ye are bought with a price: therefore glorify God in your
body, and in your spirit, which are God's*
(I Corinthians 6:19, 20).
*So ought men to love their wives as their own bodies.
He that loveth his wife loveth himself*
(Ephesians 5: 28).

ABUSE AND THE SCRIPTURES
Sexual Abuse

Sexual abuse is said to occur when... 1) one partner compels
the other to do sexual things against his or her will or, 2) physically attacks the sexual parts of that person's body, or 3) treats
a partner like a sex object, or 4) makes innuendoes, negative
comments about the partner's body, or 5) engages in any inappropriate form of touching from hugging to raping. Milder and
not as physically intrusive abuse occurs when 6) one threatens
to have an affair if sexual demands are not satisfied.

Messages Used to Support Sexual Abuse:
1.   "Women are subject unto their own husbands."
2.   "The husband needs to meet whatever sexual fantasies he has because the Bible says that the "marriage bed is honorable and undefiled."
3.   "If women don't take care of their men, there are other women who will."
4.   "If women would satisfy their husband/s sexual needs there will be less adultery."
5.   "The woman has no right to refuse her husband because she belongs to him."
We will now examine the following texts and how they are used to condone or perpetuate sexual abuse:

Ephesians 5:22-24
"Wives, submit yourselves unto your own husbands."

What is the speaker talking about?
Many husbands use this text to support their "claimed right" and desire to have sexual access to and control over their wives. When Paul wrote this letter to the Ephesians, murder, luxury, and licentiousness were rampant during this period of the Roman Emperor Nero's reign. Paul was writing to the multinational Ephesian church. The Jews and Gentiles, Asiatics and Europeans, slaves and freemen, who composed the church, needed a message that addressed the resultant diversity. Unity within the church, the family, and across races or cultures within that early group of believers was of utmost importance. "The restoration of individual unity in the life of each believer assures the unity of God's universe. The theme of unity is implicit, where it is not explicit, throughout the book."[24]

---

[24] Nichol, Francis D., *The Seventh-day Adventist Bible Commentary*, Vol. 6, p. 995.

What does the speaker say about the topic?

A close study of Ephesians 5 reveals that this portion of the message was part of Paul's larger[25] practical counsel (4:1-6:20) dealing with the foundation of a united ministry cradled in the gifts of the Spirit and the outworking of a reformed life. Beginning with verse 15, Paul turns his attention to home relationships. What is Paul talking about when he said in Ephesians 5:22, "Wives, submit yourselves unto your own husbands, as unto the Lord?" The context makes it clear that the subject of verses 15-33 is "walking circumspectly in light of the evil times in which they were living."

What does it mean?

1. The readers need to be wise, understanding the will of God (5:17).
2. The readers should be filled with the Spirit instead of being filled with wine (5:18).
3. The readers should encourage each other through music and continual praise (5:19-20).
4. The readers should mutually submit to each other (5:21).
5. The construction of 'submit yourselves' suggest that Paul is saying that wives should utilize their choice and/or will as they submit to their own husbands (5:22-24). The action is a reflexive action in that the wife is in volitional control of how her own body performs that act.
6. Husbands should love their wives as Christ loved the Church (5:25-33).

---

[25] 'Love' is the motivating factor for all actions. The use of 'Therefore' in verse 1 of chapter 5, supports the idea that Paul is tying the previous chapter to this chapter. Hence, he is saying "in the light of my exhortation to mutually love each other, imitate Christ by loving in the following way..."

Remembering the multi-ethnic composition of the church in Ephesus, and his cry for the restoration of individual, family, ecclesiastical, and ethnic unity in the life of each believer, Paul now calls for behavior that assures the inclusive unity of God's universe. What should characterize this behavior? First of all, notwithstanding the ethnic diversity, believers needed to conduct themselves in a circumspect and wise manner. Secondly, they needed to live in such a manner that it would be considered as 'redeeming the times.' This especially in the light of the uncertain, dangerous period in which they were living. Thirdly, they needed to be filled with the Spirit.

Then Paul advised all, both men and women to be mutually submitted[26] to each other. This is not a submission demanded by one of another. Rather, the construction literally carries the idea of being in subjection to oneself in an attempt to place oneself under another. The reflexive use implies that each person makes him or herself deferent to the other. This was to be voluntarily rendered if unity in the culturally diverse Ephesian Church was to be realized. Note also the idea that the experience of 5:21 was to be assumed with a mind-set of having to answer to God (in the fear of God).

What does it all mean?
Having laid the foundation of mutual submission of all believers, Paul now suggests how this submission is to be carried out on a matrimonial and relational basis. "Wives submit yourselves to your own husbands."

---

[26] 'hupotasso,' pronounced 'hoop-ot-as'-so' meaning "to subordinate; reflexively, to obey: be under obedience (obedient), put under, subdue unto, (be, make) subject (to, unto), be (put) in subjection (to, under), submit self unto." *Strong's Exhaustive Concordance of the Bible*, p. 75.

It is not all women in general to whom he addressed these words, but to wives submitting to their respective husbands. As with the previous verse, the wife assumes this submissive posture with a mind-set that implies, "I am doing this unto or for the Lord."

Paul gives his rationale for this assumed position and a working model of the concept in verses 23 and 24. What is the rationale? The headship of the husband. As has been seen, this *kephale*[27] (head) denotes that part of the organ that houses thought. Its responsibility is to house the organ of cognitive process, the brain. The idea is that just as the head is that part of the body that is taken hold of, so to the husband, as the "house-band," is that part of the family that is looked to or gravitated towards. It is a concept based on the metaphorical use of head that denotes a particular function, not primarily a type of relationship. This is further supported by the absence of the definite article *the* in reference to "head." The husband is not *the* head, meaning the final authority. He is "headish" in function as the one looked to "band the house together."

This phrase appearing twice in this verse is without the definite article in the Greek, thus emphasizing the quality of headship. Paul makes the same assertion in 1 Cor. 11:3. At the same time he emphasizes that before God there is *"neither bond [slave] nor free, there is neither male nor female."* (Gal. 3:28).

---

[27] Gr. 'kephale,' (kef-al-ay) from the primary kapto (in the sense of seizing); the head (as the part most readily taken hold of), literally or figuratively: head." *Strong's Exhaustive Concordance of the Bible*, p. 42.

"Distinctions of sex, class, or race are not found among those who are 'in Christ;' nevertheless, the different sexes, classes, and races each have their peculiar contribution to make to each other and to society by virtue of their differing qualities. The headship of the husband consists in his ability and responsibility to care for his wife, in the same way that Christ cares for the church." [28]

Further, one needs to notice that there is an explanation or clarification of both the headship and submission concepts in the two verses. This is seen by the use of the "even as" and "as" construction in the verses. What Paul is telling the reader is that the headship of the husband is to be patterned by the headship of Christ in relation to the church, His body. Submission is also to be patterned by the church's relation to its head, Christ. This relationship is one that recognizes individual functions, built on mutual respect and motivated by love.

[28] Nichol, Francis D., *The Seventh-day Adventist Bible Commentary*, Vol. 6, p. 1036.

Lastly, we notice that the Ephesian church was to walk circumspectly in the light of the evil time in which they were living by husbands loving their wives as Christ loved the Church (5:25-33). How were the husbands to love their wives? Even as Christ loved... and gave[29] Himself. Notice that Paul tells us that the goal of loving and giving is:

1. The sanctification of the church/wife (vs. 26),
2. The presentation of a glorious church/wife (vs. 27), and
3. In doing so the husband will be carrying out his obligation to love his own wife/body (vs. 28-31).

How does what is said or meant relate to the experience of abuse or domestic violence? The application of the above verses can only be carried out in light of the larger context. Paul, living in a multi-ethnic, multinational society that was characterized by individual, ethnic, and national biases, counsels his readers to demonstrate their love for God and each other by living exemplary lives evidenced in unity that would underscore the truth they believed. It would take the wisdom of the Spirit to express the truth and the new status enjoyed in the life of the believer without incurring the animosity or misunderstanding of the society in which they lived.

---

[29] 'Gave' is the Gr. 'paradidomi', (par-ad-id'-o-mee) meaning 'to surrender, i.e. yield up...' As in 'submit' in vs. 21, this is a voluntary act of participant. *Strong's Exhaustive Concordance of the Bible,* p. 54.

The truth is that all believers who have put on the "new man" are joint heirs in Christ. In this new status they are equal, blessed, free to act, free to be, and free to think. But should they demonstrate this in the society in which they lived? They would definitely make more progress if they recognized the cultural norms that existed without lowering the standard of truth. So, along with the other advice he gave, Paul tells the believers to endeavor to demonstrate their new status by being mutually submitted to each other (vs. 21). This was an important concept indispensable to the development of the growing church.[30]

From there on, he addresses wives and husbands (5:21-33); children (6:1-4); servants (6:5–8); masters (6:9) and conclusively, the entire membership (6:10-24). Nichol, commenting on the premise of mutual submission in verse 22, says: *"In this general statement of principle the apostle has prepared the way for the detailed instruction he is about to give. He proposes three areas in which the spirit of submission is to find full expression if the relationships involved are to be conducted in a Christian spirit fashion: relations of husbands and wives, of parents and children, and of masters and servants."* [31]

---

[30] *Often the demands we make of one another, even of our rights, are contrary to the spirit of loving ministry, which is the spirit of the gospel (John 13:15, 16; Gal. 5:15). In addition to submission to superiors in age and authority, and respect for those we consider equals, there is also a Christian submission due to those who may be considered inferior in position. This submission reveals itself in consideration, charity, and respect for the personality of all God's children."* Nichol, Francis D., *The Seventh-day Adventist Bible Commentary*, Vol. 6, p. 1035.

[31] Nichol, Francis D., *The Seventh-day Adventist Bible Commentary*, Vol. 6, pp. 1035-1036.

[32] Nichol, Francis D., *The Seventh-day Adventist Bible Commentary*, Vol. 6, pp. 1035-1036.

There is more to be seen in the idea of a wife's submission (vs. 22) and the husband's love for his wife (vs. 25). It is true that husbands should not demand the wife's submission with a command, but with love. Commanding submission transforms a partnership into a dictatorship. The element of mutual submission is inherent in how the husband shows his love for his wife. Paul plainly tells him to love his wife "as Christ loved the church and gave Himself for it." To give oneself to another is to surrender oneself to that person. Vis-à-vis, wives submit to your husbands and husbands love your wives by (among other things) giving or submitting to her also. *"The submission enjoined upon the wife is of the kind that can be given only between equals, not a servile obedience, but a voluntary submission in the respects in which the man was qualified by his Maker.... This principle of submission is permanent, but its specific application may vary from age to age according to custom and social consciousness."* (Compare 1 Cor. 11:3, 7–9; Col. 3:18; 1 Tim. 2:11, 12; Titus 2:5)[32] For the husband the type and quality of his love must be seen by the degree to which he is willing to give of himself to his wife.

The expressions of and rationale for verses 22 and 25 have to be understood in the framework of the chapter. Chapter 5 encourages the reader to "be followers of God." That is, the believer must act as God would act. This is the overriding precedence. This must be the molding thought that is brought to bear on evaluating what conduct is appropriate and what is not. With the husband representing how God loves, we ask, Would God demand sexual favors of his wife?

Would God use his wife's body as a play toy or merely as an impersonal sexual object? Emphatically no! Many scholars agree that *"A true husband never utters rude commands. His love will find expression in a variety of ways. It will be given in words of understanding and affection. The husband will properly provide for the wife's temporal support* (1 Tim. 5:8); *he will do everything possible to assure her happiness* (1 Cor. 7:33); *he will give her every honor* (1 Peter 3:7)." [33]

As further support of how the theology of chapters 1-4 of Ephesians expresses itself in daily life and knowing that one tends to act on what one thinks, Paul wants us to know that the "following of God" must be an out-growth of having "the mind of God."[34] In other words, how we treat our intimate partner will be based on how we view him or her. When we view each other with the mind of God, remembering how the Creator intended us to view each other, with mutual respect, that which will characterize our conduct will be mutual love (5:1, 2).

1 Corinthians 7:4
"The wife hath not power of her own body, but the husband."

What is the speaker talking about?
Paul was dealing with a church characterized by factions, incest, and litigation. His burden was twofold: (1) "reproof for the backsliding which had resulted in the introduction into

---

[33] Nichol, Francis D., *The Seventh-day Adventist Bible Commentary*, Vol. 6, p. 1036.

[34] This interpretive concept is further supported by the fact that 'children' (vs.1) is from the Gr. 'Teknon' which bears the connotation that the child is the 'begotten' or product of its parent; hence 'as children' suggests that each child will have similarities in mindset to the parent.

the church of practices that corrupted the teachings of the gospel, and (2) instruction, or explanation regarding the points of belief and practice concerning which the believers had sought for clarification."[35] In 1 Corinthians 7 he addresses questions that were sent to him. Questions are surmised based on the answers given.

It would seem that the first answered question related to the relational behavior of couples in light of harlotry and asceticism, the latter which referred to abstinence from sexual intercourse as a means of purification. In answering the question, Paul establishes three principles of marital rights that should be reciprocally recognized by the couple:
1.   The principle of need (vs. 1-3);
2.   The principle of authority (vs. 4);
3.   The principle of habit (vs. 5)

Paul said:
1.   It is good for a man not to touch a woman.
2.   To avoid fornication each individual should have his or her own spouse.
3.   The couple should reciprocally demonstrate "due benevolence" towards each other due to the fact that each have a claim on the other.
4.   The couple should not defraud each other except by mutual consent except for such things as fasting and prayer.

---

[35] Nichol, Francis D., *The Seventh-day Adventist Bible Commentary*, Vol. 6, p. 657.

What does the speaker say about the topic?
Believers who are married must stop[36] robbing each other of sexual intimacies.[37] Is that all? No. They should not deprive each other of sexual intimacies except it be with mutual consent. Are there any limitations? Yes. What are they? Paul states that it should be for a season by mutual consent. Does he give a reason? Yes. They could abstain from sexual intimacies or conjugal cohabitation for a season for the purpose of mutual prayer. After mutually agreeing to not engage in sexual intimacies for a period of time due to the mutual need for prayer, what should the couple do? Paul is clear. They are to "come together again." What is the reason for re-engaging in sexual intimacies as a part of normal marriage life? So that Satan cannot tempt them because of their inconstancy or excessive abstinence (Ex. 19:15; 1 Sam. 21:4-5; Joel 2:16; Zech. 7:3; 1Thess. 3:5).

The human body is created so that both males and females have certain biological needs. These biological needs reach a height at different times for each gender. God's expressed will is that the sexual needs of each husband and wife be met on a timely basis and in the blessed estate of marriage. Nichol states succinctly: *"Christians are told that they must stop depriving one another of the intimate privileges of marriage, except for a limited time, under special circumstances and all, by mutual consent."* [38]

---

[36] 'Stop robbing' as opposed to 'do not rob' is based on the prohibitive use of the imperative mood. It is to be remembered also that the 'cessation of the depriving' is realized by one person 'willing' the action into being.

[37] There probably were some believers who held ascetic views that led them to think that, even in the married state, they were obliged to abstain from sexual intercourse.

[38] Nichol, Francis D., *The Seventh-day Adventist Bible Commentary*, Vol. 6, p. 707.

The observance of the Principle of Habit in sexual expression is a deterrent to all forms of promiscuity, fornication, and adultery; anything outside of this principle courts sadness, unfaithfulness, and pain.

Notwithstanding this however, we must ask: Does 1 Corinthians 7:4 say that license is given to husbands to do as they wish with their wives? Should a wife feel that it is her duty to grant her husband unrestricted access to her person at all times? The honest inquirer must answer, No! While in the larger picture Paul is endeavoring to answer questions relating to concerns over abstinence and the marriage estate, the movement of the immediate passage is that both the husband and the wife must mutually will to begin and end the deprivation of sexual expression within marriage for an agreed time for the express purpose of prayer.

What does the text mean?
Notice that Paul starts his counsel by saying that it is good or appropriate for a man not to touch a woman. Understanding touch to be a euphemism representing sexual intercourse, Paul's counsel is in harmony with his general stance on "non-marriage" enunciated elsewhere and in verses 8 and 26. Being viewed from the perspective of the prevailing times in which he was living and in the light of the urgency of ministry, his counsel would be translated today as saying, "It is appropriate not to get married."

The nevertheless of verse 2 suggests that it is expected that the non-marriage stance will be deviated from in an attempt to avoid a worse condition, that is fornication. Therefore in the light of the felt need to have sexual intercourse it is imperative for each person to have a partner. This principle of need is the answer for a felt need on behalf of each spouse. The context and the phrase "let every man" makes it clear that it is having an appropriate spouse that is being addressed here not the availability of a person that is already his or her spouse. If there is a need and if you have not been given the "gift of celibacy" then it is best to have a wife. Francis Nichol concurs, *"Seeing that the condition of society in Corinth was such that immorality abounded, it was advisable for all Christians to be married."* [39] The question as to whether or not a woman has to make herself available to meet the sexual demands of her husband is addressed below.

Principle of Need: *"Let the husband render unto the wife due benevolence: and likewise also the wife unto the husband"* (1 Cor. 7:4). It is believed that "such counsel was necessary because some Christians evidently believed that there was special virtue in husband and wife living separately from each other, which at once denied them the legitimate privileges of the married condition and exposed them to the temptation to immorality." [40]

There is an interesting play on the word construction of let in verses 2 and 3 of 1 Cor. 7. It is obvious that the statement "let every man have" in verse 2 is a permissive empowerment. In other words, it is okay. In verse 3, "let the husband render[41] " is literally interpreted, "wives, empower your husband to continue

---

[39] Nichol, Francis D., The Seventh-day Adventist Bible Commentary, Vol. 6, p. 706.
[40] Ibid. p. 706.
[41] 'Render' is the permissive use of the 3rd person, singular, present imperative active of 'apodidomi' (to give an answer to a claim or expectation). It is not actually happening, but volitionally possible: that is, 'action realized by the exertion of the will of one to produce action on the part of another.'

paying you back the debt he owes you ."[42] So the entire verse suggests that there is a mutual obligation on behalf of each spouse to empower the other to pay back what is owed each other.

How is this demonstrated in the life of a married couple? Each person conducts him or herself in such a way that empowers the other to give that which is agreed on, owed, and most of all, needed. Here again, the burden and emphasis is not on one submitting to the desires or fancies of the other or one supplying the other. It is each one treating each other in such a way that it enables the other to give his or her spouse that which is matrimonially needed.

Verse 4 throws further light on the reciprocity within the relationship by outlining the **Principle of Mutual Authority**. Power in this verse is the Greek *exousiazo*, (pronounced "ex-oo-see-ad-zo") and means "to control, exercise authority upon, bring under the (have) power of."[43] The idea is that of one having the liberty of doing or acting as one pleases.... This is in contrast with *dunamis* meaning inherent power. In this verse power and control are the issues. Who has control over the body? Is it the person or is it the spouse? Paul clearly says that "the spouse does not have the liberty of doing or acting as he/she pleases in regards to his or her body" (1 Cor. 7:4). In the marriage relationship neither husband nor wife has independent control over their own body.

---

[42] Gr. 'opheilo,' pronounced 'of-i'-lo;' to owe (pecuniarily); figuratively, to be under obligation (ought, must, should)....

[43] *Strong's Exhaustive Concordance of the Bible*, p. 30.

Hence the reciprocity is seen in that each partner should enjoy liberty, action, or control in regards to the body of his or her spouse. This is a part of the larger discussion of the duty and privileges of married people in the intimate relations of marriage.

Here's an example: Jack and Jill have been married for fifteen years. They have experienced a relatively fulfilling sex life. On his 40th birthday, Jack's male friend gave him a book that deals with how sex after forty should be. As a result of digesting the contents of the book Jack wanted to have a more diverse sexual experience with Jill. His desire took Jill by surprise and left her in a quandary. After a period of disagreement and sporadic love-making they sought marriage counseling.

They decided that each would give the other the right to explore new elements in the love act that would meet their mutual comfort levels, individual growth patterns and understanding of "decency" on a reciprocal basis. Jill and Jack understood that when it pertains to the body, neither should demonstrate independence to do as one wills. At the same time, they should preserve the freedom to act in the marriage relationship.

This is not to be thought of as one spouse having absolute freedom to act or do to his or her spouse without regards for the thoughts and feelings of the other. In the new covenant relationship with God, Christians regards their bodies as belonging to God alone (1 Cor. 6:19, 20). This absolute and irrevocable ownership claim is based on Creation and Redemption. The individual manages his or her body as a steward.

John is a 27-year-old technician from a large eastern city. His wife Mary is a 25-year-old nurse who has no siblings. John is outgoing and adventurous. Mary enjoys nature and socializing. John wants to use objects when they make love which Mary feels are medically harmful to the body. Should Mary give in to the wishes or demands of John? Does he have the right to do as he wishes with Mary's body?

It would seem that Paul is resolute: the authority that is granted to the spouse is circumscribed and dictated by a higher, more absolute power which is God, the rightful Owner. The Christian must answer to his or her rightful Owner, and decide to act in harmony with the dictates of that true absolute Owner. Individuals must answer to God for any form of abuse. Temperance, decency, and the revealed will of the Creator are to be the deciding factors in relationship to the sexual acts. Paul advises a couple to observe the **Principle of Habit** as it relates to avoiding fornication. Notice verse I Cor. 7:5: "Defraud ye not one the other, except it be with consent for a time, that ye may give yourselves to fasting and prayer; and come together again, that Satan tempt you not for your incontinency."

How does what is said or meant relate to the experience of abuse or domestic violence?

When considering conjugal cohabitation and methods of sexual expression, frequency of sexual relations, and expressions of love, the Christian must make his or her decisions based on:

1. One's accountability to God as steward,
2. Compliance with God's revealed will as expressed in the Bible,
3. The preservation of individual rights and responsibility,

4.   Consideration for the other individual's growth, comfort level, and needs.

Temperance and sanctified reason should guide the couple. The possession of the Holy Spirit dictates absolute lordship and the honoring of God must be the end result to sexual acts (1 Cor. 9:25; 6:19-20; 10:31; Rom. 12:1; Phil. 4:8).

A word of caution is needed here: *"It cannot be concluded from this counsel that such refraining from the privileges of marriage is necessary in order to engage in regular daily seasons of prayer, but only that it is an allowable plan to adopt when one feels the need of a period of specially intense devotion such as suggested by the phrase, 'fasting and prayer'* (see Ex. 19:14, 15).*"*[44] It is a curious fact that must be admitted here that the stated exception in verse 5 suggests that the spiritual act of prayer takes precedence, at least for a time, over the physical act of sex. Sex is not everything. It must be an expression of selfless love or a means of procreation.

Sexual abuse is usually exhibited by men towards women. Why is this so? Why is it that men seem to have a greater sexual compulsion than do women? Could it have been in the mind of God to create the holy pair in such a way that their needs counterbalanced each other, thus establishing a balance in the male-female relationship? Could it be that the man's greater sexual need balances the woman's greater emotional need for her husband? It would appear that the reference in Genesis 3:16 *"Thy desire shall be to thy husband"* was to be in actuality, a complementation of man's higher sexual need as expressed in the frequency of the sex act.

---

[44] Nichol, Francis D., *The Seventh-day Adventist Bible Commentary*, Vol. 6, p. 707.

The essential requirement for husbands and wives then, is to recognize this dynamic and move towards creating a proper environment where marital need balance can be evident without violating an individual's right to be, to act, and to do.

1 Peter 3:1

"Likewise, ye wives, be in subjection to your own husband; that, if any obey not the word, they also may without the word be won by the conversation of the wives."

What is the speaker talking about?

Peter, like other post-crucifixion apostles, wrote in a time of persecution and fiery trials (4:2). He knew that the believers needed strengthening and encouragement. His aim in writing this passage was *"...to strengthen his readers' faith, to exhort them to blameless conduct, to exemplary citizenship, to loyal witness for Christ, and to effective preparation to meet their Lord."* [45] He counsels servants (2:18), wives (3:1–6), husbands (3:7), elders (5:1–4), and younger members (5:5–9).

1 Peter 3:1 is the beginning of specific advice to wives who lived in times of trial and under their master's watchful eye. The burden was for believers to conduct themselves in such a manner (2:12) that they would have a converting influence in their homes, the immediate community, and society at large. As we reread the verse we come to the conclusion that he is talking about "wives being in subjection to their husbands."

---

[45] Nichol, Francis D., *The Seventh-day Adventist Bible Commentary*, Vol. 7, p. 548.
[46] Literally, "submit yourselves once for all."
[47] Gr. 'hupotasso' to subordinate; reflexively, to obey:--be under obedience... in subjection (to, under), submit self unto. *Strong's Exhaustive Concordance of the Bible*, p. 75.

What does the speaker say about the topic?

1. Wives should submit to their own husbands.
2. That those husbands who are not submissive to the word of God may be won to Christ by the conduct of their wives.

What does the text mean?

To answer that question, we must look at the text more closely. Notice that the verse begins with the word *likewise*. This would suggest that the message of the passage is not only compared to the thoughts that preceded it but also conditioned by it.

The preceding thoughts in 1 Peter Chapter 2:

1. There is an appeal to the believers to lay aside certain behaviors in the light of their calling (2:1-8).

2. They were to live in their cultural setting in view of their "royal," "holy nation," and "peculiar people" status (vs. 9- 25). There were specific ways in which they were to live:

   a. All of the believers were to abstain from fleshly lusts (vs. 11), conduct themselves honestly (vs. 12), and submit[46] to all ordinances of kings and governors (vs.13-16).

   b. Believers were to honor all men, love each other, and fear God (vs. 17).

   c. Servants were to be subject[47] to, or subordinate themselves to their masters (every human institution) based on its being the expressed acceptable stance for the follower of Christ.

Therefore "wives should be in subjection to their own husbands" (3:1) in the same manner that the domestic servants were to be in subjection to their masters (2:18-25). And how were these servants to be in subjection? Peter is clear: continue to be in subjection or subordination to the morally good and reasonable, and also to the crooked, twisted mind or perverse masters with all fear. This is acceptable if it is done with a "conscience toward God, enduring grief and suffering wrongfully," and in a manner that reflects the life of Jesus. In fact, it is because of this type of wrongful suffering the believers were called to endure (see 3:21 and Matt. 22:21; 26:50–53).

Two important things are seen here. The *fear* and the *manner of subjection* Jesus demonstrated are to be the evaluative elements when determining how one must be in subjection. The subordination is acceptable if the person is conscious of God and His will in regards to enduring grief, sorrow or sadness, wrongfully (vs. 20). Additionally, Jesus kept Himself in subordination to the governing powers around Him, suffering insult and injury (vs. 21). It was not an absolute subjection, however. Whenever the will of secular powers conflicted with the will of his Father Jesus did not hesitate to obey God. In His assessment of this position when writing about the idea of subjection to every ordinance, Nichol says: *"Except where principle would be violated the Christian is to cooperate heartily with the written and unwritten laws of the society in which he lives. Peter here considers the various forms of government as man-made institutions. He does not emphasize, as Paul does in Rom. 13, the divine permission by which earthly rulers exercise their power, but stresses the human aspect of their authority."* [48] While Jesus did not fight for His rights, He was careful to maintain a lifestyle that was consistent with His mission, rights and gifts (vs. 24).

So in 1 Peter 3:1, we understand Peter to be saying: *"Wives continue to be in subordination to your own husbands just as the domestic servants were in subjection or subordination to their respective masters."* [49] Once again it is not an arbitrary subordination or even subjection based on status, class or gender. The context makes it clear for the domestic servants "...it is a voluntary subordination based on existing societal owner-employer norms."[50] It is conditioned by the believer's consciousness of the consequences, which induces fear, and by being mindful that it is a privilege to experience the same grief and unjust treatment that Jesus did. A wife is to do the same thing. That is, in the light of existing norms and with a view of winning the unbelieving spouse, she is to continue subordinating herself as was demonstrated by Jesus in his life. Peter's use of subjection and his explanation of the relationship of servants[51] as a model, colors how the wife should submit to her own husband.

Logically, this makes sense. The unbelieving spouse will reflect the values of society. It is expected that he will reflect the

---

[48] Nichol, Francis D., *The Seventh-day Adventist Bible Commentary*, Vol. 7, p. 564.

[49] Nichol, Francis D., *The Seventh-day Adventist Bible Commentary*, Vol. 7, p 564.

[50] An inference based on the continuous tense of the action. It is an action that is already going on, hence an established pattern.

[51] "Because many converts in the early church lived in physical bondage to earthly masters the church leaders found it necessary to approach the problem of slavery from a practical, rather than an ideal, point of view (see Deut. 14:26). Christian slaves were to win the esteem and kindness of their masters by manifesting faithfulness, loyalty, humility, patience, and a forgiving spirit" Nichol, Francis D., *The Seventh-day Adventist Bible Commentary*, Vol. 7, p 565.

opinion of the masses, inconsistent or unbiblical as they may be. In order to promote unity and possibly have a telling influence on her spouse it is thought to be profitable for the believing wife to work with the accepted norms wherever it does not conflict with the prerogatives given to her by her Creator.

As further support we now look at the word '*obey*' that is used in the passage. The phrase '*obey not*' used in vs. 1 in reference to the husband's stance, carries with it the idea of the husband's disbelief of the truth while '*obey*' used in reference to Sarah in vs. 6 carries with it the idea of her listening attentively or hearing.[52] Simply, it is saying that "Sarah heard—listened attentively, and obeyed." The implication is that she, Sarah, evaluated what Abraham said, saw light in it and acted accordingly. It was not a blind, submissive obedience.

Peter also addressed the husbands (vs. 7). What does he say to them?
1. Dwell with your wives according to knowledge.
2. Give honor to the wife as the weaker vessel.

These two thoughts imply that husbands should...
1. Exercise intelligence as they relate to their wives,
2. Give honor to their wives considering their limitations and their being joint depositors of God's grace, and
3. When they do the aforementioned, their prayers will not be inhibited.

---

[52] 'to hear under (as a subordinate), i.e. to listen attentively; by implication, to heed or conform to a command or authority: hearken, be obedient to, obey. *Strong's Exhaustive Concordance of the Bible*, p. 73.

How does what is said or meant relate to the experience of abuse or domestic violence? It is inconceivable that anyone would use this passage to support the abuse of a woman. Peter's appeal is that the whole church live in such a way that their lives would be instrumental in the salvation of others. Like the Savior, they all needed to be meek while suffering insult wrongly for Christ's sake. As a further support for his encouragement along this line he counsels them to move toward a unity of action or witness (2 Pet. 9; 3:8-13). All through the passage we see the elements of mutual subjection, honor, and love. Husband and wife were equal at creation, occupying the same new covenant status, enjoying the same elevated position as joint heirs and promised the same inheritance. So how could she now be placed in a relationship where she is less than he, inferior to, and dominated by a man? Anyone purporting this kind of thinking or platform is destroying the original purpose of God: to reflect His image in male and female. It is the purpose of the enemy to create distrust and confusion among the sexes. We cannot say one part of God is better than the other, male or female. We are all made in the image of God, male and female, and both to be treated respectfully and with love.

Chapter 9

WHERE DO WE GO FROM HERE?

What we know!
Throughout the preceding chapters, we have learned what domestic violence is and some of the ways it affects relationships, families, children, congregations, and communities. Studies examining the prevalence, dynamics, and social impact of domestic violence all tend to arrive at a common conclusion. Domestic violence is a social scourge often culminating in permanent physical, emotional, and sexual injuries and death. Even the casual outside observer can recognize the withered souls, drooping spirits, and intergenerational family dysfunction. As a Christian community we cannot continue to deny that domestic abuse is occurring in our homes, churches, and communities. Now is the time for our church to rise to the challenges of prevention and intervention! Domestic violence has a degenerating effect on our families and churches, compromising our witness, our mission, and our message. We have an obligation to address this issue as often as we can and in as many ways as we can.

Luke 4:18 states that Christ's mission was to preach the gospel to the poor, heal and bind up the broken-hearted, proclaim liberty to the captives, recovery of sight to the blind, and set at liberty those who were bruised. As His disciples, we are commissioned to carry on His work of healing, recovery, and restoration. Domestic violence deprives individuals of their God given rights to individuality, creativity, mobility, and spirituality. Remember, domestic violence is not just a "family feud," "personality conflict," or "private affair." It is sin, pure and unadulterated, orchestrated by the enemy to destroy the image of God in His people. When in crisis, individuals turn to sources and resources they hope will be of help. If they find the church nonresponsive, unconcerned, or unwilling to help, out of necessity they turn away from the church, and we lose the opportunity to fulfill the mission of Christ.

What we are doing!
Acknowledging that it is not exempt from the heartbreak of domestic abuse, the Seventh-day Adventist Church has taken a decisive stand to address this issue in a direct and systematic way. Each year a specific Saturday is designated as "Abuse Prevention Day." This is an opportunity for churches to design a day to raise awareness and sensitivity to domestic violence. On this day of sermons, presentations, and information-sharing, members learn about the dynamics of domestic violence, and skills for prevention and intervention.

The good news for abuse survivors is that the church has awakened to the reality of domestic violence, and to signal its humanitarian commitment, leaders are making statements, research is being conducted, and articles are being written to raise awareness. Some administrators and pastors are attending conferences and workshops where they learn to create and maintain safe church environments (especially for children), and practice skills to care for members. It is becoming more common for churches to assign a safety committee (a subcommittee of the board) to write policies, and set in place a system for monitoring sex offenders. The safety committee, in tandem with the pastor, can play a very redemptive role in the life of the perpetrator by holding him accountable for his actions. This type of direct intervention has a redemptive influence on the whole of the church.

With the support of the North Pacific Union and Upper Columbia Conference, Women's Healing and Empowerment Network serves as an interdenominational ministry through which education, resources, consultation, collaboration, and other support services are available to church leaders, members, victims, and perpetrators. The programs and services of the network address various needs and responsibilities of church members. They include:

1. *Healing Center*—a safe, temporary shelter facility, that serves as a model program helping to provide healing and empowerment for female victims and their children.
2. *Men of Compassion*—an organization that challenges men to work together to address the dynamics of domestic violence from their perspective, while holding each other accountable for healing, recovery, and restitution. They also work to develop and implement ways in which they can unite with women to minimize the occurrence of abuse in our homes, schools, churches, and communities.
3. *The "Being There" Conference*—a healing and educational conference for women, men, and service providers addressing the issues of domestic violence and sexual abuse. This conference is held in various locations annually.

4. *Healing Conferences*—conferences conducted by the network to help hurting members recognize their dysfunctional behavioral patterns, and the way to true healing in Jesus Christ (More information about the network is available on page 229).

We can make it our goal to minimize the devastation of domestic violence when we as the body of Christ unite our efforts with other organizations and institutions to address this issue. If we stand united against domestic violence, we can make a difference!

"The crisis of family violence affects people physically, psychologically, and spiritually. Each of these dimensions must be addressed, both for victims and for those in the family who abuse them. Approached from either a secular or religious perspective alone, certain needs and issues tend to be disregarded. This reflects a serious lack of understanding of the nature of family violence and its impact on people's lives. Treatment of families experiencing violence and abuse requires integrating the needs of the whole person. Thus, the importance of developing a shared understanding and cooperation between secular and religious helpers to deal with family violence cannot be emphasized too strongly" (Fortune, 1980).

What we need to do!
It is imperative that we as believers do all that we can individually and corporately to assist victims, direct abusers to services, nurture children, and support the healthy function of families in our congregations. Many are turned off from religion because of the incongruities they see in Christians who claim to believe that Jesus came to set the captives free, and yet remain

unsupportive of abuse victims. Men, women, and children suffer wherever abuse shows its ugly face. We must continue to speak out about it both in our private conversations and in our churches. Domestic abuse policies need to be written and enforced regardless of the position, role, title, educational background, or socio-economic status of the abuser or perpetrator.

Church administrators, pastors, and church leaders need to address issues of power, control, and family violence in premarital counseling. The pastor should become personally acquainted with qualified religious and secular therapists, counselors, and resources for domestic violence victims so they can make appropriate referrals. The mutual role of men and women in relationships, in the home, church, and society in general, should be encouraged from the pulpit. An abused child who grows up in a congregation that never declares its position on domestic violence will conclude that either his experience is unusual and shameful, or that the church is out of touch with real life. Either impression is problematic.

Seminaries need to incorporate an educational component for students in ministry-related degree programs. Such a curriculum should address the dynamics of domestic violence, the role that pastors play in providing safety and healing for their members, a pastor's limitations, and accountability to God for "feeding and freeing" His wounded sheep. The curriculum should help the pastor identify practical ways in which he or she can support community programs and services for victims as well as perpetrators.

Abusers, both male and female, should be referred to qualified domestic violence programs. Churches should safeguard children and abused spouses who may attend the same congregation as the estranged batterer. If the victim has a protection order, church leaders should seek to understand the court mandate and make accommodations accordingly. Church leaders such as elders, deacons, pastors, and Sabbath School teachers should meet to discuss ways to protect and incorporate victims and abusers, if possible and/or appropriate, into the life of the church.

Many of our churches sit empty for most of the week, while social service agencies are desperate for space to hold support groups, informational meetings, and planning committee meetings. When possible, churches should partner with these agencies to provide both a venue and financial support for the good work they do. This practical partnering allows the community to see that Seventh-day Adventist Christians not only speak peace, but also advocate for, initiate, and support relevant programs and services that enhance the quality of life in their communities.

Our education, service, and advocacy depend upon the adequacy of our theological vision -- the way we interpret Scripture and tradition regarding relations between women and men, sex, marriage, parenting, and violence. In this adventure of faith and thought, the victims of violence and violation can offer valuable guidance. We need to listen to their stories with an ear for the religious reflections that sustain capacities to survive, to heal and to flourish. A careful and respectful attention to the voices of the violated may also encourage the reconstruction of our theologies..." (Livezey, 1987).

In order for us to make a difference on behalf of domestically-abused victims and children, entire communities (particularly religious organizations) must accept their share of the responsibility for addressing this issue. We must give messages of liberation, hope, and empowerment to everyone created in God's image. As we put on the whole armor of God and work together, we will withstand the enemy. We will save lives, protect our children, and decrease the intergenerational cycle of abuse. As our churches become safer and more family-friendly, we will be able to maintain a quality of life that will glorify God now, and prepare us for eternity where there will be no more pain, no more sorrow, no more crying, no more isolation, woundedness, intimidation, fear, guilt, shame, blame, or death. He has promised, *"I make all things new"* (Rev. 21:5).

How we will do it!

God has provided us with the wisdom required to understand the rudiments of domestic violence, and its spiritual and relational impact through the generations. Therefore we can no longer offer excuses and allow it to continue in our homes, schools, and communities. *"But the wisdom that is from above is first pure, then peaceable, gentle, and easy to be entreated, full of mercy and good fruits, without partiality, and without hypocrisy. And the fruit of righteousness is sown in peace of them that make peace"* (James 3:17, 18).

Dear Christian,
You gave me love when I could take it.
You gave me trust when I wouldn't break it.
You gave me life when I could journey
on a path of wholeness, happiness, and safety.

You gave me peace I could depend on.
You gave me hope on which I could rely
You gave me joy to exist on
within a world of misery.

You reflected the Light that bears a signal
of the dawning of each day.
You gave me faith in the eternal
You helped me find a better Way:

The Way to truly live a new life, to love and dream,
the Way to preserve my dignity, individuality;
my right to think and do;
the Way to hope when people act indifferently.

You showed me Jesus: Love, Life,
Trust, Peace, Hope, Joy, Light, the Way.

Thank you for doing your best.
The deeds you manifested are true.
Not even angels will contest
the prize of eternity with which God will reward you.

-by Ellen, Mable's mother

References

Fortune, M. (1980). *A workshop manual for clergy and other service providers.* Seattle, WA: Center for the Prevention of Sexual and Domestic Violence, 137.

Livezey, L. (1987). Sexual and family violence: A growing issue for the churches. *The Christian Century*, 939.

◆

Helpful Information

◆

Appendix A

Crisis Intervention Directory

Agencies

Name	Contact	Phone
Community Services	_____	_____
Email _____		
Social Services	_____	_____
Email _____		
Food Bank	_____	_____
Email _____		
Local D.V. Shelter	_____	_____
Email _____		
Christian Shelter	_____	_____
Email _____		
W.H.E. Network	_____	_____
Email		
Legal Aid	_____	_____
Email _____		
Mental Health Clinic	_____	_____
Email _____		
Support Group	_____	_____
Email _____		
School	_____	_____
Email _____		

Name	Contact	Phone
Hospital	_____	_____
	Email _____	
Medical Clinic	_____	_____
	Email _____	
Dental Clinic	_____	_____
	Email _____	
Eye Clinic	_____	_____
	Email _____	
Transportation	_____	_____
	Email _____	
Prosecutor's Office	_____	_____
	Email _____	
Psychiatrist	_____	_____
	Email _____	
Other	_____	_____
	Email _____	
Other	_____	_____
	Email _____	
Other	_____	_____
	Email _____	

Personnel

Name	Contact	Phone
Doctor	_____	_____
	Email _____	
Dentist	_____	_____
	Email _____	
Lawyer	_____	_____
	Email _____	
Psychiatrist	_____	_____
	Email _____	
Psychologist	_____	_____
	Email _____	
Counselor	_____	_____
	Email _____	
Police Officer	_____	_____
	Email _____	
Other	_____	_____
	Email _____	
Other	_____	_____
	Email _____	

Incident Report Form

Name of person reporting incident_____

Date_____Address_____

_____

Telephone_____   Cell Phone_____

E-mail _____

Presenting Problem:

_____

_____

_____

_____

_____

Observations:

_____

_____

_____

_____

_____

Recommendations and/or Referrals:

_____

_____

_____

_____

_____

Additional Comments:

_____

_____

_____

_____

_____

Signed _____

Date_____

(Person completing recording incident report)

Safety Plan
(if she decides to leave the abuser)

Encourage her to:

1. Secure all important documents:
    -Birth certificates for herself and her children
    -Marriage certificate
    -Social Security cards
    -Income tax returns
    -Prescriptions
    -Medical/Insurance cards
    -Pay stubs (for herself and the abuser)
    -Credit cards / records
    -Bank statements

2. Secure transportation and a safe place (shelter, safe home, etc.) to stay.

3. Make sure her abuser is unaware of her plans to leave.

4. Leave when the abuser is not at home

Considerations about Leaving *During* an Abusive Episode

5. Create signal system with designated friend to let them know "it is time" or "call the police."

6. Stay away from places (like the kitchen) where dangerous objects are available.

7. Stay away from places small spaces (bathrooms, closets, etc) where the abuser can trap her.

8.   Call for help (911 or police) immediately. Get the names of the officers and their badge numbers.

9.   Run for help to a neighbor or friend she can trust.

10.   Take pictures of injury sites (wounds and bruises), then seek medical help.

Safety Plan
(If she decides to stay at home and the abuser has moved out)

Encourage her to:

1. Go to the court house and file for a Personal Protection Order.
2. Keep a journal and document every violation the abuser makes.
3. Call police **EVERY** time the abuser breaks the Personal Protection Order.
4. Have witnesses, if possible, other than family members go to court with her.
5. Make contact with the outside world (neighbors, church members, schools, etc.).

(Give pictures and copies of Personal Protection Order to her boss, children's school, etc. She should set up a system that will assist her if he the abuser returns. Children should not be allowed to leave school unless the individual designated to pick them up has a correct password. Neighbors can be asked to call the police if they hear strange noises, such as a bell or alarm to alert them that she needs help. She can also ask a friend or church member to stay with her.)

6. Construct alarms or other safety measures that will sound if someone tries to enter her home illegally. She could also rearrange furniture in unfamiliar ways so that the sounds of a night entry might be more quickly detected.
7. Change daily routines.
8. Change her phone number, use an unlisted number, and get caller ID to screen calls.

9. Let her children know codes so that in an emergency they can call 911 or go to neighbors and get help.
10. Keep a suitcase of copies of important papers, money, clothing, keys, etc. hidden or secured with someone she can trust.
11. Change the locks on her door.
12. Plan an escape route out of her home and teach it to her children.
13. Learn where to get help and memorize emergency phone numbers.
14. Have a safe place to go if she needs to escape. (Keep a list of religious and community resources).
15. Take a good self-defense class.

Appendix B

Case Studies

Discuss the following:
A.   What are the forms of abuse?
B.   What are the moral/ethical issues?
C.   What are the legal/religious issues?
D.   What is your Christian responsibility to the victim, perpetrator, and the church?

Apply the preceding questions to the following case studies as a way to open discussion with individuals in your congregation or church leadership.

Donna and Rob

Donna B. is 36 years old. She has been married to John B. for seventeen years. They have four children aged seven to fifteen. Donna and John began attending your church about three years ago after relocating from another city. About six weeks ago, she came and told you that she was having some problems in her marriage and wanted your advice. As she shares her story, you hear that John has been brutalizing Donna throughout their marriage. He is a truck driver and does not consistently help her to provide for the needs of the family. She tells of being beaten regularly and hospitalized three times. She reports that her husband frequently forces her to have sex, including sexual activities that she finds distasteful and perverse. When she refuses, he threatens to rape their daughter, so Donna submits to him. After one of these episodes, she left him and went to stay with her mother. But he found her and threatened to kill her mother if Donna ever left him again. As she tells her story, she begins to shake with terror. She came to you as a last resort for help. She is afraid that John might find out that she is talking with you and follow through with his threats to kill her if she reports him to anyone. She begs you to keep her secret. To compound the problem, John is the Pathfinder Director at your church.

Karen and Jack

Karen has lived with Jack for seven years. They have two children. For the past three months she and the children have been physically and verbally abused by Jack who spends his evenings in a local bar. At one point he locked the children in the basement while he beat Karen severely (almost to the point of death). She is afraid to call the police because each time they come to the home Jack blames her and the police believe him and do nothing. He has threatened to kill her, the children, and her family if she calls the police again. The house is in Karen's name, but since Jack pays half of the bills and is the father of her children, she is afraid to have him evicted because she has been told that she won't be able to make it on her own. Karen's minister told her that she should marry Jack and this would cause him to change because he would be legally bound to her and the children. He also told her that in order for her to belong to the church she and Jack would have to be married. She and the children have been attending your church for over a year and desire to be a part of your congregation.

Carol

Carol has been beaten by her husband several times during the 12 years of their marriage. He is the principal for a Christian high school. She is the church secretary for the largest and wealthiest church in the district. Both are employed by the same organization. She is afraid to get help because she feels that no one will believe that her handsome, educated, successful, and charismatic husband is an abuser. She shared her situation with two church members who encouraged her to go to a shelter. She did call the shelter program and found out that she could receive non-residential counseling. She decided to attend a support group because she did not feel strong enough to leave the relationship. When the conference president found out that she was going for counseling he asked her not to go. He told her, "They are not Christians and they only want to break up marriages."

Michael and Sue

Michael and Sue have been married for two years and Michael is attending a seminary. Michael feels that he is called to be a minster. However, Sue has her reservations about his "calling" because he frequently abuses her physically and verbally, and threatens to leave her if she ever tells anyone about his behavior. Recently Sue discovers that Michael's father, a minister of 30 years, abused him as a child and told him that he was to become a minister and not to consider any other career. Sue decided to tell a friend about her abusive relationship hoping for some emotional support. To her dismay she discovered that the friend shared the information with Michael. He became furious and made her go back and tell the friend that she exaggerated. Michael finally decided that he and Sue needed counseling. But their counselor, a pastor's wife for 20 years felt that Sue was being too emotional and suggested to her that she should be careful about "touching the Lord's anointed." Sue was devastated. She could not understand how another woman could give her such advice. She felt trapped because her husband was sponsored, well liked, a brilliant scholar, a gifted speaker, and an excellent administrator. She decided to keep on praying, hoping that God would give her the strength to endure. But after reading some articles on domestic violence and spousal abuse she decided that she should leave the relationship. Then she discovered that she was pregnant.

Ken

Ken had enough. His wife of 35 years was hitting, scratching, and kicking him. One day after an attack, he decided to call the police. They took pictures of his cuts, scratches and bruises. She was convicted in a court of law for assault and battery. For years Ken was afraid to report his wife's attacks because who would believe him? He was tall and heavy, she was short and slender. But now the truth was going to be revealed to everyone, including his church family. He was too ashamed to go to church because he felt that everyone would laugh at him and call him a coward and a wimp.

Robert C.

Robert C. is a fifty-five year old male corporate executive. He is an active member of the church. He pays a large tithe and gives a substantial offering. He is also a member of the church board and chairman of the building committee. He has been a "model" church member and you have worked closely with him for many years. Today you discover that he has been charged with molesting his seven-year-old granddaughter. He denies the accusation. You find it difficult to believe that he is capable of such a thing and feel that his granddaughter is not telling the truth. He comes to you and wants you to go to court as a character witness. It is very possible that if you testify for him the charges will be dropped.

Sally B.

It is Friday afternoon and Sally B. stops by your office after school. She attends a church school. She is thirteen years old. Her parents are both active church members. Her mother is the choir director and her father is the first elder. She has been hanging around the church more often than usual during the past eight months. She tells you that she sees her parents watching things on television, things that she doesn't like. You ask her "what kind of things?" "Just things," she replies. You ask if these things frighten her. She says "yes." You ask if the "things" are sexual in nature. She answers, "Yes." Eventually she confides in you and tells you that her parents are watching pornography and don't care whether or not she sees it too. She says that she knows that she is supposed to honor her father and mother but she feels that they should not be officers of the church if they are watching pornography.

Mr. Smith

You are a member of a rural church. Most of the church board members are related. You discover that Mr. Smith, one of the elders has been molesting his 12-year-old daughter. You decide to take this matter to the church board and request that disciplinary measures be taken. But they refuse to do anything because they don't want to discipline a family member.

◆

Appendix C

Articles to Share

"Who's to Blame?"
By Dr. Colin A. Dunbar

He stood with his hand raised high. His eyes were bright with rage. Hot blood pulsating through his now dilated veins told of frustrations and unfulfilled dreams. Should he hit her? Why not? After all, she's to blame. She doesn't understand what type of day he's had. She's not dealing with the two children, taking care of the house, and tending to his ever demanding needs. She is aggravating him with her silly answers and combative spirit. But, is she to blame? Whose responsibility is it to care for the family, to fulfill a mate's dreams, to help a mate deal with frustrations? His? Hers? Both?

In our fast paced, highly pressuring society many generations remote from the simpler lifestyle of our ancestors, it isn't easy to find a working solution that reflects the original design for healthy relationships. To find a solution we must first of all understand who "she" is. I've done some digging and have found that we come from the same stuff. She was made out of me. When our first parents were created, our Maker did not give rulership over the earth to the man alone. That's a fact. He didn't tell man to replenish and subdue everything by himself. Rather, he told both of them, male and female, to "be fruitful and multiply, replenish the earth, and subdue it; and have dominion over the fish of the sea…" (Genesis 2: 28). When was the last time you really looked at your mate? Take another look. You chose that person. You both have mutual responsibilities.

Remember that cigarette commercial? The one with the beautiful 5'6" brunette boasting 36-24-36 dimensions. She stood with the cigarette between her fingers. The commentator said "You've come a long way baby." Well, so has marriage. Because of cultural changes, successful marriage partners and others with successful relationships have found that dividing responsibilities according to strengths and capacities works best.

I took a good look at my wife, myself, and the whole man-woman scene, and I had to admit that we are tainted, yet beautiful in the eyes of God. More than that, I was excited to find that when we came from the Maker's hand, we came blessed with all the graces and aptitudes needed to grow and succeed.

So the next time he stands with his hand raised high, eyes gleaming with rage, should her hit her? No! He should take a minute and think, "She is made out of me. We are beautiful creatures of humanity, having various strengths and abilities." Men and women alike should try to understand the other's position and give their partner the privilege and freedom to be who they want to be.

The next time you want to blame or hit your mate, remember this proverb: "He that is slow to anger is better than the mighty; and he that ruleth his spirit than he that taketh a city" (Proverbs 16:32). You chose your mate. He or she is not to be blamed for your actions. You are! No one makes you do anything you don't want to do. That raised hand is a cry for help.

Get help intelligently, get help quickly, Get HELP!

◆

"Economic Abuse: Is There Such a Thing?"
By Dr. Mable C. Dunbar

Traditionally, the husband/father was considered the "bread winner" for his family. He was the financial manager for the home as well as business affairs. His role was to make sure that his family received the best he could offer with his income. Today, a working woman can have responsibility for her financial affairs and enjoy a comfortable or affluent lifestyle whether she is married or single. In some instances, she is able to earn more than her husband or partner. In mutual relationships, marriage partners seek to support each other and work together to create financial stability for their family.

In abusive relationships, one partner sometimes seeks to control or diminish the other partner's potential for financial stability. This is economic abuse. This is happening when one spouse:

1. Keeps the partner from getting or keeping a job.
2. Takes the partner's money.
3. Prevents the partner from having a say about how the money can be spent.
4. Makes the partner beg for money, or sets up conditions for him/her to get money.
5. Prevents the partner from continuing his/her education.
6. Does not provide adequately for the family.

It is important to re-emphasize that anyone can be abusive. Historically, however, the wife was dependent on her husband to take care of her economic needs while she was responsible for the welfare of the family and home. In situations where a man seeks to control the finances of the home, Ellen G. White gives some wise counsel. She states in Letter 65, 1904, *"You must help each other. Do not look upon it as a virtue to hold fast the purse strings, refusing to give your wife money." Also in Letter 157, 1903, she writes, "Give your wife a share of the money you receive. Let her have this as her own, and let her use it as she desires. She should have been allowed to use the means that she earned as she in her judgment deemed best. If she had a certain sum to use as her own, without being criticized, a great weight would have been lifted from her mind."*

Ellen White also encourages husbands to provide conveniences in the home to lighten the labor of his wife. *"I tried to show him that it was necessary for the health as well as the morals of his children that he should make home pleasant and provide conveniences to lighten the labor of his wife"* (Letter 9, 1888). For example, if a couple could afford it, a washing machine certainly lessens the burden of washing clothes by hand.

"Women should be trained to some business whereby they can gain a livelihood if necessary," according to Ellen G. White in *Adventist Home,* p. 91. Obviously this statement should be kept in proper context. I do not believe that the writer is encouraging a woman to neglect her family and take a job at any cost. There are situations where it is feasible and necessary for a woman to work, i.e., if she is a single parent, if the family is facing economic hardship, if she has no other means of support, or if she has gifts or talents that can be utilized to better humanity.

We need to keep broad principles in mind as we seek to define economic abuse. It is not necessarily the act of keeping a tight budget, or being frugal about spending. Economic abuse involves the motivation behind the act; that of diminishing the economic potential of the other for purposes of manipulation and control. Women and men should nurture and support each other's potential, encouraging one another to strive to meet goals that will build their economic power – so that they can maintain a comfortable home environment for their families. The couple should maintain an ongoing dialogue regarding ways to earn, spend, and invest their money. As trust is experienced in the relationship, they will find the freedom of relational safety, confidence, and support. When a couple joins their lives in marriage, they become as one. They share. They work together. They build together. They plan together. They reap the rewards of their labor, together.

It is God's intent that we flourish and prosper. "Beloved, I wish above all that thou mayest prosper and be in health..." (3 John 2). When Christ is abiding in the heart it does not matter who makes the most money, who has the most prestigious job, or who has the highest level of education. What matters is that each partner treats the other with respect, dignity, and forbearance while giving each other the freedom to thrive, grow, and explore the unlimited potential God has given to each individually.

Possession and Treasures:

You possess a job...you treasure your family
You possess a house...you treasure your home
You possess a bank account...you treasure your friends
You possess a car...you treasure your freedom
You possess a wardrobe...you treasure your health
You possess an appointment book...you treasure your time
You possess a heart...you treasure love
You possess net worth...you treasure the opportunity to serve

-Leonard Sweet

Treasure whatever blessings you have received from God, and use them to glorify Him and bless others.

Domestic Violence in Christian Homes
By Dr. Mable C. Dunbar

Domestic violence cuts across all racial, socioeconomic, educational, religious, and cultural lines. It is an unhappy feature
in upper-class, middle-class, working-class, and poor families.
Unfortunately, Christian homes are not exempt. As I travel
from church to church to present workshops on the dynamics
of domestic violence, both male and female members have con-
fided in me their history of abuse. Most were afraid to let others
in on their situation because they felt that the church would
reject and abandon them. Some had been warned not to "air
[their] dirty linen." They feared losing the support of family, or
being classified as "trouble-makers" who contrive stories to hurt
others or to get revenge. Others grew up in homes where abuse
was interwoven into the fabric of their lives, and did not realize that they were victims. Others were told that they should
protect the church.

I often wonder why the church (the institution) needs protection! If we serve an Almighty, All-Powerful, All-Seeing,
All-Knowing, and All-Doing God why do we need to protect
the object of His regard? Can't He protect it Himself? Why
should this responsibility be placed on a victim?

Domestic or family violence occurs when an individual in an
intimate or familial relationship attempts to gain or maintain
power and control over another through a wide range of abusive behaviors. A single act may amount to abuse. A number
of acts that form a **pattern** of behaviors may amount to abuse,
even though some or all of those acts when viewed in isolation,
may appear to be minor or trivial. Abuse can be difficult to

identify because abusive persons do not always act in ways that are abusive. Sometimes they may seem loving and kind. But if you frequently feel afraid of upsetting them, and if you change what you do to avoid their anger, these can be signs that you are being abused.

All forms of abuse – psychological, economic, emotional, religious, and physical, etc., originate in the abuser's desire for power and control. The following list can help you recognize if you or someone you know is in an abusive relationship.

Psychological Abuse
Behavior and/or comments to undermine your sense of self; name-calling or putdowns; intimidation; sulking; threatening to withhold money; disconnect the telephone; take the car away; lying to your friends and family about you; telling you that you have no choice in any decisions; threatening to commit suicide; threatening to take the children away; reporting you to welfare agencies unless you comply with his/her demands regarding the upbringing of the children.

Verbal Abuse
Constant put-downs; name calling; making harassing or threatening phone calls; saying things to scare you (e.g., telling you something "bad" would happen; threatening to commit suicide); using the children to threaten you (e.g., telling you that you would lose custody; threatening to leave town with the children).

Physical Abuse
Actual or threatened physical harm (e.g. injured you by causing bruises, cuts, broken bones, by means of punching; pushing;

choking; threatening or injuring you with objects/weapons; making threats to hurt you and/or your children; denying you sleep, warmth or nutrition; denying you needed medical care; driving recklessly while you and/or your children are in the car.

Social Abuse

Controlling where you go, who you see, what you wear; keeping you from contacting family or friends; preventing you from leaving the house; preventing you from going to a place of worship or praying; making all the 'big' decisions about where you can or cannot go; checking up on you (e.g., listening to your phone calls, checking the mileage on the car, calling you repeatedly at work); refusing to do housework or child care; trying to make you feel guilty about going to work or socializing.

Sexual Abuse

Any forced or unwanted sexual contact/activity; pressuring you to have sex when you don't want to (refusing to take no for an answer) forcing you to have sex or to do sexual acts you do not want or like; raping you. *(Forcing you to have sex is a criminal offence, even if you are married.)*

Financial or Economic Abuse

Taking control of your financial affairs when you don't want him/her to; preventing you from having access to money; stopping you from getting or keeping a job; refusing to give you enough money to live on; making all of the decisions about how the money should be spent.

Property Damage

Kicking a hole in the wall; scratching your car; taking away or breaking things that are important to you; abusing a family pet.

Stalking
Stalking is behavior intended to harass, intimidate and torment
you. Stalking includes a range of behaviors such as: repeated
phone calls; sending threatening letters, faxes or e-mails; loiter-
ing near your residence or place of work; spying on or openly
watching you; following you; harming pets.

If you are concerned about your relationship, seek help and
clarification regarding your individual rights in that relationship. No one deserves to be abused; that includes you, Christian. Anyone who deliberately tries to control, manipulate, or
hurt you is not motivated by the Holy Spirit. *"He who will
abuse animals because he has them in his power is both a coward
and a tyrant. A disposition to cause pain, whether to our fellow
men or to the brute creation, is satanic...A record goes up to heaven,
and a day is coming when judgment will be pronounced against
those who abuse God's creatures"* (Ellen G. White, *Patriarchs and
Prophets*, p. 443). If you know that you are being abused and
continue to stay in that situation, you could be perpetuating
"personal abuse." Some have noted that victims become com-
plicit in the abuser's sin if they do nothing to remove themselves from it. My prayer for you is that you will understand
how much God loves you and that His thoughts toward you
are of peace, and not of evil (Jeremiah 29:11).

O Be Careful Little Lips
By Dr. Mable C. Dunbar

She sat in front of me, a beautiful, blue-eyed brunette. She said that she was being verbally abused by her husband of ten years, a successful psychiatrist. He called her names and told her that she was so stupid she did not have enough sense to form an opinion about anything. For many years she took the verbal abuse because she thought she deserved it, after all, she had only finished high school and he was a doctor. But friends told her that she was married to an abuser and should take steps to protect herself. She did not believe them until she found out that her husband and pastor were plotting to have her admitted to a mental institution because she was "emotionally disturbed." See, she was not able to figure out how to provide meals for herself, her six year old daughter, and husband with $20.00 a week!

According to Grace Ketterman verbal abuse
1. Rejects an individual's value as a person,
2. Isolates the victim from social activities and friendships by destroying self-esteem,
3. Creates terror in the victim,
4. Ignores the basic needs of its victims,
5. Corrupts the values and behaviors of the victim,
6. Degrades the victim by robbing him/her of self-esteem,
7. Exploits its victim for the benefits of the abuser, especially from a temporary sense of power... *Verbal Abuse: Healing the Hidden Wound*, pp. 12-13.[1]

---

[1]Ketterman, Grace. (2004). *Verbal Abuse: Healing the Hidden Wound*. Ann Arbor, MI: Servant Ministries, Inc.

Victims of domestic violence often tell me that the worst form of abuse is verbal abuse because the sarcastic, negative, and scathing words repeat in their heads no matter where they go. Words like, "You are stupid," "You can't do anything right," "I wish you were never born," "You make me sick," "Why don't you act like...," "You are so fat (ugly, thin, tall, short)." These negative statements play over and over again like a broken record until the victim comes to believe them. Then the abuser's behavior reinforces her belief system.

For some this becomes a vicious cycle. What we are told about who we are contributes to the feelings we have of ourselves and then our feelings influence our behavior. We become "self-fulfilling prophets." Verbal abuse robs people of their dignity, contributing to their feelings of worthless, senselessness, and powerlessness. When an individual feels powerless, the door to their self-esteem is left open to be entered by someone who gradually gains control.

We are admonished to be careful in our speech because our words have an impact for good or for evil. Regret is most often the end product of unkind words. *"What harm is wrought in the family circle by the utterance of impatient words for impatient utterance of one leads another to retort in the same spirit and manner. Then come words of retaliation, words of self-justification, and it is by such words that a heavy, galling yoke is manufactured for your neck; for all these bitter words will come back in a baleful harvest in your soul"* (Ellen G. White, *Review and Herald*, Feb. 27, 1913).

Each one of us needs to be careful about what we say, how we say it, and the motivation behind our words. *"Let no corrupt communication proceed out of your mouth, but that which is good* to the use of edifying, that it may minister grace unto the hearers" (Ephesians 4:29). "A word fitly spoken is like apples of gold in pictures of silver" (Proverbs 25:11).

◆

APPENDIX D

Ministry Texts for the Helper

Leviticus 19:16 (New International Version)
"Do not do anything that endangers your neighbor's life. I am the Lord."

"Do not stand by idly and see your neighbor's blood spilled" (CCADA paraphrase).

2 Chronicles 7:14-15
"If my people, who are called by my name, will humble themselves and pray and seek my face and turn from their wicked ways, then will I hear from heaven and will forgive their sin and will heal their land."

Psalm 9:9
"The Lord also will be a refuge for the oppressed, a refuge in times of trouble."

Psalm 10:17, 18
"Lord, Thou hast heard the desire of the humble; Thou wilt prepare their heart, Thou wilt cause Thine ear to hear: to judge the fatherless and the oppressed, that the man of the earth may no more oppress."

Psalm 12:5 (New Living Translation)
"The Lord replies, 'I have seen violence done to the helpless, and I have heard the groans of the poor. Now I will rise up to rescue them, as they have longed for me to do? '"

Proverbs 31:9
"Open thy mouth, judge righteously, and plead the cause of the poor and needy."

Isaiah 1:17 (New International Version)
"Seek justice, encourage the oppressed. Defend the cause of the fatherless, plead the case of the widow."

"Seek justice, relieve the oppressed, and correct the oppressor. Defend the fatherless, plead for the widows" (CCADA paraphrase).

Isaiah 32:17
"And the work of righteousness shall be peace; and the effect of righteousness quietness and assurance forever."

Isaiah 35:3, 4
"Strengthen ye the weak hands, and confirm the feeble knees. Say to them that are of a fearful heart, Be strong, fear not: behold, your God will come with vengeance, even God with a recompense; He will come and save you."

Isaiah 56:1
"Thus saith the Lord, keep ye judgment, and do justice: for my salvation is near to come and my righteousness to be revealed."

Isaiah 60:18 (New International Version)
"No longer will violence be heard in your land nor ruin or destruction within your borders, but you will call your walls Salvation and your gates Praise."

Isaiah 61:1
"The Spirit of the Lord God is upon me; because the Lord hath anointed me to preach good tidings unto the meek; He hath sent me to bind up the broken-hearted, to proclaim liberty to the captives, and the opening of the prison to them that are bound."

Jeremiah 22:3
"Thus saith the Lord; execute ye judgment and righteousness, and deliver the spoiled out of the hand of the oppressor: and do no wrong, do no violence to the stranger, the fatherless, nor the widow, neither shed innocent blood in this place."

Ezekiel 3:17-19
"Son of man, I have made thee a watchman unto the house of Israel: therefore hear the word at my mouth, and give them warning from me. When I say unto the wicked, thou shalt surely die; and thou givest him not warning, nor speakest to warn the wicked from his wicked way, to save his life; the same wicked man shall die in his iniquity; but his blood will I require at thine hand. Yet if thou warn the wicked, and he turn not from his wickedness, nor from his wicked way, he shall die in his iniquity; but thou hast delivered thy soul."

Galatians 6:2
"Bear ye one another's burdens, and so fulfill the law of Christ."

Colossians 3:15
"Let the peace of Christ rule in your hearts."

Hebrews 12:12
"Wherefore lift up the hands which hang down, and the feeble knees."

Hebrews 13:3
"Remember them that are in bonds, as bound with them; and them which suffer adversity, as being yourselves also in the body."

James 5:19, 20
"Brethren, if any of you do err from the truth, and one convert him; Let him know, that he which converteth the sinner from the error of his way shall save a soul from death, and shall hide a multitude of sins."

1 John 2:29
"If ye know that He is righteous, ye know that everyone that doeth righteousness is born of Him."

Affirming Texts for the Victim

Deuteronomy 30:19 (New Revised Standard Version)
"I have set before you life and death, blessings and curses. Choose life so that you and your descendents may live."

Psalms 18:48
"He delivereth me from mine enemies: yea, Thou liftest me up above those that rise up against me: thou hast delivered me from the violent man."

Psalm 31:9, 10, 14 (New International Version)
"Be merciful to me, O Lord, for I am in distress; my eyes grow weak with sorrow, my soul and my body with grief. My life is consumed by anguish and my years by groaning; my strength fails because of my affliction, and my bones grow weak. But I trust in you, O Lord; I say, 'You are my God.'"

"Have pity on me, O God, for I am in distress with sorrow my eye is consumed; my soul also, and my body. I am like a dish that is broken... But my trust is in you, O God; I say, You are my God" (CCADA paraphrase).

Psalm 34:19
"Many are the afflictions of the righteous, but the Lord delivereth him (her) out of them all."

Psalms 103:6
"The Lord executeth righteousness and judgment for all that are oppressed."

Psalms 146:7

"Which executeth judgment for the oppressed: which giveth food to the hungry. The Lord looseth the prisoners."

Isaiah 38: 17

"Behold, for peace I had great bitterness: but Thou hast in love to my soul delivered it from the pit of corruption. For Thou hast cast all my sins behind Thy back."

Isaiah 41:10

"Fear thou not; for I am with thee: be not dismayed; for I am thy God: I will strengthen thee; yes, I will help thee; Yea I will uphold thee with the right hand of My righteousness."

Jeremiah 17:14

"Heal me, O Lord, and I shall be healed; save me, and I shall be saved; for Thou art my praise."

Jeremiah 29:11

"For I know the thoughts that I think toward you, saith the Lord, thoughts of peace, and not of evil, to give you an expected end."

Jeremiah 30:17

"For I will restore health unto thee, and I will heal thee of thy wounds, saith the Lord...."

Malachi 4:2

"But unto you that fear my name shall the Sun of Righteousness arise with healing in His wings."

John 10:10 (New Revised Standard Version)
"The thief comes only to steal and kill and destroy. I came that they may have life, and have it abundantly."

Hebrews 4:16 (New International Version)
"Let us then approach the throne of grace with confidence, so that we may receive mercy and find grace to help us in our time of need."

"Therefore let us draw near with confidence to the throne of grace, so that we may receive mercy and find grace to help in time of need" (CCADA paraphrase).

3 John 2
"Beloved, I wish above all things that thou mayest prosper and be in health even as thy soul prospereth."

Accountability Texts for the Abuser

Psalms 37:9
"For evildoers shall be cut off: but those that wait upon the Lord, they shall inherit the earth."

Psalm 37:37
"Mark the perfect man and behold the upright: for the end of that man is peace."

Proverbs 10:11
"The mouth of a righteous man is a well of life: but violence covereth the mouth of the wicked."

Proverbs 28:13
"He that covereth his sins shall not prosper: but whoso confesseth and forsaketh them shall have mercy."

Proverbs 28:17
"A man that doeth violence to the blood of any person shall flee to the pit; let no man stay him."

Zephaniah 1:9
"In the same day also will I punish all those that leap on the threshold, which fill their masters' houses with violence and deceit."

Malachi 2:16-17 (The Clear Word)
"…Guard your spirit and don't break faith with your wife; the one you married when you were young. The Lord says, 'I hate divorce. I hate it when a man is unfaithful and divorces his wife for someone else. To make things worse, he covers up his

treachery and violence by pretending to be innocent.' So guard your affections and don't break the promise you made to your wife when the two of you got married."

Matthew 18:33
"Shouldest not thou also have had compassion on thy fellow servant, even as I had pity on thee?"

2 Corinthians 9:8
"And God is able to make all grace abound toward you; that ye, always having all sufficiency in all things, may abound to every good work."

Ephesians 4:29
"Let no corrupt communication proceed out of your mouth, but that which is good to the use of edifying, that it may minister grace unto the hearers."

Ephesians 4:31
"Let all bitterness, and wrath, and anger, and clamor, and evil speaking, be put away from you, with all malice."

James 1:19, 20
"Wherefore, my beloved brethren, let every man be swift to hear, slow to speak, slow to wrath: For the wrath of man worketh not the righteousness of God."

James 1:26
"If any man among you seem to be religious, and bridleth not his tongue, but deceiveth his own heart, this man's religion is vain."

James 3:10

Out of the same mouth proceedeth blessing and cursing. My brethren, these things ought not so to be.

1 Peter 3:8

"Be ye all of one mind, having compassion one of another, love as brethren, be pitiful, be courteous."

Reference

CCADA paraphrase from Christian Coalition Against Domestic Abuse website: http://ccada.org

◆

Appendix E

Counsels to Pastors and Church Leaders/Workers Regarding
Power and Control Behaviors and/or Attitudes
(All quotations are taken from the book,
Testimonies to Ministers and Gospel Workers)
by Ellen G. White

"The Lord has not placed any one of His human agencies under the dictation and control of those who are themselves but erring mortals. He has not placed upon men the power to say, 'You shall do this, and you shall not do that'" (p. 347).

"It is not in the order of God that any man, or class of men, should assume that God has made them the conscience for their brethren, or put forth their finite hand in a patronizing manner to control the Lord's delegated workers, thus endangering the safety of the Lord's heritage as well as their own, and retarding the work of God" (pp. 208-209).

"God will not vindicate any device whereby men shall in the slightest degree rule or oppress his fellow men" (p. 366).

"When men in any line of God's work seek to bring the minds and talents of the Lord's human agents under their control, they have assumed a jurisdiction over their fellow men that they cannot maintain without injustice and iniquity. The Lord has placed no man as judge, either of the pen or the voice of God's workmen" (p. 293).

"Organizations, institutions, unless kept by the power of God, will work under Satan's dictation to bring men under the control of men; and fraud and guile will bear the semblance of zeal for truth and for the advancement of the kingdom of God. Whatever in our practice is not as open as day, belong to the methods of the prince of evil. His methods are practiced even among Seventh-day Adventists, who claim to have advanced truth" (p. 366).

"As soon as man begins to make an iron rule for other men, as soon as he begins to harness up and drive men according to his own mind, he dishonors God and imperils his own soul and the souls of his brethren" (p. 367).

"Those whom God has placed in positions of responsibility should never seek to exalt themselves or to turn the attention of men to their work. They must give all the glory to God. They must not seek for power that they may lord it over God's heritage; for only those who are under the rule of Satan will do this. But the rule or ruin system is too often seen in our institutions. This spirit is cherished and revealed by some in responsible positions, and because of this God cannot do the work He desires to do through them" (pp. 279-280).

"There will be those among us who will always want to control the work of God, to dictate even what movements shall be made when the work goes forward under the direction of the angel who joins the third angel in the message to be given to the world. God will use ways and means by which it will be seen that He is taking the reins in His own hands" (p. 300).

"The high-handed power that has been developed, as though position has made men gods, makes me afraid, and ought to cause

fear. It is a curse wherever and by whomsoever it is exercised. This lording it over God's heritage will create such a disgust of man's jurisdiction that a state of insubordination will result. The people are learning that men in high positions of responsibility cannot be trusted to mold and fashion other men's minds and characters" (p. 361).

"Satan takes the control of every mind that is not decidedly under the control of the Spirit of God" (p. 79).

"God has appointed no man to be conscience for his fellowman. It is not wise to lay so much responsibility upon an officer that he will feel that he is forced to become a dictator" (p. 477).

"Let me entreat our state conferences and our churches to cease putting their dependence upon men and making flesh their arm. Look not to other men to see how they conduct themselves under the conviction of the truth, or to ask them for aid. Look not to men in high positions of responsibility for strength, for they are the very men who are in danger of considering a position of responsibility as evidence of God's special power. Our churches are weak because the members are educated to look to and depend upon human resources, and thousands of dollars are needlessly expended in transporting finite men from one place to another, in order that they may settle little difficulties, when Jesus is ever near to help those who are needy and distressed" (p. 380).

"All the members of the church are to labor interestedly, zealously, not striving, as many have done, to see who shall be the greatest, and how to secure the highest wages, but striving to win souls for Christ, which means being a part of the firm, in partnership with Christ. Let all try to do their best" (p. 320).

◆

Appendix F

Sample Sermon Outline

Don't Keep This Secret
By Dr. C. A. Dunbar

Attract Attention:
Read First Paragraph of "Who's to Blame?" (page 191)

Create Interest:
a.   Share facts about domestic violence
b.   Define and describe various kinds of abuse
          -Physical
          -Emotional
          -Economic
          -Sexual
          -Threats
          -Intimidation/manipulation (Using children)
          -Using male privilege
          -Isolation
          -Religious (spiritual)

Establish Need:
Characteristics of abuse:
     a.   Learned Behavior – observation deepens impression
     b.   Selective – abusers choose their victims
     c.   Permissible – by ignoring domestic violence, we permit it to continue

      d.   Cyclic – occurs over and over if there is no intervention

Provide Solution:
      a.   We all have a right to exist (Gen. 2:7, 1 Cor. 7:3)
      b.   We all have a right to do (Gen. 1:28 – 2nd part)
      c.   We all have a right to think and feel (Gen. 1:28 – 1st part)
      d.   We all have a right to be ourselves – own identity and power (Gen. 1:27, 1 Peter 2:9)

The Key:
      Mutual submission (Eph. 5:21-26, 11 Cor. 7:3-4)

Visualize Benefits:
      a.   Loving relationships (Eph. 5:28, 25)
      b.   Cherishing, nurturing individuals (Eph. 5:29)

Appeal for action:
      a.   Pray for the millions of women seeking release from abuse.
      b.   Pray for impaired relationship.
      c.   Pray that we might all be what God designed us to be.
      d.   Determine to become proactive and make a difference to prevent domestic violence and abuse.

Appendix G

How Safe Is Your Church Quiz

By Norka Blackman-Richards 4 Real Seminars
(Used by Permission)

Directions: Circle the answer as it relates to your church.

1. If a woman confessed to being abused in my church, the church family (including men and leaders) would embrace her and offer compassionate concern for her situation.

   Yes   No   I don't know

2. My pastor, or someone assigned by the church is a trained counselor. He/she is accessible, offers weekly office hours, and I trust to refer situations of abuse to him/her.

   Yes   No   I don't know

3. The women in my church are, for the most part, compassionate, caring, and embracing of women who are suffering emotionally and or spiritually.

   Yes   No   I don't know

4. The Women's Ministries in my church provides several opportunities during the year, through planned activities, for women to fellowship, express their feelings and share their experiences.
    Yes   No   I don't know

5. In the past 2 years I have received some form of training, awareness workshop, or heard a sermon on abuse prevention and detection.
    Yes   No   I don't know

6. If a woman confessed to being abused in my church today, we would have an immediate plan of action to secure the victim in a safe place.
    Yes   No   I don't know

7. There are different types of support groups for women in my church, even if there is none for abused women, but these groups provide opportunities and places for women to bond and share.
    Yes   No   I don't know

8. My pastor's wife and/or the wives of my elders or others designated are accessible to listen and provide support for the women in my church.
    Yes   No   I don't know

9. In the past year the Women's Ministries of my church has sponsored at least one workshop on abuse prevention and detection for the entire church family.
    Yes   No   I don't know

10. The Women's Ministries in my church has planned more than one activity specifically targeting young girls with the goal of opening lines of communication and bonding with them.

Yes   No   I don't know

ANSWERS:

Count how many *Yes's, No's,* and *I don't knows* you answered. If you answered *Yes* more than 6 times your ministry and church are on the right track. Keep it UP! If you answered more *No's* than *Yes's* your church is NOT a safe place for abused women. You have a lot of work to do. If you answered more *I don't knows* than *No's* or *Yes's*, you need to wakc up and get involved.

◆

Appendix H

Women's Healing and Empowerment Network
(W.H.E. Network)
P.O. Box 9637
Spokane, WA 99209
Toll Free: 1-877-276-5597
Phone: (509) 323-2123
Fax (509) 323-2120
www.whenetwork.com - info@whenetwork.com

Mission

Women's Healing and Empowerment Network (W.H.E. Network) is a faith-based non-profit organization that provides education, resources, consultation, counseling, and other support services in the areas of domestic violence, sexual abuse and related abuse for churches, schools, affiliate programs, and other organizations. We assist religious organizations in establishing policies and procedures that will help to prevent child abuse, protect victims, and hold perpetrators accountable for their actions.

Programs and Services

Education on Abuse Prevention & Recovery
Educating people, families, pastors, teachers, and the community is the key to prevention of, and long-term recovery from abuse. W.H.E. Network heavily emphasizes this very import-

ant aspect of our program. Our teams of educators, counselors, clergy, and lawyers travel world-wide conducting seminars, consulting, and facilitating the implementation of Christian fundamentals into lives, churches, schools, and communities. Each year we conduct the national **"Being There Conference"** that provides a healing experience for men, women, and young adults who have been abused or are abusive or caregivers for individuals dealing with abuse.

Networking, Consultation, Collaboration, and Advocacy
W.H.E. Network is an avenue through which we network, consult, and collaborate with the community to help provide a coordinated response to domestic violence and related abuse issues. We advocate for victims of domestic violence and work with churches, religious communities, and other entities to establish and execute policies to protect victims, and hold abusers accountable for their actions.

Crisis Counseling for the Abused & Abusive
Professional Christian counseling for the abused and the abuser is available through Christian counselors and therapists. They use Biblically-based counseling practices designed to give hope, healing, and empowerment to abused and abusive individuals.

Healing Centers
When Christian women and children find themselves in an abusive situation, where do they go? W.H.E.Network healing centers and retreats wrap them in arms of love and protection.

Project: P.R.O.T.E.C.T (Preventing & Reducing Oppression to End Child Trauma)
This educational program is designed to build awareness of the prevalence of child sexual abuse in our homes and churches through educational workshops and parenting classes. Project: P.R.O.T.E.C.T's overall goal is to help empower us to do what we can to protect our children from child molesters.

EMPOWERED DVD Series
These programs feature individuals who share their history of abuse, their struggle with dysfunctional ways of thinking, feeling and living, and their experience of daily empowerment through Christ.

◆

Appendix I

National Coalitions and other Resources

Faith Trust Institute
2400 N. 45th Street #101
Seattle, WA 98103
206-634-1903 fax
E-mail: info@faithtrustinstitute.org
www.faithtrustinstitute.org

FaithTrust Institute is an international, multi-faith organization working to end sexual and domestic violence. We provide communities and advocates with the tools and knowledge they need to address the religious and cultural issues related to abuse. Faith-Trust Institute works with many communities, including Asian and Pacific Islander, Buddhist, Jewish, Latino/a, Muslim, Black, Anglo, Indigenous, Protestant and Roman Catholic.

Christian Coalition Against Domestic Abuse
850 Ives Dairy Road T-57/409
Miami, Florida 33179
E-mail: info@ccada.org
www.ccada.org

The mission of CCADA is to empower the Christian community and its leadership by bringing awareness to the issue of domestic abuse in our community so that through prayerful collaboration, education and intervention we end abusive behaviors.

FOCUS Ministries
P. O. Box 2014
Elmhurst, IL 60126
630-595-7023
E-mail: generalinfo@focusministries1.org
www.focusministries1.org

FOCUS Ministries is a not-for-profit organization devoted to offer hope, encouragement, education, and assistance to women who are struggling in difficult circumstances, especially dysfunctional marriages, spousal abuse, separation, or divorce. Based in Illinois, FOCUS Ministries provides help for women suffering the horror of domestic violence and support for those who want to help. Their mission is to encourage women who are struggling in difficult circumstances to find strength and hope in Jesus Christ.

W.A.S.H.
(Women and Men Against Sexual Harassment
and Other Abuses)
4309 Sandy Spring Road, Burtonsville, MD 20866-1139
301- 384-3727, 800 - 433-WASH.
Fax 301-421-4431
Website: www.tagnet.org/wash/aboutwash.html

———⊛———

*Through educational means, W.A.S.H. will help church members
and leaders stop harassment and abuse. This will involve training
and utilizing the resources of experts in the field to interrupt the
cycle of denial and facilitate healing.*

The National Domestic Violence Hotline
1-800-799-SAFE (7233)
1-800-787-3224 (TDD)

American Institute on Domestic Violence
PO Box 2232
Ruidoso, NM 88355
Phone: 505-973-2225
E-mail: info@aidv-usa.com
Website www.aidv-usa.com

National Coalition of Anti-Violence Programs
240 W. 35th Street #200,
New York, NY 10001
Phone: 212-714-1184
Website www.ncavp.org

National Network to End Domestic Violence
2001 S Street NW, Suite 400,
Washington, DC 20009
Phone: 202-543-5566
Fax: 202-543-5624

The National Domestic Violence Hotline is staffed 24 hours a day by trained counselors who can provide crisis assistance and information about shelters, legal advocacy, health care centers, and counseling. The number is 1-800-799-SAFE (7233).

The Rape, Abuse, Incest National Network (RAINN)
200 L Street, NW, Suite 406
Washington, DC 20036
Phone: 202-544-3064 or 1-800-656-HOPE
Fax: 202-544-3556
Website: info@rainn.org

RAINN will automatically transfer you to the rape crisis center nearest you, anywhere in the nation. It can be used as a last resort if people cannot find a domestic violence shelter.

National Center for Victims of Crime
2000 M Street, NW, Suite 480
Washington, DC 20036
Phone 202-467-8701
Website: www.ncvc.org

Family Violence Prevention Fund
E-mail: info@endabuse.org
Website: endabuse.org

———❦———

Main Office
Family Violence Prevention Fund
383 Rhode Island St., Suite #304
San Francisco, CA 94103-5133
Phone: (415) 252-8900
Fax: (415) 252-8991
TTY: (800) 595-4889

Washington, DC Office
1101 14th Street NW, Suite 300
Washington, DC 20005
Phone: (202) 682-1212
Fax: (202) 682-4662

Boston, MA Office
67 Newbury Street. Mezzanine Level
Boston, MA 02116
Phone: (617) 262-5900
Fax" (617) 262-5901

The Family Violence Prevention Fund works to prevent violence within the home, and in the community, to help those whose lives are devastated by violence because everyone has the right to live free of violence.

Family Violence Department
National Council of Juvenile and Family Court Judges
P.O. Box 8970
Reno, NV 89507
Office: (775) 784-6012
Toll free: (800) 527-3223
Fax: (775) 784-6628
E-mail: staff@ncjfcj.org
Website: www. ncjfcj.org

National Clearinghouse on Marital and Date Rape
2325 Oak Street
Berkeley, CA 94708

**American Bar Association Standing Committee
on Pro Bono and Public Service**
*This site provides information on pro bono legal assistance as well
as a directory of pro bono programs.*
www.abanet.org/legalservices/probono

Appendix J

State Coalitions on Domestic Violence

Alabama Coalition Against Domestic Violence
P.O. Box 4762
Montgomery, AL 36103
(334) 832-4842 Fax: (334) 832-4803
(800) 650-6522 Hotline
Website: www.acadv.org
Email: info@acadv.org

Alaska Network on Domestic and Sexual Violence
130 Seward Street, Suite 214
Juneau, AK 99801
(907) 586-3650 Fax: (907) 463-4493
Website: www.andvsa.org

Arizona Coalition Against Domestic Violence
301 East Bethany Home Road, Suite C194
Phoenix, AZ 85012
(602) 279-2900 Fax: (602) 279-2980
(800) 782-6400 Nationwide
Website: www.azcadv.org
Email: acadv@azcadv.org

Arkansas Coalition Against Domestic Violence
1401 West Capitol Avenue, Suite 170
Little Rock, AR 72201
(501) 907-5612 Fax: (501) 907-5618
(800) 269-4668 Nationwide
Website: www.domesticpeace.com
Email: kbangert@domesticpeace.com

California Partnership to End Domestic Violence
P.O. Box 1798
Sacramento, CA 95812
(916) 444-7163 Fax: (916) 444-7165
(800) 524-4765 Nationwide
Website: www.cpedv.org
Email: info@cpedv.org

Colorado Coalition Against Domestic Violence
1120 Lincoln Street, Suite 900
Denver, CO 80203
(303) 831-9632 Fax: (303) 832-7067
(888) 778-7091
Website: www.ccadv.org

Connecticut Coalition Against Domestic Violence
90 Pitkin Street
East Hartford, CT 06108
(860) 282-7899 Fax: (860) 282-7892
(888) 774-2900 In State DV Hotline
Website: www.ctcadv.org
Email: info@ctcadv.org

Delaware Coalition Against Domestic Violence
100 West 10th Street, #703
Wilmington, DE 19801
(302) 658-2958 Fax: (302) 658-5049
(800) 701-0456 Statewide
Website: www.dcadv.org
Email: dcadv@dcadv.org

DC Coalition Against Domestic Violence
5 Thomas Circle Northwest
Washington, DC 20005
(202) 299-1181 Fax: (202) 299-1193
Website: www.dccadv.org
Email: info@dccadv.org

Florida Coalition Against Domestic Violence
425 Office Plaza
Tallahassee, FL 32301
(850) 425-2749 Fax: (850) 425-3091
(850) 621-4202 TDD
(800) 500-1119 In State
Website: www.fcadv.org

Georgia Coalition Against Domestic Violence
114 New Street, Suite B
Decatur, GA 30030
(404) 209-0280 Fax: (404) 766-3800
(800) 334-2836 Crisis Line
Website: www.gcadv.org
Email: info@gcadv.org

Hawaii State Coalition Against Domestic Violence
716 Umi Street, Suite 210
Honolulu, HI 96819-2337
(808) 832-9316 Fax: (808) 841-6028
Website: www.hscadv.org
Email admin@hscadv.org

Idaho Coalition Against Sexual and Domestic Violence
300 E Mallard Drive, Suite 130
Boise, ID 83706
(208) 384-0419 Fax: (208) 331-0687
(888) 293-6118
Website: www.idvsa.org
Email: thecoalition@idvsa.org

Illinois Coalition Against Domestic Violence
801 South 11th Street
Springfield, IL 62703
(217) 789-2830 Fax: (217) 789-1939
(217) 242-0376 TTY
Help Line: (877) 863-6338
Website: www.ilcadv.org
Email: ilcadv@ilcadv.org

Indiana Coalition Against Domestic Violence
1915 West 18th Street, Suite B
Indianapolis, IN 46202
(317) 917-3685 Fax: (317) 917-3695
(800) 538-3393 In State
Website: www.violenceresource.org
Email: icadv@violenceresource.org

Iowa Coalition Against Domestic Violence
515 - 28th Street, Suite 102
Des Moines, IA 50312
(515) 244-8028 Fax: (515) 244-7417
Website: www.icadv.org
Email: admin@icadv.org

Kansas Coalition Against Sexual and Domestic Violence
634 Southwest Harrison Street
Topeka, KS 66603
(785) 232-9784 Fax: (785) 266-1874
Crisis Hotline: (888) 363-2287
Website: www.kcsdv.org
Email: coalition@kcsdv.org

Kentucky Domestic Violence Association
P.O. Box 356
Frankfort, KY 40601
(502) 209-5382. Phone/Fax (502) 226-5382
Website: www.kdva.org
Email: info@kdva.org

Louisiana Coalition Against Domestic Violence
P.O. Box 77308
Baton Rouge, LA 70879
(225) 752-1296 Fax: (225) 751-8927
Website: www.lcadv.org
E-mail: sheila@lcadv.org

Maine Coalition To End Domestic Violence
104 Sewall St.
Augusta, ME 04330
(207) 430-8334 Fax: (207) 430-8348
Website: www.mcedv.org
Email: info@mcedv.org

Maryland Network Against Domestic Violence
6911 Laurel-Bowie Road, Suite 309
Bowie, MD 20715
(301) 352-4574 Fax: (301) 809-0422
(800) 634-3577 Nationwide
Website: www.mnadv.org
Email: info@mnadv.org

Jane Doe, Inc./Massachusetts Coalition Against Sexual Assault and Domestic Violence
14 Beacon Street, Suite 507
Boston, MA 02108
(617) 248-0922 Fax: (617) 248-0902
(617) 263-2200 TTY/TDD
Website: www.janedoe.org
Email: info@janedoe.org

Michigan Coalition Against Domestic and Sexual Violence
3893 Okemos Road, Suite B-2
Okemos, MI 48864
(517) 381-4663 Phone/Fax: (517) 347-1060
(517) 381-8470 TTY
Website: www.mcadsv.org
Email: general@mcadsv.org

Minnesota Coalition For Battered Women
Leo Plato Blvd E, Suite 130
St. Paul, MN 55107
(651) 646-6177 Fax: (651) 646-1527
(866) 223-1111 Crisis Line
Website: www.mcbw.org
Email: mcbw@mcbw.org

Mississippi Coalition Against Domestic Violence
P.O. Box 4703
Jackson, MS 39296
(601) 981-9196 Fax: (601) 981-2501
(800) 898-3234
Website: www.mcadv.org

Missouri Coalition Against Domestic and Sexual Violence
217 Oscar Drive, Suite A
Jefferson City, MO 65101
(573) 634-4161 Fax: (573) 636-3728
Website: www.mocadsv.org
Email: mocadsv@mocadsv.org

Montana Coalition Against Domestic & Sexual Violence
P.O. Box 818
Helena, MT 59624
(406) 443-7794 Fax: (406) 443-7818
(888) 404-7794 Nationwide
Website: www.mcadsv.com
Email: mcadsv@mt.net

Nebraska Domestic Violence Sexual Assault Coalition
1000 "O" Street, Suite 102
Lincoln, NE 68508
(402) 476-6256 Fax: (402) 476-6806
(800) 876-6238 In State Hotline
(877) 215-0167 Spanish Hotline
Website: www.ndvsac.org
Email: help@ndvsac.org

Nevada Network Against Domestic Violence
220 South Rock Boulevard, Suite 7
Reno, NV 89502
(775) 828-1115 Fax: (775) 828-9911
(800) 230-1955
Website: www.nnadv.org

New Hampshire Coalition Against Domestic and Sexual Violence
P.O. Box 353
Concord, NH 03302
(603) 224-8893 Fax: (603) 228-6096
(866) 644-3574 Domestic Abuse Hotline
(800)-277-5570 Sexual Abuse Hotline
Website: www.nhcadsv.org
Email: info@nhcdsv.org

New Jersey Coalition for Battered Women
1670 Whitehorse Hamilton Square Rd.
Trenton, NJ 08690
(609) 584-8107 Fax: (609) 584-9750
(888) 252-7233 TTY
(800) 572-7233 In State Hotline
Website: www.njcbw.org
Email: info@njcbw.org

New Mexico Coalition Against Domestic Violence
201 Coal Avenue Southwest
Albuquerque, NM 87102
(505) 246-9240 Fax: (505) 246-9240
Website: www.nmcadv.org
Email: info@nmcadv.org

New York State Coalition Against Domestic Violence
350 New Scotland Avenue
Albany, NY 12208
(518) 482-5465 Fax: (518) 482-3807
(800) 942-6906 English-In State
(800) 942-6908 Spanish-In State
Website: www.nyscadv.org
Email: nyscadv@nyscadv.org

North Carolina Coalition Against Domestic Violence
123 West Main Street, Suite 700
Durham, NC 27701
(919) 956-9124 Fax: (919) 682-1449
(888) 232-9124 Nation wide
Website: www.nccadv.org

North Dakota Council on Abused Women's Services
418 East Rosser Avenue, Suite 320
Bismark, ND 58501
(701) 255-6240 Fax: (701) 255-1904
(888) 255-6240 Nationwide
Website: www.ndcaws.org
Email: ndcaws@ndcaws.org

Action Ohio Coalition For Battered Women
5900 Roche Drive, Suite 445
Columbus, OH 43229
(614) 825-0551 Fax: (614) 825-0673
(888) 622-9315 In State
Website: www.actionohio.org
Email: actionoh@sbcglobal.net

Ohio Domestic Violence Network
4807 Evanswood Drive, Suite 201
Columbus, OH 43229
(614) 781-9651 Fax: (614) 781-9652
(614) 781-9654 TTY
(800) 934-9840
Website: www.odvn.org
Email: info@odvn.org

Oklahoma Coalition Against Domestic Violence and Sexual Assault
3815 North Sante Fe Avenue, Suite 124
Oklahoma City, OK 73118
(405) 524-0700 Fax: (405) 524-0711
Website: www.ocadvsa.org

Oregon Coalition Against Domestic and Sexual Violence
380 Southeast Spokane Street, Suite 100
Portland, OR 97202
(503) 230-1951 Fax: (503) 230-1973
(877) 330-1951
Website: www.ocadsv.org

Pennsylvania Coalition Against Domestic Violence
6400 Flank Drive, Suite 1300
Harrisburg, PA 17112
(717) 545-6400 Fax: (717) 545-9456
(800) 537-2238 Nationwide
(800) 553-2508 TTY
Website: www.pcadv.org

The Office of Women Advocates
Box 11382
Fernandez Juancus Station
Santurce, PR 00910
(787) 721-7676 Fax: (787) 725-9248

Coordinadora Paz Para La Mujer, Inc.
(By Puerto Rican Coalition Against Domestic Violence and
Sexual Aggression)
Apartado 193008
San Juan, Puerto Rico 00919-3008
(787) 281-7579 Fax: (787) 767-6843
Website: www.pazparalamujer.org
Email: pazmujer@prtc.net

Rhode Island Coalition Against Domestic Violence
422 Post Road, Suite 202
Warwick, RI 02888
(401) 467-9940 Fax: (401) 467-9943
(800) 494-8100 In State Hotline
Website: www.ricadv.org
Email: ricadv@ricadv.org

South Carolina Coalition Against Domestic Violence and Sexual Assault
P.O. Box 7776
Columbia, SC 29202
(803) 256-2900 Fax: (803) 256-1030
(800) 260-9293 Nationwide
Website: www.sccadvasa.org

South Dakota Coalition Against Domestic Violence & Sexual Assault
P.O. Box 141
Pierre, SD 57501
(605) 945-0869 Fax: (605) 945-0870
(800) 572-9196 Nationwide
Website: www.southdakotacoalition.org
Email: chris@sdcadvsa.org

Tennessee Coalition Against Domestic and Sexual Violence
2 International Plaza Drive, Suite 425
Nashville, TN 37217
(615) 386-9406 Fax: (615) 383-2967
(800) 289-9018 In State
Website: www.tcadsv.org

Texas Council On Family Violence
P.O. Box 161810
Austin, TX 78716
(512) 794-1133 Fax: (512) 794-1199
Website: www.tcfv.org

Utah Domestic Violence Council
205 North 400 West
Salt Lake City, UT 84103
(801) 521-5544 Fax: (801) 521-5548
Website: www.udvc.org
Email: admin@udvc.org

Vermont Network Against Domestic Violence and Sexual Assault
P.O. Box 405
Montpelier, VT 05601
(802) 223-1302 Fax: (802) 223-6943
(802) 223-1115 TTY
Website: www.vtnetwork.org
Email: info@vtnetwork.org

Women's Coalition of St. Croix
Box 2734
Christiansted
St. Croix, VI 00822
(340) 773-9272 Fax: (340) 773-9062
Website: www.wcstx.com
Email: wcsc@pennswoods.net

Virginia Sexual and Domestic Violence Action Alliance
5008 Monument Ave, Suite A
Richmond, VA 23230
(804) 377-0335 Fax: (804) 377-0339
Website: www.vadvalliance.org
Email: info@vsdvalliance.org

Washington State Coalition Against Domestic Violence
711 Capitol Way, Suite Suite 702
Olympia, WA 98501
(360) 586-1022 Fax: (360) 586-1024
(360) 586-1029 TTY

Washington State Native American Coalition Against Domestic and Sexual Assault
P.O. Box 13260
Olympia, WA 98508
(360) 352-3120 Fax: (360) 357-3858
(888) 352-3120
Website: www.womenspiritcoalition.org
Email: info@womenspiritcoalition.org

West Virginia Coalition Against Domestic Violence
5004 Elk River Road South
Elkview, WV 25071
(304) 965-3552 Fax: (304) 965-3572
Website: www.wvcadv.org

Wisconsin Coalition Against Domestic Violence
307 South Paterson Street, Suite 1
Madison, WI 53703
(608) 255-0539 Fax: (608) 255-3560
Website: www.wcadv.org
Email: wcadv@wcadv.org

Wyoming Coalition Against Domestic Violence and Sexual Assault
P.O. Box 236
Laramie, WY 82073
(307) 755-5481 Fax: (307) 755-5482
(800) 990-3877 Nationwide
Website: www.wyomingdvsa.org
Email: info@mail.wyomingdvsa.org

◆

Part 4

Helpful Resources

◆

Selected Books

Adams, C., & Fortune, M. Eds. (1995). *Violence against women and children: A Christian theological sourcebook.* New York: Continuum.

Advisory Committee on Social Witness Policy of the General Assembly Council: Presbyterian Church (U.S.A.). (2001). *Turn mourning into dancing! A policy statement on healing domestic violence.* Louisville, KY: The Office of the General Assembly.

Allender, D. (1990). *The wounded heart: Hope for adult victims of childhood sexual abuse,* Colorado: NavPress.

Alsdurf, J. & Alsdurf, P. (1989). *Battered into submission: The tragedy of wife abuse in the Christian home.* Downers Grove, IL: Intervarsity Press.

Andersen, J. (2007). *Woman submit: Christians and domestic violence.* One Way Cafe Press.

Berry, D. (1995). *Domestic violence sourcebook.* Los Angeles: RGA Publishing Groups, Inc.

Bingham, C. (1986). Doorway to response: *The role of clergy in ministry with battered women.* Springfield, IL: Illinois Conference of Churches.

Blanco, J. (1994). *The clear Word: An expanded paraphrase of the Bible to nurture faith and growth.* Hagerstown, MD: Review and Herald Publishing Association.

Borg, M. (1997). *The God we never knew: Beyond dogmatic religion to a more authentic contemporary faith.* San Francisco: Harper San Francisco.

Branson, B. & Silva, P. (2007). *Violence among us: Ministry to families in crisis.* Valley Forge, PA: Judson Press.

Brewster, S. (2000). *To be an anchor in the storm: A guide for families and friends of abused women.* Seattle: Seal Press.

Brock, R. & Parker, R. (2001). *Proverbs of ashes: Violence, redemptive suffering, and search for what saves us.* Boston, MA: Beacon Press.

Brown, C. & Bohn, C., Eds. (1989). *Christianity, patriarchy, and abuse.* New York: Pilgrim Press.

Brown, L. (2008). *Happily never after.* Frederick, MD: PublishAmerica, LLLP.

Bussert, J. (1986). *Battered women: From a theology of suffering to an ethics of empowerment.* New York Division for Mission in North America, Lutheran Church of America.

Chagee, P. (1997). *Accountable leadership: A resource guide for sustaining legal, financial, and ethical integrity in today's congregations.* San Francisco, CA: Jossey-Bass.

Cooper-White, P. (1995). *The cry of Tamar: Violence against women and the church's response.* Minneapolis: Augsburg Fortress.

Couden, B., Ed. (1999). *Understanding intimate violence.* Hagerstown, MD: Review and Herald Publishing Association.

Dobash, R. & Dobash, R. *Violence against wives: A case against the patriarchy.* New York, NY: Free Press (Macmillan).

Domestic Violence Awareness Task Force, Office of Justice and Peace, Catholic Diocese of Richmond, VA. (2003). *Circles of healing: A support group curriculum for abused Christian women.* Seattle, WA: Faith Trust Institute.

Dopke, C. (2002). *Creating partnerships with faith communities to end sexual violence.* Olympia, WA: Washington Coalition of Sexual Assault Programs.

Dunbar, M. (2004). *The truth about us: How to discover the potential God has given you.* Lincoln, NE: Advent*Source*, Church Resources Consortium (2002).

Dutton, D. (1998). *The abusive personality: Violence and control in intimate relationships.* New York and London: The Guilford Press.

Dutton, D. & Golant, S. (1995). *The batterer: A psychological profile.* New York, NY: Basic Books, a Division of Harper Collins Publishers.

Eugene, T. & Poling, J. (1998). *Balm for Gilead: Pastoral care for African American families experiencing abuse.* Nashville, Abingdon Press.

Flowers, R. & Flowers, K. (1998). *Peace & healing: Resource kit for making homes abuse free.* Lincoln, NE: AdventSource.

Fortune, M. (1987). Keeping the faith: Questions and answers for the abused woman. San Francisco: Harper San Francisco.

Fortune, M. (1999). *Is nothing sacred? When sex invades the pastoral relationship.* Cleveland: The United Church Press. (Available from FaithTrust Institute, (www.faithtrustinstitute.org).)

Fortune, M. (2005). *Sexual violence: The unmentionable sin.* Cleveland, OH: Pilgrim Press, (Available from FaithTrust Institute, (www.faithtrustinstitute.org).)

Gaddis, P. (1996). *Battered but not broken: Help for abused wives and their church families.* Valley Forge, PA.: Judson Press.

Gafke, A. & Scott, L., Eds. (1996 & 2000). *Living the sacred trust: Clergy sexual ethics—A resource on clergy misconduct of a sexual nature for cabinets and boards of ordained ministry of the United Methodist Church.* Nashville, TN: The General Board of Higher Education and Ministry.

Graetz, N. (1998). *Silence is deadly: Judaism confronts wifebeating.* Northvale, NJ: Jason Aronson.

Haegen, C. (1993). *Sexual abuse in Christian homes and churches.* Scottdale, PA: Herald Press.

Hollies, L. (2006). *Inner healing for broken vessels: A domestic violence survival guide.* Cleveland, OH: Pilgrim Press.

Holt, V., Coombs, V., Coombs, B., & Dunbar, M. (2008). *We Suffered In Silence.* Longwood, Florida: Xulon Press.

Hopkins, N. & Lasser, M., Eds. (1995). *Restoring the soul of a church: Healing congregations wounded by clergy sexual misconduct.* Bethesda, MD: The Alban Institute.

Horton, A. & Williamson, J. (1990). *When praying is not enough.* Lexington: Lexington Books.

Jantz, G. (2000). *Healing the scars of emotional abuse.* Grand Rapids, MI: Fleming H. Revell, a division of Baker Book House Company.

Johnson, D. & Vonderen, J. (1977). *The subtle power of spiritual abuse: Recognizing and escaping the spiritual manipulation and false spiritual authority within the church.* Minneapolis, MN: Bethany House Publishers.

Jones, A. (2000). *Next time she'll be dead: Battering and how to stop it.* Boston: Beacon Press.

Ketterman, G. (1992). *Verbal abuse: Healing the hidden wound.* Ann Arbor, MI: Servant Publications.

Kroeger, C., and Beck, J., Eds. (1996). *Women, abuse, and the bible: How Scripture can be used to hurt or heal.* Grand Rapids, MI: Baker Books.

Kroeger, C., & Beck, J., Eds. (1998). *Healing the hurting: Giving hope and help to abused women.* Grand Rapids, MI: Baker Books.

Kroeger, C., & Nason-Clark, N. (2001). *No place for abuse: Biblical & practical resources to counteract domestic violence.* Downers Grove, Ill: InterVarsity Press.

MacDonald, B. (1993). *Surely heed their cry: A Presbyterian guide to child abuse prevention, intervention, and healing.* Louisville, KY: Presbyterian Child Advocacy Network.

McClure, J. & Ramsey, N., Eds. (1998). *Telling the truth: Preaching about sexual and domestic violence.* Cleveland: United Church Press.

Melton, J. (1998). *Safe sanctuaries: Reducing the risk of child abuse in the church.* Nashville, TN: Discipleship Resources.

Miles, A. (2000). *Domestic violence: What every pastor needs to know.* Minneapolis: Fortress Press.

Miles, A. (2002). *Violence in families: What every Christian needs to know.* Minneapolis: Augsburg Books.

Morris, M. (1993). *Sins of the father.* Boise, Idaho: Pacific Press Publishing Association.

Murphy, N. (2003). *God's reconciling love: A pastor's handbook on domestic violence.* Seattle, WA: FaithTrust Institute (www.faithtrustinstitute.org).

Nason-Clark, N. (1997). *The battered wife: How Christians confront family violence.* Louisville: Westminister John Knox Press.

Nicarthy, G. *Getting free: You can end abuse and take back your life.* Seattle: Seal Press.

Patterson, M. (1995). *Broken by you: Men's role in stopping woman abuse.* Etobicoke, Ontario: The United Church Publishing House.

Poling, J. (1991). *The abuse of power: A theological problem.* Nashville, TN: Abingdon Press.

Poling, J. (2003). *Understanding male violence: Pastoral care issues.* St. Louis, Missouri: Chalice Press.

Poling, J. & Cozad Neuger, C., Eds. (1997). *The care of men.* Nashville, TN: Abingdon Press.

Sanford, P. (1988). *Healing victims of sexual abuse.* Oklahoma: Victory House Publishers.

Schechter, S. & James, A. (1993). *When love goes wrong: What to do when you can't do anything right.* New York: Perennial Publishing.

Shantz, K. (1994). *Lord, hear our prayers: Domestic violence worship resources.* Kitchener, Ontario: Mennonite Central Committee, Canada.

Stangler, M. (1995). *Striving to be...violence free: A guidebook for creating a safety plan.* St. Louis Park, MN: Perspectives, Inc.

Swagman, B. (2002). *Responding to domestic violence: A resource for church leaders.* Grand Rapids, MI: CRC Publications.

White, E. (1952). *The Adventist Home.* South Africa: Southern Publishing Association.

White, E. (1940). *The Desire of Ages,* Boise, ID: Pacific Press Publishing Association.

White, E. (1962). *Testimonies to Ministers and Gospel Workers,* Boise, ID: Pacific Press Publishing Association, 1962.

Wilson, K. (1997). *When violence begins at home: A comprehensive guide to understanding and ending domestic abuse.* Alameda, CA: Hunter House.

Selected Study Guides, Brochures and Media Resources

---⟨◈⟩---

A Sacred Trust: Boundary Issues for Clergy and Spiritual Teachers (Video). This exciting new video series, designed for clergy and seminarians, consists of four training videos (approximately 22 minutes each) and a comprehensive facilitator's guide with background information, discussion questions, and suggestions for role-plays and other interactive exercises. This video series is closed-captioned. *Available at the FaithTrust Institute, formerly Center for Prevention of Sexual and Domestic Violence, www.faithtrustinstitute.org.*

Bibliography on Sexual and Domestic Violence, FaithTrust Institute. This selected bibliography, presented in alphabetical order according to authors, is a resource for congregations, clergy and other religious leaders, secular and faith advocates, counselors, victims and survivors, students, and everyone seeking understanding of religious issues related to sexual and domestic violence. *Available at www.faithtrustinstitute.org.*

Broken Vows: Religious Perspective on Domestic Violence (Video & Study Guide). Inclusive of various denominations in the religious community, this one-hour video is an effective resource for bringing awareness to religious leaders and their congregations regarding the devastating effects of domestic violence. Weaving together the stories and viewpoints of battered women, clergy, psychologists, and shelter workers, it shows ways congregations can work on prevention; educates secular workers about spiritual issues that may arise for battered women; and illustrates ways that secular and religious communities can work together to bring spiritual support and physical safety to women experiencing domestic violence. Also available in Spanish. *Available at the FaithTrust Institute, www.faithtrustinstitute.org*

The Preachers: Working to End Sexual and Domestic Violence (Video). This educational video features sermons by ordained clergy who have survived partner violence. Each sermon contains insightful discourses into domestic violence as it relates to issues of faith. Includes a companion study guide. *Available at The Black Church and Domestic Violence Institute, www.bcdvi.org/index.htm.*

Engaging the Faith Community In Violence Prevention: A Tip Sheet for Practitioners, National Funding Collaborative on Violence Prevention (Tip Sheet/Brochure). NFCVP, 2000. This tip sheet covers all the basics for the prevention advocate looking to collaborate with the faith community. This is a good checklist for starting your project or initiative. Additional readings and information about other national organizations are included in this effort.

Enhancing Collaboration: Increasing Action in Preventing Domestic Violence in California (Trainer's Guide & Workbook), by Transforming Communities: Technical Assistance, Training and Resource Center (TC-TAT), 2004. This workshop curriculum for domestic violence advocates and faith community leaders is currently being revised, and will be re-named "Faith in Violence-Free Families: Building Partnerships for Change." The current curriculum focuses on collaboration between faith communities and domestic violence prevention advocacy communities. Topics such as "what faith leaders and domestic violence advocates need to know about each other," "identifying shared values," "deepening the dialogue," "developing common language," and "creating strategic plans" are addressed in this curriculum. Both versions of the curriculum are available through TC-TAT at info@transformcommunities.org (415) 526-2536.

Love - All That and More (video & six session curriculum), FaithTrust Institute. *Love – All That and More* is a 3 part video series that includes curriculi for use with youth and young adults in classrooms, community and religious groups and other settings. It is designed to inform young people about the elements that make up healthy relationships, increase awareness and understanding about violence and abuse, and motivate youth and young adults to seek relationships based on equality and mutual respect. *Available at the FaithTrust Institute, www.faithtrustinstitute.org.*

Religion and Domestic Violence: Books, Useful Web Sites and Organizations, Compiled by Nancy Flanakin, Librarian, National Center on Domestic and Sexual Violence, 2004. *PDF available atwww.ncdsv.org.*

Resources from a Religious Perspective on Issues of Domestic Violence, Safe Haven Ministries. Available at http://www. safehavenministries.org/bookstore_resource_list.cfm.

What Every Congregation Needs To Know About Domestic Violence (Brochure). FaithTrust Institute, 1994. This brochure contains good information for clergy, members of congregations, battered women's programs, and human service providers. It is designed in a question and answer format to answers basic questions about domestic violence and the faith community. Also available in Spanish at *www.faithtrustinstitute.org.*

Working Together: To Prevent Sexual and Domestic Violence (Newsletter). This newsletter includes articles, editorials, book reviews, resources and information about local, national and international prevention efforts addressing domestic violence, sexual violence, child abuse, and sexual abuse by clergy. *Available at www.faithtrustinstitute.org/Newsletter/mailing_list. htm.*

Internet Resources

Enter key words such as "domestic violence," "religion and domestic violence," "religious abuse," "spiritual abuse," etc. in your search engine. You will find many helpful links and information, including support groups, books, and organizations that address the issue of domestic violence and abuse from a religious perspective. You can also access information relating to what the church can do to prevent domestic violence and how to provide intervention for victims as well as perpetrators.

EDUCATING THE
LIBRARY USER

EDUCATING THE LIBRARY USER

JOHN LUBANS, JR.

R. R. Bowker Company
New York & London, 1974
A Xerox Education Company

XEROX

Published by R. R. Bowker Co. (A Xerox Education Company)
1180 Avenue of the Americas, New York, N.Y. 10036
Copyright © 1974 by Xerox Corporation
Printed and bound in the United States of America

Library of Congress Cataloging in Publication Data

Lubans, John.
    Educating the library user.

    Bibliography: p.
    1.   Libraries and readers—Addresses, essays,
lectures.   I.   Title.
Z711.2.L83   021   74-11794
ISBN 0-8352-0674-2

Dedicated to
J.A.L.

CONTENTS

PART II
FACULTY INVOLVEMENT IN LIBRARY-USE INSTRUCTION

PART III
IMPLEMENTATION AND EVALUATION OF LIBRARY-USE INSTRUCTION PROGRAMS

PREFACE

Educating the Library User is a collection of original essays, case studies, and research reports on the problems, hopes, and techniques of instructing library users and nonusers, from the kindergartener to the preschool adult, in the effective use of libraries and their resources. Merging the library-use teachings of school, public, and academic libraries, this book demonstrates the need for a consistent, sequential plan of library-use instruction that crosses traditional library boundaries. The contributors, librarians and teachers from varied backgrounds and types of libraries, all have expertise in the problems and progress of educating the library user.

Until now journal articles have provided the only forum for discussion of current issues in library-user education. This is the first book on the subject from a total systems point of view and it offers a wealth of information and experience which will be of interest to many readers, from eager library students, to practiced librarians, to all professionals—librarians, educators, and administrators—who are committed to bringing new insights to new users and to extending the library's reach beyond its traditional audience to the nonuser.

To place this subject in perspective, *Educating the Library User* opens with a comprehensive overview of the research to date on library-user education. Articles in Part I, "Rationale for Educating Library Users," probe the special problems in dealing with children and young adults, undergraduates, and the postschool adult. Concepts for instruction in elementary, middle, and high schools, two- and four-year colleges, technological universities, and the public library are discussed individually. In "Faculty Involvement in Library-Use Instruction," Part II, authors explore the significant and often neglected role of the teacher in educating students to use the library. Various approaches to library-use instruction are presented in Part III, "Implementation and Evaluation of Library-Use Instruction Programs." Library tours, videotapes, handbooks, computer-assisted instruction, films, and other methods suggest models adaptable to individual needs. Finally, the library school's responsibility in preparing librarians who can successfully introduce the library to potential users is considered.

Appreciation and acknowledgement is expressed to the following for their help in putting this volume together: the editors at R. R. Bowker Company; Aileen Gray, Heidi Boggs, and Lenore Martinez for preparing numerous typed drafts; the Interlibrary Loan Department at the University of Colorado; Lisa Paddock for bringing order out of chaos in the bibliography, and to the many others who have provided inspiration and ideas for this book. Recognition is also made of the librarians of the University of Colorado for creating and participating in a variety of stimulating library-user education programs that not only benefit library users but also shed light on the process of library-use instruction. In addition, the Council on Library Resources is recognized, for their Fellowship program, which provided the initial impetus for the development of *Educating the Library User.*

JOHN LUBANS, JR.
Assistant Director for Public Services
University of Colorado Libraries, Boulder

INTRODUCTION

Although little emphasis is placed in the library school curriculum on educating the library user, a large amount of interest and activity has been and is taking place in the field. Practically every library, from the most understaffed to the most affluent, offers the user some kind of instruction; oftentimes it is a library handbook or some other type of printed bibliographic aid. In academic libraries a formal, credit-bearing course in bibliographic instruction is no rarity. Many multimedia programs for library orientation now exist. School libraries doggedly pursue the library's involvement in the student's life: in some elementary schools the library is part of the curriculum and various state boards of education have established standards for student library performance.

Conferences are a measure of the practicing librarians' interest in the matter. In May 1971 the first conference on "Library Orientation for Academic Librarians" was given at Eastern Michigan University. In 1970 the fourth triennial meeting of the International Association of Technological University Libraries, at Loughborough, England, was devoted to "Educating the Library User," [1] and in the same year the New York Library Association sponsored a conference on "Use, Mis-Use and Non-Use of Academic Libraries." [2] In 1972 the exhibition sponsored in Chicago by the American Library Association's Committee on Instruction in the Use of Libraries program displayed much of the best work done in educating the library user in all types of libraries by using graphics and other media, such as tape/slide presentations, filmstrips, videotapes, and computer-based instruction. At the end of 1973 the University of Denver hosted a Conference on Evaluation of Library Instruction; proceedings of this meeting are to be published.

To note yet another indicator of interest and commitment: the Council on Library Resources and the National Endowment for the Humanities have funded a number of experiments meant to make the library central to colleges and universities. Many of these programs are described in the July and October 1971 issue of the *Drexel Library Quarterly* on "Integrating Library Instruction in the College Curriculum." Results are already evident and an important realization is becoming prevalent in campus libraries—unless teachers emphasize the library, librarians *alone* will not be able to significantly change the situation of poor use. And this is by no means a domestic problem, but one that is international in scope, which librarians in England, Denmark, Australia, South Africa, and elsewhere are exploring and attempting to define. [3, 4, 5, 6]

Do the users think they need instruction in library use? In a February 1971 study students were asked: "Should the University of Colorado offer instruction in the use of the libraries and their resources?" Eighty-seven percent of the sample of 600 library users said *yes.* [7] At the University of California, Berkeley, enrollments for a course in bibliography often exceed the class size limit. Many students appear to feel a personal need to know more about libraries and do seek out instruction.

Yet the problem of misuse and nonuse of libraries exists. A 1969 study estimated the nonuser population on campuses at 30 to 40 percent of the total enrollment in any one semester.[8] In another, more recent study of school children the conclusion was: "While only one percent of Philadelphia's fourth graders did not visit a library during the first two months . . . almost 16 percent of the 12th graders failed to visit a school or public library even once." [9]

We assume that significant solutions to problems of library use can occur by working through and with the teacher and the classroom. Although librarians can and do affect a student's knowledge of library use with their initiative and innovative programs, it is the teaching practices at most levels (with of course some outstanding exceptions) that directly affect the student's use or nonuse of the library. Under the present system few students have the opportunity to learn how to evaluate sources of information or how to transform information into knowledge.

In order, then, to make better, more effective use of the learning resources at any library level, closer working relationships must be developed between librarians and teaching faculty. A strong liaison between librarians and teachers can result in some changes in current teaching methodologies that should increase and improve the students' use and understanding of libraries.

NOTES

1. International Association of Technological University Libraries, *Educating the Library User: Proceedings of the Fourth Triennial Meeting* (Loughborough, England, April 1–3, 1970), ed. by C. M. Lincoln (Loughborough, University of Technology Library, 1970), various pagings.

2. New York Library Association, College and University Libraries Section, *Use, Mis-Use and Non-Use of Academic Libraries: Proceedings of Spring Conference, May 1–2, 1970* (New York, The Association, 1970).

3. Charles Crossley, "Education in Literature and Library Use," *Library World* 7 (May 1970): 340–341+.

4. D. B. Scott, "Training for Educational Self-Reliance," *Australian Library Journal* 19 (October 1970): 329–333.

5. D. E. Haag, "The Teaching Function of the University Library," *South African Libraries* 37 (April 1970): 272–279.

6. Danish Library Association, "Materials and Aids to Library Orientation," A Committee Report, *Bogens Verden* 52 (1970): 234–241.

7. University of Colorado, "Users and Uses of Norlin Library—Preliminary Report, May 4, 1971" (Boulder, University of Colorado, Norlin Library, 1970). Comprises 2 pages and questionnaire.

8. John Lubans, Jr., "Student Use of a Technological University Library," *IATUL Proceedings* 4 (July 1969): 7–13.

9. John Q. Benford, "The Philadelphia Project," *Library Journal* (June 15, 1971): 2041–2046.

EDUCATING THE
LIBRARY USER

RESEARCH ON LIBRARY-USER EDUCATION:
A REVIEW ESSAY

Arthur P. Young
Research Associate, Library Research Center, University of Illinois at Urbana-Champaign

If publication activity is a reliable indicator of professional interests, library instruction is generating considerable attention. In the six years from 1967 through 1972, 309 citations under the heading "instruction in library use" have appeared in *Library Literature* index. Not surprisingly, most of the articles and reports are of the "how we do it in our library" variety. Research on library instruction (or library user education), a small fraction of the published literature in any given year, has been reviewed here when it has met one or more of the following criteria: statement of hypothesis, use of statistical inference, experimental design, intensive case study, and multi-institutional surveys. No claim is made for exhaustive coverage. Chronological limits range from the 1930s to the present, with special emphasis on the past ten years. User education research relating to academic libraries and elementary and secondary school libraries falls within the scope of this review. Research literature pertaining to the formal education of librarians and orientation to automated information retrieval systems is specifically excluded.

LITERATURE SURVEYS AND BIBLIOGRAPHIES

For historical perspective on the educational aspects of librarianship, the reader should consult Helen Butler's still valuable literature survey prepared in 1942.[1] In 1960 George S. Bonn examined the literature on library instruction relating to all types of institutions from 1876 to 1958.[2] With citations to and commentary on over 300 articles, monographs, and theses, Bonn's work is the most comprehensive attempt to summarize the literature in this field. A valuable synthesis of 25 library-use studies from 1930 to 1964 was completed by Woods in 1965.[3] While library use studies do not often deal directly with library instruction, user behavior patterns are essential considerations in the design of library user education programs. The most detailed discussion of library tests, library proficiency, and academic performance is found in chapter two of Felix Snider's seminal dissertation on library ability and academic achievement.[4] Henne has written a perceptive paper on library instruction that includes an analysis of the literature, summaries of use studies, and proposals for future research.[5] Elementary and secondary schools, and higher education are covered in her review. Various media and technological approaches to library instruction are reported by Wendt in a summary of the research literature appearing from 1960 to 1966.[6]

A general survey of research and programs in library user education, with particular emphasis on British practices, is provided by Tidmarsh.[7] Davis reviewed selected research studies on the relationship between library use and academic achievement, library use and scholastic aptitude, and library use and class level.[8] A review by Bates of 181 user studies in many areas (e.g., circulation, information service, catalogs), including some references to library instruction, is highly recommended for those desiring a solid introduction to the literature of user behavior.[9] Scrivener's discerning comments on instructional practices and research merit serious attention.[10] Research studies pertaining to school librarianship for the period 1950–1967 have been summarized by Lowrie,[11] and for the years 1967–1971 by Aaron.[12] Especially valuable are the many references to theses and dissertations. Research on library use and effectiveness, user education, and user informational requirements is sifted and reported by Ford.[13]

The cornerstone bibliography of use studies is by Davis and Bailey.[14] Brief annotations accompany the 438 entries on a variety of information use topics. DeWeese has updated, and to some extent duplicated the Davis and Bailey bibliography through 1967.[15] A serviceable, annotated bibliography of use studies covering the period from 1950 to 1970 was compiled by Atkin.[16] This work is slightly marred by some inaccurate entries due to secondary verification from other bibliographies. A recent bibliography by Mirwis is devoted exclusively to user education studies for the decade 1960–1970.[17] Periodical coverage is adequate, but the section on research reports and theses omits many relevant titles.

For continuing bibliographic coverage of use studies and library instruction literature, the following indexes/abstracts, and annual reviews should be consulted: *Library Literature, Library and Information Science Abstracts, Information Science Abstracts, Research in Education* (ERIC documents), *Education Index,* and *Annual Review of Information Science and Technology. Dissertation Abstracts* often includes dissertations not recorded by the above abstracts and indexes.

ATTITUDINAL STUDIES

Few investigators have attempted to measure the attitudes of librarians, users, and instructors toward library user education. Attitudinal studies as defined here relate to general perceptions of the library's instructional role in contrast to opinions about a specific, ongoing program.

In 1970 British chemist T. A. Whitworth authored a major report on attitudes toward the centrality/marginality of the librarian's role, with particular emphasis on tutorial and educational advisory activities.[18] A mail questionnaire, with a return rate of 71 percent or more for each category, was answered by 290 technical college librarians, 188 academic staff, and 200 students. One item probed the essentiality of instructing students in the use of the library and found positive support for the proposition from librarians, staff, and students in descending order. When asked if library projects should be an essential part of student learning, librarians supported the proposition with 94 percent, staff 75 percent, and students 49 percent. To the question that no further library instruction is needed by students after an initial orientation, librarians, staff, and students agreed 1 percent, 9 percent, and 22 percent, respectively. Role conflict and incompatible perceptions regarding the library's instructional mission between librarians, faculty, and students are clearly documented. Replication of Whitworth's survey in the United States would probably elicit similar conclusions.

User opinion on library instruction has been explored by Lubans in two studies. Analyzing 27 nonusers at Rensselaer Polytechnic Institute, the author found 56 percent of the students were satisfied with their previous exposure to library instruction, 57 percent indicated that librarians were helpful and effective, and 100 percent said they would consult the literature if assigned to develop a new process.[19] And yet, when asked if they would take an optional course in library instruction, 80 percent of the students responded negatively.

Lubans conducted a more extensive survey in 1971–1972, involving 375 students (users and nonusers) at the University of Colorado.[20] Freshmen through doctoral students, although not in exact proportion to the school's population, were represented in the voluntary sample. Students were generally aware of the need to be familiar with certain library tools as well as techniques for retrieving information. At least 55 percent of each respondent category (undergraduates, master's and doctoral students) favored the availability of library use instruction courses. However, when queried on whether they would take such a course, affirmative undergraduate responses ran 56 percent, 42 percent, 31 percent, and 30 percent from freshmen through senior years. A series of questions on faculty attitudes toward library use and knowledge from the student's point of view are illuminating. Less than one third of the undergraduates agreed with the statement that professors encourage student use of the library while 60 percent of the graduate students concurred. No more than 21 percent of any student category thought that professors graded papers in any relation to student expertise or lack thereof in library use. From Lubans's responses one can infer that student estimates of the value of information-seeking competencies mirror the faculty's assessment of the library's contribution to instructional goals. Widespread student acceptance of the need for library user education is unlikely without a faculty and curriculum committed to bibliographically oriented learning.

A user education survey of New York State academic libraries by Young, Boone, and Salverson drew responses from 125 institutions.[21] Two-year colleges, undergraduate schools, and universities participated in the mail study. Although an aggregate 89 percent supported the value and relevance of some form of library instruction program, 78 percent indicated unhappiness with their present instructional efforts. Lack of sufficient library staff was rated as the major difficulty in developing and implementing educational services. Only 55 percent believed that a full-time instructional librarian should be an essential component of a user education service.

Divergent faculty-librarian opinions over the provision of user education were manifested in a model sociological study of area specialist bibliographers by Stueart.[22] When bibliographers (Number = 27), faculty (N = 131), and library administrators (N = 77) were asked to comment on whether bibliographers should instruct students in library use of area program materials, affirmative replies were 96 percent, 63 percent, and 67 percent, respectively. Since 60 percent of the bibliographer sample held at least two master's degrees, comprising an elite subset of the profession in terms of educational attainment, the significant degree of role dissonance is especially disquieting.

THE LIBRARY AS AN EDUCATIONAL AGENCY

The library's degree of influence in the educational setting is conditioned by many factors. Four facets of this influence will be examined: (1) patterns of library use as they relate to various student characteristics; (2) effect of the level of library service on academic achievement; (3) role of the instructor in impelling library utilization; and (4) teachers' knowledge of and preparation in library skills. Although some of these studies contribute only indirectly to our comprehension of user education dynamics, they do illuminate the library's impact on the educational process, and useful inferences can be drawn regarding the most effective directions for library instruction.

Research on the relationship between library use and class level, academic achievement, and scholastic aptitude has failed to identify any causal connections.[23] With some exceptions, surveys reveal a consistent increase in book borrowing from freshmen to senior years. For five decades, investigators have been pursuing the elusive quest of establishing a high correlation between academic achievement and library utilization. Correlation coefficients of library use against grade-point averages are invariably low when large numbers of students from many majors, or class levels, or both are manipulated as an ungrouped sample. However, some modest, positive associations have been demonstrated when the percentage of student withdrawals is matched against specific grade-point ranges. Evidence of a positive association between student library use and scholastic aptitude, or intelligence ratings, is inconclusive. In a vintage study, Thompson and Nicholson reported a slight relationship between circulation and intelligence scores.[24] Knapp, in her seminal study of Knox College, found statistically significant associations between student aptitude test scores grouped in quartiles and course-related borrowing. The per capita borrowing from the general collection by students in the top quarter outranked all other groups.[25]

At least three researchers have examined the impact of the level of precollege library services on subsequent academic accomplishment. Walker, using a rigorously controlled and statistically sophisticated research design, set out to determine the contribution of the availability and level of library service in the student's community of origin to his academic performance as a University of Illinois freshman.[26] Indexes of school and public library services were constructed out of such quantitative indicators as resources, circulation, expenditure per capita and applied to a sample of 552 graduates of Illinois public schools. No evidence was found that the level of library service was positively correlated with college grade-point averages. In a variant replication of the Walker study, Ladner compared the public and school library services available to 565 Georgia State College freshmen and their scores on a library orientation test.[27] There was only a slight positive relationship ($r = .31$) between available precollege library service and ability to use the library. Investigating the relationship between media–student ratios in secondary schools and collegiate academic performance among 200 students, Harkin concluded that the amount of available media resources did not significantly influence subsequent scholastic performance.[28]

Moving from the impact of antecedent library service to the value of contemporaneous library programs and their effect on student achievement, a number of studies have produced mixed results. Positive influence was found by Hale, whose investigation involved 50 twelfth grade students from two matched classes.[29] The experimental group was provided with library instruction, maximum library service, and an opportunity for independent study under the supervision of a librarian. Library services were incidental and provided upon demand for the control group. Moderate gains for the experimental group in performance on the College Board Scholastic Aptitude Test and a locally devised library skills test were recorded. Library familiarization and use may contribute to measurable improvement in reading skills, subject matter competence, etc., but the successful experiments invariably incorporate sufficient collections, quality library staffing, and teacher encouragement and/or participation in the library experience.

The dominant role of the instructor in influencing library use is beyond question. Student borrowing is highly related to course assignments and instructor attitudes. At Knox College, Dr. Knapp reported 94 percent of all books borrowed were for course-related purposes and that 52 courses, or 32 percent of course offerings, accounted for nearly 90 percent of the borrowing.[30] Hostrop's evaluation of a community college led him to conclude that "the instructor is the prime factor motivating students to use the library." [31] He then elaborated on library-oriented instructors:

> Library-impelling instructors shared certain common characteristics which included explicit assignments, provision of specific titles or bibliographies, continual follow-up on library assignments, requirement that sources be cited in student papers, insistence upon high standards, and expression of their own fondness for books.[32]

Two important studies, both originating as doctoral dissertations, probed the connection between teacher attitudes, actions, backgrounds, and student library behavior. Analysis of elementary school teachers' ($N = 18$) reading habits and library backgrounds as possible determinants of sixth grade pupils' ($N = 161$)

reading habits and mastery of library skills prompted el-Hagrasy to assert a positive relationship.[33] Blazek employed an experimental design to test the hypothesis that "the greater the teacher utilization of library resources in his teaching, the greater the use of the library by pupils because in their recognition of the teacher as a subject matter authority they will emulate his manner of acquiring knowledge. . . ." [34] Seventeen high school students in a mathematics course were assigned to experimental and control groups. Teacher encouragement to use library materials was prominent in the experimental class and mentioned only incidentally to the control group. Library use was not required for either group. During the six-week test period the experimental group withdrew twice the number of titles as the control group. Teacher influence over library use, even for nonrequired materials, was certified beyond reasonable doubt.

If we accept the premise that teachers are pivotal influences on the nature and extent of most student library use, it is important to know the amount of library knowledge possessed by prospective teachers. Several studies have uncovered serious deficiencies. Perkins administered two tests (*Peabody Library Information Test* and the *Library Orientation Test for College Freshmen*) to nearly 4,000 college seniors enrolled in secondary school teacher training curriculums in 63 colleges and universities representing 38 states.[35] The author concluded that prospective teachers were not capable of using library materials satisfactorily, and that their knowledge of available library resources was limited. Exposure to library fundamentals, said the author, should be required of future teachers.

Lee administered the *Library Orientation Test for College Freshmen* to University of Georgia freshmen and seniors preparing for teaching careers and identified deficiencies similar to the Perkins study.[36] Lee also queried 94 teacher training institutions in the Southeastern United States and found that while 70 schools supported the idea of a required library orientation course for prospective teachers, only 11 institutions actually offered such courses. Additional studies dealing with other academic disciplines and different educational levels are clearly warranted.

Generalizing from research, especially when much of it is narrowly conceived and statistically simplistic, is a risky undertaking. However, when studies in certain areas continue to suggest similar conclusions, it is appropriate to extract the essential findings and consider their implications. In the foregoing synthesis of research pertaining to the educational potency of the library, the cumulative evidence places the library in a nonvital, somewhat reactive posture. The judgment is not meant to disparage an aggressive, innovative approach to user education on the part of librarians, but does recognize the constraints of promoting library use and inculcating library skills. The data do not support a rationale for user education that attempts to equate library use as a predictor of academic achievement. Acquisition of particular library-related skills and improved retrieval efficiency, all of which beg for more investigation, would perhaps form the nucleus of plausible reasons for user education. That library use escalates as students progress through college, and that teacher influence is paramount lend indirect, but strong support to the concept of integrated library instruction. In this approach, as exemplified by the Earlham College staff, instruction is course-related, graduated, and premised on close faculty-librarian cooperation.[37]

MEASURING LIBRARY COMPETENCE

Tests for measuring student proficiency in library skills have been used for two main purposes. They have been utilized as diagnostic tools to determine the need for library instruction (pretesting to identify exemptions) and as predictive instruments to ascertain the relationship between knowledge of library skills and a variety of student characteristics. About a half-dozen nationally distributed tests applicable to the elementary, secondary, and college levels have appeared during the past 35 years. Several instruments have been subjected to a degree of statistical validation, but no published library test has undergone the rigorous evaluation required for complete standardization. For an example of the intensive analysis that a library test should receive, the early and still unsurpassed investigation by Reed on a test that was never published should be consulted.[38]

Perhaps the best-known tests are the multilevel *Peabody Library Information Test* (1938–1940) by Louis Shores and Joseph E. Moore and the *Library Orientation Test for College Freshmen* (1955) by Ethel M. Feagley, et al. The *Peabody Test* appeared in three forms for use at the elementary, high school, and college levels. In 1940 Deer examined the reliability and validity of this test using 1,322 freshmen and junior subjects from nine colleges and reported satisfactory results.[39] However, Scates noted in a review that the Deer study notwithstanding, "the three levels of the test give the impression of a fairly good idea poorly executed." [40] Feagley's test has received less than enthusiastic reviews.[41]

Interminable criticisms can be leveled at the major library tests: lack of standardization, excessive reliance on memory, faulty test item construction, and so on. The greatest limitation, however, to the prominent as well as to the numerous locally developed paper-and-pencil tests of library knowledge is their artificiality as devices for ascertaining a user's ability to negotiate the complex bibliographic structure of a library. Paper-and-pencil tests, according to Knapp, are easy to administer and inexpensive, but are only useful as a "gross measure of fairly elementary library knowledge and skill." [42] To move beyond the abstractions inherent in the available tests, Knapp and her associates developed a series of five performance tests as a more realistic approach to assessing actual student competence.[43]

A few researchers have examined the relationship between proficiency in library knowledge and such variables as sex, academic achievement, class level, and scholastic aptitude. Special consideration will be given to a comprehensive study by Snider, but related investigations by Louttit and Patrick,[44] Moore,[45] Joyce,[46] Riley,[47] and Lee,[48] are commended to those desiring a fuller perspective.

Between 1957 and 1959 Snider administered a locally developed library ability test to 1,490 freshmen students at Southeastern Missouri State Teachers College.[49] Library competence was compared with a host of other variables commonly used to predict success in college. The 100-item objective test used to determine library ability registered an internal reliability coefficient of .83. Snider reported a correlation coefficient between library ability and cumulative four-year grade-point averages of .56, significant at the .01 level. The library test outranked or equalled such traditional predictors of collegiate performance as high school percentile standing and precollege educational achievement. While the relationship between library proficiency and grade-point averages at the college level is the strongest yet reported in the literature, a caveat is still in order. Abilities reflected in a library test may well be symptomatic of more generic attributes, such as problem solving and intelligence.

INSTRUCTIONAL STRATEGIES FOR USER EDUCATION

The challenge of educating library users has generated a multiplicity of instructional approaches. Most of the research under review in this section involves the utilization of multimedia materials and technological devices for the purpose of orienting users to basic library services and sources.

It has been nearly a decade since the first reports began to appear about the experimental library program at Monteith College.[50] An exploratory study to design and evaluate a four-year integrated sequence of library use instruction for a liberal arts curriculum, the project was operational during 1959–1962. Dr. Knapp and her able colleagues developed library assignments that exposed students both to the traditional bibliographic organization of the library and to the specialized tools that form the scholarly bibliographic structure. The project staff tried several ways of relating to the faculty and gaining access to the decision-making process. Faculty were provided with bibliographic assistants for research and course needs. As a pilot project, the results (and failures) from the Monteith experience are not easily generalizable beyond the original setting. Among the enduring contributions of this study may be counted the perceptive sociological analysis of the academic environment and the well-conceived library assignments.

Logistical and time problems associated with providing library orientation to large numbers of students have led to some experimentation with television. Hertel reported a television experiment in which 200 freshmen were divided into four groups, each receiving some combination of a three-part TV lesson, or the traditional live classroom lecture, or both.[51] Library use assignments were incorporated into the test situation. No significant differences were noted between the television presentation and the standard lecture. Subsequent investigations by Holley and Oram [52] and Moffett [53] confirmed that television is a satisfactory, although not demonstrably superior, substitute for the lecture as a vehicle for teaching basic library skills. In a 1971 survey of 81 colleges and universities, Melum found that only five libraries were using television while six libraries had discontinued its use.[54]

The teaching effectiveness of programmed instruction compared to conventional classroom instruction has been profusely investigated in the educational and psychological literatures. Generally, programmed instruction is a viable alternative to personalized teaching when the subject being taught comprises discrete, factual knowledges and skills. The principal advantages of programmed instruction are its self-pacing capability, provision for immediate reinforcement, and reduction of instructor time once the material has been prepared.

Wendt conducted the first major experimental study of the application of programmed instruction to teaching basic library skills.[55] Twelve sections of a freshman English course were randomly selected and divided into three groups. The experimental group received programmed instruction via slide projectors, the control group received conventional instruction, and a zero group did not get any instruction. Both the experimental and control groups excelled the zero group, but no significant difference was noted in the achievement scores between programmed instruction recipients and the lecture group.

Earlham College was the site of an excellent study to determine the value of self-contained instruction.[56] Two classes of biology students were divided into groups, the control group to receive a lecture-demonstration form of presentation and the experimental group to work its way through a performance-oriented type of programmed instruction called a guided exercise. Students in the experimental group were actively engaged in the search process, whereas students in the control group were not. Class papers were assigned and attitudinal tests administered to ascertain the impact of the two instructional strategies. According to investigator Kirk, neither instructional method proved superior to the other. One particularly interesting finding related to the amount of assistance requested from a librarian during the assignment phase. The lecture group, having the benefit of instruction from a librarian, sought out librarians for help more often than students learning through the guided exercise.

Several researchers have compared the effects of multimedia presentations against conventional instruction and have arrived at quite similar conclusions. Wassom, employing an experimental design, exposed 84 freshmen subjects taking library orientation to one of three treatments: multimedia presentation, lecture and tour, and no instruction.[57] Neither form of instruction produced marked differences in library-skill achievement. Faster retrieval time for the group receiving extensive audiovisual exposure was the only significant finding. In an experimental study consisting of 715 ninth grade students, Evans concluded that the use of slides was as effective as the lecture method.[58] A randomized block design was recently used by Kuo at Portland State University that manipulated one or two variables in six different versions.[59] Variables included conventional lectures, slides, audiotapes, television, overhead transparencies, and self-pacing. The slide/tape method was more effective than audio instruction, the conventional library lecture, and television instruction. Students who prepared themselves by the audiotutorial method prior to a 50-minute follow-up session by a librarian using overhead transparencies and allowing for a question and answer period achieved the highest mean score of the six versions. This study represents the most elaborate experimental research on instructional strategies to date, but the sample was small (about 200 students divided into seven groups), and the procedures for ensuring sample randomness were not described in sufficient detail.

Machine applications such as computer-assisted instruction (CAI) have been used to facilitate the delivery of user education. Axeen set up an experimental study to compare the effectiveness of computer-based programmed instruction with the conventional lecture.[60] Both methods resulted in gains in knowledge of library use, but no significant differences were noted between the two groups due to the experimental variable. Many other valuable insights are enumerated concerning student completion times and demands on the teacher for each type of instruction. A major flaw in Axeen's use of programmed instruction was the failure to extensively field test the frame sequences prior to the experiment. For a good analysis of the complexities involved in the formulation and evaluation of behavioral objectives and programmed instruction materials, see the report by Wiggins and Low.[61] Additional user education projects with various mechanized systems have been reported by Genung [62] at Mt. San Antonio College and Culkin [63] and Hansen [64] at the University of Denver.

Computer-assisted instruction appears to be suitable for introducing large numbers of students to basic library knowledges, but the evaluations to date are rather primitive. Students' intermediate and long-range library use behaviors will need to be examined before a definitive judgment can be rendered. Finally, worth underscoring is that the preparation of user education programs, manual or automated, beyond the beginner level requires librarians conversant with subject literatures as well as bibliographic tools.

TOWARD A RESEARCH AGENDA

Librarianship seems to be nurturing a more evaluative cast of mind, and this proclivity is having some effect on research in user education. Although the quality of user education research has improved over the past decade, there is ample room for methodological and statistical refinements. Rather than recapitulate or further analyze the studies covered in this review, the remaining remarks will center on a few recommendations for future research. Most of the recommendations apply equally to different types of libraries and to all educational levels.

There is a priority need for longitudinal (long-term) studies that trace the impact of user education programs on subsequent academic achievement and selected occupational variables. Many researchers have evaluated the effectiveness of a variety of mechanized and media strategies. We should not neglect the importance of developing and testing instructional programs that aim for high learner achievement levels. One could speculate that many user education presentations often fail to reflect the findings of information-seeking, shelf-failure, and catalog use investigations. Research into this hypothesized deficiency is required to ascertain if user education programs are incorporating current knowledge about the library-user interface. There is little empirical evidence about the relative emphasis that should be accorded to knowledge of the search process and specific bibliographic sources in user education programs.

Research focusing on classroom teachers and curriculum decision makers to elicit attitudes regarding the need for and optimum configuration of user education deserves attention. The relationship, if any, between librarians possessing full academic status and the extent and quality of user education programs should be explored. Little is known about the views of library school educators toward library instruction in the field.

It may be debatable whether standardized tests of library knowledge should be constructed. An obvious problem is that a test designed for national application must necessarily be a compromise. On the other hand, it is probably a waste of staff resources to develop generally mediocre tests at the local level. And standardized tests provide an external criterion against which to gauge the results of local test administrations. Existing published tests, with dated norms and lack of performance provisions, hardly qualify as sound instruments.

In the process of reviewing scores of studies, this writer has been struck by the large amount of redundant content and frequent failure to cite relevant prior investigations. Perhaps it is time to initiate periodic state-of-the-art reviews and even to produce a comprehensive, interpretive history of user education encompassing different types of libraries.

NOTES

1. Helen L. Butler, "The Library in Education," *Review of Educational Research* 12 (June 1942): 323–335.
2. George S. Bonn, "Training Laymen in the Use of the Library," in *The State of the Library Art,* vol. 2, pt. 1, ed. by Ralph R. Shaw (New Brunswick, N.J.: Rutgers University, Graduate School of Library Service, 1960).
3. William E. Woods, "Factors Influencing Student Library Use: Analysis of Studies" (Master's paper, University of Chicago, Graduate Library School, 1965).
4. Felix E. Snider, "The Relationships of Library Ability to Performance in College" (Ph.D. diss., Urbana, University of Illinois, 1965), pp. 12–42.
5. Frances Henne, "Instruction in the Use of the Library and Library Use by Students," in *Conference on the Use of Printed and Audio-Visual Materials for Instructional Purposes,* ed. by Maurice F. Tauber and Irlene R. Stephens (New York: Columbia University, School of Library Service, 1966), pp. 164–190.
6. Paul R. Wendt, "New Library Materials and Technology for Instruction and Research," *Library Trends* 16 (October 1967): 197–210.
7. Mavis N. Tidmarsh, "Instruction in the Use of Academic Libraries," in *University and Research Library Studies,* ed. by William L. Saunders (London: Pergamon Press, 1968), pp. 39–83.
8. Elmyra Davis, "The Unchanging Profile—A Review of the Literature," *Library-College Journal* 3 (November 1970): 11–19.
9. Marcia J. Bates, "User Studies: A Review for Librarians and Information Scientists," Educational Resources Information Center (ERIC) document, 1971 (ED 047 738).
10. J. E. Scrivener, "Instruction in Library Use: The Persisting Problem," *Australian Academic and Research Libraries* 3 (June 1972): 87–119.
11. Jean E. Lowrie, "A Review of Research in School Librarianship," in *Re-*

search Methods in Librarianship: Measurement and Evaluation, ed. by Herbert Goldhor, University of Illinois Library School Monograph no. 8 (Urbana: University of Illinois, Graduate School of Library Science, 1968), pp. 51–69.

12. Shirley L. Aaron, "A Review of Selected Research Studies in School Librarianship: 1967–1971: Part 1," *School Libraries* 21 (Summer 1972): 29–46. Part 2 is in *School Media Quarterly* 1 (Fall 1972): 41–48.

13. Geoffrey Ford, "Research in User Behavior in University Libraries," *Journal of Documentation* 29 (March 1973): 85–106.

14. Richard A. Davis and Catherine A. Bailey, *Bibliography of Use Studies,* Drexel Library School Series no. 18 (Philadelphia: Drexel Institute of Technology, Graduate School of Library Science, 1964).

15. L. Carroll DeWeese, "A Bibliography of Library Use Studies," in Aridman K. Jain, *Report on a Statistical Study of Book Use,* U.S. Department of Commerce PB 176525 (Lafayette: Purdue University, 1967).

16. Pauline Atkin, *Bibliography of Use Surveys of Public and Academic Libraries, 1950–Nov. 1970* (London: The Library Association, 1971).

17. Allan Mirwis, "Academic Library Instruction: A Bibliography, 1960–1970," *Drexel Library Quarterly* 7 (July and October 1971): 327–335.

18. T. A. Whitworth, "The Centrality of the Librarian's Role in the English Technical College," *Research in Librarianship* 3 (January 1970): 7–36.

19. John Lubans, Jr., "On Non-use of an Academic Library: A Report of Findings," in New York Library Association, College and University Libraries Section, *Use, Misuse and Non-use of Academic Libraries* (Woodside, N.Y., 1970), pp. 47–70. For an abbreviated version see *College and Research Libraries* 32 (September 1971): 362–367.

20. John Lubans, Jr., "Report to the Council on Library Resources on a Fellowship Awarded for 1971/72," mimeographed (Boulder: University of Colorado Library, November 28, 1972).

21. Arthur P. Young, Morell Boone, and Carol Salverson, "Survey of User Education in New York State Academic Libraries" (Paper delivered at the New York Library Association, College and University Libraries Section, October 6, 1971), Educational Resources Information Center (ERIC) document (ED 055 621), pp. 6–20.

22. Robert D. Stueart, "The Area Specialist Bibliographer: An Inquiry into His Role" (Ph.D. diss., University of Pittsburgh, 1971), pp. 159, 196.

23. See Note 8 for a review of library use studies that explore the relationship between library utilization and these student characteristics.

24. Russell I. Thompson and John B. Nicholson, "Significant Influences on General Circulation in a Small College Library," *Library Quarterly* 11 (April 1941): 182.

25. Patricia B. Knapp, *College Teaching and the College Library,* ACRL Monograph no. 23 (Chicago: American Library Association, 1959), p. 24.

26. Richard D. Walker, *The Availability of Library Service and Academic Achievement,* Research series no. 4 (Springfield: Illinois State Library, 1963), pp. 46–49.

27. Mary M. Ladner, "The Relationship Between Available Pre-College Library Service and Ability to Use the College Library" (Master's thesis, Atlanta, Emory University, 1966), pp. 13–43.

28. Willard D. Harkin, "Analysis of Secondary School Library Media Programs in Relation to Academic Success of Ball State University Students in Their Freshman and Sophomore Years" (Ed.D. diss., Muncie, Ind., Ball State University, 1971), pp. 90–98.

29. Irlene W. Hale, "The Influence of Library Services Upon the Academic Achievement of Twelfth Grade Students at Crestwood Senior High School, Chesapeake, Virginia" (Athens: University of Georgia, Department of Library Education, 1969), Educational Resources Information Center (ERIC) document (ED 047 694), pp. 3–6, 13–14.

30. Knapp, op. cit., p. 39.

31. Richard W. Hostrop, *Teaching and the Community College Library* (Hamden, Conn.: Shoe String Press, 1968), p. 161.

32. Ibid., p. 163.

33. Saad M. el-Hagrasy, "The Teacher's Role in Library Service: An Investigation and Its Devices," *Journal of Experimental Education* 30 (June 1962): 347–354.

34. Ronald D. Blazek, "The Influence of the Teacher on Pupil Use of Nonrequired Library Materials in Mathematics—An Experimental Study," *Illinois Libraries* 53 (September 1971): 528–544.

35. Ralph Perkins, *The Prospective Teacher's Knowledge of Library Fundamentals* (New York: Scarecrow Press, 1965), pp. 15, 194–199.

36. Chi Ho Lee, "The Library Skills of Prospective Teachers at the University of Georgia" (Ed.D. diss., Athens, University of Georgia, 1971), pp. 85–89.

37. James R. Kennedy, Jr., Thomas G. Kirk, and Gwendolyn A. Weaver, "Course-related Library Instruction: A Case Study of the English and Biology Departments at Earlham College," *Drexel Library Quarterly* 7 (July and October 1971): 277–297.

38. Lulu R. Reed, "A Test of Students' Competence to Use the Library," *Library Quarterly* 8 (April 1938): 236–283.

39. George H. Deer, "The Peabody Library Information Test: A Study of Its Statistical Validity and Reliability," *Journal of Experimental Education* 9 (March 1941): 233–236.

40. Douglas E. Scates, quoted in Oscar K. Buros, ed., *The Third Mental Measurements Yearbook* (New Brunswick, N.J.: Rutgers University Press, 1949), p. 565.

41. See reviews by Janet G. Afflerbach and J. Wayne Wrightstone in Oscar K. Buros, *The Fifth Mental Measurements Yearbook* (Highland Park, N.J.: Gryphon Press, 1959), pp. 787–789; and the review by Morey J. Wantman, in Buros, *The Sixth Mental Measurements Yearbook* (Highland Park, N.J.: Gryphon Press, 1965), p. 1144.

42. Patricia B. Knapp, *The Monteith College Library Experiment* (New York: Scarecrow Press, 1966), p. 71.

43. Ibid., pp. 64–72.

44. C. M. Louttit and James R. Patrick, "A Study of Students' Knowledge in the Use of the Library," *Journal of Applied Psychology* 16 (1932): 475–483.

45. Joseph E. Moore, "The Relationships Between Library Information and Elementary School Attainment," *Peabody Journal of Education* 18 (July 1940): 27–31.

46. William D. Joyce, "A Study of Academic Achievement and Performance on a Test of Library Understandings," *Journal of Educational Research* 54 (January 1961): 198–199.

47. Louise E. Riley, "A Study of the Performance on a Library Orientation Test in Relation to the Academic Achievement and Scholastic Aptitude of a Selected Group of Freshmen College Students at Tuskegee Institute" (Master's thesis, Atlanta University, 1962).

48. Lee, op. cit., pp. 95–114.

49. Snider, op. cit., pp. 43–115.

50. Patricia B. Knapp, "The Methodology and Results of the Monteith Pilot Project," *Library Trends* 13 (July 1964): 84–102.

51. Robert R. Hertel, et al., "TV Library Instruction," *Library Journal* 86 (January 1, 1961): 42–46.

52. Edward G. Holley and Robert W. Oram, "University Library Orientation by Television," *College and Research Libraries* 23 (November 1962): 485–491.

53. Thomas J. Moffett, "A Comparison of Two Methods of Familiarizing Students with Library Materials and Methods" (Ph.D. diss., Gainesville, University of Florida, 1965), pp. 26–53, 89–90.

54. Verna V. Melum, "1971 Survey of Library Orientation and Instruction Programs," *Drexel Library Quarterly* 7 (July and October 1971): 234.

55. Paul R. Wendt, et al., *A Study to Determine the Extent to Which Instruction to University Freshmen in the Use of the University Library Can Be Turned Over to Teaching Machines* (Carbondale: Southern Illinois University, 1963), pp. 1–14.

56. Thomas Kirk, "A Comparison of Two Methods of Library Instruction for Students in Introductory Biology," *College and Research Libraries* 32 (November 1971): 465–474. For a fuller discussion of this experiment and a copy of the guided exercise, consult the author's identically titled Master's thesis, Indiana University (1969).

57. Earl E. Wassom, "A Study of the Effects of Multimedia Instructional Techniques on a College Freshman Library Orientation Program" (Ed.D. diss., Stillwater, Oklahoma State University, 1967), pp. 48–53.

58. Roy W. Evans, "Using Slides for Library Orientation," *Illinois Libraries* 51 (April 1969): 300–303. Based on the author's 1969 Ph.D. dissertation, Southern Illinois University, entitled "An Experimental Study to Determine the Effectiveness of Using Slides with Ninth Grade Students in Six Randomly Selected Schools in Southern Illinois to Teach Library Usage."

59. Frank F. Kuo, "A Comparison of Six Versions of Science Library Instruction," *College and Research Libraries* 34 (July 1973): 287–290.

60. Marina E. Axeen, "Teaching the Use of the Library to Undergraduates: An Experimental Comparison of Computer-Based Instruction and the Conventional Lecture Method" (Ph.D. diss., Urbana, University of Illinois, 1967), pp. 1–78. Also available as Educational Resources Information Center (ERIC) document (ED 014 316).

61. Marvin E. Wiggins and D. Stewart Low, "Use of an Instructional Psychology Model for Development of Library-Use Instructional Programs," *Drexel Library Quarterly* 8 (July 1972): 269–279.

62. Harriett Genung, "Can Machines Teach the Use of the Library?" *College and Research Libraries* 28 (January 1967): 25–30.

63. Patricia B. Culkin, "Computer-Assisted Instruction in Library Use," *Drexel Library Quarterly* 8 (July 1972): 301–311.

64. Lois N. Hansen, "Computer-Assisted Instruction in Library Use: An Evaluation," *Drexel Library Quarterly* 8 (July 1972): 345–355.

PART I
RATIONALE FOR
EDUCATING LIBRARY USERS

THE TEACHING PROGRAM IN THE ELEMENTARY SCHOOL LIBRARY

MELVYN K. BOWERS

Formerly Director, Curriculum Materials Center, Cuyama Unified School District, California. Currently Director, Library Services, Konocti Unified School District, Lower Lake, California

The elementary school library is where most students usually begin their education in library use. As with any beginning, this is an important one and will likely form the basis of the students' favorable or unfavorable attitudes toward libraries. In view of this, significant effort should be put into the library instruction program so that each student's understanding of the library is meaningful and useful.

SOLVING THE SPACE PROBLEM

Before any purposeful education of library users may be accomplished in the elementary school, certain minimum physical and material requirements must be present, one of which is space: adequate library space for a single student to browse or study, for a small group to work, for an entire class to meet.

The most satisfactory space is that which is specially designed and constructed for library purposes. Functional construction plans and knowledgeable resource people are readily available to any school district interested in planning such permanent additions to its plant.

The portable, self-contained unit, when designed properly, is also very satisfactory, and school districts using these facilities usually find the cost is about one-half that of permanent constructions.

Another facility may be created out of an unused classroom. The converted classroom, however, seldom has sufficient space for a workroom, storage room, or conference rooms, yet it could prove adequate while other arrangements are being completed.

Some schools are installing shelving in a multipurpose room or along the wall of a wide corridor and calling that facility a library, but because of the multiple-use nature of these areas arrangements of this kind are inadequate for anything except a book depository. The interruptions caused by other activities do not allow a library atmosphere to develop, scheduling is almost impossible, the space is seldom enough even for library furniture that can accommodate any more than a small group, workroom and storage space is inadequate, and both lighting and ventilation may not be satisfactory.

The temptation is to advise school districts that cannot provide better facilities than makeshift ones to ask the public library or the county library service to schedule bookmobile visits to the school and save the district the expense of acquiring its own collection until more desirable facilities may be found.

Another solution to the space problem might be to merge the school library and the public library into one facility. Possible advantages of this merger would be reduction in land acquisition, plant construction, and maintenance, since materials, services, and personnel would be shared and thus duplication of facilities would be eliminated. Although problems might occur in such a merger, its singular advantages should be worthy of serious consideration.

ACQUIRING A SUITABLE COLLECTION

Another necessity before a library-user teaching program may begin is a materials collection that meets the minimum standards set by the American Library Association. Acquiring this collection will take awhile, though, and teaching will probably begin before the minimum standards are reached, but will probably be somewhat limited.

Providing an adequate materials collection is primarily a problem of budgets. Some districts rely on gifts and donations from the Parent Teachers Association and other "friends of the library." But this dependency is unrealistic since there is no assurance of dollar amounts that might be received, and the librarian is unable to plan purchases to either build a collection or properly maintain an already existing one.

The school must provide the library with a budget that has three categories: the first should cover purchases of new and replacement materials, and this provision should be inviolate; the second and smaller category should be for necessary repairs and maintenance of the collection; and the third should provide for periodic replacement of encyclopedia and similar reference tools that need to be kept current.

Though gifts and donations are always welcome, it is only through a regular budget that the librarian is able to plan the collection, keep it in balance and maintain it properly.

HIRING COMPETENT STAFF

Another library program necessity is personnel. Some districts still consider the position of a librarian as clerical, and instead of a trained teacher or librarian they employ a secretary or volunteer aide to manage the library. While such people may become quite competent in charging, shelving, repairing, and other routine library duties, they cannot perform the services that require the judgment and knowledge of the person professionally trained in library service. Purchasing, technical processing, teaching, teacher assistance, and resource and reading guidance are just a few of the library service areas that are usually beyond the abilities of the secretary or volunteer; the library thus staffed cannot operate on a level much above an expensive book depository.

Other schools attempt to staff their library by assigning library duty as an extra task for a teacher, often with only a small addition in salary. This is hardly a satisfactory arrangement, because the teacher is usually not a trained librarian, does not have adequate time to give to the post's many responsibilities, and is not always available when needed (making a full-time library operating schedule an impossibility).

Librarianship is a highly skilled profession, requiring the skills of librarianship combined with the expertise of a competent, experienced teacher. It is only through the utilization of all this training and experience that a school is able to realize a full return on its investment in a library program.

ACHIEVING A COOPERATIVE PHILOSOPHY

Closely allied with personnel is the teaching philosophy of the school staff. Effective utilization of library services occurs when mutual agreement and cooperation between the library and classroom teachers are achieved. In school systems where the teachers teach page one today, and page two tomorrow, where education is blocked out in units with time schedules for mastering each new step, and the manual is the "bible" of methodology, not too much use may be made of the library and its resources. The librarian is faced with a difficult task, and any program developed will most likely be the program of the library and not of the school.

Contrast this with the system where the kindergarten teacher sends the little boy to the library with his butterfly, for identification by picture comparison, or where children in the fifth grade group come to the library to search out an answer to an argument they have been having. That school system's staff is making wiser use of its library facilities, and the students cannot help but benefit. Librarians in systems like this will work harder, but their professional life will be more rewarding and the libraries more worthwhile ventures.

Teacher training institutions, particularly in their methods courses, should also accept at least a part of the responsibility for teachers' nonuse of library facilities, for they seldom mention the role of the library as one of the teaching tools available to the teacher. While it is true that some courses lend themselves to the use of library resources more than do others, a library can perform services for teachers in all areas of the school curriculum that can help with their teaching. Discussions on the use of library services should be included in the course content of educational methods classes for teachers. In the meantime, inservice workshop courses on information resources that are not costly (and may carry college credit) might be of some help to teachers.

Textbook authors and publishers may also be guilty of contributing to the teachers' nonuse of library resources. Seldom do they place any stress on the use of library resources and services as a teaching tool, other than an occasional mention of a short bibliography of related materials. For an interesting experiment in library utilization, educators might develop a textbook, probably in the social sciences, that offers students an outline to use as a guide, with the details of the study to be worked out by the students themselves, through research and reference.

DEVELOPING THE LIBRARY STUDY COURSE

Once staff, space, and materials are acquired, it is time to decide on the course of study for the library.

While the library has little to teach of its own, many areas of the curriculum might be better taught in the atmosphere of the library. Since the library teaching will probably include subject matter traditionally taught in the classroom, it is of vital necessity for the entire teaching staff, the librarians, and the administration to cooperate in developing the library course of study. The bibliography lists a number of publications that will be of value to a school system planning its library teaching program. Knowledgeable resource people, too, are usually readily available. The course of study, when completed, should be incorporated into the school's curricular plan as one of its regular course subjects.

SCHEDULING THE LIBRARY PROGRAM

Scheduling the library instruction can be a bit difficult since it is one of the few subjects in the school that involves planning by all members of the teaching staff. The teaching schedule must interlock with blocks of library time needed for other library activities. An approach used in some California schools is simply to include the teaching time in the library as part of the regular reading program, and one period a week is scheduled for this purpose. The teachers usually plan their program so that each grade level has its reading period at the same time, and there are no period conflicts between the various grades.

Another method sets the reading schedules, including the library instructional period for the school, and the teachers construct the balance of their program around this. A more dictatorial situation occurs when the administration simply sets up the instructional schedule for the school.

No hard and fast rules can be established to solve scheduling problems for all school systems; each must solve its own problems in its own way. No matter how the question of scheduling is resolved, however, no library can operate at maximum benefit to the school system if its schedule is constantly preempted by other school activities.

A few rules and regulations concerning the library and its operations should be established. Those involving the school system, the staff, or the administration should be included in the school policies. It is almost impossible to suggest a list of rules and regulations, for each school will have different needs, and will meet them in different ways. Whatever rules are developed must be understood by both staff and young patrons of the library, and be within the framework of school policies.

The following outline of the library course of study in use in the Clearlake

Oaks and Burns Valley Elementary Schools in Northern California is offered as an illustration of what two systems are doing in this area. Each school must tailor its own plans to meet its own particular needs; no single plan will probably ever be developed that could be adopted by all school systems.

A SAMPLE LIBRARY STUDY COURSE

Kindergarten. The kindergarten offers the library its greatest opportunity and responsibility since many of the youngsters starting their school career may be experiencing their first encounter with books, pictures, and the other varied and interesting materials housed in the library. It is of the utmost importance that these children find pleasure in the experience, for this will help ensure the beginnings of a desirable attitude toward library materials, services, even knowledge itself.

The kindergarten program places its emphasis on storytelling, sharing, browsing, and some elementary research that stems mainly from classroom needs. A minimum of basic rules of library conduct and materials use are also discussed.

First Grade. Both the objectives and activities of the first grade are extensions of the kindergarten program. In addition the children will learn the correct procedure for charging material from the library and how to properly care for this material. These activities also include the rules governing charging privileges.

The last half of the year will introduce the children to the parts of the book, and they will practice their alphabet by reading the call numbers on the backs of the titles in the E section (none of these contain Dewey Numbers) and playing shelving and location games with these and the easier-to-read titles.

If a class is accelerated, they may be introduced to the easier picture dictionaries, but this should be left to the discretion of the classroom teacher.

Second Grade. While the library instruction program in the second grade is largely a continuation of the past two years, the story hour is expanded to include easy drama that the children may read in parts or walk through, some simple jokes and cartoons, and an introduction to the easier children's magazines. The children are also introduced to the tape recorder and encouraged to do one of their reports or share something with the class by using this medium.

Work is started with the picture dictionary, or continued if already begun in the first grade, and the title page and table of contents are added to the children's vocabulary, with some work done on their use as a selection aid.

Third Grade. The third grade continues many of the activities of the lower primary years with an introduction to the easier-reading materials in the general collection as a means of encouraging an expansion of variety in their selections.

The story hour is expanded to include such activities as a visit by the music teacher to share one of the children's operas and play a few of its selections or a visit by a guest who shows and tells an interesting hobby, thus presenting the opportunity to introduce some of the easier materials in a particular subject area of the library collection.

Work is continued with the dictionary, and the children are introduced to the use of the primary encyclopedia, pictures, models, filmstrips, tapes, realia, and other items from the library collection that may be charged for use in their reporting.

Fourth Grade. The fourth grade begins with a general review, and the story hour is given over to more discussions of varied materials and their use. The children are introduced to the vertical file and to other audiovisual aids not already presented and are encouraged to use them as an aid to research as well as for personal pleasure or information.

Shelving games are expanded to include all the library as a means of becoming familiar with shelf location before starting to learn the use of the card catalog. While this is being done, the purpose of the call numbers is also discussed, and the children usually enjoy the story of Mr. Dewey and his number system.

The second half of the year introduces the use of the card catalog. The Subject Card is the first one used because it is the most frequently used by the children. The Analytic (or Added Entry) Card is taught along with it, with little distinction made between them. The Title Card is next introduced, followed by the Author Card. These are the only cards taught, since they are the only ones the children use with the exception of the cross-references mentioned here. Cross-references are emphasized during the use of indexes, where they occur with greater frequency than in the card catalog.

Work with the dictionary is extended, and if time permits, some work may be done with the encyclopedia and atlas. These are generally left to the fifth grade where their use becomes more popular.

Fifth Grade. The story hour is continued, but the actual reading of stories grows less, while greater emphasis is placed on sharing good materials and attempting to increase the range of interest by presenting many different types of materials.

The year will begin with a review of what has gone before, with emphasis on the rules of the library, charging procedures, and use of the card catalog in materials location. In addition, the children will study the various parts of a book, including the purpose and use of the table of contents and the index. They will do some map work and drawing (in preparation for the more detailed study of the atlas to come in the sixth grade), extend the use of the encyclopedia, and be introduced to the use of the opaque projector and filmstrip-slide projector for use in reporting.

By this time the children should be fairly efficient users of the dictionary, and the extension of these skills should be planned by the librarian and the classroom teachers.

Sixth Grade. The last year in the elementary school is a very busy one. After completing a general review to refresh memories and bring any newcomers up to date, the children plunge right into the use of the atlas, its maps, charts, graphs, and detailed information. When they are so sufficiently adept at using this reference source that the classroom teacher may begin using it as a reference in their classroom work, the children are introduced to the unabridged dictionary. Though some have been using it, few will have discovered its wealth of information, and this needs to be pointed out to them.

Such specialized reference tools as the encyclopedia of sports and the subject index to poetry are introduced in this grade, though almanacs, biographical dictionaries, and yearbooks are generally left to the junior high school. Along with the continued practice with the card catalog, the children should also learn the general Dewey divisions and a bit about how these numbers are selected in book processing.

When time permits, the children may also be introduced to the use of the overhead projector for use in reporting, and the setup for a simulated radio-type presentation. The use of the tape recorder may also be extended to include sound effects, background music and the use of several people for effective voice changes.

It sometimes happens that classes do not have time to complete all the activities suggested in any given year. This is all right. The librarian simply picks up the next year where the children left off and continues with the work. A conference between the elementary school and junior high school librarians will acquaint the latter with the work that has been done in the elementary grade, so that the children may continue in the program without interruption.

CONCLUSION

While a school without efficient library services may present an adequate program of education to its youngsters, it cannot attain that level of teaching which can achieve excellence. Though many problems may be involved in establishing an effective library program in the elementary school, these problems can be solved—and the children of the district are the beneficiaries.

BIBLIOGRAPHY

"An Outline of Library Instruction for Elementary School Libraries." Mimeographed. Albuquerque, N. Mex., Public Schools, Division of Library Services, 1968.

Baechtold, Marguerite, et al. "Library Instructional Skills Program—K–12." Mimeographed. New Jersey School Library Association. Trenton, N.J.: State Department of Education, 1964.

Bowers, Melvyn K. *Library Instruction in the Elementary School*. Metuchen, N.J.: Scarecrow Press, 1971.

Boyd, Jessie, et al. *Books, Libraries and You*, rev. ed. New York: Scribners, 1965.

Curriculum Materials Center for Sacramento City Schools. "Library Education in the Elementary Schools." Mimeographed. Sacramento, Calif.: Superintendent of Schools, n.d.

Mott, Carolyn, et al. *Children's Book on How to Use Books and Libraries*. New York: Scribners, 1948.

"School Library Instruction." Mimeographed. Riverside, Calif.: Office of the City Schools Superintendent, n.d.

State Library Service Committee, Curriculum Improvement Commission. *Curriculum Guide for the Teaching of Library Skills: Grades K–12*. Tulsa, Okla.: State Department of Education, 1969.

IS LIBRARY INSTRUCTION IN A MUDDLE IN THE MIDDLE SCHOOL?

Estella E. Reed
Associate Professor of Educational Media, Purdue University, Calumet Campus; recipient of Delta Kappa Gamma International Scholarship 1972–1973

In collaboration with Charles A. Walker, Media Specialist, Scott Middle School, Hammond, Indiana

Critics of the middle school point to the lack of clear goals and call it the muddle school. Instruction in the use of media centers for grades five through eight may be contributing to the muddle. It behooves the profession to abet education in general, and the 10- to 14-year-old user in particular, by arriving at some goals for the upper elementary years. Each discipline in the United States school system advocates a progressive learning process from kindergarten through grade twelve; we believe in a developmental theory. The ungraded school, independent study, and the instructional media center, all militate *toward* the personalized learning process. What, then, are librarians doing to help clarify goals of the middle school?

THE MIDDLE SCHOOL CONCEPT

What is the middle school? In short, it is a revision of the administrative unit called the junior high school. The middle school was brought about to capitalize on earlier onset of puberty, the redistricting needed for integrated education, and different physical facilities that will accommodate greater curriculum experimentation. The middle school philosophy should evoke a different program for learning; the librarians must calculate their teaching role. Swarthout has named three definite instructional concerns of the elementary and junior high school librarian: "a literary concern, a study skill concern, and a library skill concern." [1]

Judith Murphy, author of *Middle Schools*, defines middle school as "a school in between elementary and high school, housed separately and ideally, in a building freshly designed for its purpose, and covering at least three of the middle school years, beginning with grades 5 or 6." [2]

There is no general agreement on whether the initial year of the middle school should be grade 5 or grade 6, but opinion is nearly unanimous that the ninth grade should be part of the high school. The Committee on Junior High Education of the National Association of Secondary School Principals recommends three years for the middle unit, but it does not oppose four years. It does, however, oppose a two-year school. The Carnegie Unit for graduation credit from high school and the greater maturity and social sophistication of ninth graders have been factors ruling out ninth grade from the middle school.

Theodore C. Moss, in his 1969 publication *Middle School,* states that the junior high school failed to achieve its purposes.[3] Junior high schools have tried to mimic the activities of the high school. The functions of a junior high school, as described by William T. Gruhn and Harl R. Douglass, are as follows: integration, exploration, guidance (educational and vocational), differentiation, socialization, and articulation (gradual transition from preadolescent to adolescent needs and programs).[4] The areas of exploration and differentiation seem intrinsic to instruction in the use of libraries in the middle school. In close coordination with the classroom teacher, the librarian will set goals that facilitate the exploratory function for each student.

THE MIDDLE SCHOOL STUDENT

What are the characteristics of the middle school library users? Their period of rapid physical growth and dramatic bodily change has been called the awkward age in child development. It is also the awkward period in library instruction as students from various "feeder" schools reach the middle school. Library skills may vary widely. Historically, the diversity of interests, limited attention span, and physical activism of preadolescents have tested the mettle of teachers.

Eichhorn has termed the 10–14-year-old a "transescent," defining transescence as

> the stage of development which begins prior to the onset of puberty and extends through the early stages of adolescence. Since puberty does not occur precisely at the same chronological age in human development, the transescent designation is based on the many physical, social, emotional, and intellectual changes that appear prior to the puberty cycle to the time when the body gains a practical degree of stabilization over these complex changes.[5]

Eichhorn stakes the ultimate progress of the middle school upon the ability of educators to develop programs in which the middle school "transescent" is the focal point for change. The media center program, or curriculum, will rise or fall on this same effort. We agree with Eichhorn in his statement about changing the teaching process: "The traditional lecture-recitation method must give way to more appropriate methods involving seminar and individually directed learning experiences."[6]

Strickland and Alexander also refer to "transescent" in explaining the development of the middle school: "The newer organization also reflects many previous efforts to find a better way to serve children, in this case the transescent stage of development."[7]

DETERRENTS TO LIBRARY USAGE

Certain classroom practices may dissipate the media program. The hard emphasis on reading skills has often tapered off by grade 5; many reading problems exist in the middle schools. Good procedures in the classroom should fire interests that can be satiated in the library.

Hoyt and Blackmore investigated the reading achievement of 50 pupils who had been in continuous attendance from grades 1–7 in the same California school system.[8] They assumed "reading achievement" to be the outgrowth of total experiences in the seven school grades. The researchers found that during the first three grades the pupils achieved above expectations. A decline in achievement beginning in grade 5 persisted through grade 7 where 85 percent of the cases did not reach expected achievement level.

The Right-to-Read effort is based on this very issue. National literacy is a school concern. Motivating reading is a joint responsibility of teachers and librarians. Very special bait will have to be used to lure transescents to sedentary tasks. *Introducing Books: A Guide for the Middle Grades* [9] will be helpful in this capacity, as will *Subject Guide to Children's Books in Print* [10] and *Resources for Learning.*[11]

Further evidence that classroom practices deter library usage is supplied by Brekke who found that grades 4, 5, and 6 spent less time than recommended on teaching reading skills.[12] If students cannot read, what enticement does the library offer? The middle school program should recognize these weaknesses and initiate individualized activities that encourage all modes of learning, radiating from the classroom. Starr recommends an approach that any teacher could implement wherein a student proposes his learning activities via written format.[13] If students *can* read, who is motivating them?

These studies, and others, raise questions about the nature of reading instruction in the upper elementary grades. Could well-stocked media centers, plus instruction in the art of discovering pertinent materials, offset aggravated apathy that develops in schools toward lifetime reading habits? Only with teacher-librarian teamwork can this be tested. The isolated reading laboratory in another part of the building is a poor physical arrangement. Swarthout has observed that "both the classroom teacher and the librarian should approach instructional goals with experimental attitudes that are analytical of outcomes and that promote continuing inquiry." [14] A program of perfunctory skill-building in the classroom will not produce creative readers or inquirers.

Instruction in the use of libraries has commonly been effected through routine scheduling of classes to the media center. Where does the classroom teacher go during this period? Fleischman studied the influence of the classroom teacher's presence on pupils' learning of library skills in Central Elementary School, Long Beach, New York, during the fall semester 1970–1971.[15] Ten lessons on the following topics were administered to two sixth grade classes: the production of a book; the parts of a book; general arrangement of books in the library; use of the Dewey Decimal System; how to use the card catalog; rules for filing in the card catalog; how to use an encyclopedia; how to compile a bibliography;

how to use the *World Almanac;* how to use other reference books: atlases, gazetteers, and *Index to National Geographic.*

Although the researcher found no significant difference in the mean scores of the experimental (teacher present) and the control (teacher not present) groups, she did find a significant change in the standard deviation of scores, favoring the experimental group. Fleischman concluded the presence of the teacher had some influence on achievement of library skills by sixth graders who were tested.

The greatest area of growth for both groups of sixth grade students in the Fleischman study, between the pre- and post-test, was in the "use of reference books." When both groups were considered, sixth grade students in this study got 32 percent of the pretest questions correct; after instruction, the post-test showed 49 percent correct. Judging from this study, the "use of reference books" category seems to signal increased instruction for middle school students. The "bibliography" category also indicated an area of student need. In the program proposed later in this chapter, we have harkened to the Fleischman research.

Group instruction is not an adequate method in the middle school. Thoughtful administrators have deemed the new administrative unit, the middle school, a necessity for preadolescent learners. Library instruction must be devised that takes cognizance of what the student has learned before middle grades, what library usage is appropriate to the middle school curriculum, and what content is expected to be handled in grade 9. Barton shows ways to loosen up the school continuum.[16] In truth, we are in the middle!

Emmett L. Williams has pointed out: "Still another observable common characteristic of middle schools is the definite, planned emphasis on greater student self-direction and self-responsibility for learning. Nearly all of the new middle schools have some form of independent study plan." [17] Clearly, this is the alarm that signals media specialists to action. We need library instruction programs that place greater emphasis on "student self-direction and self-responsibility for learning."

The Learning Activity Package of Nova School in Ft. Lauderdale, Florida, described by Prostano and Prostano is a good example of how the learner assumes an active role in his learning.[18] Library usage must be an outgrowth of classroom needs.

Prostano and Prostano also offer a scope-and-sequence array for introducing media and skills.[19] In grade 5 they suggest abridged and special subject dictionaries; almanacs and yearbooks; atlases, maps, and globes; periodicals and *Abridged Readers' Guide.* In grade 6 the stress is on special reference sources: biographical, English, science, and social studies.

Albeit the need exists for professional cooperation in school programs, certain monoliths have been erected in education that preclude the easy integration function of middle schools. These stonelike blocks include learning centers in classrooms that never extend into the library; the encyclopedia syndrome that views a set of encyclopedias as the acme of learning; the isolationism that rests in reading labs, science, guidance, and health departments; traditionalism that admits learners to the media center only during their scheduled periods; and the "disadvantaged" principal who grew up *before* the era of IMCs in elementary schools and *during* the era of lack of IMC treatment in school administration textbooks.

TEACHER DEFICIENCIES

Unless there have been great strides since Perkins wrote *The Prospective Teacher's Knowledge of Library Fundamentals*,[20] the teacher-training institutions are not sending out teachers who can transmit library know-how. After surveying 4,170 college seniors in sixty-nine institutions in thirty-eight states to sample the prospective teacher's knowledge of library fundamentals, Perkins concluded, "The greatest potential source of education for today's youth, the library, is being wasted." [21]

Hartz, discussing faculty responsibility in training students to develop library skills, said, "Since a majority of the faculty themselves have to be prodded into making better use of the library, it is doubtful whether they could stimulate better student use." [22]

el-Hagrasy found a positive relationship between sixth grade teachers' backgrounds in (1) library skills and (2) reading, and the achievement of their students in these two areas.[23]

In reviewing the Fordham Publishing Co. kit for teaching library skills in grades 7–9,[24] Daniels recommends using this sequence for teachers, and she says, "The teacher's unsophisticated use of library tools is a common frustration for librarians, though hardly the teacher's fault." [25]

Furneaux, principal of a school for disturbed and psychotic children, speaking about troublesome letters of inquiry from college students, points out that training in how to locate information should start very early, and that "the further implications are even more serious, because these students are so soon to become teachers themselves. If they really do not know 'where to look' for information, how can they be ready to assume the responsibility of the education of children?" [26]

Again, the librarian is in the middle—right between the materials and the user—and the user whose need is greatest is not always the 10–14-year-old. But, for the transescent, perhaps we can generalize from Moss who says the middle school should foster:

> learning specifically geared to immature and maturing students in an atmosphere which challenges but does not pressure the individual. Such programs recognize that there are many different learning styles and that large numbers of this age group cannot tolerate huge doses of subject matter because of their rapid physical metamorphosis.[27]

SELECTED EXAMPLES OF INSTRUCTION FROM THE LITERATURE

Although it is impractical to design content for user instruction in the use of library materials that will fit every middle school, some help may be derived from selected programs in the literature. The measure of best fit will be assured by local adaptations by librarians and teachers.

Helen Smith, librarian in St. Louis County, lists nine basics in "What Every Seventh Grader Should Know About Libraries." [28] These include knowing a system for arranging a library; the difference between fiction and nonfiction; the definition of biography; how to use a card catalog; that call numbers direct users to library shelves; the term "reference" as libraries use it; some library rules; some basic library vocabulary; and that magazines are also called periodicals. Here is a librarian who looked at her users and spelled out some essentials for a program. Other schools might need more sophisticated skills. More of this introspection will improve the instructional program.[29]

Joseph Mersand, chairman of the English department of a Jamaica, New York, high school, wrote an article for *The Principal* entitled "How To Teach Library Skills" that listed the following eight aims of library instruction: (1) knowledge of the general arrangement of the library, (2) use of the card catalog, (3) use of the encyclopedia and other reference books, (4) use of the *Readers' Guide to Periodical Literature,* (5) knowledge of the magazines and newspapers in the library, (6) knowledge of the parts of a book, (7) knowledge of the dictionary, and (8) skill in following a topic through various references and cross-references and in extracting only the pertinent information.[30]

Mersand offers the following principles, which seem to be valid guidelines at any grade level, in organizing a program of library instruction:

1. Library skills are learned best when they are needed for help with problems faced by students.

2. Library skills are best acquired through the laboratory method, with the student going through each procedure, rather than just listening to a talk.

3. Instruction should be gradual, sequential, and cumulative. The intricacies of the card catalog cannot be mastered in one lesson. Several lessons spaced over several terms are more effective. The same principle holds true for all other library skills.

4. Once a library skill has been taught, students should put it to use in solving a problem, and should be expected to use that skill on all future occasions where it is necessary.

5. Since the teacher knows best which classroom situations will require a knowledge of the library facilities, she should be equipped to give the greater part of instruction in library usage. Although the school librarian can best give instruction in certain aspects of the library, she does not have time nor the energy to give all the lessons to all the students, particularly in a large school.[31]

In view of some of the teacher deficiencies cited earlier in this chapter, in-service training or additional media staff seems requisite. According to "Policies, Principles, and Standards for the Approval of Junior High Schools," issued by the North Central Association of Colleges and Secondary Schools in 1967, "In-service training programs for students and staff for making effective use of the services of the instructional materials center shall be provided" (p. 31, Code 9.31).

The technology of videotapes, audio cassettes, and learning modules could be employed to assure individualization of learning with staff efficiency. Such devices allow for repetitive instruction needed by some students.

Blau takes an opposing stance from Mersand. In discussing the perennial "reports" or "research papers" required of students as an element in independent study, Ms. Blau writes:

> The steps required for carrying out this type of study involve the subject field teacher as mentor. It is the subject field teacher who sets the guidelines, approves the topics, indicates the format for the bibliography and footnotes (if any), suggests the length of the research project, and checks on the progress. But after these initial steps have been taken, the student himself must start the search for the raw material of his paper. At this point, he should turn to the person trained to help him. That person is the forgotten teacher—the librarian.[32]

The collaboration between teacher and librarian is tantamount to the user's success in middle school library skills.

McAteer views the library as a teaching asset. He says to the teacher:

> Having inventoried the library for its strength and appropriateness to your area, why not use the facility as a teaching asset? Engage the librarian's assistance when planning your learning or resource units. Recall that the librarian is a professional educator, more frequently than not holding the same teaching certificate which authorizes your presence in the school. They are products of the same preparation process which you experienced and in many cases are former classroom teachers themselves. . . . The librarian may become an active teaching partner by examining your objectives in light of the resources with which he is most familiar. . . . The librarian has an overview of all subject areas and may recommend supplementary aids and references. You may use him as a sounding board for ideas, interact with him on questions of technique, and secure his insight for suggestions regarding your planning. By sharing your thoughts and objectives with the librarian, he may better assist your students as they seek to complete the tasks which you have designed for their intellectual development.[33]

Some school systems, e.g., Barrington, Illinois, have provided liaison staff members between the library and the grades or departments. Perhaps when teachers are convinced of the teaching alliance that can be formed with media staff, the "lone-ranger librarian" will be flanked with released-time teachers who can speak and plan for specific team areas.

Many middle schools offer exploratory shop courses. John A. Striepling, an electronics teacher, who advocates a minilibrary as a mode of developing the "library habit," writes: "Open your library with a demonstration lecture on the uses of the index, table of contents, etc., found in most books. Encourage the students to help one another to locate and use the source materials. This is the method of learning used in industry—asking for assistance from another employee before interrupting the supervisor. . . ."[34] Striepling believes that the shop library will help students to use materials that are available to them on all levels, "from the elementary through the graduate school."[35] Rotating collections might stimulate readers who do not come to the library.

Weller provides an example of teacher-librarian cooperation:

The media generalist and the classroom teacher must often exercise their ingenuity in using media and integrating them in the classroom curriculum. Perhaps
early in the school year when the fifth grade teacher is beginning a unit on
maps, she works with the media specialist on ways of using the media center to
introduce the study. The media generalist plans lessons on maps and globes.
The class becomes acquainted with the atlases in the center, learning about their
differences and likenesses, and the main features of each. Transparencies and
filmstrips reinforce the study of atlases; the use of the index, the different types
of maps, legends, and information in each type of atlas. Mercator, equal-area,
and polar maps are defined, illustrated, and discussed. The media generalist gives
specific lessons on how to read maps and globes; the classroom teacher reviews
these and the children apply their learning through assignments.[36]

Wehmeyer,[37] Hopkinson,[38] and Lieberman [39] have compiled lists of commercially available teaching aids, including map skills, for teacher and librarian.
David L. Shepherd cites five major map skills for junior high school and provides
examples of research-directed questions that a teacher might use.[40] Thralls makes
additional suggestions.[41]

Rupp investigated the effectiveness of instruction in card catalog skills.[42]
After examining courses of study for elementary schools, books treating library
instruction, and curriculum guides from nine large city school districts, Ms.
Rupp devised a test to assess the impact of card catalog skills. She found that
children who have access to an elementary school library program exhibit higher
educational gain in grades 4–6 than do children who do not have access to library
instruction.

The optimum time to teach the card catalog seems to be "Muddled." In examining a variety of materials on library instruction, much disparity exists. The
curriculum guide from Seattle Public Schools [43] and Palovic and Goodman [44]
suggest card catalog instruction in grade 3; Freund [45] advocates grade 4; Cleary's
handbook for students in grades 5–8 [46] includes it. Since not all schools have a
program of library instruction, or perhaps not even a library, Mott and Baisden
have included the card catalog in their very easy guide that children may do by
themselves, as verified by field-testing "with real children in a real school situation." [47] Nevertheless, as Mersand has pointed out earlier, "The intricacies of
the card catalog cannot be mastered in one lesson." However, by the time children reach grade 6, they should be somewhat adept in the use of the card catalog. We do not construe the card catalog as suitable content for large-group
instruction in the middle school; tutorial aid may be necessary. Kreigh [48] and
Peterkin [49] suggest games as a mode of application of learnings.

The whole theory of the middle school rests on the belief that transescents are
in a period of varying maturation rates and that exploration and differentiation
are functions of the curriculum for this age group.[50] Therefore it seems only
reasonable that instruction in the use of the library should avoid the conventional block scheduling to cover material that may already be learned. What,
then, are some alternatives?

First, a flow of information to and from the classroom teachers must be initiated. This may be facilitated by request forms issued to teachers three or more times a semester. The form should ask for topics of study that could lead to library usage. It could ask for additional materials needed in units of work, or personal interests of students that have been expressed in the classroom. A pack of simple "query forms" could lie atop the card catalog where students could uniformly indicate problems of locating materials on personal pursuits of learning. The queries could lead to brief bibliographies that librarians would prepare for the learner. The queries will also indicate to a perceptive librarian the kinds of individualizing instruction that middle school students need.

After the anxiety of asking for help is reduced, students might be encouraged to increase their prowess by sharing information in student-designed seminars. In Heather Hill Elementary School in Flossmoor, Illinois, students post a topic of information they would like to share with other students. If as many as five or six students sign their names beneath the topic, the originator is then allowed to plan a seminar. The student must work with the resource center teacher in preparing the presentation. He or she researches the topic, prepares an outline on a ditto master, and assembles the visuals before conducting the small group seminar. Two such presentations were on "Furs" and "Origami."

In the same way, students could recruit small groups of learners for demonstration of library skills that were "taught" in earlier grades. Teacher domination can be reduced in the skill-building process by releasing student power. More responsibility is shifted to the learners—at least in the decision about when they want to learn specific skills. The teacher and library staff become the resource people; Bubeck amplifies this theory that the emphasis is on learning—not instructing.[51]

We need local user-surveys, more teacher-librarian planning keyed to curriculum, more library staff to individualize instruction, and tests for "entering" skills at the middle school level,[52] and a scope-and-sequence chart for K–12 emphases. The classroom teacher must be actively involved in the process.

An assortment of tests, written or practical, should be accumulated to establish that the following skills have been acquired before grade 6:

1. An operational ability to locate materials and equipment within the physical arrangement of the media center or school plant.

    (a) *Print*—books, pamphlets, card catalog, map case, picture file, periodicals,

    (b) *Software*—filmstrips, recordings, transparencies, tapes, cassettes, globes, kits,

    (c) *Hardware: housing and operation*—cassette player, filmstrip projector, record player, overhead projector, slide projector, opaque projector, CAI terminals.

2. An operational skill to use card catalog drawer labels and call numbers on catalog cards and book spines.

3. Performance skill in checking out all types of media.

4. Applied skill in using parts of a book in locating information within a textbook; the parts of a book.

5. Expository skill in illustrating the ten general classes of the Dewey Decimal Classification System.

6. Operational skill in locating information in general encyclopedias via index, volume, page, and page position.

7. Skill in using the telephone directory (as a prelude to understanding filing in card catalog and using indexes).

8. Skill in using an abridged dictionary.

RECOMMENDATIONS FOR LIBRARY INSTRUCTION ACTIVITIES IN THE MIDDLE SCHOOL

1. With classroom teacher assistance, design proficiency modules that include (a) goal, (b) precise directions for performing each skill, and (c) a proficiency test on the skill. The directions may incorporate cassettes, transparencies, filmstrips, videotapes, models, or print.

2. Requisition a shallow-drawer filing cabinet that will accommodate 8½ x 11-inch paper stored flat. Label each drawer with the grade level and separate skill. File the proficiency modules for open access to students. Scott has given some practical suggestions in physical management of filed exercises.[53]

3. Divide each classroom into learning teams of two or three pupils; or, implement the volunteer seminar learning mentioned above.

4. Provide each student with ten media goals and time options for demonstrating proficiency.

5. Provide incentive by posting names of "Media Magnates" in the library. Allow these pupils with demonstrated skill to check the proficiency tests of other students. To stay in step with classroom topics, let Media Magnates supply new questions continuously, for proficiency test items.

6. Enlist teacher assistance to record achievement of library skills on report cards and in cumulative folders. Excellent, average, and poor achievement could be noted. Some record of attainment might underscore the significance of library skills.

Goals must arise from curricular content and methodology. In one school we have found the following pursuits appropriate:

Grade 6
1. How to interpret the second schedule of Dewey Classification.
2. How to use an atlas and gazetteer.
3. How to use *Merit Encyclopedia* (designed for grade 5 up).
4. How to use *Abridged Readers' Guide*.
5. How to make a bibliography, drawing from indexes in books when the subject is not listed in the card catalog.
6. When to use almanacs.
7. How to use a thesaurus (beginning with a junior thesaurus and rhyming dictionary).
8. When to use the *Lincoln Library* and *Columbia Encyclopedia*.
9. How to locate quotations.
10. How to locate a state flag.

Grade 7

1. How to write a precis of a magazine article.
2. How to make a bibliography including references from at least four different sources: books, magazines, encyclopedias, filmstrips, personal interview, etc.
3. How to read and interpret the decimals in Dewey Decimal Classification.
4. How to locate information about authors (at least four different biographical sources).
5. How to locate information in special encyclopedias on music and art.
6. How to locate references in science and health.
7. How to locate material in applied arts.
8. How to use special references in social studies.
9. How to nurture an interest in a hobby or sport.
10. How to interpret the various kinds of information in an unabridged dictionary entry.

Grade 8

1. Investigating book reviews for style and organization.
2. Distinguishing between primary and secondary sources in historical documents.
3. Locating facsimiles of art masterpieces.
4. Finding material about individual states, rivers, climate, etc.
5. Finding puzzles, secret codes; planning parties; conducting games.
6. Using collective biographies; study of analytics in card catalog; *Index to Young Readers' Collective Biographies.*[54]
7. Using specialized dictionaries: foreign language, space, mathematics, *D.A.B.*, etc.
8. Using concordances: Shakespeare, Bible.
9. *Famous First Facts* and inventions; copyrights and patents.
10. Full schedule of Dewey Classification in 900s.

CONCLUSION

Yes, library instruction may be in a *muddle* in the middle school. There is no Elysium in programming; we have no national curriculum. Just as the range of abilities grows wider as students progress up the educational ladder, so the range of library skills diverge. Routine classes in library skills become redundant and dull. To enlist teacher concern is basic. To meet each learner's needs requires diversity.

The answers to an effective program will never be singular; solutions will never be resolved by librarians alone. The uniqueness of the middle school concept must be understood by the total staff, and classroom teachers must be involved in a program of exploratory and differentiated activities that releases the transescent in self-directed learning, harmonious with curricular and personal goals.

Research findings, successful practices in the literature, and a wealth of commercial media are available as aids to a specialized program. Local assessment of needs will determine the program of best fit. Obstructive monoliths in the educational program should be torn down as teachers and students discover the joy of learning through ready access to all forms of information in a well-stocked, well-staffed middle school library.

NOTES

1. Charlene R. Swarthout, *The School Library as Part of the Instructional System* (Metuchen, N.J.: Scarecrow Press, 1967), p. 235.
2. Judith Murphy, *Middle Schools* (New York: Educational Facilities Lab., 1965), p. 6.
3. Theodore C. Moss, *Middle School* (New York: Houghton Mifflin, 1969), p. 18.
4. William T. Gruhn and Harl R. Douglass, *The Modern Junior High School* (New York: Ronald Press, 1956), p. 421.
5. Donald H. Eichhorn, "Middle School Organization: A New Dimension," in James E. Hertling and Howard G. Getz, eds., *Education for the Middle School Years: Readings* (Glenview, Ill.: Scott, Foresman, 1971), p. 103; inclusive reading, pp. 102–105.
6. Ibid., p. 104.
7. JoAnn H. Strickland and William Alexander, "Seeking Continuity in Early and Middle School Education," in James E. Hertling and Howard G. Getz, eds., *Education for the Middle School Years: Readings* (Glenview, Ill.: Scott, Foresman, 1971), p. 10; inclusive reading, pp. 9–14.
8. Jeanne S. Hoyt and Dorothy S. Blackmore, "Fifty Seventh Graders: A Comparison of Their Reading Achievement and Expected Achievement in Grades One through Seven," *Journal of Educational Research* 53 (January 1960): 163–171.
9. John Gillespie and Diana Lembo, *Introducing Books: A Guide for the Middle Grades* (New York: R.R. Bowker, 1970), p. 318.
10. *Subject Guide to Children's Books in Print* (New York: R.R. Bowker, revised annually).
11. Roderick McDaniel, ed., *Resources for Learning: A Core Media Collection for Elementary Schools* (New York: R.R. Bowker, 1971).
12. Gerald Brekke, "Actual and Recommended Allotments of Time for Reading," *The Reading Teacher* 16 (January 1963): 234–237.
13. Robert J. Starr, "A Suggestion for Individualizing Instruction within a Traditional School Organization," *Audio-Visual Instruction* 16 (October 1971): 68–69.
14. Swarthout, op. cit., p. 111.
15. Helen Fleischman, *A Study of the Classroom Teacher's Role in Library Skills Lessons* (Brookville, N.Y.: Long Island University, Graduate Library School, 1971), p. 77.
16. Anthony Barton, "The Continuum: How to Analyze Your School Environment—and Loosen it Up," *Library Journal* 95 (December 15, 1970): 4317–4323.
17. Emmett L. Williams, "The Middle School Movement," *Today's Education* 57 (December 1968): p. 42.

18. Emanual T. Prostano and Joyce S. Prostano, *The School Library Media Center* (Littleton, Colo.: Libraries Unlimited, 1971), p. 226.
19. Ibid., p. 223.
20. Ralph Perkins, *The Prospective Teacher's Knowledge of Library Fundamentals,* (Metuchen, N.J.: Scarecrow Press, 1965).
21. Ibid., p. 199.
22. Frederic R. Hartz, "Library Instruction in the Secondary School," *Journal of Secondary Education* 41 (May 1966): 201–205.
23. Saad M. el-Hagrasy, "The Teacher's Role in Library Service: An Investigation and Its Devices," *Journal of Experimental Education* 30 (June 1962): 347–354.
24. Diana L. Lembo, John J. Gillespie, and Ralph J. Falcarelli, *The School Library and Its General Reference Tools,* Seeking and Finding: Library Instruction Program III (Bronx, N.Y.: Fordham Publishing Company, 1969).
25. Leona M. Daniels, "Library Learning Laboratory III," *School Library Journal* 17 (December 1970): 28–29.
26. Barbara Furneaux, "I Do Not Know Where to Look," *The Times Educational Supplement,* no. 2,698 (57th year), February 3, 1967, p. 345.
27. Moss, op. cit., p. 21.
28. Helen Smith, "What Every Seventh Grader Should Know About Libraries," *School and Community* 58 (February 1972): 7.
29. Paul R. Daniels, "Learning Centers and Stations: A Different Concept," *Audio-Visual Instruction* 15 (November 1970): 29.ˑ
30. Joseph Mersand, "How to Teach Library Skills," *The Principal,* (New York: Yeshiva Principals Association, February 1971).
31. Ibid.
32. Eleanor W. Blau, "The Forgotten Teacher," *Independent School Bulletin* 31 (May 1972): 66–67.
33. John F. McAteer, "The Library as a Teaching Asset," *Clearing House* 45 (April 1971): 510–512.
34. John A. Striepling, "Keep Them Using the Shop Library," *School Shop* 30 (October 1970): 88.
35. Ibid.
36. Elizabeth Weller, "The Elementary School Media Center in Action," *Contemporary Education* 41 (November 1969): 77–78.
37. Lillian Wehmeyer, "Library Media Center Skills," *The Booklist* 68 (May 15, 1972): 808–814.
38. Shirley L. Hopkinson, *Instructional Materials for Teaching the Use of the Library: A Selected, Annotative Bibliography of Films, Filmstrips, Books and Pamphlets, Tests and Other Aids,* 4th ed. (San Jose, Calif.: Claremont House, 1971).
39. Irving Lieberman, "A Working Bibliography and Commercially Available Audio-Visual Materials for the Teaching of Library Science," Occasional Paper No. 94, mimeographed (Urbana: Illinois University, Graduate School of Library Science, December 1968).

40. David L. Shepherd, *Comprehensive High School Reading Methods* (Columbus, Ohio: Merrill, 1973), p. 108.

41. Zoe A. Thralls, *The Teaching of Geography* (New York: Appleton-Century Crofts, 1958), pp. 59, 62–63.

42. Bette H. Rupp, "The Effectiveness of Card Catalog Skills," *Contemporary Education* 41 (November 1969): 79–81.

43. Seattle Public Schools, Curriculum Development Division, *Library Experiences for Elementary School Children,* n.d., p. 32.

44. Lora Palovic and Elizabeth B. Goodman, *The Elementary School Library in Action* (West Nyack, N.Y.: Parker Pub., 1968), p. 240.

45. Freund, op. cit, p. 180.

46. Florence Damon Cleary, *Discovering Books and Libraries* (Bronx, N.Y.: H. W. Wilson, 1966), p. 119.

47. Carolyn Mott and Leo B. Baisden, *The Children's Book on How to Use Books and Libraries* (Scribners, 1961), pp. 207, 8.

48. Helen Kreigh, "It's Elementary, My Dear Dewey," *School and Community* 55 (January 1969): 29, 31.

49. Helen M. Peterkin, *Individualized Library Instruction for Fourth Graders Through a Multi-Media Game* (Brookville, N.Y.: Long Island University, Graduate Library School, 1968), p. 99.

50. Neil P. Atkins, "Rethinking Education in the Middle," in James E. Hertling and Howard G. Getz, eds., *Education for the Middle School Years: Readings,* (Glenview, Ill.: Scott, Foresman, 1971).

51. Robert H. Bubeck, "The Emphasis Is on Learning—Not Instructing," *School Management* 15 (August 1971): 29–31.

52. Frances Hatfield and Irene Gullette, National Test of Library Skills (American Testing Co., 6301 S.W. Fifth St., Ft. Lauderdale, Fla. 33314).

53. Helen E. Scott, "The Preparation of a File of Exercises for Developing Study Skills in the Middle Grades," *Journal of Education* 136 (November 1953): 40–45.

54. *An Index to Young Readers' Collective Biographies* (New York: R. R. Bowker, 1970).

EDUCATING LIBRARY USERS IN THE SENIOR HIGH SCHOOL

RUTH ANN DAVIES
Coordinator of Library Services, North Hills School District and Faculty member, Graduate School of Library and Information Sciences, University of Pittsburgh, Pennsylvania

Today's school librarian "is a teacher whose subject is learning itself."[1] As a teacher, one of the senior high school librarian's major responsibilities is to design and implement a program for teaching the use of the library with purpose, profit, challenge, and satisfaction. Learning how to use the library is a basic component of each high school's instructional program for "the purpose which runs through and strengthens all other educational purposes—the common thread of education—is the development of the ability to think."[2] Learning how to use the library goes far beyond the traditional program of being introduced to library resources, services, and facilities; it involves developing the student's rational powers and encompasses learning how to think, how to communicate thought, and how to master the skill of lifelong learning.

Learning to use the senior high school library is the final stage of a school district's developmental study skills program. Such a program is far too important to be left to chance or whim. Because the study skills program is a basic component of the total instructional program, it must be both scientifically planned and systematically implemented.

A scientifically planned study skills program (1) is based on sound psychological principles; (2) identifies fundamental skills, tools, and terms; (3) arranges the skills, tools, and terms in a continuum: kindergarten through grade 12.

The following psychological principles have been identified by The National Council for the Social Studies as essential for undergirding a developmental study skills program:

1. The skill should be taught functionally, in the context of a topic of study, rather than as a separate exercise.

2. The learner must understand the meaning and purpose of the skill, and have motivation for developing.
3. The learner should be carefully supervised in his first attempts to apply the skill, so that he will form correct habits from the beginning.
4. The learner needs repeated opportunities to practice the skill, with immediate evaluation so that he knows where he has succeeded or failed in his performance.
5. The learner needs individual help, through diagnostic measures and follow-up exercises, since not all members of any group learn at exactly the same rate or retain equal amounts of what they have learned.
6. Skill instruction should be presented at increasing levels of difficulty, moving from the simple to the more complex; the resulting growth in skills should be cumulative as the learner moves through school, with each level of instruction building on and reinforcing what has been taught previously.
7. Students should be helped, at each stage, to generalize the skills, by applying them in many and varied situations; in this way, maximum transfer of learning can be achieved.
8. The program of instruction should be sufficiently flexible to allow skills to be taught as they are needed by the learner; many skills should be developed concurrently.[3]

A study skill, reference tool, and basic terminology continuum provides three levels of emphasis: (1) introducing the specific skill, tool, or term through planned experiences; (2) developing the skill and the use of tool or term within a context of functional utility and need; (3) reteaching, maintaining, and extending the skill or reference tool as part of the ongoing instructional program. The Appendix to the Thirty-Third Yearbook of the National Council for the Social Studies, *Skill Development in Social Studies*,[4] presents an excellent model of a comprehensive study skills continuum, K–12. A school district desiring to initiate or strengthen its study skills program can well begin by studying the study skills analysis chart included in this Appendix.

If a district study skills program has not been spelled out, then the high school librarians must take a leadership role in designing and implementing a plan for integrating learning how to use the library with the school's instructional program. Florence Cleary, in *Blueprint for Better Reading: School Programs for Promoting Skill and Interest in Reading*, provides in Chapter 7, "Reading for Information and Knowledge," and in Chapter 8, "A Framework for Teaching the Investigative Skills," a step-by-step procedure to follow in organizing and implementing a library-based study skills program.[5] Cleary suggests organizing instruction in the use of the library under the following categories:

I. LOCATIONAL SKILLS

The supplementary skills for locating information that should be taught and retaught in high school include:

Using library tools to locate books and other informational materials
Locating ephemeral material through indexes

Gaining facility in the use of a number of special reference books in different subject fields—history, biography, literature, music, art, social science, science

Acquiring facility in the use of magazine indexes, such as *Readers' Guide to Periodical Literature,* and other specialized indexes as sources for locating current materials

Gaining acquaintance with all parts of the book: the title page, preface, introduction, table of contents, lists of maps and illustrations, notes, appendix, bibliography, and glossary

Learning about the arrangement and special features of dictionaries, encyclopedias, annuals, almanacs, yearbooks, atlases, and maps

Using special indexes of poetry, plays, costumes, essays, songs, and biography to find materials in collections

Acquiring ease in the use of handbooks, manuals, directories, and yearbooks for locating a variety of types of information

Locating information from many sources and acquiring essential skill in observing, listening, and viewing in order to obtain relevant information

II. SELECTION AND ORGANIZATIONAL SKILLS

Regardless of the amount of emphasis given to skill development in the elementary and junior high school, the high school staff cannot assume that the pupils need no further guidance in selecting and organizing information. Instruction should continue, with emphasis on the following intermediate skills:

Identifying the purposes for acquiring the information

Skimming to ascertain if the selection contains information pertinent to the problem

Choosing a number of important topics under which the information may be grouped

Selecting and classifying less important facts under the main topic

Examining large or major topics to determine the most systematic arrangement as they relate to the problem

Selecting all the facts that bear on the problem

Jotting down sources of information and looking up unfamiliar words

III. INTERPRETIVE SKILLS

A number of intermediate skills are basic to the interpretation of what is read:

Understanding what the author means

Relating and evaluating pertinent ideas

Evaluating the reliability of sources and recognizing and analyzing propaganda

Distinguishing between fact and opinion and recognizing and tracing pertinent relationships and time and place sequences

Willingness to evaluate one's own attitude on the subject being examined

IV. GENERALIZING AND CONVERSION SKILLS

As instruction continues in the high school grades, there are numerous questions that teachers and librarians may use to give directions for reaching generalizations and conclusions and for evaluating decisions:

What are the possible conclusions and generalizations which can be drawn from an analysis of the information?
Have you taken into account your own biases and prejudices which might have influenced the reaching of these conclusions?
Have you gone beyond your information in reaching conclusions?
What do your conclusions indicate? Have they changed or clarified any of your previously held opinions or judgments?
Can you use this information in making judgments and reaching decisions in other areas or with other problems?
May further information make necessary a possible reconsideration of conclusions? [6]

Cleary identifies the abilities, facilities, and skills in locating and gathering information, in organizing, evaluating, interpreting, and using information, and in reaching conclusions, solving problems, and sharing information. She groups these basic learning experiences under the following eleven headings:

I. GETTING ACQUAINTED WITH THE SOURCES OF INFORMATION AND KNOWLEDGE

Desirable learnings for pupils:

Acquaintance with the many and varied sources of information
Understanding of the skills involved in locating and gathering information
Knowledge of the resources and services of the school library—as a vast source of information and knowledge
Development of wholesome attitudes and habits in using the sources and resources of knowledge and appreciations

II. ACQUIRING INFORMATION AND KNOWLEDGE THROUGH THE SKILLFUL USE OF BOOKS

Desirable learnings for pupils:

An understanding and appreciation of books as sources of information, as the record of man's cultural heritage and creative ideas and thoughts
Knowledge of how books are written, illustrated, printed, published and distributed
Appreciation of literary, aesthetic, and human values in books
Acquaintance with books that provide for the enrichment and integration of the curriculum

Knowledge of and facility in the use of the books as a source of information

Facility in using such special features in books as graphs, charts, illustrations, maps, and bibliographies

III. LOCATING BOOKS AND OTHER LEARNING MATERIALS IN THE LIBRARY

Desirable learnings for pupils:

Understanding of the opportunities for acquiring and utilizing knowledge through skillful use of books and libraries

Knowledge of the various resources in the modern school library, and their location and use

Acquaintance with and facility in using the Dewey Classification system in locating books on library shelves

Skill in using the card catalog to locate books and other learning materials in the library

Skill in the use of indexes and lists for locating poetry, plays, biography, short stories, songs, fiction, and other materials in collections

Facility in locating films, filmstrips, records, flat pictures, and other audio-visual materials—those available in the school and those available through other agencies

IV. LOCATING AND USING CURRENT MATERIALS

Desirable learnings for pupils:

Understanding the value of current ephemeral materials as sources of information and knowledge

Acquaintance with and facility in reading and using magazines as sources of information

Skill in using magazine and newspaper indexes

Facility in using and evaluating newspapers as sources of information

Facility in using TV programs in documentary films as sources of information and knowledge

V. USING REFERENCE BOOKS TO LOCATE INFORMATION

Desirable learnings for pupils:

Acquaintance with and ability to use reference books that supply concise information about places, things, people, events and progress

Ability to use general encyclopedias efficiently in gathering information

Ability to use handbooks, almanacs, yearbooks, manuals, directories, and government and state documents in locating statistical information

Ability to use appropriate reference books in securing information on special subjects and in special fields

Facility in securing geographical information: location of place names, statistics concerning commerce, population, industry resources, and other pertinent data

VI. LOCATING AND GATHERING INFORMATION ABOUT PEOPLE

Desirable learnings for pupils:

Acquaintance with the many sources of information about people, and facility in choosing the source appropriate to the purposes of the reader and investigator

Knowledge of general biographical dictionaries and encyclopedias and facility in their use

Knowledge about and facility in the use of many special biographical encyclopedias, dictionaries, and directories

VII. LOCATING INFORMATION ABOUT WORDS, PHRASES, QUOTATIONS, LITERARY ITEMS, AND REFERENCES

Desirable learnings for pupils:

Identification of the letters of the English alphabet and skill in alphabetizing

Facility in the use of dictionaries to obtain information about words

Ability to use word books and supplementary English language sources in gaining facility in writing and speaking

Knowledge of and skill in locating literary items and references

Skill in finding sources of quotations

Ability to locate brief information about foreign words, phrases, items, and allusions

VIII. GATHERING AND SELECTING INFORMATION FROM MANY SOURCES

Desirable learnings for pupils:

Ability to determine what information is needed and the appropriate and pertinent sources for locating it

Skill in observation—the ability to obtain clear and vivid perceptions and to learn from direct experience

Ability to listen and learn from the experience

Skill in interviewing and using people as authoritative resources for gathering information

Facility in locating printed, audio-visual and symbolic materials in libraries, museums, galleries, and institutions

Ability to read with understanding and to select appropriate and pertinent materials

Ability to record the sources of information in approved bibliographic form

Skill in recording sources of information in footnotes

IX. ORGANIZING INFORMATION AND KNOWLEDGE

Desirable learnings for pupils:

Facility in selecting information pertinent to a topic or problem

Skill in organizing information in outline form

Ability to take notes and record sources

Skill in organizing information gained from observing and listening, from manipulating objects and examining symbolic materials

X. ANALYZING, INTERPRETING, AND EVALUATING INFORMATION

Desirable learnings for pupils:

Ability to read for meaning—to understand what is read
Perceptiveness in evaluating the authoritativeness of the sources of information and knowledge
Ability to differentiate between fact and opinion
Skill in recognizing and evaluating propaganda
Skill in analysis and interpretation of information and knowledge

XI. USING INFORMATION: REACHING GENERALIZATIONS AND CONCLUSIONS, AND SHARING INFORMATION

Desirable learnings for pupils:

Facility in summarizing information, reaching conclusions, and generalizations
An understanding of how information is used in solving problems and in making decisions, in thinking deductively as well as procedurally
Skill in sharing information, in reporting the facts, and in participating in discussion
An understanding of the difference between memorizing facts and using the method of inquiry and investigation
Insight into the processes through which the individual sharpens, clarifies, or changes beliefs and values as the evidence comes in.[7]

Having compiled the checklist of basic skills to be introduced or reinforced in the high school, the next logical step is to compile two companion checklists: a checklist of basic reference tools to be introduced or reinforced (see Appendix 1) and a checklist of basic terminology to be integrated with the high school skill development program (see Appendix 2). These two companion checklists are essential components of the high school's instructional program in how to use the library.

The next step is to plan for the systematic integration within the instructional program for the introduction, the reinforcement, and the practice of each of the basic skills, tools, and terms. It is the high school librarian's responsibility to blueprint an integration chart that pinpoints exactly where within the framework of the existing courses of study it is most appropriate to introduce, reintroduce, or reinforce the teaching of each of the fundamentals. Such a blueprint should identify by subject, by grade, by unit, and, where appropriate, by topic or concept where each fundamental can best be integrated. An example of an integration chart follows.

After compiling the "Skill/Tool/Term Integration Chart," the next step for the high school librarian is to utilize the chart as a guide and reminder when planning with teachers for the integration of library support with the ongoing,

SKILL/TOOL/TERM INTEGRATION CHART

Skill/Tool/Term	Grade	Subject	Unit or Topic Tie-In
Skill:			
Gaining facility in the use of a number of special reference books in different fields	10	Science	**Unit:** Man's Fight Against Pollution
Tools:			**Topics:**
Biography Index			John Muir
			Gifford Pinchot
Current Biography Yearbook			Rachel Carson
			Walter Hickle
Encyclopedic Dictionary of the Environment			Air monitoring
			Noise pollution
Reference Shelf			Land Use in the United States
			Water crisis
Term: "Cross-reference"			
Essay and General Literature Index			Ecology, *see also:* Environment
			Industrial waste
			Pollution
Readers' Guide to Periodical Literature			Ecology, *see also:* Environment
			Fishes
			Food chains
			Human ecology
Terms: "Cross-reference"			Conservation, *see also:*
"Thesaurus"			Air pollution
International Thesaurus of Quotations			Environment
			Trees

day-to-day teaching and learning program. Each time the librarian plans for course or unit development he or she must consistently plan to incorporate appropriate specific skills, basic tools, and special terminology.

The following problems have traditionally prevented the full implementation of a planned program of instruction in the use of the library:

1. Lack of a school district K through 12 developmental study skills program that mandates the integration of library skills as an integral component of the program

2. Limitation of instruction in the use of the library being limited to a brief orientation session

3. Failure to include in state or locally developed courses of study, specific learning experiences requiring library support and specific reference to the necessity of integrating instruction in the use of the library within the framework of the teaching-learning program

4. Isolation of the librarian from curriculum study and revision activities

5. Failure of teacher-training institutions to include in their basic training programs an adequate understanding of the function of the school library as a learning laboratory and the role of the school librarian as a fellow teacher

6. Failure of the teacher to expand class knowledge beyond textbook contents and classroom confines

7. Reluctance of the teacher to preplan with the librarian for the class or group to use library media, facilities, and services before a unit is introduced to the class

8. Lack of sufficient staff—both professional and paraprofessional—to adequately support a comprehensive, diversified instructional program in the use of the library.

Resolution of the above problems, except for number 5, begins with administrative understanding, concern, and direct support. Dr. Edward D. Kruse, 1970 recipient of the American Association of School Librarians' Outstanding Administrator of the Year Award, told his fellow administrators that there is little hope of an educationally strong library program without their backing. He said:

> Dr. George Brain, Dean of the College of Education at Washington State University, believes, as I do, that developing and supporting a quality school library program is an imperative administrative responsibility. In his book, *Increasing Your Administrative Skills in Dealing with the Instructional Program,* Dr. Brain makes the statement: "The library program in your school will be a creative, dynamic one only if you understand and discharge your obligations to it." In my opinion, your school or district's instructional media program will be a creative and dynamic one only if you, the administrator, will bring to your school library program your administrative understanding, your administrative concern, and your administrative backing. Such understanding, such concern, such backing comes under the heading of "administrative accountability." [8]

CONCLUSION

The responsibility of the senior high school library program is to teach students how to learn; learning how to use the library with purpose, profit, challenge, and satisfaction must be assigned top priority in any list of library functions. For far too many students graduation from high school marks the end to their formal education—for many young people graduation from high school is the point of no return. For all students high school is the threshold of adulthood, for the right to vote is theirs at age eighteen.

A functionally literate adult knows how to find the answers to problems, knows how to keep informed and intellectually alive. Educating for functional literacy is the overriding goal of the school's instructional program; learning how to learn and how to use the library is the senior high school library's contribution to helping students achieve a high level of functional literacy. A program of such import can never be left to whim or chance. It must be scientifically planned and systematically implemented; the library must function as a learning laboratory, and the librarian must serve as a teacher whose subject is learning itself.

NOTES

1. Douglas M. Knight, Foreword, *Library Services for the Nation's Needs: Toward Fulfillment of a National Policy,* Report of the National Advisory Commission on Libraries, 1968, as quoted in *Libraries at Large,* ed. by E. Shepley Nourse (New York: R. R. Bowker, 1969).
2. Educational Policies Commission, *The General Purpose of American Education* (Washington, D.C.: National Education Association, 1961), p. 12.
3. Helen M. Carpenter, ed. *Skill Development in Social Studies,* 33rd Yearbook (Washington, D.C.: National Council for the Social Studies, 1963), pp. 311–312.
4. Ibid., pp. 310–327.
5. Florence D. Cleary, *Blueprints for Better Reading: School Programs for Promoting Skill and Interest in Reading* (Bronx, N.Y.: H. W. Wilson, 1972).
6. Ibid., pp. 195–201. Reprinted by permission of the publisher.
7. Ibid., pp. 207–224. Reprinted by permission of the publisher.
8. Edward D. Kruse, "Manpower and Media for the Use of the Minority and the Majority," address presented to the American Association of School Administrators' Convention, Atlantic City, N.J., February 24, 1971.

APPENDIX 1
CHECKLIST OF BASIC REFERENCE TOOLS

GENERAL REFERENCE BOOKS

Almanacs
Information Please Almanac
Official Associated Press Almanac
(*formerly* New York Times . . . Almanac)
Reader's Digest Almanac
World Almanac and Book of Facts

Atlases
Goode's World Atlas
Hammond Medallion World Atlas
Muir's New School Atlas of Universal History
National Geographic Atlas of the World
Rand McNally Commercial Atlas and Marketing Guide
Shepherd's Historical Atlas

Biographical Tools
Biography Index
Current Biography
Dictionary of American Biography
Webster's Biographical Dictionary
Who's Who
Who's Who in America

Dictionaries
Acrononyms and Initialisms Dictionary
Concise Oxford Dictionary of Current English
Funk and Wagnalls Modern Guide to Synonyms and Related Words
Funk and Wagnalls New Standard Dictionary of the English Language

New Language Dictionary
Roget's International Thesaurus
Webster's Seventh New Collegiate Dictionary
Webster's Third New International Dictionary of the English Language
World Book Dictionary

Encyclopedias
Collier's Encyclopedia and Yearbook
Compton's Encyclopedia and Yearbook

SPECIAL REFERENCE BOOKS
Art
Dictionary of Contemporary American Artists
Encyclopedia of World Art
Larousse Encyclopedia of Modern Art

Business, Economics, Statistics
Dictionary of Modern Economics
Economic Almanac
The Economics Reference Book
Guinness Book of World Records
Historical Statistics of the United States
Statistical Abstract of the United States
Statistical Yearbook

Education
American Junior Colleges
American Universities and Colleges
Occupational Outlook Handbook

Etiquette
Amy Vanderbilt's New Complete Book of Etiquette
Emily Post's Etiquette

Geography
AAA Tour Guides
Larousse Encyclopedia of World Geography

Encyclopaedia Britannica and Book of the Year
Encyclopedia Americana and Annual
New Book of Knowledge
Our Wonderful World
The World Book Encyclopedia and Year Book

Indexes
Essay and General Literature Index
New York Times Index
Readers' Guide to Periodical Literature

National Register of Historic Places
Webster's Geographic Dictionary
Worldmark Encyclopedia of the Nations
Words on the Map

History
American Negro Reference Book
Civil War Dictionary
Dictionary of American History
Dictionary of Events
Documents of American History
Great Documents of Western Civilization
The Indian Heritage of America
The Negro in Our History
Oxford Classical Dictionary
Oxford Companion to American History
Words from History

Literature (See also *Poetry, Theater*)
American Authors, 1600–1900
British Authors Before 1800
British Authors of the Nineteenth Century
Contemporary Authors
Cyclopedia of Literary Characters
Cyclopedia of World Authors
European Authors, 1000–1900
Literary History of the United States

Masterpieces of World Literature
in Digest Form
Oxford Companion to American
Literature
Oxford Companion to Classical
Literature
Oxford Companion to English Literature
Reader's Digest of Books
A Reader's Guide to Literary
Terms

Mathematics
James and James Mathematics Dictionary
Universal Encyclopedia of Mathematics

Music
Baker's Biographical Dictionary of
Musicians
Concise Oxford Dictionary of Music
Dictionary of Music and Musicians
Encyclopedia of Jazz
Great Composers: 1300–1900
International Cyclopedia of Music
and Musicians
Milton Cross' Encyclopedia of the
Great Composers and Their Music
Popular American Composers, from
Revolutionary Times to the Present

Mythology
Bulfinch's Mythology
Classic Myths in English Literature
and Art
Dictionary of Mythology
New Larousse Encyclopedia of
Mythology
Words from the Myths

Philosophy and Religion
Concise Encyclopedia of Western
Philosophy and Philosophers

Handbook of Denominations in
the United States
Masterpieces of World Philosophy
in Summary Form
Story of Philosophy
Yearbook of American Churches

Poetry
Complete Rhyming Dictionary
Encyclopedia of Poetry and Poetics
Granger's Index to Poetry
Home Book of Verse, American
and English
Poetry Handbook: A Dictionary of
Terms
Poet's Manual and Rhyming Dictionary

Politics, Government, Current Events
America Votes: A Handbook of
Contemporary Election Statistics
Book of States
Congressional Digest
Political Handbook and Atlas of
the World
Statesman's Year-Book
United States Government Organization Manual
Yearbook of the United Nations

Quotations
Bartlett's Familiar Quotations
Dictionary of Quotations
Home Book of Quotations
International Thesaurus of Quotations
Oxford Dictionary of Quotations

Science
American Men of Science
Basic Dictionary of Science
Collegiate Dictionary of Zoology
Dictionary of Biological Sciences
Dictionary of Biological Terms
Discovering Natural Science
Encyclopedia of Oceanography
Encyclopedic Dictionary of the Environment

Handbook of Chemistry and Physics

Harper's Encyclopedia of Science

Larousse Encyclopedia of Animal Life

McGraw-Hill Encyclopedia of Science and Technology

More Words of Science and the History Behind Them

Science Year: The World Book Science Annual

Van Nostrand's Scientific Encyclopedia

Words of Science and the History Behind Them

Speeches

Reference Shelf

Treasury of Great American Speeches

Treasury of the World's Great Speeches

Vital Speeches

Theater

Digests of Great American Plays

Guide to Great Plays

Oxford Companion to the Theatre

Reader's Encyclopedia of Shakespeare

Reader's Encyclopedia of World Drama

APPENDIX 2
CHECKLIST OF BASIC TERMINOLOGY

abridged
abstract
adaptation
almanac
annotation
anonymous
anthology
appendix
archive
author entry
author index
bibliography
bibliophile
biographer
biography
blurb
book note
boxed edition
call number
card catalog
chronicle
circa
classic
classification system
collective biography
colophon

compendium
content
contributor
copyright
criticism
cross-reference
cyclopedia
definitive edition
diary
dictionary
document
documentation
dust jacket
edit
editor
editorial
encyclopedia
epilogue
essay
excerpt
expurgate
facsimile
fiction
folio
footnote
foreword

format
frontispiece
gazette
gazetteer
ghost-writer
glossary
half title
id est
imprint
incunabula
index
introduction
joint author
journal
lexicographer
lexicon
limited edition
main topic
manuscript
media
memoir
microform
nonfiction
nota bene
outline
pamphlet

part title
pen name
periodical
preface
primary source
prologue
pseudonym
publisher
quid vide
report
research

resume
review
revision
sequel
serial
series
sic
subject index
subtitle
sub topic
summary

supporting detail
syllabus
synopsis
table of contents
thesaurus
title index
trilogy
unabridged
unexpurgated
vertical file
volume

LIBRARY INSTRUCTION FOR YOUNG ADULTS IN PUBLIC LIBRARIES

PENELOPE S. JEFFREY
*Branch Librarian, Clason's Point Branch,
The New York Public Library*

Since public school libraries are now nearly universal in the United States, Young Adult (YA) Specialists in public libraries no longer give formal instruction in the use of the library.

Class visits to public libraries are used to give a brief introduction to basic tools and a tour of locations of materials, but generally no attempt is made to do in-depth library instruction.

The usual practice in public libraries is to give individual assistance. Ideally, when a young person presents a specific title or subject request, she or he is accompanied to the catalog and the librarian explains its function. Then when the classification is located, the young person is directed or accompanied to the shelf. When using tools other than the catalog, the same explain-as-you-go technique is used.

For young adults attempting to do research on their own, the subject approach may be particularly frustrating. Few young people are able to think in the same channels as Library of Congress subject headings. In most cases, subject headings are more helpful to librarians than to library users. Therefore, librarians should be alert and helpful to young adults trying to use subject headings.

Of course, the above procedures are not always possible. Some public libraries lack YA Specialists, or sympathetic staff, or both, or there is often a lack of time to do as much explanation as we would like.

There are many indications that teachers are in as great a need for library instruction as their students. They still often fail to realize that no contemporary library has the budget or space to stock 90 copies of a given title, or 400 different titles on any subject taught in secondary school. In addition, assignments involving library use often work against meaningful research. Topics are frequently too general to cover in a short term paper, students are forbidden to use encyclopedias, or assignments are so poorly phrased that students must be taken by the hand in order to dig up what they really need. Also, whole classes are forced to compete for materials that could be easily duplicated by the teacher, e.g., the words to "The Star-Spangled Banner."

Some public libraries (Enoch Pratt of Baltimore is one example) have forms and brochures giving teachers the opportunity to notify the public library of forthcoming assignments. All librarians serving young people are required to make a great effort to obtain such warning. It usually is incumbent upon librarians to initiate a dialogue in which teachers can learn of the library's assets and limitations. Frequent visits and telephone calls are the rule in initiating and continuing this type of dialogue.

Since many assignments come in a blitz, and material is quickly exhausted, the New York Public Library has developed a "last-resort" form (see Appendix) for students to give to their teachers. If possible, besides checking the form, we suggest an alternative to a title or ask the teacher to give a substitute assignment. This form serves to excuse the students from completing the assignment, but we have no way of measuring whether it has any real impact on the teacher. Certainly, no teachers have ever called me in response to any of these forms I have distributed.

In an increasing number of libraries, book catalogs are replacing drawers of catalog cards. This seldom means that a community's libraries will have the same type of catalog. If the school library uses a card catalog and the public library uses a book catalog, librarians in both types of libraries must be willing to explain the differences to their clients.

For libraries that use the Dewey Decimal system, radical changes in numbers are also confusing to the public.

Greater communication between school/public/university/community college libraries serving young people is a must for effective service. How many librarians are ignorant of mechanical differences between their libraries and yet continue instructing students as if all libraries are the same?

There is a trap in educating clients to use the library: the neglect of an important library resource, the librarian. Too many people may think that we *teach* catalog use (or the use of any tool) so that they will not bother us anymore. They try the subject approach on their own, find nothing and leave without consulting a librarian, and possibly even give up the whole attempt of ever finding anything in a library. Librarians can clear up incorrect interpretations of library resources, suggest other approaches, and refer to other libraries, institutions, and individuals providing information.

Based on what some see as the library's awesome image and a prevalent lack of education in library use among library users, we need to educate young people in the help that is available from people who work in libraries.

APPENDIX
ONE LIBRARY'S "LAST RESORT" TECHNIQUE

When research proves fruitless the librarian fills out a form such as this and the student takes it to his or her teacher, in the hope of appropriate follow-up.

THE NEW YORK PUBLIC LIBRARY
Circulation Department

TO THE TEACHER: DATE _____

_____ came to this library today. We regret we were unable
to fill the request for "_____."

Reasons:

_____ All circulating material is in use because of the large student demand
for material on this subject

_____ Reference material in this area is limited

_____ A reasonable amount of research failed to turn up the desired information
tion

_____ The book is not available at this branch

_____ The book is no longer in print and cannot be repurchased.

We hope you will come into the branch library named below to discuss with the
branch librarian the availability of materials.

_____ Librarian
_____ Branch Library

THE PUBLIC LIBRARY AND YOUNG ADULTS: A VIEWPOINT

MARGARET A. EDWARDS
Formerly Young Adults Coordinator, Enoch Pratt Free Library, Baltimore, Maryland

Ever since Dewey invented the catalog, librarians have had a compulsion to teach the general public, especially the young, to master its intricacies because, they felt, learning to use the catalog was in itself a fine educational experience; but more than that, they told themselves, it would enable students to support their continuing self-education.

Before the public library embarks on any more projects to educate young adults in the use of the catalog and other library resources, we might well ask why we should do this and if it is likely to prove fruitful. To this end, it might be helpful to review our past efforts in library-user education. After teaching the use of library tools had been going on for years, ALA, in 1967, appointed an Ad Hoc Committee on Instruction in the Use of Libraries that included in its report this statement: "The great majority of students do not master library skills, and do not feel impelled to gain proficiency in them." Other surveys also testify to the failure of library-user-education efforts.

Teenagers are not so dumb. They know the catalog is primarily the librarian's tool, not theirs. They do not wish to make the independent use of the catalog and library tools an essential part of their formal education—and since they do not wish it, they cannot be taught to do so.

As for learning the use of library resources in support of their continuing self-education—that concept is obviously for the birds. The typical young adult is not planning (if he or she ever gets out of school) to pursue self-education—certainly not to the extent of doing research. In fact, many high school students have been so burned out by lessons in the catalog that they have no intention of ever setting foot in a library when they leave school. Very few adults in this country ever use the public library, and when they do it is seldom to do research. In our large cities, probably about one in every thousand adults make use of the hours, months, and years of library instruction they have received.

Is it possible that there are other, Freudian reasons for the librarians' obsession, this apparent love affair librarians have, with the catalog? Despite all our arguments to the contrary, too many librarians are frustrated people who secretly find satisfaction in giving young people a hard time. Their favorite slogan is: "Look it up in the catalog," and though they could easily give the youngsters what they ask for, they find more fun in making people pull out a drawer, write down a number, and then, in great bewilderment, try to find the book among the hundreds of titles on the shelves. Our inflexible discipline has become a trademark. If this were not so, we would not be so mercilessly cartooned, to the amusement of the general public who never take exception to all the lampooning.

Another possible reason for all this effort to teach the use of the library is that, though difficult and fruitless, it is a whole lot easier than introducing young people to the joy and enrichment of voluntary reading. To persuade young adults to read requires dedication, a love of people and of books and reading, wide-ranging reading, a sense of humor, an emotional adjustment, and a warm heart that inspires confidence. The librarian with these qualities can change many an apathetic young person into a patron of the public library and better citizen of the republic. But since they find it far easier to set up a lesson in the catalog, that is the route most librarians choose.

When classes from nearby schools come to the public library for a visit, all too often the librarian prepares for their visit by putting together a lesson on the use of the catalog. Yet that librarian might instead have found out ahead of time the interests, capabilities, and experience of the prospective audience and, drawing on his or her rich reading background, set up a colorful display of books the class would enjoy. There could be posters and music and book lists and books that could be borrowed without a library card if necessary. But above all, there would be a well-prepared presentation of the books, with clever thumbnail sketches for some and at least one bang-up good book talk.

The class's visit should be the high-water mark in the school day that will lead students to regularly use both the school library and the public library and be for many their introduction to the joys of reading. A visit of this type should literally impel young people to return to the library, where they know there is a friendly, resourceful librarian who can dissipate the impersonal, institutional air of the public library and make reading a "fun thing."

With Zindel's *Pigman*, Remarque's *All Quiet on the Western Front*, Wright's *Black Boy*, and Tolstoy's *Anna Karenina* crying out for an introduction to eager youth, what a waste to anesthetize kids, who possibly are already numbed by their experience in the school library, with a deadening shot of the Novocaine of the catalog.

College-bound seniors might profit from a few hours of instruction in the use of library tools, though colleges should be able to orient their freshmen to the use of the college library. Both school and public libraries might set up film and slide programs showing how to use the library, for those who wish to learn, but not forcing the matter. Nor should we overlook the possibility that computers may one day give students material on all school assignments at their mere pressing of a button, and thus do away with the need to "look it up in the catalog."

In any event, the public library should not become a part of the gigantic, up-hill, fruitless efforts of the schools. Instead, the public librarians should help young adults with their assignments with kindness and grace and spend their remaining time inspiring young people with the joy and enrichment of reading and with a love of libraries and books.

INSTRUCTING THE OUT-OF-SCHOOL ADULT IN PUBLIC LIBRARY USE

RUTH T. NEWMAN

Coordinator, Adult Services, Denver Public Library

This paper devotes itself to the premise that many out of school adults need to be oriented to the public library and instructed in using it and its information resources, and that little is being done about it. The first half of the discussion will focus first on several recent surveys and studies of librarians' attitudes on the need for adult library-user instruction and then on some specific library programs of adult instruction. The remainder of the paper is an overview of the Denver Public Library's activities in the area of adult user education.

SURVEY/STUDY FINDINGS

In her keynote address to the American Library Association Joint Adult Services Division/Reference Services Division preconference on library orientation in San Francisco on June 23, 1967, Kathleen Molz commented on the joint study the ASD/RSD made in the mid-1960s.[1] A feature of the study, a questionnaire asking librarians to define the problems and needs of adult patrons, elicited some interesting answers that reflected librarians' attitudes toward the adult library user.

One question was: "In general, do you believe there is a need for a coordinated effort to study public library orientation of adults and develop a program of action?"[2] Most of the librarians who responded agreed that a study and program were necessary to better acquaint the public with what the library is really about. They frequently described the adult patron as hesitant, bewildered, reluctant, fearful, and showing ignorance, and the comment was made that "library nonusers and even users regard the library as formidable, frustrating, or time wasteful."[3]

One librarian wrote: "We feel that it is important that any adult be permitted to have relative freedom in his use of the library, without having to rely on a librarian every step of the way."[4] Most librarians would agree with this, but the patrons must have some knowledge of the library and how to use it before they are ready for "relative freedom" to work on their own without help from the librarian. Many librarians agree that adults fail to use the library, most especially the large library, from their sheer awe and bewilderment at its arrangement.

In 1966, an extensive survey of library users was made in a seven-county, largely metropolitan area centered around Baltimore, Maryland, and Washington, D.C. The survey attempted to find out who the library patrons were; what they came for and why; what they did while in the library; whether they got what they wanted; if not, why not. Ninety-nine libraries cooperated in collecting the data, and though the survey was done several years ago, many of its answers can still be applied to most metropolitan areas. The following information is summarized from Mary Lee Bundy's report on the study: More than 135,000 adults entering all types and sizes of libraries were given questionnaires. Of this number, 21,385 patrons responded. As expected, the survey covered the entire spectrum of ages, occupations, and all levels of educational background. Almost half of the patrons were out-of-school adults, most of them college educated. Of these, only a very small percentage used library tools or asked for staff help. Browsing seemed to be the way most materials were located. Relatively few patrons reported using the card catalog to locate materials. With the above information, we can probably assume that a very small percentage actually received professional help.[5]

Bundy points out that failure of a patron to turn to a librarian for help does not indicate that the user doesn't need help. Undoubtedly, many patrons who fail to get material could have had greater success had they had some library orientation or assistance from library staff. Not only do they not know how to use the tools, they also are unaware of the many services offered and made available by public libraries.

Several studies have recently been done on teaching the adult library user. Among these is the 1970 study of Indiana libraries by Edwin E. Olson, School of Library and Information Services at the University of Maryland.[6] Olson found that providing instruction was thought to be important for users of public libraries, but there was wide variance among the libraries, and some librarians were uncertain what was meant by instruction in specific areas or for specific projects.

Olson did find that more than half of the large public libraries in Indiana provide extensive "instructional" service, compared to only 10 percent of the smaller public libraries. About half of the smallest public libraries do not provide any general instruction and three-fourths of the small libraries do not provide any specific instruction. He observed that "formal courses in the optimal use of information resources are rarely given in any but the largest public libraries." [7]

Olson further found that most libraries provide directional services of some kind for the user, such as pamphlets or maps describing the layout of the library, and signs to guide the user to appropriate sections of the library.[8]

It is evident that optimum provision is not made for teaching programs in library resources.

In 1973 a committee chaired by Margaret Knox Goggin, dean of the Graduate School of Librarianship, University of Denver, completed a "Report on the Instruction in the Use of Libraries in Colorado for the Colorado Council on Library Development." [9] The section of the report dealing with the study of library instruction in public libraries in Colorado is brief. Of the 68 public libraries whose questionnaires were analyzed, only three offer formal instruction, while 27 have informal instructional programs, and the majority, 32, offer no library instruction whatsoever. Self-learning through instructional materials is emphasized in 14 libraries. This survey apparently includes all levels of instruction and is not confined to adults.

In the introduction to its report the committee states that in the provision of instructional services "major difficulties arise from the complexity of the public library's role in the community. . . . Furthermore, in its role as a community service institution, the public library is . . . concerned with the activities of public relations which overlap the activities of instruction." [10] According to the report, the same activities carried out by different libraries may be considered a part of different programs and labeled differently, yet be identical.

Citing variance in users' backgrounds as a difficulty the report states: "The out-of-school adult as a library user poses many problems to the public librarian since it is particularly difficult to find a commonality of background of library use and understanding among adults. In the last two decades there has been a shift from individual adult reader guidance toward group services." The committee found that talks by librarians, in conjunction with displays or tours combined with lecture and/or discussion, are the most popular form of instructional program, that "tailoring of lecture tours to particular needs of an individual group makes this an effective means of library use instruction." [11]

The two state reports are not very encouraging, but surely as other states conduct surveys, preferably similar to the Maryland-Washington, D.C., one in 1966,[12] an evaluation will come forth of the real needs for instruction in library use or some formalized orientation. Although many librarians seem to be ignoring the problems of the adult library user, they would be the first to admit that the user is not competent in library use.

In a smaller survey recently done by the author, inquiries were sent to 25 libraries, comparable in size to the Denver Public Library, asking about their active or past programs in teaching adults to use the library or in orienting the adult patron. Seventeen responded, and while all agreed that such a program was needed, seven said they offered no program of any kind, and ten said they had no formal program but did, upon request, give some instruction to special groups and tours. Most of the libraries have informative materials to give to patrons. One library said it has plans underway for a formalized orientation program for adult library users.

SOME SPECIFIC PROGRAMS FOR ADULTS

In the mid-1960s the staff of the Dayton-Montgomery County (Ohio) Public Library ran a very interesting library instruction seminar for its users.[13] The training was held in three sessions on successive Saturday mornings. While the program was concerned primarily with the out-of-school adult, some response was expected from upper-level students, both high school and college. After much deliberation, the staff decided that the adults could probably profit most from learning how to use the card catalog, the periodical indexes, and the basic reference tools and how to approach a library research problem. A tour of the library was optional. As it turned out, these were wise and useful choices: the program was well worked out, it had good publicity and received good response, and several interested groups went through the training. The training seminars were thus deemed highly successful, and they were continued until it appeared that all potential users had been reached. Plans are now in progress to offer the program again.

The Detroit Public Library has an interesting program underway, the "Info-Tour," which it is promoting via a bookmark. The Info-Tour covers: (1) How to use the card catalog; (2) How to use periodical indexes; and (3) How to find the books and other materials needed. The bookmark circular advertises the facts, noting that the Info-Tour is for students in grades 9–12 and is held on Sundays from 2 to 3 P.M. Adults are not urged to take the tour, but may do so.

The Detroit Public Library Friends' volunteers take groups on informational tours and, on request, the group may receive more detailed orientation from the Reference Department staff. Librarians speak at adjacent educational institutions to give pointers on making the best use of the library in their special fields. Special orientation sessions are given. The Burton Historical Collection and the Detroit Genealogical Society hold periodic sessions at which they instruct participants in how to do ancestor research in the Burton Archives.

Enoch Pratt Free Library, Baltimore, Maryland, has a 15-page booklet, complete with map and index, for use by tour leaders with groups, that has excellent descriptive materials and appears to be helpful.

Tulsa (Oklahoma) City-County Library System offers slide shows—presentations of which are apparently heavily used in orienting both adults and young adults. They also have "Focus"—a seminar the Business and Technology Department presents to businessmen, upon request—that is an in-depth orientation into library materials directly related to their fields.

Several libraries reported much the same kind of instructional service as Tulsa's, not only in business but in other areas, such as art appreciation, black history, and real estate.

The Malaga Cove Plaza Branch Library in California has used a slightly different approach.[14] When a large new library was opened nearby, users of the

Malaga Cove Plaza Branch changed and decreased in number, and the staff decided to take measures to promote library use. Starting with mothers who brought their children for story hours, the staff designed a series of half-hour programs that would introduce the public to the library's services, facilities, and staff. The programs featured various forms of media, tours, and information on periodicals, as well as a workshop on the use of the card catalog and other simple reference tools. All this was interspersed with talks about books—all kinds of books. This small start has grown into a full-fledged series of meetings that are popular and well attended. The community itself has taken over the meetings, planning them around various topics as well as library services, and "the program has evolved from the traditional librarian's book talk to lectures by and for the community."

DENVER PUBLIC LIBRARY'S ADULT PROGRAMS

All of the foregoing concepts are interesting ways of informing the library user. Their results are encouraging and make one ready to accept the premise that many adults want orientation and guidance in the use of public libraries and information about services offered.

The Denver Public Library became aware of this premise many years ago, but it wasn't until Henry G. Shearouse, Jr., became assistant librarian that it was given serious thought. Our long-time observation of adults trying to use the library and embarrassed at not knowing procedures had made us increasingly aware of the adult users' real need of help, and we decided to try to do something about it.

Early in 1968, Mr. Shearouse invited the coordinator of adult services, the public information officer, and one of the division heads from technical services to meet with him to plan a program of instruction in library use for our adult patrons. We knew from our observation that our patrons could use some help; the question was, exactly what kind of program would serve them best. It should be able to meet user needs as well as improve patron service, and a further expectation, increase library use.

INFORMATION BOOKLET

The four of us set about planning. Deciding that an informational booklet was necessary to help patrons, we compiled a 25-page one entitled, "How to Use the Library: A Guide to the Denver Public Library." It included a glossary of so-called library jargon, e.g., "folio," "hardback," "phonodisc," "serials," "shelflist," and many other words librarians constantly use, frequently to the patrons' dismay and incomprehension. Each word was given a full, but simple definition, and in some instances, the use of the word was explained, e.g.: "*Transaction card:* sometimes referred to as a 'T-card.' A numbered IBM card which records the loan of a book from a library. This card is slipped into a pocket inside the book cover at the time a library patron borrows a book. The transaction card is stamped with the date on which the book is due back at the library."

Also in the booklet was a list of abbreviations and shelving symbols used by this library—more library jargon clarified.

Several pages defined, located, and described the card catalogs used throughout the system. We clearly identified the parts of the various catalog cards—author, subject, title cards; analytic, series, reference cards of all kinds—using the simplest possible language. The circulation call slip and its use were fully explained, and a summary of Dewey was broken into 10s. Locations of the various classifications within DPL were given, including nonbook materials.

A page was copied from the *Readers' Guide to Periodical Literature* and its items within entries and references identified. Sample pages from several frequently used reference books were also included, and each book was briefly annotated and its location in the library was given.

WORKSHOP SERIES

As well, we decided to sponsor a series of "How to Use the Library" workshops, to be introduced in the fall of 1968. The workshop design called for four sessions of approximately two hours each, held on the same evening each week. Advanced registration was required, with membership limited to 30. Registration forms were printed and made available in all library agencies, and newspaper publicity was received. The workshop series was an immediate sellout, with a long waiting list.

We bought an overhead projector and made numerous visuals of sample catalog cards and sample pages from books and indexes. Tables were set up in the large meeting room we used so that everything was visible to all participants. Informality was emphasized and coffee was available throughout the meetings.

The first session was given by the assistant librarian. In addition to brief histories of books and printing, libraries and public libraries, Mr. Shearouse presented an overview of the Denver Public Library, including a detailed description of its organization, holdings, and staff; the library commission and its functions; the budget and book-buying policies; the many services offered, and just about anything that could help make the patron aware of the many activities that make a library function. The patrons were fascinated and asked many, many questions, all of which were answered with complete honesty.

The second session featured the card catalog and was conducted by Josephine Shepard, one of the division heads from technical services. Visuals were used with the overhead projector, and much of the session involved the arrangement of the catalog and what the patrons should be aware of—not the rules, but some of the common exceptions that frequently keep patrons from finding what they want. The details of a catalog card were explained and explanations of guide cards were given. The participants followed the procedures and made notes in their "How to Use the Library" booklets.

The third session, about frequently used reference books, was conducted by Beverly Walker, an enthusiastic staff member from the literature and history department. She covered such items as encyclopedias, dictionaries, *Essay and General Literature Index, Book Review Digest, Readers' Guide to Periodical Literature* (as an example of a Wilson index), *New York Times Index,* handbooks, almanacs, and ready-reference books from every department. The "investment services" were briefly described. The overhead projector was used to show sample pages from some of the items discussed. No attempt was made to teach the complexities of index arrangement; only brief descriptions of content were given, with emphasis on scope.

The fourth session was a complete tour of the main building, from the fourth floor to the subbasement. In addition to having participants visit the open and familiar areas, we made a point of taking them on tour of all library areas that were generally closed to the public or that the public was unaware of. These included the Rocky Mountain Bibliographical Center for Research, lower stack areas, book lift, pneumatic tubes, army maps, and the vault where many rare books and other items are kept. This tour was the highlight of the meetings.

The considerable response to these seminars has continued, and we have conducted either two or three each year since 1968. There is always a waiting list. Each seminar has followed much the same format, but with updated material, and we have continued to use the same staff. Mr. Shearouse has become the city librarian, and the division head from technical services has become the director of technical services, but each continues to do his or her one session because each believes strongly in the program.

At the end of each workshop series the participants are asked for a brief evaluation. Everyone has been enthusiastic and has requested additional sessions. As a result, and at the suggestion of various groups, we have added a fifth session: by dividing the tour into two parts, we now can show the patrons more and they have more time for questions.

Staff members have become personally involved with each group and have watched the members' reactions and encouraged their participation. No question has gone unanswered. There is great satisfaction in seeing workshop graduates in the library sometime later, going about their business like veterans, sure of themselves, but never afraid to ask for help.

The participants in these sessions have ranged in age from a teenager to an 80-year-old, and in occupation from a laborer to a Ph.D. candidate. Many budding writers have enrolled, along with professional genealogists, nurses, a taxi driver, and an executive housekeeper for a large hospital. Many of the participants have been housewives just wanting to learn. In every session approximately one-third of the group has been male. We have had a total of about eight black participants, but only two or three Spanish-speaking persons.

PROGRAM FOR SPANISH-SPEAKING ADULTS

The large Spanish-speaking population's reluctance to use the library's services and facilities is the Denver Public Library's constant concern. In his article, "Workshop on Library Services and Materials for Mexican Americans," Austin Hoover notes that the Mexican American is one of our largest underserved publics, and he gives reasons for hesitancy on the part of Mexican Americans to use public libraries.[15] Many of these reasons are the same as those given for reluctance on the part of the out-of-school adults: fear, differences in culture, confusion, bewilderment, and so forth. There are great differences between an Anglo and a Spanish-speaking group of adults, but many of their library needs would appear to be the same.

The Denver Public Library is presently involved in a federally funded adult basic-reading program, "The Right to Read," that is primarily for the Spanish-speaking adult to whom English will be taught as a second language. The program is based in one of the branch libraries located in the Spanish-speaking community where materials of all kinds are readily available and reading materials for the new *adult* reader are emphasized. The counselors and some tutors working with the program have shown interest in the library and have been given some orientation along with the "How to Use the Library" booklet. The "Right to Read" program may be just the vehicle for drawing more Spanish-speaking persons to the library.

OTHER DPL ACTIVITIES

We are also involved in several of the types of orientation mentioned by other libraries, reported on earlier in this paper, including specialized seminars for specialized groups, for instance, members of the Denver Police Academy. These groups are given a very detailed tour of the building, and then a day of concentrated effort is spent in familiarizing their members with the tools they may find useful in their profession.

Tours, usually in small groups, are also given for adults with special interests, and individual training is provided at this time, especially in the use of the card catalog, the *Union List of Serials, British Books in Print,* or almost any tool housed adjacent to the card catalog. At all times when the Denver Public Library is open to the public, one or two librarians or library assistants are on duty at the general catalog to help patrons to use the catalog and other tools housed nearby and to direct them to proper areas for further help. We have been considering producing a description of the library on cassette tape. Used in a small cassette player with ear plugs, it would be made available to patrons who might care to make a self-guided tour of the library.

All of Denver Public Library's adult education programs are grouped under the collective title "On Your Own," the banner for all self-directed learning programs offered by the library. Under this heading, in addition to its seminars on library use and the federally funded "Right to Read" project directed toward the functionally illiterate, the library has several other self-directed learning programs: the Great Books program (and similar group projects); the College Level Examination Program (CLEP); an Independent Study Project sponsored by the College Entrance Examination Board and the Office of Independent Study and Guidance, and a new, experimental offering entitled "Time[a]live."

As noted earlier, the "Right to Read" program at Denver Public Library is directed toward Spanish-speaking as well as Anglo nonreading adults. Bilingual tutors work on a one-to-one basis with the participants in the program.

CLEP is designed to help individuals earn and receive college credits through self-directed study. The library both serves as a referral center and provides readers' guidance for persons who wish to prepare for and/or take qualifying examinations in a number of subjects. All colleges and universities in the metropolitan area are cooperating in this project. Participants are not required to take the examinations.

"Timealive" is designed to illuminate selected time periods, from theories on the earth's origin to the present, through learning packages comprising books, films, artwork, recordings, and local museum exhibits. Emphasis is on man's cultural heritage and the connective themes of history. Both the Denver Art Museum and the Denver Museum of Natural History are cooperating in this endeavor, along with the State Historical Museum.

SOME EVALUATIONS

The "On Your Own" concept and its several applications have enriched both library services and patron response, and in so doing, have underlined the importance of an ongoing orientation program, with more seminars and more in-depth training. The "How to Use the Library" seminars are effective public relations tools, and the people who attend them become avid supporters of our library. The seminars are carried on as part of the regular Denver Public Library program, funded from the library budget of this tax-supported institution.

Denver Public Library has received little negative criticism from its publics and few efforts have been made to institute any form of censorship. Through the years every bond issue has been passed, including one in 1972 for $1.5 million (carried by a large majority). Many of the active workers for the bond issue were DPL Friends' volunteers, a large number of whom had attended one of the workshops on library use.

It is our conviction, because of the emphasis on user services, that more of Denver's adults do use the library more frequently and with greater ease than formerly because they are no longer "bewildered" by its arrangement. They have not always mastered "the intricacies of the subject headings or the vagaries of filing rules," [16] but they have a headstart and are no longer afraid to ask the librarian for help. That alone is a significant stride toward real success.

NOTES

1. Kathleen Molz, "The 'State of the Art' of Public Library Orientation," *Maryland Libraries* 34 (Winter 1968): 10–17.
2. Ibid., p. 11.
3. Ibid.
4. Ibid.
5. Mary Lee Bundy, "Metropolitan Public Library Use," *Wilson Library Bulletin* 41 (1967): 950–961.
6. Edwin E. Olson, "Survey of User Policies in Indiana Libraries and Information Centers," Indiana Library Studies Report No. 10, Peter Hiatt, gen. ed. (Bloomington: The Center, 1970).
7. Ibid., p. 99.
8. Ibid., p. 103.

9. "The Report on the Instruction in the Use of Libraries in Colorado," presented to the Colorado Council of Library Development by the Committee on Instruction in the Use of Libraries, Margaret Goggin, chairman, February 9, 1973, n.p. Only one chapter from the report was used, "Introduction in the Use of Public Libraries."

10. Ibid.

11. Ibid.

12. Bundy, op. cit.

13. Mildred T. Stibitz, "Library Workshop for Adults," *ALA Bulletin* 60 (1966): 937–941.

14. "Aware," *American Libraries* 1 (1970): 619. Group programs revive dying branch library.

15. Austin Hoover, "Workshop on Library Services and Materials for Mexican-Americans," *Texas Library Journal* 46 (Winter 1970): 206–208.

16. Molz, op. cit.

EDUCATING LIBRARY USERS IN TWO-YEAR HIGHER EDUCATION INSTITUTIONS

SHERYL ANSPAUGH
Chief Librarian, Learning Resources Center, South Oklahoma City Junior College

INTRODUCTION

With the declining birthrate and a resulting reversal of the population trend, colleges and universities need to revise and reevaluate their educational programs to include the entire social, educational, and economic environment.[1] In former years educational institutions have failed to evaluate adequately the needs and desires of the students or the surrounding community. Today it is imperative for these institutions to be highly sensitive to the new concept of society in order for them to have a successful existence. This problem should be examined in depth by each educational institution, and concrete, practical solutions need to be found.

The role or purpose for attending college and obtaining a degree is changing. During the era of the 1950s and 1960s affluent society considered a college degree the magic door to social and economic success. The acquisition of the college or university degree assumed greater importance than the education obtained. Recognition is now being given to a responsive criteria in education that includes the ability of educators and educational institutions to adjust to cultural and environmental needs.

Einstein said imagination and curiosity are more important than knowledge. Ideally, as librarians and educators we will work toward the goals of inspiring the curiosity and imagination of the individual and, secondarily, serving cultural and environmental needs of the individual and his community.

Another element to consider is the spiraling upward cost of education. Monetary return as a result of education and career training is important and vital to most students. The communities supporting education also want an economic return on their investments through curricula that provide for jobs, occupations, and a higher living standard.

Most acknowledge that education is a lifelong process. However, our institutions of higher learning should realize that with the reversal of population growth the number of 18- and 19-year-olds attending college will decrease. Educational institutions ought to be able to serve adequately the needs of those returning to school. These people, generally from 25 to 40 years old, need job retraining, self-development, or improvement in job skills. Not only should class schedules be flexible to allow them the benefits of education, but specifically designed classes should be developed to meet their needs. Schooling can enhance their self-esteem and sense of self-satisfaction.

The two-year postsecondary institution can and should be the most adaptable and varied of the higher educational institutions in the United States. These schools should use the valuable resources in personnel available in the community and ought to develop the fine skills of public and community relations. The two-year college should share in the design of community needs and aid in supplying these needs. This includes actively seeking community response, eliciting answers and determining attitudes in order to develop a responsive institution of education.

TWO-YEAR INSTITUTIONS

There are basically four types of two-year institutions: (1) two-year associate degree; (2) vocational-technical; (3) two-year college transfer program; (4) community colleges with strong continuing education programs.

Generally a college combines two programs and sometimes three into its goals as a higher educational institution. The two-year junior college offers an associate of the arts degree to students who complete the requirements stipulated for graduation. These courses are usually the basic programs designed to give students the background to succeed upon transfer to a four-year institution. On occasion, the two-year degree will qualify and train personnel for immediate job entry, thus coinciding with the objectives of vocational-technical schools.

Vocational-technical schools are contributing to the community and serving the needs of students by offering training in skilled or semiprofessional work. Valuable on-the-job training and experience are often an important aspect of the schooling, and this enhances the students' occupational ability and also benefits the employer.

Continuing education, the youngest area of educational development, is exciting and wide open. The new progressive community colleges are making a concerted effort in establishing courses in this area of education. They are succeeding because an obvious need is being recognized and filled.

All four types of institutions have basic similarities in their learning resources centers (LRC), which includes the traditional print-oriented library. Generally the LRC areas include reference and reserve materials, books or materials circulated for a specific time length, and a periodical section. All learning resources centers (libraries) seek to assist patrons in fulfilling their information needs. Two problems in junior college libraries are of constant concern to the LRC staff. First is the instructors' attitude toward the LRC. If the instructors' attitude is favorable toward the LRC and its use they will encourage the students' use and exposure to the library and its many benefits. Or, if the instructors see little benefit from the library their students will develop minimum use of the library.[2] This seems to be especially true in two-year colleges that are not oriented toward extensive research.

The second problem is the development of a library orientation or introduction that fits the needs of the student. As with all subject areas, students are at different levels of learning. It is important to begin library instruction at a point the students are capable of understanding and to proceed at a rate that prevents boredom or frustration.

LIBRARY INSTRUCTION

JUNIOR COLLEGES

Students beginning their college career in a two-year junior college institution will in most cases come from a print-oriented high school and enter a print-oriented college. Not only will they remain print-oriented, but if they transfer to a four-year college or university they will need to know the many benefits of the print material held by the LRC.

Library orientation will be more meaningful if the values of the LRC are clearly understood by the students. They should learn the value of the LRC in reducing their time and effort in researching and/or writing a paper or giving a report. In seeking material they should be able to find it rapidly and without frustration, thus making assignments easier and quicker to handle. They should learn that many varied resources are available for their use.

The instructors encountered during the students' college career will be a determining factor in their use of the library and their desire to further their understanding of library facilities. Also, library literature indicates that the subject approach seems to work most successfully in library orientation. The university-bound students need to know so many aspects of the library that the job of instructing them can be quite complex. However, the approach needs to be slow and steady and taught at the time the students need the information. First-semester freshmen need to know the location of the library, where to find a set of encyclopedias, how to check out a book, and where to find magazines available for browsing and relaxation between classes. A general mood evoking slide/tape presentation may be most effective at this time. This could be shown during a general orientation week or through freshman classes. If a formal orientation program is developed, it can be made more effective and more personalized with greater self-actualization if the students can be given a pretest as a self-assessment. This allows the students to determine their individual needs, to analyze their areas of weakness and strength, and to proceed with some guidance to their library instruction. To be hoped is that the librarian has worked with the counselors and instructors and all are aware of the reading level of the students. Some students will need concentrated training in reading skills in order to gain a minimum college reading level. Library acquisitions should reflect an awareness of the students' abilities in the reading skills. Materials acquired are most useful at the level of understanding by the majority of students.

In later semesters students can begin to increase their expertise of library knowledge. If the librarian and instructing faculty can work together, they can develop several A-V self-paced module units that the students may repeat as needed. These units could be shown as desired for general classroom instruction in a variety of subject fields. This would acquaint the students with the material available to them. To increase the use of this A-V module and the material, a pretest and self-assessment can be distributed in a learning packet (library handbook, information sheets, or library workbook) that lists the objectives of the library material, its value, location, scope, and the A-V unit available for review to assist the students in mastering the use of the material. This pretest can be a self-discovery of what the students need to learn and where their learning should begin. The students need to acquire information concerning the card catalog and the vertical file, to become familiar with a variety of periodical indexes, the interlibrary loan, reference materials, and generally to feel at ease in the LRC situation. The students do not need to know the meaning of "collation" or "tracing," nor do they need to know the cumulations of an index or specific information of any particular encyclopedia or almanac. They need to understand methods of procedures, where to look for directions, to observe dates of the material, and to check for author information. They must realize that at times it will be advisable to ask for help and the hope is that they will.[3] With encouragement from their instructors they may develop a sense of importance in their LRC training that will be continued throughout their college career.

Objective learning systems may be desirable and can be designed by the library staff with instructional assistance. Some librarians might like to try the "pathfinder" method as developed and used at M.I.T.[4] The pathfinder method of citing a library's introductory references and materials on a specific topic could be applied to basic courses at a junior college. This would provide a quick and helpful guide to students unfamiliar with primary reference and material sources.

Orientation to the myriad of LRC materials should be in a simply written form (learning packet) that can be glanced at for easy referral, such as *Pathfinders* or a library handbook. Included in this should be information on location of materials, purpose of the material, a listing of the materials' scope and limitations, and a general description of how the materials are used as reference tools, with one or two briefly outlined examples in each case. Not only would it be best to approach orientation to LRC materials by print but also by an A-V method—a hearing-and-seeing method. This approach should give the students a well-rounded orientation to the LRC and, it is hoped, should make their college career easier.

One aspect that cannot be stressed enough is the tremendous personal relations work that the librarians must do. They will need to develop rapport with the instructors and the students since both are vital to the success of the LRC and should be shown every interest and consideration. They are the users and the LRC is user oriented—or it should be. As in any business, public relations are necessary and the customer all-important.

VOCATIONAL-TECHNICAL SCHOOLS

Vocational-technical students are primarily interested in learning a job skill for immediate job entry. They need to know the latest information in their specialized areas and how to locate this information. They need to know references relating to their occupational fields. They may or may not be good readers. With these aspects in mind the orientation to the LRC should be very specific and subject oriented. A subject-oriented videocassette or slide/tape program might be the most effective method to introduce the students to their subjects. The program could begin with a tour of the library to describe the book stacks, periodicals, reference material, and circulation desk. After this introduction to the library the specific subject should be the focus point of the film—where to locate basic guides, encyclopedias, manuals, how to use the card catalog, vertical file, and periodicals, special libraries in the specific field and availability of government documents and how to obtain them.

The students will need information on indexes to the variety of technical magazines. A super-8mm silent or sound continuous filmloop set up alongside the indexes might well serve the students' basic needs for information concerning the use of the indexes and location of the periodicals. As training progresses and the students become aware of their needs for more information, a series of A-V material may be developed for their use. Not only can their information of sources be increased but they can be taught to evaluate critically the information they find and to examine the literature in their field.

Library Pathfinders would work well in a vocational-technical institution where materials are more specific and technical. Although this would be a large task, the instructor and librarian could work together to develop a fine bibliography and "how to use" sheets for these students. Reading, plus hearing, seeing, and doing can be most effective in successful learning.

COMMUNITY COLLEGES

The (new and innovative) community college offers a special challenge to librarians. To have a successful LRC the community college librarians must perform many tasks. Their students will be citizens from the community seeking enrichment courses or retraining for a job or increasing present job skills. The librarians will serve the students who may transfer to a university after two years of study. They will serve the students who are vocationally inclined and seeking education as a means to a better financial end. They must educate all these users to the LRC, and to each one the LRC will represent something quite different.

Definitely these librarians must know their learners and their learners' reading skills and capabilities. Generally, the reading level in a community college will be considerably lower than in a traditional two-year college institution. This will be especially so if the college has an "open door" policy of admittance.

Instructors should offer librarians guidance to the needs of their students and the requirements of their curricula. The LRC should be prepared to offer a basic library education. "Pathfinder" materials could be used and included in the learning packets or syllabi of the course outline. Two-year students who are training in a specific career would find a bibliography of basic LRC material helpful. This bibliography can go a step further by succinctly describing library materials by location, scope, and objective. An invitation for LRC personnel to visit the classroom could provide one means of introducing students to the materials. This classroom time allows a librarian to explain material uses and gives the students an opportunity to see, hold, and use the materials. An A-V production of other materials available by subject areas could be presented to the students. Later students can refresh their memories by individually reviewing the A-V material as they want to use it. They also need to learn about the specialized indexes, magazines, and government document material available in their career area.

The university-bound students can learn the many benefits of the library through subject-related courses on library use. These should be developed with the instructor's assistance and be available for review at any time by students on an individualized basis. Students and faculty should be aware of the many library facilities in the community. Public, private, and special libraries can be valuable to the student. Interlibrary loan service can be invaluable, especially to the instructor who needs some special materials for a class. The availability of these services and any others should be publicized on bulletin boards and in newsletters or student papers. If bibliographies are exchanged and materials are readily available from other sources, they should be placed into the catalog system, either incorporated or separate. The important point is to make the patrons aware of their many, many resources.

In a community college it is vitally important for the librarian to develop public relations with LRC patrons. Asking users if their needs are being met or distributing a short, but exact survey of the LRC effectiveness, orientation, courtesy, and helpfulness of staff are ways of measuring the effectiveness of the library. Making sure instructors' needs are being met may be the easiest way to ensure students' use of the LRC.

THE NECESSITY OF PUBLIC RELATIONS

Today, education and libraries are in the process of renovation because in the past they have met the needs of relatively few people. The image and use of our educational facilities should develop and evolve to meet the changing needs of our changing society. A progressive and concerned library staff will develop a feeling for and a rapport with the community and with other libraries in their area.

The combination of audiovisual materials and know-how (seminars on A-V uses and methods are held around the country) contribute to the beginnings of a dynamic library that can become a college library on the line with Dr. Shores's dreams.[5] If the college library desires to make a total commitment and become a *community college library,* it must meet the needs of the community and students. Desire and commitment are the first steps.

Secondly, the library staff should share its ideas with the faculty, public and special libraries in the area, and other community services and develop their ideas and viewpoints. This is a slow process, but the results can be a total sharing and responsibility for educating not only the students in the two-year college but the people of the community. (This can also be beneficial to the college as a recruitment possibility.) We all know that it takes careful planning, desire, and a rather daring attitude to break the traditional bonds of education that we allow to influence our decisions, but there are improvements that can be made and we are progressing.

As noted earlier, faculty support of the LRC is absolutely necessary. This constitutes a selling job that the LRC must perform well. Student use and nonuse can be directly related to the instructor's attitude toward the library, as several studies have shown. Librarians cannot expect people to appreciate services about which they are not informed or educated. In several library use and nonuse studies, librarians conclude that a number of instructors make extensive use of the facilities and too many instructors make no use or very little use of the same facilities. This attitude is, of course, reflected in student use. Before an LRC can develop a successful library orientation for students, the library needs to have a successful record with instructional staff. A library staff that has confidence in its program should talk with instructors about class and curriculum needs. A number of things can be done for and with the faculty: talk with them about materials in their field that are important and available; ask their advice and guidance in purchasing the best books for their needs; discuss over an extended time the variety of A-V material available; set up a workshop on A-V material and have a guest media specialist assist and demonstrate possibilities; send and discuss new book lists, including information on available films that are free or easily accessible, tapes or TV programs that are of interest in their subject area. The key to good personal relations is simply consideration and demonstrating concern and thought for the instructors and their instructional problems. The response from most instructors will be increased concern for library development, both holdings and staff, and an increase in their students' use of the LRC.

In the vocational schools and community colleges, instructors generally know the value of A-V materials and make extensive use of the learning resources center in the teaching of their courses. Librarians should be trained in the many uses and advantages of A-V material (seminars are valuable for short, intensive training) and promote new approaches and ideas to their instructors. An individually paced instructional module on many aspects of library use and instruction is natural in these colleges. Some progressive colleges have developed individually paced instructional modules by which students become familiar with the library and this new concept of learning.

Although librarians know that knowledge of the library is the key to further learning, students tend to be shortsighted in the value they place on the LRC. Most students use the library to fill an immediate need, and they like an easy and all-encompassing book when writing a paper or report. Librarians need to realize this and approach students with this understanding. Softsell the library and its benefits. Give the students what they need and in the process show them how to find it themselves, plus giving them just a little more. Competent guidance is necessary. Be kind and understanding and give the users special attention. (How important attention is!) Before the student leaves make sure his or her needs have been fulfilled. The LRC can be a physically formidable place for students to enter.

Making the library as physically attractive as possible is also important. Libraries need carrells equipped to handle available A-V materials adequately. Also lounge areas, quiet study areas, and group study areas help to entice and please the students. A central campus location is helpful to the students. Visiting displays of art, sculpture, or other interesting materials add attractiveness to the LRC and draw users into the library.

DEVELOPING AN ORIENTATION PROGRAM

Many orientation systems are available, for example general tours of the library, classroom lectures about the library, handbooks, guide sheets, and audiovisual presentations. To have an effective orientation, a spectrum of media and nonmedia should be employed. People learn at different rates and in different ways. No longer should students be punished by carrying the stigma of failure for inability to learn at a rate or method set by someone else. Individually paced instruction can be a reality.

In planning a library-learning resources center the goals of the institution need to be specifically defined. With the philosophy stated in learning objectives the library staff can plan and coordinate a successful learning program with the instructional staff.

The instructor and librarian need to know the learners and how they learn.[6] They need to know each learner's general reading level. They need to know the methods each student learns best by. And they need to know why the students are there.

The content of the course must be decided upon. The instructor needs to determine before further preparation just what each student needs to know. The librarian needs to know what materials can best assist the instructor and students in order to insure their availability. The instructor, by setting forth the goals and objectives of the course, explains the course standards to be met and the procedure for meeting these standards. Ideally the students can then concentrate on the stated course material and no longer play "out-guessing the instructor."

With assistance from the librarian or A-V personnel the instructor needs to determine the media to be used. By knowing the learners and their capabilities, selection of the type or types of media to be used will be facilitated. If A-V material is selected, it should be of quality material and be workable for hours and hours of student use and also be simple to use. Reading material or script material should also be available for home study and on the level of the student's reading ability. To keep costs reasonable, select the most desirable type of A-V equipment and use it extensively. Avoid obtaining media in many forms because of the resulting expense. Select one or two forms the student can readily learn to operate and use these exclusively. Librarians will find that courses that are individually paced will require lesser amounts of hardware and software because students' needs are extended over a larger time unit.

Along with the selection of media will come the design of material to be offered. Software, printed handouts, and books should be cataloged for easy retrieval, storage, and circulation. Media software will be the most difficult to handle, and plans for cataloging, storing, and circulation must be carefully designed. This is especially true if student help is employed and relied upon for much of these library skills and duties. Planning is essential and flexibility necessary.

Finally, when the hardware is to be purchased check for durability, ease of use, procedures for repair and maintenance of equipment, and of course, cost. Remember to orient library tools to the needs of the student. This is also true of printed matter. As carefully as possible check book requests for feasible use by the students. An instructor's graduate-level textbook that he or she has requested to be bought should be reviewed and points of use discussed tactfully.

The most important aspect is to involve the students directly and overtly, to insure successful learning. Seeing, hearing, and reading plus actively responding to questions will increase the students' learning ability and motivation. A single sheet of explanation added to a workbook (depending on the course or lesson to be learned) that corresponds to the available A-V material is beneficial for listing goals and objectives, lesson material, reviews, and self-assessments. This is illustrated in the Appendix. Successful and continuous use of the library by students, faculty, and community will be demonstrative of a job well done by the library staff. That is our goal. Any orientation to a library system is only as successful as the students who use and appreciate the attributes of the library.

Finally, seek the opinion of the students. Get their personal reaction to the media they have used. Make them important and the basis of the library's many services.

NOTES

1. Lyman A. Glenny, "The Changing Milieu of Postsecondary Education—A Challenge to Planners," mimeographed (keynote address delivered to the National Higher Education Management Seminar, October 16, 1972, Washington, D.C.), p. 24.
2. Joan M. Bechtel, "A Possible Contribution of the Library-College Idea to Modern Education," *Drexel Library Quarterly* 7 (1971): 190.
3. Verna V. Melum, "Library Orientation in the College and University," *Wilson Library Bulletin* 46 (1971): 65–66.

4. Marie P. Canfield, "Library Pathfinders," *Drexel Library Quarterly* 8 (1972): 287–300.
5. Fay M. Blake, "The Library-College," *Drexel Library Quarterly* 7 (1971): 175.
6. Beatrice D. Simmons, "Librarian: Instructional Programmer," *Drexel Library Quarterly* 8 (1972): 250.

BIBLIOGRAPHY

Allen, Robert F. *Fundamental Biological Concepts.* Oklahoma City: South Oklahoma City Junior College Press, 1972.

Barton, Anthony. "The Continuum—How to Analyze Your School Environment —And Loosen It Up." *Library Journal* 95 (1970): 4317–4323.

Bechtel, Joan M. "A Possible Contribution of the Library-College Idea to Modern Education." *Drexel Library Quarterly* 7 (1971): 189–201.

Benford, John Q. "The Philadelphia Project: 10,000 Students Tell What's Wrong and What's Right About Their School and Public Libraries." *Library Journal* 96 (1971): 2041–2047.

Blake, Fay M. "The Library-College Movement." *Drexel Library Quarterly* 7 (1971): 175–188.

Brown, Helen M. "ALA Activities to Promote Better Instruction in the Use of Academic Libraries." *Drexel Library Quarterly* 7 (1971): 323–326.

Canfield, Marie P. "Library Pathfinders." *Drexel Library Quarterly* 8 (1972): 287–300.

Culkin, Patricia B. "Computer Assisted Instruction in Library Use." *Drexel Library Quarterly* 8 (1972): 301–311.

Ellsworth, Ralph E. "The Contribution of the Library to Improving Instruction." *Library Journal* 94 (1969): 1955–1957.

Evrard, Connie F., and Waddington, Charles C. "The Undergradaute Survey: Its Roles in Changing Patterns of Reference Service." *Drexel Library Quarterly* 7 (1971): 351–356.

Gardner, Jeffrey J. "Point-of-Use Library Instruction." *Drexel Library Quarterly* 8 (1972): 281–285.

Geller, Evelyn. "This Matter of Media." *Library Journal* 96 (1971): 2048–2053.

Hackman, Martha. "Proposal for a Program of Library Instruction." *Drexel Library Quarterly* 7 (1971): 299–308.

Hansen, Lois N. "Computer Assisted Instruction in Library Use: An Evaluation." *Drexel Library Quarterly* 8 (1972): 345–355.

Hare, Robert P. "College Libraries for Students." *Library Journal* 94 (1969): 2207–2208.

Henning, Patricia A. "Research of Integrated Library Instruction." *Drexel Library Quarterly* 7 (1971): 339–341.

Hinchliff, William E. "Urban Problems and Higher Education: Federal City College." *Wilson Library Bulletin* 36 (1969): 527–533.

Howison, Beulah C. "Simulated Literature Searches." *Drexel Library Quarterly* (1971): 309–320.

Knapp, Patricia B. "Guidelines for Bucking the System: A Strategy for Moving

Toward the Ideal of the Undergraduate Library as a Teaching Instrument."
Drexel Library Quarterly 7 (1971): 217–221.

Larson, Dale M. *Library Instruction in the Community College: Toward Innovative Librarianship.* ERIC (Educational Resources Information Center) Report ED 054 765, 1971.

Line, Maurice B. *Library Surveys: An Introduction to Their Use, Planning, Procedure and Presentation,* rev. ed. Hamden, Conn.: Shoe String Press, 1969.

Lubans, John, Jr. "Evaluating Library User Education Programs." *Drexel Library Quarterly* 8 (1972): 325–343.

Mager, Robert F. *Preparing Instructional Objectives.* Belmont, Calif.: Fearon, 1962.

Melum, Verna V. "Library Orientation in the College and University." *Wilson Library Bulletin* 46 (1971): 59–66.

Palmer, Millicent C. "Creating Slide-Tape Library Instruction: The Librarian's Role." *Drexel Library Quarterly* 8 (1972): 251–267.

Simmons, Beatrice D. "Librarian: Instructional Programmer." *Drexel Library Quarterly* 8 (1972): 247–250.

Stillman, Mary E. "A Program for Action." *Drexel Library Quarterly* 7 (1971): 375–378.

Vogel, J. Thomas. "A Critical Overview of the Evaluation of Library Instruction." *Drexel Library Quarterly* 8 (1972): 315–323.

Williamson, John G. "Swarthmore College's 'Teaching Library' Proposals." *Drexel Library Quarterly* 7 (1971): 203–215.

APPENDIX
A SAMPLE UNIT FOR LIBRARY-USER INSTRUCTION

INTRODUCING THE COURSE

There are few areas of study as helpful as the study of the retrieval and function of written material. Adequate coverage of both print and nonprint materials in a single course places severe limitations on successful learning of the Learning Resources Center (LRC). Learning of the many materials that are available in your libraries will be a continuous study throughout your college career.

The purpose of this course is to provide a means for those who have not had a basic course in LRC use or who feel the need for additional preparation, to acquire and demonstrate proficiency with certain key concepts, materials, and equipment that are basic to your college study and attainment of general or specific knowledge.

The modular organization of this course is designed to lead you from one concept to another in a logical and continually expanding manner. For this reason it is important for you to follow the sequence of the units that are provided. Much of the information in each unit is either prerequisite to or will facilitate your understanding of subsequent subjects. Please do not feel that your use is limited to the information presented in the tape-slide materials of the materials in the LRC. You are encouraged to seek out additional information from current literature in each area according to your interest.

Self-paced individualized instruction is intended to provide the maximum amount of flexibility possible in your study. This does demand an added degree of responsibility and maturity on your part, to apply yourself consistently and enthusiastically so that your time and money are not wasted.

You have noted from the class schedule that this course is by class and individual arrangement. Before you proceed with the LRC portion of the course I expect to have a brief meeting with you. I will be happy to answer further questions in our first meeting.

UNIT 1: READERS' GUIDE TO PERIODICAL LITERATURE

Rationale

Since man has had the ability to write, written knowledge has become the source and basis to further one's intellect and knowledge. Man's learning has increased so rapidly that it is difficult to keep abreast of the developments in just one subject field.

Objective

The objective of this unit is to become familiar with the *Readers' Guide to Periodical Literature.* You will have fulfilled this objective when you accomplish the following with 90 percent accuracy:

1. Locate the periodical and periodical index section of the library. Do not hesitate to seek help from a librarian.

2. Locate and identify the "how to use" page and the listing of periodicals indexed by the *Guide.*

3. Pick an entry and identify author, title, periodical, volume, pages, and date.

4. Pick a subject of concern and find three entries listed for that particular subject.

5. From the three entries successfully locate in the library the three periodicals and articles.

6. Given a particular person, find the entry listed by name.

7. Successfully use and identify a cross-reference.

Procedure

1. Read the rationale and objective to determine what will be expected of you and how you will be evaluated.

2. Take the self-assessment test in this workbook as a pretest to determine the areas, if any, in which you need to concentrate your study for the final assessment.

3. View the tape-slide unit for *Readers' Guide to Periodical Literature* and complete the active response sheet.

4. Study the *Guide to Periodical Literature* located in the LRC and finish completing the active-response sheet.

5. Take the self-assessment test.

6. When you feel confident of your ability to complete the objectives of this unit, take the final assessment.

Active Response Sheet:

Complete the active-response sheet as you study the tape-slide show. Stop the tape at any time to complete the response sheet.

1. The *Readers' Guide to Periodical Literature* is _____

_____

_____

2. The *Readers' Guide* is located in _____

_____

3. Identify the parts of the following entry:
Dolphin myth is really true![1] R. Claiborne.[2] il Nat Wildlife[3] 10:[4]28–31[5] F '72[6]

1. _____   2. _____   3. _____

4. _____   5. _____   6. _____

4. A cross-reference is _____

_____

5. Go to the LRC and pick one entry of your choice from the *Guide* and carefully rewrite the entry here.

_____

_____

6. Now find two additional entries and write the pertinent information that enables you to correctly and easily find the periodical articles to which they refer.

1. _____

_____

2. _____

_____

Self-Assessment:
1. The *Readers' Guide to Periodical Literature* is found in

_____

2. The *Readers' Guide* is a current listing of _____

_____ materials.

3. Entries are listed by _____   a. date
                                             b. subject
                                             c. geographic area

4. Label the following entry:
   Let's de-fuse dogdom's population explosion.[a] C. R. Holmes.[b] il Sci Digest[c]
   71:[d] 68–73[e] My '72[f]

   a. _____   d. _____

   b. _____   e. _____

   c. _____   f. _____

5. A cross-reference indicates _____

   _____

   _____

6. For an explanation of abbreviations or how to read the entry you should

   _____

   _____

Answers to the Self-Assessment:
1. The center isle of the LRC or periodicals' section.
2. Periodical.
3. b.
4. a. title
   b. author
   c. periodical
   d. volume number of periodical
   e. pages of article in periodical
   f. date of periodical
5. Related subjects under which additional material may be found or more generally accepted forms, names, or subjects.
6. Turn to the front pages and review the introduction and suggestions for use or ask a librarian for assistance.

PROBLEMS IN LIBRARY INSTRUCTION IN FOUR-YEAR COLLEGES

Thomas G. Kirk

Science Librarian, Earlham College

The average college student . . . is ignorant of the greater part of the bibliographical apparatus which the skilled librarian has in hourly use, to enable him to answer the thousand queries of the public. A little systematic instruction would so start our students in the right methods, that for the rest of their lives all their work in libraries would be more expeditiously accomplished. . . . In fact, it is hardly an exaggeration to say that now students often . . . spend half their time in the library finding out what they don't want to know, and the remaining half in getting confused notions of what they do want to know.[1]

The equipment of the library will not be finished until it shall have upon its staff men and women whose entire work shall be, not the care of books, not the cataloguing of books, but the giving of instruction concerning their use.[2]

These passages, written over 70 years ago, were once viewed as lofty, unattainable goals to which academic librarians gave lip serivce. Now such goals are being achieved in a number of colleges throughout the country. Furthermore, many other college librarians are taking up the challenge and developing programs of library or bibliographic instruction.[3]

Librarians, faculty, and students have made a serious mistake in assuming that to know about the physical layout of the library and the services the library provides is enough to be able to use the library. The result of this misconception has been the dull library tours crowded into the New Student Week schedule. Orientation to a library's organization and services is only the first stage of instruction. More important, and more difficult, is the development of a sound library instruction program that recognizes the library as "a highly complicated system, or better, a network of interrelated systems, which organizes and controls all kinds of communication." [4] It is this latter aspect that I call library, or bibliographic instruction.

The term "integrated library instruction" has been used several times in the literature to refer to library instruction that is incorporated into the regular academic program.[5, 6] Furthermore, the literature almost unanimously states that integrated library instruction is more effective than other patterns of instruction, e.g., separate courses or volunteer programs. (This point remains to be "proven" by any systematic research.) It may be easier to develop separate courses on use of the library or to mount a public relations program on what the library has to offer. However, unless effective use of the library is made part of a college's expectations for graduation, and the effective use is frequently practiced by the students, the program will not reach most students (especially those who need it) and will eventually disappear from the library's plan of service to the college. It is this integrated library instruction that I believe is the most desirable approach. Later sections of this paper will discuss some of the problems of developing this integrated instruction.

That bibliographic instruction is now an important and vital concern to the academic library profession can best be demonstrated by reviewing the current status of the literature, recent meetings on library instruction, and the work of ALA committees. The growth of the literature on library instruction has been nothing short of phenomenal. As Table 1 indicates, the rate of publication from the founding of ALA up to 1921 was about eight articles per year while the period 1958–1971 produced an average of 35 articles per year, an increase of 440 percent.

Equally significant has been the number of recent meetings that were devoted to the topic of academic library or bibliographic instruction. The recent list begins with the Workshop/Conference at UCLA in 1970 and the conference on Confronting the Undergraduate Environment at the 1971 ALA convention in Dallas. Over the past three years state library organizations in Michigan, New York, and Washington have had conferences on library instruction, and in the academic year 1972–1973 no less than four regional or state conferences were devoted to academic library instruction. Special mention should be made of the series of conferences held at Eastern Michigan University. Although the conference titles include the term "library orientation," the conferences have not been restricted to or even primarily concerned with orientation. This series, which has been held annually since 1971, has attracted wide interest and participation from around the country.[10] The conferences have not been a forum

Table 1. *GROWTH OF THE LITERATURE ON LIBRARY INSTRUCTION*

Years	Number of citations	Average per year
1876–1921	360	8 [7]
1921–1945	432	18 [7]
1945–1958	338	26 [7]
1958–1971	450	35 [8]
1972	52	52 [9]

NOTE: for [7], [8], [9] see chapter notes.

for the development of new ideas but have served primarily to convey information informally about what librarians are doing in their library instruction programs. The conferences have usually tried to review all aspects of library instruction and as a result have not permitted detailed exploration of specific problems.

A growing interest in academic library instruction is in evidence in the American Library Association and the Association of College and Research Libraries. ALA has had an Instruction in the Use of Libraries Committee since 1967. The meetings and programs of the committee have been most heavily attended by academic librarians. The 1972 program meeting, a "Show and Tell" clinic, demonstrating audiovisual materials for library instruction, was attended by over 2,000, of which many were academic librarians.[11] At the 1971 ALA conference the ACRL Committee on Bibliographic Instruction was formed "to consider the possibility of establishing a clearinghouse for information on instructional programs currently in operation; to explore methods of evaluating existing programs and materials; and to investigate the need for research into problems connected with instruction programs."[12] This committee has been collecting information on library instruction[13] and is currently developing a statement of instructional objectives that library or bibliographic instruction programs should be striving to achieve. These objectives, along with a model evaluation program, are expected to be available late in 1974.

These activities are testimony to the increasing interest and activity in developing library instruction programs and associated instructional materials. As a result, one of the major problems academic librarians face is staying abreast of new developments. It was the awareness of just such a problem that created some of the impetus for the formation of the ACRL committee. Since the formation of the committee an organization has developed that can serve the vital clearinghouse function that is needed to keep the profession alert to new developments. Project LOEX (Library Orientation EXchange), launched in 1972 and located at Eastern Michigan University, was established to facilitate communication among libraries with instructional programs, to assist libraries interested in developing such programs, and to aid librarians in their research endeavors. To become a member, a librarian simply completes a brief questionnaire (even if one does not have a library instruction program) and sends it to the LOEX director. As a member, one may make written or telephoned requests for information or referral on matters relating to academic library orientation and bibliographic instruction. The membership's responsibilities are to deposit information and materials and to provide information to other members who are referred to them. Project LOEX publishes an occasional newsletter, *LOEX News*. If Project LOEX can get adequate financial support it may become a major force in the development and improvement of academic library orientation and bibliographic instruction.[14]

Is the increased concern for library instruction an irrelevant passing fad? The answer would be "maybe" if certain new thrusts in higher education are themselves a fad. But there is little evidence that the concept of student-centered education, with the associated concepts—independent study, self-teaching, "university without walls," and continuing education—is about to go out of style. If the concept is here to stay, then the problem of information access, which is at the heart of student-centered education, remains a crucial concern to the academic community. The result is to force the library profession to forthrightly address itself to the relevance of the library to the academic program. If college libraries are to fulfill their mission in the new educational context, then an active program of library instruction becomes mandatory.

GETTING STARTED

Although there has been a substantial increase in the development of library instruction programs, there remain many college libraries that do not provide library instruction and college librarians who do not recognize its value. This lack of interest no doubt is partly a result of a traditional view of the academic librarian's role as passive. But another, more insidious factor is the entrapment of college libraries by what has been called the "university-library syndrome." [15] While the university-library syndrome has affected many aspects of college librarianship, there are two main areas that affect the library's attitude toward library instruction, and these must be changed before a library instruction program can be fully developed.

The emphasis on materials collection and processing to the detriment of reference and public services in college libraries is a significant symptom of the syndrome. It could be said that this is another form of the perennial problem of finding the proper balance of technical and public services. A much more fundamental problem, however, is the librarian's failure to recognize the primary mission of the college library—that is, support of the educational program. This support, of course, does include the prompt ordering and rapid processing of materials, but it also includes reference service. But this does not mean merely that staff members should be available to answer questions while they go about other apparently more important tasks. Rather, library staff assignments should recognize the need to have available during most of the library's hours professional staff whose primary job is assisting library users. This staff should be situated so that they are visible when one enters the library and so that they can see the card catalog and reference area easily. While on duty they should be actively aware of students who need help so that they can offer assistance.

Special emphasis should be placed on the importance of actively seeking out students who appear to be having problems. Unless librarians take the attitude that they must reach out and anticipate student needs and approach library patrons and offer to help, then the library remains a storehouse of books that only the most aggressive or knowledgeable students use effectively. College librarians too frequently assume that students will ask for help when they need it. This attitude is partly the result of the librarian's experiences in university libraries where graduate students and faculty ask for specific information when they are unable to find it in the specialized sources of which they were aware. The undergraduate students' problems are of a very different nature. They know nothing of specialized sources or of the bibliographic apparatus to which Dr.

Knapp alludes.[16] Their knowledge is confined at best to encyclopedias, the *Readers' Guide,* and a card catalog that uses Sears subject headings. Furthermore, students have the attitude, possibly passed on to them by their teachers, that they know how, or should know how, to use the library. The result is that students will not ask for help for fear of admitting they do not know how to use the library, or they do not recognize their own inadequacies. Therefore, when they enter the library, students will no doubt begin with the card catalog. It is here the librarian can begin a program of library instruction, because the student, in this situation, needs more than specific information. Instead, he or she needs a careful introduction to search strategy and to the use of the reference collection: encyclopedias, the card catalog, bibliographies, indexes, etc. If one has had experience working at a reference desk, one knows the practical limitations that time places on this type of service. Furthermore, repetition of the same minilecture is an inefficient use of librarian's time and soon results in boredom for the librarian. But it is in the attempt to provide good individual reference service (the *how* of finding information, as well as the actual location of the needed information) that one most readily recognizes the practical need for library instruction.

The university-library syndrome is also evident in the attitude of new faculty toward the library and the role of the library in the educational program. As emerging scholars from graduate school, new faculty quite naturally look to the library to provide those services they were accustomed to receiving at the university: acquisition of research materials, handling of reserve materials, and interlibrary loan for faculty. It is these services they inquire about when they are new to a college faculty, rather than asking about how students use the library, what instructional and reference services the library provides, or how faculty and librarians cooperate to involve the library in the educational program.

The two major problems that college libraries must solve then, if library instruction programs are to be developed, are (1) a reordering of priorities within the library and (2) a change in faculty attitudes toward the role of the library in liberal arts education.

REORDERING PRIORITIES

A reordering of the college library's priorities will require serious examination of the library's policies and procedures. This examination should be done with two guiding principles kept constantly in mind. First, technical services activities should be streamlined and original cataloging reduced to the absolute minimum. College libraries simply must stop redoing what the Library of Congress has already done: original cataloging and maintenance of a subject authority file. College libraries can better spend their resources for public services personnel who will be serving students and faculty in ways they are not now served rather than for technical services staff who at worst will be duplicating the efforts of others and at best will only slightly increase the quality of the card catalog. The limitations and weaknesses of the card catalog for undergraduates are serious and are adequately described in the professional literature.[17] Because of these weaknesses and the emphasis on the card catalog in high school libraries, one of the main objectives of college bibliographic instruction should be to place the card catalog use in proper perspective in relation to bibliographies and other reference tools. (The subject approach of the card catalog should be used only after encyclopedias and bibliographies have been consulted and have failed to provide an adequate bibliography.) Given this need to de-emphasize the use of the card catalog, it is imprudent for the library to spend scarce funds on duplicating Library of Congress efforts or to attempt to improve on the L.C.'s work.

Second, the reference staff must be upgraded and staffed by professionals whose choice of occupation is based not only on a respect and enjoyment of books and education, but on a desire to work with and help people. The college library should no longer be viewed as a comfortable haven from teaching. College libraries must have, particularly on their reference staffs, persons who are concerned about student access to information and the role of information in the educational program of their institutions.

CHANGING FACULTY ATTITUDES

To change faculty attitudes toward the library is a much more difficult objective to achieve, first because people with Ph.Ds will have to be reeducated, and second because the library has little institutional power to reinforce the theoretical ideas with practical changes in the classroom and curriculum. So much has been written on the present state of college education and the need to remodel teaching practices, curriculum, and even the very nature and rationale of college education, that by now faculty feel embroiled in incessant battle.[18] It therefore behooves librarians to tread softly. More will be gained by low-keyed person-to-person discussion than by jumping into a battlefield where lines are drawn among faculty, students, and administrators. Library instruction can be eased into the curriculum through gentle, but persistent pressure. The faculty who are already the most library conscious can be approached first, and as the program develops they will be the best salespeople for library instruction.

In the rhetoric about independent study, seminars, honors programs, preparation for lifelong learning,[19, 20, 21] all of which have a substantial impact on the library's relation to the educational program, little has been said about the library's relationship to these new developments. Therefore, one of the major tasks of educating faculty is to demonstrate the relationship of libraries, library use, and library instruction to these new ideas about educational methods.

The basic premise of much of the discussion on change of teaching patterns and new directions for curricula seems to be that a concentrated and forthright effort should be made to wean the student from specially prepared, prepackaged information. An educational program founded on this premise should contain components designed to improve students' capabilities to collect information effectively and efficiently, evaluate critically, and communicate with others effectively. When education is put in these terms, it becomes quite obvious that the library and library instruction are an absolute must if the objectives are to be achieved.

What is implied here is a comprehensive unified program that is likely to exist only where extensive curricular changes and experimentation have been implemented. When this occurs, library involvement is likely. (The Model Library Grant Program of the Council on Library Resources and the National Endowment for the Humanities are good examples.) On the other hand, the more typical situation will be an individual faculty member or the faculty of a department, a division, or in a few cases, a whole college, who in their day-to-day activities are continually trying to improve their teaching and who will be experimenting with new patterns. It is with these faculty that the librarian can most fruitfully work. As a team they can interact and from their different perspectives mold subject matter and library instruction into a coordinated instructional program.

I have not dealt with the practical aspects of getting a library instruction program established. Little has been said or written about such practical matters simply because situations differ so much from one institution to another. If one is interested in present programs of academic library instruction, three recent surveys may be consulted.[22, 23, 24] If one operates in sympathy with the comments made above and the literature cited, and uses diplomacy, then the librarian has the tools for bucking the system and moving toward the ideal of the college library as a teaching instrument.

WHAT TO TEACH

THE "RESPONSE" APPROACH

The content of almost all presently operating programs of college library instruction has been the result of practical considerations. Generally, college librarians in their situations have responded by providing instruction aimed at meeting the student needs that they have perceived from their vantage points at the reference desk. This instruction (the "response" approach) has focused on the use of reference tools that are particularly helpful to the specific assignment that students are working on. As a result the students' perception of library use after four years is that of a patchwork of assignments that required library use of varying types and that were generally accompanied by some practical comments and/or bibliography designed to expedite the location of relevant material on a desired topic. There is much to be said for this response approach. It is the easiest form of instruction to work into already established courses. The faculty are required only to give up an hour or two of lecture time for the librarian to make his or her presentation, or, at least, to mention the library instruction services that are provided in the library. This response approach is the easiest for librarians because their attention is clearly focused on the specific assignment being given, and thus comments can be directed toward giving the most practical advice on how to find the desired information. For the student this form of instruction is also desirable. The direct payoff in better grades is a highly motivating factor that makes students receptive to what the librarian has to offer.

One serious weakness of such a response approach is the view of the library that such instruction fosters.[25] The student views the task of library use as one of checking a list of reference tools and the card catalog for relevant literature. The list of reference tools is prepared for the student and given to him or her with instruction on how to use the tools, and there usually is not instruction on the concepts of classes of reference tools (handbooks, encyclopedias, dictionaries, bibliographies, indexes, union catalogs), the selection of the relevant title from each class, and the proper sequence in which the classes of reference tools should be consulted.

THE "BIBLIOGRAPHIC" APPROACH

The "bibliographic" approach, as referred to earlier, is one in which the instructor recognizes the intricacies and complexities of the library.[26] The bibliographic approach and the response approach of library instruction are not mutually exclusive. But if the bibliographic approach is used in specific course assignments there is the practical problem of time that limits what can be accomplished in one or two sessions. The result is that students get repetitive instruction in basic search strategy, but never progress beyond it. Because search strategy is a conceptual framework for logically organizing use of the library and for explaining the organization of recorded literature, teaching search strategy needs more time and requires practice in using it. This need for time demands attention to a number of other problems and details on the development of a bibliographic instruction program; greater coordination with the faculty member's course structure is required, coordination between one course and another is needed, and most difficult of all, a plan of course assignments and library instruction must be developed that will achieve both the subject matter objectives and intellectual skill objectives (reading, writing, critical thinking, information gathering) set by the professor, the librarian, and the institution.

This idealistic pattern is deliberately emphasized because it is the direction in which college library instruction should be going. The response approach has been widely used in college libraries with some success. But where it has been extensively used throughout the college's curriculum the result has been that, at best, the basics of search strategy and general reference tools have been repeated frequently and the more sophisticated tools and strategies are skimmed over or ignored, or at worst, the students only know about and can use a few dozen reference tools. It is time for the profession to tackle the difficult task of developing an appropriate search strategy or strategies in which undergraduates should be competent, and to develop ways of teaching them. This is not meant to imply that we should be making undergraduates into junior reference librarians; that would be a major blunder. On the contrary, we must recognize the student as a novice both in the subject matter and in the use of sophisticated bibliographic apparatuses, and develop a strategy that takes these factors into account.

The search strategy diagrammed in Figures 1, 2, and 3 is an example of one such strategy, and while it appears simple, it is deceptively so. The strategy can be taught in three stages, each building on the previous stage and making the competent students more and more self-sufficient in their library use. Stage 1 is the solid portion of Figure 1. This is a simple strategy predicated on these assumptions: the student is working on his or her first scholarly paper in the discipline (biology); the student is still being oriented to the library's facilities and services; [27] all students have generally the same basic library competence; [28] and all students are doing much the same kind of assignment, although not necessarily on exactly the same subject. This stage is designed to emphasize six ideas or skills:

1. Library searches in subject areas unfamiliar to the student should begin with a general source. (During Stage 1 of the instruction these sources are stated: e.g., *McGraw-Hill Encyclopedia of Science and Technology,* 3rd ed., 1971, and its text. This is Option I in Figure 1.)

2. The bibliographies of general reference sources are important because they are selective guides to the best available secondary literature.

3. Tracings should be used to establish appropriate subject headings for card catalog searches.

4. The subject approach to the card catalog has several limitations and therefore is *not the first* place to look for material. (Weaknesses are: lack of specificity in subject headings, problems of synonymity, inconsistency in heading structure, and time-lag for new subjects. Limitations are: does not cover entire collection, government documents, periodical articles, nor does it index parts of books.)

5. Secondary sources should be reviewed and read for pertinent vocabulary and bibliographic references.

6. Serials indexes are important tools in library research.
    (a) the use (when and how) of *Science Citation Index*
    (b) the use (when and how) of *Biological Abstracts*

Note that the strategy is based on specific reference tools and that teaching Stage 1 will necessarily involve the method of using specific titles. This is not unlike the best instruction that would be given in the response approach. The actual use of the library via this strategy by a novice undergraduate has been described in the literature.[29] Stages 2 and 3 make this bibliographic approach qualitatively different from the response approach.

Stage 2 consists of the side branches (printed with double lines) of the strategy in Figure 1. It emphasizes that while there are general reference tools that are the most important for the subject field in general, there are a vast number of specialized sources that are more useful for a given specific topic. It is important to recognize that the instruction does not emphasize titles but categories of literature and how to locate the most useful title in each category. (Note that this stage examines only the task of selection in the reference-tool categories—encyclopedias, texts, reviews, and bibliographies—and omits the problem of selecting the best indexing or abstracting tool.) The techniques taught for locating the useful titles in a reference-tool category are listed in Table 2.

Table 2. *TECHNIQUES FOR LOCATING RELEVANT, USEFUL REFER-ENCE TOOLS: ENCYCLOPEDIAS, DICTIONARIES, BIBLIOG-RAPHIES, HANDBOOKS, AND INDEXES*

Technique 1. Use bibliography produced by library. This is a selective, anno-tated list of titles held by the library that are considered especially suitable for undergraduates. The list should be organized by ref-erence-tool types and then by special subjects in and related to the major field of study. An index of titles, reference-tool types, and subjects should be included.

Technique 2. Use of guides to the literature (listed in the above bibliography) or suggested by the reference librarian.

Technique 3. Use of subject-form approach to the card catalog.

Stage 3, illustrated in Figures 2 and 3, is presented to students who are doing more advanced work, including independent laboratory research. It is designed to help them categorize the type(s) of information they need and to match that type with the proper class of reference tool. Stage 3 also extends the idea of techniques for selecting appropriate specific titles in a reference-tool class to indexing and abstracting services. The same techniques (Table 2) are to be used.

This search strategy provides a framework for both the student and the librarian. For the student it is a superstructure on which the bits and pieces learned can be arranged. For the librarian it serves as an organizing device to avoid some of the weaknesses of the response approach. If this bibliographic approach has any validity, the student who receives it should be able to transfer his or her concepts of search strategy from one subject area to another and be able to do a competent library search in a new subject area. This transferability needs to be demonstrated experimentally if the bibliographic approach is to be justified. Whether this approach makes the student a more independent library user than does the response approach is another area of study that needs attention.

CHARACTERISTICS OF GOOD TEACHING METHODS FOR LIBRARY INSTRUCTION

While librarians have done little research on teaching methods (e.g., lecture, programmed instruction, audiovisual devices, etc.), educational researchers have churned out vast quantities of research data. The conclusion we can draw from these data is that no one method is superior. In fact, one suspects that it is not method itself but some other characteristics that determine teaching effective-ness, such as efficiency, personal attention to the student, and "hands on" ex-perience for the student.

EFFICIENCY

Efficiency is listed first not because it is most important but rather because it is usually thought so. Frequently, efficiency is cited as an important reason for

Figure 1. Search Strategy for Undergraduate Biology Students

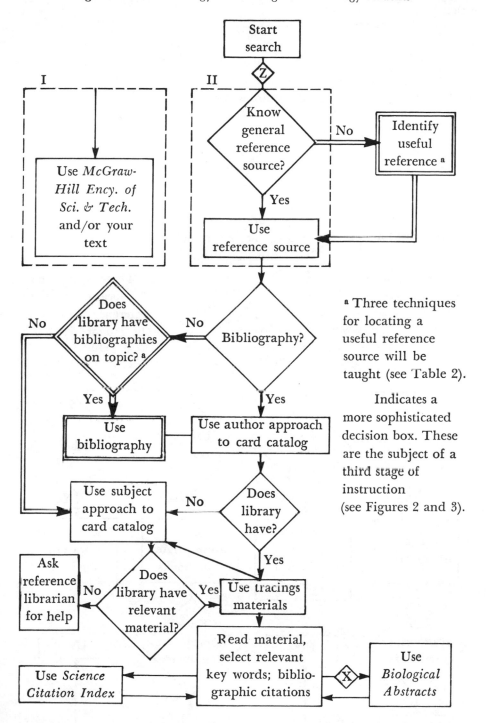

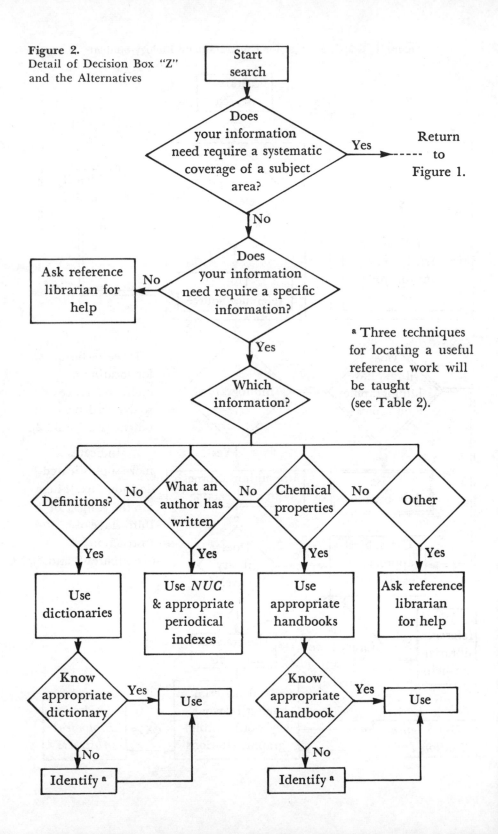

Figure 2.
Detail of Decision Box "Z" and the Alternatives

Figure 3. Detail of Decision Box "X"

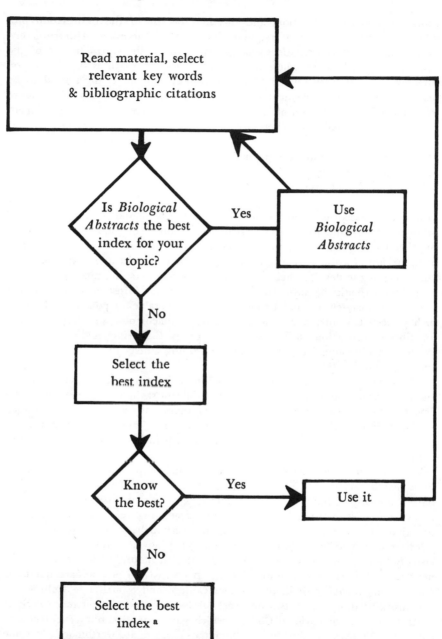

Read material, select relevant key words & bibliographic citations

Is *Biological Abstracts* the best index for your topic?

Yes → Use *Biological Abstracts*

No

Select the best index

Know the best?

Yes → Use it

No

Select the best index [a]

[a] Three techniques for locating the best index will be taught (see Table 2).

using programmed instruction, and this may be true if the information programmed remains fixed and frequent change is not necessary. Unfortunately, library instruction content does change—especially if the instruction is of the response approach. Even where a more systematic approach is used that presumably is not directly related to course subject content, changes need to be made because of rearrangement of the library, changes in format of reference tools, inclusion or exclusion of various reference tools, and general improvement resulting from experience. Therefore, when any kind of programmed instruction or audiovisual material is contemplated it is important that the life-expectancy of the material be estimated and the cost of revision be included in any overall cost estimates.

Librarians should also be cautious about getting involved in the technical aspects of instructional materials development. Unless the college has media production specialists, a librarian's time would be better spent in personal reference service and live library instruction. A librarian should not be spending time taking pictures, creating layouts, etc., etc. That is the job of the library media technical assistant or comparable personnel. Instead of individual librarians struggling to develop their own slide/tapes, films, etc., funding agencies and foundations should be supporting the development of instructional materials that are deliberately created to be as widely adaptable as possible. The only such projects currently operating are the development of a slide/tape package for library instruction in English literature by Catherine Schlichting (Ohio Wesleyan University), the work at Brigham Young University,[30] and the Project Intrex *Pathfinders* (M.I.T.).

When individual college libraries develop their own programmed or audiovisual materials, the major advantage is not the cost savings but rather that their development can be pursued during quieter times, such as summer or between semesters, instead of during the semester, as the "live" approach requires. However, if this is to be done and course relatedness is to be maintained, the librarian must know something of the faculty's plans for the course.

While talking about efficiency and economy it is important to dispel any notions that library instruction will reduce the need for reference staff and thus reduce the cost of public services. While it is true that basic instruction will relieve reference personnel from the mind-deadening repetition of basic instruction on how to use the card catalog and certain basic reference tools, over a longer period of time library instruction generates more reference questions. Usually these questions are of a more sophisticated nature, which results in the need for additional staff time in reference. A comparison of reference questions asked at the reference desks of Earlham College and Swarthmore College has demonstrated this. During two one-week periods in 1969 the reference desk at the Lilly Library of Earlham College, which gave extensive library instruction, handled 277 questions asked by undergraduates. While at Swarthmore's McCabe Library, where little instruction is given, 111 questions were asked.[31] Furthermore, a higher percentage of Earlham's questions were of the reference type as opposed to the locational type. Table 3 shows the breakdown of the questions by type for the two colleges. R-1, -2, etc., are reference question types defined

Table 3. *COMPARISON OF REFERENCE QUESTIONS ASKED BY UNDERGRADUATES AT EARLHAM'S LILLY LIBRARY AND SWARTHMORE'S McCABE LIBRARY*

	Earlham		Swarthmore	
	No.	*%*	*No.*	*%*
Information	52	17.5	26	23.4
R-1	143	48.2	28	25.2
R-2	0	0.0	1	0.9
R-3	15	5.1	36	32.4
R-4	57	19.2	12	10.1
R-5	11	3.7	2	1.8
R-6	14	4.7	6	5.4
R-7	1	0.3	0	0.0
Search	4	1.4	0	0.0
Totals	297	100.1%	111	99.2%

SOURCE: Billy R. Wilkinson, *Reference Services for Undergraduates* (Metuchen, N. J.: Scarecrow Press, 1972), pp. 270, 314.

by Wilkinson for his study. Generally speaking, higher number categories require more time and professional skill, except category R-7, which is a miscellaneous category. The "Search" category is for questions that require between 30 and 60 minutes of time and the use of several library resources. Except for the R-3 category ("bibliographic verification of material not on campus") Earlham had a greater percent of questions in categories R-1, -4, -5, -7, and "Search," and about the same in categories R-2 and R-6. These results show that development of a library instruction program is not an alternative to reference service but a complement to it. No library administrator should promote library instruction solely on the basis of economy, because in the long run it will be more expensive. What is decisive is that through library instruction it is economically feasible to improve reference service.

PERSONAL ATTENTION TO STUDENTS

It's no secret that some of the difficulties the large universities have found in recent years have been the result of student feelings of depersonalization and a resulting alienation. Small colleges, on the other hand, have played up smallness as desirable for a meaningful, personalized education. This should not, however, ipso facto, eliminate the use of audiovisual and other nonpersonal instructional materials. The use of programmed and audiovisual materials for certain tasks will provide more time for personal attention in other aspects of library instruction. If there are areas of instruction that change little, are repeated frequently, and cost-wise compare favorably with live presentations, then prepared instructional materials should be considered. But there should be built into the system adequate personal contact between students and librarians so that students can identify persons they know to be sympathetic to their problems.

At least one study has clearly indicated that students use librarians least as a source of information.[32] One of the most important things that libraries must do is begin to change that pattern. It can be done best by exposing librarians to students in a way that illustrates their primary role: providing guidance in the location of needed information. What better way than through library instruction of the type discussed above? When this exposure occurs, the personality of the librarian giving the instruction will have an important influence on the effectiveness of the instruction. It would be desirable to describe the personality of the perfect teacher, but that is not possible, as any academic administrator can quickly tell you. What is important is that in the selection of new personnel for the reference department, consideration should be given to the candidates' qualifications and professional interests in: library instruction, the relevance of the library to the curriculum, and the kind of education the institution is trying to provide. As stated earlier, the library must not be viewed as a comfortable haven from college teaching. Therefore, the selection of new reference personnel must recognize the dynamic role that must be filled if a library is to be relevant to the college's educational program.

"HANDS-ON" EXPERIENCE FOR STUDENTS

The third important factor to be considered is that of providing first-hand experience for the student. Because effective library use involves a constellation of intellectual tasks and manipulative skills (of files, books, indexes, etc., abstract numbers, references, etc.), effective library instruction should contain some element that requires actual use of the library. Such use can take many forms, such as Earlham's guided exercises,[33] UCLA's library skills program,[34] * or Sir George Williams University's library experiences. These forms, which I call "involvement" instruction, are related to programmed instruction in that they provide a planned course of activity that the student must become involved in by responding to questions about the material. Involvement instruction differs from programmed instruction in that the involvement required is a response not to material on how to use the library but to using the library itself. Appendixes 1 and 2 show examples from two of the three types of involvement instruction mentioned above.

In each case the questions asked require actual use of the library in order for the student to respond. This feature helps ensure that the student will become familiar with the physical layout of the library (orientation), the layout and organization of the reference materials themselves, as well as the whys, whens, and wherefores of the use of the reference materials.

Only three elements of instructional method have been discussed in detail. Others, such as course-relatedness, timing, etc., have been written about in the literature [35, 36, 37] or elsewhere in this paper, and there is no need for restatement here. Institutional context is another important factor that must be recognized,

* Discussed in a paper by Miriam Dudley in Part III of this book.—EDITOR

but that cannot be discussed in any detail. Suffice it to say, the methods of library instruction will be determined partially by the instructional methods of the faculty in whose courses the library instruction is being given. In any case, the methods chosen should provide as much contact between student and librarian as is economically feasible and should provide the student with much experience in trying to use the library. No one method (in-class lectures, programmed texts, slide/tape presentations, etc.) will solve all the instructional problems. The choice of methods will depend on the particular combination of factors that exist in a librarian's institution.

CONCLUSION

Much of what I have said in this paper is based on my experience in day-to-day attempts to provide good library instruction, my personal contact with fellow librarians, and what others have written about their experiences. Little of what I said can be supported by any type of comparative research data. Library instruction is now widely discussed as a professional concern by academic librarians and there have been many well-intentioned, but groping efforts to find ready-made answers. There are none. While I have tried to state some fair generalizations about what quality library instruction is or should be, these statements can only be guidelines, guidelines within which the institutional context must be considered. Regardless of what is taught, or how it is taught, the ultimate goal is to enable students to become effective library users, both for their classroom assignments and for their life to come, i.e., after graduation.

NOTES

1. Columbia University, *Annual Report of the President,* 1883, p. 46.
2. W. R. Harper, "The Trend of University and College Education in the United States," *North American Review* 174 (1902): 458.
3. If a defense for library instruction is needed, see: Millicent C. Palmer, "Why Academic Library Instruction?" in *Library Orientation,* ed. by Sul H. Lee, papers presented at the First Annual Conference on Library Orientation, Eastern Michigan University, May 7, 1971, Library Orientation Series no. 1 (Ann Arbor: Pierian Press, 1972), pp. 1–17.
4. Patricia B. Knapp, *The Monteith College Library Experiment* (Metuchen, N.J.: Scarecrow Press, 1966), p. 40.
5. James R. Kennedy, "Integrated Library Instruction," *Library Journal* 95 (1970): 1450–1453.
6. "Integrating Library Instruction in the College Curriculum," *Drexel Library Quarterly* 7 (1971): 171–378.
7. George S. Bonn, "Training in the Use of the Library," in *The State of the Library Art,* vol. 2, pt. 1 (New Brunswick, N.J.: Rutgers University, Graduate School of Library Service, 1960), p. 1.
8. J. E. Scrivener, "Instruction in Library Use: the Persisting Problem," *Australian Academic and Research Libraries* 3 (1972): 87.

9. Total count from *Library Literature* 1972.

10. Proceedings of the first two conferences are available from Pierian Press, Ann Arbor, Mich.

11. A catalog of the audiovisual materials present is available from ALA headquarters.

12. *ALA Handbook of Organization 1971–72* (Chicago: ALA, 1972), p. 36.

13. The result of this work has been the report of the Association of College and Research Libraries Committee on Bibliographic Instruction, "Academic Bibliographic Instruction, Status Report 1972" (ERIC Report ED 072 823, 1973), pp. 1–75.

14. All correspondence with Project LOEX should be addressed to Project LOEX, University Library, Eastern Michigan University, Ypsilanti, Mich. 48197.

15. This idea is the subject of a paper by Evan I. Farber, which will soon be published by Scarecrow Press in a *Festschrift* for Guy Lyle. I wish to acknowledge his cooperation in permitting me to read his manuscript and to use his main ideas.

16. Knapp, op. cit., p. 40.

17. Palmer, op. cit., pp. 9–11.

18. Patricia B. Knapp, "Guidelines for Bucking the System: A Strategy for Moving Toward the Ideal of the Undergraduate Library as a Teaching Instrument," *Drexel Library Quarterly* 7 (1971): 217–221. While written about the university situation, it contains salient comments pertinent to the nature of college faculty.

19. Paul L. Dressel, *College and University Curriculum* (Berkeley: McCutchen, 1968).

20. Philip Runkel, Roger Harrison, and Margaret Runkel, eds., *The Changing College Classroom* (San Francisco: Jossey-Bass, 1969).

21. Lewis B. Mayhew, *Colleges Today and Tomorrow* (San Francisco: Jossey-Bass, 1969).

22. Association of College and Research Libraries Committee on Bibliographic Instruction, op. cit.

23. Verna V. Melum, *Wilson Library Bulletin* (1971).

24. Verna V. Melum, "1971 Survey of Library Orientation and Instruction Programs," *Drexel Library Quarterly* 7 (1971): 225–253.

25. Another weakness of the "response" approach, which will not be discussed in this paper, is the failure, again for lack of time, to show how the library can be used to locate *quality* literature on a topic. So many times students are so desperate for literature on their topic that they will grab at anything related to it. Library instruction should include elements that indicate the techniques for locating the best material and not just any material.

26. Knapp, *Monteith College Library Experiment*, p. 40.

27. By discussing only bibliographic instruction, I do not mean to imply that orientation is not important or that it can or should be separated from the early stages of bibliographic instruction.

28. If this assumption is to be justified, the library must take steps to assure, as nearly as possible, this homogeneity. One possibility is the testing of all incoming students.

29. Thomas G. Kirk, "The Role of the Library in an Investigative Laboratory," in *The Laboratory: A Place to Investigate,* ed. by John W. Thornton (Washington, D.C.: Commission on Undergraduate Education in the Biological Sciences, 1972), pp. 127–130.

30. Marvin E. Wiggins, "The Development of Library Use Instructional Programs," *College and Research Libraries* 33 (1972): 473–479.

31. Billy R. Wilkinson, *Reference Services for Undergraduates* (Metuchen, N.J.: Scarecrow Press, 1972), p. 336.

32. Colleen Coughlan Amundson, "Relationships Between University Freshmen's Information Gathering Techniques and Selected Environmental Factors" (Ph.D. thesis, Minneapolis, University of Minnesota, 1971), p. 248.

33. Thomas G. Kirk, "A Comparison of Two Methods of Library Instruction for Students in Introductory General Biology," *College and Research Libraries* 32 (1971): 465–474.

34. Miriam Dudley, "Teaching Library Skills to College Students," *Advances in Librarianship* 3 (1972): 83–105.

35. Kennedy, op. cit., p. 1450.

36. Millicent C. Palmer, "Library Instruction at Southern Illinois University, Edwardsville," *Drexel Library Quarterly* 7 (1971): 255–276.

37. Scrivener, op. cit., pp. 87–119.

APPENDIX 1
TWO FRAMES FROM EARLHAM'S GUIDED EXERCISE

Frame X

Normally you would check any important reference in all years of *Science Citation Index* from the time the article was published up to the present. However, to make the exercise less tedious and lengthy you are asked to check only one year for each reference. Using the articles listed below and following the steps illustrated on pages *32a* and *32b* (instruction on the use of *Science Citation Index*), establish which articles have cited Sutherland. List only the first two articles listed under each.

Year of *S.C.I.*
to be checked

Sutherland, N. S.	1963.	*Nature*, London	197:118–122.	1967
Sutherland, N. S.	1960.	*Nature*, London	188:1092–1099.	1966

Frame Y

Under each of the articles the first two articles found are:

Sutherland, N. S. 1963. *Nature,* London 197:118–122 (in 1967)
    Ganz, L. *J. Com. Physl.* 63:258.
    Hershens, M. *Psychol. B.* 67:326.

Sutherland, N. S. 1960. *Nature,* London 188:1092–1099 (in 1966)
  (only one is listed)
  Wells, M. J. *Adv. Mar. Bio.* 3:1.

If you had no trouble finding these in the *Science Citation Index,* you may
skip over to page 36 and begin with the statement *"Science Citation Index. . . ."*
If you are having trouble, follow the step-by-step process that follows.

If you will look up Sutherland, N. S. in the 1967 *Science Citation Index,* volume
4 (NICH to TANA), you will find his name first in column 20999 (numbers at
bottom of page) of the citation index. Note that below his name are a number
of broken lines, each of which represents his name, and a different article. What
determines the sequence of the articles?

APPENDIX 2
EXAMPLE FROM SIR GEORGE WILLIAMS UNIVERSITY'S
LIBRARY EXPERIENCE, MONTREAL, P.Q.

Name _____

Class _____ Section _____

Research Topic _____

LIBRARY EXPERIENCE—PHILOSOPHY

1. Encyclopedias

   Use an encyclopedia for general background reading on a subject. Multi-
   volume sets usually include an index volume. You should always begin your
   search for information in the index.

Encyclopedia of Philosophy	*Ref B 51 E5*
International Encyclopedia of the Social Sciences	*Ref H 41 15*
Encyclopedia of Religion and Ethics	*Ref BL 31 E4*

   Use one of these encyclopedias and look for background material that will
   assist you in your research topic.

   Title of encyclopedia used _____

   Subject heading (term) used in the *index* volume? _____

   The article is in volume number _____

   Is there a bibliography at the end of the article? _____

   (You should look in the card catalogue to see if the library has any of the
   books listed in the bibliography.)

2. Essays

You may not be able to find what you want in the card catalogue or the topic you are researching may be so popular that all of the books on the subject may be already checked out. It is at this point you can turn to essays.

The *Essay and General Literature Index* is a guide to essays. It is located on the index tables in the Reference Room. *Index AI 3 E8*

It is arranged by subject. If, for example, you are researching a paper on ecology: find the heading in the *Index* and choose one essay appropriate to your topic.

An example of the information as it appears in the *Index:*

ECOLOGY
    Crook, J. H. *The nature and function of territorial aggression.* In *Montagu, A., ed. Man and aggression. p. 141–78.*

Subject heading you used in the *Index?* _____

Author of essay _____

Title of essay _____

Title of book that contains the essay (follows word *In*) _____

_____

Editor or author of book of essays _____

Page numbers of the essay _____

Now look in the author/title section of the card catalogue to see if the library has this book of essays (section 28).

INSTRUCTION IN THE USE OF THE UNIVERSITY LIBRARY

MARGARET KNOX GOGGIN
Dean, Graduate School of Librarianship,
University of Denver

Librarians have been concerned about instruction in the use of university libraries for many decades. Kenneth Brough traces the interest back to Harvard and discussions there in the 1920s.[1] Others point to the statement by Columbia's president in his annual report of 1883, when he suggested that "a little systematic instruction would so start our students in the right methods, that for the rest of their lives all their work in libraries would be more expeditiously accomplished."[2] One may record the start of serious concern with the initiation of the first elective course in bibliography at the University of Michigan in 1882, or with the first planned instruction at Columbia University in 1909 and at Maryland in 1919. Whatever the benchmark, the hundreds of articles that have been published describing programs of instruction, problems encountered in attempts to teach students how to use the university library, individual experiences and differing techniques used to accomplish learning, all attest to the intense preoccupation librarians have had with this facet of their responsibilities through the years.

Several analyses of the published literature in this field have been made, the most complete being George Bonn's *Training Laymen in the Use of the Library* published in 1960, and covering the period up to and including 1958.[3] Allen Mirwis provided a bibliography of articles on academic library instruction from 1960 to 1970,[4] and Verna Melum brought a 1971 view to the field through a survey of programs existing at that time.[5]

Access to information in a university library is complicated by many factors. By its sheer size it baffles the beginning student who finds it an incomprehensible mass of materials. The librarian may try to compensate for the size of the collection by relocating certain resources to areas where they may be readily accessible as she or he assists users. But the users find the numerous special locations and special collections an additional barrier to their use of the library.

The resources of a university library are found to be in a variety of formats. Microcards, microprint, microfiche, microfilm, and ultramicrofiche may be housed in special areas, even separating one microform from another. Report literature, data files, and documents are recognized formats to the librarian as items to be separately handled, but to the users they may be simply difficult-to-locate answers to their questions.

A third characteristic of a university library is the dispersion of resources throughout the campus. A few universities have centralized libraries, but most institutions have library systems composed of the central library and a number of branch or departmental libraries located around the campus. In addition to the resources within the library system, university campuses frequently have institutes, laboratories, and research centers (i.e., Urban Studies Center, Laboratory for Ornithological Studies, etc.) with libraries of technical studies and data banks of value for the researcher. Awareness of all of these resources may be essential to students and faculty of the university.

To the library staff the university community presents a complex array of students, faculty, and research staff as potential users of the library. Not only does the large number of students make individual assistance difficult, but also the varied preparation and library experience represented by the student body make group instruction difficult. Students enter the university not only in the freshman year, but in increasing numbers transfer from the community college into the junior year. An orientation program tied to a freshman English class no longer can be expected to fulfill the needs of all new students. Graduate students at the masters, doctoral, and postdoctoral levels, faculty and research staff present to the library a diverseness of education and experience and exhibit varying levels of sophistication of need.

These, then, are some of the characteristics of the university library and its clientele, characteristics that indicate the challenge to librarians in a university system to provide relevant instructional programs for users amid the complexity of the need for knowledge.

Programs of library instruction for the university community are generally based on the following assumptions: (1) that students need information in order to successfully complete their university education; (2) that the library can best satisfy their information needs; (3) that information is so packaged and stored in libraries that few people can find the information they need without some instruction; and (4) that when users learn how to locate information for one need, they will be able to apply the same or a similar strategy to find other information when the need arises.

Nowhere in the literature or in the field does there appear to be disagreement concerning the levels of instruction required if the university's clientele is to be efficient in accessing the library's storehouse of knowledge. First, there is the orientation to the physical library, its environs, and how to use its services. Coupled with this is a modicum of library instruction needed by the beginning freshman who, in most universities, needs to cope with limited assignments involving the use of the library. Second, at the time when students select their major and start taking courses requiring the research and the writing of term papers, there is need for an instructional period or series of sessions to acquaint them with the general body of literature in their subject field and the search strategies that might be employed to locate information. At the graduate level the need is for more sophisticated bibliographical guidance and instruction directed to the specialized students.[6]

ORIENTATION

Orientation to the library is defined here as the introduction of students and faculty to the library, to locations of essential areas and resources, basic elements of using the library, and the services provided by librarians.

There appears to be general agreement that library orientation is a vital part of the students' introduction to their academic career, although a cause-and-effect relationship between the use of the library and academic success may not be assumed.

Articles and surveys of university libraries testify to the vast amount of experimentation conducted over the years by librarians in their attempts to find a perfect method of orientation. Unfortunately, the factual data of many of these experiments are lost in the files of annual reports of reference departments, and the reasons for abandoning one mode for another are lodged in the memory of the librarians.

The tour of the library building has been the prevalent mode for introducing new students to the university library. Modifications from one campus to another and on the same campus from one year to another relate to the proper time to schedule the tour and to the most effective format. Thus, some librarians plan tours during summer orientation periods, others during new-student week prior to the opening of school, and still others during the first three or four weeks of the term. The physical touring of a building may be done in small or large groups led by librarians, the library's student assistants, or by student orientation leaders. The leaders may have a prepared script and have had one or more inservice training sessions, or taped messages may be set up at identified stops along the route, and the leader's responsibility is to take the group to each area and activate the taped messages at each stop.

Dissatisfied with the results achieved by a required tour of the library by a captive audience of students, many librarians have made the tour voluntary. Advertisements on bulletin boards and in the packets for new students express the willingness of librarians to take students through the library at certain times during the first few weeks of each semester. In the last few years, the self-guided tour of the library has been introduced, using either the individual cassette, which the student borrows from the circulation desk, or a programmed text. This has the advantage of allowing each student to pace himself or herself and to become as involved in learning about the library as he or she wishes.

Some libraries have abandoned the tour, replacing it with a slide/tape presentation of the library that may be shown to groups during an orientation program, or to selected classes at the beginning of the semester. The production may be set up in an area of the library where it may be viewed individually by students as they feel the need to learn. Some use the slides as an introduction to the physical tour of the building, and others follow it with assignments to be accomplished through using the library. Videotape programs have been prepared by a few universities, to be shown to large groups of new students either in orientation meetings or in classes, or through closed circuit into the dormitories. The expense of production coupled with the need for frequent revision makes this too costly for many libraries.

INSTRUCTING FIRST-YEAR STUDENTS

Orientation and instruction of first-year students in the use of basic reference tools is sometimes combined as a part of the first-year, freshman English courses, with faculty administering the program entirely, or with faculty and librarians sharing the teaching, or with librarians assuming the responsibility for library-use instruction. While some universities are abandoning their programs, other institutions are initiating new programs, while still others are pleased with successful cooperative experiences that have lasted over a number of years.

The most effective programs are found to be those developed by faculty and librarians together, for this approach relates the ability to use libraries with the academic program. Library assignments become a way of fulfilling classroom objectives rather than being a series of isolated exercises. As Palmer wrote: "Instruction must be a joint concern, with the classroom teacher providing the need-motivation and standards for quality sources, and the library faculty providing, by any possible means, a knowledge of the best ways to find the quality sources." [7]

Reinforcement of the value of library instruction within the first-year English program should be provided by faculty-librarian discussions at frequent intervals. It is easy for faculty to be disenchanted with such a program, or be caught up in some new topic that demands the time previously given to library instruction. Without faculty support and reinforcement, library instruction risks being eliminated from the schedule.

THE LECTURE

Next to the orientation tour, the single lecture to a class on resources in a subject field is the most common method of instruction on university campuses. While in past years the first-year students were the main target for this information, in more recent years librarians have learned that in most universities these students may not recognize their need for this knowledge and may successfully complete required courses without much use of the library beyond the reserve book room. It is at the time the students begin their major fields of study that the need to know how to access that literature appears relevant. Thus librarians, while continuing to provide basic lectures to first-year English classes when requested, offer their services to faculty in the form of lectures on search techniques and resources in particular subject areas. The Melum survey indicates that almost every university surveyed uses this mode of instruction,[8] and while

Blakely found that "no department reported that it was overburdened by such faculty requests" for class lectures,[9] annual reports from university librarians record a growing number of class lectures provided by the reference staff over the past five years.

A program of lectures to classes in the students' major fields of study demands an aggressive outreach program on the part of the reference staff, and a continuing plan for working with faculty. The lectures should provide the information most needed by the students for their class assignments, and should reach the largest number of majors in the specific field.

SEPARATE COURSE

The separate course in "Bibliography" or "How to Use the Library" is offered by some university libraries for one or two hours of credits. It may be primarily for first- and second-year students, for example at Arizona State University and the University of California at Berkeley, or for upperclassmen, as at the University of Florida. As an introduction to the library, the course given to first- and second-year students generally includes lectures on the card catalog, filing in the catalog, bibliographies and subject guides, abstracts and indexes, government documents, and reference sources. Generally, the assignment is the compilation of a bibliography on a topic.

As an upperclassmen's course, "The Use of the Library" presupposes a basic knowledge of the catalog, the *Readers' Guide,* encyclopedias, and a few other basic reference sources. Starting from the students' need to locate information, such as book reviews or statistical data, the instructor outlines search strategy and the resources that are available. Weekly assignments unique to each student reinforce the instruction with practice.

Either course may be given in the traditional classroom setting, in the library, or by closed-circuit television. Where television courses have been offered results have proven that teaching is as effective or more effective than that gained through traditional lecture method, as long as a librarian is available for discussion. While expensive to produce, the TV programs reduce the demand on staff and ensure a more uniform presentation of information. Experiences at the University of Illinois and the University of Florida illustrate the fact that the television lectures do become outdated and need to be replaced, the Florida experience indicating a five-year maximum lifetime expectancy for these videotapes. Despite the methodology used it has been learned that lectures must be followed by assignments to be completed by the student if learning is to take place.

On some campuses, notably University of California at Los Angeles under Miriam Dudley and the University of Alaska with Millicent Hering, the library course has become a self-directed study, with objectives to be accomplished for each unit and individual assignments to implement the learning process. Students proceed at their own pace and earn credit when they have completed the specified number of assignments.

At the graduate level many academic departments offer a required course in research methods and resources for masters and doctoral students. While these are generally taught by faculty of the department, evidence indicates that, as information sources are becoming more complicated, librarians are being asked to contribute lectures or to assume responsibility for some of these courses. As an example from one campus, courses on "Music Bibliography," "Bibliography and Methods in Scandinavian Literature," and "Latin American Studies: Source Material" are all taught by librarians at the University of Minnesota. Legal bibliography and medical bibliography are courses generally taught by law and medical librarians on most campuses.

INDIVIDUALIZED INSTRUCTION

Convinced that the best instruction is still that given to individuals when each recognizes his or her need, librarians have been seeking ways to provide this type of opportunity for the large numbers of students found on university campuses. The "Library Resources Day" at the University of Michigan, the "Solution Sessions" at Pennsylvania State University and the "Term Paper Clinics" at the University of Pittsburgh and the University of Colorado are examples of some of the efforts to provide individual assistance.

The provision on some campuses of Library Instruction Librarians,[10] Tutor-Librarians,[11] Outreach Librarians,[12] or Consultants for Library Research[13] is another attempt to individualize instruction. Such a title identifies for students and faculty a person or a group of people specifically dedicated to their needs for tutorial help in the library. On the other hand it isolates from general reference duties certain librarians for the sole purpose of identifying and serving the instructional needs of library patrons, and thus helps to ensure time for planning and developing the educational program.

Computer assisted instruction (CAI) has been tried as an individualized learning-teaching mode and presents a successful way of providing a number of learning packages on a variety of subjects, and all available to the students whenever they desire them. The experience of the University of Denver Libraries with 21 courses ranging from the use of indexes and abstracts to how to do research for a term paper attests to the popular acceptance of CAI.[14]

From Project Intrex Model Library Program at M.I.T. has emanated audio-visual programs, each limited to instructing the user on how to use one single reference source and each located beside the tool to be explained.[15] Slide/tape instruction for *Engineering Index* and audio programs are available to assist the students after they have selected the resources they need to use. The modest cost of preparing and using audio programs recommends this type of individualized instruction to university libraries.

Finally, librarians should recognize that the library's graphics program and its publications, such as the library handbook and individual leaflets, are essentially tools for individual instruction. Specialized bibliographies and subject guides to the literature, such as the M.I.T. *Library Pathfinders,* form a highly useful educational function within the university library's total instructional plan.

NOTES

1. Kenneth J. Brough, *Scholar's Workshop* (Urbana: University of Illinois, 1953), p. 152.
2. Columbia University, *Annual Report of the President,* 1883, p. 46.
3. George S. Bonn, *Training Laymen in the Use of Libraries* (New Brunswick, N.J.: Rutgers University, Graduate School of Library Service, 1960).
4. Allen Mirwis, "Academic Library Instruction—A Bibliography, 1960–1970," *Drexel Library Quarterly* 7 (1971): 327–335.
5. Verna V. Melum, "1971 Survey of Library Orientation and Instruction Programs," *Drexel Library Quarterly* 7 (1971): 225–253.
6. Note for example: Millicent C. Palmer, "Library Instruction at Southern Illinois University, Edwardsville," *Drexel Library Quarterly* 7 (1971): 255 ff.; A. Graham Mackenzie, "Reader Instruction in Modern Universities," *Aslib Proceedings* (July 1969): 271–279, and L. C. Pugh, "Library Instruction Programmes for Undergraduates," *The Library World* 71 (March 1970): 267.
7. Millicent C. Palmer, "Why Academic Library Instruction?" in *Library Orientation,* ed. by Sul H. Lee, papers presented at the First Annual Conference on Library Orientation, Eastern Michigan University, May 7, 1971. Library Orientation Series no. 1. Ann Arbor: Pierian Press, 1972.
8. Melum, op cit.
9. Florence Blakely, "Perceiving Patterns of Reference Service: A Survey." *RQ* 11 (Fall 1971): 35.
10. Found at Southern Illinois University at Edwardsville, Arizona State University, and many others.
11. Used in many British universities.
12. Eastern Michigan University, for example.
13. Ohio State University.
14. Patricia Culkin, "Computer Assisted Instruction in Library Use," *Drexel Library Quarterly* 8 (1972): 301–311.
15. Jeffrey J. Gardner, "Point-of-Use Library Instruction," *Drexel Library Quarterly* 8 (1972): 281–285.

LIBRARY INSTRUCTION IN COLLEGES AND UNIVERSITIES IN THE SEVENTIES: A VIEWPOINT

VERNA MELUM BEARDSLEY
*Formerly Library Orientation Librarian,
Swen Parson Library, Northern Illinois
University*

Cries of the futility of attempting to provide library orientation and instruction programs to soaring enrollments have been replaced by the conviction that new methods *must* be developed to introduce users to the libraries of the 1970s. Re-evaluation of old methods considers many factors: motivation, timeliness, relevance, grade levels, automation versus live instruction, cooperation with faculty, service to faculty, librarians as teachers, staff time, sharing of materials, and feasible goals.

MOTIVATION

Are first-year students motivated for library instruction? No! They do not realize the complexities of college and university libraries: the vast and varied resources, the many types of bibliographic control, new and varied methods of searching, the organization of the Library of Congress Classification System, computer-produced catalogs and indexes. In short, they do not expect to encounter problems in the library. They will be self-motivated to seek or to listen to assistance only when problems arise in connection with their assignments.

Therefore *instruction* should be left until it can be correlated with course work. But first-year and other new students can be *introduced* to the library in ways that will motivate future instruction. What can be included in such an introduction?

First of all, a warm welcome, to offset fears of going to the library and exposing their ignorance by asking for direction and assistance.

Second, an introduction to *people* and to *services,* to let students know that there are *people* as well as books in a library—people who are not too busy to help them; people who are not stern and unapproachable but smiling and friendly.

Third, the introduction of a *few* titles of reference sources and indexes for the purpose of awakening students to the wealth of resources beyond what they knew in high school.

Fourth, announcements of future opportunities to learn more about the library.

Brief, simple orientation of this type can be expected to motivate a desire for further assistance in using the library.

TIMELINESS

There is unanimous recognition today of the fact that library instruction is effective only at the time of need. General orientation of the type just discussed can be effective early in a term, but instruction in the use of specific references must be relevant to assignments of the moment. Library instruction in a vacuum has been abandoned. Keeping in mind the distinction between "orientation" and "instruction" is helpful in deciding what to present under different given circumstances.

RELEVANCE

What not to teach is a major factor in selection of content for any library instruction. Librarians need to post a warning to themselves: Give instruction in the use of the library; do not teach library science! Students will retain only the instruction that is followed up immediately by purposeful use. Librarians should consider carefully what details are essential to the students and which are irrelevant to them.

LEVELS OF INSTRUCTION

One lecture or even one unit of library orientation/instruction is not enough. The new concept calls for a continuing program, through the undergraduate years and also at the graduate level. Instruction to graduates is imperative also (and is the most fully appreciated, when related to specific needs).

AUTOMATED VERSUS LIVE INSTRUCTION

Point-of-use equipment and programs seem to be the best answer to current problems of library instruction. Students become self-motivated when they find a program of explanation adjacent to the index or reference they are about to use, and their retention will be in proportion to their need.

Automated programs for group instruction are efficient and time-saving once they have been worked out. All media programs can have the advantage of being thoroughly prepared, with meticulous attention to accuracy and choices of effective examples.

But the best automated programs cannot compete with the effectiveness of direct communication between librarian or teacher and students. Live teaching will always be highly desirable; automation is an expedient alternative.

COOPERATION WITH TEACHERS

Cooperation between teachers and librarians is essential to effective library instruction, whatever its plan and form. Both informal and formal contacts are needed, from casual conversations at coffee hours to scheduled meetings and written communications. Again, personal contacts are the most effective. Staff assignments for responsibility for certain departments provide the framework for successful liaison communication.

Librarians need to take the initiative in making these contacts, and take it repeatedly. Confidence and faith in the importance of library instruction and a willingness to be of service must be combined with discretion, diplomacy, and tact. Faculty too often are unaware of the services that the library and the librarians are prepared to give. Cooperation may range from checking the availability of materials before they are assigned to consultations in planning assignments and assistance in making bibliographies. How much better for librarians to work with teachers in setting up problems to be presented without relation to any context or interest. Only with the cooperation of faculty can librarians be assured of meeting student needs.

Cooperation is a two-way street. Librarians have much to learn from faculty too. Teachers think of concepts, content, and methods of inquiry rather than of subject headings, facts, and indexes. Consultations with faculty help librarians to look beyond the details of bibliographic search to the intellectual content and the ultimate goals of a course, thus making their contributions worthy of greater intellectual respect.

SERVICE TO FACULTY

Service to the faculty is essential in order that they may serve the students. Library instruction programs are student-centered, but the faculty are the greatest motivating force. Most faculty members appreciate notification of new materials and of changes and developments in the library, and they are impressed with good service for their own study and research. But repeated suggestions and encouragement may be necessary in order to win some of them to the library. Once won over, their attitudes are reflected in those of their students.

LIBRARIANS AS TEACHERS

All librarians are deeply involved in the learning process. The procurement and the organization of library materials are essential to the academic climate. Reference librarians interpret books and search strategies; often they interpret assignments. They are consultants; they are tutors; they are instructors. Whether they work with individuals, prepare automated programs of instruction, or lecture to classes, they contribute immeasurably to the teaching program. Furthermore, they are in a position to see the academic picture as a whole rather than in course segments.

STAFF TIME

Should not these above facts dignify library orientation and instruction to a position of top priority in the planning of staff time and duties? The planning, development, and presentation of programs of orientation to the library and instruction in its use can well be a full-time job; half-time would seem to be a minimum. It is gratifying that more libraries are finding it possible to allocate more staff time for a phase of their overall programs that is receiving more and more recognition as being essential in the libraries of the 1970s.

SHARING OF MATERIALS

Why should every library work out its own programs on resources that are found in every college and university library? *Orientation* has to be local, but instruction on the use of basic references has to be similar everywhere. Some libraries are making their productions available to others. This development would seem to help solve the problem of lack of time and budgets to develop effective programs. With some basic materials to start with, librarians should be in a better position to put programs into operation by adding a minimum of local orientation.

FEASIBLE GOALS

The writer is well aware of the many difficulties and obstacles to carrying out these concepts, from student (and yes, sometimes librarians') apathy due to lack of time, budgets, and technological difficulties. But she has observed with great satisfaction the impetus and the steady gains of library orientation and instruction programs during recent years. The literature of the field and this book attest to the fact that successful programs are now in operation. Librarians cannot hope to reach every student, but they are finding ways to provide higher quality assistance to the students who will benefit the most from it and thus are stimulating intellectual curiosity. Each library must find the methods most feasible within its own limitations. The growing realization that *something* must be done to help the library users of the 1970s is a big step in the advance of library orientation and instruction.

BIBLIOGRAPHY

Melum, Verna V. "Library Instruction in a University." *Illinois Libraries* 51 (1969): 511–521.

————. "Motivating Students and Faculty." In *Library Orientation,* ed. by Sul H. Lee, papers presented at the First Annual Conference on Library Orientation, Eastern Michigan University, May 7, 1971. Library Orientation Series, no. 1. Ann Arbor: Pierian Press, 1972.

————. "1971 Survey of Library Orientation and Instruction Programs." *Drexel Library Quarterly* 7 (1971): 225–253.

————. "Survey to Aid Your Fall Planning: Library Orientation in the College and University." *Wilson Library Bulletin* 46 (1971): 59–66.

PROGRAMS OF UNDERGRADUATE LIBRARIES AND PROBLEMS IN EDUCATING LIBRARY USERS

ANNE B. PASSARELLI
Reference Librarian, Odegaard Undergraduate Library, University of Washington

MILLICENT D. ABELL
Associate Director of Libraries, State University of New York at Buffalo; formerly Assistant Director of Libraries for Undergraduate Library Services, University of Washington

In the report entitled *Reform on Campus* (June 1972) the Carnegie Commission on Higher Education cites, as one of the forces requiring change in higher education, a vast increase in human knowledge. No longer is it possible for a college education to provide more than a modest sampling from this tremendous body of knowledge. Moreover, the rate at which old knowledge is being supplemented or even supplanted by new makes it imperative that students learn how to keep abreast of change—not only while in school but throughout their lives. As the commission asserts:

> The teaching of existing knowledge . . . becomes comparatively less essential to the task of higher education and the imparting of skills for continuing self-education comparatively more, particularly in independent study and through the library.[1]

This proliferation of knowledge in its recorded form is clearly one of the factors that has contributed to the development of undergraduate libraries on university campuses. As the increased size and complexity of the research library collection created problems of both physical and intellectual access, a separate, smaller collection to meet the undergraduate's more limited needs was seen as a desirable solution. Robert Muller expresses a common view when he states:

> The distinctive characteristic of an undergraduate library on a large university campus is not only that it serves undergraduates but that the collection of books, periodicals, and other library materials is (or should be) of a highly selective and "choice" nature.[2]

Since 1965, when Irene Braden made a study of the first six undergraduate libraries in the country, the number of such libraries has quadrupled at least. For the most part, these libraries are found in large university systems with undergraduate enrollments of over 10,000 students.

The "core collection" was basic to all undergraduate library designs, but other elements also contributed to the original concept. Braden identified six distinctive characteristics of these libraries: (1) provision of open access to the collection; (2) centralization of services needed by undergraduates; (3) a selective collection of required, recommended, and recreational reading materials; (4) a center of instruction in library use; (5) special services for undergraduates, such as media centers, discussion areas, and exhibits; (6) a physical plan adapted to the habits of undergraduates.[3]

Closely related to the concept of a "select" collection for undergraduates is the idea of a special service function emphasizing the teaching of skills in the use of academic library resources. Braden quotes Keyes Metcalf, librarian at Harvard during the 1940s whose planning gave birth to Lamont, the first of the undergraduate libraries, on the concept underlying reference service at Harvard: "A large part of a liberal education is learning how to use the library." [4] Again and again in the years following the founding of Lamont, librarians have cited, as an important element in the undergraduate library planned at their institutions, the instructional function that would be incorporated into these libraries. Based on her six-library survey Braden stated that this function involved

> attempting to make the library an instructional tool by planning it as a center for instruction in library use, to prepare undergraduates for using larger collections, and by staffing it with librarians interested in teaching the undergraduate the resources of a library and the means of tapping these resources.[5]

She further states that the undergraduate library

> was envisioned as a workshop in which the undergraduate could learn on a relatively small scale those library skills which could later be applied to larger and more complex collections. The staff was seen as having a teaching function as one of its most important tasks.[6]

The undergraduate library, then, was originally conceived as having an inherent teaching function. This teaching function was not often described in detail; however, some articulate spokesmen for undergraduate libraries suggested that it included considerably more than person-to-person service at the reference desk. At the 1970 San Diego Conference on Training for Service in Undergraduate Libraries, John Haak, defining an undergraduate library, included as an essential ingredient "a staff and services which promote the integration of the library into the undergraduate teaching program of the university." [7] Haak saw undergraduate libraries as committed to "a program which, as a result of library-academic planning, would contribute forcefully to the educational experience of undergraduates." [8] At this same conference, Patricia Knapp advocated the challenging conception of the undergraduate library as a teaching instrument, totally involved in undergraduate education.[9]

Among its basic recommendations for change in higher education, the Carnegie Commission includes:

A greater emphasis on the library as an active participant in the instructional process.[10]

Elaborating upon this recommendation, the commission notes that libraries are often seen as passive centers, although on a few campuses they are developing an active instructional operation. The report calls for librarians themselves to shift their outlook from the traditional role of custodian of knowledge to "a more aggressive orientation toward the distribution of information," [11] a role that might include among its activities: supervision of independent study projects, teachng of seminars, and giving courses on research methods, as members of the instructional staff. It must also be noted that the commission recommends an increase in the proportion of the library budget allocated for instructional purposes, perhaps even double present funding levels.

So far, so good. A need exists for undergraduates to learn independent study skills to cope with the expansion of information that faces them now and will continue to occur during their lifetimes; a prestigious report reiterates the frequent call upon practitioners of the library profession to get out and provide active service in teaching these skills; and, with nice timing, a new institution has evolved, right where the need is most pressing, in the large unversities—an institution ostensibly dedicated to responding to this need. It would appear that everyone will live happily ever after.

In fact, however, no such millennium has arrived. Instead, undergraduate library staffs have found themselves on an obstacle course of such dimensions that some have given up the battle before it was even begun. Of those libraries that have taken up the active service challenge, most have met undergraduates' instructional needs only on the most superficial level and in accustomed modes. To suggest how undergraduate librarians can identify and deal with the real obstacles is the purpose of this paper.

In an attempt to assess the instructional programs currently provided by undergraduate libraries, the authors made an informal survey of 18 of the major undergraduate libraries.[12] The information received indicates that actual commitment to the teaching function in the undergraduate library ranges through four basic positions:

1. Regardless of original intentions, this function is not presently seen as a principal goal of the undergraduate library.

2. This function is viewed as important, but is not considered feasible in present circumstances except for a few efforts.

3. Attempts are being made to exercise this function, but there is no comprehensive plan.

4. Thought is being given to a systematic approach to a broad-scale instructional function.

Considering that most of these libraries have been established for several years, that the San Diego Conference with its clear challenge for library activism is now three years in the past, and that the goal of active programs has been legitimized repeatedly in the literature, it is alarming to find so few in this group actually responding to the challenge, or even considering a response in the immediate future. The paucity of evidence regarding programs that reach beyond the library's walls or transcend its traditional service patterns gives rise to a number of disturbing questions: Is there any relationship between this situation and the fact that some observers of the undergraduate library phenomenon see it as a passing fad? Does a relationship exist that might explain, or even predict, the decline and fall of the undergraduate library, a development no longer in the realm of sheer speculation since the demise of South Carolina's undergraduate unit? Is it significant that South Carolina's staff had, at the time of Braden's report, the vaguest statement of its reference service philosophy among the six institutions studied, and no apparent plans to differentiate its reference service in kind or degree from the traditional academic model? [13] What will happen in those undergraduate libraries still in existence whose professional staffing has been cut, an act which usually affects the reference section? To implement a significant teaching library role in a large university, generous staffing appears to be essential. Staff decreases may indicate library administration priorities, a demonstrated lack of activity in the undergraduate library reference section, or perhaps both.

MODES OF UGL INVOLVEMENT IN
UNDERGRADUATE EDUCATION

There are several ways to categorize the instructional activity carried on by undergraduate librarians. One approach is to consider activities developed on librarians' initiative and those developed in response to external demands. The active-service concept espoused by participants in the San Diego conference favors library initiation of programs, but includes programs initiated in direct response to curriculum needs. In examining the various types of programs identified through the survey of undergraduate libraries, the emphasis will be on library-initiated programs, above and beyond the basically responsive service that most libraries offer as a matter of course to both faculty (when a request for course-related bibliographic assistance is received) and students (in the form of one-to-one instruction in the reference area).

The emphasis is on library-initiated programs for two reasons. The first is that most of the action in those libraries with a vigorous commitment to instruction comes in programs generated within the libraries. Second, librarians view students' information and retrieval skill needs from a unique perspective that affords them a much broader view than an individual instructor or student could achieve.

Within this framework, programs will be categorized according to whether they offer instruction to students through cooperative contacts with the faculty as an intermediary (as in a bibliographic lecture in an academic course), or to students directly (as in library-developed self-guided tours, audio programs, or the library-generated course in research techniques).

The nature and degree of contact between librarians and faculty in a university depends on such variables as the official status of librarians on that campus, the extent of informal library/faculty relations, the degree of faculty prestige and conservatism, and the strength of the university's commitment to undergraduate education and its improvement. That there should be widespread contact between librarians and faculty, few librarians would dispute. It is doubtful that a goal of supporting the undergraduate teaching effort could be implemented without some mechanism for communicating with teachers, even if the communication is no more than handling requests for reserve materials. In fact, in some libraries it appears that this is the only form of communication taking place. Wilkinson's study, *Reference Services for Undergraduate Students,* in which he contrasted the service in two undergraduate libraries with two small, liberal arts college libraries, tested several hypotheses, among them

> that communications between librarians in undergraduate libraries and their faculty concerning reference services for their students have been minimal when contrasted with communications between liberal arts college librarians and faculty members concerning available reference services for their students.[14]

Communications in this context is defined as conferences with chairmen of departments and with individual faculty members; informal discussions between librarians and faculty in an academic or social situation; orientation sessions given by librarians for new faculty, brochures, letters, memoranda, or other written material sent to faculty by librarians, and other similar methods.

Analysis of the data proved this hypothesis, at least in the institutions under study, to Wilkinson's satisfaction. He attributes different degrees of communication in part to the degree of acceptance of librarians as peers by the faculty.[15] While faculty status would seem to contribute to increased contacts, not all undergraduate librarians who have such status feel that they are viewed as peers by their classroom colleagues or that communication has improved significantly. Changing attitudes will follow only after a vigorous demonstration of the library's teaching capabilities.

Several of the undergraduate librarians surveyed identified faculty attitudes as one of the major obstacles in providing instruction in library use. Patricia Knapp describes thoroughly the problems that confront a library attempting to establish an active service image in a traditional institution. She warns that faculty attitudes, such as placing "a high value on 'knowing one's subject' and . . . a corresponding lack of interest in teaching methodology [as well as a] limited perception of what real understanding and skill in the use of library resources means" act to undermine library efforts in instruction.[16] Her "guidelines for bucking the system" are required reading for librarians planning strategic approaches to this problem.[17]

Turning to a consideration of actual programs in use in undergraduate libraries to instruct students through formal curriculum channels, it is not surprising to find that most programs are attached to first year, English or, in some cases, its successor in the undergraduate curriculum. Where a required course of this type exists, it is still seen as an appropriate place to provide an initial round of instruction in library use.

Library orientation in conjunction with first-year English has an unattractive reputation as the largely irrelevant "library lecture" or its technological off-spring, the slide/tape program. Actually, such approaches are on the decline now, at least in undergraduate libraries, as librarians develop an increased sensitivity to student needs, preferences, and communication styles. Unfortunately, in abandoning such programs some librarians have thrown out the baby with the bath water, leaving nothing in the area of course-related instruction. In fact, where lower-division students can be "caught" in a required course that involves appropriate library activity, librarians have an excellent opportunity to provide meaningful instruction.

However, at many institutions, first-year English has been either disbanded or made optional. Where this is the case, librarians who seek to offer course-related instruction have to identify appropriate courses, in terms of both content and student level, in which to concentrate their instructional efforts. At the University of California at San Diego, a module on library use has been incorporated into a program of urban and rural studies; the University of California at Berkeley provides term paper help for students in a junior-level history course; Washington gives assistance in English 172, College Writing. Obviously, none of these support activities reaches an entire class of students after the fashion of first-year English; but, if the right combination of courses could be selected, it would be possible to cover a significant proportion of the student body without too much duplication.

In an endeavor like library instruction where they tend to be the exception rather than the rule, good programs are bound to be imitated. The example of intensive subject-oriented reference service to classes offered by the Earlham College Library (itself influenced by Patricia Knapp's Monteith College Library experiment) has inspired many librarians, though its measurable effects on undergraduate libraries with their massive student populations have so far been negligible. The Michigan Undergraduate Library cites Earlham's influence in connection with a projected plan for giving intensive support to an Asian studies program. At Washington, special funding made it possible for the undergraduate library to offer intensive library support to a few classes during spring 1973; this support included joint library-faculty preparation of assignments that would develop library skills while introducing the content of the course, formal instruction by the librarian in the classroom, librarian-prepared bibliographic guides to accompany assignments, and the development of a variety of multimedia guides to literature of the field. The amount of staff time required for the planning and preparation of materials for this level of course support prohibits rapid widespread application for most libraries. If applied to the right courses in the curriculum, however, it could have considerable impact on both student research skill and faculty attitudes.

Another influential program, designed to meet the challenge of large student population and limited librarian time, is the Library Skills course developed at UCLA College Library by Miriam Dudley.[18] In this program, which was initiated by a request from the Chicano Studies office and is currently administered through the Office of Recruitment and Development, students complete a series of assignments in a workbook at their own pace. It has been adapted by the Michigan and Washington undergraduate libraries for use primarily with disadvantaged students.

The importance of working to develop programs of library instruction within the regular curriculum cannot be overstated. These programs, when carefully planned and implemented, would seem to provide the most efficient and attractive type of library instruction in terms of real student needs. They offer the additional benefits to the library of: (1) increasing faculty-library communication; (2) legitimizing the librarian as a participant in the formal instructional process; and (3) affecting the curriculum itself by reforming teaching methods. The potential payoff for the library that cares about improving the quality of undergraduate education is tremendous. So are the obstacles. But it is an avenue that librarians—particularly undergraduate librarians—cannot afford to ignore; nor, having been rebuffed in the past, can they afford to give up trying this approach.

In contrast to cooperative efforts with faculty in specific courses, or with administrators, as in the self-paced Library Skills program, the other major category of instruction in undergraduate libraries includes all programs developed by the library staff for direct use of students. The advantages of multimedia approaches to this type of instruction have been recognized for some time, and undergraduate libraries, typically serving large populations and also frequently housing audiovisual facilities, have made use of media in a variety of ways. The audio tour for building orientation has been well received at Tennessee and UCLA; multimedia orientation programs are currently in use or in preparation at several institutions; Michigan State has a slide/tape program that instructs students in the use of basic reference tools. Several institutions report having tried videotape programs of one sort or another, but all cite problems with their programs, perhaps indicating that this medium has less applicability to library instruction than a simple audio or sound-with-slide approach. At Washington, for example, videotapes are used for physical introduction to library collections, services, and routines, though probably not as effectively as small-group tours. The videotapes are time-consuming to make, require considerable technical expertise to do well, and quickly become outdated.

Two influential programs in direct librarian-to-student instruction had their origins at M.I.T., as part of the CLR-funded Project Intrex. For instruction in the use of individual library tools, the "point-of-use" audiotape approach has been adopted by several undergraduate libraries.[19] These programs offer the advantage of relative ease of preparation and maintenance and provide independent self-instruction to large numbers of users at the time when instruction is needed. Washington currently has seven of these tapes in the reference area; the subjects range from use of the card catalog to explanations of *PAIS* and *Bibliographic Index*. Maryland is producing audiotapes to be located in several reference clusters spread throughout the building.

Library Pathfinders also originated at M.I.T. These bibliographic guides to principal information sources on a narrowly defined topic have been expanded to cover topics in the humanities and social sciences as well as science-technology.[20] A number of undergraduate libraries have subscribed to *Pathfinders* and some are also engaged in their preparation.

Special sessions on research paper techniques, offered to individuals or groups at appropriate times during the academic term, constitute another promising mode of direct library-student instruction. However, few of the librarians queried were engaged in such programs. Indeed, one institution had abandoned the practice of in-library lectures because of light attendance. On the other hand, Indiana considers its well-known program of "Reference Raps," individualized instruction by appointment, highly successful.

The most expensive form of library-to-student instruction in use in undergraduate libraries is the formal, nonrequired course in bibliography, taught by one or more library staff members for regular academic credit (two–three credit hours as a rule). Stanford's course, the oldest among the libraries surveyed, was started in 1967, and is presently being examined for possible revision with an eye to building in a greater degree of self-instruction. Michigan and Washington have also offered such a course. At UC-Berkeley, "Bibliography I" was developed in 1968 and has had remarkable success in terms of student response and institutionalization; it is now under the official auspices of the Library School.[21] However, this course was not initiated by the undergraduate library (which was not yet in existence in 1968), and it is not currently an undergraduate library program, although some of the undergraduate librarians participate in its teaching, along with librarians from other parts of the system. The UC-Berkeley course has been particularly influential in contributing to the resurgence of interest in credit courses. The major advantage of formal courses is the in-depth bibliographic instruction that can be given, in many cases tailored to each student's particular needs and interests. Their greatest disadvantage is that they reach a relatively small number of students in proportion to the investment of librarians' time. UC-Berkeley's course, by far the largest operation, accepted 500 pre-enrollments in Winter Quarter 1973, out of an undergraduate population of approximately 20,000; 12 librarians received 10 hours a week released time in order to participate in the program.

The two elements that seem most likely to ensure successful programs of direct library-student instruction are (1) instruction available at the time of need and (2) instruction that carries academic credit. Other factors that certainly affect the development of programs are staff interest, capabilities, and time. At Washington, special funding was successfully sought outside the library's budget to release an undergraduate reference librarian to work on point-of-use tapes and the formal course.

A number of undergraduate libraries are offering instruction concurrently in several of the modes described above. The general belief is that different kinds of library instruction are needed to respond to a variety of student needs. Other librarians explain that they keep trying new approaches, with the hope of finding the magic combination that will solve all problems without further ado. Still another factor that contributes to the multiprogram approach is the predisposition of individual librarians who carry their favored methods with them when they move to new positions or who value novelty.

There is very little evidence, however, that institutions with variety in their instructional program are acting in accordance with a master plan. Coherent and ordered goals in the area of undergraduate library-use competence are conspicuously absent. The typical approach instead, where there is any thought given to the matter at all, seems to be to look at one's programs and justify them in terms of the user needs that each fills. John Haak speaks directly to this problem, pointing out that undergraduate libraries have typically expressed their service function in intangible goal statements, but have avoided the real challenge of translating these general aims into tangible, operating goals that can serve as guides in program development.[22]

One dimension of the development of a comprehensive plan for library use education of students is the identification of student needs. The survey of library users, which measures types of users, user attitudes toward the library, or what users perceive as their needs, is a fairly common exercise. Surveys of nonusers like those of John Lubans, while more difficult in execution, can also be of value. In the final analysis, however, surveys depend for their validity and applicability on skills of construction, administration, and analysis that most librarians lack.

A more common method of gauging user needs in libraries is simply by observing the demands made on the library staff at the various service points. The tricky part here is that librarians must be certain that they are, in fact, identifying these needs correctly, not merely accepting the superficial need expressed by the student when he or she approaches the reference desk. One of Wilkinson's personal observations based on his study was that of the institutions under his scrutiny; Earlham librarians did a better job than the others of ascertaining and responding to the real needs of students asking reference questions.[23] Undergraduate librarians, with their idealistic statements about giving service especially attuned to the undergraduate's information requirements, should examine closely their reference techniques, in the light of Wilkinson's observations, to see whether they are really performing adequately in the one-to-one confrontations that for most undergraduate libraries constitute the major area of instructional contact with students.

The sequential nature of an effective library instruction program has been recognized for many years. It formed the basis of Patricia Knapp's Monteith experiment and is one of the themes that Verna Melum Beardsley found running through the responses to her 1971 survey of library orientation and instruction programs.[24] Among undergraduate libraries, its articulation can be observed at Tennessee where a five-part program is being developed that includes (1) an audio tour, (2) *Library Pathfinders,* (3) point-of-use instruction cassettes, (4) bibliographic search guides for the different disciplines, and (5) individualized course-related bibliographic lecture-demonstrations.[25] At Washington, programs are operating or being planned for each of the four levels of need that have been recognized: (1) general orientation, (2) use of specific tools, (3) search strategies for different kinds of information needs, and (4) subject-related bibliographic understanding.

The current activity of the Association of College and Research Libraries' Ad

Hoc Committee on Bibliographic Instruction is directly concerned with planning a sequential program of library instruction. The committee is presently working to identify, in behavioral and attitudinal terms, the specific components of library competence that should be mastered by undergraduates. Once these objectives are specifically defined, the committee hopes to develop techniques for measuring progress in meeting objectives. It is the committee's intent that libraries planning instructional programs will benefit from this information and that more widespread attention to a planned sequence of effective library instruction will be facilitated by its work.

PROBLEMS IN UNDERGRADUATE LIBRARY INSTRUCTION

Undergraduate librarians explain lack of activity in the instructional area, notwithstanding their avowed interest in developing programs, in terms of a variety of external and internal constraints.

SIZE OF STUDENT BODY

Most institutions mention the size of the student population as a major problem. There is no question but that Earlham, with something over 1,000 students and five librarians, can reach more of the student body in class-related instruction sessions than can the five librarians at Michigan State's undergraduate library, with 35,000 students. Student populations of 18,000 to 30,000 undergraduates are characteristic of institutions with separate undergraduate libraries. However, there appears to be no correlation between the degree of activity in developing course-related instruction and size of student body. Maryland, Michigan, Tennessee, and Washington are all examples of large institutions trying to provide such instruction; Harvard, with a far smaller undergraduate population, is making no such effort. Size of student population, then, may require new approaches to class-related instruction, but it is not a decisive factor in determining whether the library will enter into such activity.

CURRICULUM

The nature of the undergraduate curriculum presents difficulties also. Although the priorities at large universities have for some time tended to favor graduate and research programs, there is evidence at many institutions of real concern for improving the quality of undergraduate education. The Stanford undergraduate librarian described a study of education at Stanford (1967–1968), for example, that resulted in a set of recommendations that in many parts anticipates the Carnegie Commission's report. At the University of Washington, a much larger institution, an Office of Undergraduate Studies provides leadership, advice, and funding to instructors who are experimenting with curricular offerings or teaching methods.

An increase in flexibility in the undergraduate curriculum is one effect of educational reform; another is the introduction of new courses and majors on broad, interdisciplinary subjects. Both of these changes have implications for the undergraduate library's instructional activity. Curriculum flexibility, as such, does not appear to be an inhibiting factor for undergraduate libraries initiating course-related instruction, except, as mentioned above, in making it more difficult to identify key courses. The introduction of new courses into the curriculum may well represent an opportunity for the library. Michigan and the University of California at San Diego, as described above, have developed instructional programs in conjunction with interdisciplinary programs. Instruction in such courses is often (1) nontraditional in mode and (2) inhibited at the outset by a lack of appropriate materials. An alert undergraduate library can, at this point, be very effective in establishing continuing partnerships with classroom faculty.

THE ADMINISTRATION'S VIEWS

Administrative attitudes toward the undergraduate library are not so much described as implied in the statements of individual librarians. Two elements are to be considered here: the library administration and the university administration. Meaningful support of undergraduate library goals by the library administration must include adequate budget for staff as well as materials. When the undergraduate library staff is reduced to a skeleton level of two or three, the library administration usually has no expectation that instructional services are to be offered. Several librarians mention that they have requested a position in their libraries of orientation or instruction librarian without success. If the library administration does not recognize the peculiar capabilities of the undergraduate library, but sees it primarily as a study hall, the library's chances for survival, to say nothing of effectiveness, are greatly reduced.

The university administration may also be relatively unconscious of or insensitive to the unique qualities of the undergraduate library. Two libraries report funding for large staffs and special projects that stems directly from the university administration's interest in greater involvement of the libraries in undergraduate education. However, often the library (and not just the undergraduate library) suffers from relative invisibility on campus. Two undergraduate librarians state that university committees appointed to study problems directly relating to undergraduate activities failed to include undergraduate library representation.

STAFF ACTIVITY AND ATTITUDES

There appears to be a positive correlation between undergraduate library staff size and stated commitment to instructional goals. Whether this situation reflects the administrative view of the undergraduate library or whether the library has, in effect, earned its staff size by its degree of activity is not always clear. What is apparent is an intriguing coincidence: that undergraduate libraries that are actively carrying on instructional programs have managed to keep up their staffing levels, while others have often found their staffs cut.

Other staff characteristics may also affect library success in initiating instruction programs. One characteristic that clearly does is the commitment and enthusiasm of individual staff members. Just as the library's attention to instruction depends on staff commitment, so the quality of programs developed depends on the resourcefulness and originality of the entire staff. Where undergraduate library staff members are recruited with this goal in view, the chances for success are greatly increased.

Many undergraduate libraries sport a young staff; in at least one case an age limitation was written into the original job description. Most would probably agree that age per se is not the most important factor, but that a youthful staff makes it easier to establish rapport with the student body. One of the consequences of concentrating on a young staff is that it increases the likelihood of staff turnover. For those libraries with a clear set of operating goals, such turnover can have a positive effect. In other cases, frequent changes of staff may mean frequent changes of direction with little evidence of achievement.

Another staffing characteristic present in several of the libraries is the utilization of librarianship students, through a cooperative agreement with either the institution's own library school or a nearby school, to assist in the undergraduate library reference area without drawing on library payroll funds. Of the eight institutions having this resource available, four had established relationships with these students, in most cases on a fieldwork basis. Any means for augmenting personnel in the reference area should be explored. Library school students who have learned the basic skills of reference assistance can be an asset to the library while gaining for themselves invaluable practical experience. Inasmuch as insufficient staffing is one of the major obstacles to expansion of instructional services outside the library, every effort should be made to develop a mutually advantageous arrangement of this kind with schools of librarianship wherever they exist on or near campuses with undergraduate libraries.

FACULTY RESPONSE

Faculty attitudes are cited as a major problem in developing instructional programs at a number of institutions. Significantly, the libraries that are trying to initiate course-related instruction recognize that faculty are often hesitant about accepting a librarian as a teaching partner, while at institutions where service is primarily responsive, the problem is perceived as "getting the faculty to ask for help." Librarian initiative and diplomacy, particularly along the lines suggested by Knapp, offer the best potential for effecting attitude change among the faculty. Faculty status, while perhaps helpful, is not the end of the matter. Constructive and mutually profitable contacts with faculty in any form—to discuss collection development, clarify an assignment, or consider library policies —should be encouraged among all staff members.

FUNDING

Finally, since inadequate funding is one of the librarian's most common complaints in explaining inactivity, the effect of special funding sources on library instruction activity merits consideration. Several of the programs described here were made possible through special institutional funds reserved for innovative educational programs. The current surge of interest in undergraduate education and its improvement means that such funding sources will probably continue to be available at many institutions. The resourceful undergraduate library will seek to identify such sources wherever they may be found and work actively for a share to support its instructional efforts.

A second theme, which recurs in undergraduate library program descriptions and has implications for funding sources, is the program that operates not through an academic department but through administrative channels, to develop skills needed by disadvantaged students for success in college. Most universities are actively committed by now to the encouragement of minority student applicants through special-admissions policies. These students often receive extra orientation and tutorial assistance during their first year. Generally, a special office or administrative department on campus is charged with academic services to these students. Where this is the case, the undergraduate library can often tap funds allocated to this office if it can offer a well-planned program for these students. This is how the UCLA Library Skills program has been used in several instances, for disadvantaged students are a particularly appropriate target group for the very basic instructional level of this program.

COMMITMENT OF UNDERGRADUATE LIBRARIES TO INSTRUCTIONAL GOALS

A basic question that recurs throughout any study of undergraduate library instructional programs is: To what extent are undergraduate libraries actually committed to the goal of providing active service to students in the form of library instruction over and above reference-area service? Braden's survey, as well as others of the late 1960s, described undergraduate libraries primarily in terms of their physical characteristics and, to a lesser extent, in terms of the services (often, as John Haak notes, confused with resources) that were available within the building. Reference service within the undergraduate library has been scrutinized—and criticized—by Wilkinson. But up to 1970, the question of whether undergraduate libraries should be doing more and different kinds of things in the area of instruction had not really been faced.

At the 1970 San Diego conference, two papers in particular attacked this question head-on. For John Haak:

> Problems of purpose associated with undergraduate libraries are related to a lack of definition of whom these libraries are to serve and how. While there may be no such thing as a purely undergraduate level book or even book collection, there are services which are more appropriate for undergraduates than for other members of the academic community. It is these services that make the library uniquely an undergraduate library.[26]

Haak further breaks down appropriate undergraduate library services into two areas: self-service and active-service capabilities. By self-service, he refers to the services described by Braden as inherent in the building plan. He defines the active-service capability as

> one which revolves around the concept of the undergraduate librarian as teacher rather than technician. Active library service is totally dependent on the library staff and on its ability to work with faculty and students, and requires the participation of the librarian inside and outside of the library building. It is with these active services that the librarian binds the library to the curriculum and guides the student in the use of the library's resources.[27]

Patricia Knapp, using the same terminology, describes the elements (including faculty and student attitudes, the curriculum, the library system, and the university administration) in a large university system that affect the implementation of "active library service in collaboration with the teaching faculty," [28] and suggests practical methods by which librarians can counteract negative influences inherent in these elements. Knapp identifies four commonly held views on the undergraduate library: (1) as an administrative sop for the neglected undergraduate; (2) as an instrument for pure efficiency in providing mass service; (3) as a gentlemen's library with select materials and an ambiance of cultural stimulation; and, finally (4) as the perspective, endorsed by Knapp, of a teaching library.[29] Describing this fourth point of view as it has been articulated by library spokesmen, Knapp writes:

> Some of these statements (goals) use phrases like "instructional tool" or "learning workshops" which suggest something more than or different from mere retrieval skills, that is, the ability to *locate* books and articles and information.
> Presumably that "something more" occurs to some extent in the teaching emphasis in undergraduate library reference service. . . . But the phrases suggest, also, a more general and total involvement in undergraduate education, a role which is well-described in the terms "active service capability" and "the concept of the librarian as teacher" which were used in the proposal for this Institute.[30]

Knapp concludes: "The teaching perspective is probably the least realistic of the four suggested. But it is also the most challenging. So let us take up the challenge." [31]

The intangible goals statements that Knapp refers to are, as Haak points out, not generally supported by corresponding sets of tangible goals. Furthermore, evidence of actions that indicate a working, as opposed to a purely theoretical commitment to these goals, is entirely lacking in several undergraduate libraries. The phenomenon of goal displacement that Haak describes so well is apparently widespread in these institutions.

Wilkinson's study confirmed for him the hypothesis that

> no effective means of stimulating use of reference services (such as integrating bibliographical lectures or discussions by librarians with courses at the exact time students have need of such assistance) have been developed by reference librarians in separate undergraduate libraries.[32]

Wilkinson, of course, based his study on only two such libraries, and his data are already four years old. Of the undergraduate libraries in the study, one has since then initiated a variety of service activities in this area (the Library Skills workbook for disadvantaged students, a formal two-credit course, and, in preparation, more course-related instruction with the English and Asian studies departments); the other is still essentially at the planning stage, although instruction is recognized as a high-priority undergraduate library concern. Of the 18 libraries surveyed for the present report, three apparently give no thought to this kind of instruction, and the others are about equally divided between passive-commitment and active-commitment stances. Clearly, the San Diego conference and the Wilkinson report have had some influence, but not enough undergraduate libraries are working on this problem to tip the balance toward active programs.

John Haak warned in 1970: "For many undergraduate libraries the honeymoon period is now ending . . . the day finally dawns when the issue of the undergraduate library's effectiveness is raised, and the honeymoon is over." [33] When this day arrives, undergraduate libraries must be able to justify their existence, to point to the element or elements that make them not just distinctive but indispensable in the university library system. Can the library possibly hope to base its self-defense on its attractive building, full of built-in student appeal? Can it cite with pride its "select" collection—which may not have grown according to the same careful criteria that it was originally assembled with? Can it honestly believe that a research-oriented faculty will be convinced that students should have a buffer library full of easy-use features, to wean them gently to the realities of large research collections? Will its vast compilation of statistics on building and collection use stand it in good stead? It is more likely that undergraduate libraries will be judged in terms of the necessity of what they do within the university system. They must have a visible and significant impact on the educational process.

At this point, it is essential that undergraduate libraries be able to measure and produce evidence of the qualitative elements of their programs. This includes, as a first step, clear definition of the library's objectives in operational terms; it also involves assessing program costs and giving high priority to the development of techniques for measuring program effectiveness.

SOME GUIDELINES

In planning programs appropriate to its resources and the needs of its users, the undergraduate library must not lose sight of institutional factors that dictate program limitations. It cannot hope to imitate in toto such programs as Earlham's; but it can borrow features from this and other successful programs, to the extent that these features are compatible with a large university environment. Some guidelines include:

1. Be constantly alert to effective applications of media, to counteract the overwhelming ratio of library users to library staff.

2. Seek out the "best" courses for library support activities, while continuing to offer limited support to any course that requests or demonstrates the need for it. ("Best" should be defined in terms of course content; extent to which library instruction can be integrated with this content, rather than superimposed upon it; student composition; potential for reaching a large group of students over a period of time; appropriateness in terms of sequential skills development; and faculty cooperativeness.)

3. Emphasize library-initiated development of programs that help the users to help themselves independently at their point of need.

4. Seek any potential staff resources that might be locally available and that could help to free the professional staff for greater involvement in outreach activities.

5. Find funding sources on the local and national level to finance experimental programs.

6. Invest time, thought, and energy in developing a rationale and plan for instructional programs, including elements of assessment of need, objective setting, program development and implementation, analysis of costs and effectiveness, and evaluation.

An undergraduate library that tries to define its uniqueness and indispensability to the academic community in terms of resources, or by citing some special mystique in its reference service is only deceiving itself. Wilkinson's study should dispel any notions held by undergraduate librarians that their reference service is automatically superior or more attuned to student needs than reference service given elsewhere.

In the last analysis, the undergraduate library will stand or fall on the extent to which it is uniquely identified with the undergraduate teaching/learning process. To develop the special facets of this, involvement should be the prime goal of the undergraduate library staff. It will not derive from faculty initiative in methodologies of teaching, or from students' increasing involvement in independent study, or from a sudden rise of interest in learning and reading among students. Librarians who await such developments to start generating a rush for their services will have a long wait. Commitment to the improvement of undergraduate education, individual initiative, and clear operating objectives are the prime and necessary ingredients in the full realization of the potential value of the undergraduate library.

NOTES

1. Carnegie Commission on Higher Education, *Reform on Campus: Changing Students, Changing Academic Programs* (New York: McGraw-Hill, 1972), pp. 23–24.
2. Robert Muller, "The Undergraduate Library Trend at Large Universities," in *Advances in Librarianship* I, ed. by Melvin J. Voigt (New York: Academic Press, 1970), p. 113.
3. Irene Braden, *The Undergraduate Library* (Chicago: American Library Association, 1970), p. 2.
4. Ibid., p. 21.
5. Ibid., p. 2.
6. Ibid., p. 3.
7. John R. Haak, "Goal Determination and the Undergraduate Library" (paper presented at Institute on Training for Service in Undergraduate Libraries, University of California, San Diego, August 17–21, 1970), p. 10.
8. Ibid., p. 2.
9. Patricia B. Knapp, "The Library, the Undergraduate and the Teaching Faculty" (paper presented at Institute on Training for Service in Undergraduate Libraries, University of California, San Diego, August 17–21, 1970).
10. Carnegie Commission on Higher Education, op. cit., p. 4.
11. Ibid., p. 50.

12. Cornell, Harvard, Illinois, Indiana, Maryland, Michigan, Michigan State, Nebraska, North Carolina, Southern Illinois (Carbondale), Stanford, Tennessee, Texas, University of California at Berkeley, University of California at Los Angeles, University of California at San Diego, University of Washington, and University of British Columbia.

13. Braden, op. cit., pp. 73–74.

14. Billy R. Wilkinson, *Reference Services for Undergraduate Students: Four Case Studies* (Metuchen, N.J.: Scarecrow Press, 1972), pp. 5–18.

15. Ibid., p. 339.

16. Knapp, op. cit., p. 6.

17. Patricia B. Knapp, "Guidelines for Bucking the System: A Strategy for Moving Toward the Ideal of the Undergraduate Library as a Teaching Instrument," *Drexel Library Quarterly* 7 (1971): 217–221.

18. Miriam Dudley, "Teaching Library Skills to College Students," in *Advances in Librarianship,* vol. 3, ed. by Melvin J. Voigt (New York: Seminar Press, 1972), pp. 95–104.

19. Jeffrey J. Gardner, "Point-of-Use Library Instruction," *Drexel Library Quarterly* 8 (1972): 281–286.

20. Marie P. Canfield, "Library Pathfinders," *Drexel Library Quarterly* 8 (1972): 287–300.

21. This course is described by Dudley, "Teaching Library Skills . . . ," pp. 92–95.

22. Haak, op. cit., pp. 5–9.

23. Wilkinson, op. cit., p. 343.

24. Verna V. Melum, "1971 Survey of Library Orientation and Instructions Programs," *Drexel Library Quarterly* 7 (1971): 227–228.

25. Tennessee University Library Orientation Committee, "A Proposal for the Development of a 5-Level Program of Library Instruction," mimeographed (October 27, 1972).

26. Haak, op. cit., p. 3.

27. Ibid., p. 15.

28. Knapp, op. cit., p. 1.

29. Ibid., pp. 33–37.

30. Ibid., pp. 36–37.

31. Ibid., p. 37.

32. Wilkinson, op. cit., p. 6.

33. Haak, op. cit.

A HISTORIC LOOK AT LIBRARY INTEGRATION IN TECHNOLOGICAL UNIVERSITIES

EDWARD A. CHAPMAN
*Director of Libraries Emeritus, Rensselaer
Polytechnic Institute*

Faculty use of the library in teaching continues more the exception than the rule, though lately library research efforts on the subject have been intensified.[1] In all fairness it must be said, an appreciable number of technological university faculty would utilize the library were its resources and services adequate for developing well-rounded reading and reference support to their teaching efforts. Until recently the progressive inadequacy of more than a few technological university libraries stemmed from parsimonious and reluctant funding, which far from improving service and collection competence could not even support the status quo. Indeed, it caused consistently gradual erosion and retrogression of such competence as did exist, through cancellation of subscriptions, the bypassing of newly appearing and obviously important periodicals and monographs, unsuccessful recruitment of new and replacement professional personnel at noncompetitive salaries, and reduction in hours of service. Under this circumstance individual pleas for needed library support went unheeded by the administration, with the faculty member backing off muttering "you can't beat city hall." For reasons given later this sorry pattern is gradually giving away to fairly active administrative fostering of library resources and services development.

Again, until recently, college and university presidents, feeling little or no organized pressure from their faculties, have said for the record that their libraries are indeed essential to their educational and research facilities and

This paper describes an innovative library-use instruction program undertaken more than 20 years ago. Its approach is as viable today as then in trying to solve the information-use problems in the technological fields as well as other disciplines. The author was chairman of the Engineering School Libraries Committee of the American Society for Engineering Education when the national program described here was initiated and developed.—EDITOR

132

services; that they thought of libraries as centers of information; and that there is no question but that their libraries are important components of their institutions. All such pious and vague bromides are usually modified by some such statement as that the main problem is the amount of money required in relation to *other institutional obligations* (euphemism for income-producing activities in which the library is regarded as not qualifying since its contribution is not readily measurable on the balance sheet).

A solution to the long-time problem of library integration with instructional and research activities has been sought by the library profession over many years, as attested by the appended bibliography to selected early readings containing discussions on library use and user training. However frustrating it has been for college and university libraries in general, perhaps the greatest difficulty has been and is being experienced by those serving sci-tech educational institutions or technological universities.

This state of affairs is traceable as far back as the earliest times of technological education. From the beginning until beyond the 1950s technological institutions were largely dedicated to turning out engineers to fill specific vocational requirements, to supply industry with instant engineers trained in the practices of specific industries, that is, trained in the current state of industrial arts. As late as the 1920s a teaching practice dating from the beginning of engineering education in this country early in the nineteenth century was common: that of the students writing their course "textbooks" based upon the oracular lectures of their teachers. Published textbooks for given courses played a secondary role to the lecture, a couple of handbooks of technologic data, the slide rule and the drawing board.[2, 3]

The library simply was not a student's learning resource—far from it—and, as late as the 1940s it was the rare engineering teacher who promoted literature use.[4] Thus the library existed merely as a gesture toward the requirements of accreditation and respectability, receiving support commensurate with that attitude and enjoying recognition only to the extent that nobody was against it. This attitude has begun to fade in the last decade or so due to technical education's changing tendency, away from vocational training and toward the teaching of theory and principle basic to technologic results. This change in teaching methods is requiring engineering students to consult the "literature" in order to make their own judgments and to learn by inquiry rather than from authority. Another factor of not inconsiderable impact has been the federal incentive grants for college and university resources under the now moribund (1973) Title II-A of the Higher Education Act requiring schools to show fiscal improvement in library support and interinstitutional cooperation to qualify for year to-year grants.

Professional concern about the tenuous position of library services in science and technology and the apparent apathy toward library utility in such educational institutions crystalized in a pioneering effort, in late 1949, by the then Engineering School Libraries (ESL) Committee of the American Society for Engineering Education (ASEE): a long-range study of the elements of library service vital to science and technology. The governing objective of the program was to generate common recognition of the library as a dynamic factor in high-level student learning, in teaching, and in successful research.

Library literature is studded with many accounts of individual efforts directed toward identifying libraries with teaching and research and the problems encountered in trying to reach this goal. Faculty apathy and disregard resulting in student disinterest, lack of administrative policy, and financial support were a few deterrents. What was pioneering about the ESL Committee's program was its approach to this perennial library problem on a *nationally coordinated* scale designed to involve all the librarians and concerned faculty of science-technology universities in a concerted group effort to establish the role of the library as an integral agency in sci-tech education.

The committee proceeded on the well-founded premise that faculty involvement in library-use instruction, literature-use promotion, and library resources development under strong library professional leadership was required if library identification with teaching and research was to be achieved. It further was held that librarians must take the initial steps in establishing cooperation between faculty and librarians in defining library services and facilities that will contribute directly to the execution of instructional programs and research at all levels and in planning the application of these library services and facilities. Only in this way could the library be transformed into an active participant in educational and research programs, instead of having to abjectly solicit that use be made of its resources and services.

In the begining ESL Committee discussions centered around the problematical situation of faculty and student apathy toward library utility. Typical observations and arguments were: [5]

1. Time and efficiency which are so important to the success of any engineering endeavor, too often are sacrificed where even a small amount of literature-searching skill on the part of the investigation would have saved both.

2. The ability to find information quickly can be an asset of high economic value. Such ability will be found to be of measurable value from the first year of college through an engineer's entire career.

3. The potentialities of library techniques and resources are seriously overlooked by the studying, the teaching and the practicing engineer alike.

4. It is the librarian's responsibility to advertise these potentialities and to give the library's community an opportunity to take advantage of them.

5. This advertising must be done on a nationwide basis. It must be striking, persuasive and sufficiently forceful not only to dissolve existing barriers of apathy but to inspire active interest in the library as a concrete aid in teaching, in investigation, and developmental work.

The plan for generating maximum integration of library services and resources with teaching and research activities included the following major facets:

1. ESL groups were organized in the 16 regional sections of the ASEE; these comprised technical librarians and faculty irrespective of their affiliation with ASEE. This, in the main, was accomplished with the cooperation of the association's section chairmen who appointed chairmen for the ESL section groups.

The ESL National Executive Committee supplied ESL section chairmen with suggestions and instructions designed to standardize the format of the group organization and the content and pattern of group meetings including the annual conferences of the national ESL Committee.[6]

Since attainment of the goal sought would necessarily involve faculty, it was specified that the basic organization should be a mix of librarians and faculty members with known interest in library use. Similarly, programmed conferences were to include faculty members at large, practicing engineers, and others with technologic interests and not be conducted as librarian discussion sessions. Without the views, opinions, and advice of such people, without acceptance of and participation in library-use promotion and instruction by faculty particularly, there was little chance of reaching any meaningful level of integration with teaching, student learning, and research.

Examples of programmed conferences applying the foregoing policy included a meeting on "The Present State of Engineering Literature" discussed by three representatives of publishers of technical literature and a leading technological university library director, with an audience of engineering educators, engineering writers and librarians; a meeting on "The Importance of Engineering Literature to Practicing Engineers" as seen by a quality-control supervisor, a consulting engineer, a director of research, and a government engineer; a meeting on "Technical Information Services" as related to engineering education with three discussants from the Atomic Energy Commission and the Brookhaven National Laboratory; and a meeting on "Teaching the Use of the Engineering School Library" with discussion papers given by a faculty member and an engineering school librarian.

To assist sectional ESL groups in thinking through these matters the ESL Executive Committee supplied memoranda detailing all possible elements conceivably applicable to reaching the program's overall goal. The points covered such matters as librarian-faculty and library-faculty relationships, services to faculty, faculty participation in the development of library services and resources, library-student and general relationships of a promotional or "advertising" character.[7]

ESL's governing objective was this: to effect recognition of the library as a coordinated agency of education with as much responsibility and significance in teaching and research as any department of instruction; an objective whose realization depended directly upon the individual librarian's acceptance of responsibility and the conviction that the integration of library services with teaching and research is a significant phase of successful professional work in libraries serving educational institutions.

2. A survey was made of a group of 1,000 practicing engineers to test the validity (and, hopefully, find confirmation) of the need of instruction in library and literature use for technical students. This questionnaire survey of opinion was conceived with the objectives of determining whether practicing engineers regarded literature use as a factor in job skill, and if so, whether this constitutes a directive to technical schools and possibly to industrial self-improvement training. The 11-item questionnaires asked opinions on the following points:

(a) What value do you place on library-use or literature-use "know how"?
(b) What training have you had in this direction?
(c) Do you think such training is desirable or even essential for prospective engineers?
(d) What ideas do you have on the sort of training, if any, that should be given?

The mailing list for the survey consisted of 200 names randomly selected from each of the 1952 membership directories of the following five societies: American Institute of Chemical Engineers, American Institute of Electrical Engineers, American Institute of Mining and Metallurgical Engineers, American Society of Civil Engineers, and the American Society of Mechanical Engineers.

Concurrently, to gain notice for the project in the engineering profession at large, a release—"Do Engineers Need Literature-Use 'Know-How'?"—was sent to the editors of some dozen technical journals. It was favorably received and published by the majority.

Of the 966 engineers actually receiving the questionnaire, 495 or 51.2 percent replied. Analyzed by society the percentage returns varied from 40.1 percent to 56.9 percent in the case of A.S.M.E. members. In general, here is what the composite engineer believed, at that time, about the use of engineering literature and the need of knowing how to use it:

(a) He apparently felt that library-use and literature-use skill is an asset and an essential requirement for fully effective practice by *any* engineer.
(b) In school he didn't learn much of what he felt he should know about getting at engineering results reported in the literature; and since then had had to do some digging in unfamiliar ground applying uncertain, uneasy methods. In school also, he was given no inkling of the importance of engineering literature, how to use it, and how to get at it, as a needed tool in engineering practice.
(c) If he had had the decision, he would have recommended that his school give emphasis to the teaching techniques in library use and literature use, and in the basic literature resources of specific engineering fields resulting in easy familiarity with such resources on the job.

Detailing the composite engineer's interest a bit, he considered awareness of literature that reports activities and developments in fields related to his own specialty as of first priority value; how to use guides to printed information, bibliographic, abstracting and indexing services, was his second ranking need; and given equal emphasis was knowledge of how to ask for specific information in a library and an understanding of library catalogs, subject classification schemes and other literature-locating devices.

The project yielded only the foregoing generalized information suggesting investigation of specific elements entering into the respondent's reactions. Detailed analysis of the raw data was not completed and left unanswered such questions as the following: Were length of practice and age factors in the replies and what was the "interest pattern" based on these factors? Did particular professional society affiliation have any bearing on attitudes toward the subject? What, if any, were the programs indicated for technical schools and companies to meet the need evidenced by respondents for systematic knowledge of technical literature and of how to use it? Nevertheless the project did confirm emphatically the need of instruction in library use and literature use for the technical student as well as for the practicing professional man.

3. Existing types of library training in engineering colleges were surveyed. The questionnaire survey of the 150 schools with accreditation in 1952 yielded 122 replies. As was more or less anticipated, results showed that only a few schools and their libraries were using anything beyond passive training devices, such as tours, exhibits, and handbooks, and that still fewer were achieving any very real library integration with educational programs. In the majority of schools faculty interest and motivation appeared practically nonexistent.[8] However discouraging this report, the survey did bring in a collection of course outlines numbering some 70 pages, indicating that some progress was being made in user training and toward the goal of the ESL Committee.

4. Preparation of a generally applicable syllabus for user library training was planned. The objective was to outline the basic kinds of library information that are most useful to the engineer and scientist in and out of school. The project was not brought to fruition, although a considerable amount of preliminary work was done by the assigned subcommittee.

A synthesizing analysis of the course outlines received in connection with the survey of existing library instruction programs was planned. Using such innovative and effective course elements as could be found in that analysis, it was intended to pattern the proposed syllabus after the proven one-hour, one-credit course, "Instruction in the Use of the Library and the Bibliographical Tools of Research" (Engineering 3) whose beginning at the Columbia University School of Engineering dates back some 40 years.

William S. Budington, onetime engineering librarian at Columbia, describes this course and its approach:

> In general, the form-of-publication approach is used. Subject emphasis is possible since each curriculum—mechanical, industrial, electrical, etc.—has its own section of Engineering 3. The first hour is devoted to an introductory survey of purposes and methods of the course. Three periods are occupied by the principles of classification, the various uses and vagaries of the card catalog, and the making of references. Guides to the literature . . . are explained. Encyclopedias and handbooks are followed by a view of general book publishing, the national bibliographies and review sources. Then come technical bibliographies of general and special natures. The importance and use of serial literature brings in the general and special technical indexing and abstracting services. Bibliographies of bibliographies are explained. . . . The use of standards and the enormity of government documents are explored. Trade literature and a word on microfilm and documentary production and reproduction conclude the fifteen lecture periods.
>
> Each student, as his project for the course, completes a bibliography on a topic of his choosing and in his field, subject to the instructor's approval. The number

of references and the number of sources from which they are obtained are specified. The intent is not to obtain comprehensive bibliographies, but a fairly comprehensive covering of sources; the paydirt for today's subject may be worthless for tomorrow.[9]

Other projects that made preliminary progress, but were not completed by appointed subcommittees, included development of a standard minimum bibliographic reference notation for documenting engineering papers, and the setting up of a clearinghouse of information on methods and results of individual institutional work toward the goal of library integration with teaching and research through user training, faculty participation, and library-use publicity generally.

The archives of the committee also contain section ESL group reports of progress, particularly in the area of faculty participation in planning methods of library-use promotion and training. An outstanding example of library-faculty cooperation in user training resulting from ESL Committee influence, is reported in the proceedings of the conference on "Use, Mis-Use and Non-Use of Academic Libraries." [10] In this instance, sessions of a laboratory course during the entire semester were scheduled for "library research" under joint instructor-librarian guidance. The teacher of this highly specialized course, dealing with the technology of joining metals by the welding process, helped students lay out nonduplicating areas of search on the history and development of this technology. With the reference librarian assigned to assist the students, pertinent indexing and abstracting services and technical bibliographies were identified, as well as those serial publications regarded as of first importance, nationally and internationally, in the fields of metallurgy or materials science. Finally, instructions for the students' "library work" periods were prepared jointly by the instructor and the librarian.

The high measure of success of this cooperative teaching program is traceable to at least two factors: (1) the librarian took the initiative to discuss with the instructor the course content and requirements and suggested ways that the librarian thought library services could fit into the instructor's teaching activities, and (2) subsequently, students' recognition of library-use skill as a means to reach course objectives ensured their interest in the required library-use training.

It may be observed in connection with the first of these two factors that the librarian can only engage in a one-for-one persuasion campaign of long duration, looking for the help of a chain reaction when a sufficient number of faculty accepts library participation as support for their teaching and research functions.[11] The second factor mentioned involves the generating of a student motivation that cannot be uniformly expected in the "dry run" type of library-use training. Student evaluation of the briefly described course-related library-use training was unanimously and enthusiastically favorable: "Why didn't somebody tell me about this before?"

Although the aim of this paper has been to supply a brief, albeit incomplete historical sketch of the ramifications of the ESL program, the question of its effectiveness logically arises. What were the results of three years of intensive effort, beginning in late 1949, to mobilize technical school librarians nationally in this campaign to give more meaning and significance to the technical library services? The results have not been systematically measured, assessed, or quantified with respect to the scope of the program's effect and success. The following estimation is based upon personal observation and direct involvement in the program from its inception.

In the years since, it cannot be claimed that this national effort, which continues to an appreciable extent today in the ASEE, was or is electrifyingly successful. The success that has been attained is traceable to a gradual lessening of the apathy and discouragement of technical librarians in ever getting very far toward the stated goal; to a perceptibly, if slowly increasing level of faculty insistence upon the supporting functions of the library and its resources in student learning; and to increasing institutional administrative support, resulting from the foregoing pressure of the modern academic community, to the upgrading of the library's ability to function as an integral agency in the technical education process. Particularly in the last decade, due to the pressure of faculty applying the referred to modern teaching principles, governing administrations of technical institutions by and large have become concerned about the place and importance of their libraries rather than complaining about the cost of maintaining these "nonincome-producing" operations or "financial sinkholes" in their organizations.

For these reasons it is felt with some conviction that the goal of the Engineering School Libraries Committee is, after some 20 years, being attained at an accelerated degree as older faculty and librarians, bred to the vocational approach in sci-tech education, are replaced by those committed to the modern philosophy of such education emphasizing the teaching of the principles basic to technologic developments and their sociologic impact. The need of library use, literature use, and training in these skills, having assumed importance under this new technical educational philosophy, seems to be reflected by the fact that the original and somewhat ignored Engineering School Libraries Committee was accorded, in 1970, divisional status in the American Society for Engineering Education representing technical school faculty and research people nationwide.

The proposed United Engineering Information Service (1969) [12] and the Report by the Committee on Scientific and Technical Communication of the NAS—National Academy of Engineering (1969) [13] both undergird and seemingly validate the efforts of the ESL Committee initiated several years before. Emphasis in these two programs, as it was in the ESL program, is placed on lack of proper and sufficient use of published information resources by engineers, the causes of this situation and how to overcome them, determination of user needs, and required training in library use and literature use for engineering students, faculty, and practicing engineers alike.

A limitation of progress in the ESL program doubtless is the total dependence on "volunteer" participation, which under even circumscribed circumstances is not easy to mobilize in a concerted and steady effort. With the auspicious sponsorship, support, and sophisticated approach of the above programs with assigned staff, the chance to solve the pressing national problem of inadequate use of technical information in sci-tech education, research, and practice should be vastly better.

NOTES

1. Namely, the efforts promoted by grants from the Council on Library Resources and the National Endowment for the Humanities. Recipient schools include Wabash College, Dillard University, University of Colorado, Hampshire College, among others. The intent of the grants is to make the library more central to the academic life by involving administrators, teachers, students, and librarians in grant activities.
2. William S. Budington, "Training in Library Usage—The Formal Course Method" (unpublished paper, June 1949), p. 1.
3. H. L. Hazen, "The Engineering Library in Teaching, Science and Technology" (unpublished paper, June 1947), p. 1.
4. Ibid., p. 2.
5. American Society for Engineering Education, "Library Identification with Teaching and Research," report of the Executive Committee, Engineering School Libraries Committee, 1950–51 (unpublished, September 1950), pp. 1–2.
6. American Society for Engineering Education, Engineering School Libraries Committee Executive Committee, "Suggested Program for Section Meetings," supplement (The Society, February 1951).
7. American Society for Engineering Education, Engineering School Libraries Committee Executive Committee, "Possible Elements of Library Integration with Teaching and Research" memorandum (The Society, December 1950; June 1951).
8. American Society for Engineering Education, Engineering School Libraries Committee, "Survey of Existing Types of Library Training in Engineering Colleges Tabulation," in *Annual Meeting Proceedings, June 1952* (unpublished), pp. 31–34.
9. Budington, op. cit., pp. 3–4.
10. Robert A. Wyant, "Use and Non-Use of the Library in Teaching Engineering Courses," in *Use, Mis-Use and Non-Use of Academic Libraries* (Woodside, N.Y.: New York Library Association, College and University Libraries Section, 1970), pp. 21–29.
11. Edward A. Chapman, "Non-Use of an Academic Library," in *Use, Mis-Use and Non-Use of Academic Libraries* (Woodside, N.Y.: New York Library Association, College and University Libraries Section, 1970), pp. 84–85.
12. "Description of the Proposed United Engineering Information Service," *Scientific Information Notes* 1 (1969): 253.
13. National Academy of Sciences—National Academy of Engineering, Committee on Scientific and Technical Communication, *Scientific and Technical Communication* . . . (Washington, D.C.: The Academy, 1969), p. 62.

BIBLIOGRAPHY

Bonn, George S. "Bibliodynamics Laboratory." *Journal of Engineering Education* 42 (1951): 173–6.

Budington, William S. "Teaching the Use of Engineering Libraries." *College and Research Libraries* 12 (1951): 268–72.

Chapman, Edward A. "Engineers Need the Plus Factor." *Library Journal* 74 (1949): 784–787.

———. "Librarians Cannot Require Library Usage by Students." *Library Journal* 76 (1951): 275.

Cole, Betty Joy. "Library vs. Laboratory as a Basis for Research." *Journal of Chemical Education* 21 (1944): 319–321.

Connolly, A. G. "Library vs. Laboratory Research." *Journal of Chemical Education* 20 (1943): 531–533.

Johnson, B. Lamar. *Vitalizing a College Library*. Chicago: American Library Association, 1939.

Lancaster, John H. *The Use of the Library by Student Teachers*. New York: Columbia University Teachers College, 1941.

Lane, Ruth McG. "The Place of the Library in Engineering Education." *Journal of Engineering Education* 28 (1938): 571–581.

Lyle, Guy R. *The Administration of the College Library*. New York: H. W. Wilson, 1944.

McCrum, Blanche P. *An Estimate of Standards for a College Library*. Lexington, Va.: Journalism Laboratory Press, 1937.

Randall, William M., and Goodrich, Francis L. D. *Principles of College Library Administration*. Chicago: American Library Association and the University of Chicago Press, 1936.

Sprague, M. D. "Limiting the Objectives of the Course in Instruction in Library Use." *College and Research Libraries* 10 (1949): 140–144.

Whitford, R. H., and O'Farrell, J. B. "Use of a Technical Library." *Mechanical Engineering* 70 (1948): 987–993.

Wilson, Louis R., and Tauber, Maurice F. *The University Library: Its Organization, Administration and Functions*. Chicago: University of Chicago Press, 1945.

PART II
FACULTY INVOLVEMENT
IN LIBRARY-USE INSTRUCTION

LIBRARY INSTRUCTION THROUGHOUT THE CURRICULUM: EARLHAM COLLEGE PROGRAM

EVAN IRA FARBER
Librarian, Earlham College

Although Earlham, in its highly developed library programs, may not be characteristic of even most liberal arts colleges . . . [it has] shown ways in which other librarians could begin to improve reference services for undergraduates.[1]

It may be immodest to begin with such words of praise, but there are two reasons for citing them. First, like the story of the mule whose owner must first hit him over the head with a stick before giving him directions, it gets the reader's attention; second, it puts me on my mettle to show that those statements are still warranted since they were based on observations made in 1969.

Earlham's program is unique, and one must know the institutional context in order to understand it and appreciate it: our program—as indeed is true of most educational programs—was designed for and has been shaped by its context; it is not an exportable package. Furthermore, because library instruction at Earlham has been so intimately related to the total program of library development and administration during my decade as librarian, much of the following will necessarily be described in somewhat personal terms. Despite the special character of the program and the personal viewpoint, certain features and experiences should be helpful to others.

THE INSTITUTIONAL CONTEXT

In the parlance of college catalogs, Earlham is a small (1,200 students), midwestern (Richmond, Indiana; population 45,000), church-related (Society of Friends) four-year liberal arts college. For the purposes of this discussion, its most characteristic features are that it is primarily a residential college, rather selective in its admissions, with a closely knit sense of community and a very informal relationship among students, faculty, administration, and staff. The curricular structure and teaching program could hardly be termed radically experimental, but they combine innovation and tradition in a happy mix.[2]

Because of the method by which Quakers carry on organizational matters—that is, by consensus—there is rarely an extreme change in program or curriculum. By the same token, however, the way is easier than at most colleges for experimenting with parts of the program or trying new approaches. Though students are not highly competitive with one another, the academic atmosphere is serious and the work is demanding. Most classes are relatively small, and there is an emphasis on various modes of independent study, with a concomitant emphasis on research papers and heavy use of library materials.

Library facilities consist of Lilly Library, which is the main library, and the Ernest A. Wildman Science Library. The former was opened in 1963, has three levels comprising altogether about 43,000 square feet, and a capacity of about 180,000 volumes. It is an unusually attractive and comfortable building, with a variety of seating and study accommodations, and a relaxed atmosphere that students enjoy and appreciate. In discussing its role in the program of library instruction, two design features are especially important. One, it has a projection room, with a seating capacity of about 50 (very few classes are larger than this), that was intended primarily for film and slide presentations, but is ideal for classes in library instruction. Second, it is a "reference-centered" library: this characterizes not only its program and educational involvement, but is manifested by the location of reference facilities—the reference desk ("the least formidable reference desk ever seen by this writer" [3]) is just to the right of the main entrance, about ten feet from the nearest point of the card catalog, about 25 feet from its farthest point, and in clear view of all users of the card catalog. Behind the reference desk are the reference offices; beyond it is the reference collection, with the periodical indexes on counter-height shelving (also visible from the reference desk) and the other volumes on standard steel shelving. The entire reference area is fairly compact, but quite attractive, comfortable, and with sufficient seating for users of the collection. The area was intended to be convenient, inviting, and easily supervised, and it has, I think, succeeded.

The Ernest A. Wildman Science Library was completed as part of a new science complex in 1972. It is located between the two science buildings, off the enclosed corridor that joins the two, contains 8,400 square feet on two levels, with a capacity of 50,000 volumes and space for 125 readers, and its facilities were designed and arranged to achieve much the same ambience and effective reference service as the main library. Taking both libraries together, the collection consists of about 190,000 volumes, with some 1,200 periodicals currently received.

The attitudes and practices of the professional staff are of course a crucial—perhaps the most crucial—factor in giving effective reference service. Wilkinson observed: "When the five Earlham librarians were asked in individual interviews 'Do you consider reference services for undergraduates to be one of the most important functions of the library?', they all replied that this was *the* most important function of a college library." [4] All six professional librarians, including the science librarian, take regular turns at the Lilly Library reference desk. In staff meetings they frequently discuss such matters as the reference interview, problems with particular groups of students, recent reference tools, new approaches to instruction in individual courses, and other aspects of reference work. All but one of the staff (who prefers not to) lecture to classes, but the load varies greatly according to interest, availability, and inclination.

Relationships with the teaching faculty are excellent. "Earlham librarians," Wilkinson noted, "have, to an extraordinary degree, become part of the whole college. This uncommon rapport with faculty has made possible the development of a highly successful library instruction program which in turn has greatly influenced the reference service for students." [5]

This happy relationship, growing partly from the Quaker ethos that permeates the college in many subtle ways and partly from the individuals—Quaker and non-Quaker—concerned, is manifested in other ways that are important to the librarians and consequential for the library program: the librarians teach occasional courses and serve on all faculty committees, including those weighty ones that shape the academic program and help determine the character of the college. And as far as library instruction is concerned, this becomes important since one or another of the staff is almost certain to be involved when new courses or programs are planned. The common complaint of librarians elsewhere that they are the last to know about matters that may affect the library is unheard of at Earlham, and the injection of library instruction into a new course or program becomes an immediate possibility. This relationship between teaching faculty and librarians regarding library instruction has now reached the stage where, on occasion, even when librarians are not involved initially in course planning, a faculty member will call upon one of us to see how the library should be related to the course.

A recent example of this happy relationship is the report presented in April 1973 to the faculty "for encouraging a review of the ends and means of our educational efforts," and a revision of "the organized educational program." The proposal accepts "as general goals for the curriculum":

> encouraging each student to take greater initiative for planning and carrying through his educational program; requiring him to take greater responsibility for his program's, and his own, lack of success, but also giving him chance for greater credit for success; and encouraging greater independence in learning, more self-education.

To accomplish this, 13 "educational aims" were enumerated, such as "competence in a second language and knowledge of its culture" and "knowledge of the history, philosophy, and methods of the natural and social sciences." But the one of most interest here is number ten: "competence in the skills of information retrieval and the use of the library for research purposes." The inclusion of knowing how to use the library as a basic educational objective is interesting enough, but the fact that no librarian was on the committee when the report was written makes it especially significant, and indicates that the teaching faculty and students who *were* on it didn't even need to be reminded of the importance of that objective. Whether this particular proposal, or a variation of it, is adopted, there's not much question that the idea of library instruction as a part of the educational program is now generally accepted.

The college administration's attitude is also important, not just in regard to finances, but other supportive actions and attitudes. Prospective faculty members who are being interviewed have a session with the librarian as part of their interview schedules, and his opinion is considered in the overall evaluation. In the week before each new academic year begins, new faculty go through a number of orientation sessions, meeting with the various administrators and certain faculty committee chairmen; a session with the librarian occupies one of these sessions, and in it the program of library instruction is described, along with the procedures—book ordering, reserves, etc.—in which faculty are traditionally interested.

We have, then, a context for library instruction that is almost ideal: a curriculum and approach to learning that invite it; a building that facilitates it; a staff dedicated to it; a faculty that in the beginning were receptive and have become increasingly cooperative; and finally, an administration that is supportive. Some of this just happened, but most of it has resulted from planning, patience, and hard work. Nor has any outside assistance contributed; almost all of the staff time and materials have come from the regular budget.

THE PROGRAM

Before I came to Earlham, I had had no professional experience with library instruction. Indeed, I had done little thinking about it. Perhaps, though, one incident, which happened in the late 1950s while I was at Emory University, engendered later thinking. Surely it was not uncommon, and it seemed insignificant at the time. I had asked a student who was wandering around in the stacks what he was looking for, since he was obviously puzzled. I don't remember his exact question, but it had something to do with articles in biological journals. "Did you look in *Biological Abstracts?*" I asked. This drew a blank look, and I asked him what year student he was. When he told me he was working on his M.A. in biology, I was incredulous—a graduate student in biology who didn't even know *Biological Abstracts!* I urged him to speak to the science librarian, but when talking the matter over later with other staff members, I found out that this sort of thing was not at all unusual.

After coming to Earlham and working my turn at the reference desk, I realized that despite the very good teaching, there were many students who didn't know how to find information; at the same time, as an administrator, I also realized that requiring the reference librarian to answer approximately the same question 20 different times for the students in one class was a terribly inefficient use of professional time. With this latter observation as an appeal, I asked a member of the English department if I could talk to his class. He agreed, and the results were sufficiently encouraging for me to approach other faculty.

There was another incentive to my growing interest in instruction. As librarian, I had to justify (in a practical way) to the college administration and to myself my budget requests for additional materials—especially new subscriptions and back files of periodicals—that my training and experience had convinced me were essential for a good academic library. But if they were not being used much, why were they essential, and how could the request for funds be justified?

The answer, of course, was that they were not used—or at least not used enough —because students didn't know about the indexes, bibliographies, and abstracts that would lead them to these periodicals, and if students were only shown the existence and usefulness of these tools, then the periodicals would be used.

At the same time as these ideas were percolating, several other events were taking place that abetted library instruction. First, we had just moved into a new building that, because of its fine facilities and atmosphere, rapidly became a center for many students and faculty, so that the library—along with its mate- rials—began to play a more important role in campus activity and thinking. Second, the college was considering and initiating a variety of new programs and educational approaches, many of them appropriate for library instruction. Third, the library was designated a government depository library, and because of my experience working in a documents department, I was determined that federal documents would not become the unused and unknown collection I'd seen in so many institutions, but would be a vital part of the library. Fourth, the occasion to replace and add staff members gave me the opportunity to hire a reference librarian, Jim Kennedy, and a science librarian, Tom Kirk, who would share and reinforce these objectives. Over the succeeding years, the three of us have talked more about the theory and practice of library instruction than any other single subject, and the present program has been shaped largely by these discussions.

CONTENT

The program as it existed in 1968 has been described in an article by James Kennedy,[6] so that the following discussion will describe in detail mostly the changes since then.

We have no "library orientation"; during Freshman Week the entire group of first-year students (about 330) is addressed by the librarian for ten or 15 minutes, simply as a welcome and an explanation of why they are all about to take the brief library test. That is, to let us know which students have such a deficient knowledge of library use that they will need special help. When these students are identified, they are contacted through their advisers and urged to attend a few instructional sessions. A couple of lectures and a few individualized exercises focus on the card catalog and the *Readers' Guide* so the students can use the library and comprehend the later instruction that assumes this level. During these talks and sessions, we stress the important role of the library in their academic life, and it is crucial at this juncture to present a serious, but pleasant and helpful attitude.

All first-year students are required to take a two-term humanities course. The first term is devoted to reading a book a week, then writing essays on the books and discussing them in small tutorial groups. It entails no use of critical mate- rials—even discourages it—so there is no need for library instruction. The second term is topic oriented. In groups of 20 or so, students read and discuss assigned works on their group topic, but they spend most of the final four or five weeks of the term working on a research paper related to that topic. Originally, an hour's lecture on basic reference sources beyond the high school level was given by a librarian who then met with the smaller tutorial groups to discuss their individual papers and point out particularly appropriate bibliographies and other reference tools. Now, the hour lecture describes some of these general reference sources, but the emphasis is more on pointing out the differences between using a high school library and this library. (I have come to think that perhaps the biggest problem in giving college library instruction is correcting library skills learned in high school; it is, in some ways, easier to instruct students from foreign countries or from schools where no library instruction was given.) It is pointed out that in high school knowing how to use the card catalog and the *Readers' Guide* was enough, simply because most of the available materials could be found through them. But using college libraries is something else. First, by depending on the *Readers' Guide,* one gets to only one-eighth (in Earlham's case) of the library's current periodicals, and not even the most useful ones; then the variety of other periodical indexes is described, with some emphasis on the *Social Sciences & Humanities Index.* Second, we show why the card catalog is primarily a location device: it doesn't tell which books are important, or which are useless. While in high school this generally may not make too much difference since there were so few sources for any one topic, in this library one has got to use bibliographical guides to know which items are going to be most useful. Third, we show that there is an enormous body of material that one can't even find through the card catalog—government publications, articles in the *New York Times,* essays, book reviews (as well as, of course, periodical articles), and we mention the indexes one can use for these. All the while, the limitations of subject headings are pointed out in a number of ways: their lack of specificity, their complicated and unpredictable forms, their outmoded terminology, their inconsistencies—though at the same time it is shown how to make the best use of them (since they're the only ones we have) through the use of subject tracings and the *Subject Headings Used in the Dictionary Catalog of the Library of Congress* plus the 1966–1971 cumulations of supplements published by the University of California and later supplements issued by LC. Knowing how to use these is essential at Earlham, since there are almost no subject cross-references in the card catalog.

The importance of encyclopedias is the other point of contrast between how students are taught to use high school libraries and how they should use the college library. Students smile knowingly when asked if using encyclopedias for term papers was not discouraged or even prohibited in high school, and this leads to our pointing out the value of encyclopedias and handbooks: they not only provide the background and context for an unfamiliar subject but also often suggest the most useful books to use in investigating a topic. And from there, one proceeds logically to a discussion of the variety and usefulness of subject bibliographies, with examples appropriate for the particular class. Some of these are listed on the sheet that is given the class and that consists mostly of annotations for the reference tools mentioned above, plus perhaps a selected listing of appropriate subject headings.

The concluding comment to students is also a summarizing one. In writing high school papers, it is pointed out, a major problem is finding enough information on a topic. The problem now, on the other hand, is having so much information available that the main consideration is getting to the best or most useful information—selecting, in other words, from the material available. One must now use the library not only efficiently but effectively, and that means intelligently and that, in turn, means taking advantage of bibliographical works, especially selective and annotated ones if possible, which provide expert guidance through the mass of material.

At the end of the lecture (which, it should be noted, is given in as spontaneous and informal a style as possible), individual appointments are set up with members of the reference staff to discuss approaches and particular reference tools for the individual topics. This is obviously a time-consuming job, and in a sense contravenes one of the original reasons for giving library instruction (that is, in order to instruct an entire class at one time rather than individual students asking the same question over and over), but the circumstances *are* different, and the development of student library skills is significant. This is the time when we can talk about search strategy, about comparing different sources, about using the bibliographical recommendations of authorities, rather than simply finding answers to questions. Moreover, since these conferences are related to topics the students are actively interested in, their motivation is high and more is learned than ordinarily. Putting the conferences on the same level as an assignment means that students who would ordinarily be reluctant to ask for help—and they are often the ones who need it most—are given the structure for receiving that help. This is a point that should not be minimized. Even a strong student will not ask a question that could easily be answered by a reference source simply because the student assumes no such source exists. Students don't ask because they don't know what they don't know, and it is helpful to provide the occasion for this to be pointed out.

Working with first-year students in the humanities course has proved one of the foundation stones of the entire library instruction program. Originally the primary purpose of the beginning instruction was to introduce college students to college-level reference materials, to get them away from almost sole dependence on the *Readers' Guide* and the card catalog. The evolution of instruction in that course, however, has led us to go far beyond the original purpose. The card catalog is examined much more closely, in order to show not only its limitations but features of it that make it a more precise and versatile tool. Some guidelines for search strategy are indicated, attempting to get students to look not for quick answers, but to work from the general to the specific, to depend on bibliographical authorities, to use the knowledge and opinions of experts, and to realize that there is an enormous amount of information, much of it fairly well hidden from the average user, and that one needs to know the keys to this information, or at least to ask if there are keys. Finally, the combination of relatively informal lectures and individual conferences has helped turn around the attitudes most students have of libraries and librarians; they no longer fear the library or ignore the staff, but come to realize that both can be of enormous help if used well.

Even before they have taken Humanities 12, many first-year students (about one-third of the total of 330) take General Biology. Built into this course is a library component, which requires students to use primary source materials, especially articles in scientific journals, to document certain biological phenomena. In order to find such materials students are taught the purposes, structure, and mechanics of such bibliographical tools as *Science Citation Index* and *Biological Abstracts.*[7] In one sense, then, they learn to run before learning to walk, but it does have the advantage that, when they take humanities, they have a real appreciation of how helpful library instruction can be, as well as some knowledge of bibliographical parlance and structure.

By the time students have gone through their first college year, they presumably know how to use the card catalog fairly well with the aid of the Library of Congress *Subject Headings* list and subject tracings. They also know the various Wilson indexes and the *New York Times Index,* and many students, depending on the topics they've worked on, know other, more specialized indexes. Just as, or perhaps even more important, by now they realize that there is a whole world of other indexes, bibliographies, and reference tools that are unknown to them, and they also recognize that the library staff is knowledgeable and approachable. At the next level, then, library instruction concentrates on sources important for all majors in particular disciplines. For example, all English majors take English 60, Introduction to the Study of Literature, in which each student writes a lengthy research paper. The library instruction to this class consists of a general lecture on the structure of bibliography of English and American literature, the search strategy to cope with that structure, and some comments on the handbook given each student, the latest revision of which contains 60 pages and annotates some 280 reference works in all areas of English and American literature. Each student then schedules a meeting with a reference librarian to discuss sources for his or her particular paper.

All psychology majors take the two-term course, Basic Psychological Processes, which is devoted to methodology and research design and analysis. As part of the course students devise an experiment that will test a psychological concept; in order to do this they must make a thorough search of the literature on the topic. This is an ideal situation for library instruction, and a lecture is given consisting of the following two levels: First, the structure of psychological literature is described, using a diagram that shows the steps by which the results of research are disseminated—preliminary findings to individuals, reports to meetings, submission of the manuscript to a journal, publication of the article, the abstract appearing in *Psychological Abstracts,* a summary in the *Annual Review of Psychology,* then appearing in a bibliography of another article, and finally in a textbook—each step showing the time lapse.[8] Second, a bibliography that has been compiled on a topic is shown, and the steps followed by which the bibliography was compiled, emphasizing the use of handbooks, encyclopedias, and the *Annual Review of Psychology,* to provide the key books and articles on the topic, and then stressing *Psychological Abstracts* and *Science Citation Index* and other abstracting or indexing services related to the topic in order to update the key items. A 23-page handbook listing and annotating in some detail almost all reference works in psychology in the library's collection is given all students. As psychology majors, they are supposed to keep this, and in later, more specialized courses they are given supplements listing recent additions to the reference collection. Presumably little further instruction is necessary, since the literature of psychology is so well structured, and once students learn how to find materials for one area of psychology, they should, with the aid of the annotated bibliography of reference works and perhaps a brief lecture on a few unique sources, be able to conduct a literature search in any area of psychology.

Though the instruction in Basic Psychological Processes is on the same level as English 60—that is, they are both courses in which students are introduced to the basic bibliographical tools of a discipline—it seemed to us that because of the logical structure of the bibliography of psychology and the lack of structure for the bibliography of literature, individual sessions with psychology students were not nearly as important for them as they were for English majors. But to be sure that psychology students were finding their way and making a fairly systematic and thorough search of the literature, the last time the course was given, students were asked to keep a log of their literature searches. Though keeping the log was optional for each student, the two professors who taught the course agreed to give extra points for it and practically all students participated. The willingness of these faculty members to modify their grading pattern, which is almost sacrosanct to most teaching faculty, indicates again the cooperative attitude of the faculty. The psychology department, we have found, is one of the most receptive and helpful departments in library instruction. It is not simply that its members are willing for us to come to their classes, or to bring their classes to the library, but they work with us in planning the instruction and its integration into their assignments. The results are impressive, indicated not only by the students' familiarity with the bibliographic apparatus of the field but by their intensive and extensive use of psychological journals in the library, their interlibrary loan requests, and their willingness to travel to other libraries out of town. Faculty members have been pleased with the results, so that their cooperation and involvement is assured.

The more specialized courses in the disciplinary sequences offer little problem. By the time most students take them they realize that while library lectures may not be terribly exciting, their usefulness in helping locate materials is something to be appreciated. Lectures for such courses may consist of the full treatment—a lengthy, annotated bibliography, the use of projected transparencies to illustrate pages from reference tools that may be especially useful or unusual, with comments on these and on search strategy for that subject, all taking place in the library's projection room; or it may just be a ten- or 15-minute presentation of a very limited nature, depending on the nature of the assignment or project and the bibliographical knowledge of the students. Consultation with the faculty is essential in these lectures in order to determine the thrust of the assignment and when the instruction would be most timely in terms of students' preparation and motivation.

By far the largest number of library lectures don't fit into any sequence because the courses themselves are not built into the major sequence, or because they are interdisciplinary; they are, for one reason or another, special. These are perhaps the most problematical courses to deal with since the students in any one course may range from first-year to seniors, with a variety of previous library experiences. There may be some who know science bibliography thoroughly, but don't know their way around government documents or the literature of the humanities. Those who are already quite knowledgeable cause special concern because they have had so much library instruction there is both a real and an imagined danger of overkill. If students are subjected to materials and concepts they're already familiar with, they may be so turned off that they will be inattentive when new things are presented, or they may not even come to a session on library instruction because they think they've heard it all before, and perhaps they have. In such situations the usual lecture pattern may be altered: by having separate sections for the less knowledgeable ones and for those who are already familiar with most of the materials; or by beginning the lecture with reference sources that are new to even more advanced students, and then excusing them from the remainder of the lecture that is devoted to more basic materials. The important point is that since instruction in use of the library and library materials is by its very nature rather matter-of-fact and systematic, with not much room for the play of ideas, whatever repetition can be eliminated without vitiating the purpose of the instruction should be; if repetition does seem necessary, it should be camouflaged with somewhat varied presentations.

In order to insure that all courses needing library instruction are covered, at the beginning of each term the library staff contacts each faculty member who is teaching a course in which it seems likely that students will be doing some library work that should entail the use of bibliographical sources. If instruction seems appropriate, a tentative date is set up. The timing of this is crucial, since the instruction must come not just when there happens to be an open date in the course schedule, but when the students are beginning to look for materials. If there is a term paper, it is helpful if the students have been asked to submit a preliminary bibliography, and we encourage faculty members to do this; when students have struggled with this, their motivation is high, and they are eager for (or at least receptive to) help in showing them ways to find additional materials.

If, for one reason or another, we miss contact with a faculty member or are assured that no instruction is necessary, only to find at the reference desk later that some student in the class has no idea how to find the most appropriate materials, then the instructor is notified to see if a session can be arranged. Often we find that the instructor felt instruction wasn't necessary because on being asked, the class had assured the instructor they knew the sources. It is discouraging at such times to realize that even though most students come to realize that there must be reference sources they'll need but don't know about, some still feel that whatever library instruction they already had is sufficient. Fortunately, such cases are relatively infrequent.

Perhaps the most interesting—and certainly the most fun—is library instruction that is planned along with the course as an integral part of it, rather than just as an attachment or addition. The instruction can be structured so that it not only ties in with the course content, but exercises can be shaped so that the student proceeds from one assignment to another in a logical sequence that instills a growing sophistication in library knowledge and use. A case in point was the experimental PIE (Program for Integrative Education) course on Post-war Japan.

This course was taught by three faculty members: a historian, a political scientist and a philosopher, all with strong backgrounds in Japanese studies. The course occupied a student's full time during one term and counted for three courses, the usual student load. The basic purpose of PIE was to show how each discipline approaches a similar set of circumstances or body of knowledge, or social phenomenon, or creative work—how each approach differs and yet interacts and contributes to a common understanding. A librarian participated in the planning sessions for the course and it was decided to make library instruction a continuing part of it, culminating in the preparation by each student of a critical, annotated bibliography.

The first step, it seemed to us, was to make students aware of the information overload, to impress upon them just how much material was available on the subject and from a wide variety of sources—sources that are sometimes difficult to use, are often arranged differently from other similar sources, yet can lead to important materials that would never have been found otherwise. To accomplish this each student was assigned an event in recent Japanese history, a list of 11 varied sources, including the card catalog, the *Readers' Guide,* the *Monthly Catalog of U.S. Government Publications, PAIS,* the *LC Catalog—Books: Subjects* and the *New York Times Index,* and asked to find one reference to their event in each of the 11 sources, plus five other sources of their own choosing. At various stages of the course, other reference sources were explained thoroughly and compared—for example, the extraordinary usefulness of the *CIS* (Congressional Information Service) compared with the *Monthly Catalog* and *PAIS.*

Whenever a new aspect of Japan was introduced the librarian would talk about special reference sources for investigating it. By the time the course was over, the students knew the whole variety of reference tools useful for the study of Japan and also knew how to approach these in an effective manner. Our hope is that they can now extrapolate this knowledge to other fields.

THE DEFINING POINTS

In the details and background material presented above, the essential features of the library instruction program may have gotten lost. Here, then, are the underlying points that define the present program.

Flexibility and variety. Perhaps the outstanding features of the program, flexibility and variety, are made possible by the size of the institution and the close relationships the library staff has with students and faculty. These relationships enable us to know when library instruction is needed and to find out what the situation demands in time, format, and purpose. The willingness, even eagerness, of the librarians to try new approaches and presentations also contributes to this flexibility. And so we have formal lectures and informal discussions; lectures to large classes at one extreme and individual conferences at the other;

instruction spread over almost an entire term, building from basic techniques to sophisticated concepts, and spot lectures, some only ten minutes long, focusing on particular reference works. Some instruction is given through written exercises, but most by demonstration and oral directions. The locale may be the library's projection room, the reference area, the regular classroom, or even the librarian's office. The materials used include transparencies, brief bibliographies, lengthy handbooks with annotated entries, and sample pages from complex reference works. The determining criteria are simply what is feasible and what will be most effective, and since the two are sometimes in conflict, the result is often a compromise.

During the 1972–1973 academic year we gave some 70 lectures for 48 different courses, divided among the social sciences, natural and physical sciences, and humanities. These do not, of course, include conferences with individual students or discussions with small groups.

Use of structured examples and illustrations. Whereas at the start of the program most lectures merely described and explained the various reference tools appropriate for particular subjects, we've come to realize that going over one reference work after another—no matter how fascinating they are to librarians —is for students fairly tedious and mostly ineffective; only by *using* the reference works can students really know and appreciate them. And so we have more and more used the process of compiling a sample bibliography, step by step sometimes, and let the annotated listings of reference works that are handed out to classes serve to point out specific works.

What we are trying to do, then, is to get across concepts by way of example. The *Pathfinders,* developed by Project Intrex at M.I.T. and now being published by Addison-Wesley, use a similar approach, but most of their topics are too broad for our use. Our hope is that what students learn from the *Pathfinders* by inference, and more directly from our lectures, is a workable search strategy that begins with introductory works—encyclopedias, handbooks, and other guides —and then proceeds to selective bibliographies and other reference works that give more specific information, and finally takes them to the card catalog for items in the library.[9] The idea of search strategy is reinforced in the individual sessions with students, which leads to the next feature of our instructional program.

Personalized reference service. One of the major benefits of giving lectures to classes is the rapport established with students, who come to realize that librarians are approachable, knowledgeable, and interested in students' library problems. Because of this rapport, it is easier than in most library situations to make responses to reference questions an element of library instruction and, whenever possible, to show how looking for the particular information requested fits into a pattern of search strategy. At the same time, when individual reference works are consulted, their nature and uses are explained. The reference interview, then, is viewed as a potential educational experience and an important part of library instruction.

Librarians as instructors. In view of these features and the concepts mentioned below, it seems almost superfluous to say that we feel the teaching faculty cannot give adequate library instruction. On the other hand, we encourage—almost insist upon—faculty members attending the library instruction sessions for their courses, not only because their absence would say something to the class about the lack of importance they attach to the sessions but because they can, and often do contribute to the discussions by their knowledge of particular items that come up in the lectures, and by relating points in the lecture to aspects of the course and its assignments.

But teaching faculty are discouraged from giving library instruction, and even from preparing explanatory material for assignments that entail bibliographic tools, without consulting with librarians. For too many times we've found such explanations incomplete or incorrect, and while talking about this with some faculty members takes a good bit of discretion, the message can usually be gotten across by pointing out that there are additional sources they may have overlooked, or that some reference works they were familiar with have changed their nature or been superseded by newer, more useful ones, and—most important—that it takes someone who knows how students use and misuse these sources to guide them in using the reference sources. We disagree strongly here with some devotees of the library-college concept. We feel that while the teaching faculty have the central responsibility in the educational enterprise, librarians can help them carry out that responsibility much more effectively and at the same time enhance it. While the two groups—teaching faculty and librarians —can and should work together, neither one can do the other's job.

There is really no way of determining how much staff time is used—though we know it's considerable—since the lecturing time is only the tip of the iceberg. The other five-sixths (nine-tenths?) of the iceberg is taken up in discussing the approach and specific materials with the teaching faculty and with the staff, and then preparing the bibliographies and transparencies, in which several staff members are involved. To make the computation even more difficult, the load is spread irregularly throughout the academic year, with most of the lectures coming in the third through the sixth week of each (11-week) term, while the preparation for these weeks of lectures is carried on sporadically during the preceding weeks. If I were asked to give a rough estimate, I would guess that about ten to 15 hours a week are given to class presentations during those weeks of lectures, but as indicated, this is a small portion of the total staff time.

Extending the library's resources. If students are going to be shown how to use indexes, abstracting services and other bibliographical tools, the library must be willing to provide, as far as it is possible, the materials discovered through these tools. Otherwise, the frustration of finding just the right item in a bibliography, and then not being able to examine it—a frustration encountered again and again—will soon cause students to return to dependence on the card catalog, so they can be sure of having the materials available. Obviously, a college library must lack many important items, but it can give priority to materials that are indexed, and even more helpfully can provide ways for students to use the resources of other libraries by a number of means: improving interlibrary loan service and making its availability known; providing union catalogs; joining periodicals banks and state or regional systems; cooperative arrangement with local or nearby libraries. We have done all these.

OBJECTIVES

By using these features and applying these precepts, what are we trying to convey to students? How do we want them to act, and what do we want them to understand and put into practice? Do we want them, really, to become junior reference librarians?

The last question can be answered very quickly: No—though we do want them to know how reference librarians approach a search for answers or information. To imply that we should even try to do much more than this would be to severely denigrate the professional training and role of reference librarians, to indicate a very restricted notion of what reference librarians are and a very simplistic notion of what they do. We would be attempting a dangerous thing, the substitution of second-class knowledge for first-class skills.

What, then, do we want?

At first, we want students to be struck by the difference between a high school library and a college library. Perhaps this was not such a difficult assignment years ago when there was little or no library instruction in the school systems, but now most of our students know—or think they know—how to use a library when they get to college, and after all, what is the difference on first sight? A college library is larger, of course, and the call numbers are different, but there's the card catalog and near it the *Readers' Guide*—what else do you need? What we librarians must do, in some way, is convince students that an entirely new approach is called for, a new approach that makes use of a bibliographical apparatus they never dreamed existed and techniques that may have been unknown to them, but are necessary to make the most of that apparatus.

Leading directly from this, we want them to realize that there are relevant reference sources for almost any topic. Since their biggest problem is rarely going to be a lack of material, but rather identifying the most important and pertinent items, the ability to find and use these reference sources is essential.

A third point is that certain principles comprise a search strategy that can be applied to almost any library research topic. The details of course will vary from topic to topic, but if one has grasped these basic principles, materials can be found much more effectively and efficiently.

And fourth, students should realize that no student, no matter how well trained, can be aware of all the useful reference sources. Students should work with a reference librarian when exploring new territory.

Finally, because the information one wants may appear in so many places, and because our library is necessarily limited in its resources, the library should be used for doing the bibliographical searching, but one should be prepared to go outside it, either by borrowing materials or using other libraries.

EVALUATING OUR EDUCATIONAL THEORY

The function of philosophy, it has been said, is to find questions to answers. If whatever I've claimed or described above indicates that we think we have all the answers, it was not so intended. What we do have is a program that has been devised and revised to meet certain perceived needs, and it has, within recognized limitations, succeeded. But we do have serious questions about it.

How do we know it has succeeded? Only recently, a doctoral candidate interviewed some Earlham students as part of his dissertation, his subject being the use of historical journals by students in liberal arts colleges. Comparing them with students in a group of other colleges of approximately the same size, he found our students were more familiar with the bibliographical materials in American history, yet, paradoxically, they did not feel as confident as the others in their ability to use the library. One may think it strange that I found this satisfying, but I did, simply because it indicated to me that though our students know and use the reference materials we present to them, they are also painfully aware of the complexity and extensiveness of library reference tools. And this, it seems to me, is really one of the most important things one can get across to undergraduates. "To be conscious that you are ignorant is a great step to knowledge," said Disraeli, but most students have no concept of this ignorance—in many areas, certainly, but especially in using the library. Our students are, we hope, beginning to ask themselves, "What indexes or bibliographies should I be using?"

We do know that students who have gone on to graduate school have come back and told us how much they benefited from the program; we have had students transfer to Earlham who contrasted what they were now learning about the library with their previous lack of exposure. We can tell something from faculty response and the repeated requests for instruction. We can compare the sources students use now with those they used several years ago, attested to by the sharp increase in the use of interlibrary loans as well as by looking at the bibliographies submitted with papers. An increased use of "logs" or "library experience" work sheets should help us to determine even better how good or how poor students' library procedures are. But we don't know *how* effective the program is; perhaps this sort of quantitative evaluation can never be obtained.

While we know students are able to find more and better materials, is this what our basic objective should be, or should it be something more? Should we be trying to do what Patricia Knapp advocated as a result of the Monteith experiment: to teach, through a sequence of specific assignments coordinated with the curriculum, critical bibliographical thinking based on concepts and processes rather than a more applied knowledge based on specific library tools? [10] We hope we're doing some of this—that is, teaching concepts and processes—but it *is* only a hope, because we are depending on students' abilities to draw inferences.

To ask the question another way: Do we want students to understand the organization of knowledge, or should we be satisfied with wanting to teach them to be able to find the most useful information related to particular subjects? There's no question that we want them to learn to work more or less independently, but for which end? Perhaps the two purposes are not incompatible, or maybe can't even be separated. In any case, a tentative—and probably unsatisfying—response may be provided by the realities of academic life, specifically the autonomy and territoriality of the disciplines (represented by departments) and the lock they have on most curricula. At almost every established college and university the curriculum is not so much based on educational principles as it is on political compromises among departments, and this prerogative is guarded jealously. Certainly, part of the reason for the demise of the Monteith program was that departmental limits, though breached, even removed for a time, reasserted themselves, and the cooperative spirit that led to a library instructional program that crossed or ignored disciplines—a program that, in a sense, was an end in itself but benefited all departments—was lost.

Given the realities of the situation—that college or university faculty and their administrators are highly discipline oriented, that this is reflected in the structure of the curriculum, and that students are primarily interested in doing well in their courses, courses corresponding to the units into which the separate disciplines are broken—one must come to the conclusion (regretfully, perhaps) that only by working through the courses, and that means through individual faculty members, can the objectives of library instruction presently be achieved.[11] This conclusion is possibly underscored by the fact that the educational theory behind library instruction is not generally agreed upon, whereas the purposes of courses in the traditional disciplines, while they are beginning to be questioned and modified, have at least historical justification. One might respond that this is a fairly flimsy justification, but one must also recognize the traditionalism, the educational conservatism of academia.

Working with the faculty, then, becomes a given. This should not imply any betrayal of a higher or different purpose, but rather it means working toward that purpose while a clearer and better-grounded theory for library instruction can be worked out, and/or until the teaching faculty wholeheartedly accept library instruction as a valid part of the curriculum. If such a theory cannot be worked out—that is, if the real justification for library instruction is indeed primarily to permit students to do better work in the disciplines—then we still may have lost nothing and even gained in experience. Moreover, if we can have demonstrated our contribution to better course work, we will have justified our services and materials beyond the warehouse/custodial concept that so many faculty now have of libraries and librarians. I say "*may* have lost nothing" because we should recognize that if we do give library instruction only through other courses, it becomes difficult to teach concepts in order to focus on the specific tools that will permit better papers.

If, for the sake of peace of mind, one feels it necessary to look for unapparent advantages in giving library instruction through more or less traditional courses, there are some. Since courses vary in organization, method, and purpose, as well as subject matter, the library instruction given for each course must necessarily differ if it is to be effective. While this requires new preparations and continual rethinking, both of which entail time and discussion, it also means the presentations to classes are more likely to be fresh (if not always successful), a characteristic probably lacking in much library instruction, to say nothing of other instruction; it also means that librarians should become more intimately involved with the teaching faculty in the construction of course library assignments in particular, and perhaps in the planning of course objectives in general. Whether or not these potential advantages are realized depends very much on how effective the initial library instruction is—that is, the better it is, the larger contribution it will make toward general course objectives, and the more readily will librarians be welcomed, even courted, into participation in the teaching and learning process.

This is very much what's happened at Earlham. As one can see from the description of our program above, librarians play a substantial role in the curricular process, both at the level of program planning and course preparation, simply because the faculty has come to appreciate what the library has done and can do for their students. This is enough for the time being to keep us busy and to make us feel that we are making an important contribution to the educational program. We are still talking about our theoretical objectives. Continued discussion and experimentation will indicate the direction we want to go, and our present program, with its faculty support and involvement, is helping prepare the way.

NOTES

1. Billy R. Wilkinson, *Reference Services for Undergraduate Students: Four Case Studies* (Metuchen, N.J.: Scarecrow Press, 1972), p. 348.
2. It is, of course, impossible to convey the ambience of an institution in a few sentences. For a more extensive and quite perceptive view of what Earlham is like—and it is important for understanding the role of the library— see Thomas J. Cottle, "A Learning Place Called Earlham," *Change Magazine,* January–February 1971, pp. 52–9.
3. Wilkinson, op. cit., p. 308.
4. Ibid., p. 312.
5. Ibid., p. 304.
6. James R. Kennedy, Jr., "Integrated Library Instruction," *Library Journal* 95 (1970): 1450–1453.
7. For a more detailed description of this instruction, see the article by James R. Kennedy, Jr., Thomas G. Kirk, and Gwendolyn Weaver, "Course-Related Library Instruction: A Case Study of the English and Biology Departments at Earlham College," *Drexel Library Quarterly* 7 (1971): 277–297.
8. This diagram is based on the one appearing in the article "Scientific Communication: Its Role in the Conduct of Research and Creation of Knowledge," by William D. Garvey and Belver C. Griffith, *American Psychologist* 26 (1971): 349–362. The diagram is on p. 353.
9. A notion we have toyed with is moving the subject portion of our card catalog from its present location adjoining the author-title catalog to a part of the reference collection, so that it will be regarded by students for what it

should serve as—a bibliographical tool—rather than for what too many students now use it for, the first place to look for books on any subject. Would this encourage students to search for materials in a more logical way? We're not sure, and because of this uncertainty as well as the logistic problem entailed, and perhaps the radical nature of the move, we have done nothing more with the idea.

10. Patricia B. Knapp, *The Monteith College Library Experiment* (Metuchen, N.J.: Scarecrow Press, 1966).

11. If questions on library use were part of the Graduate Record Examinations, students (and faculty) would insist that library instruction be an integral part of their programs. Library-use questions would seem a perfectly logical inclusion on the GREs, since such knowledge is so important to graduate work, but the Educational Testing Service has been unresponsive to my suggestions.

THE HIGH SCHOOL LEVEL: EXAMPLES OF PLANNING, PREPARING, AND IMPLEMENTING LIBRARY-USER INSTRUCTIONAL PROGRAMS

CORINNE P. CLENDENING
High School Librarian, North Hills School District, Pittsburgh, Pennsylvania

Educating the library user at the high school level today is infinitely more complex than just a rigidly structured "library science" course. *Genuinely educating* the library user means nurturing his or her ability to think. Such an educational goal can only be implemented by a philosophy of dedication, by ingenuity of method, and by flexibility of approach.

A philosophy of dedication concerns itself with two major thrusts:

> [1] the nation's educational goal of providing equally rich opportunity through open-ended learning for each student to achieve a quality, optimum education of excellence in order to become a humane human being as well as a functionally literate United States citizen at the age of 18; and [2] the school library's educational goal of being a learning laboratory where students learn how to learn under the guidance of a librarian who is a teacher whose subject is learning itself.[1]

For enriched understanding of the philosophy undergirding such a functional library media program, *The School Library Media Center: A Force for Educational Excellence* by Ruth A. Davies [2] and *To Improve Learning: An Evaluation of Instructional Technology* [3] by the Commission on Instructional Technology, are highly recommended reading.

ORIENTATION

The student's orientation to the high school library should not be an all-at-once, singular occurrence, but rather an evolving experience covering the years of high school, which in turn should be an extension of the elementary and junior high school library programs. Students should not be overwhelmed with

163

a record-breaking 42-minute instruction period of graduate school level intensity in the art of Dewey—which is far more likely to tune out than to interest. Instead, the initial orientation visit should be viewed as a golden opportunity for students, whether coming as an entire English or social studies class at the beginning of the year or as individuals registering later in the term, to build a positive, receptive attitude toward the library based upon three fundamental concepts:

1. The library is a learning laboratory, richly provisioned with an array of unsuspected resources and services designed to meet the students' developing interests and emerging needs during their high school career.

2. The librarian, rather than a forbidding and possessive curator of the archives, is instead a friendly, knowledgeable teacher, who makes students feel welcome and who comes off as someone who wants to be genuinely helpful to them in maximizing the success of their high school life.

3. The library's circulation policies, its manner of organizing and locating the various types of media, and its simple rules and common sense procedures, are designed as an open invitation to each student to maximize his or her use of all library services, resources, and guidance; and that further, individual recreational uses of the library, such as browsing through the collections of fiction and records, flipping through magazines, or just enjoying the morning newspaper are library activities just as welcome as more purposeful research and directed study.

LIBRARY TOUR

The simplest manner to achieve these initial attitudinal goals is for the librarian, after introducing herself or himself and the library staff, to conduct an informal walking tour of the library facilities, taking time to call attention to as many of the following aspects of the library program as time and resources will permit:

1. the arrangement and uses of the various physical facilities of the library such as main reading room, browsing area, open stacks of the general collection, librarian's office, work room, audiovisual room, individual study carrels, seminar rooms, library classroom, and the television studio;

2. the circulation desk as the busy hub of the library for the borrowing and returning of materials (here circulation routines and policies are briefly explained within the governing principle of *making all materials readily available to all students* and an invitation is extended to any interested students to submit an application for work as library aides);

3. the card catalog as the *key* to the library's holdings;

4. the location of fiction, nonfiction, reference, periodical, newspaper, filmstrip, slide, recording, microfilm, study print, and vertical file collections;

5. the various machines and equipment available, including the typewriter and the photocopier;

6. the function of the library as a learning laboratory and the willingness of the librarian(s) to assist individually any student in locating materials, making suggestions or advising, teaching the use of any library reference tool, instructing how to use any of the listening and viewing equipment, or just being helpful to the student as the situation or problem presents itself.

Librarians striving to cope with extraordinary numbers of entering students might try videotaping the orientation tour. Such a tape can be used repeatedly and minimizes the drain on staff time and energy.

No attempt should be made during the library orientation tour to teach in depth the use of any library key or reference tool. Within the courses of study prescribed by the English and/or social studies curriculums—or ideally within the context of the school's entire curriculum—will be found many opportunities to teach the use of library keys and reference tools as well as accompanying information use techniques, procedures, and action patterns. In a well-developed library program, it is axiomatic that utility or need generated by a specific assignment or personal quest will build receptivity to learning. In *The New Library Key* Margaret G. Cook states her belief that "it is a serious mistake to require a student . . . to learn about books in which he has no present interest, just because they are important books." [4]

TEACHING THE LIBRARY RESEARCH PAPER

Although differences of professional opinion abound concerning the wisdom and necessity of having librarians teach about the formal high school library research paper, the paper still continues to be the favorite vehicle of many English and social studies teachers for teaching and/or evaluating student proficiency in research study skills. The following questions should be considered in collaboration with the teacher before the high school librarian undertakes a research paper project:

How should the research paper be taught? Should the unit be taught as a single, in-depth paper requiring a lengthy period of investigation? Or should the unit employ several developmental papers of limited scope? Should both research and writing take place in the library? Or should only the research take place in the library and the writing take place in the classroom?

When should the research paper be taught? Should the research paper be taught at the beginning of tenth grade as a diagnostic means of assessing the degree of student competence? Or should the paper be taught during the twelfth grade as a culminating activity in preparation for collegebound students and as a final evaluative assessment of student mastery?

Should the research paper be taught to all students? Should the research paper be required of all students? Or should the paper be required only of those students who are collegebound? Can the research paper be justified as a worthwhile learning experience for the less than able learner?

Where within the school's curriculum can the research paper most effectively be taught? Should the research paper be considered a logical responsibility of the English program? Or should the teaching of the research unit be the shared responsibility of a teaching team representing several or more subject areas?

OUTLINE PLAN: 10 BASIC STEPS IN RESEARCH

The following research paper outline is adapted from an article on research procedure in *The World Book Encyclopedia.*[5]

   I. Choosing a subject
     A. A subject that interests you
     B. A subject you know something about
     C. A subject treated in *available* resource sources
     D. Limit subject to a specific topic
     E. A topic not too elementary
     F. A topic about which you have an open mind
     G. When to stop researching
  II. Reading for background
     A. Reliable encyclopedia for overview of topic in perspective and unexpected suggestions for exploration
     B. Discussion with teacher and librarian for background reading possibilities
 III. Preliminary outline
     A. Must give purpose or main idea of paper
     B. Must show relationship between facts
     C. Must develop a logical conclusion
     D. Can be either topic outline *or* sentence outline
     E. Possible later to refine topic outline into sentence outline
 IV. The preliminary, or "working" bibliography
     A. List of sources to use in researching topic
     B. Gives idea of previous research on topic
     C. Helps discover what library has on topic
     D. Will grow and change
     E. Includes sources given in encyclopedia articles
     F. Includes likely sources in bibliography in books
     G. Includes likely sources in magazine and newspaper indexes
     H. Includes likely sources given under appropriate headings in card catalog and vertical file
     I. File cards used for working bibliography
     J. Necessary information on typical bibliography card
  V. Where to find information
     A. Start search with card catalog
     B. Reference books for specific information
     C. Additional library and other information resources
 VI. Using sources of information
     A. Judging reference sources—know *what* you are using and *why*
     B. Using a reference book

C. Using other sources of information
D. Taking notes
VII. Preparing report
    A. Review and organize notes
    B. Compare statement of purpose from preliminary outline with scope of notes
    C. Evaluate, revise, and refine statement of purpose
    D. Evaluate, change, revise, and refine preliminary outline to reflect what you have learned
    E. Research necessary topics from preliminary outline that you may have omitted
    F. Arrange and rearrange notes to suggest ways to present report
    G. Final arrangement of note cards provides basis for writing final outline
    H. Prepare final outline
VIII. Writing and revising
    A. Use final outline and note cards assembled in proper order to start first draft of paper
    B. Let your ideas pour out
    C. Write from notes, but avoid copying word for word
    D. Concentrate on organization, building from one idea to the next
    E. Plan now for footnotes and quotations
    F. Use clear statements, logical development, proof by examples, definite references, and acknowledgment of sources
    G. Write or type rough draft on standard-size paper
    H. Copy quotations exactly, enclosing them within quotation marks
    I. Begin revision by checking organization of ideas, sentence structure, paragraphing, word choice, mechanics of grammar and correctness of spelling
    J. Check that quoted material has been accurately copied and correctly documented
IX. Documenting your report
    A. Credit the source in a footnote for any borrowed words, ideas, facts, or statistics, and then fully identify source in the bibliography
    B. Use of footnotes
    C. The bibliography is a complete and fully documented list of *all sources actually used in report:* books, magazines, interviews, letters, audio-visual materials
X. Preparing the final report
    A. Let a day or two pass before reading rough draft for last time and before typing final report
    B. Observe particular typing and preparation rules required by the teacher
    C. If teacher prescribes no special preparation rules or manual, consult a good style manual such as Turabian
    D. Final report has logical order of pages within folder or binder
    E. Final report *must be handed in to the teacher on time*

Librarians who teach the use of the high school library effectively employ the same sound principles of teaching and learning that undergird successful classroom teaching. Today's high school librarians utilize all types and kinds of instructional media—print and nonprint—just as the classroom teachers support their teaching programs with myriad appropriate instructional resources. Fortunately, a wealth of appropriate media is commercially available to support teaching the use of the library. The instructional resources noted in the Bibliography and Nonbook Media lists at the end of this discussion have proved effective for teaching students how to use the high school library.

It should be emphasized that the research paper is just one extremely important use the English and social studies departments make of the library and that these departments are in turn just two of the curricular areas integrating their instructional program with the resources, facilities, and guidance of the high school library program. It should also be emphasized that the research unit is but one of many library-based units designed cooperatively by teacher and librarian to provide high school students with content-skill integration. Integration of the library program with the ongoing instructional program presupposes the following:

1. There will be preplanning between teacher and librarian concerning unit goals and objectives, topics to be explored, teaching strategies to be employed, special student needs to be accommodated, special skills to be introduced or reinforced, and when the teacher anticipates scheduling the class, groups, or individuals to work in the library. These preliminary planning sessions should take place far enough in advance of the introduction of the unit to enable the librarian to search for appropriate media to meet the developmental needs of the unit as well as the individual learning needs of the students.

2. The librarian will introduce the unit to the students either in the library, in the large group instruction room, or in the classroom. The librarian orients the students not only to the materials but especially to how best to work with the different types of resource materials. Such orientation to a new unit is a vital part of teaching the students how to learn to use the library efficiently and effectively. The students, the teacher, and the librarian will evaluate the success of the library support program and critically appraise areas of strength and weakness so that the library support program can be adjusted to meet more realistically the implementation and support needs of the curriculum.

Teaching the use of the library is a continuous concern of the librarian, and the librarian should scrutinize each instructional unit and each learning experience for potential opportunities to teach appropriate library materials, skills, and techniques to students. In unit building, it is helpful to develop a form, such as the following one, to use in preplanning sessions with teachers.

Greater depth, breadth, relevance, and creativity are added to the teaching program when the teacher has informed access to the resources of the library. The following instances of actual teacher-librarian planned units demonstrate the value to be realized from the face-to-face exchange of ideas:

SAMPLE TOPIC/FUNDAMENTAL ANALYSIS FORM:
TEACHER-LIBRARIAN UNIT PLANNING GUIDE

Subject _____   Teacher _____
Grade _____   School _____
Unit _____

PLEASE INDICATE UNDER THE APPROPRIATE HEADING
EACH SPECIFIC TOPIC OR FUNDAMENTAL REQUIRING
LIBRARY MEDIA SUPPORT.

PERSONS	PLACES	THINGS	EVENTS	IDEAS AND CONCEPTS	SKILLS

Each of three English teachers introducing Chaucer employed three different library support/enrichment strategies. Preparatory to beginning the Chaucer unit one teacher worked with the librarian to develop a library unit entitled "Religion, Myth, and Legend in Elizabethan England." The class enjoyed working in the library with materials supporting and developing topics, such as Knights of the Round Table, Chivalry, the Druids, the Mystery of Stonehenge, and King Arthur on Broadway. A second teacher brought her class to the library to work with a unit entitled, "Man Meets His God and Confronts His Spiritual Being," a richly developed unit with topics supporting a range of student interest running from the historical to the contemporary. Students elected study topics, such as Jesus Christ, Pope John, Martin Luther, Confucius, Martin Luther King, Jr., and Evangelist Billy Graham, and religious societies, such as Old Economy and the Jesus Freaks. Especially effective material for this unit was found by teaching the use of indexes to popular magazine articles and paperback books, and biographies. A third teacher preferred reserving a shelf of background readings and critical works about Chaucer and the *Canterbury Tales* for students to consult during their individual study hall periods. Each approach was different and unique to the teaching style and needs of the individual teacher.

The social studies department most closely rivals the English department in its consistent utilization of the resources and services of the library media center. Library units were developed to support and enrich each period and/or movement in the unfolding of American history: Exploration, Colonization, Revolution, War of 1812, etc. Because modern social studies teaching methods call for student awareness of various and often conflicting views of specific events or historic periods, the librarian seized this opportunity to teach the concept of "primary sources," using such tools as *The Annals of America* and the microfilm collection of *Harper's Weekly* in order to show contrasting contemporary views of important historic events. In addition, course bibliographies are constantly being revised to aid individual students with selection of independent auxiliary reading. "Minorities in the United States" is a newly developing social studies unit that has great appeal and is constantly being extended and enriched by new media appearing on the scene all reflecting the achievement and culture of the various minority groups: collections of primary source materials, such as *Black Annals of America;* compilations of information relating to specific minorities, such as *The Negro Almanac* and *The Indian Almanac;* motion pictures, such as Coronet's series on different minority groups, sound filmstrips on minority groups, as well as new biographies and collective biographies of important minorities figures; new anthologies of poetry, painting, drama, short stories.

The foreign language department makes good use of the library in enriching language courses. The Spanish teachers have enthusiastically pursued, among others, three particularly popular units: "The Aztecs," "The Incas," and "The Mayas." Good rapport between the Spanish faculty and the librarians has resulted in a fine, comprehensive library collection of Spanish print and non-print support and enrichment media. In the most popular Spanish unit, "Trip to Mexico," which is taught toward the end of the school year preparatory to the annual student trip to Mexico, the *AAA Tour Guide of Mexico* receives much more than just academic interest. Likewise, Latin is making a significant comeback because a gifted teacher, through preplanning with the librarians, exploited every teaching-learning media within the library's resources to enhance understanding of and appreciation for our Latin heritage. Her library-based units: "The Punic Wars," "Life in Republican Rome," "Life in Imperial Rome," "Roman Social Life and Customs," are profitably studied by the students. The two Latin units most popular with students have been the year-end units, "The Bacchus Bugle" and the "Trip to Rome." In the "Bacchus Bugle" unit students research all aspects of Roman life in preparation for writing journalistic articles for a gazette of the day as a culminating activity of the course.

Contrary to popular belief about library nonuse by science departments, the mathematics department throughout the year brings classes to the library for work on carefully preplanned units. These include "Applied Math in Everyday Life," which utilizes materials as widely divergent as chess instruction manuals; *Popular Mechanics* magazine articles explaining bicycle gear ratios; mathematical diversions and puzzles, and materials illustrating the application of mathematics in art, science, and music. Of particular interest was a challenging "Advanced Placement Calculus" unit. The librarian wisely "called for help" from the systems-wide library coordinator who agreed with the librarian's assessment that the library mathematics collection could not support the teacher's sophisticated assignment, inasmuch as the course was only in its second year of development.

After extensive preplanning, a positive library learning experience was made possible for this small group of bright students who were rather skeptical of the assignment. The first thing the library coordinator did was to administer a pretest of library skills normally given by many colleges to entering first-year students who, if they pass it, are automatically exempt from a college library orientation course. The high school students' interest became keener after the test when they found out, much to their surprise, that they knew less than they thought they did.

Having captured their interest, the library coordinator explained that the science and technology fields of higher education (which they in all probability as calculus students would enter) demand a more sophisticated research expertise than those research skills learned in high school. She explained that some science and technology library resources were organized in collections using a "classified catalog" as opposed to the dictionary catalog they were accustomed to. To their genuine surprise, she also pointed out that one of the greatest science and technology holdings in the world is the famous science and technology department of the Carnegie Library of Pittsburgh. Arranging a car pool with the calculus instructor and a student-teacher, the library coordinator conducted a two-day field trip of orientation and research work at the Carnegie Library of Pittsburgh, exploring the intricacies of the classified catalog for science and technology.

In addition to providing library education for entire classes of students, examples of library instruction to faculty members, to groups of students, and to individual students demonstrate the flexibility of approach and ingenuity of method mandated by a school library program of excellence. Some examples of educating the individual library user include:

1. preplanning with a social studies teacher and a student committee to insure the success of a new "Minorities" unit before bringing the entire social studies class to the library to work on the project;
2. preplanning with the teacher of Advanced Placement English to provide reserve shelves in the library for media supporting, widening, and deepening the teaching of the "Tragic Drama" unit, and to supply those shelves with appropriate materials to support the subsequent units of the course;
3. instructing individual students, coming in to bone up for tests on Shakespeare's *Hamlet, Macbeth,* and *King Lear,* in the use of recording resources available for individual listening and also pointing out the excellent commentary and criticism to be found on the slipcases of the records as well as the study guides;
4. arranging with the faculty sponsors of the school newspaper and senior yearbook to build collections of newspapers and other journalism materials and

organize them to aid students in perfecting the development of their student publications;

5. teaching students how to use quotation reference books, mathematical puzzles books, and books about optical illusions as sources of information and inspiration in order to take advantage of badly needed extra credit points awarded by one mathematics teacher to students who would complete an interesting and informative mathematics display bulletin board;

6. acquainting boys and girls who are interested in repairing cars with the recognized automobile repair manuals;

7. building interesting displays (and changing them frequently) of books and media within the library, to reflect and capitalize on student interests and fads and to encourage wider reading interests pertaining to nationally topical subjects, such as ecology, political scandals, and drugs.

And so on and on, the examples will multiply—each new instance of successfully educating the high school library user suggesting new strategies and triggering improved methods and techniques. A school district must first adopt, morally support, and financially back a school library program that proclaims the philosophy that the library is, indeed, a learning laboratory and that the librarian is a teacher whose subject is *learning* itself. Such a program must then be staffed with qualified teachers dedicated to the imaginative implementation of that rich philosophy. The school district will then be well on its way to building a school library program of excellence dedicated to widening, broadening, and deepening learning.

NOTES

1. Douglas M. Knight, Foreword, in *Library Services for the Nation's Needs: Toward Fulfillment of a National Policy,* Report of the National Advisory Commission on Libraries (Washington, D.C.: The Commission, 1968).

2. Ruth A. Davies, *The School Library Media Center: A Force for Educational Excellence,* 2nd ed. (New York: R. R. Bowker, 1973).

3. Sidney G. Tickton, ed., *To Improve Learning: An Evaluation of Instructional Technology* (New York: R. R. Bowker, 1970).

4. Margaret G. Cook, *The New Library Key,* 2nd ed. (New York: H. W. Wilson, 1963), p. v.

5. Abraham H. Lass, "How to Do Research," in *Research Guide/Index,* The World Book Encyclopedia, copyright © 1973 Field Enterprises Educational Corporation. Adapted and used by permission of the publisher Field Enterprises Educational Corporation, Chicago. "How to Do Research" provides the librarian with a fine tool for guiding student learning of the basic research techniques and procedures. It is available in reprint form from the publisher, modestly priced at 25¢ each when bought in multiple copies of ten or more; thus most schools can afford to purchase sufficient copies so that each student may have an individual guide to follow while completing his or her research assignment.

BIBLIOGRAPHY AND OTHER RESOURCES

NOTE: Prices listed are subject to change.

HANDBOOKS AND GUIDES

Carman, Robert A., and Adams, W. Royce. *Study Skills: A Student's Guide for Survival.* New York: John Wiley, 1972. $2.95, paper. A self-teaching guide.

Cleary, Florence D. *Discovering Books and Libraries,* 2nd ed. New York: H. W. Wilson, 1972. $2.50, paper.

Lass, Abraham H. "How to Do Research." Chicago: Field Enterprises Educational Corporation, 1973. Single copy, $1.00; multiple copies of ten or more, 25¢ each. Reprint of the article in the *Research Guide/Index* volume of The World Book Encyclopedia.

McCormick, Mona. *Who-What-When-Where-How-Why Made Easy: A Guide to the Practical Use of Reference Books.* New York: New York Times Company, 1971. $5.95.

Rossoff, Martin. *Using Your High School Library,* 2nd ed. New York: H. W. Wilson, 1964. $1.50, paper.

Turabian, Kate L. *Student's Guide for Writing College Papers,* rev. 2nd ed. Chicago: University of Chicago Press, 1970. $3.75; $1.25, paper (134, Phoen.).

Using Almanacs

"Fun in Finding Facts." World Almanac, P.O. Box 489, Radio City Station, New York, N.Y. 10019. Single copy free; quantity prices on request.

"How to Use the Almanac." World Almanac, P.O. Box 489, Radio City Station, New York, N.Y. 10019. Single copy free; quantity prices on request.

Using Indexes

"The Cataloging and Indexing Services of the H. W. Wilson Company." New York: H. W. Wilson, annually. Multiple copies free on request.

"How to Use the *Readers' Guide.*" New York: H. W. Wilson, annually. Multiple copies free on request.

Using Quotations

Mersand, Joseph. *A Guide to the Use of Bartlett's Familiar Quotations,* 2nd ed. Boston: Little, Brown, 1962. $1.25, paper.

NONBOOK MEDIA

Bookmarks

Dewey Decimal Bookmarks. Sturgis Library Products, P.O. Box 130, Sturgis, Mich. 49091. $5.75 for 500.

Catalog Cards

Enlarged Wilson Catalog Cards. Sturgis Library Products, P.O. Box 130, Sturgis, Mich. 49091. Sets range in price from $1.50 to $15.00.

"Vicalog." Eye Gate, 146–01 Archer Ave., Jamaica, N.Y. 11435. $8.00. A flip-over enlargement of a catalog card designed to stand on the top of the card catalog.

Charts

Guide to the Library. Josten's Library Supplies, 4070 Shirley Drive, S.W., Atlanta, Ga. 30336. $9.50.
"A Story About the Dewey Decimal System of Classification." National Library Week, 58 W. 40th St., New York, N.Y. 10018.

Filmstrips

The Card Catalog: Dewey Decimal Classification (sound). Library Filmstrip Center, 3033 Aloma, Wichita, Kan. 67211. $21.00.
Encyclopedias: Basic Knowledge (sound). Library Filmstrip Center, 3033 Aloma, Wichita, Kan. 67211. $21.00.
Encyclopedias: Usage Techniques (sound). Library Filmstrip Center, 3033 Aloma, Wichita, Kan. 67211. $21.00.
Reference Collection (sound). Library Filmstrip Center, 3033 Aloma, Wichita, Kan. 67211. $21.00.

Motion Pictures

Critical Thinking: Making Sure of Facts. Coronet, 65 E. South Water St., Chicago, Ill. 60601.
Effective Writing: Research Skills. Coronet, 65 E. South Water St., Chicago, Ill. 60611.

Multimedia Kits

Your Library Resources and How to Use the Readers' Guide. New York: H. W Wilson. $99.00.

LIBRARY-USE INSTRUCTION: A COLLEGE TEACHER'S VIEWPOINT

JOHN D. STARKEY
Professor, Department of Secondary Professional Education, Northern Illinois University

My viewpoint on library use instruction for the college student is that of a faculty member. From this perspective I am offering ideas that college teachers may use, adopt, adapt, change, improve, and yes, even reject—and all are aimed at putting enthusiasm in library study for the undergraduate and especially for the graduate.

The procedure for teaching library use and the success of a research methods course depends largely on the purposes, needs, and relevancy of the teaching. There are many different methods and techniques for helping students become aware of the importance of the library in their college work and eventually in their professional life. Procedures vary from university to university and from teacher to teacher, but it is doubtful if success is attained by very many students unless the method suits individual student needs. My procedure is described here, and no assumption is made that it is the best procedure in existence; rather it is presented as one successful way of teaching library usage to the college student that has generated enthusiasm for library study and use.

"The Starkey Individualized Brainstorming Method" begins in the very first class meeting when the teacher sets the stage for the need and relevancy of library study. In this example the class was an educational research methods class at the graduate level. In the initial session each student talks with a neighboring student and after about 15 minutes of conversation attempts to describe to the class the research project and literature search techniques of this neighbor. This accomplishes two things: it forces one student to listen and it forces the other student to make precise his or her ideas. The role of the teacher in this first phase is to guide the students' development of search strategy. The students are not allowed time to go home, mull over their fears and inadequacies, but each must tell a neighbor what research he or she intends to do in the library. Students do not have to defend their ideas before the class, but their neighbor must be able to explain the project. This gives both students and their neighbors some realization of the limits of their knowledge of the information resources in the particular field and leads them to seek more knowledge of how to use their library.

Often one hears about students plagiarizing or using other people's research projects. With this method, plagiarism is almost impossible because the class and the instructor are so familiar with what the student is attempting. While a student may use a paper prepared in another class, but not published, we expect the student to improve upon it, by using library research, experiment, or survey. The creative impetus involved in researching a phase of knowledge the student feels most expert in helps to give relevancy and motivation for the student to do in-depth library research that may help him or her to reach intellectual heights not otherwise attempted.

The important aspect of this exercise is to create an enthusiastic and relevant approach to library usage and study. The individualized technique encouraged an interest in a course in library usage that was formerly mundane. Many of the students' creative ideas are published in various journals, not as a course requirement but as a result of knowledge gleaned from relevant and meaningful library study.

Too many of our college students lack library proficiency. All students should have some library use instruction so that they can competently and confidently deal with information resources. "Who knows only his own generation remains a child" is the inscription engraved over the front of the University of Colorado library. Over one of the entrances is an inscription that reads: "Enter here the timeless fellowship of the human spirit." It is in the library the students ideally should begin their quest for social, cultural, and intellectual maturation. In this spirit each professor should strive to stimulate each student toward library use.

The eagerness and resolution the student approaches the library with depends largely on the attitude of the college instructor. The students who miss this aspect of knowledge may miss the lesson altogether because they know only what they can memorize and regurgitate, but not where to look for information and how to intellectualize it once they have it.

The size of the university and the library are important correlates to library use. The larger the university, the larger the library must be to take care of the divergent needs of the intellectual community. In order to engagingly introduce the library, there must be adequate student space and a sufficient supply of library materials. Too many of our libraries are so steeped in tradition and regulations that what should be a leisurely, enjoyable field trip to the library often fails to be so for the user.

With the explosion of knowledge, it becomes increasingly apparent that faculty members are faced with the difficult and important task of helping students to be self-reliant in gathering and using information for personal or professional use.

First, in spite of some teachers who believe that education "just happens," it is necessary to set the stage for library instruction and usage. This can be done by handouts, pamphlets, or question-and-answer periods, but a well-organized lecture supported by media can still be highly efficient. The plethora of gimmicks, motivators, and exhortations employed to increase library use are not necessary stimuli for the intelligent and motivated students. They have the desire for knowledge, but like Tolmanian theory, they want to take the easiest path.

If questions arise during the lecture, the teacher should switch to a discussion in order to generate enough feedback to answer general, troublesome unknowns. In a discussion, it is important to watch for all signs rather than just the simple verbal questions. Alert teachers ask themselves questions, such as: Are the students interested? Do they respond with nods, smiles, or perplexed looks? Are they alert and interested in the instruction because of its relevancy and usefulness?

Discussions with the entire group or with members of various small groups are an important way of getting ideas across to the students. Discussions should be carried on by the teacher at the student level and usually are more successful if the teacher makes an effort to listen and get at the root of the problems. Teachers using these discussion techniques should arrange students in circles, at tables, or informally. There should be eye-level communication, laughter, smiles, stories, body movement, restive expression, interest in the discussion, leaning forward and back, crossing legs, crossing and uncrossing arms, notetaking by the instructor, and courtesy and politeness toward the discussant. This is in contrast with the more formal lecture presentation that uses such media as filmstrips, overheads, slide projectors, charts, and the chalk board. Discussion techniques when used properly can help greatly in creating enthusiasm in library study and usage.

Another way of instructing in library use is by a panel discussion involving two or more persons presenting an idea to a larger group and with a question-and-answer period following it.

Videotaping is an excellent method of teaching library usage. The advent of inexpensive videotape makes it possible to show some students in action. It is definitely better to show real people in a situation rather than an actor, because the task then becomes relevant. Movies fall into the same category and should be used whenever a meaningful film can be found.

Another recent aspect of library instruction is the use of microform and photocopy machines. A demonstration is necessary to teach both graduate and undergraduate students how to use the machines in the library. One method is to give out short, individual assignments that include use of microreaders and printers and the photocopier. A demonstration or lecture on the machines could be supplemented with slides depicting the various machines and their operation.

Instructor-supervised visits to the library are a must, especially for classes in graduate research, and they should take the form of an orientation session—a short talk, demonstration, lecture, slide presentation, and then some on-site use of the library by students. The following activities have been successfully used in a library-use instruction program:

1. Self-guided tour. Northern Illinois University has a tour that is thorough and aids many students in their library orientation and usage. The tour must be well planned, with maps, locations, rooms clearly marked, and have the cooperation and help of the library staff.

2. Subject experience. Give individual students a particular subject and have them find as many sources as possible. This experience is designed to help the students with the card catalog, and indexes, such as *Readers' Guide* and *Psychological Abstracts*.

3. Author search. Give the student an author's name to investigate. This will provide an experience with the author card and the various listings in which the author location is of prime importance.

4. Event search. An interesting experience can arise from the search for information on a current event. The students are asked to look in periodicals, books, newspapers, etc., to uncover all the details.

5. A person search. The students are individually assigned to a personality, such as Lyndon Johnson, and challenged to find references to this particular individual in as many places as possible. This search, especially when related to class subject matter, can be very rewarding.

6. Small group visitation. Have one librarian escort each group of five people on a guided tour of the library. Small group visitations are often failures if the preorientation procedures are inadequate or the assignment is mere busywork, or there is no meaningful dialogue, discussion, and followup. This exercise really should be one of the college teacher's most effective instruments.

7. Large group conducted library tour. A large group tour is difficult to conduct in many libraries because of the heavy demands for quiet and serenity in the research areas.

8. Interlibrary loan. Students often need materials and books not available in their own library, which may lead them to the interlibrary loan department. A discussion about and a visit to the interlibrary loan department would be of benefit to the students.

9. A specific exercise
    (a) Each student chooses a subject.
    (b) The student is required to list four types of library material:
        (1) Three books from the card catalog
        (2) Three periodicals
        (3) One review of research studies found on microfilm or microfiche
        (4) One article from Educational Research Information Center (ERIC)
        (5) One review of research read by the student in a reference work, such as *The Encyclopedia of Research*
    (c) The student could bring one of the books and one of the periodicals listed to class for use in studying and reviewing current articles.

10. The Educational Research Information Center. The student must become familiar with ERIC, which is fast becoming one of our major document-holding sources in the world. In this exercise ask the student to research ERIC for a specific kind of information and report back to the class.

11. Thesis and dissertation exercise for the graduate student. Assign the student to find and read six research papers. Two historical, two descriptive, and two experimental papers should give the student ample experience in this very important library function.

12. A treasure hunt. The above exercises can be incorporated in a scavenger-type treasure hunt in which several items are given out for location. This can turn into a farce if all students are given the same task, and many libraries tend to frown on any activity that seems to be frenzied or noisy.

IN SUMMARY

The successful teaching of library study usage can be compared to successful teaching in other subject areas. The Florida studies, especially the one by Arthur Combs noted in the bibliography, have pointed out the characteristics of the effective teacher. This is certainly appropriate for the college teacher of library instruction. While the following description based on the Combs publication has been published in many places, it is particularly apt for teachers of library usage: The successful teacher perceives students as able, rather than unable. He sees them as friendly and worthy rather than unfriendly and unworthy. He believes that they are internally motivated, dependable, and helpful. The successful teacher sees himself as worthy, wanted, dependable, able, and with people rather than apart. He sees the teaching task as an encouraging process.

This certainly is appropriate for library study, which is, in the final analysis, a do-it-yourself project. The successful teacher's general frame of reference is internal rather than external, geared to people rather than things, and emphasizing perceptual meanings rather than facts and events. If each teacher of library usage can follow some of these proven and researched tenets along with the techniques listed in this chapter, his or her chances of helping students will be increased considerably.

BIBLIOGRAPHY

Ahlers, Eleanor E. "Instruction in the Use of the Library." Mimeographed. Chicago: American Association of School Librarians, 1962, pp. 1–4.

American Library Association. "Show and Tell: A Clinic on Using Media in Library Instruction." Presented during ALA's Annual Convention, Chicago, June 1972. Chicago: The Association, 1972, pp. 28–29.

Beeler, Richard. "Library Orientation and Instruction at the University of Denver." *Colorado Academic Library* 8 (Spring 1972): 20–24.

Combs, Arthur W., et al. *Florida Studies in the Helping Professions.* University of Florida Monographs Social Sciences No. 37. Gainesville: University of Florida Press, 1969, pp. 10–71.

Griffin, Lloyd W., and Clarke, Jack A. "Orientation and Instruction of Graduate

Students in the Use of the University Library: A Survey." *College and Research Libraries* 33 (November 1972): 467–472.

Knapp, Patricia B. "A Suggested Program of College Instruction in the Use of the Library." *Library Quarterly* 26 (July 1956): 224–231.

Lee, Sul H., ed. *Library Orientation.* Papers presented at the First Annual Conference on Library Orientation held at Eastern Michigan University, May 7, 1971. Ann Arbor, Mich.: Pierian Press, 1972.

Perkins, Ralph. *The Prospective Teacher's Knowledge of Library Fundamentals: A Study of the Responses Made by 4,170 College Seniors to Tests Designed to Measure Familiarity with Libraries.* Metuchen, N.J.: Scarecrow Press, 1965.

Schnucker, R. V. "For New Stars Through Learning." *Learning Today* 6 (Fall 1973): 55–64.

THE LECTURE-TEXTBOOK SYNDROME
AND LIBRARY USE

ROBERT A. POIS

*Associate Professor, History Department,
University of Colorado*

Today, the phrase "crisis in education" is a much favored one, and probably for very good reason. Through teach-in and dropout, the 1960s called into question the relevance of virtually every field in the Arts and Sciences (with the possible exception of sociology) in a world that for those young in heart—or at least hoping to be—seemed to be characterized by plastic indifference and mechanized brutality. At the same time, the more-or-less traditional "lecture-textbook syndrome" was condemned by students and—although perhaps somewhat disingenuously in many cases—by professors alike as being somehow representative of the gross depersonalization and alienation that seemed to characterize modern, industrial bourgeois society. Now, in the 1970s, administrators, professors, and some students as well declare with obvious relief that the great period of disruption is over. To be sure, students are as alienated as ever before; but, the trivia bowls have replaced the teach-ins, withdrawal has replaced activism, alcohol has been staging a heroic comeback against drugs. However, the 1970s has seen the emergence of yet another educational crisis. Partly in reaction to the events of the 1960s, partly due to the drying up of state and federal funds, the American public, as accurately represented in the various state legislatures and in the person of chief executive Jedermann, has displayed a perhaps unwonted sense of cupidity and impatience with at least the system of higher education in the United States. Now, the heat is on, and perhaps for the first time in recent memory, bemused professors are being told by equally bemused administrators that they are expected to produce not tomes, or even so-called liberally educated students; but, rather, increased credit hours. The very things against which the student rebel of the 1960s was rebelling, the large classroom and the lecture system, are now seen by legislatures and, perhaps most important of all, by many parents as somehow constituting the backbone of the American system of higher education. The capitalist principle, previously kept on the sidelines in the form of semisecret projects for industry and defense, has suddenly emerged full-blown as the pedagogical leitmotif of the American college and university. The professors are no longer to be ivory-tower pedants grinding out monographs on subjects of almost perverse obscurity. Each is now to be a sort of esoteric plant manager, watched over by an administration possessed of the paternalistic concern of an army of bookkeepers. Education must justify, i.e., pay for, itself. These have been the major pressures upon higher education during the 1960s and the early 1970s. How these have affected the so-called lecture-textbook syndrome and, in turn, the use of libraries will be explained later. For now, there is yet one more general force (or pressure) that we must concern ourselves with. This is the American tradition of mass higher education.

For at least the past 50 years or so, the "American dream" of providing higher education for the masses has been in the process of realization. At first, of course, realization of this dream largely was confined to those white of skin and relatively well-off; but, the last decade has witnessed an opening of university doors to minority students as well, although the speed that this has taken place with has not been, on the whole, precipitous, at least in the eyes of the minorities. Presumably, this is all to the good and the country can derive some measure of satisfaction from this translation, however partial, of American hypothetical egalitarianism into reality. Both of the two major events considered above, i.e., the student revolt of the 1960s and the rise of a sort of public resentment against "freeloading" faculty and students that has characterized the 1970s have to be considered against this general development. Indeed, as we shall soon see, all three forces hang together. Or, perhaps one should say that the two more *zeitgebunden* phenomena of the past decade and a half flow logically out of the more general one of the emergence of mass education during the past 50 years.

It is the concentration of this writer that the new result of all of this has been to create a general pressure upon professor and librarian that can only have —at least in the immediate future—deleterious results insofar as true educational advancement and improved use of libraries are concerned. First of all, I would like to consider the overall effect of the trend toward mass education upon the lecture-textbook syndrome and secondarily upon the use of libraries. The effect(s) of the events of the 1960s and early 1970s then will be considered in detail.

Perhaps it would be somewhat of an exaggeration to claim that the American Myth always has implied that everybody in the United States, outside of hopelessly depraved felons and confirmed idiots, has to be educated. The notion that women are deserving of a higher education has received broad dissemination and acceptance only in this century, and as mentioned before, minority students, at least in large numbers, have not been encouraged to seek an education until very recently. However, mass education as a pedagogical, political, and even moral concept has provided a heuristic point of departure not only for educators and legislators but for the public as a whole ever since the establishment of land-grant colleges. To be sure, many of these were so-called agricultural schools, self-consciously designed to produce a more efficient yeomanry. At the same time, however, the notion of a "higher" education, however baldly practical, for a substantial number of citizens regardless of class was a fairly unique one. Furthermore, as indicated above, that traditional object of parental concern and scrimping, the "college education," has become, if certainly not *the* usual, then most certainly *a* usual follow-up to high school.

As suggested by the late Richard Hofstadter, it is quite probably true that the United States can be generally considered anti-intellectual. However, a curious dialectical corollary to this mood has been the notion that everybody should, or ought to be able to be, exposed to the college or university experience. (Perhaps, however, this is not so curious. In a country where the university degree is hardly an object of veneration, simply because there are so many people holding it, an at least indifferent attitude toward things intellectual can be expected.) At the state universities and larger, privately endowed schools, this has had a decisive impact on pedagogy and the use of libraries.

It is obvious—or ought to be—that in large universities attending to the needs of thousands of students, mass education compels the professors to try and reach as many students as possible per given period of time. The most efficacious method of doing this—particularly when one bears in mind the differing backgrounds and abilities of the students with which the faculty are confronted—is through the traditional lecture and textbook syndrome. To be sure, this approach can be avoided in smaller classes or in "special" classes in which rigorously controlled enrollment ensures the entrance of exceptionally bright or well-trained students. Also, there are professors who insist that larger classes, e.g., Western Civilization, can be broken up into study or discussion sections, textbooks and lectures abolished (or at least reduced to a happy minimum), and students left to seek out their own respective levels and interests, assisted from time to time by their brotherly minded mentor. In such a fashion, it is maintained, will education become more "relevant" to the student. However, if a professor thinks that it is of importance for a student to learn the significance of the nominalist/realist controversy as well as the significance of Nat Turner's revolt or the Warsaw Ghetto uprising, and if this professor wants to be quite certain that the student will be at least *exposed* to the awesome panoply that constitutes the content of a discipline, he or she will then have to fall back upon: (1) the lecture and (2) the textbook(s). Relevance might well be of importance in determining what one chooses to apply to the task of dealing with contemporary issues or problems. However, the pool of knowledge that one draws example or allusion from has to be both wide and deep. In a mass education type of environment, the best way to assure width (or at least the possibility of such) is through the lecture-textbook syndrome, however impersonal this process might seem. Again, it is well to emphasize that smaller institutions of higher learning, or professors teaching relatively small classes consisting of students with more uniform backgrounds, might well be able to avoid this syndrome. However, if large numbers of students are to learn that which is considered necessary to provide either rudimentary knowledge of a discipline or that elementary substructure from which more specialized knowledge can be gained, then the lecture-textbook syndrome will remain, pathetic cries of irrelevance and authoritarianism notwithstanding.

Nevertheless, there can be no gainsaying that such an approach can have and, in large measure, *has had* a very bad effect upon library usage. The reasons for this are not too hard to fathom. First of all, the ordinary lecture course is set up in the following manner: lectures are written, dealing with those areas or issues of a subject considered important by the professor. Either as complements to or adjuncts to these lectures, textbooks are assigned. Possibly, a certain number of books are put "on reserve" as well, with the pious, and usually unfounded hope that at least a majority of those in the class will be motivated enough to investigate these books as well as the texts. To be sure, most upper-division courses, i.e., junior level and above, do formally require students to make use of a library. However, the extent to which students actually make substantive use of reserve materials, to say nothing of books other than those placed on reserve, is open to some question.

Of course, the student is not solely responsible for this situation. Another reason—and perhaps in some ways the most important—is the failure of a large number of professors (particularly and understandably those with classes of 50 or more students) to assign papers that call for the use of library resources beyond the *Book Review Digest* or the several fine and amply illustrated encyclopedias most libraries are happily endowed with. Besides lecturing, the professor generally has things to do other than taking the time to grade 50 or more papers of between ten and 30 pages in length. Furthermore, an unfortunate effect of the dropping of the first-year English composition requirement (plus, of course, the general loosening of standards at the secondary school level) has been the decline in quality of students' written work to the point where reading large numbers of undergraduate papers serves only to bring out the Calvinism in even the most mild-mannered instructor. At any rate, the overall effect of mass education has been to greatly restrict the assigning of papers that call for the *substantive* use of library resources. Again, one must emphasize that in smaller colleges, or in smaller or so-called honors classes in larger schools, this condition often does not or, at least, *need not* obtain.

In and of itself, then, that mass education hallowed by American egalitarian sentimentalism (if not really by American active involvement) has been in part responsible for a situation in which the lecture-textbook syndrome has become a pedagogical necessity. This has had the effect of necessarily inhibiting truly meaningful use of the library, both because of the very structure of the lecture course itself and because of the simple mechanics of dealing with the large number of students generally found in such courses. The burden of deciding whether or not "their" students, i.e., those students in the larger lecture-style classes, make extensive use of library resources obviously rests upon the professors. If they are willing and able to take the time necessary to advise students on papers and to read such papers, student use of library resources obviously will be fairly extensive. It must be seen, however, that the overall effect of the lecture-textbook syndrome—a *syndrome* in large measure necessitated by the traditional demands imposed by mass education—insofar as library use is concerned has been and is negative.

All this is certainly bad enough. Yet, events of the past ten years have exacerbated the situation to a really extraordinary degree. First of all, we must consider the so-called student revolt, one which is usually dated from the Free Speech Movement in Berkeley in 1964 and which played itself out (or perhaps this phase of it) in the 1970 uprisings against the U.S. invasion of Cambodia. (Often, the spring uprisings in Paris in 1968 are seen as apotheosizing student activism against the bureaucratic, indifferent state.) That, at least at this time and place, students and proletarians manned the same barricades has endowed these activities with an almost romantic aura in the eyes of young American and European radicals.

The Columbia uprisings of the same year saw no such alliance. While political motives bulked large in the activities and goals of "radicals" at this time, a good part of the revolt was directed against irrelevant and authoritarian aspects of both secondary and higher education. Higher education, however, no doubt due to the higher level of consciousness of those supposedly victimized by it, was on the receiving end of the brunt of such attacks. The American university—with its established ties to defense industries and defense research, almost imperialistic attitude toward the surrounding community (e.g., Columbia to upper Manhattan), stultified administrators and research-oriented faculty—found itself up against the ivy wall, dependent, in some cases, upon the most easily stereotyped forces of social reaction, the police and the national guard, for protection against those whom it was attempting to educate. Anger against the university for neglecting minority groups was also expressed by the young rebels, as well as a more general, somewhat less well-defined anger against the "system" as a whole, with its "irrelevant" requirements and demands, requirements and demands that seemed to reflect the compulsive and tyrannical pressures of an acquisitive bourgeois society.

What the rebels of the 1960s really wanted—even some of those who, being Marxists, should have known better—was the translation of the "American dream" into reality. The generation of the late 1960s, post-World War II either by birth, consciousness, or both, had been weened on a sugar-coated democratic/egalitarian pap both at school and at home. Now, the American college and university were confronted by a generation of largely middle-class idealists, people who had known no hardship to speak of and, being idealists, wanted the world. The logical corollary at the university level to "Power to the people" was "Democracy in the classroom." Implicit in such a demand, of course, was an attack upon the lecture-textbook syndrome. Professors were being told that the days of force-fed knowledge were over, and that the students had to be given a say in such things as subject matter treated and choice of books. Presumably, demands of this nature, if acted upon, would have allowed for a higher degree of student participation in their own education, thus entailing greater, or at least more sophisticated use of the library. Such was not the case, however.

The student movement of the 1960s is dead, at least for the moment. It was an active force in educational change for too small a period to be as effective as some wished it to be, or as disruptive as others feared. There was an aspect to it that has lingered on, however, an aspect that cannot be conducive to more sophisticated library use. A very strong anti-intellectual posture was part and parcel of the student upheaval of the 1960s. The manifesto was to replace the book, and street action was to take the place of contemplation. Indeed, calls for action for action's sake, appeals to the heart rather than to the mind, combined with a strong emphasis upon changes in "lifestyle" seemed to point to an ideology (if such it can be called) more akin to right-wing romanticism than to left-wing revolutionary action. The radical left traditionally has rooted itself in the enlightenment principle of reasoned action in terms of one's own self-interest. Some of the slogans of the student movement—"Up against the wall, mother-fuckers!"; "Down with the intellectuals!"; etc.—sounded more like the early twentieth-century cries of the proto-Fascistic Italian Futurists than anything else. The anti-intellectualism that manifested itself in the student movement of the 1960s hardly augured well for greater use of libraries. Indeed, libraries were, more often than not, viewed as being part of the same oppressive machinery that embraced the lecture-textbook syndrome.

This anti-intellectualism is probably the single most residual aspect of the turbulent 1960s. Today, just about any educator who has any contact at all with students has been confronted with the following declaration: "I am going to become a leatherworker," or "I am going to take a trip by jeep through Central America." Why? "Because I want to find out about the real world." How it is more "real" to punch laceholes in shoe leather or hack one's way through a tangle of lianas and bushmasters than it is to read a book has never been terribly clear, at least to me. To be sure, such attitudes are hardly new. Never-theless, the rise of a sort of *Lebensphilosophie* à la nineteenth-century Roman-ticism seems to have taken place in recent years, and more than ever before. Of course, this mood does not mean that instructors have accommodated it, i.e., by not assigning books and periodical articles. However, it certainly has inhibited use, by students, at least of academic libraries. Naturally, it would be most inaccurate to suggest that reading just enough to "get by" is something new among college students. However, the formidable anti-intellectual rationaliza-tions supplied by the Timothy Learys and Abbie Hoffmanns of today were lacking in previous years. Thus, both the anti-intellectual activism and the anti-intellectual quietism, products of the 1960s and the lethargic sequel to this period, have had a somewhat debilitating effect upon library use, while the denouement of the original revolt against academic formalism and the attendant lecture-textbook syndrome has been to leave the latter generally unaffected, except to the degree that individual faculty members, out of conviction or out of a disingenuous desire to be loved by students, have capitulated to the some-what strained concern for "relevance."

As far-reaching as the effects of the student revolt seem to have been upon student attitudes toward education, and thus secondarily upon the library, they pale in comparison to those produced, in part, in reaction to this revolt. Never before, at least in recent history, has the basically conservative nature of the average citizen been revealed so clearly as today. This could be seen in the reaction of John Doe to the Kent State and Jackson State shootings in 1970. "Elitist" news commentators and columnists, as well as a few "soft-headed" politicians might have decried the shootings. However, the average citizens were as little disturbed by them as they were by the events in Southeast Asia that were responsible for the ugly mood of that terrible summer. In the overwhelming election, two and one half years later, of a man almost belligerently committed to the status quo, the public mood of anger against all those forces that threatened domestic order and tranquillity achieved its zenith. This mood of conservatism is probably the most important fact of life today, both for higher education and for the academic library that serves it.

Now, the American public and the legislatures that represent it are demanding that colleges and universities perform the "traditional" role of servicing large numbers of students. Faculty research, except, perhaps, that in the sciences and in engineering, is being called into account and—albeit for different reasons—parents are agreeing with their children that professors really ought to be spending more time in the classroom and less time involved in specialized projects of their own. Smaller, perhaps more esoteric classes are to be abandoned, or at least reduced in number. In brief, the American institution of higher learning is being called upon to take account of itself, to prove that it is providing a given amount of educational credit per dollar spent on this institution.

The result of all of this has been, or will be, to place an increasing demand upon the professor to teach larger numbers of students. Naturally, the result of this demand can only be a further strengthening of the lecture-textbook syndrome. For now colleges and universities are being told that, if they are to be financed by a public increasingly wary of such extracurricular activities as sit-ins, teach-ins, and the like, they must "service" the community or state in much the same fashion as a business office or a factory. Obviously, the most efficacious way of doing this—if not in the eye of public opinion, then at least in that of the harassed professor—is through the traditional lecture-textbook syndrome. Again, it is obvious that some professors, i.e., those teaching smaller classes (those smaller classes that survive the recent more obvious intrusion of the capitalist method into education) or those teaching at smaller institutions, will be able to avoid the lecture method, or at least to supplement it with such things as discussion sections, tutorials, and so on. However, the professor teaching at a large state university, especially a professor who is in any way conscientious about teaching, will have to fall back upon the tried—if not exactly "true"—lecture-textbook syndrome. Only this way will the now heightened demand for "mass" education be met. Naturally, if such is the case, the problems we have seen earlier, i.e., during the salad years of unchallenged mass education, will intrude all the more onto the library scene. Professors, as before, will rely on texts of one sort or another, library readings will be confined to those relatively few books put on reserve, and truly meaningful use of the library will be reserved for the professor and for the graduate student. Here again, though, we face another problem.

Due to the drying up of previously substantial public and private funds, and due increasingly to government efforts in the direction of economy (sic), monies formerly available to graduate students have been reduced to penny-ante proportions. At the same time, the job market has shrunk in proportion to declining funds available for full-time employment positions. Across the country, admissions officers, under these pressures of vanishing funds and shrinking job markets, are naturally cutting back on admissions to graduate programs. All this, if it has not already, will add up to fewer and fewer students electing to do graduate work, at least in the formal sense. There will be more students going into such fields as law, government service, or business. Perhaps some of this is a good thing, in that many of those who entered graduate school in the 1960s were doing so either to escape the draft or to escape the challenge of steady employment or marriage.

However, outside of its very obvious hardship upon bright young people who are eager to do graduate work, the general cutback in graduate programs has had, or will have, an extremely bad effect upon substantive library usage. For it is obvious that any major college or university library worth its salt is characterized as a "good research library." With the demand for research sharply reduced, the demand for the "research library" will follow suit. Whether legislatures in general will actually cut back on funds allocated to library research purposes is uncertain. However, the immediate (if not long-range) effect of the recent glorification of capitalism in the modern university cannot help to be a bad one, particularly insofar as the research library is concerned. The cutting back of graduate programs in the liberal arts, combined with the previously mentioned emphasis upon an education that "pays for itself," poses a rather baleful challenge, both to the professor who seeks at least an adjunct, if not an alternative, to the lecture-textbook syndrome, and to the librarian who sees valuable library resources and potentially innovative programs go down the drain, due to an educational system inherently inimical to mature use of libraries.

It is customary for historians, those most gloomy of pedagogues, to offer gloomy predictions for the future. Is there any way *out* of the dilemma facing professor and librarian alike? Actually, in the opinion of this writer, several things can be done to salvage American higher education and the library. First of all, the American public must be persuaded to accept the fact that mass education, at least at the level of so-called higher education, not only is impossible in any meaningful sense but is in fact a somewhat undemocratic way of doing things. Not everybody belongs in a four-year liberal arts program. To be sure, matters of color or class have no roles to play in deciding who goes to college. However, the notion that each citizen needs to be exposed to a smattering of Thackeray, or that he or she has to be aware of the historical debate concerning the role of the Girondists during the French Revolution is absurd. To precisely the same degree is it unnecessary that this citizen observe a paramecium waving its cilia. Certainly, it is of immense importance, if we are indeed to have a culture, that some people, i.e., those who are genuinely interested in such matters, have the opportunity to participate in the activities mentioned above. To say that every citizen of the land has to do this, however, is insulting both to the average citizen and to the disciplines concerned. This surprisingly parochial notion in turn stems from probably one of the most dangerous ideas ever to be imposed upon education; viz., that the goal of education is good citizenship. To be sure, higher education ought to provide opportunities to sharpen one's critical faculties and thus, indirectly, to allow one to participate more meaningfully in such things as political decision making. However, if higher education actually accomplished the purpose of educating one toward good citizenship, it would serve the purpose of educating one toward acceptance of the status quo. Fortunately, there is little evidence to suggest that American education, if such indeed is its purpose, ever has succeeded in inculcating students with those virtues that, taken together, constitute good citizenship. Views toward politics and social change seem more to be functions of class, occupation, and region rather than anything else. Nevertheless, especially today there is an increasing demand that colleges and universities produce the well-rounded "good Joe" (or Josephine), studious, industrious, and above all, content with his (or her) lot. Thus, in a curious way, the American notion of "education toward citizenship" could well have effects as dangerous as the more obviously insidious attitude—traditionally strong in Germany—that the realms of culture and politics are distinct, one from the other. Each of these respective attitudes different as they are, in content and origin, posits the political eunuch as the highest form of social life. Whether the vast mass of citizenry view this as bad is, of course, open to some question. Somehow, they must be made to see this, a so-called mass education, with citizenship as its rationalization, if not its goal, is undesirable. First of all, they must be made to see that mass education does not work. Rather, it serves to stifle creativity in the classroom and in the library. Second, they must see that mass *indoctrination*, i.e., education toward citizenship, even if it can work, is undesirable.

Since the nefarious attitude described above is part and parcel of that more general attitude described earlier, viz., that education has to be "useful" (i.e., it must pay for itself in terms of service and utility) and since these attitudes are in turn due to the general capitalistic orientation of American society, one could well argue that only the most radical of social changes could dispose of, or at least alter them. However, there is little hope of this for the future. What has to be done is that educators and librarians, through the media and the legislatures, must present more of a case for radical educational reform. Education must be respected in and of itself and not because its existence constitutes a pillar of some ill-defined and potentially dangerous sense of utility/citizenship. Furthermore, through expanded programs of technical and vocational education—and through such devices as more sharply separating such institutions as business schools from liberal arts institutions—resources must be placed at the disposal of those who do not wish or need to go to college. Naturally, institutions of higher learning can and should have extension classes available for those who want them. However, the nauseating charade of attempting to educate the bored and ill-motivated undergraduates on an assembly line basis, something which, as we have seen, necessitates the preservation of the lecture-textbook syndrome, has to end. At the same time, though, greater support than ever before must be provided for graduate education. As a rule, the graduate student is reasonably committed to forwarding the cultural integrity of the community. He or she will be the teacher, political analyst, or librarian of tomorrow (whether or not he or she is a "good citizen" is beside the point). The ending of our ludicrous system of mass education, coupled with a strengthening of the graduate programs, is absolutely essential if meaningful change and innovation are to take place in the university classroom. These changes and innovations are of imminent importance if the, at this time, needed predominance of the lecture-textbook syndrome is to be broken and more substantive use of library facilities is to be made.

The notion that the university and its library somehow lead ivory-tower existences is both absurd and dangerous. Unfortunately, far too many educators and librarians seem to think this to be the case. Educators and librarians are both guilty of viewing their relationships to public and legislature as being ad hoc in nature. Administrators, faculty members, and librarians grind out long-range proposals, to be sure. However, truly meaningful educational *change* is seldom mentioned. Education cannot maintain a lobby like those proffered by lumber, oil, and steel interests, or by American riflemen. For if it confines itself to seeking to obtain "its share" of tax revenues and the GNP, it will merely act to justify the public attitude that education is a business like all other businesses. Paradoxically, if American education is to be able to justify itself *an sich,* it must become more involved, and on a *long-range* basis, with the very community from whose rigorous control it seeks to escape. Only in such a way can the tyranny of a poorly rationalized and perversely applied system of mass education end; and only through the ending of this tyranny can the alarming trends of the past 15 years be reversed.

In this essay, the writer has attempted to point out two facts: (1) that the lecture-textbook syndrome and poor use of library resources go together, and (2) that both the professor and the librarian are ensconced in a society whose incredibly parochial and disingenuous views of the role of education are inimical to truly meaningful use of classroom and library resources. Whether this society wants or indeed is able to alter these views is uncertain. What is certain is the *necessity* of librarian and teacher working together in a truly meaningful attempt to persuade the American public of the need of educational change. If such a change is not forthcoming, the American university classroom will either be ruled by the lecture-texbook syndrome or pedagogical chaos. The library would stand in either case, not even as a monument to societal waste and educational decay, but rather as a dust-filled and ill-served mausoleum.

INSTRUCTING COLLEGE FACULTY IN THE BIBLIOGRAPHIC RESOURCES OF THEIR SUBJECT FIELD: A CASE STUDY

MARGERY READ
Media Utilization Advisor, Bergen Community College, Paramus, New Jersey

SARAH KATHARINE THOMSON
Chairman of the Library and Learning Resources Department, Bergen Community College, Paramus, New Jersey

For the past three years, the library faculty at Bergen Community College Library Learning Resources Center have offered graduate courses to Bergen teaching faculty.[1] Because we are a learning resources center dealing with print and nonprint materials, we give a course in the use of audiovisual materials in the classroom and a course in the bibliography of a faculty member's subject specialty. The bibliography course concentrates on developing skill in the subject bibliography of the faculty-student's discipline. Primarily it covers doctoral and professional research methodology and bibliography, but the course also includes selection of texts and reading material for community college students. "Special Topics in Bibliography" is a three credit graduate course of the University Extension Division, Graduate School of Library Service, Rutgers University.[2]

The faculty at a community college are often students themselves. Librarians give advice on first-year (English) composition on the one hand and doctoral dissertation proposals on the other. The Library Learning Resources staff at Bergen has always taught general and specialized library orientation classes to students, and in the spring of 1972 formal instruction for faculty members was offered as well.

Probably no self-respecting faculty member would admit to being bewildered by a library, but the fact is that an amazing number do not know where to begin with library research. They have little idea what bibliographic tools exist or how to use them; they cannot organize a search strategy; some of them are even baffled by the Library of Congress classification scheme. The reference desk has been coping with this problem since the college opened; however, we had been unable to give individual faculty members the time and organized instruction they needed.

In 1971 Professor Peter A. Helff began offering a course with William Paterson College, which he taught at Bergen, on the use of audiovisual materials for community college students. The reference librarians saw the need for a similar course on bibliography for our faculty.

In the first year that "Special Topics in Bibliography" (see Appendix 1) was offered the goal was twofold: to teach people how to organize library research and to teach people what bibliographic tools are available. Although the structure of the course has been modified in the past three years, the goal remains the same. The course is not intended to turn out instant librarians. Instead, it is concerned with a researcher's questions: How can I start my research? Where do I begin? How will I know what is available and where it is located? How can I tell if I covered everything? What is bibliography? What is research? These are not easy questions to answer even for a homogeneous group. The classes have consisted of from 15 to 25 people whose interests have ranged from Spanish mysticism to sports medicine. They have had their own special problems and areas of concern. The greatest problem is how to deal with such variety.

To assess these varied interests, the course begins by asking the students to fill out individual detailed profiles of their research interest. They are asked: What do you hope to get out of the course? What graduate studies are you engaged in? What other research courses have you had? What subjects do you teach at Bergen? What special topic would you like to work on for your term project? Why does that subject interest you? Not all of the students are Ph.D. candidates: some are interested in exploring bibliography in a broad area to assist in teaching; others are writing books or developing specific subject skills. Through assessing the student interest profiles, we are able to shape the course specifically to that year's students, modifying the specific subject sessions and aspects of the general sessions to suit their needs.

After a tour of our library, the class meetings are divided into two parts: sessions that deal with the first objective—teaching students how to do organized research—and with bibliographic tools and subject areas of general interest, such as the *National Union Catalog* or the bibliography of education. Then we arrange the class in specific subject sessions and explore in detail the literature of science and medicine, the humanities, social sciences, business, or whatever the students require. An arrangement such as this still does not deal adequately with individual interests. Students whose unusual subject areas do not fit neatly in the class plan meet with instructors individually. We do not feel we can fill all their needs unless we actually tutor them individually throughout the semester.

In the first year of teaching "Special Topics in Bibliography" we invited four speakers to supplement our own staff in specialized subject areas. In 1973 we relied heavily on our reference and media staff to cover subject areas. In 1974 to insure continuity in the class and subject coverage two instructors taught all but two classes: one on audiovisual bibliography and one on selection of materials for community college students, which specialists on the college faculty taught. Handling such diverse subject areas requires considerable class preparation on the instructor's part. While each of us brings subject expertise to our instruction, teaching the social sciences, sciences, and humanities classes has forced us to enlarge our professional capabilities and to explore new areas. In several cases, we have traveled with students to libraries in the Metropolitan New York area to explore with them the bibliographic tools in a specialized field. We both return having learned something.

Unless we enlarge our staff beyond all necessary proportion for a community college, we will never fully solve the problem of subject specialization. Nevertheless, the majority of our students are our own teaching faculty members who naturally reflect the subject areas taught at the college, and in turn reflect the library skills required of our own staff. In addition, our students realize we cannot be specialists in everything, and they are grateful for our cooperation and efforts on their behalf.

Teaching research methodology is the most difficult part of the course. Among our behavioral objectives in teaching research are that the students:

1. define specifically the topic of their interest;
2. locate and read some general information on the topic;
3. outline all the parameters of this topic;
4. assess this topic in terms of the type of library research that it will require: book, journal, manuscript, and so on;
5. create a subject headings array of all possible terms involved with this topic;
6. begin their search using the subject headings array in a single *genre* source, such as books;
7. progress logically through all the source *genres,* expanding the subject headings array as necessary;
8. document every step: every index, subject heading, and date searched; every tool used.

Students are expected to demonstrate these proficiencies by producing a comprehensive bibliography of their topics accompanied by a log describing the steps and rationale of the decisions made in searching.

The students are shocked at the inconsistencies they find in indexing, bewildered at the idea of bridging the index gap and meeting the indexer's mind, unsure and unable to explore related and synonymous terms.

The first year we began with a philosophical lecture on search strategy that proved to be much too sophisticated. The second year we began with a very detailed example of what we expected them to do by exploring all the research possibilities of the topic *Noise;* unfortunately, most of the students were so distracted by our attempted explanation that we lost them. This year we are breaking down the steps of research outlined above in the eight behavioral objectives and are dealing with each individually, building carefully until the students understand what research must include. Assignments for these first general sessions follow the eight objectives and include constructing a thesis statement, locating a general article, and creating an ever-growing subject headings array. Lecture/demonstrations in search strategy cover citation and documentation, the development of a citation style manual based on examples from major journals in each student's discipline, analyzing the boundaries of the search topic, and the development of the subject headings array. Students finally grasp what research means when they complete the term assignment, the bibliography and the log. These first basic classes can only describe the process of research and simulate the various aspects step by step, but the whole process gels for each student when each prepares his or her final product and understands how the components of search strategy fit together and contribute to each other.

In the meantime, the course progresses from generalizations on research to specific searching tools that will be useful to the entire class. The basic bibliographic tools in the reference collection are covered, beginning with the *National Union Catalog*. Since we are not trying to produce librarians, the approach to the tools is somewhat different from that of the traditional reference course. Unlike librarians, our students don't need to know all the details about each tool. Instead, we concentrate on how certain types of tools can contribute to research and what kinds of tools a researcher can expect to find, such as bibliographies, union lists, handbooks, and books on the research of a specific area. In the past three years we have been building our reference collection with the course in mind, adding bibliographies and guides to the literature in many areas. Most of our students are amazed at tools like *NUC, Besterman,* and *Winchell*. We have fought the temptation to produce these tools like magicians; instead we discuss the shape of bibliography in general and what tools they should logically expect to find, as well as those that are missing. We point out analogies and differences between general and specific subject-area bibliography. Our students learn what questions are critical about bibliography in a subject area.

After dealing with general tools, we move to descriptive bibliographic works dealing with periodicals, followed by a period with the *New York Times Index* and the first lesson in actually matching wits with an indexer. In an article on searching the chemical literature, Julian F. Smith has described the processing of index research as two engineers tunneling from opposite sides of the mountain using all the skill and all the charts they possess to meet in the middle.[3] The *New York Times Index* is a fairly difficult index to begin with, but it is a tool of general interest with information on everyone's subject. After a brief look at Lincoln's assassination on microfilm and the first copperplate attempt at indexing, we discuss the problems of indexing something as complex as the *New York Times* and how these difficulties are passed on to the searcher. We consider the thesaurus, why it is helpful, and how it could be more helpful. Then for the laboratory period in the second hour of class, students begin homework on locating different types of information in the *New York Times Index* and then actually finding it in the paper. Hands-on experience with this rather difficult index illustrates to the students the need for a flexible subject-headings array in their approach to research. Also, they all learn how to use the *New York Times Index* and what a thesaurus can do.

A session is spent on the indexes and reference books in education, including

ERIC, dissertation lists, and computer searches. We encourage students to request a computer literature search and to obtain relevant documents from ERIC or on interlibrary loan.

Although some of the class have already taken the course in audiovisual instruction offered at Bergen, and know how to search for nonprint materials, the bibliographic control sources for nonprint materials are reviewed, and the students include citations for films, tapes, etc., in their final project.

Toward the end of the term, Professor Louis Piccininno from the Developmental Program at Bergen Community College joins the class as instructor for two sessions on evaluation of the reading level of materials for the community college student. He reviews various methods that have been used to evaluate reading level. Faculty members pair off to evaluate selections from texts actually being used at the college.

At this point the class breaks up into small groups, each dealing with a specific subject. These small groups have varied annually in aim and composition. They meet in separate seminar rooms in the library to discuss general and specific tools in a discipline. We try to vary the approach, using discussion groups, student lectures, and audiovisuals; some classes are videotaped so that all the students can see them. As the small subject groups interact, the tempo relaxes; students ask more questions and explore more on their own. We try to go on field trips to specialized libraries in the area with strong collections in the subject the students are researching. Students without the courage or credentials to study at the Engineering Society Library or the New York Academy of Medicine travel with us singly or in small groups on weekends. By arranging ahead by telephone, and occasionally purchasing a library membership, we are usually able to get warm receptions from librarians and full cooperation in our exploration of their reference tools.

The major project for the term is developing an extensive documented bibliographic search of a topic. Each student decides on a topic when the course begins, usually selecting a subject related to his or her dissertation or a major paper, occasionally to a new course he or she is developing at the college. Each week an assignment is given which represents a step in the process of assembling the final term project. These steps, which reflect the behavioral objectives outlined above, include: (1) a search problem statement; (2) an analysis of the scope of the subject and the form the research will take; (3) location of an overview article; (4) a table of subject headings; (5) a diary of progress through bibliographic sources; (6) three types of documentation: citation cards, contents notes, and a list of subject headings searched in each bibliographic source.

These written assignments give feedback on how well the students understood the lecture/demonstrations. In developing any new course, a continual cycle of problem diagnosis, teaching, and reevaluation occurs. We learned early that we were trying to cover too much material in too many titles; we strive to simplify our presentations as much as possible. The staff makes every effort to remember that we are not training librarians, but competent subject specialists with expertise in their subject fields. It is especially important to avoid library jargon. The faculty-students work hard to achieve a comprehensive working knowledge of the bibliography of their subject fields, but they are highly vocal about not wanting busywork. We assign and explain all our assignments very carefully, demonstrating their relevance to the objectives of the course and their subject interest.

At the last session of the course each faculty member is given a rating sheet (see Appendix 2) listing each unit of the course and asked to rate how effective the presentation was and the amount of emphasis the topic should be given. We also ask for comments, criticisms, and suggestions. From this feedback we revise and improve the course each year. This final session is devoted to an uninhibited, free-for-all exchange on these problems and solutions. Students have expressed their realization of research complexity, a greater appreciation of the library staff, and frustrations with the system. Some of their suggestions on the running of the Library Learning Resources Center have been tried and proven valuable.

One of the major reasons for the success of this course at Bergen Community College is that it has consistently had the support of the college administration. During new faculty orientation the LLRC staff is given the opportunity to describe the course, and the college president, Dr. Sidney Silverman, urges the faculty to enroll. Tuition is reimbursed for members of the full-time Bergen faculty. The dean of instruction, Dr. George Charen, has followed the development of the course and has observed several sessions. The most effective publicity has been by word-of-mouth from faculty colleagues who have taken the course.

In any kind of academic library, faculty stimulate a high proportion of student use. This is especially true at a community college where many of the entering students read at the tenth-grade level or below. If the library staff can teach the faculty to use libraries with greater ease and productivity, their students should benefit also. The course in bibliography has improved our own teaching methods for student library orientations: we have learned to simplify and explain the process of research much more effectively, and to deal with problems common to both faculty and students. The faculty at Bergen have learned to appreciate the members of the Library Learning Resources Center and the profession of librarianship. They accept us more readily as teaching colleagues and as professionals. The course in bibliography has increased the respect and friendship of the faculty; this achievement alone makes it worthwhile.

NOTES

1. Bergen Community College, Paramus, N.J., a suburban comprehensive community college 40 minutes from mid-Manhattan, began offering instruction in 1968. By fall 1973 the enrollment had grown to 7,254 students (4,954 full-time equivalent). There are 233 full-time and 103 part-time faculty. The student population is divided approximately 60/40 between liberal arts transfer and two-year career programs. The college has a library collection of over 50,000 volumes and access to rich bibliographic resources of New

York City and the New Jersey interlibrary loan network, which includes Princeton and Rutgers.
2. Professor Dorothy F. Deininger, director of Professional Development Programs, has been very helpful in developing and revising the course.
3. Julian F. Smith, *How to Search the Chemical Literature,* Advances in Chemistry, vol. 30 (Washington, D.C.: American Chemical Society, 1971).

APPENDIX 1
EXCERPTS FROM STUDENT COURSE OF STUDY: SPECIAL TOPICS IN BIBLIOGRAPHIC ORGANIZATION AND DESCRIPTION

To begin: Thursday, February 7, 1974—16 sessions—5:00–7:00 P.M.
Location: Bergen Community College Library, 400 Paramus Road, Paramus, N.J.

Open to college faculty to increase their bibliographic skills as doctoral candidates, researchers, and writers; teachers of college students; advisors to library and learning resources centers in the selection of materials; nonprint media specialists interested in developing library bibliographic skills; graduate librarians only with permission.

Laboratory periods will develop skill in subject bibliography of the student's discipline. These laboratory periods will include small group sessions in a number of special areas. In each of the disciplines study will include survey of bibliographic structure and controls, evaluation of the principal reference tools and resources.

Instructors: Sarah K. Thomson and Margery Read, Library and Learning Resources Center, Bergen Community College.

COURSE OBJECTIVES
  I. Each student shall demonstrate comprehension of bibliographic search strategy methods by:
    1. Specifically defining his topic: problem statement.
    2. Delineating search strategy in terms of format of research literature.
    3. Locating and reading general information on the topic with a review of the research literature/overview article.
    4. Creating a subject array of all the possible headings involved in the topic.
    5. Progressing logically through the bibliographic sources.
    6. Documenting his progress with full citations, search matrices, and a diary recording the rationale of decisions made in his progression.
    This comprehension shall be demonstrated by preparing and documenting an extensive bibliographic search on a specific topic of interest to him in his subject field.
  II. Each student shall locate and document relevant bibliographic items in a specific list of *general* indexing and bibliographic tools and the card catalog.
 III. Each student shall examine and describe the bibliographic characteristics of the major indexing and abstracting sources in his subject field, the major journals, review annuals, and guides to the literature.

IV. Each student shall evaluate comprehension level, readability, and interest level of print and nonprint materials for use with his community college students, based on a list of criteria.

WRITTEN WORK

I. *Term project:* The major project of the term will be the development of an extensive documented bibliographic search of a topic. This project is described in the packet "Term Project Requirements and Evaluation."

II. *Field trip:* Each student is expected to visit and use at least one major library with a strong collection in the subject he is investigating.

III. *Written assignment:* There will be 10 written assignments, most of which will be done in a library. These assignments are outlined with due dates, and percentage of term grade, in the "Assignments" packet. Some of these assignments, indicated by an asterisk, will be incorporated into the term project, and it is suggested that the student retain a photocopy for his use while the assignment is evaluated by the instructor.

TEST

There will be one short test on February 21 on the material covered in the lecture of February 14. The questions will be:

1. Show exactly how the following material would be cited in a major journal in your field:
    (a) A given citation from *Readers' Guide* (or other H. W. Wilson index).
    (b) A periodical article from a given journal.
    (c) A book.
    (d) A card catalog book citation. Also, indicate what subject headings list this book in the BCC card catalog.
2. Given ten LC call numbers, show how these items would be arranged on a correctly ordered shelf.

GRADING

All grades will be marked in terms of the percentage of that test or assignment to the course; for example, Assignment III [see "Semester Calendar," below] represents 3% of the course grade. A satisfactory completion of this assignment would be marked "3"; less than satisfactory will receive a grade lower than 3. Any student who receives less than the maximum grade and who wishes to rework and submit any written work or test for a higher grade may do so.

SEMESTER CALENDAR

Student Interest Profile. This profile was distributed to each class member through local mail on February 4. Please fill it out and return it during the February 7 class period if possible, or no later than February 14.

I. *February 7*
    1. Discussion of the content and requirements of the course.
    2. Discussion of the term project, to illustrate the contribution of each activity to the cumulative expertise in the search.
       Demonstration of hypothetical subject: Noise.
    3. Tour of Bergen Community College Library and Learning Resources Center.

HANDOUT: Library Handbook.
ASSIGNMENTS: I. Student Interest Profile, if not already in.
II. Preliminary Analysis of the Problem and Delineation of Search Strategy.

II. February 14—Search Strategy:
Documentation, citation, review/overview article.
1. Documentation. Matrix preparation.
2. Bibliographic data elements.
3. Available data elements type of index or bibliography.
4. Citation format, bibliography cards, serial and nonserial.
5. How to take notes.
6. How to find an overview article.
HANDOUTS: Citation formats.
Abbreviations lists for bibliographies.
ASSIGNMENTS: III. Citation Style Manual.
IV. Review/Overview Article.

III. February 21—Search Strategy:
Analysis of topic by format of literature and the relevant types of indexes and bibliographies.
TEST: See Student Course of Study, page 2. [See above, under "Test"—Editor]
ASSIGNMENT: V. Expanded analysis of types of tools.

IV. February 28—Search Strategy: Subject arrays
1. Brainstorming, subject headings (descriptions, indexing terms, etc.), thesauruses.
2. Relationship of subject array to table of contents classifications, etc.
ASSIGNMENTS: VI. Expanded Table of Contents/Topical outline and parallel subject array.

V. March 7
1. General Periodical Indexes.
2. Ulrich and other subject lists of periodicals.
3. Union lists and other locating lists.
4. *New York Times Index.*
5. Interlibrary loans.
ASSIGNMENT: VII. *New York Times Index.*

VI. March 14
Bibliographies in Education, ERIC, computer searching, dissertation lists.
ASSIGNMENT: VIII. ERIC.

VII. March 21
1. National and trade bibliographies.
2. General guides to reference books.
3. Evaluation of reference sources.
4. Subject guides to books.

ASSIGNMENT: IX. Location and evaluation of a guide to the literature of instructor's discipline.

VIII. March 28
Guides to literature of specific disciplines.

IX. April 4
Periodical indexes in specific disciplines.

X. April 11
FIELD TRIP.

April 18—NO SESSION/BCC SPRING RECESS.

XI. April 25
Journals in specific disciplines.

XII. May 2
Subject bibliography.

XIII. May 9
How to select materials for use with your students.
ASSIGNMENT: X. Evaluation of textbooks.

XIV. May 16
1. TERM PROJECT DUE
2. How to select materials (continued).
3. Problems of teaching students to use library materials.

XV. May 23
Bibliographic control of nonprint materials.

XVI. May 30
You, the Library, and the Learning Resources Staff.
1. General discussion.
2. Criticism, evaluation, and suggestions about the course.

APPENDIX 2
1973 EVALUATION SURVEY

Stress much more	Stress more	About right	Stress less	Omit from course		Explanation satisfactory	Explanation unsatisfactory	COMMENTS
					Search Strategy			
					Overview article, how to find and use			
					Developing a subject array			
					Documenting what subject headings were searched in which bibliographies			
					General Periodical Indexes			
					New York Times Index			
					Bibliographic data elements and citation format			
					Card catalog			
					How books are arranged by call number on the shelves			
					Guides to reference books			
					Guides to subject literature			
					Indexes and bibliographies in specific disciplines			
					Education indexes and research tools			
					Computer-based information banks			
					How to find audiovisual materials			
					How to select materials for your students			
					Term projects			
					Journals in specific disciplines			

Other comments, particularly things you wish had been included, whether you think the course should be given again, strengths and weaknesses, satisfactions and dissatisfactions (can be continued on reverse side):

ONE BUSINESS LIBRARY'S APPROACH TO USER EDUCATION: A CASE HISTORY IN FACULTY INVOLVEMENT

MARJORIE A. BROWARD

Visiting lecturer, Department of Librarianship, Royal Melbourne Institute of Technology, Australia; 1973/74 Business Librarian, University of Colorado

For more than fifty years librarians, especially those in colleges and universities, have been concerned with the need to teach readers how to use libraries. Recently this concern has begun to take on the features of an obsession and the professional literature has been increasingly burdened with opinions, theories, surveys and accounts of practice.[1]

From experience as a visiting lecturer in several library schools one becomes painfully aware of this proliferation of material. However, as one of the librarians struggling with the problem for at least half of these 50 years, the temptation to recount personal theories and practice is overwhelming. This paper is therefore presented as a case history of the methods evolving in one particular school of business library over a period of years. Conversations with colleagues in other business libraries have confirmed that neither our problems nor our solutions are unique. In this case study of the University of Colorado's College of Business Administration library the library has the dual responsibility of teaching not only the use of the library but, *in cooperation with the teaching faculty,* the use of the subject literature of business. The effectiveness of any library in an academic setting seems dependent upon the mix of three major elements: the physical environment, the human resources, and the educational climate.

PHYSICAL ENVIRONMENT

The library came into existence in 1964 as a department within the main university library. During the six years prior to the move to the new College of Business Administration building the library staff and the faculty were exploring areas of mutual concern: how to encourage students to ask questions and search for answers; how to aid students to evaluate information by reading critically rather than with blind acceptance of the printed word; how to structure assignments to avoid straining limited resources of books, space, staff; how to free teaching staff from dependency upon lengthy reading lists by devising a more flexible approach to the "reserve" problem.

A brochure, prepared in 1970 for the dedication of the William M. White Business Library at the University of Colorado, stated that the plan for this library reflects notable changes in the character of business and went on to identify some of these changes as:

> the professionalization of management; increasing interaction between business and the surrounding society; major advances in decision-making and problem-solving techniques; heightened concern for the place of the individual in the corporate activity; greatly increased informational requirements for effective management and the proliferation of informational forms; the increasingly critical need for creative and imaginative enterprise; the imperatives to social responsibility in the conduct of business affairs.[2]

The brochure noted that these changes dictate a new kind of intensified study experience and further stated:

> The library is the work center and academic "home" for business students, and is located in the center of the Business Building, within a minute of all classrooms and faculty offices. The facilities are intended to enhance student efficiency through easy access to study materials offering a considerable range of subject matter in widely varying form.[3]

The library, which occupies about 14,500 sq. ft., has a seating capacity for 285 and a present book stock of about 40,000 volumes, with a growing collection of microforms, audio- and videotapes, financial reports, and numerous files of ephemeral materials. Concentrated in this library are the university's principal collections of materials for the fields of management, business finance, accounting, marketing, banking, transportation, insurance, and real estate.

HUMAN RESOURCES

The user population is estimated at 1,200, based on a faculty of about 60 full-time members and a student body of undergraduates, and graduate students in the master's and doctoral programs in business, as well as a sprinkling of users from other departments on campus.

The library staff consists of one professional librarian, two paraprofessional assistants, and an average of ten students working approximately 100 hours per week. In addition, a doctoral candidate, financed by the college, is assigned to the library on a half-time basis to serve as liaison with the faculty, in the development of course-related materials. In the selection of staff, emphasis is placed on the importance of working with users and on the service aspect of the library organization.

EDUCATIONAL CLIMATE

The dedicated interest and concern of the dean of the college has been a primary factor in establishing the central position of the library. His interest has been matched by the enthusiastic support of department heads, the Library Committee, and the majority of the faculty. It is this cooperative spirit that has enabled the library staff to implement its programs within a supportive framework.

From the beginning the library staff has operated on the philosophy that it is our responsibility to anticipate user needs and to organize the library so that its use will be simple, and self-evident. We believe in a marketing approach that is consumer and use oriented. Our basic goal is to satisfy the needs of the user. We are not interested in making would-be librarians out of everyone. We know the library is overwhelming to the uninitiated, that it can loom as a failure threat, a source of frustration. Students are encouraged to understand the basic arrangement of the material in the catalog and on the shelves so they can do their own searching. But the special library in industry is geared toward providing the information for the patron rather than the source only, and our staff attempts to respond to faculty and student requests in a similar fashion when necessary. Our heterogeneous mix of products and services is not static— it is a viable set of tools for problem solving.

A recent survey showed that the number of papers required of business students during a semester ranged from one to 22, with an average of eight. While these papers are not necessarily of the scale of a humanities term paper and may include marketing reports, solutions to case problems, reviews, or reports on independent research or reading, they usually require some use of the library for facts, figures, or simply verification of an idea or a name.

Students majoring in business are taught to analyze facts, to compare, to simulate, to weigh alternative solutions in decision making. It follows then that these students should be directed toward utilizing this training in evaluating sources of information.

TYPES OF INSTRUCTIONAL PROGRAMS

Recent studies have proved what we discovered early on—students learn best when there is a *need to know*. Our programs have been based on an inverted-pyramid concept for the undergraduate. That is, we begin with a limited amount of basic information and build on this in the amount and complexity of content each year until by the fourth year the bachelor's degree candidate will have been exposed to the full range of our products and services.

Andersen has succinctly stated his views on what should be covered in a user education program:

> The details will necessarily vary in different situations but teaching should establish and promote those traditional skills without which no student can make adequate use of his library. First, an understanding of library arrangements, physical, bibliographical and conceptual. Secondly, a knowledge of sources and of which will be appropriate in any given situation. Thirdly, the ability to in-

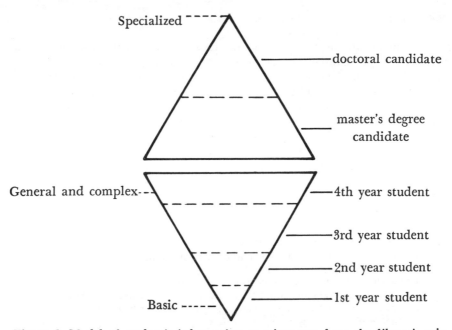

Specialized

doctoral candidate

master's degree
candidate

General and complex

4th year student

3rd year student

2nd year student

1st year student

Basic

Figure 1. Model of student's information requirements from the library's mix of products and services.

terpret his own need so as to frame a relevant question. Fourthly, an awareness of search techniques including the ability to devise serviceable routines. Finally, the student needs skill in the art of evaluating his sources and presenting his material.[4]

These statements summarize the objectives of our program. The students who continue work toward graduate degrees are expected to have this broad foundation of knowledge and will then continue library research in a narrowing specialized approach until the doctoral candidate reaches a point of the pyramid in specialization. This model (see Figure) illustrates not only the students' need for the products of the library but also the need for the services provided by the library staff. As the student's subject horizons expand so do his or her informational needs and need for supportive library services. Graduate students, having once absorbed this broad spectrum of resource information, hone and refine their needs until they become sophisticated and selective consumers of the library's wares.

Of the standard techniques, well documented elsewhere, we have used library tours, point-of-use instruction, handbooks, and handouts of bibliographies on specific topics. These are useful as introductory orientation efforts. Our major thrust for the undergraduate comes when the student is enrolled in core subjects. By this point we can assume that he or she has attained our first objective—that is, an understanding of library arrangements—and can use basic tools, such as the card catalog, periodical indexes, general handbooks, and directories. Early in the semester the lecturer sets an assignment that will require extensive library use and invites the librarian to visit the class and discuss the methodology of the search. The librarian arrives for the class pushing a truck of books and visual aids for the show-and-tell portion of the session. The librarian's preparation for the class has included a study of the course outline, the reserve list, and text, as well as a preliminary conference with the lecturer to discuss course content and approach and the specific details of the assignment.

The purpose of the class visit is not only to introduce students to basic reference tools useful in conjunction with that particular course (e.g., marketing, or finance) but through the dialogue between professor and librarian to relate the use of these sources to typical projects in the "real" world as well as in future course work. In the informal setting of the small classroom the librarian can identify students' subject interests and can encourage free discussion of library-related problems.

Sara Lou Whildin compares library instruction in most college classrooms with the desperation of sudden-death overtime in professional sports. She comments:

> If realism is necessary to determine what a student knows about the library, it is also essential in evaluating what he needs to know . . . librarians with "only one chance at the students" feel compelled to dump the whole library on them when they really need only a few basic tools.[5]

Knowing that we will have a number of chances to reach a student makes it possible to concentrate on a limited quantity in any one session.

The location of a series of group study rooms within the library encourages groups to meet there to work on cases or prepare class presentations and to settle controversies directly from source materials. We have also noticed the effectiveness of the one-teach-one method where the member of the group responsible for searching the literature will impart his or her newly acquired skills to fellow students.

Upper division classes or seminars usually request a continuation of the show-and-tell session using more advanced materials.

Graduate students are provided with the usual introductory materials, but are then expected to determine for themselves the amount of additional help needed. Those students who embark on a master's degree in business administration with the background of an undergraduate degree in a nonbusiness subject are provided with evening library-use instruction classes at the level of presentation of materials to the undergraduate core courses. This places the graduates nearer the level of their peers (in information-use ability) and the level of expectation of their professors. From this point on classroom visits are presented on a request basis. However, working with the officers of the master's and doctoral candidates' own student organizations, we can pinpoint areas where the library can increase or adapt services that will be more beneficial for these groups.

Most doctoral candidates doing preliminary literature searches on a proposed dissertation topic usually spend some time discussing the subject with the librarian to determine if any potential sources have been neglected. Graduate faculty members and the librarian have been working toward a proposal to formalize this approach in order to make certain that the candidate, the candidate's advisor, and the librarian have reviewed together the bibliography and references used before the final draft of the dissertation is written.

ANALYSIS

User education is not just a series of programs—it is a constant ongoing process, a teaching/learning experience that *every* member of the library staff plays a vital part in (shelvers and desk clerks included). Our efforts are based on these considerations:

1. The library does not operate in a vacuum; it is an integral part of the instructional and research programs of the college.

2. Students come to us with varying levels of library competence; programmed teaching is of necessity geared towards broad generalities rather than specific needs and we have not yet found the teaching aid which is more effective than eyeball to eyeball contact between the student and the "live" librarian.

3. A teacher's attitudes condition student attitudes; our services must be of proven value to the faculty.

4. There must be active outreach plans that anticipate student and faculty needs.

5. We should send out to industry and government students who can cope with the changes in the character of business, not the least of which is the greatly increased informational requirements for effective management.

This is one library's response. Obviously such an extensive effort is practicable only when numbers of patrons are limited and when the patience and energy of library staff members are limitless.

NOTES

1. J. E. Scrivener, "Instruction in Library Use: The Persisting Problem," *Australian Academic and Research Libraries* 3 (June 1972): 87.

2. The William M. White Business Library, School of Business, Graduate School of Business Administration, University of Colorado (privately printed, 1970).

3. Ibid.

4. Lillemot Andersen, "Training in the Use of Libraries," in *Changing Concepts of Librarianship*, Proceedings of the 14th Biennial Conference, Library Association of Australia, Brisbane, 1968 (Brisbane: The Conference Committee, 1968), p. 20.

5. Sara Lou Whildin, "Plimpton Prepares: How to Win the Library Instruction Game," *Drexel Library Quarterly* 8 (1972): 234.

PART III
IMPLEMENTATION AND EVALUATION OF
LIBRARY-USE INSTRUCTION PROGRAMS

OBJECTIVES FOR LIBRARY-USE INSTRUCTION IN EDUCATIONAL CURRICULA

JOHN LUBANS, JR.
Assistant Director for Public Services,
University of Colorado Libraries

Some indicators of progress being made in library instruction are in evidence. Several of the existing (locally developed) guidelines for instruction in library skills are a step forward in making such skills specific and are of potential benefit to the teaching process. These guidelines are rarely based on specific objectives, however. One definition of an *educational objective* suggests that the term

> essentially refers to *statements* of what learners should be able to do when instruction has been completed. When educational objectives are stated with sufficient detail to permit valid measurement they are now called behavioral objectives.[1]

There is some difference in the use of the terms *goals* or *objectives*. Objectives are sometimes seen as the more specific or narrow of the two, while goals tend to be overriding concepts. One performance *objective* of library instruction reads:

> The student will apply his understanding of numerical arrangement to find specific materials in a given category, and locate classes of nonfiction books by using the Dewey Decimal System.[2]

The broader aspect of a *goal* is exemplified in:

> The student recognizes the library staff, particularly the reference staff, as a source of information and is comfortable seeking assistance from staff members.[3]

This chapter deals with various librarians' attempts at establishing educational objectives and striving to integrate these objectives into the teaching curriculum. The concern with the merging of library-use instruction within the established curriculum is based on many librarians' belief that there is no other avenue for making significant improvements in the knowledge of the library by both students and faculty.

A difficulty in arriving at specific objectives for library-use instruction is that it is not a separate discipline but rather a skill that requires integration with established disciplines, such as English or social studies or mathematics. These regularly taught courses create library use or the lack of it. The amount of library use emphasized in a course of study is what generates use among students, and through this *use* students learn about information resources.

Another related difficulty is that since library-use instruction is not a separate course of study in most curricula but reliant on its objectives being promoted in other courses, its effect may be diluted and not easily measured.

Obviously, the objectives (or goals) of any library need to be established. If one of these goals is to supply information that will satisfy the information needs of its active and potential clientele, then some form of instruction for users would appear to make sense.

Librarians in all types of libraries make some efforts at library-use instruction, and many librarians have even a strong and open commitment to the notion of educating the library user. A basic question that may be asked is: Why do we have this concern?

J. E. Scrivener has cataloged some of the reasons he discovered in his survey study on why library-use instruction is offered:

(1) Students should be educated to solve intellectual problems themselves without overmuch dependence on mentors.
(2) This cannot be done effectively unless they draw as widely as possible on resources held in libraries.
(3) Without instruction they will not begin to tap these resources.
(4) The independent approach to problems should continue after tertiary education is completed, at which time library skills are even more important.

In addition to these long-range arguments there are a number of more immediate ones:

(1) The student will get more from his studies if he can find out for himself.
(2) He will perform better in exams because of wider learning possibilities opened up.
(3) Information-gathering techniques will be vital for many in their occupations, particularly for scientists and technologists.
(4) The costly resources of libraries will be more fully utilised.
(5) There will be less pressure on library staff to answer minor enquiries.

The logic of these arguments seems unexceptionable but this tends to mask the fact that they are hypotheses whose validity in practice has never been tested.[4]

It is becoming increasingly evident that empirical research needs to be done to *prove* the need for educating library users in information use. Several factors of the day, economic and political, dictate that quantification be applied to any educational effort. No longer are intuitive concepts (based on observation and experience) adequate by themselves to justify the needed investment of hours and resources into instruction. Ideally, the effect of library instruction should be a change in the user's information-seeking behavior. Empirical studies may be able to successfully demonstrate such changes. Once this is done and published, it would appear that a good chance exists for faculty and administrative support to move beyond lip-service levels into active application.

In the meantime, while the necessary research, it is hoped, gets underway, an examination of existing objectives may be relevant, since these objectives (or hypotheses) are what need to be shown as scientifically valid. Philosophies of library instruction and its valid objectives have been published at various times. The following are cited as examples of some of the thinking behind library-use instruction:

General objectives of library instruction:
A. Creating a love of books and reading
B. Integrating the library in the school program so that the work of the classroom is enriched and made increasingly vital
C. Equipping the student with an understanding of the use of books as tools
D. Aiding the student in building attributes of good citizenship through the use of the library
E. Developing responsibility and good work habits through library service contributed by students.[5]

Among the objectives to be expected from a well-formulated program of instruction in library skills are: to emphasize the importance of good library behavior, to motivate good citizenship through respect for library rules and proper care of library materials, to explain how to locate materials and to encourage independence in research, to increase awareness and enjoyment of the great variety of subjects and materials in libraries, and to stimulate creativity in sharing time.[6]

Each student should be guaranteed a minimum exposure to basic library procedure. Those who learn to use research skills successfully will find that they can satisfy curiosity, do independent reading, and enjoy books, recordings, and other materials without continued guidance of teachers and librarians. If this knowledge is acquired early in life, children will feel secure in their approach to school and public libraries and later in college and university libraries.[7]

The quality of the citizen as a person must be of prime concern to educators in a free society. Decency, integrity, and dedication to the ideal cannot be legislated. The fate of democracy rests not on the documents written to direct the function of the government but rests on the thoughts and actions of each citizen. Each generation holds the fate and the future of the American way of life.[8]

To expand the use of all types of libraries for information, recreation, and inspiration.
To create a love for and a permanent interest in good books; and to form the habit of reading printed material critically and appreciatively. To develop discrimination in the selection of materials for individual use.
To help students become skillful users of library materials and resources of all types.
To guide students in pursuing self-directed learning of all kinds.[9]

In detail, upon leaving the university the student would measurably understand: major physical arrangements of libraries (the classification and cataloging systems); major tools of reference such as indexes and abstracts in general and specifically those in his area of endeavor; and the intellectual aspects of searching out and using information. (Also the love of reading with which the student arrived on campus should be no less upon his leaving it.) [10]

The validation of any one of these objectives will be a difficult task, but not impossible. It should be obvious, though, that the more specific the objective is the better the chance of demonstrating its achievement.

Several library skills guides (similar to lesson plans) have no statement of philosophy or objectives. They are apparently based on the self-evident or implied righteousness of the mission of educating the user.

A close examination of several of the guides reveals or suggests they have one or more of the following ailments that may hinder achieving their stated or implied objectives.[11]

One evident problem is that certain elements of the instructional plan (such as the card catalog) are highly repetitive. This may indicate progressive expansion of the topic, or it may be a repeat of the same lesson. Some major topics are taught as many times as eight grades out of 12 on the elementary and secondary school level.

The repetitive nature of library instruction can be seen in the example taken from a library skills chart (see tabulation).

The worrisome factor is the apparent lack of any guarantee that the development of skills is emphasized instead of the same lesson being repeated each year. Redundancy may be necessary because of uncertainty in the students' ability to use the library (their progress may not be evident). If this is the case there may also be need of teacher motivation that would stimulate library skills development.

Another seeming dilemma is the apparent lack of direction in integrating library instruction into the established curriculum. There seem also to be significant difficulties in coordinating progressive library instruction even with courses that tend to encourage library use. In line with this, although suggestions for cooperation do exist, there is a lack of teacher/librarian cooperation in making library instruction valuable to students. This situation may be based on inertia on one or the other side or on actual unacceptance by the teacher of the need for effective library use. Another facet of the problem could be that the objectives and specific skills are often prepared in a vacuum by librarians without input from the teacher. Some of the problems in librarian/teacher cooperation can no doubt be traced to the image the teacher has of the library and its purpose. In her recent interesting study, Virginia Sadler examined the image of the library as presented in 25 selected teacher-training textbooks used in Kentucky. Her findings are revealing:

> The picture of the public school library presented by these selected textbook authors was a blurred and faint likeness of the institution we tout as the heart of the instructional program. What emerged was not a dynamic service organization upon which all instruction was dependent, but a shabby insignificant "place" where teachers might find some supplementary books.[12]

K–12 LIBRARY INSTRUCTION CHART

Grade of Introduction	Library Skills	Review in Grades
5	Atlases Unabridged dictionary Poetry indexes Card catalog	Grades 5–12
4	Dewey decimal class Card catalog (intro.) Encyclopedia (intro.) Making a bibliography	Grades 4–12
1 & 2	Selecting suitable books Care of books Citizenship in the library	Grades 1–12

If this finding is typical for other states, then it stands to reason that the teacher and librarian start off on an inadequate basis for cooperation.

Difficulties are inherent in the upward movement of students, in many instances from one school building to several others, as they progress through their schooling. The library-use skills they've developed and practiced in one phase of their school life may not be called upon in another, which makes the retention of learning difficult for them. That librarians generally find it necessary and expedient to begin on a *basic* level with most users of libraries is an indicator of the lack of developmental growth on the part of the user. National norms for library-use knowledge by students could be instrumental in reversing this trend. There is an indication of the beginning of national standards on the elementary school level for some bibliographic skills. Science Research Associates, Inc., has established national percentiles for a category called *Use of Sources* in their SRA [student] Assessment Survey. This category includes *dictionary, table of contents, index, references, catalog cards* and *maps, charts* and *graphs.* Students who take the achievement series tests are shown how they stand on a percentile basis with a national grouping and also the local student percentile. This is of possible interest because teacher and student awareness of these tests and their requirements could have a positive effect on the teaching and learning of library-use skills. In a sense these skills become *necessary* and valid by being on such a test.

Additional problems in applying library skills guides may lie in that many states do not have a central curriculum planning agency with power to change curricula in school districts. In fact, any suggested revision of a course and the way it is taught is decided locally by dozens of school districts in each state. A similar situation exists in colleges and universities where teaching methodologies are apt to be as difficult to modify as at the elementary or secondary levels. In a centralized system there are even difficulties in imposing lesson plans on uncommitted teachers. Only through teachers' becoming convinced of the value of library use will library skills become important in their teaching.

Along with the difficulties listed above is the problem of the pressures inherent in the mass-education system, both on students and teachers. Students realize they have to perform certain *things* to achieve passing or better grades. Teachers often teach students so that students can demonstrate achievement on tests. This is required by the curricular structure. Library use is not a consistent, integral factor in many courses, and as a result students are not required to get a good grade or the faculty is not required to test the students' achievement in library skills. A situation like this can easily lead to student and teacher apathy to effective information use. Their apathy may also be based in the demands of mass education. Tutorial-style instruction is not possible in mass education where large numbers of people are *processed* through educational channels. Reserve reading, large lectures, multiple-choice examinations, and textbooks rarely encourage students to go beyond course requirements on their own.

Some librarians (at least in universities) confronted by massive student enrollments and the diverse needs of student bodies have not reacted with increased library and information-use programs. Instead, many university libraries (until recently) have not gone far beyond providing the traditional reference desk-type service. Rogers and Weber, in their text on university library administration, acknowledge the difficulties of students using libraries effectively, stating that

> service policies . . . can follow the basic principle that the staff should help readers to learn to use the library but not in general answer questions for them. Readers should be given every aid to serve themselves through signs, simple means to locate materials, and an easily evident and logical pattern of staff service points.[13]

Unless the library makes a concerted effort to promote effective use of its resources, the users' dilemma in library use can only increase. Since the teaching faculty is not trained to teach in-depth use of libraries, and if the library fails to make genuine efforts to promote library use, the users are literally stuck in the middle to fend for themselves.

The students' motivation in the mass-education system may be relevant. It may be on social pressure alone that they are in school. Getting the degree and getting out may be the underlying operating philosophy for many students. On this basis it would be surprising for some students to make any extra efforts, such as using the library, to work beyond course requirements. If the use of the library is perceived by students in their course work as a frill or an educational nicety, then it will quickly become unnecessary as they grind their way toward the degree.

Librarians who recognize this attitude can still do much to aid the students and perhaps even help them develop some library skills. The important part in this is to understand the varying levels of need among students for library use. These needs should dictate the amount and level of library instruction the students receive.

For librarians to attain effective library use among their users will probably mean that faculty and students are subscribing to the objectives of library-use instruction. As stated above, these objectives need to be practical and specific—to the point of measurability. Their concern should not be merely with the specifics of library tools, such as the card catalog or the *Readers' Guide,* but with the idea of *problem solving* through the use of the library. The student is to be seen as one developing considerable self-reliance in library use.

Significant changes in information-use patterns of students can be developed through an enlightened faculty. To attain this, obviously, the teacher/librarian relationship must be developed to such a level that the teacher considers library-use skills as important as the other thought-process abilities that the students demonstrate in completing assigned course work.

It is feasible that a strengthening of the teacher/librarian partnership will develop if librarians can demonstrate to the teacher the desirable qualities of effective information use by students versus the situation where library use is minimal or nonexistent.

Four observers, Patricia Knapp, Ralph Perkins, Guy Lyle, and I, have stated their attitudes on the need for faculty involvement in solving the problems of the misuse and nonuse of libraries. Their conviction is that improvement of a significant scope can come only through the faculty and classroom.

> Competence in the use of the library is one of the liberal arts. It deserves recognition and acceptance as such in the college curriculum. It is furthermore a complex of knowledge, skills and attitudes not to be acquired in any one course but functionally related to the content of many. It should therefore be integrated into the total curriculum. But it cannot be so integrated until the faculty as a whole is ready to recognize the validity of its claim and to implement this recognition through regularly established procedures of curriculum development.[14]

> Librarians seem to be the sole interpreters of the library. Long ago it should have been recognized that the masses of students are too great to handle in such a teaching program. Administrative heads of the public schools and colleges must be fully convinced of the values to be contributed by the proper use of the library. Next teachers must be taught—all teachers in all areas of the curriculum —and let the teachers teach. Granted this is to be no easy task, but the present practices have proved that current methods are at an impasse.[15]

> As a solution for limiting non-use it is recommended that faculty involve the use of the literature by students in research or problem-solving assignments whenever possible. In other words, it is hoped that improvements continue to be made over the time of Abelard when: "successive generations of laborious and studious men . . . consented for centuries to grow pale over a small number of texts, always the same, reread and commented on to satiety, gnawing as it were the same bone forever." [16]

> The faculty have the primary responsibility for structuring the academic courses for independent study. Present teaching practices would appear to provide little incentive for students to do substantial and rewarding reading. If professors are wedded to the idea of using textbooks and reserve readings there

is little the librarian can do about making changes. He should, however, continue to exert his influence in working with individual professors to promote independent library use and to this end he should create a library atmosphere conducive to tutorial instruction.[17]

Quoted below is a list of questions for school teachers about their use of the learning resources center; this listing stresses the need for faculty involvement in effecting effective library use:

Teachers should ask themselves these questions:

1. Do I know how to use library tools and resources? If not, am I attempting to obtain this knowledge?
2. Do I discuss the materials with the librarian before beginning a unit?
3. Am I acquainted with the resources of the library, their arrangement and use?
4. Do I assume responsibility for instruction of students in the use of the library? Should I?
5. Do I check carefully the library skills already possessed by students in my class and those that are needed to carry out assignments?
6. If I am not well qualified to teach library skills, do I seek help?
7. Do I plan my class work and schedule so that there is an opportunity for students to work effectively in the library?
8. Am I well informed about materials in my field, and do I keep up-to-date?
9. Do I continue to read books interesting to the children whom I teach so that I am able to work with the librarian in both individual and group reading guidance?
10. Do I participate in the selection of materials for the library media center? [18]

This can be read as a blunt statement on the many difficulties to be overcome before the teacher/librarian relationship can become effective.

Similar problems exist on the university level. Patricia Knapp described what librarians need to do to win over the faculty to making changes in teaching methodology to emphasize information use.[19] The following is a paraphrase of the guidelines she suggests:

Librarians will need to:

1. Demonstrate how poorly students use the library to faculty who may respond constructively.

2. Persuade these instructors to involve "library" in problem-solving assignments given to students.

3. Make library resources generally available through promotion to students and faculty.

4. Stress the overall value of library competence.

5. With the help of the departmental faculty draw up proposed solutions to the problem of library misuse and nonuse.

6. Work through curriculum committees for changes in teaching methods and objectives.

The attainment of any of these tasks is going to be difficult. Apart from employing librarians with charming and winning personalities the need is to systematically demonstrate the differences between effective use and the misuse of libraries not only by students but, obliquely, by the teaching faculty. No doubt there will be a need to quantify the findings and to demonstrate them since the *evident-need* concept (that is, librarians *knowing* that teachers would do better by their students if library use were stressed more often) has not had the desired effect except that practically everyone agrees that libraries are *good* and *necessary*. But few nonlibrarians seem to have caught on to the notion that creative problem solving or research should start in the library in order to save time and effort on everyone's part.

Quantification is part of the answer. Another aspect is that of the library having something to offer if anyone is willing to listen. This may be termed the *crying in the wilderness technique,* but the payoff, if it catches on, could be considerable. In other words, librarians must get the attention of the teacher and then be able to follow through with instructional programs.

The input of students and teachers should be sought, particularly in library use instruction matters. This can be achieved through either selective interviews or questionnaires. As well, an advisory committee on integrating library instruction into curricula could have student (where practicable) and teacher representation.

An interesting example of teacher/librarian cooperation is the booklet, published as a joint effort by the Oklahoma [state] Library Resources Division, and the Oklahoma Curriculum Improvement Commission, entitled: *A Guide for Teachers and Librarians with Suggestions for Teaching Indian Students.* The intelligent use of this type of literature could lead to utilization of library resources (both material and personnel) at a high level, along with a deepened appreciation of library use by teachers and students.

NOTES

1. Jack V. Edling, "Educational Objectives," in *The Teacher's Handbook,* ed. by Dwight W. Allen and Eli Selfman (Glenview, Ill.. Scott Foresman, 1971), pp. 207–219.
2. Allene J. Guinyard, *Where the Books Are: English* (Miami: Dade County Public Schools, 1971; also ERIC document, ED 061 988).
3. American Library Association, Association of College and Research Libraries, (ad hoc) Committee on Bibliographic Instruction, "Preliminary Draft of Objectives," mimeographed (n.p., August 1973).
4. J. E. Scrivener, "Instruction in Library Use: The Persisting Problem," *Australian Academic and Research Libraries* 3 (1972): 87–119.
5. Carolyn Crawford and May Chun, *Hawaii School Libraries: A Manual for Organization and Services,* rev. ed. (Honolulu: State of Hawaii, Department of Education, 1964).
6. New Jersey School Library Association, "Library Skills Instructional Program —K–12," prepared by Marguerite Baechtold, et al., Instructional Skills Committee, mimeographed (Trenton: New Jersey State Department of Education, Division of the State Library, Archives and History, Public and School Library Services Bureau, 1964).

7. Oklahoma Curriculum Improvement Commission, Library Resources Division and the State Library Service Committee, "Curriculum Guide for the Teaching of Library Skills: Grades K–12" (n.p., Oklahoma State Department of Education, 1969).

8. Ruth Ann Davies, *The School Library: A Force for Educational Excellence* (New York and London: R. R. Bowker, 1969).

9. Indiana Department of Public Instruction, *Digest of Courses of Study for Secondary Schools of Indiana* (Indianapolis: State Department of Public Instruction, 1961).

10. University of Colorado Libraries, Library Use Instruction Committee, "Draft —Objectives in the University of Colorado Libraries Provision of Instruction in Use of Libraries," mimeographed (Boulder: University of Colorado Libraries, October 1973).

11. Including: Albuquerque, N. Mex., Public Schools, Division of Library Services, "An Outline of Library Instruction for Elementary School Libraries," mimeographed (n.p., The Division, 1968). District of Columbia Public Schools, Department of Libraries. "Proposed Schedule for Teaching the Use of the Library and Books: Kindergarten Through Grade Six," mimeographed (n.p., n.d.). Virginia Department of Education, "School Library Instruction in Use of Materials," mimeographed (Richmond: The Department, n.d.), reprinted from: Virginia Department of Education, *School Library Guide for Grades One through Twelve* (Richmond: The Department, 1961). New Jersey School Library Association, op. cit. Oklahoma Curriculum Improvement Commission, op. cit. "Nevada Elementary Course of Study: Library Skills," mimeographed (n.p., n.d.).

12. Virginia P. Sadler, "Role of the Library in Education; the Library Image as Presented in Selected Teacher Training Textbooks in Use in the State of Kentucky," mimeographed (Barbourville, Ky.: Union College, 1970; also ERIC document, ED 073 789).

13. Rutherford D. Rogers and David C. Weber, *University Library Administration* (New York: H. W. Wilson, 1971), p. 204.

14. Patricia B. Knapp, "A Suggested Program of College Instruction in the Use of the Library," *Library Quarterly* 26 (1965): 230.

15. Ralph Perkins, *The Prospective Teacher's Knowledge of Library Fundamentals* (Metuchen, N.J.: Scarecrow Press, 1965), p. 196.

16. John Lubans, Jr., "Non-use of an Academic Library," *College and Research Libraries* 32 (1971): 364.

17. Guy R. Lyle, "Use and Mis-use of the College Library," in Guy R. Lyle, *The President, the Professor and the College Library* (New York: H. W. Wilson, 1963), p. 56.

18. Idaho Department of Education, "Library Resource Center (and) Library Resource Skills: Capabilities and Know-How," mimeographed (Boise: The Department, 1972).

19. Knapp, op. cit., pp. 224–231.

TESTING FOR LIBRARY-USE COMPETENCE

MASSE BLOOMFIELD

Supervisor, Culver City (California) Library, Hughes Aircraft

The literature leads us to believe there are numerous local tests of library ability administered both independently and in association with programs of instruction, but only a half-dozen or so have been published for national distribution. The published tests are all subject to serious criticisms on various details and particularly because there has been inadequate validation and standardization. The unanimous conclusion from the testing done and from personal observation is that most students are seriously lacking in knowledge and ability to use books and libraries effectively.[1]

Librarians' concern with measuring the students' competence in library use is revealed in the several tests designed for this purpose. Ostensibly, the motivation for these tests is to diagnose students' library skills and to indicate the gaps, if any, in their learning of these skills. However, since the tests repeatedly demonstrate the students' inability to use libraries, they may also serve to dramatize for the students their need for library-use instruction.

This paper analyzes 16 library-use tests.[2] These and several other tests are listed in the accompanying Bibliography of Tests, according to those that are divided into parts and those that are not. About half the tests listed were written during the 1930s, the rest during the 1940s to 1960s, which may indicate a greater interest in test design and use during the 1930s than presently.

THE MOST POPULAR TEST

The most popular test in use, as determined by a survey of over 100 colleges taken by Barbara H. Phipps in 1965,[3] is *A Library Orientation Test for College Freshmen,* the so-called Feagley test (see Bibliography). There is little evidence that Phipps's finding has changed.

Phipps states that the Feagley test

is devised for diagnostic, or pre-testing. Norms are available for uninstructed students. It seems adequate as a guide to what and how much instruction is needed. Some of the questionnaire respondents suggested instructing only those students who fell below a predetermined passing mark on this test. For local comparison the test might be used again, unannounced, after the instruction program. No norms are provided for this use of the test.4

Reasonable standards for the Feagley test are provided by Perkins in *The Prospective Teacher's Knowledge of Library Fundamentals.*5 The book gives the entire Feagley test along with the results of the testing, and the standards are in percentage terms for each question of the test.

Since the Feagley test is the one most used, since it is still available and since it has both norms and standards, it will receive the most attention in this discussion.

THE FEAGLEY TEST ANALYZED

The Feagley test manual provides a percentile score and a standard score from the raw scores. The manual states that over 4,000 first-year college students in various parts of the country were selected between 1956 and 1959 for testing to produce the norms. The test itself is divided into nine sections:

Part I. Definition of terms.
Part II. Interpretation of information on a catalog card.
Part III. Choice of subject headings in the card catalog.
Part IV. Arrangement of headings in the card catalog.
Part V. Literature reference works.
Part VI. Sources of biographical information.
Part VII. Choice of indexes.
Part VIII. Interpretation of information in periodical indexes.
Part IX. Abbreviations.

Figure 1 is a representation of the construction and content of the Feagley test. The Feagley test represents a philosophy quite acceptable to most college and university librarians of what content should appear in a test given to beginning first-year college students. The test has a liberal arts and humanities background, which is obvious.

Certain parts of the test may be questioned. The portions of it that may be oblique to the *performance objectives* of a library-use instruction course are most typified by Part IX, "Abbreviations." There may be little reason why first-year college students should be tested on library skills with questions dealing with the abbreviations given below:

Abbreviation	*Answer*
et al.	and others
ibid.	the same
e.g.	for example
f., ff.	and following pages
q.v.	which see
o.p.	out of print
v.	volume

Figure 1. Feagley Test, Part II: Interpretation of Information on a Catalog Card. From Ethel M. Feagley et al., *A Library Orientation Test for College Freshmen*, copyright © 1955 by Teachers College, Columbia University, p. 4. Reprinted by permission of the publisher, Teachers College Press, New York.

DIRECTIONS: An author card is reproduced below. Identify **each** point of information listed below by selecting the correct item on the card. Write the **number** of the item in the space on the Answer Sheet.

EXAMPLE: Author   Answer ___8___

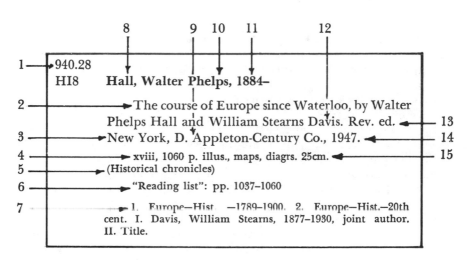

Points of Information

10. Bibliographical note
11. Edition
12. Joint author
13. Key to location of book in library
14. Name of series
15. Other headings under which cards for this book may be found in catalog

DIRECTIONS: Refer to the same catalog card to determine whether **each** statement below is true or false. Write a plus sign (+) in the space on the Answer Sheet if a statement is true. Write a zero (0) if a statement is false.

16. The book was published in 1884.
17. The book has been published in more than one edition.
18. The title of the book is *Historical Chronicles*.
19. The book is less than one thousand pages in length.
20. The book contains references to additional material on European history.

These are seven representative questions of the 12 given in Part IX. It is difficult to relate the ability to use a library with knowing that *e.g.* means *for example* or that *et al.* means *and others* or that *v.* means *volume. V.* under other conditions could also mean volts or velocity or vanadium or verse or verb. Because the matching list does not contain any of the variant definitions of *v.*, it can be assumed that the *v.* in the Feagley test stands for *volume.* In fact, only one word beginning with the letter "v" appears among the definitions, which should make the right answer to this abbreviation obvious. Also *f.* and *ff.* stand both for *following* and for *folios.* The restricted meanings given in the test preclude any misunderstanding, but even so, the inclusion of Latin abbreviations in a library skills test may be out of place.

Perkins's book (mentioned above) provides the results of testing about 2,500 college seniors with the Feagley test. Figure 2 is a selection of the results obtained with Part III of the Feagley test, "Choice of subject headings," which is used to test student knowledge of the subject headings in the card catalog. Both the correct answers and the percentage of correct answers are given for each question noted. The percentage figure given with each question of the Feagley test in the Perkins book provides a standard by which to measure the ability of other groups taking the test.

An intelligent student, in most instances, should be able to figure out the correct answer. What this type of exercise does not do is test the students on their ability to think of the appropriate subject heading or approach when confronted with an information problem. This is not to suggest the students should memorize the L.C. catalog of subject headings but rather that they have the ability to approach their information needs in a systematic manner.

One area of library skills that should be included in a test of library skills is the ability to locate government reports. Nothing in the Feagley test alludes to the existence of an enormous literature available in government documents and government-supported reports.

In trying to define library skills test design, one must mention objectives. The test should define the learning the librarians want college students to have. If

---

21. A critical study of drama in various countries
    (7) 82 percent correct
23. A book with the title *A History of Art*
    (3) 91 percent correct
24. An anthology of plays by English authors
    (11) 70 percent correct

1. ART, ENGLISH — BIBLIOGRAPHY
3. ART—HISTORY
5. DRAMA—BIBLIOGRAPHY
7. DRAMA—HISTORY & CRITICISM
8. DRAMATISTS
11. ENGLISH DRAMA—COLLECTIONS, ETC.

Figure 2. Feagley Test, Excerpt from Part III: Choice of Subject Headings in the Card Catalog, with Correct Answers and Percent Correct Answers from the Perkins Study.

we librarians want the average college student to know and understand Latin abbreviations, these abbreviations should be included in a course on library skills. If we want college students to know the definition of the words *copyright, edition, italic, bibliography,* and *series* (definitions asked in Part I of the Feagley test), then the Feagley test is designed to determine the effectiveness of such a course. But if we want students to have the ability to use various information resources and to intellectualize a library-use problem, then a different test will need to be designed.

A LOOK AT SOME OTHER TESTS

As noted earlier, additional tests have been examined, including those that were organized into parts and those that were not, and the eight tests organized into parts have been compared. Tables 1, 2, and 3 show some of the characteristics of these tests. According to Table 1, an analysis of each of the tests by

Table 1. *NUMBER OF QUESTIONS FOR EACH TEST BY SUBJECT AREA*

	Feag-ley	UNH	Per-fec-tion	Hurt	Ben-nett	Pea-body	PEA	Tyler-Kim-ber	Totals
Definition and General Information	9	13	40	28	10	0	0	0	100
Subject Headings	9	0	0	0	10	0	0	0	19
Reference Books	13	0	13	26	50	24	30	30	186
Maps and Graphs	0	0	0	0	0	0	0	55	55
Indexes to Periodicals	21	15	0	11	10	20	15	0	92
Abbreviations	12	0	0	0	0	0	0	20	32
Card Catalog	11	7	0	31	15	24	15	20	123
Filing Rules	5	10	0	0	10	0	0	0	25
The Book	0	0	0	0	15	24	25	20	84
Classification and Arrangement of Books	0	0	10	0	10	28	0	0	48
Periodicals	0	0	18	0	0	0	0	30	48
Oral and Written Reports	0	0	10	0	0	0	0	0	10
Dictionaries	0	0	9	0	0	27	20	0	56
Encyclopedias	0	0	0	0	0	24	10	0	34
Bibliography	0	0	0	0	0	23	0	0	23
Totals	80	45	100	96	130	194	115	175	935

Table 2. *NUMBER OF TESTS COVERING SPECIFIC*
SUBJECT AREAS

Subject Area	Number of Tests
Reference Books	7
Card Catalog	7
Indexes to Periodicals	6
Definitions and General Information	5
The Book	4
Filing Rules	3
Classification and Arrangement of Books	3
Dictionaries	3
Subject Headings	2
Abbreviations	2
Periodicals	2
Encyclopedias	2
Maps and Graphs	1
Oral and Written Reports	1
Bibliography	1

the subject areas covered, the Feagley test does not cover such areas as maps and graphs or dictionaries or encyclopedias. None of the tests cover all the subjects defined, nor did any test appear to consider that any one subject was essential.

Two of the nine parts of the Feagley test were consolidated into other subject categories to reduce the number of its subject areas shown on Table 1 from nine to seven. Part VII, "Choice of Indexes," and Part VIII, "Interpretation of Information in Periodical Indexes," were included in the category "Indexes (Periodicals)" and Part V, "Literature Reference Books," and Part VI, "Sources of Biographical Information," were merged in the "Reference Books" category. The Feagley test covers those seven of the 15 subjects listed.

The Feagley test omits questions to eight subject areas. One of these that may be of some importance in the design of a library skills course, is instruction on the elements of a bibliographic entry, particularly periodical citations.

One qualification to be made in the general analysis shown in Table 1 is that there is no attempt here to determine the relevance of individual questions. It is assumed that each question of every test has the same value as any other question on a different test.

The results from Table 1 show the lack of consensus among librarians about the design of a library skills course. If librarians have so much difficulty in finding any agreement in the construction of a library skills test, there will likely be the same disagreement in the elements of the instruction to be given.

In a different analysis of the information given in Table 1, the subjects the test designers thought the most important are listed in Table 2. This is a list

Table 3. *NUMBER OF QUESTIONS FOR EACH TEST BY KIND OF QUESTION*

	Feagley	*UNH*	*Perfection*	*Bennett*	*Peabody*	*Hurt*	*PEA*	*Tyler-Kimber*	*Totals*
Matching	52	11	47	20	80	0	10	80	300
Diagram	13	20	0	10	10	0	0	65	118
True or False	10	0	0	55	0	20	0	30	115
Filing Arrangement	5	0	0	0	0	0	0	0	5
Multiple Choice	0	14	53	45	64	0	105	0	281
Completion	0	0	0	0	40	76	0	0	116
Totals	80	45	100	130	194	96	115	175	935

of the number of tests which have parts pertaining to the different subject areas.

The Feagley test scores well in Table 3 in the items most designers of library tests feel are important. It is among those with questions covering the first four subject areas. However, only Feagley and Tyler-Kimber have sections on abbreviations and only Feagley and Bennett have sections on subject headings.

Table 3 shows the type of questions asked on library skills tests. The most popular is the matching answer type and the second most popular, the multiple choice. True and false, diagram, and completion questions are almost tied for third place.

SOME SAMPLE QUESTIONS FROM RECENT TESTS

UNIVERSITY OF NEW HAMPSHIRE/LIBRARY COMPETENCE QUIZ

1. A catalog card for William J. Lederer's book *A Nation of Sheep* (New York: Norton, 1961) is shown with arrows identifying pertinent items, as is done on the Feagley test. Seven matching questions on locating the following bibliographic elements are asked:
   (a) Title.
   (b) Date the book was published.
   (c) Call number, which locates the book.
   (d) Number of pages in the book.
   (e) Year the author was born.
   (f) Place of publication.
   (g) Publisher.
2. A bibliography (*multiple choice*)
   (a) is a list of writings relating to a particular subject, period, or author.
   (b) gives facts about an author's life.
   (c) gives quotations for one or more books.
   (d) makes a book authoritative.
   (e) lists topics arranged in alphabetical order.

BROOKLYN COLLEGE/FRESHMEN LIBRARY TEST

Section III, Part 2 (true or false)

1. A bibliography may be defined as a systematically arranged list of printed matter on a given subject, or the works of an author.
   True _____   False _____
2. *Who's Who in America* gives brief biographies of living persons.
   True _____   False _____
3. *Essay and General Literature Index* refers to material in books.
   True _____   False _____

Section IV (multiple choice)

1. An account of the life of George Canning, nineteenth-century British statesman, will be found in
   (a) *Essay and General Literature Index.*
   (b) *Who's Who.*
   (c) *World Almanac.*
   (d) "DNB" (*The Dictionary of National Biography*).
2. The imprint refers to the name of publisher, place or publication, and
   (a) pagination.
   (b) name of editor, if any.
   (c) date of publication.
   (d) illustrations.

PERFECTION FORM CO./LIBRARY SURVEY TEST

Test 1 (multiple choice)

1. A book in which the author tells the life story of another person is called
   (a) a biography.
   (b) a character sketch.
   (c) a bibliography.
   (d) a personality profile.
2. For your convenience, all the books in a library are recorded in
   (a) *Books in Print.*
   (b) the card catalog.
   (c) the accession book.
   (d) *Readers' Guide.*
3. A book in which the author tells the story of his own life is called
   (a) an autobiography.
   (b) a vignette.
   (c) a biography.
   (d) a personality profile.

The above questions were chosen at random to represent the subject matter covered by the various library skills tests. These questions with those from the Feagley test provide a cross-section of the information felt to be important for first-year college students to know about library use. At the same time these questions should be answerable by secondary school students, since these tests are generally designed for entering students.

TESTING THE TEST OBJECTIVES

In the development of any test, the major objective of the test designer is usually to evaluate instruction taught to the student or information the student has learned from other sources. The test therefore represents the objectives the test designer feels are important and covers those salient elements that should be covered by an ideal course of instruction. It is impossible to separate the instruction from the test.

Librarians have assumed the role of test designers. The foregoing materials outline to some degree the instructional philosophy of those test designers. In the way we have constructed our tests on library skills it appears that we librarians have shown a poor understanding of the value of the library to our students.

We need to teach each student how to find books, how to find periodical articles, and how to find government documents. From an analysis of the results in Table 1, the most popular way the test designers think students should find books is through the card catalog (questions on subject headings, card catalog, filing rules, and abbreviations totaled 199). The Feagley test follows this trend. Librarians have exalted the card catalog as the major source for locating books. The card catalog is one of the most useful library tools we have, but it certainly is not the only one. There are many other tools for locating books. The emphasis placed on the use of the card catalog suggests that librarians are convinced that a thorough knowledge of the card catalog is essential to the efficient use of a library. Test designers for library skills evaluation should use a little more imagination in their development of both test and course materials.

In testing students' ability to locate periodical articles, the test designers have been more generous. There usually is a section on the *Readers' Guide to Periodical Literature*. However, there are few references to other periodical indexes.

There is practically nothing at all in the tests on the locating of government reports. None of the tests represented in Table 1 show any section devoted to questions on government documents, an area that has grown in importance in the last 20 years. Since many of the tests were developed prior to 1950 when scientific and technical government reports were in an early stage of development, it would be expected there would be no questions or few questions dealing with them. Any new test should, however, be concerned with them.

According to Table 1, the most popular topic for instruction is the use of reference books, such as handbooks, dictionaries, encyclopedias, biographical works, and quotation works. In spite of this emphasis, no reference is made anywhere in library skills tests to Winchell's *Guide to Reference Books*. There seems to be an unstated opinion among librarians that Winchell is a librarian's private tool and not meant for students.

Students should have some idea of bibliographic entries before they write dissertations. Too many doctoral dissertations demonstrate that these most advanced students have little facility with bibliographic citations. Nor do they have an adequate skill in literature searching to understand the true value of a library.

Our educational institutions should design library skills instruction that would quickly tell students how to find books through the *Subject Guide to Books in Print* as well as the card catalog; how to find periodical articles through the *Readers' Guide* as well as many other periodical indexes, such as *Business Periodicals Index, Education Index, PAIS,* and *Psychological Abstracts,* plus a smattering of the scientific indexes, such as *Chemical Abstracts.*

In terms of government documents and reports, we ought to be able to teach students about the *Monthly Catalog,* and the *NTIS U.S. Government Reports Announcements.* The Congressional hearings listed in the *Monthly Catalog* are as informative and important as any article listed in the *Readers' Guide.*

The design of both library skills tests and courses tend to reflect what may be confused understanding on the part of test designers of how users need to use a library. Before we can design what are effective learning experiences in terms of either courses or tests, we are going to have to determine our library skill objectives and the needs of students as prescribed by teachers with more understanding than we have had in the past.

NOTES

1. Felix Eugene Snider, "The Relationship of Library Ability to Performance in College" (unpublished thesis, Urbana: Graduate College of the University of Illinois, 1965).
2. These tests were collected to try to determine the effectiveness of a proposed library-use training course for engineers and scientists, the result of which is: M. Bloomfield, *How to Use a Library: A Guide for Literature Searching* (Reseda, Calif.: Mojave Books, 1970).
3. Barbara H. Phipps, "Library Instruction for the Undergraduate," *College and Research Libraries* 29 (1968): 411–422.
4. Ibid., p. 422.
5. Ralph Perkins, *The Prospective Teacher's Knowledge of Library Fundamentals: A Study of the Responses Made by 4,170 College Seniors to Tests Designed to Measure Familiarity with Libraries* (Metuchen, N.J.: Scarecrow Press, 1965).

BIBLIOGRAPHY OF TESTS

TESTS ORGANIZED INTO PARTS

Bennett, A., and Schrammel, H. E. *Bennett Use of Library Test, High School and College.* Emporia, Kansas: Bureau of Educational Measurements, Kansas State Teachers College, 1947.

Feagley, Ethel M., et al. *A Library Orientation Test for College Freshmen.* New York: Teachers College Press, Teachers College, Columbia University, 1955.

Hurt, P. *An Examination to Test Student Ability to Use a Library.* Berkeley: School of Librarianship, University of California, 1933.

Kirkpatrick, Mary S., et al. *The Use of Library and Study Materials, Grades 9–16.* Austin, Texas: The Steck Co., 1939–41.

Perfection Form Co. *Library Survey Test.* Logan, Iowa, 1967.

Progressive Education Association. *Test on the Use of Books and Libraries, Grades 7–12.* Chicago: University of Chicago, 1939.

Shores, L., and Moore, J. E. *Peabody Library Information Test, Grades 4–8, 9–12, 13-16,* rev. ed. Minneapolis: Educational Test Bureau, Educational Publishers, Inc., 1940.

Smith, Elmer R. *Library Usage Test, Grades 11–13.* Atlanta, Ga.: Turner E. Smith Co., 1940.

Tyler, H. T., and Kimber, G. C. *Tyler-Kimber Study Skills Test.* Stanford, California: Stanford University Press, 1937.

University of New Hampshire, University Library. *Library Quiz.* Durham, N.H.: 196?.

TESTS NOT ORGANIZED INTO PARTS

Brooklyn College. Library. *Freshmen Library Test.* Brooklyn, 196?.

Clatworthy, L. M. *Library Test for College Students.* Denver: University of Denver, 1932.

Colorado State Teachers College. *Test on the Use of Books and of the Library.* Greeley, Colo.: The College, 193?.

Pierson, S., and Gilbert, A. W. *Comprehensive Examination in the Use of the Library.* Kansas City, Mo.: Teachers College of Kansas City, 1939.

Quiz on Units. In: Toser, M. A *Library Manual: A Study-Work Manual of Lessons on the Use of Books and Libraries.* 6th ed. New York: Wilson, 1964.

Reed, L. R. *Test on the Use of the Library for Colleges.* n.p., 1936.

Sample Tests Covering All Divisions of Library Instruction. In: Ingles, M., and McCague, A. *Teaching the Use of Books and Libraries: A Manual for Teachers and Librarians.* New York: Wilson, 1944.

White, C. M. *Test.* Nashville, Tenn.: Fisk University Library, 1936.

OTHER TESTS

Lindquist, E. I., and Feldt, Leonard S. *The Iowa Test of Educational Development, Test 9, Uses of Sources of Information.* Chicago: Science Research Associates, 1960.

Melville, S. D., et al. *Cooperative Dictionary Test, Grades 7–12.* Princeton, N.J.: Cooperative Test Division, Educational Testing Service, 1951–52.

Spache, George D. *A Test on Use of the Dictionary, High School and College.* Gainesville, Fla.: Reading Laboratory and Clinic, University of Florida, 1955.

Stephenson, Claude E. *Senior High School Library and Reference Skills Test, Grades 9–12.* Logan, Iowa: The Perfection Form Co., 1960.

EVALUATING LIBRARY-USER EDUCATION PROGRAMS

John Lubans, Jr.
Assistant Director for Public Services, University of Colorado Libraries

Instructional programs in all types of libraries have been infrequently evaluated; their need and effect have not been measured except in a few isolated cases. Measurement or evaluation that has taken place has been largely heuristic, that is, not scientifically established, but useful nevertheless to explain observations made in library-use instruction. There are a few statistically valid studies, but these deal with *methods* of instruction rather than the success or lack of success on the part of the user in learning about information use.

The evaluations that have been done reflect to a certain extent the prevalent uncertainty that exists around what the objectives of library-use instruction are or should be.

Most library-use instruction is based on what we as librarians *think* library users need to know. It is this educated guesswork or *perceived need* on which many programs (tours, orientation lectures, a multitude of multimedia presentations, and formal courses in bibliography) have been based. Since we are prompted to action by what we observe is lacking in the library users at the time of the user's need, our response is apt to be a type of bibliographic first aid. This may explain some of the lack of long-range objectives in educating the library user. That there *is a need* for library instruction can be vouchsafed by most librarians working with the public. Probably the major errors in basing programs only on perceived need is the redundancy inherent in such an approach and that such a shortsighted view does not generally get to the source of many information-use problems: the teacher/librarian relationship. Invariably, the beginning user gets the greatest amount of attention, while the slightly advanced user is offered little. This situation is changing somewhat, and evaluation of programs (including surveys of user/nonuser needs) will do much to redirect instruction—in collaboration with the teacher—toward the other levels where it can be substantive.

We should be able to measure the impact of instruction. The results of evaluation not only present possible alternatives for better programs but should also provide some standards of performance for such instruction and demonstrate to funding agencies the libraries' role in effective information use.

Several attempts at evaluation will be examined in this chapter. Through these examples and illustrations a general directon is provided.

PROBLEMS OF EVALUATION

We may be able to measure the immediate effects of library-use instruction, but have no means at present to measure the long-range, lasting effect. For that matter the short-term result is just as difficult to grasp, since very few school, public, or academic librarians get to see the completed research paper or report or whatever the end result may be of the question they assisted the user with. Even in the school environment few librarians are consulted by teachers regarding the bibliographic quality of research papers.

Another problem of evaluation, particularly when the users are asked for their opinion, is the users' almost certain lack of experience (and resulting inability) to effectively compare one learning situation with another. They can react to what is at hand (that is, did it help when they needed it?) but generally have little understanding of the broader perspectives of information use.

One particular concern in use instruction is the users' apparent redundancy and lack of retention. It is not uncommon for persons to be instructed in the use of the *Readers' Guide* several times during their student life and for them never to retain the information. As a research paper deadline approaches, the library instruction cycle restarts. This is indicative of the lack of continuity in library-user education and of the uneven emphasis on bibliographic skills by classroom teachers.

A study of library-use instruction at a high school and its feeder schools concluded that instruction offered by these schools was not developmental (that is, it did not build and expand upon skills previously taught) and that instruction tended to be concentrated at one or two grade levels.[1] Since it is likely these conditions result from a lack of strong and consistent identity for library use in the curriculum, this role should be emphasized in planning library-user education programs.

EVALUATING THE NEED FOR LIBRARY-USE INSTRUCTION

A number of studies have stated and attempted to demonstrate that a relationship exists between scholastic grade-point averages and library use.[2-8] Research findings have indicated that the higher the grade-point average the student has the more likely and frequently the library is used. Some even venture to say it is because the library *is* used that the student's grade point is higher than when the library *is not* used. It would seem to follow that since the library at least has a marginal effect on students' scholastic effectiveness there is justification for the library to provide library-use education programs, since by doing so we are contributing at least tangentially to the students' success in their studies.

Another measurement of the need for library-user instruction can be gained by questions on this topic in a general library survey. One such survey asked whether the library should offer instruction.[9] Table 1 charts the college students' apparent awareness of a need for a deeper understanding of how to use libraries.

As illustrated, over 80 percent of each class of students sees a need to be filled by the library. A similar question was asked of a group of library nonusers at a technological university, and the response even from this sample was 48 percent in favor of library-use instruction.[10] Availing themselves of library-use instruction is, of course, another matter, but the interest appears to be there.

Another indication of the need for library-user education is the findings of a number of researchers who have tested students' level of library-use knowledge.[11-13] The results of these tests, as a rule, have shown a very low basic knowledge of bibliographic skills. The extensive study and analysis by Perkins [14] paints a particularly dismal picture of library users' knowledge. In testing thousands of graduating seniors of teachers' colleges he found them seriously lacking in library skills. One may quibble about the standardized tests used in any of these studies, since the tests do include some superfluous technical items (e.g., questions on "tracings"). Even so, the students missed many of the most fundamental questions, such as what basis (size, color, binding, subject, or date) is used for library classification. Elsewhere in this book is a discussion of library tests, of their positive aspects and limitations. At present levels of users' and nonusers' skills a basic homemade library-use test can be (and has been frequently) utilized to measure the library users' bibliographic knowledge. This is of some value in determining the type and level of library-use instruction program. The tests further verify that it is generally safe to assume that the instructional program start at the *basics* level.

USER NEEDS IN LIBRARY-USE KNOWLEDGE

In a recent survey of user needs the student union was deliberately chosen as the distribution point so that a more representative group of library users and nonusers could be queried than just the users entering a library. To take this a point further, Table 2 offers a revealing comparison of an in-library study with one done in a student union regarding frequency of library use.[15]

It is probably safe to say that the sample group at the student union is a better representation of use and nonuse of the library for librarians to study

Table 1. *SHOULD THE LIBRARY OFFER LIBRARY-USE INSTRUCTION?*

	Graduate	Senior	Junior	Sophomore	1st Year
No. Responding:	94	86	95	79	49
Yes	83%	84.8%	81.1%	95%	92%
No	17%	15.2%	18.9%	5%	8%

Table 2. *HOW OFTEN DO YOU USE THE LIBRARY?*

	In-Library Survey	Student Union Survey
%		%
65	More than once a week	31
19	More than eight times a semester	27
12	A few times	25
4	Infrequently or not at all	16

than is the in-library group. Parenthetically the nonusers are an important group to study. A lot can be learned from this often overlooked group, since understanding its difficulties in finding information could do much to provide clues to help convert instructors teaching courses not conducive to library use.

The "Assessment of Student Needs in Knowing How to Use Libraries" (Appendix 1) questionnaire was designed to find out (1) information about the respondents; (2) the history of user/nonusers' library-use instruction in libraries; (3) user/nonusers' attitudes toward libraries and librarians; (4) respondents' self-appraisal of their library skills/knowledge; (5) respondents' awareness and use of the library, and (6) students' view of faculty attitudes toward library use and know-how.

Among the study's findings, the analysis of the history of user/nonusers' library-use instruction reveals that when the respondents were high school students almost all (85 percent and above) of them had access to a library and made some use of it (some 27–42 percent made *more* use of it than of the university library).[16] The public library appears to have been used about as much as the high school library.

Also evident is that the respondents (and by extrapolation most students) had used libraries before their arrival on campus and that their use had been in some depth. The survey further showed that the majority of these users had had some instruction in library use, as indicated by the following two tallies (note that the amount by which a column fails to add up to 100 percent is equal to the nonresponse to that question):

"Were you given an introduction to the use of the high school library?"

	1st Yr.	Soph.	Jr.	Sr.	Mast.	Doct.
Yes	58%	74%	75%	71%	64%	54%
No	26%	24%	20%	23%	32%	23%

"Was any library-use instruction given you in the public library?"

	1st Yr.	Soph.	Jr.	Sr.	Mast.	Doct.
Yes	28%	19%	17%	21%	15%	13%
No	63%	76%	76%	77%	77%	80%

The other side of this is that the "no" line is fairly high for both high school and, particularly, public libraries. Discounting failure of the respondent's memory, it is particularly discouraging that 26 percent of the first-year-college-student respondents did not receive library-use instruction in high school. This, it seems, is tantamount to the student missing out on a major portion of his or her education.

An interesting response is noted to the evaluated statement:

"My course work has benefited from the introductions, orientations, tours, etc., I've had":

	1st Yr.	Soph.	Jr.	Sr.	Mast.	Doct.
Agree	5	18	19	15	7	30
Neutral	26	24	24	16	21	8
Disagree	30	21	26	25	7	15
Don't know	33	34	34	47	69	46

From the groupings above the doctoral students seem to have felt the most beneficial effect of the library-use instruction that they have had. The majority either think it has not helped or have no opinion on its effectiveness. This opinion is, of course, somewhat clouded by many of the students' not having had to use libraries except on a cursory basis and as a result their *need to know* has not been there consistently enough to create a memorable learning experience.

Certainly, asking what students expect and need and how they see the library is an important step toward understanding students better, and as a result providing more effective information and educational services.

EXAMPLES OF EVALUATION STUDIES

Hansen has described the evaluation of computer-assisted instruction (CAI) in the use of an academic library.[17] Through questionnaires she studied the attitude of users toward the University of Denver's CAI library program. Within Hansen's original research paper is a brief literature search on the topic of evaluation that notes the doctoral dissertation by Donna Jean Corlett entitled: *"A Correlational Analysis of Study Skills and Attitudes, Library Skills and Reading Skills with the Academic Success of Education Students at the University of Portland"* (1969). She also cited a recent paper by Kirk wherein he makes a comparison of two methods of library instruction for students in introductory biology.[18] Employing control groups, of which the one was given guided exercises in library use and the other was lectured to in the conventional manner about library skills, Kirk found that "neither method is superior" in effectiveness for teaching library instruction. Frank Kuo, in his recent report on which of six methods of library instruction are best, states that the "self-paced audio-visual tutorial study followed by a summary and question/answer session was the most effective way of increasing student achievement" on a test.[19]

Hansen also points out Axeen's thorough study at the University of Illinois that involved control groups for a lecture presentation and an electronic programmed instruction series in library skills.[20] Both groups made essentially the same progress in learning about libraries.

The literature reveals an early document: a paper by Barkley published in 1939 that describes the program in user education at the Towson Teachers College Library where a pretest was given to all incoming students.[21] The results of this pretest were used to tailor instruction for those showing the greatest unfamiliarity with libraries.

In 1968 Carey carried out tests to measure the library knowledge of first-year college students after they had had orientation to the library for two weeks.[22] The tests used were the standardized *Library Orientation Test for College Freshmen and Library Proficiency Test.* In 1969 the tests were given again, this time to new students without any orientation. Table 3 gives the interesting comparison of the two years. This experiment does indicate the likely effect of library orientation: the "with instruction" mean is above the mean for "without instruction" mean by almost 15 percent.

An open-space elementary school's school-wide survey asked the students to respond to statements about the school by either *agree, undecided,* or *disagree.*[23] Although the statements are not specifically library-use instruction ones, they do provide some insight into what success the overall library program may be having. For example, the student response to the statement "Our library is a friendly place" showed 55 in agreement, 23 undecided, and 22 disagreeing. Other, more specific questions could be included in surveys of this type.

At the University of Colorado Libraries evaluations of instructional programs have been done for two slide/tape programs, "How to Find a Book" and "How to Find a Periodical," for the library tours, and for a film loop on the *"Readers' Guide:* How to Use It." The questionnaires for the slide/tape programs and the *Readers' Guide* loop are reproduced in this chapter as Appendixes II and III, respectively.

A number of the critical comments on the slide/tape programs were used in producing the new editions. For example, to the question "What did you *not* like about the program?" responses such as these were received:

Table 3. *MEASURING THE LIBRARY KNOWLEDGE OF FIRST-YEAR COLLEGE STUDENTS*

	1969: Without Prior Library-Use Instruction (%)	*1968: With Two Weeks' Library-Use Instruction* (%)
Median	50.5	49.0
Mode	60.0	66.0
Mean	51.72	65.3

"The sick music in the background and sitting in the middle of a hallway listening to it."

"They were quite boring; the voice was irritating."

As a result of this evaluation the machines were moved to a different location, and in the new production a different voice and livelier music were used and the dialogue was extensively shortened.

A questionnaire on library tours was distributed to find out why as many as 1,000 users take them each year when no one is compelled to do so. Tours have been much disparaged in critical evaluations of library orientation in the literature. The questionnaire showed that first-year students were the largest group taking the tours—over one half. Close to all the respondents said they took the tour because they felt a need to know what the library *is*. A number also checked the slot next to "I think it will help my grade average."

The questionnaire on the *"Readers' Guide:* How to Use It" film loop is designed to measure the educational effect of this experimental, homemade, silent, program. The 4.5-minute film is next to the actual set of the *Readers' Guide*. The questionnaires were placed there also. Here are some of the questions and some of the responses:

Have you learned something from the film?

40%   Yes, I did learn.
30%   Yes, I learned some things but still have questions.
30%   No, the film didn't help me learn.

How interesting was this program?

30%   Interesting.
60%   O.K.
10%   Very dull.

Would it have helped to be able to stop the program at certain places or to repeat certain parts?

10%   Yes.
90%   No.

How would you prefer to get information about library tools?

60%   Watching this kind of program.
40%   Asking a librarian.

Comments to "How could this program be improved?" included:

"More explanatory frames (graphics) . Less light overhead. Means of sitting close to screen. It seems like a really usable medium for library instruction."

"Nothing was said of volume coding, date coding." [There was, but viewer must have missed it.]

Another example of before-and-after evaluation is provided in the recent Brigham Young University programmed instruction manual on using the card catalog.[24] The pretest student score was 32 percent, and after completing the workbook the posttest score went to 84 percent. The tests are included in the text of the workbook.

The point in all these examples is that evaluation, however one might arrive at it (questionnaires, tests, observations [hidden or open], suggestion or comment notebooks) is a necessary part of any program in library-use instruction. Not only is it necessary for an understanding of where our efforts are going and what educational (teaching/learning) effect they are having but also for making improvements. User feedback is valuable and highly desirable to have on practically all aspects of the library.

EVALUATING FORMAL BIBLIOGRAPHIC SKILLS COURSES

Formal (credit-bearing) library-user education classes are frequently evaluated by students like any other course offered at a university. As with other academic courses the evaluations probably first originated with students as they sought to publish guides on what classes were good, indifferent, or bad. Evaluation of this sort is generally done through questionnaires. This method can be used to test the effectiveness of a bibliographic research or library methods class. (It is assumed that the amount that the students learn is realized through the grading of term papers and examinations.) As with other questionnaires a number of approaches are possible and available. An essay-type questionnaire could involve asking for an opinion on the course; an evaluation of the amount of the student's personal participation and involvement in the course; an opinion about the instructor, and specific suggestions for improving a given course.

One device employed at the School of Education of the University of Colorado is the "Course Evaluation Inventory," using a 1–5 rating scale. A representation from the 40 questions asked reveals how thorough and forthright a survey like this can be:

The instructor avoided
   confusing or useless jargon: always 1 2 3 4 5 never
His reaction to difference
   of opinion was: encouragement 1 2 3 4 5 intolerance
The assignments were
   necessary (not busy work):   always 1 2 3 4 5 never
The subject matter was
   intellectually stimulating: always 1 2 3 4 5 never

A computer-based-course-evaluation procedure has been done at the University of Colorado. Each student was requested to fill out 34 questions on a *mark-sense* form, each question to be answered on a scale of five (0 = not at all; 4 = always). Some of the questions asked were:

In this course the instructor:
Emphasizes conceptual understanding: 0 1 2 3 4
Has a genuine interest in students: 0 1 2 3 4

This course:
Was boring: 0 1 2 3 4
Inspired me to do required
study, reading, or thinking: 0 1 2 3 4

In this case the questionnaires were tabulated and the information returned to the instructor to provide him with information about how students feel about various aspects of their courses. The analysis tries to measure how open the instructor is with students, how broad an approach is taken in course presentation, how enthusiastic the presentation of the course is, how well prepared, thorough (clear) the presentation of materials is, and how meaningful the instruction received is. Given good questions and responses it would seem much can be learned from students about what they think about a course and most of what is related to it.

CREATING EVALUATION QUESTIONNAIRES

Questionnaires are a convenient way to gather opinion and probably allow the respondents the greatest freedom in their responses (particularly if response is anonymous). The methods of constructing questionnaires, whether for use by users alone or for structured interviews, have been discussed in a number of books, some of which are particularly good to consult before starting out.[25-28]

EXAMPLES OF QUESTIONNAIRES

FROM UNIVERSITY OF COLORADO LIBRARIES

"Slide/Tape ["How to Find a Book" and "How to Find a Periodical"] Programs Questionnaire" (Appendix 2). This questionnaire is short and easy to fill out. Again, the effectiveness of the program is questioned and users are asked how it could be made better.

"The *Readers' Guide:* How to Use It Questionnaire" (Appendix 3). This borrows heavily from other questionnaires of its type. It seeks a statement from the users on whether they learned from the film-loop program. Comments are also solicited for improvements, for use in other programs like this that may be created.

"Term Paper Clinic Questionnaire" (Appendix 4). This questionnaire is a bit different from the others in that it asks for an evaluation of *librarians* rather than media techniques. Following a Brown University study, some attention is also paid to how and/or if users heard about the Term Paper Clinic (by giving users a variety of publicity media to choose from), so that future publicity efforts may be refined for best effect. The Term Paper Clinic involves stepped-up reference service and the manning of all public information desks on weekends. Frequently, two or three librarians are in the card catalog area to assist library users.

FROM MASSACHUSETTS INSTITUTE OF TECHNOLOGY, BARKER ENGINEERING LIBRARY

"Audio-Visual Aids Questionnaire" (Appendix 5). This questionnaire measures the educational effectiveness of the AV programs in the Barker library. A good amount of candor is evident; there is no holding back on types of criticism for which the users have options.

FROM COLORADO STATE UNIVERSITY LIBRARIES

"Keys to CSU Libraries Questionnaire" (Appendix 6). Designed for key-punching, for ease of tabulation, this questionnaire serves essentially the same purposes as those above—i.e., to measure the effectiveness, both mechanical and educational, of a program and to solicit users' advice on how such programs may be improved.

NOTES

1. Louise Crosby and Sherril Totemeier, "Library Skills Instruction at Alameda Senior High School and Its Feeder Schools: Is It Developmental?" (Research Paper, Graduate School of Librarianship, University of Denver, 1971).
2. Patrick Barkey, "Patterns of Student Use of a College Library," *College and Research Libraries* 26 (March 1965): 115–118.
3. Floyd Cammack and Donald Mann, "Institutional Implications of an Automated Circulation Study," *College and Research Libraries* 28 (March 1967): 129–132.
4. Patricia Knapp, "College Teaching and the Library," *Illinois Libraries* 40 (December 1958): 828–833.
5. Lloyd A. Kramer and Martha B. Kramer, "The College Library and the Drop-out," *College and Research Libraries* 29 (1968): 310–312.
6. John Lubans, Jr., "Student Use of a Technological University Library," *IATUL Proceedings* 4 (July 1969): 7–13.
7. E. W. McDiarmid, "Conditions Affecting Use of the College Library," *Library Quarterly* 5 (1935): 60–63.
8. Ralph Perkins, *The Prospective Teacher's Knowledge of Library Fundamentals: A Study of the Responses Made by 4,170 College Seniors to Tests Designed to Measure Familiarity with Libraries* (Metuchen, N.J.: Scarecrow Press, 1965).
9. John Lubans, Jr., "The Use of a Large Academic Library by Undergraduate and Graduate Students" (unpublished draft, February 21, 1972, University of Colorado, Boulder).
10. John Lubans, Jr., "Non-use of an Academic Library," *College and Research Libraries* 32 (September 1971): 362–367.
11. Peyton Hurt, "The Need of College and University Instruction in Use of the Library," *Library Quarterly* 4 (1934): 436–448.
12. Knapp, op. cit.
13. Perkins, op. cit.
14. Ibid.

15. John Lubans, Jr., "Non-users and Library Surveys," *The Colorado Academic Library* 7 (Summer 1971): 1–3.

16. John Lubans, Jr., "Report to the Council on Library Resources on a Fellowship Awarded for 1971/72," mimeographed (Boulder: University of Colorado Libraries, November 28, 1972).

17. Lois N. Hansen, *Computer Assisted Instruction in the Use of an Academic Library: Success or Failure* (Research Paper, University of Denver, March 1972).

18. Thomas Kirk, "A Comparison of Two Methods of Library Instruction for Students in Introductory Biology," *College and Research Libraries* 32 (1971): 465–74.

19. Frank F. Kuo, "A Comparison of Six Versions of Science Library Instruction," *College and Research Libraries* 34 (1973): 287–290.

20. Marina E. Axeen, "Teaching the Use of the Library to Undergraduates: An Experimental Comparison of Computer-Based Instruction and the Conventional Lecture Method," *Report R-361* (Urbana: University of Illinois Coordinated Science Laboratory, 1967, AD 657216).

21. Margaret Barkley, "Arrows for freshmen," *Library Journal* 64 (May 15, 1939): 402–404.

22. Faye Carey, Memoranda *To:* Instructors in E100 and E110, *From:* Faye Carey, Reference Librarian, *Subject:* Library Orientation (Temple Buell College, 1968 and 1969), 3 pages and 2 pages, respectively, n.d.

23. "School Survey," Eisenhower [School] Newsletter (Boulder, Colorado) 3 (June 1973): 2–7.

24. Charles I. Bradshaw et al., *Using the Library: The Card Catalog* (Provo, Utah: Brigham Young University Press, 1971).

25. Robert L. Kahn and Charles F. Cannell, *The Dynamics of Interviewing, Theory, Techniques and Cases* (New York: Wiley, 1957).

26. A. N. Oppenheim, *Questionnaire Design and Attitude Measurement* (New York: Basic Books, 1966).

27. Stanley L. Payne, *The Art of Asking Questions* (Princeton, N.J.: Princeton University Press, 1951).

28. Maurice B. Line, *Library Surveys: An Introduction to Their Use, Planning, Procedure and Presentation* (London: Clive Bingley, 1968).

APPENDIX 1
UNIVERSITY OF COLORADO LIBRARIES: ASSESSMENT OF STUDENT NEEDS IN KNOWING HOW TO USE LIBRARIES

QUESTIONNAIRE

A1. What is your status at CU?

a. ☐ Freshman   e. ☐ Master's Program
b. ☐ Sophomore   f. ☐ Doctoral Program
c. ☐ Junior   g. ☐ Other
d. ☐ Senior

A2. What is your major field of study?

    a. ☐ Humanities
    b. ☐ Social Sciences
    c. ☐ Sciences
    d. ☐ Engineering
    e. ☐ Other

A3. How often do you use the CU Libraries (Norlin and/or the branches):

    a. ☐ More than once a week
    b. ☐ More than 8 times a semester
    c. ☐ Few times a semester
    d. ☐ Very seldom, or never

If you checked either of the last two categories ("c" or "d"), what in your opinion is the reason?

    a. ☐ My courses don't require library use
    b. ☐ The library is inadequate for my purposes
    c. ☐ I don't care for the library environment
    d. ☐ Other

B. In this section please make your ratings using the following scale:

IF YOU CIRCLE   IT MEANS YOU

    1 .... strongly agree with the statement
    2 .... moderately agree with the statement
    3 .... feel neutral about the statement
    4 .... moderately disagree with the statement
    5 .... strongly disagree with the statement
    6 .... do not know or the question does not apply

a. 1 2 3 4 5 6   My course work has benefitted from the introductions, orientations, tours, etc., I've had to using libraries and their resources.

b. 1 2 3 4 5 6   I think the main function of the CU Libraries is to store books and periodicals. Basically it is a store house.

c. 1 2 3 4 5 6   My professors, in general, encourage students to use the library.

d. 1 2 3 4 5 6   My expertise or lack of it in library use is taken into account by my professors when they grade my papers.

e. 1 2 3 4 5 6   Knowing how to use the library is over-rated. You can get along without instruction in library use.

f. 1 2 3 4 5 6   I generally find that a bibliography at the end of my papers is graded on quantity rather than quality of the citations.

g. Each of these items is important to me in a library:
   - 1 2 3 4 5 6 good lighting
   - 1 2 3 4 5 6 comfortable study carrels and other furniture
   - 1 2 3 4 5 6 ease of locating materials
   - 1 2 3 4 5 6 comfortable inviting interior
   - 1 2 3 4 5 6 low noise level
   - 1 2 3 4 5 6 good ventilation—and temperature quality control
   - 1 2 3 4 5 6 privacy and lack of crowding

h. 1 2 3 4 5 6 My undergraduate training (so far) has given me all the preparation I need for finding information in the libraries.

i. 1 2 3 4 5 6 My professors, in general, do not give a high priority to knowing how to use the library.

j. When I walk into a library I feel:
   - 1 2 3 4 5 6 relaxed, want to pick up an interesting book and read.
   - 1 2 3 4 5 6 curious, want to browse through the books.
   - 1 2 3 4 5 6 purposeful, want to do some serious work.
   - 1 2 3 4 5 6 frustrated, want to get what I need without being there half a day.
   - 1 2 3 4 5 6 cooped-up, want to get outside and breathe deeply.

k. 1 2 3 4 5 6 I am at a loss when faced with doing a term paper in the library.

l. Each of the following I consider valuable to a student regardless of his study areas:
   - 1 2 3 4 5 6 knowledge of use of bibliographies, abstracts, and indexes.
   - 1 2 3 4 5 6 awareness of pertinent literature in fields related to his own field.
   - 1 2 3 4 5 6 knowledge of how to look for specific information.
   - 1 2 3 4 5 6 knowledge of one or more foreign languages.

m. I think librarians are:
   - 1 2 3 4 5 6 possessive of their books.
   - 1 2 3 4 5 6 reluctant to tell you about library services.
   - 1 2 3 4 5 6 over-worked, too busy to help me.
   - 1 2 3 4 5 6 resentful of any intrusion.
   - 1 2 3 4 5 6 really interested in my problems.

n. 1 2 3 4 5 6 I feel well able to do research in the library.

o. 1 2 3 4 5 6 The library should offer courses, clinics, etc., in how to use libraries and their resources.
   - 1 2 3 4 5 6 I would take such courses, clinics, etc., if offered at a convenient time.

p. 1 2 3 4 5 6 "The library is the heart of the university."

q. 1 2 3 4 5 6 Whenever I do research for a paper in the library I get the feeling that there are information resources on my topic which I'm somehow missing.

r. 1 2 3 4 5 6 Instructors assume that I know already enough about using libraries to do an in-depth term paper.

C1. Which of these library services/facilities have you used (check all that apply):

____ reserve books	____ government documents
____ current periodicals	____ records
____ bound periodicals	____ audio-visual material
____ newspapers	____ reference books in reference
____ periodicals indexes or abstracts	department
	____ microforms
____ specific single books	____ term paper clinic
____ information desk	____ other

C2. In addition to the above I've used the following (check those that apply):

____ card catalogs	____ interlibrary loan
____ study areas (to study my own material)	____ photocopying service
	____ serials book catalog
____ the help of reference librarians	

C3. Regarding the services/facilities you have not used, was it because you (check those that apply):

____ didn't know they even existed	____ figured it wasn't worth the time spent using them
____ were aware of them but didn't have time	____ thought only librarians were supposed to use them
____ didn't want to ask about how to use them	____ couldn't locate the service even though I knew it existed
____ felt no need to use them	

C4. Do you feel that you would like more information and/or explanation on any of these services/facilities (check as many as apply)?

____ card catalogs	____ interlibrary loan
____ periodicals indexes or abstracts	____ special collections
	____ audio-visual materials
____ government documents	____ other
____ reference books (bibliographies, encyclopedias, etc.)	

C5. If the library staff included an information specialist in your subject area would you use that person?

_____ Yes
_____ No

C6. Do assignments in your courses usually involve using library resources other than just books placed on reserve by professors?

_____ Yes
_____ No

C7. Please check one of the following:

_____ I generally feel about 50–75% successful in using the library

_____ I generally feel above 75% successful in using the library

_____ I generally feel below 50% successful in using the library

C8. Did your high school have a library?

_____ Yes
_____ No

If yes, did you use the high school library more than you use the CU Libraries?

_____ Yes, more
_____ No, less
_____ No, about the same

Were you given an introduction to the use of the high school library?

_____ Yes
_____ No

C9. Did you use the public library in your community?

_____ Yes
_____ No

If yes, did you use the public library more than you use the CU Libraries?

_____ Yes, more
_____ No, less
_____ No, about the same

Was any library use instruction given you in the public library?

_____ Yes
_____ No

PLEASE RETURN TO THE BOX AT DOOR

APPENDIX 2

**UNIVERSITY OF COLORADO LIBRARIES: "HOW TO FIND A BOOK"
AND "HOW TO FIND A PERIODICAL" SLIDE/TAPE PROGRAMS**

QUESTIONNAIRE

PLEASE FILL OUT QUESTIONNAIRE AND LEAVE IN BOX

1. Did you find the slide/tape programs helpful?   Yes _____ No _____

2. What did you like about the programs?

3. What did you *not* like about the programs?

4. Were they too long?   Yes _____   No _____

5. Which of the following types of programs would you prefer (check one)?
   _____ (a) six or seven shorter programs on more specific topics such as the card catalog, the *Catalog of Serials,* the classification systems, etc.
   _____ (b) one short introduction to the library omitting the details of how you actually locate materials.
   _____ (c) the two programs as they are or with slight modification.

6. What changes would you make in the programs now on the machine?

7. What other ideas would you like to see implemented in teaching use of the library?

APPENDIX 3

**UNIVERSITY OF COLORADO LIBRARIES: "THE READERS' GUIDE:
HOW TO USE IT" FILM-LOOP PROGRAM**

QUESTIONNAIRE

PLEASE FILL THIS OUT. IT WILL HELP US IMPROVE OUR SERVICES.

1. Did you learn how to use the *Readers' Guide* after viewing this film. (Please mark the most appropriate answer.)
   _____ Yes, I did learn.
   _____ Yes, I learned some things but still have questions.
   _____ No, the film didn't help me learn.
      If No, please explain why _____
      _____

2. Have you ever used the *Readers' Guide* elsewhere (for example in high school)?   _____ Yes   _____ No
If Yes, do any of the following apply after seeing the film?
_____ I learned things about it I didn't know before.
_____ The program refreshed my memory about using it.
_____ I didn't learn anything I didn't already know.

3. How interesting was this program?
_____ Very interesting.
_____ Interesting.
_____ O.K.
_____ Dull.
_____ Very dull.

4. Was the program _____ too long, _____ too short, or _____ just right?

5. Would it have helped to be able to stop the program at certain places or to repeat certain parts?   _____ Yes   _____ No

6. Do you think the film would have been better with narration and background music?   _____ Yes   _____ No

7. How would you prefer to get information about library tools?
_____ Watching this kind of program.
_____ Asking a friend.
_____ Reading about it.
_____ Asking a librarian.

8. How could this program be improved _____
_____
_____

THANKS

PLEASE LEAVE THIS QUESTIONNAIRE IN BOX BY THE PROJECTOR

APPENDIX 4
UNIVERSITY OF COLORADO LIBRARIES: TERM PAPER CLINIC

QUESTIONNAIRE

	YES	NO
1. Are you in the library because of the Term Paper Clinic?	_____	_____
2. Did you discover the Term Paper Clinic through:		
friends	_____	_____
newspapers	_____	_____
faculty announcements	_____	_____
posters	_____	_____
or did not discover	_____	_____

3. Are you a:

graduate student	____	____
senior	____	____
junior	____	____
sophomore	____	____
freshman	____	____
special student	____	____
other	____	____

4. Are you using the library today in order to write a paper?   ____   ____

   subject _____

5. What is your major? _____

6. Where were you *initially* assisted by the library staff?

Information Desk?	____	____
Public Catalog?	____	____
Reference Department?	____	____
College Library?	____	____
Education Library?	____	____
Government Documents?	____	____
Periodicals Room?	____	____

   or other _____

7. Was the guidance from the library staff:

more than adequate	____	____
adequate	____	____
inadequate	____	____

8. Was the attitude of the library staff:

friendly	____	____
unfriendly	____	____
indifferent	____	____

9. Did you find the material you needed?

books	____	____
periodicals	____	____
microfilms	____	____

10. Was the material you found sufficient for your need?   ____   ____

11. What do you think "Term Paper Clinic" means?

help in writing a paper	____	____
help in finding material for a paper	____	____
help in organizing a paper	____	____
help in picking a topic for a paper	____	____

12. Would you hesitate to request the services being offered during the Term Paper Clinic at other times during the year? _____ _____

13. Would you use the Term Paper Clinic again? _____ _____

14. Please make any further comments you might have on the back.

RETURN: AT THE GUARD DESK EXIT FROM NORLIN *or* MAIL TO:
REFERENCE DEPARTMENT, NORLIN LIBRARY.

APPENDIX 5
MASSACHUSETTS INSTITUTE OF TECHNOLOGY, BARKER ENGINEERING LIBRARY: AUDIO-VISUAL AIDS

QUESTIONNAIRE

Name (optional) _____

1. What is your current status at M.I.T.?
   _____ Undergraduate _____ Graduate student _____ Staff _____ Faculty
   _____ Other

2. Which reference source was described by the audio-visual aid you used?
   _____ Author-Title Catalog   _____ Subject Catalog
   _____ Engineering Index   _____ NASA STAR
   _____ Science Citation Index

3. Why did you use the audio-visual aid?
   _____ Wanted to use the reference source described.
   _____ Started to use the reference source and couldn't understand something.
   _____ Curious about the audio-visual aid.
   _____ Other (please explain): _____
   _____

4. How helpful was the aid?
   _____ Extremely helpful _____ Very helpful _____ Moderately helpful
   _____ Slightly helpful _____ Not helpful

5. Check one or more of the following to explain the above rating.
   _____ The aid made me aware of a reference source I did not previously know about.
   _____ I learned things about the reference source that I didn't know before.
   _____ The aid refreshed my memory about the reference source.
   _____ The aid was too elementary in its description of the reference source.
   _____ Other (please explain): _____
   _____

6. How interesting was the program?
_____ Very interesting   _____ Interesting
_____ Neither dull nor interesting   _____ Dull   _____ Very dull

7. If the program included humorous material, did you approve of its inclusion?   _____ Yes   _____ No

8. Was the presentation: _____ too long   _____ too short, or _____ about right?

9. Were any parts of the presentation: _____ too fast, or _____ too slow? Please specify, if you can, which parts were too fast or too slow.

10. Would it have helped to be able to stop the program at certain places or to repeat certain parts?   _____ Yes   _____ No

11. Would you prefer audio accompanied by slides or audio accompanied by actual samples?
_____ audio with slides   _____ audio with sample catalog cards (or pages from index)

12. Do you prefer some different means for learning how to use reference tools?
_____ Yes   _____ No
If yes, please check which you prefer:
_____ individual assistance   _____ written instruction
_____ library orientation tour
_____ other (please explain): _____
_____

13. What other reference sources, if any, would you like to have described by audio-visual aids?

14. Please make any additional comments on the back of this sheet. Thank you.

PLEASE DEPOSIT THE COMPLETED QUESTIONNAIRE IN THE BOX PROVIDED

APPENDIX 6
COLORADO STATE UNIVERSITY LIBRARIES: KEYS TO
CSU LIBRARIES

QUESTIONNAIRE

This opportunity for self-instruction in the use of the library was made possible by a grant from the CSU Office of Instructional Development. It involves NO FUNDS from the CSU Libraries' budget. By completing this questionnaire, you will help us evaluate this type of library instruction.

Please mark squares with an X to record your answers (☒).

0. In what category are you? Please mark one.

fresh-man	sopho-more	junior	senior	gradu-ate stu-dent	faculty	staff	other
1 ☐	2 ☐	3 ☐	4 ☐	5 ☐	6 ☐	7 ☐	8 ☐

1. What best describes your reason for listening to this program? Please mark one.

    1 ☐ for curiosity satisfaction
    2 ☐ for general information
    3 ☐ for specific information (for term paper, etc.)
    4 ☐ for class assignment to use this program
    5 ☐ other _____

2. Did you understand this program?

    1 ☐ yes
    2 ☐ no
    3 ☐ not completely

3. How much of the information presented did you already know?

    1 ☐ none   3 ☐ most
    2 ☐ some   4 ☐ all

4. Do you think you will find this program helpful in using the library?

    1 ☐ yes
    2 ☐ no
    3 ☐ somewhat

5. How many times did you watch this program today?

    1 ☐ once
    2 ☐ twice
    3 ☐ more

6. Did you enjoy this program?

    1 ☐ yes
    2 ☐ no
    3 ☐ no comment

7. How did you find the mechanical performance of this device?

    1 ☐ satisfactory
    2 ☐ unsatisfactory

8. How would you prefer to get this kind of information about the library? Please mark one.

    1 ☐ watching or listening to this kind of program
    2 ☐ asking a friend
    3 ☐ reading a library handbook
    4 ☐ asking a librarian

9. Please feel free to use this space and the back for any additional comments which may help us evaluate this type of library instruction.

PLEASE RETURN THE QUESTIONNAIRE TO THE BASKET NEARBY

LIBRARY TOURS: THE FIRST STEP

MARY JO LYNCH

Doctoral student, Rutgers University School of Library Service; formerly Assistant Professor, University of Michigan, School of Library Science

Batches of students—I have seen as many as thirty in a group—are herded through a dozen or so stations. The guide is not always a librarian, nor is he always well-prepared. "This," he says, with a wave of his hand, "is the Periodicals Room." "That," with a nod, "is CBI, a universal English language bibliography, dictionary arrangement, with author, title, and subject entries. You must remember that the main entry is author." Then with the thirty students standing five deep around a card catalog drawer, the guide proceeds to dispatch with main entry, tracings, call numbers, etc., all of which are the product of a system, the convolutions and subtleties of which would call forth the admiration and envy of a Byzantine administrator. Small wonder that at the third or fourth station, most of the students stop listening. Libraries and librarians, they conclude, are as bad as anticipated. Obviously one's efforts are best applied in finding ways of avoiding, not utilizing the library.[1]

Thus did Robert Harlan of the University of California School of Librarianship at Berkeley, describe one of the "meaningless ways" used in the past to instruct students in the use of the academic library. What he is describing is, of course, a library tour—that much used and much maligned form of educating the library user.

PRACTICES OF THE PAST

Over 20 years ago when Mary Case Marquis studied user education she learned that tours were one of the three methods of library instruction prevalent at that time (the other two were: a series of lectures and a separate course with or without credit).[2] Since Marquis, several other surveyors have reported similar findings.[3] But most of them, and many others who have written about various aspects of user education in specific libraries, also report that tours are unsatisfactory and use such words as "deadly" or "ghastly" or "herded" or "amorphous mass" to describe them.

In reporting the results of her 1965 study of 200 colleges, Barbara Phipps made the following observations concerning tours:

> The respondents to the questionnaire rated the library tour the least effective [method of instruction] if used alone. Eighty-nine of the librarians (56.7 percent), however, still use the library tour. Chief objection to the tour seems to be that it usually comes before the student has need to use the library, and in the midst of much other orientation, rendering the student glassy-eyed and saturated with information and admonitions.[4]

Later in the article she comments:

> While the tour has generally been rated ineffective as an instructional device in teaching the use of the card catalog, reference books, periodical indexes, and the like, it has been fairly effective in familiarizing students with locations of departments and services.[5]

Somewhere in that last statement is a notion that comes up frequently in comments about tours and seems to underlie the negative attitudes often expressed toward them—a notion that a tour *ought* to do more than familiarize the library user with locations of things in the library building. Too often, librarians have acted as if users could learn all about a library in a brief tour and, therefore, have tried to cram into users' heads all kinds of information about using the card catalog, the periodical indexes, the reference collection while they are on a walk through the building. Very little of this is comprehended or remembered, and so librarians become discouraged about the value of tours. Once those great expectations are abandoned, however, and the tour is seen simply as a means of introducing people to a complex physical structure with a collection of material organized for their use and a staff ready and willing to offer many services, the tour can be assessed realistically as a valuable part of the user-education program.

"Library tours" does not appear as a separate heading in *Library Literature* so one must look for material under the heading "Instruction in the Use of Libraries." In recent years the largest number of articles listed here fall under the subheading "College and University Students." Evidently it has always been this way, for George Bonn reported in his 1960 *State of the Library Art* study on "Training Laymen in the Use of the Library" that "the greatest number of articles on instruction in the use of libraries has appeared in the college and university field."[6] He explains this by noting that "college libraries are much older than any other kind [and that] it was in colleges that the idea of research and reference use of libraries first developed."[7] A logical explanation for the absence of commentary on tours in libraries other than academic is that tour programs complicated enough to write about are probably found only in large, complex libraries that are used with some regularity by a substantial number of identifiable persons.

The most perceptive analysis of why tours might be needed in large libraries can be found in a speech addressed not to academic librarians but to public librarians concerned with orientation for the out-of-school adult. Kathleen Molz, who gave the keynote address to the American Library Association Preconference on Orientation at San Francisco in 1967, criticized some of the comments made by public librarians in a questionnaire sent to some 1,730 libraries by a joint Adult Services Division/Reference Services Division committee charged with finding out what was being done to train the out-of-school adult in the use of library materials. Molz argues that the "bewilderment," "frustration," "hesitance," and "fear" that librarians noted in adult patrons was entirely justified, that

> all mature people feel qualms and uncertainty in entering a strange building, or learning new routines. The subway system in New York City inspired me with absolute dread, and yet I cannot say that I am ignorant, or confused, or even frustrated. I was anxious not to lose my way or get off at the wrong stop or take the uptown train when what I wanted was the downtown one, and I am sure that my face reflected the tenseness of a person bent on not making a mistake. To interpret that kind of tension as ignorance, especially manifest when the individual is surrounded by people, all of whom look like they know what they are doing, is, I think, a grave error of judgment. Libraries, like banks, or department stores, or train stations, or a host of large and imposing public structures, can be intimidating.[8]

Molz does not specifically recommend tours, but she would probably agree that they can be an important part of library orientation, which she describes as "part of the library's entire public relations program [and] a way by which unfamiliarity can be lessened, by which anxiety and tension can be allayed." [9]

NEW IDEAS

For many years the library tour meant a conducted tour that involved one member of the library staff or a college's orientation staff leading a group of the uninitiated around the building. In recent years, however, as library buildings and holdings have become more complex and as the number of users has grown, new methods have been tried. Librarians now use self-guided tours, either in printed leaflets or on audiocassettes. Some, having abandoned the physical tour altogether, use slide presentations or, in a few cases, a film or videotape to move the newcomers around the building vicariously. Melum reported some of these innovations in her 1971 survey of user education programs; [10] some appeared at the Clinic on Using Media in Library Instruction that the ALA Committee on Instruction in the Use of Libraries sponsored at the 1972 Annual Conference in Chicago; [11] others are mentioned in the Status Report of the ACRL Committee on Bibliographic Instruction.[12] At the Third Annual Conference on Library Orientation for Academic Libraries at Eastern Michigan University in May 1973, Mary Butterfield summarized the reports she had received from the 140 libraries who had joined Project LOEX (Library Orientation EXchange).[13] Those reports show that 99 libraries use conducted tours, 24 use self-guided tours, 13 use self-guided cassette tours and 11 use synchronized slide/tape programs to perform the function of a tour (some used more than one of these techniques).

Since the literature on the subject of library tours is so scanty, this writer sent questionnaires to approximately 75 libraries, known to use one or more forms of the tour, asking for information that could be presented in this paper. All libraries listed in Melum's article were contacted, and questionnaires were also sent to additional libraries mentioned in one of the other three sources noted above, so that answers from a substantial number of libraries using each type of tour could be studied. Almost all librarians contacted responded promptly and generously. In addition, the writer examined the 178 reports sent to the ACRL Committee on Bibliographic Instruction.

BACK TO THE BEGINNING

The conducted tour has been such a standard part of user-education programs in so many libraries for such a long time that it seems unnecessary to talk about it in any detail. But conducted tours are still with us today, and since this volume is a study of all aspects of user-education programs, a rough summary of the common patterns revealed in completed *questionnaires on conducted tours* received from 22 libraries may be pertinent.

In most of these libraries (16) the responsibility for tours rested with the Reference Department. Tours were conducted by the professional staff either entirely (11) or with assistance from supportive staff. Most (20) reported that tours are given whenever requested by a group or, in colleges, by an individual faculty member. In addition, several libraries reported that they offer tours on a regular basis throughout the year (5) or during the first few days of a semester (6). The length of a tour may vary anywhere from ten minutes to one hour. The largest number (12) are offered independently of any other part of the user-education program, but some libraries offer tours in connection with various other kinds of orientation or instruction. Three librarians said that their tours covered only a physical orientation to the building; the rest noted that some instruction in the use of materials was offered. Attendance at the tours was voluntary in 12 cases, required in four, and varied in the others. Undergraduates (19), graduates (17), and faculty (15) were invited to take the tours, and several academic libraries reported that they conducted tours for high school classes and for people in the community. The number of persons usually included in each touring group varied from ten to 50 with ten and 15 being the most popular sizes. Only two libraries reported that the same route was followed by all tour guides, and most reported that the commentary always varies. Many noted that the route and the commentary were adjusted to the needs of the group on tour. The campus paper was most likely to be the medium used for publicizing the tours. Several other methods frequently cited were posters, a flyer sent to all new students, and faculty announcements.

Obviously, the preceding summary is not based on a scientific study of the conducted tour in libraries. It is doubtful that such a study is worth doing, though it does seem unfortunate that only in a few libraries are conducted tours carefully planned. Since tours often make the all-important first impression on potential users, someone on the staff should see to it that the impression is the one the library wants to make. Contrary to popular belief, it is not a simple matter to conduct an effective tour. Anyone who doubts that should take time to read Robert Pierson's witty account of "A Jaundiced Approach to the Guided Tour." [14]

Although an article devoted exclusively to the conducted tour has probably never been written, the subject does come up frequently in articles about other techniques used in library orientation programs and in general articles on library orientation. The most detailed advice on conducting tours comes from a British source—Hazel Mews's study of *Reader Instruction in Colleges and Universities*. She describes introductory talks on the library followed by tours of the building and warns:

> These tours can become wild scrambles of small parties on the run around a large institution, anxious only to head off the party in front and avoid involuntary fusion with the party behind. An obvious way to avoid this is to space the tours out during the orientation week or the first few days of term, putting up notices about them in all possible places and letting the students' union know well in advance so that the tours can be listed in the programmes circulated to all freshers. Then, for example, six tours a day can be offered to all who assemble at a given point and a set time (e.g., on the hour) and members of the library staff can be at the ready to act as guides, with some kind of briefing given beforehand to new members of the library staff.
>
> It is easy to expect too much of such tours, but they do perform one service of inalienable value—they give the student the actual physical and psychological experience of being in the library building—for him it can never again be the first time of entry into what may be regarded as a large and forbidding edifice. He can also at least be shown where to enroll as a reader and where to make his enquiries, and he can be handed a copy of the library's *Handbook* or *Guide,* which is still standard practice for academic libraries to print, or near print each session.[15]

The above presents a neat summary of much of the advice about conducted tours available in articles written in the United States. Usually, comments on conducted tours are buried in general articles on orientation programs. When Verna Melum reported on her sabbatical visits to over 50 academic libraries during the spring of 1969 she noted that

> a surprising number of academic libraries continue to give tours to new students. The obvious advantage of getting students into the library seems great enough to warrant tours until a satisfactory substitute is worked out. Furthermore, students come back to the librarian who conducted a tour, and they identify with student leaders. Yet many librarians question the value of tours to the student. Difficulty of hearing the guide, misinformation given out by student guides, fatigue and inattention often mitigate the major purposes. Furthermore, library patrons sometimes complain about the disturbing traffic, and tours take staff time.
>
> Subject-oriented tours to class groups, scheduled upon request of faculty and followed by instruction, are more effective because they are motivated by class assignments. But again the problem of interrupting patrons must be considered and justified.[16]

Although the conducted variety is the most widespread form of library tour in use at present, there is some evidence to indicate it is on the way out, at least in the largest institutions. Several librarians who responded to our questionnaire and reported to the ACRL Committee mentioned increased enrollment and heavier staff loads as reasons why they had to stop what someone once called "student cattle drives," unpopular with staff and students alike. Luckily there are other ways of achieving the same ends.

TOURS IN PRINT

One of these ways is the self-guided tour using a printed tour "guide" (see illustration). This very simple technique was first described by Dr. R. R. Ronkin, a biology professor at the University of Delaware.[17] Ronkin explained that tours of the library had for some time been part of an intensive four-week study program for biology graduate students. Groups of from eight to 12 students would spend an hour touring the library, guided by a member of the library's professional staff. Answers to a questionnaire revealed, however, that this program was inadequate for several reasons: librarians emphasized some services of little use to biology students and overlooked a few very necessary items, some students in each group could not see or hear the librarian, students did not get a chance to actually handle the books and journals that the librarian pointed out, and an individual could not spend time with an item that especially interested him or

Figure 1. The cover from a printed library tour guide. Cover drawing by Edward Koren, Associate Professor of Art, Brown University, from "A Walking Tour of the Rockefeller Library" by Connie Evrard, Reference Librarian; cover lettering and drawings accompanying text by Lucy Commoner, Brown University Class of 1972 (Providence: Brown University, 1972). Reproduced and used by permission of Edward Koren.

her. For these reasons, and because planning and conducting the tours was absorbing too much library staff time, a new approach to library orientation was developed.

Directions for self-guided tours of the library were written by biology instructors who used the "detailed, pedantic style of the European tourist guidebooks." [18] After review by librarians in the Reference Department, these tours were duplicated and distributed to students. The tour began at the main entrance and ended with instructions that sent the students through the exit turnstile. In between, the students examined some 78 features of the library, including seven specific publications. They were also encouraged to browse. The tour was supplemented by a plan of the main floor of the library and some easy retrieval problems.

Observations during the first year that these tours were used revealed that students spent about twice as much time on them as they had on the traditional conducted tours. There were also indications (the nature of these "indications" was not explained in the article) that many students remembered better the items they saw on the tour. Other obvious advantages are that the tour can be scheduled entirely at the convenience of the student and that, once the instructions are written, the tours take little or no time away from instructors or librarians. Ronkin suggested that similar self-guided tours could be designed for graduate students in other disciplines and even for undergraduates in courses that depend upon library research.

The present writer read Ronkin's article several years later and decided to experiment with the self-guided-tour approach to first-year students' orientation. Successful use of this technique at the University of Detroit and at the University of Massachusetts was reported in *RQ*.[19] At the same time, but in another place, Melum reported that several libraries were trying this technique:

> A new approach which seems expedient for any library is a self-guided tour. Several libraries have developed such a guide. This may be tried out in mimeographed form then printed. Overall floor plans may be augmented by a segment of a floor plan on each page with numbered explanations and directions. The use of color enhances the usefulness and the attractiveness. Such a tour may be made available on portable cassette tape recorders.
>
> Once worked out, no further staff time is required, and this tour is available to anyone who enters the library—students, faculty members, visitors—at any hour all year.[20]

Everything seems to indicate that this technique works in many libraries. One of the 16 library recipients of a questionnaire on printed tours responded that they had tried the technique, but had given it up, while another library reported that the idea had to be abandoned after a trial run because one of the library administrators did not like the "irreverent" cartoons used to make a monumental building seem less forboding. But most librarians who have tried a self-guided tour seem to like it—not as *the* answer to the problem of orientation but as one effective way to help people get used to a new building. A few report that they have not abandoned the conducted tour altogether, but use the self-guided tour as a supplement for those who prefer this form for one reason or another.

Martha Hackman recommended the self-guided tour in her "Proposal for a Program of Library Instruction." She believes that a user education program geared to the process that an individual student learns by would begin with a *Library Handbook* distributed to the student outside the library; then,

> once in the Library, he needs help in orienting himself. Here I recommend a self-guided tour, following a marked path through the building. A sheet giving a brief explanation of the major points along the route would be provided. The student could take this tour at a time convenient to him and proceed at his own pace.[21]

Another favorable comment on the self-guided tour comes from Miriam Dudley:

> Several institutions report having developed successful printed, self-guided tours; and these do have the very decided advantage of walking the student through the building at his own pace and allowing him the opportunity of a personal confrontation with the books, the facilities, and the people. . . . A well-written, self-guided tour can be warm and welcoming and can introduce some of the more obvious uses of the most obvious reference tools, as well as their locations. This seems to work especially well as part of the organized freshman orientation courses, which many colleges and universities conduct in the summer. In one such program, the student is directed into the reference room and various facilities are pointed out as he stands in the doorway. Then: "You see the Reference Librarian at the desk ahead of you, you nod pleasantly, but since you don't need assistance just now, you turn to the card catalog to your left." The librarians reported that, inevitably, students with the guide in hand walk in, look around, nod pleasantly, and turn to the left. It does seem to be a better response than the glazed, bored expressions so often seen on the faces of those being toured through the library.[22]

The active role that users play in taking the self-guided tour is one of the most attractive aspects of the technique. One appreciative user of the self-guided library tour at the University of Massachusetts wrote on a questionnaire: "This was more than a tour—it was an experience."

This special tour for biology majors is still used at the University of Delaware, but it appears that the idea of self-guided tours for students in a particular field has not been tried in other libraries. A tour for a music appreciation class was described by Miriam Dudley in a paper presented at the Berkeley conference in 1970,[23] but the literature is otherwise silent on the subject. To the question: "Do you use only a general tour leaflet or have you also developed tours for students majoring in particular fields?" only three libraries reported any of the latter, and two of these were prepared for students using a departmental library on a large campus. However, several librarians commented that they liked the idea of a self-guided subject tour and intended to try it.

Some libraries have tried to incorporate "problems" in using the library into the self-guided tour. That may be acceptable to some students on some campuses, but the "problems" this writer has seen seem to be versions of the Mickey

Mouse library assignment that has been with us for too long. One tour that included problems had them so arranged and marked that the tourers could easily omit doing them if they so desired, and continue on their way—a nice touch in a form promoting self-direction. A few libraries report that signs have been posted in the building to indicate stops on the tour. At the University of Illinois at Chicago Circle numbered cubes that hang from the ceiling are readable from four directions. With regard to posting signs one reference librarian made a familiar complaint: "Sure wish we could, but our librarian doesn't like signs."

One item on the questionnaire on printed tours asked: "Do you have any advice for librarians wishing to use this form of orientation?" Some of the answers to that question may be useful to readers:

> Make the instructions clear and specific. Avoid referring to north, south, east, and west, but do tell the reader how to move around the building.

> Make it attractive through use of color and interesting pictures.

> Keep all explanations brief. If additional information is required, utilize supplemental pamphlets or special orientation booklets for those more complicated areas.

> Keep the approach light, even though the material covered is not necessarily so.

> Be careful to keep the tone warm and cheerful, to avoid any feeling . . . that this is a complete replacement for living human beings as guides. It is good to have it [the guide] displayed someplace where a person can hand it to the students with some welcoming comment, or suggestion that they stop back for further information.

TOURS ON CASSETTE

In some cities the "pedantic, European style tourist guidebook" that Ronkin used as the model for his self-guided library tour has been replaced by cassette tapes (which may be rented) to tell you how to get around the city and to describe the attractions at each stop. Libraries are successfully using audiocassettes for similar purposes—a development anticipated a dozen years ago by Ralph McCoy who suggested that "tours might lend themselves to automation with the installation of a short-wave device such as those used in a number of art galleries." [24]

Brigham Young University uses this type of tour for reasons clearly outlined by Marvin Wiggins:

> Alternative methods in instruction were examined, such as physical tours given by librarians, slide-tape and videotape presentations, and cassette tapes with hand carried playback units. The cassette taped tour was adopted for four reasons:
> *First,* a taped tour can be an effective, yet inexpensive, way to introduce 4,000 or more students a year to a large library complex. Students simply check out a cassette tape player and the information on the tape will do the rest. Slide-tape and videotape presentations are best for showing fixed locations but present a difficulty in linking one location to another.

Second, cassette players can be obtained for less than $20. Students may come at their own convenience throughout the day and large numbers of students can be handled throughout a semester without much notice of their presence.

Third, cassette tapes can be easily and quickly updated by either splicing or making a new master. Videotapes are expensive to produce, particularly if the final project is to have a professional polish, and are often out-of-date before production is completed.

Fourth, minimal personnel are needed for distributing and repairing cassette player units.[25]

Although the cassette tour is not used in a great many libraries today, those that do use it seem to be satisfied and the number of its users appears to be growing. All 13 librarians who responded to our questionnaire were pleased with this method, and several librarians who are not now using a cassette tour commented they intended to try it sometime soon. Most who are using a cassette tour noted that the information on the cassettes involved only a physical orientation to the building, though a few did explain that some instruction in the use of the card catalog or periodical indexes was included. As one might expect, the cassette tours are used mainly by first-year students, transfer students, and visitors to the library. The cassette tours are usually available at all times, although they seem to be most used at the beginning of the term. Reference librarians typically prepare and record the tour, occasionally with some help from students in the speech department or someone in the audiovisual center. Signs marking stops were often reported. What was not reported was any problem with security. Several librarians did note that they held an ID card or driver's license while the student used the machine, but vandalism was not a problem, contrary to what might be expected with equipment of this kind.

Occasionally the cassette tour is used as one element in a multifaceted orientation program. Ronald Powell has described such a situation in his article on what is done at Prince George's Community College:

Currently being favorably received by both faculty and students is a two-part program: a self-guided tour of the LRC, followed by an assignment which takes the student through the motions of using such basic tools and materials as the card catalog, vertical file, *Readers' Guide,* the LRC's periodicals directory, and microfilm. The program does not utilize any class time; each student is to come to the LRC on his own time when the orientation is assigned by his English teacher, and is to work at his own pace until the concepts to be learned are mastered. A student to be oriented checks out, at the circulation desk, a cassette player, a head set, and the taped program; he is told where to begin the program, and is given a number-coded floor plan of the LRC along with a work sheet to complete for the assignment segment of the program, this to be returned to his English teacher for evaluation. The tour portion of the program is not too unlike the tours being offered in so many museums; the student, following taped directions, and aided by the number-coded floor plan as well as strategically placed tour-guide markers, takes himself through the LRC to be familiarized with the physical facilities, materials, and equipment available to him. The follow-up assignment is designed to give the student an experience in utilizing vital retrieval tools.[26]

Librarians who used the cassette tours had much to say in response to the question: "Do you have any advice for someone considering this form of tour?" There were so many suggestions that they have been grouped below in four categories: planning, script writing, recording, and miscellaneous.

PLANNING

Figure out how long it's going to take to do it. Then multiply by ten.

Plan carefully *precisely* how you are going to administer the tour—before even beginning to write it.

Do have a rough version. Try it out on a number of students and get their ideas and suggestions. Then do a final version.

SCRIPT WRITING

After 20 minutes of recorded time/40 minutes of walking time, we find a loss of retention of information. Some locations must be omitted.

Give more directions than you feel you need because you are familiar with the library and the patron is not.

Keep it short and funny (but not cute).

Don't say where you are going to go until you actually want the patron to go there.

RECORDING

Tapes must be professional in quality.

Have professional readers do the recording.

Music volume needs to be balanced and located so as not to distract from what is being said.

Do the recording in a sound-proof room or better yet in a radio studio.

Remember to save a master copy of the original tape made.

Use simple declarative sentences, keep the delivery slow and clear and invite the user to shut off the player where appropriate so that he may explore on his own.

Musical background distracts from the information being conveyed.

MISCELLANEOUS

Accompanying maps get in the way.

We have found the use of shoulder straps on our tape players a convenience for those who take the tour.

ARM-CHAIR TOURS

When Verna Melum described some of the "new approaches" to orientation that she had seen on her sabbatical visits, she noted that "arm-chair tours" of various kinds were being used in several libraries.[27] Films and television tapes have been tried for this type of tour, but have not been notably successful so far. What does seem to work are synchronized slide/tape programs. These can be and have been used for many different aspects of the user-education program. They seem to work especially well, however, for introducing newcomers to the physical building, its services, and its staff. One feature that particularly recommends the slide/tape is that it can be revised easily and at little expense when some change has been made in the library. A film or videotape is not revised so readily.

In academic libraries most often the slide/tape tour is used in connection with first-year-student orientation and is shown either before the term begins or during the first few weeks. A few librarians reported that the program was set up somewhere in the library and ran continuously during the first few weeks of a term. Others reported that the package (or part of it) is available whenever it is needed by a librarian who might want to use it as part of a class lecture. At Plymouth State College (New Hampshire) the program is available at all times on the remote access system.

A large number of librarians noted that the slide/tape was introduced primarily as a substitute for a conducted tour. One wrote that they wanted "to avoid walking students in a mob around the library, half of them being unable to see or hear." Some noted that they reinforced the slide/tape with some kind of conducted or self-guided tour of the library. The program at Southern Illinois University, "a 20 minute color-slide, synchronized sound production," has been described by Millicent Palmer:

> The content is strictly limited to (a) physical arrangement of our three-level library which includes four subject libraries, (b) general concepts of varieties and quantities of resources, and (c) general patterns of physical arrangement of these resources. Music bridges are used and the narration is read by a senior, who introduces himself as the guide for the visual tour of the Library.
>
> This production is used before the summer and fall quarters as one unit of an all-day pre-orientation system sponsored by the Dean of Students Office. In our first two years of these pre-orientation sessions, we followed the slides with guided tours led by student volunteers, whom I attempted to train to give accurate tours. Even though the groups were kept as small as eight per guide we all had doubts about the value of the tours. Again—too much too soon! And there were complaints from library faculty that the information dispensed was not always either accurate or adequate. Finally, we offered the students a choice of a student-guided or self-guided tour for which we provided floor maps with suggested tour routes. Forty-five percent chose the self-guided tour, and on an evaluation check sheet turned in after the tour, 84 percent of these answered "Yes" to the question, "Would you recommend the self-guided tour to other new students?" Tour guides, always enthusiastic and capable volunteers, reluctantly decided that of the 55 percent who still wanted guided tours, a large percent appeared to be disinterested or too tired to show interest. Since then we have discontinued guided tours, but kept tour maps at the entrance to the library during the opening weeks of each quarter. Although a sign says, "Please return after use," very few do, and the map box has to be refilled frequently.[28]

Another form of self-guided tour follows the slide/tape at North Dakota State University. Here the visual tour is a package that can be viewed on an individual basis in carrels designed for the program. Afterwards the student is "encouraged" to take a self-guided tour on cassette tape.[29]

Detailed advice on how to produce a synchronized slide/tape is available in several sources.[30] Librarians who might want to use the slide/tape as an arm-chair tour of the library could benefit from the suggestions made above for cassette tours and these responses:

> Allow for trial runs before audiences not familiar with the building.

> Make it visually stimulating and entertaining and not merely a poorly disguised effort to make instant librarians out of the students.

> I would recommend that this type of program not be too lengthy, probably no longer than 20 minutes.

> If background music is used, it should be music which will not distract.

> Give the student some time to absorb by using relief slides of social/human interest.

> Maps are difficult to grasp in a slide.

> Use a variety of voices in the narration rather than one person throughout.

> The whole world of photography, past and present, is at your disposal so it is important to be as imaginative and creative as possible.

WHAT'S NEXT?

When Richard Parsons opened the ASD/RSD workshop on Orientation of the Out-of-School Adult to the Use of Public Libraries in 1967 he quoted an acquaintance of his who was in electronics: "You librarians build modern-looking buildings out of brick or stone, with picture windows. You have wall-to-wall carpeting, restful colors, and nice teak furniture. But your orientation methods are still in the nineteenth century." [31] That may have been true at the time, but librarians have come a long way into the twentieth century during the years since then. A number of new techniques for orientation have been tried and one just has to talk for a few minutes to a group of librarians in the orientation and instruction "movement" to know that they are still experimenting, looking for better ways to help people use libraries.

What's next? Who knows? But it is doubtful that libraries will get any simpler, so it is likely that more effort will have to be expended in helping people deal with complexity. Tours are only one small part of educating the library user, but they are an important beginning.

NOTES

1. Robert Harlan, "Welcoming Notes," in *Instruction in the Use of the College and University Library—Selected Conference Papers* (Berkeley: University of California, School of Librarianship, 1970), p. 2.

2. Mary Case Marquis, "A Study of the Teaching of Library Facilities to College Students" (unpublished thesis, George Peabody College for Teachers, 1952), summarized by Barbara H. Phipps in "Library Instruction for the Undergraduate," *College and Research Libraries* 29 (1968): 412–413.

3. See the article by Phipps cited above. Also see: E. J. Josey, "The Role of the College Library Staff in Instruction in the Use of the Library," *College and Research Libraries* 23 (1962): 492–498; Lloyd W. Griffin and Jack A. Clarke, "Orientation and Instruction of Graduate Students by University Libraries: A Survey," *College and Research Libraries* 19 (1958): 451–54 and "Orientation and Instruction of Graduate Students in the Use of the University Library: A Survey," *College and Research Libraries* 30 (1972): 467–472; Verna A. Melum, "1971 Survey of Library Orientation and Instruction Programs," *Drexel Library Quarterly* 7 (1971): 225–253 and "A Survey to Aid Your Fall Planning: Library Orientation in the College and University," *Wilson Library Bulletin* 46 (September, 1971): 59–66; Arthur Young et al., "Survey of User Education in New York State Academic Libraries," Paper presented at the New York Library Association Annual Conference in New York City, 6 October 1971.

4. Phipps, op. cit., p. 413.

5. Ibid., p. 414.

6. George S. Bonn, "Training Laymen in the Use of the Library," in *State of the Library Art,* vol. 1, pt. 1, ed. by Ralph Shaw (New Brunswick, N.J.: Rutgers University, Graduate School of Library Service, 1960), p. 27.

7. Ibid.

8. Kathleen Molz, "The State of the Art of Public Library Orientation," *Maryland Libraries* 34 (Winter 1968): 15.

9. Ibid., p. 17.

10. Verna Melum, "1971 Survey of Library Orientation."

11. American Library Association, Committee on Instruction in the Use of Libraries, "Show and Tell: A Clinic on Using Media in Library Instruction," mimeographed (American Library Association Annual Conference, Chicago, June 28–29, 1972).

12. ACRL Committee on Bibliographic Instruction, *Academic Library Bibliographic Instruction Status Report 1972,* ED 072 823.

13. The report will appear in the proceedings of the conference to be published in 1974 by Pierian Press, Ann Arbor, Mich.

14. Robert Pierson, "A Jaundiced Approach to the Guided Tour," *RQ* 11 (Fall 1971): 55–58.

15. Hazel Mews, *Reader Instruction in Colleges and Universities* (Hamden, Conn.: Linnett Books, 1972), pp. 18–19.

16. Verna Melum, "A Survey to Aid Your Fall Planning: Library Orientation in the College and University," *Wilson Library Bulletin* 46 (September, 1971): 60.

17. R. R. Ronkin, "Self-guided Library Tour for the Biosciences," *College and Research Libraries* 28 (1967): 217–218. Although Ronkin was first to describe how a self-guided tour was developed and used, the idea of a self-guided

tour to a library did appear in the literature a few months earlier when the Friends of the Detroit Public Library published a tour that had been prepared after the expansion of that library. See Arthur Woodford's "A Walk Tour of the Main Library," in *Among Friends,* No. 45 (Winter 1966–67).

18. Ibid., p. 218.
19. Mary Jo Lynch, "A New Approach to the Guided Tour," *RQ* 11 (Fall 1971): 46–48.
20. Verna Melum, "A Survey to Aid Your Fall Planning," pp. 62–65.
21. Martha Hackman, "Proposal for a Program of Library Instruction," *Drexel Library Quarterly* 7 (1971): 299–308.
22. Miriam Dudley, "Teaching Library Skills to College Students," *Advances in Librarianship,* vol. 3, ed. by Melvin Voight (New York: Seminar Press, 1972), p. 89.
23. Miriam Dudley, "Instruction in Library Skills at UCLA," in University of California, Berkeley, School of Librarianship, *Instruction in the Use of the College and University Library: Selected Conference Papers* (Berkeley: University of California, School of Librarianship, 1970), p. 25.
24. Ralph McCoy, "Automation in Freshman Library Instruction," *Wilson Library Bulletin* 36 (1962): 468.
25. Marvin E. Wiggins, "The Development of Library Use Instructional Programs," *College and Research Libraries* 30 (1972): 473–479.
26. Ronald H. Powell, "Library Orientation," *RQ* 11 (Winter 1971): 148.
27. Verna Melum, "A Survey to Aid Your Fall Planning," p. 62.
28. Millicent Palmer, "Library Instruction at Southern Illinois University, Edwardsville," *Drexel Library Quarterly* 7 (1971): 262–263.
29. "North Dakota State University Is Solving Its Library Orientation Problem," *Mountain Plains Library Quarterly* 17 (Spring 1972): 22–24.
30. See Carl F. Orgen, *Production of Slide-Tape Programs* (Iowa City: University of Iowa, School of Library Science, 1972) and Millicent C. Palmer, "Creating Slide-Tape Library Instruction: The Librarian's Role," *Drexel Library Quarterly* 8 (1972): 251–267.
31. Quoted by Margaret C. Hannigan, "Orientation of the Out-of-School Adult to the Use of Public Libraries," *ALA Bulletin* 61 (1967): 829–830.

POINT-OF-USE LIBRARY INSTRUCTION

CHARLES H. STEVENS
Director, SOLINET, Southeastern Library Information Network; formerly Associate Director, Project Intrex, and Director, Project Intrex Model Library Program

JEFFREY J. GARDNER
Management Research Specialist, Office of University Library Management Studies, Association of Research Libraries; formerly Director, Project Intrex Model Library Program

Library-use instruction as an integral part of library service has begun to receive the recognition it has always deserved. For as libraries, and particularly research libraries, have become larger and more complicated, the bibliographic research task facing the undergraduate or beginning graduate student has become correspondingly complex and tedious. The problem is perhaps most acute in the sciences where the rapid expansion of literature has been matched by the proliferation of bibliographic aids marked by their distinctive functions and formats. From reference sources relying on controlled vocabularies, to KWIC indexes, to citation tracers, the users of today's research libraries are faced with an array of bibliographic searching tools designed for that rare creature: the literature specialist.

Under a grant from the Council on Library Resources, Inc., the Model Library Program of Project Intrex at the Massachusetts Institute of Technology developed, evaluated, and shared with the library community two responses to this problem. Using M.I.T.'s Barker Engineering Library as a laboratory, the Model Library staff directed its efforts toward alleviating two inextricably related problems: (1) the orientation problems of that library's users and (2) the repetitive, instructional demands placed on that library's staff. The latter problem was accentuated at the Barker Library because that library was serving as the working environment for the Project Intrex experiments. These experiments required a significant commitment of staff time to working with users of the Intrex computer-based information system and led the Model Library staff toward attempting to train users to become more self-reliant in both the traditional and the advanced modes of library research.

One intent of the Model Library experiments was to provide library-use instruction in such a way that the very specific information needs of individual users could be met without the constant assistance of the professional staff in giving basic bibliographic instructions. How many users need to be told that engineering journal articles are indexed in *Engineering Index* or that *Science Citation Index* is really an effective subject searching tool, and "this is how it is used"? What happens to the evening or weekend user who usually cannot draw on a professional's expertise? And what of the users who would prefer not to exhibit their ignorance of the library system by asking for help?

One answer to these questions is the utilization of what in business is called point-of-sale marketing and what libraries can call point-of-use or point-of-need instruction. The Model Library staff developed a series of nine short audiovisual programs, each discussing one reference source, such as *Engineering Index* or *Science Citation Index*. The lengths of the programs varied from two to ten minutes, with all but two running under seven minutes; each was designed for simple, on-demand use. Since each was located on a table or shelf next to the reference source discussed, users were provided library instruction at the time *and* place of actual need; there were no restrictions due to library staff schedules and no need to proceed to a special location. In addition, a variety of media and equipment was used and evaluated for both ease of production and effectiveness.

The key to the program, then, was the design of a modular system of library-use instruction; each module available to any user at the place of need, at anytime the library was open. The only demand placed on the users was that they lift a phone, or, in some cases, push a button.

SOME PROGRAMS IN USE IN 1973

BARKER ENGINEERING LIBRARY SUBJECT CATALOG

A 2½-minute synchronized sound-filmstrip designed as a brief introduction for the new user of the library, this program is not intended to cover the wide range of individual, complex problems that may arise, but does cover the basic information all users need to know in order to use the catalog. The program is set up in a commercially available rear-screen sound projector (Labelle Sentinel) with standard headset and single-button operation (see Figure 1). Since the unit utilizes a continuous-loop format, the program shuts down automatically at its conclusion and is then ready for the next user.

BARKER ENGINEERING LIBRARY AUTHOR-TITLE CATALOG

This 2½-minute synchronized sound-filmstrip is similar to the subject catalog program in intent, format, and in the equipment used to present it to the user.

ENGINEERING INDEX

This 3-minute introduction discusses the scope and arrangement of *Engineering Index*, emphasizing subject headings, citation content, and the author index. It is a synchronized sound-slide program and is presented to the user in a rear-screen unit designed and fabricated at M.I.T. The unit consists of a Kodak Carousel projector with Buhl right-angle lens and a Labelle Plamatic audio system in a rear-screen cabinet small enough to fit easily into a typical library environment (see Figure 2). The program is activated by lifting a standard phone from a cradle, the slides are advanced by inaudible signals on the audiotape,

Figure 1. Labelle Sentinel sound-filmstrip unit in use with author-title catalog program. The unit is located on a table connected to the author-title catalog

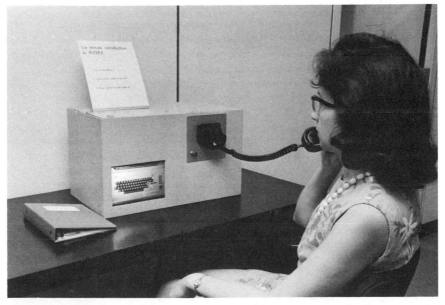

Figure 2. M.I.T.'s sound-slide unit in use with program on the Intrex system. The program is activated by lifting the phone and shuts down automatically at the program's conclusion

and the program shuts down automatically at the end. The equipment utilizes a continuous loop format, and therefore is always ready for the next user.

NASA STAR

This 5-minute program was an audiotape accompanied by sample pages from the *STAR* index; it has been replaced with the "International Aerospace Abstracts/NASA *STAR*" program (see below). The audiotape discussed the scope and arrangement of *Scientific and Technical Aerospace Reports* and described its use both for current awareness and for retrospective searching. The program utilized a continuous-loop cassette and standard cassette player in a unit constructed at M.I.T. (see Figure 3). The equipment was activated by lifting a phone; shutdown was automatic at the program's conclusion. The audio track referred the user to premarked sample pages from *STAR* placed in a notebook located with the unit.

INTERNATIONAL AEROSPACE ABSTRACTS/NASA STAR

This 9-minute audiotape program with sample pages replaced the program on NASA *STAR* by combining it with a discussion of *International Aerospace Abstracts*. The similarities in format and in subject orientation of the two publications are discussed and the differences in coverage emphasized.

SCIENCE CITATION INDEX

This 5½-minute audiotape program with sample pages emphasizes the *Citation Index,* and it discusses the *Source Index* and *Permuterm Index* in some

Figure 3. The NASA Star audio unit is activated by lifting the phone and shuts down automatically at the end of the program. The unit is located on the table that houses copies of NASA Star

detail. The equipment used is similar to that used for the NASA *STAR* program discussed above.

CHEMICAL ABSTRACTS

That this program was in many ways the most challenging to write is indicated by its length—10 minutes. This audiotape program with sample pages provides a brief introduction to the major indexes of *Chemical Abstracts* and describes its scope and format. The equipment used is similar to that described above under NASA *STAR*.

GOVERNMENT REPORTS INDEX

This 7-minute audiotape program with sample pages discusses access to report literature via both *Government Reports Announcements* and *Government Reports Index*.

INTRODUCTION TO INTREX

This 6-minute sound-slide program was presented using a unit similar to that used for the *Engineering Index* program (noted above) and described the features and use of the Intrex computer-based information system.

EVALUATING THE PROGRAMS

An important part of the Model Library Program was to evaluate these programs with respect to their adaptability to other libraries and, more importantly, with respect to their utility to users.

HARDWARE ASSESSMENT

While each format offers some advantages, most libraries will find audio programs with sample pages to be easier and less expensive to produce than audiovisual screen presentations. The availability of the M.I.T. programs for loan and duplication in either cassette or ¼-inch tape format makes them easily adaptable in other institutions. Since the programs are located on shelves or index tables with the reference sources discussed, the size of the audio unit offers an additional advantage; it requires approximately a quarter of the space needed for the sound-slide unit or the filmstrip unit. Continuous-loop equipment, programmed for automatic start and stop, such as M.I.T.'s loop cassette units, are still rather expensive—approximately $300—but an inexpensive ($30) cassette player with rewind capability could be used instead. This method requires that the user rewind the cassette, play the tape through, and turn the machine off at the program's conclusion. This process, while certainly not burdensome, is likely to reduce the number of uses a program receives. Automatic rewind was considered, but not devised for the M.I.T. experiments.

Sound-slide programs will be less widely adopted by libraries because of the time and expense involved in scripting an audiovisual program, doing the art work and photography, and constructing a continuous-loop projection unit (the M.I.T. hardware cost was approximately $800). However, the sound-slide units themselves have been relatively troublefree, and the slide format permits editing individual visual frames.

Table 1. *TOTAL COMMENTS FOR ALL PROGRAMS* (*N = 430*)

Categories	Number of Responses	% of Total
1. Uncritically favorable	137	32
2. Favorable with reservations	117	27
3. Favorable to the concept; unfavorable to specific program	35	8
4. Totally unfavorable	31	7
5. Irrelevant comments	70	16
6. Equipment problems	40	9

Sound-filmstrips have all the disadvantages of sound-slide programs along with two of their own. It is virtually impossible to edit single visual frames without refilming the entire strip, and filmstrips tend to deteriorate after prolonged use. On the positive side, sound-filmstrip projection equipment is commercially available for approximately $350.

PROGRAM USERS' ASSESSMENT

Of more importance than the staff's evaluation was the evaluation provided by the program's users. This assessment was carried out in two stages. Initially, users were asked to comment, in whatever way they chose, in notebooks placed with the audiovisual units. When they were coded and tabulated these comments provided general indications of the programs' utility and effectiveness. The totals are given in Table 1.

The comments in category 5 provided some comic relief and those in category 6 led to improvements in equipment, but neither group was relevant to the concept of using audiovisual point-of-use instruction. Removing those two categories, the percents in categories 1 through 4 shift as indicated in Table 2.

The figures in Table 2 clearly indicate that point-of-use instruction was an

Table 2. *TOTAL RELEVANT COMMENTS FOR ALL PROGRAMS* (*N = 320*)

Categories	Number of Responses	% of Total
1. Uncritically favorable	137	43
2. Favorable with reservations	117	37
3. Favorable to the concept; unfavorable to specific program	35	11
4. Totally unfavorable	31	10

acceptable technique to 90 percent of the users, and that it was enthusiastically welcomed by nearly half. The two audiotape programs with sample pages included in these statistics (*Science Citation Index,* and NASA *STAR*) scored appreciably better than the sound-filmstrip catalog programs; the sound-slide *Engineering Index* program scored higher than the catalog programs, but not as well as the audio with sample page programs.

Because many comments were of a general nature, users were later asked to complete a questionnaire designed to elicit more specific information. The results from this questionnaire are summarized in Table 3.

The questionnaires reinforced the general conclusions reached by analysis of the previously discussed notebooks and provided answers to a number of specific questions.

The percent of users who utilized programs because they were curious about the audiovisual units was significantly greater for the sound-slide and sound-filmstrip programs (74 percent) than for the audiotapes with sample pages programs and their less intriguing equipment (48 percent). While the original concept of point-of-use instruction was to present information at the time the user actually required it, the serendipitous acquiring of instruction would clearly be a benefit.

However, in nearly every other measurable way, the audiotape programs with sample pages scored higher than sound with visuals. Ninety-three percent of the users of the audio programs found them at least moderately helpful; the corresponding percent of users of slide and filmstrip programs was 71. Forty-five percent of those using the slide and filmstrip programs would prefer a different means of library-use instruction; this figure dropped to 29 percent of those who used the sample pages programs. Finally, 53 percent of the total sample indicated a general preference for the audiotape with sample pages format.

The response to the question regarding the inclusion of humorous material indicated that only 17 percent disapproved of its inclusion. But it should be pointed out that there was no indication that the majority of users preferred humor, only that they did not mind if it was there. One discovery was that the humor used should be devoid of sociopolitical implications. An early program that included humor at the expense of student political action was rather violently objected to by many students; another program that compared using a complex reference source to riding with a woman driver did not utilize the wisest of metaphors in this age of women's liberation.

User acceptance did not depend on the length of the programs. Since length of program was largely a function of the complexity of the reference source described, this was not surprising. In any case, a strong effort was made to keep programs as short as possible while providing essential introductory information. In the range from two minutes for the catalog programs to ten minutes for the *Chemical Abstracts* program, there was not a significant decrease in user acceptance.

Forty-two percent of the respondents indicated the desirability of being able to stop programs or repeat parts of programs. The chief problem in supplying

Table 3

Questions	No.	% of Total
1. *Why did you use the audiovisual aid?* (N = 200; 24 answered twice)		
Wanted to use the reference source described	60	30.0
Started to use the reference source and couldn't understand something	11	5.5
Curious about the audiovisual aid	135	67.5
Other	18	9.0
Total	224	
2. *How helpful was the aid?* (N = 200)		
Extremely helpful	14	7.0
Very helpful	63	31.5
Moderately helpful	90	45.0
Slightly helpful	23	11.5
Not helpful	10	5.0
Total	200	
3. *Check one or more of the following to explain the above rating:* (N = 200; 44 answered twice)		
The aid made me aware of a reference source I did not previously know about	87	43.5
I learned things about the reference source that I didn't know before	78	39.0
The aid refreshed my memory about the reference source	36	18.0
The aid was too elementary in its description of the reference source	27	13.5
Other	16	8.0
Total	244	
4. *How interesting was the program?* (N = 200)		
Very interesting	14	7.0
Interesting	108	54.0
Neither dull nor interesting	70	35.0
Dull	5	2.5
Very dull	3	1.5
Total	200	

Table 3 (*Cont.*)

Questions	No.	% of Total
5. *If the program included humorous material, did you approve of its inclusion?* (N = 87)		
Yes	72	83.0
No	15	17.0
Total	87	
6. *Was the presentation:* (N = 200)		
Too long?	15	7.5
Too short?	20	10.0
About right?	165	82.5
Total	200	
7. *Would it have helped to be able to stop the program at certain places or to repeat certain parts?* (N = 178)		
Yes	75	42.0
No	103	58.0
Total	178	
8. *Would you prefer:* (N = 152)		
Audio with slides?	71	47.0
Audio with sample pages?	81	53.0
Total	152	
9. *Do you prefer some different means for learning how to use reference tools?* (N = 153)		
Yes	56	37.0
No	97	63.0
Total	153	
If yes, please check which you prefer: (N = 56; 15 answered twice) [a]		
Individual assistance	29	52.0
Written instruction	24	43.0
Library orientation tour	15	27.0
Other	3	5.0
Total	71	

[a] *Note:* In this last question the 29 users who indicated a preference for individual assistance represent only 19 percent of the total respondents to question 9.

this capability is related to equipment; while not technically impossible, it is difficult and therefore expensive without sacrificing on-demand, continuous-loop performance.

SUMMARY OF PRACTICAL ADVANTAGES

The practical advantages of point-of-use instruction within libraries have proven to be worth the time and effort required for developing and maintaining the programs. The major qualification for a commitment to point-of-use instruction is that it be used in conjunction with other methods. The need for general instruction in library use is not completely fulfilled by point-of-use, and libraries will want to consider various possibilities including class lectures, tours, and printed guides. Another approach, which is utilized at the Barker Library, is the use of a brief, on-demand audiovisual introduction to the library that emphasizes the range and types of services and sources available, without describing any in detail. This kind of program can provide an awareness of what is available in a library; point-of-use programs and, of course, librarians can then provide the more detailed instruction on the specific sources and services required by individual users.

A final advantage to at least partial reliance on point-of-use instruction is related to the changes in educational philosophy and methodology that are apparent at many, if not most, colleges and universities. Prominent among these are: more flexible course requirements; an emphasis on independent research, and a striving for intellectual endeavors more pertinent to students' actual needs and interests. On-demand, point-of-use instruction is one response to these trends and can help place the library in the mainstream of educational philosophy and practice.

FORMAL COURSES IN BIBLIOGRAPHY

HANNELORE B. RADER
*Orientation Librarian, Eastern Michigan
University Library*

One of the various methods employed to instruct users in the use of the library, especially in academic situations, is to offer a formal bibliography course that can be packaged in a variety of ways. It may be either a noncredit course or offer anywhere from one to four credit hours; it may be an elective or a requirement with any one of the following titles: *library orientation, bibliography, library skills, research methods, guide to reference sources,* or *seminar in library instruction.* Such a course may be general and open to any student or be subject-oriented and limited to students with appropriate prerequisites. On occasions the formal course may even take the form of a series of minicourses.

Often the various graduate departments in a university will include a course in the bibliography of their particular discipline and require it for all their graduate students. Such courses are almost always taught by nonlibrarians and concentrate on the literature of a particular discipline to prepare the advanced-degree candidate for the research required in writing a thesis.

This discussion's focus is the formal bibliography course usually offered to undergraduates.

SURVEYS

The formal course in bibliography has of course been part of the curriculum in numerous colleges and universities around the country for many years, and surveys tell us that varied formats of the course are still being offered in many academic institutions, and that the inherent problems of providing such a course continue for the librarians teaching it. In spite of its problems, the course has met with success in several institutions.[1]

Barbara Phipps found, in a survey of library instruction programs for the undergraduate taken in 1965, that 29 percent of the 157 reporting institutions offered some type of orientation course.[2] Included in this 29 percent were general university orientation courses that contained a unit on the library.

In 1971, a survey taken of New York State academic libraries showed 9 percent of the 125 reporting institutions offering a formal course in bibliography.[3]

According to the latest survey of library instruction programs in academic libraries, undertaken by the Association of College and Research Libraries (ACRL) Committee on Bibliographic Instruction (Ad Hoc) in 1972 and published in 1973, 20 percent of the 174 reporting institutions offer some type of formal course in bibliography. Most of these are credit courses; only 6 percent are noncredit.[4]

The files of Project LOEX (Library Orientation Exchange) at Eastern Michigan University present a similar finding: 22 percent of the 139 reporting institutions offer a formal course in bibliography.[5]

PROBLEMS

Most courses are elective, and possibly because of this only a small percentage of the student body are reached; as a rule, on the average less than 1 percent to 5 percent of the students enroll in an elective course on bibliography. There are, of course, exceptions to this rule, such as the University of California at Berkeley where relatively large numbers of students have enrolled in the elective course called Bibliography I.[6]

If the bibliography course were a requirement, it would reach all students, and many advocates of a formal course in bibliography endorse this approach.[7] But the assurance of university administration cooperation would be needed, to enforce the requirement, to grant academic credit, and to provide additional teaching personnel. In many reported instances, teaching the course places an extra burden on the librarian to whom it is assigned, since he or she has to assume this responsibility in addition to regular job duties.[8]

Another factor to consider is that in these days of relaxed basic requirements for students, an added requirement in the form of a library instruction course would probably do more damage than good in motivating students toward bibliographic instruction. Much would depend on how well the course is presented and how meaningful it is for the students. (Too often, required courses carry the onus sometimes attributed to *compulsory chapel.*) If no academic credit is offered for the course in bibliography, enrollment will probably be too small to warrant its teaching; students kept busy with their normal course work usually will not add on courses without credit. It is possible that a minicourse in bibliography may attract certain students who are particularly motivated toward research or who need to do an extensive term paper. Some libraries have experimented successfully with minicourses or "intensive care" for term papers, such as the Term Paper Clinic offered at the University of Colorado.[9]

A course offering some academic credit would appeal to students more than one that does not. The credit hours offered for a bibliography course vary. A one-credit course seems practical, especially for the beginning student: the class meets for an hour once a week during the term or semester, and course work can be combined with the other courses the student is taking. A one-hour elective course in bibliography may offer a student the extra hour needed to graduate. Admittedly, this is not the best intellectual reason for enrollment in the course, but it does work to the student's advantage.

Enthusiastic promoters of formal courses often state that students need more than one or two lectures about bibliographic materials and that a separate course is the answer, especially in large and complicated library systems. The opponents of such a course maintain that an entire course on bibliography is excessive because it is too often patterned after a library science reference course and provides only busywork for students instead of course-related bibliographic instruction.

Another pro argument is that students will not use reference material unless it is required as part of their course work and that a course in bibliography will teach them bibliographic search methods for their future needs. The opposing side counters that most students do not feel the need for a course in bibliography and that enrollment in such an elective course will be minimal.

PLANNING THE COURSE

Initial course planning may take from a few months to a year. A committee may be the entity responsible for planning the course objectives and content.[10]

Course objectives will vary depending upon the level and type of course desired. For a first course in bibliography aimed at undergraduates, the objectives are not difficult to determine. They may be stated as follows: Students who have completed the course should be familiar with their particular library, its organization, and its services. They should be aware of and familiar with basic reference tools and be able to use them effectively for future research problems. Students should be able to produce a representative bibliography on a topic of interest by using proper *search strategy*.

From these objectives, it is not difficult to determine the content of the course. Instruction in the use of such items as the card catalog, the classification scheme, indexes, basic reference works, and bibliographic form should be contained in the course.

Establishing evaluation procedures for the students is also necessary. Objective or essay tests, library searches on a topic, or a term project consisting of an annotated bibliography are some types of evaluative measures used in a bibliography course.

Next, the materials to be used in teaching the course must be determined. Usually, a syllabus is prepared by a planning committee or the librarian/instructor. Often the latter will write his or her own textbook, but some commercially available texts are also used, such as *Guide to the Use of Books and Libraries* by Gates.[11] A text may be supplemented with locally created bibliographic guides, slides, films, transparencies, or other handouts.

TEACHING METHODS

A formal course in bibliography can be taught in several ways, for example in the traditional manner, by having the librarian present lectures to the class followed by related assignments (a method that may prove unstimulating to many students) or with information presented by the best qualified person (e.g., the cataloger presents the unit on the card catalog and classification, the serials librarian talks about periodicals, the reference librarian about reference works, the documents librarian about documents, and so on). The latter teaching method provides variety and expertise, but because of the manpower involved it may be costly as well as difficult to coordinate.[12]

The course may also be presented via videotape or slide-tape, which makes it possible for students to take the course any time, in groups or individually. The need for a teaching staff would be reduced to someone to read and correct assignments. The obvious disadvantages to this method are the initial expense of putting the course into the audiovisual form along with postproduction changes, which are costly in time, materials, and manpower. A lack of interaction between students and teacher must be weighed when making this decision.

A course may occasionally be taught on an individual basis, either with or without credit, by providing programmed or packaged instruction for each student. This method is utilized at the University of Alaska: each student completing a series of 16 tasks in sequence during the semester receives one credit.[13] Miriam Dudley at the University of California, Los Angeles, developed the prototype of the program used at the University of Alaska, and it is now available in published form.[14] This instructional program—which must be adapted to each particular library—has much potential in individualized library instruction, particularly in a large college or university.

EVALUATION

Whether or not the course is given for credit, the students should be evaluated and course planning should include the evaluative measures to be used. Many of the reported courses in bibliography require the students to prepare some type of bibliography at the end of the course, evaluated according to the varieties of items included. Students are often required to hand in with the bibliography a paper describing how it was compiled, noting their search strategy. Sometimes students are evaluated by so-called worksheets or tests that gauge their knowledge of the library.

Then there is the student evaluation of the course, and most librarians teaching a course in bibliography are concerned about how the students value the course. Many institutions of higher education have a mechanism for student evaluations of all courses taught. But many librarians may want more in-depth evaluation of the course, particularly when it is new and changes must be instituted. Librarians may ask for additional student feedback—their reaction to the course, was it useful, which changes would they suggest, would they recommend it to other students, etc.

HELPFUL HINTS FOR COURSE PLANNERS

These thoughts should be borne in mind by those planning a course in bibliography:

1. The course should be at least a one-credit elective.

2. It should be administered by one or more librarians.

3. It should be well advertised on campus in student and faculty publications, on campus radio, by posters, and in catalogs. It should also be promoted by all student advisors.

4. Planning the course should be done well in advance.

5. The objectives of the course should be clearly stated and communicated to the students.

6. A variety of materials should be used to make the course more appealing and to stimulate continuous interest. Audiovisual materials, such as transparencies, slides, films, posters, etc., are good supplementary instructional aids.

7. The course should be taught as much as possible on the basis of the individual student's needs and should be made course-related for all students. Each student should be able to relate all course assignments, such as work sheets, literature searches, and bibliography to term projects in other classes or to a topic of personal interest.

8. Caution should be exercised to keep the course from becoming a *library science* course. It is very important to eliminate any materials that are not absolutely essential to the understanding of search strategy and bibliography. After all, most students enrolling in a course on bibliography are not library science majors. Emphasis should be on basic materials—the card catalog, classification system, indexes, dictionaries, encyclopedias, yearbooks, maps, handbooks, abstracts, documents, and perhaps some subject bibliographies.

9. Instruction on each reference tool should be followed by practical application of it by the student.

10. Care should be taken that each student understands one unit before progressing to the next. Students should be graded on their ability to find their way around the library and to compile a representative bibliography on a topic of their individual choice by using effective search strategy.

11. The students should be made continuously aware of the interrelationship between information sources and the possibility of transferring search strategy principles from one subject to another. The course in bibliography can be the one that relates all other courses for the students.

12. Through the course, the students should become aware of the importance and potential value of libraries for their future information needs.

CONCLUSION

While a bibliography course may not be the only method of bibliographic instruction, it certainly has a place in any library instruction program that hopes to reach as many library users as possible. In order to develop an effective library instruction program, all types of instruction must be utilized, and a bibliography course is a definite inclusion. While proportionately few students are reached through a course, it is likely that students who do enroll would not have been reached in any other way. There are always library users who find the idea of the formal course appealing either because they need the credit or because they like learning things in a formal and systematic manner. The formal bibliography course is an ideal method of library instruction for these students.

NOTES

1. Verna Melum, "Library Orientation in the College and University," *Wilson Library Bulletin*, September 1971, p. 61.

2. Barbara Phipps, "Library Instruction for the Undergraduate," *College and Research Libraries* 29 (1968): 413.
3. Arthur Young et al., "Survey of User Education in New York State Academic Libraries," Paper presented at the NYLA Annual Conference October 6, 1971. Mimeographed.
4. ACRL Committee on Bibliographic Instruction, *Academic Library Bibliographic Instruction Status Report 1972* (ERIC document, 1973, ED 072 823), p. 8.
5. Mary Butterfield, "Project LOEX Means Library Orientation Exchange," *RQ,* Fall 1973, pp. 39–42.
6. John Lubans, "Report to the Council on Library Resources on a Fellowship Awarded, for 1971/72." Boulder, Colo.: University of Colorado Library, November 28, 1972. Mimeographed.
7. James Kennedy, "Question: A Separate Course in Bibliography or Course-Related Library Instruction?" *Library Orientation* (Papers presented at the First Annual Conference on Library Orientation held at Eastern Michigan University, May 7, 1971, Ann Arbor: Pierian Press, 1972), pp. 19–20.
8. Charles Shain, "Bibliography I: The U.C. Berkeley Experience," *Instruction in the Use of the College and University Library* (Selected Conference Papers, July 13–14, 1970 Conference Workshop, Berkeley, University of California, 1970, ED 045 103), pp. 4–5.
9. Lubans, op. cit.
10. Ibid., p. 10.
11. Jean Gates, *Guide to the Use of Books and Libraries,* 2nd ed. (New York: McGraw-Hill, 1969).
12. Mary Jo Peterschmidt, "Experiences: Team Teaching Library Instruction at San Jose State College," *Instruction in the Use of the College and University Library* (Selected Conference Papers, July 13–14, 1970 Conference Workshop, Berkeley, University of California, 1970, ED 045 103), pp. 3–4.
13. ACRL Committee, op. cit., pp. 11–12.
14. Miriam Dudley, *Workbook in Library Skills: A Self-Directed Course in the Use of UCLA's College Library* (Los Angeles: University of California Library, 1973).

APPENDIX 1
SAMPLE OUTLINE FOR A LIBRARY ORIENTATION COURSE OPEN TO ALL STUDENTS—AN ELECTIVE, ONE-CREDIT COURSE IN BIBLIOGRAPHY

Each student will take three quizzes, give one five-minute oral report on a library-related topic, and do an annotated bibliography on a topic of his or her choice.

Text: Gates, Jean K. *Guide to the Use of Books and Libraries.* New York: McGraw-Hill, 1969. $3.95.

Week 1 Introduction to course: Organization and Services of the Library
Assignment: Read chapter 3.
Study library handbook.

Week 2 Card Catalog
Classification systems
Assignment: Read chapters 4 and 5.
Do worksheet on the card catalog.

Week 3 Research methods
Bibliographic form for research papers
Assignment: Read chapters 2 and 3.
Do worksheet on bibliographic form.

Week 4 Quiz
Parts of the Book
Types of reference works
Assignment: Read chapters 2 and 16.

Week 5 Indexes
Assignment: Read chapter 9.
Do worksheet on indexes.

Week 6 Encyclopedias
Assignment: Read chapter 8.
Do worksheet on encyclopedias.

Week 7 Dictionaries
Assignment: Read chapter 7.
Do worksheet on dictionaries.
Final choice of topic for individual talk is due.

Week 8 Quiz
First talks will be given on a voluntary basis.

Week 9 Biographical sources
Assignment: Read chapter 10.
Do worksheet on biography. [See Appendix 2.—EDITOR.]

Week 10 Atlases and Gazetteers
Yearbooks and Handbooks
Assignment: Read chapters 11 and 12.
Do worksheet on atlases and gazetteers.

Week 11 Bibliographies
Assignment: Read chapter 13.
Do worksheet on bibliographies.

Week 12 Quiz
More talks may be presented on a voluntary basis.
Assignment: Read chapter 14.

Week 13 Special Reference Materials, including nonprint materials and documents

Week 14 Review
Annotated Bibliographies are due.

Week 15 Optional final exam to improve grade if desired.

APPENDIX 2
SAMPLE WORKSHEET FOR THE ELECTIVE, ONE-CREDIT COURSE IN BIBLIOGRAPHY—THE ASSIGNMENT FOR WEEK 9

Name: _____

Biography Worksheet

For the following person: _____

List this information:

Date of birth: _____

Date of death (if applicable): _____

Nationality: _____

Profession or occupation: _____

Major accomplishments or publications: _____

_____

Place of residence: _____

Indicate sources in which you found the information (as many as possible):

THE REFERENCE/ADVISORY INTERVIEW: ITS CONTRIBUTION TO LIBRARY-USER EDUCATION

MARCY MURPHY
Planning Librarian, U.S. Air Force Academy Library

NANCY MILDRED NILON
Head, Reference Department, University of Colorado Libraries

The basic question addressed here, and the topic of this paper, is: Just how does the reference/advisory interview contribute to educating the library user? It is suggested that the interview can contribute to the user's education in a number of special ways, that learning the skills and techniques that encourage open interpersonal communication channels are of significant importance to public service librarians, and finally, that this vital field of librarianship, conducting the actual interface with the patron, remains to be systematically developed in the library schools, on the job, and in continuing education courses.

Who are the users we educate? In this paper, we are speaking of all adult users who approach librarians for assistance. Traditionally, the "education" of the user has meant teaching use of the card catalog—just as though it really provided a systematic, organized approach to the collection [1]—or use of periodical indexes or abstracting journals. We also think of more specialized classes or tours in which users are introduced to subject bibliographies, guides to the literature, and occasionally to critical methods of identifying and evaluating bibliographical sources. There is also the traditional one-to-one instruction in the sources available on a specific topic.

However, the concern here is not with librarians' knowledge of information sources or its transmission to the users. The focus is rather on the interview itself as an educational medium, that crucial exchange which takes place between the librarian and the user *before* the retrieval of the information begins.

As a further illustration, we might briefly define three parts of any interview. The first part could be considered that which establishes the climate in which good interpersonal communication can occur. In the profession, we have sometimes used the word "approachability," which is certainly a part of what we are talking about here. The second part of the interview consists of the actual question negotiation, when the users try to communicate to the librarian what their respective needs are and the librarian attempts in each case to be open, perceptive, and empathetic. In this stage, particularly, professional expertise is required in order to help the users clarify their needs, possibly even their thinking, and to check constantly for feedback, in order to assure that the message received by the librarian is in fact the one intended to be conveyed.[2] The tendency in the past has been to believe that librarians are all-understanding and to emphasize that confusion, or "noise," in the communication channel is due to the user's lack of definition and communication skills. Research now suggests a more humble approach, that librarians, as a middle-class professional group, have very definite limitations in their abilities to comprehend and an even greater need to sharpen their perceptual skills, since their role as interpreter is crucial. Finally, the third part of the interview is the follow-up, the actual search for information, that is subsequent to the first two stages. It is here that the knowledge of library and community resources is essential, and it is also to this purpose that most library school reference courses address themselves.

The style or type of interview, as well as its component parts, can also be categorized. All share the same requirement for a skilled communicator or counselor who can get to the heart of the problem before turning to resources which will answer it. However, although these definitions are greatly oversimplified, "reference" interviews could probably be considered as negotiation of often one-time requests for quite specific information—regardless of the unspecific form the original inquiry may be wrapped in. "Advisory" interviews often extend beyond one session, as in reading courses tailored to meeting individuals' interests that may extend over a period of time; also, sometimes "advisory" interviews help people to develop interests that were vague and unarticulated before they came into the library. Just by talking with a patron, or rather listening to him or her, a librarian may offer a valuable social service. In both types of interviews, most of the needs of the user can be supplied by library resources. "Counselor" librarianship interviews, the third type, cover a much wider range of subjects and issues that can, and typically do, extend beyond the library walls to the entire range of community resources: political, social, and economic. Referral to other agencies in the total community services network, in which the library plays but one of many roles, is basic to counselor librarianship.[3]

Will all users benefit in the same way and to the same degree from these different kinds of interfaces? While it is likely that all interactions will be the better for the services of a skilled interviewer, it seems even more likely that some users will benefit far more than others because their need for understanding is greater and their use of library resources may be totally dependent on perception on the part of the librarian.

There is nothing new in the idea that the library has served a middle-class elite; the Public Library Inquiry stated that some 20 years ago.[4] What is newer is the effort made in recent years by an increasing number of "socially responsible" librarians to reach out to other subcultures within our society and mount campaigns to heighten awareness and raise public consciousness regarding the kinds of services libraries are capable of offering, beyond their traditional confines. Implicit in these efforts are attempts to encourage among the economic and culturally disadvantaged a more informed and responsive lifestyle that can contribute to upward mobility, open up the possibility of greater participation in determining societal goals, and equip people with wider options. The impact of this trend has been particularly visible in the experimental outreach programs of public libraries and the notable High John project of the University of Maryland Library School.

To help these clients is to perceive their needs with minimal assistance from them. And even before aiding them directly, somehow they must be encouraged to ask for help by the librarian's attitude. It is not easy to ask for information, even at a sophisticated level. Librarians who have assisted experts in one field search for answers outside the experts' own area of expertise have noted the struggle to define precisely what is wanted on an unknown subject—theoretically, an almost impossible task—and noted also the sense of humiliation a user can feel at not knowing and having to ask. Both this inability to cope and this feeling of embarrassment may well be intensified in the user who lacks sophistication in knowledge of libraries and may feel even more proud and reluctant to ask.

While the importance of the "reference interview" has long been acknowledged by librarians, there has also been a feeling that good reference or public services librarians are born, not made. Their necessary virtues and attributes have been listed by such authorities as Margaret Hutchins [5] on down through the ages, but not much has actually been taught about either how to acquire or how to practice the skills of communication with the user. Library schools have taught titles: their graduates have been propelled into public service positions in libraries where they received little or no in-service training and often have less than perfect examples before them on which to model their behavior.

"There has been little or no research (in communication skills) and the only current interest centers around the University of Pittsburgh, a few writers in Great Britain, and, more recently, the present innovative program at the University of Denver, which provides students . . . with an opportunity to work in speech/mass communication area." [6] This recent, rather pessimistic statement can be tempered somewhat in view of the survey reported later in this paper that presents still more recent knowledge of some programs currently underway in the field and in the library schools.

In what further ways do we hope to educate our library users in any interview? How can we help them to change? How will their behavior be altered? First, we would hope to help them focus on structuring answerable questions from what was earlier perhaps only a nebulous feeling or thought or even anxiety. Implicit in the interviewing process, also, is a problem-solving technique, which may instill in the users a growing sense of confidence both in the person who is willing to become really involved with them in their quest and, more important, a sense of confidence in themselves and their ability to communicate successfully with another human being. Users may also perceive a methodology that this success was achieved by the interviewer through certain successive steps of expansion, clarification, and finally, definition of an emerging construct. With this feeling of increased ability, the users may, in the future, more freely approach informational sources with increased expressive capacity.

How does the librarian accomplish this? A few examples of checklists or guidelines for interviewers and counselors might serve as helpful examples of communication theory. Blocker suggests 12 steps for "tracking behavior," which may be used for evaluative purposes:

A good interviewer:

1. Allows the client to select the topic for the interview.
2. Listens for a considerable period of time without commenting.
3. Seems alert to problems or difficulties other than the first one mentioned by the client.
4. Responds with an economy of words; does not ramble or repeat himself unnecessarily.
5. Asks clear and relevant questions; does not use a standard catalogue of questions.
6. Uses a wide variety of leads to help the client talk about his situation.
7. Phrases questions in an open-ended manner, i.e., cannot be answered yes or no—why, rather than what, when, etc.
8. Follows abrupt shifts in topic by the client and seems able to tie these into a common theme.
9. Frequently restates content of client statement.
10. Frequently reflects feelings of the client.
11. Usually waits during silences for the client to respond—does not interrupt or overtalk the client or rush the pace of the interview.
12. Phrases summaries or interpretations of client statement in tentative ways inviting client feedback—what you mean, or client hears it this way.[7]

Penland suggests that if the librarians tend to talk as much as the patron, or more, they are likely blocking the patron's communication. He cites several factors important to the librarian/user relationship:

1. Any show of intellectual brilliance or superiority on the part of the interviewer should be avoided.
2. Any show of haste is to be avoided if the patron's small sense of self-importance is to be preserved.
3. Reference to the interviewer and his private affairs is to be avoided.
4. The use of an illustration from another information case history is to be avoided.
5. The method of putting facts and information in juxtaposition that the patron is able to draw obvious conclusions, is preferable and avoids the need for duplication.
6. Any contact of one individual with another involves suggestion. The librarian's attitude, statements, questions, and even his very inactivity carry the power to influence information seeking behavior.[8]

Other techniques of helping users and also evaluating performance are suggested by scales for "Cognitive Flexibility," [9] "Consistency of Behavior Between Verbal and Nonverbal Behavior," [10] "Perceptual Sensitivity," [11] and "Involvement with the Client." [12] While these scales were not established either by or for librarians specifically, many points are covered that librarians will find useful. These same scales also serve as inferential examples or introductions to the wealth of material available today on the topic of interpersonal communication.

In summary, it can probably be said that if public services librarians fail to communicate with users, then in a large sense all the resources of the library, print, nonprint, and people, have come to very little purpose. Some librarians have become extremely adept at interviewing, through a combination of natural ability and experience; however, many more continue to function at a level considerably lower than they could achieve if they learned and practiced some basic interviewing techniques.[13] It would seem that in order to educate the users, we must first educate the librarians.

SURVEY OF CONTINUING EDUCATION IN COMMUNICATION SKILLS

If educating librarians is of such significance, then it follows that it would be useful to inventory efforts underway on a national level to promote teaching communication skills to library staff and library school students. In order to gather such data on the present state-of-the-art, a survey was designed and a report of that survey and its findings follow.

METHODOLOGY

There were certain limitations to the scope of the study. First, only the dyad, or one-to-one relationship, was covered, not group interactions. While the major topic was the interview between librarian and user, interviewing skills in related professions, such as counseling and guidance and social work, and in related circumstances, such as job interviews or counseling troubled employees, were considered to have bearing on and application to the problem. Therefore, when the relationship of interviewing skills in any field seemed marginal to the subject, the policy was one of inclusiveness.

The chief requirement of the sampling technique was to poll the greatest number of librarians with the fewest possible questionnaires. For this reason, the three largest public libraries in each state were selected, in addition to the members of the Association of Research Libraries. It is worth noting that larger institutions, by their very nature, are often slow to initiate change; it seems likely, therefore, that the findings reported here are biased toward the traditional.

Since interviewing skills seem increasingly so basic to effective communication, it seemed feasible to investigate whether a majority of librarians and library educators shared a current concern for learning and developing expertise in this area. Two questionnaires on interpersonal communication skills with cover letters were sent out: one (see Appendix 1) went to the 58 accredited library schools in the United States and Canada. Its purpose was to determine what programs were underway for formal instruction in techniques of interpersonal communications.

The other questionnaire (see Appendix 2) was designed and sent both to the 89 member libraries of the Association of Research Libraries and 145 public libraries that represented the three largest public libraries in each state as listed in U.S. Office of Education *Statistics of Public Libraries Serving Areas with at Least 25,000 Inhabitants, 1968*.[14] Since there are 50 states, the sample should have numbered 150 public libraries; however, two were members of the Association of Research Libraries; one had merged into a regional system; the two others were represented by the State Library. The purpose of this questionnaire was to determine what, if any, efforts were being made to train staff, both professional and support, in interviewing skills and other techniques of interpersonal communication, either within the library or by contracting for such training through outside agencies.

A third category, state library agencies, was also polled by letters (see Appendix 3) which requested any printed materials on continuing education courses relating to interpersonal communication which the agency had been involved in during the last two years.

The Bureau of Library Services at the U.S. Office of Education provided lists of workshops and institutes funded under Title IIB of the Higher Education Act from 1967 through 1973. The lists were used to identify any possible programs relevant to the area of concern of this paper that might not be reported through other channels, and to identify resource personnel.

In addition, the U.S. Civil Service Commission, Personnel Management Training Center sent sample listings of programs available both on national and regional bases.

Table 1 shows the type and number of institutions polled and the percent of the response. Of the total of 342 requests for information, 248 responses, or 73 percent, were returned.

FINDINGS

The Library Schools

Forty-eight of the 58, or 83 percent, library schools responded to the questionnaire. Fourteen do not offer instruction in interpersonal communication skills and 34 schools offer some instruction. Of the 34, nine offer separate courses, such as: Interpersonal Communications for Public Services Librarians, Services

Table 1. *QUESTIONNAIRES SENT TO AND RECEIVED FROM NATIONAL SAMPLE, WITH PERCENT OF RETURNS*

Universe	Sent	Received	% Returns
Library Schools	58	48	83
Research Libraries	89	62	69
Public Libraries	145	107	74
State Libraries	50	31	62
Totals	342	248	73

to Individuals, Social Communication Systems, Group Dynamics, Human Relations in Organizations. (A complete list of library schools offering courses is given in the Resources section.)

The remaining 25 library schools offer instruction in interpersonal communication skills as a unit in the teaching of courses as follows:

Administration (43): Principles of Library Administration (15); Academic Library Services (6); Public Library (7); Special Services (7); School Media (4); Management of Information Services (1); School Library Administration (2); Seminar in Administration (1).

Communications (5): Communications (3); Libraries and Multisensory Communication Media (1); Seminar in Communication (1).

Resources (29): Basic Reference (12); Advanced Reference (7); Literature of the Humanities (1); Literature of the Social Sciences (1); Literature of the Sciences (1); Government Documents (1); Reader's Services (3); Seminar in Adult Education (1); Seminar in Reference Librarianship (1); Services to the Disadvantaged (1).

Other (8): Special topics, such as Group Processes, Professional Seminars, and Tutorials; Research Methods; Seminar on Interviewing; Adult Education Services; Foundations of Librarianship; Master's Seminar, and User Services.

Only one school reported a separate course basic to interpersonal communications skills as a degree requirement. The course, entitled "Introduction to Communication," has been a requirement for two years. One other school commented that such a course should be required and that it is in their curriculum planning for the future. While others do not have such a requirement, per se, they reported a number of available options, such as courses in Management, Communications, Counseling and Guidance, Intercultural Speech Communication, Process of Persuasion, etc. One school reported recommending highly to their students a Human Relations in Organizations course offered in the School of Business.

Library educators seem to be generally aware of the need and importance of training in interviewing skills and in the techniques of interpersonal communication. However, only two of the graduate library schools teach formal communication theory in separate courses.

Academic and Research Libraries

Of the 89 questionnaires sent to members of the Association of Research Libraries, 62, or 69 percent, were returned. Not one reported a formal on-the-job-training program required in interpersonal communication skills or interviewing techniques. Five libraries had optional programs available that were not required of their staffs. Of these five, training was offered to support staff only, not to professionals, in two of the libraries. Training was offered to both support staff and librarians in the other three.

Financial support for continuing education programs was offered by 45 of the 62 libraries responding. The respondents apparently interpreted this question broadly to include *all* areas of continuing education, not just those limited to interpersonal communication and interviewing. Seventeen libraries offer no financial support. The "no financial support" response, however, could be interpreted to mean "no, not in interpersonal communication skills only," so the results are not clearcut. Possibly, these 17 would underwrite training in other subjects, although the evidence suggests otherwise.

Of the 45 academic libraries offering support for continuing education, five offer this support to professionals only; the other 40 report supporting both groups in this endeavor. More support was given to professionals during the past two years, however.

Libraries were asked to indicate what classes, seminars, or institutes their staffs had participated in and to give the job title or position of the participant. Only one academic library reported widespread staff participation in a training program in the area of concern offered through the University Training Office. Other choices available through the same office included classes in Interpersonal Communication, Advanced Interpersonal Communication and Communication Seminar (Transactional Analysis). A General Office Practice course also had a section on dealing with the public. Eighty-six members of the library staff participated in the program during the last two years.

Other libraries reported continuing education participation in managerial techniques only.

Public Libraries

Of the 145 public libraries queried, 107, or 75 percent, responded. Thirteen of the respondents had a formal on-the-job-training program in interviewing techniques or in interpersonal communication skills that was required. In only one of the 13 libraries was this training available to professionals, and in only one to support staff. Eleven libraries reported training available to both. Six libraries offered the program more than twice a year; five, twice a year; two, once a year.

An outside agency conducted training in one public library; staff members and an outside agency shared training in six others and the library staff alone conducted sessions in the six remaining libraries. Personnel from nearby universities, particularly from psychology and social sciences faculties, often conducted the library courses. Personnel from local telephone companies provided instruction in telephone etiquette. Generally speaking, administrators and department heads conducted courses internally.

Fifteen libraries reported that training was available, but not required. In only one was it restricted to professionals; the other 14 offered training to librarians and associates alike.

Administrative support, financial and otherwise, for continuing education of staff was available to 84 of the 107 libraries responding. Again, this question was frequently interpreted to mean education in any area, not just the one specified. Twenty-three libraries indicated no support.

Continuing educational opportunities were restricted to professionals in seven libraries; support was limited to associates or paraprofessionals in one. The questionnaire returns indicated that all staff receive support in 76 of the libraries.

More professional than support staff were involved in continuing educational opportunities. In only 12 libraries did the number of training programs for paraprofessionals surpass that of the librarians. Four libraries reported 100 percent participation of the entire staff in continuing education, but they did not specify the subjects studied.

Respondents seemed eager to report all their educational activities, whatever the subject, so varied was the response, even though the questionnaires were clearly labeled "Interpersonal Communication Skills Questionnaire." Of course, in some instances, it can be assumed that some aspect of interviewing or communication was touched on, in greater or lesser degree, that only a participant could identify. For these reasons, findings were ambiguous.

The public libraries were asked to give the title of classes, seminars, or institutes. It is difficult, often impossible, to judge course content by title alone. However, title was the only access available. On this basis, then, the courses were divided into three categories: those that seemed to be directly related to interpersonal communications or interviewing; those that were possibly related; and those that seemed unrelated. The courses judged to be of either direct or possible relevance are listed on the following page. The names of the sponsoring libraries are available from the authors on request.

In summary, it would seem, first, that public services staffs are currently receiving very little training, either on the job or through continuing education courses, in interviewing skills for negotiations with users. Academic and public libraries were sent 234 questionnaires, and 169 of these questionnaires were returned. Only 35 libraries reported programs in this area: five academic and 15 public libraries had optional programs; 15 public libraries had required programs.

Second, public libraries demonstrate much more interest. Not one academic library required on-the-job training; only five expressed concern. This is disappointing, since it would seem that academic institutions should be more actively responsive to the needs of students involved in the wide span of experimental programs, such as the "minicollege," "midcareer," "over sixty," "free university," and the like. Open enrollment, too, poses other communication problems: varied needs of clientele, such as that of different ethnic groups, require very special perceptions on the part of the librarian for facility in understanding, let alone educating.

Third, although several academic and public libraries seem committed to the concept of continuing education, their course offerings seem almost exclusively dedicated to improving managerial and technical skills rather than communication with users. Courses for supervisors were the most common.

State Libraries and Their Programs

Letters, without questionnaires, were sent to 50 state libraries (see Appendix III) from the list included in the current *American Library Directory*.[15] The letters inquired if continuing educational programs in interviewing techniques had been offered by the state agency within the last two years. The librarians were specifically asked whether any printed publications or brochures were

PUBLIC LIBRARY CONTINUING EDUCATION PROGRAMS IN COMMUNICATION SKILLS

Related	Possibly Related
Customer Relations	IST Programs for Staff
Conference on Interpersonal Communications	Images and Realities
	Telephone Etiquette (3)
Conference on Group Processes, Communication Skills and People to People	Reaching Out to the Spanish Community
	Reaching Out to the Black Community
PNLA Workshop on Interpersonal Communication	Reaching Out to American Indians
	Black Writers of the United States
Improving Communications with the Public	Outreach (Prisons)
	Telephone Manners
Operation Reachout Institute	Telephone Courtesy
Seminar on Communication Barriers in Public Libraries	Community Outreach Services Institute
Outreach Leadership Network	"Don't Bother Us, We Can't Cope"
Readers' Advisory Institute	Additudinal Workshop on Relations with the Public
Workshop on Social Interaction	Conversational Spanish
Serving the Underserved	Service to the Disadvantaged
Videotape on the Reference Interview and Desk Behavior	
Group Dynamics Exercises	
Communication	
Human Relations	
Communicating with the Disadvantaged	
Communication and Counseling Tips	
Personal and Interpersonal Relationships of the Librarian/Patron Interface	
Interpersonal Communications (3)	
Group Leadership (2)	
Effective Listening	
Interviewing Techniques (3)	
Public Relations	
Reference Methods	
Interviewing	

available and could be sent. This was intended to spare writing lengthy answers; however, several librarians did respond in considerable detail, sometimes in addition to sending printed materials.

Thirty-one of the 50, or 62 percent, of the state libraries responded. Ten of the 31 reported no such programs presently underway. One of the ten said, however, that such a program would be highly desirable, and two more indicated that instruction in interviewing and interpersonal communication skills was on the drawing board for the future.

Twenty-one state agencies reported workshops and seminars. Again, not all of them directly, or even indirectly, related to the topic. Since most agencies did send programs and prospectuses, there was more opportunity to evaluate course content than when course titles alone were given (as was the case with the returns from most of the library schools and libraries).

Affirmative responses were divided into four categories and tallied: (1) *Directly related* to advisory counseling and interviewing skills; (2) *Possibly related;* (3) *Not related but with some potential* in subject, and (4) *Not related.* The programs that seem to have some relationship to the area of communications with users are included in the accompanying list.

Judging from the information received, six workshops or institutes seemed to belong in category 1: "Directly related." Category 2, "Possibly related" contains 20 programs (nine programs with less expressive names, but with course content were described in accompanying letters and were judged eligible for inclusion).

Several state librarians mentioned the opportunities that were available through neighboring colleges, universities, or extension courses. One state said it depended entirely on WICHE (Western Interstate Commission on Higher Education), located in Boulder, Colorado, to structure all of its continuing education courses for librarians. The influence of this commission seems widespread indeed. According to its director, all WICHE programs are funded by and through the state libraries only, and are generally not available to libraries within a state where WICHE has not been funded.

In addition to WICHE, some regional library associations have been very influential in promoting training in interviewing techniques and interpersonal communication skills. Two associations deserve special mention: the Pacific Northwest Library Association and the Southwest Library Association. Their efforts were frequently cited in letters from state agencies.

Civil Service Commission Programs

Several federal government agencies offer workshops and institutes for federal employees that provide insights into client "advisory" interviews, although none directly zero-in specifically on library interactions. General Services Administration, Veterans' Administration, and Action (which now handles the functions of the Peace Corps and Vista) are examples. Probably most closely identified with and utilized by librarians are the offerings of the Civil Service Commission, which span a very wide subject spectrum. Two courses specifically cited by the Civil Service in Washington as applicable to the topic were: Personnel Interviewing and Counseling, Principles and Practices (September 25–28, 1973); Techniques in Motivational Interviewing and Referral: the Troubled Employee

STATE LIBRARY CONTINUING EDUCATION PROGRAMS IN COMMUNICATIONS SKILLS

Directly Related	*Posssibly Related*	*Unrelated, but with Some Potential*
Interpersonal Communications Workshop, sponsored by WICHE, 1973 (Alaska)	Problem Solving Techniques (Alaska)	Training Skills for Office and Management (Alaska)
Workshop on Building Client and Consultant Skills, 1971 (California)	Developing Reference Skills (Colorado)	Motivation and the Right to Read Workshop, 1972 and 1973 (Indiana)
Seminar on Communication across Cultural Lines, 1971 (Florida)	Outreach Leadership Networks (Maine and New Hampshire)	Management Seminar (Minnesota)
Workshop on Interpersonal Communications, sponsored by PNLA and presented three times	Workshop for Personnel Utilization (Montana)	CLEP (College Level Examination Program) (SUNY, Albany)
	The Human Side of Libraries (Oklahoma)	Seminars in Communication, Management and Change for Public Librarians (SUNY, Albany)
Seminar on Communications Management and Change for the Library Profession, 1971, 2 seminars (Pennsylvania)	The Reference Game (Oklahoma)	
	Evaluation Seminar (Pennsylvania)	Leadership Style (Ohio)
	Reaching the Adult (Michigan)	Understanding Motivation and Leadership Behavior
Annual State Convention had several sessions dealing with stereotyping and role playing (Michigan)	Open Forum in Human Relations (Michigan)	Workshop for Mexican Americans (Texas)
	Interactive Movement and Pairing (Michigan)	Personnel Management (Texas)
Project Planning and Development Workshop Groundwork for Good Communications (Ohio)	Understanding Individual Values and Needs (Ohio)	
	Others (9)	

Program (August 27–31, 1973).[16] Regional offices of the Commission provided more lists of opportunities and specific titles; an example is Understanding and Managing Human Behavior (Transactional Analysis) offered out of the Training Centers in Missoula, Rapid City, Billings, and Denver, in fall and winter 1973–1974.

Institutes Sponsored by the Higher Education Act of 1965
Since 1968, the federal government has funded institutes for training in librarianship under Title IIB of the Higher Education Act of 1965.

Over the six-year period, eight institutes were identified that seem to relate directly to the topic: Interpersonal Communication, Adult Services and Change (University of Wisconsin, 1973–1974); Strengthening Librarians' Capabilities to Elicit and Respond to the Felt Needs of the Majority/Disadvantaged Persons and Groups (University of Oklahoma, 1973); Library Services to Inner City Communities (University of Pittsburgh, 1971–1972); Improving Communication Skills of School Library Supervisors (University of Michigan, 1970–1971); The Floating Librarian in the Underprivileged Community (University of Pittsburgh, 1970–1971); Interpersonal Relationships in Libraries (Immaculate Heart College of Los Angeles, 1969–1970); Interpersonal Group Communications for Libraries (State University of New York at Buffalo, 1969–1970); Readers' Advisory Services to Adults (University of Pittsburgh, 1969–1970).

Forty institutes were offered that seemed to relate in part or indirectly to the topic, again judging from title alone. Only one list from the Bureau of Library Services, U.S. Office of Education, that for fiscal year 1973, had annotations that facilitated selection. The distribution of these institutes by years is shown in Table 2.

The biggest year was 1969–1970—both overall, in the total number of institutes offered, and specifically, for interpersonal communications seminars. Eighteen communications institutes, the greatest number, were aimed at unspecified disadvantaged groups, including the unreached in the innercities; the second largest group, numbering 11, offered training in services to specific minority groups: Black, Indian, Spanish-speaking, Aged, Handicapped, Young Children. The remaining 11 were addressed to developing communication skills in various special contexts.

Table 2. *DISTRIBUTION OF INSTITUTES OFFERED UNDER TITLE IIB, HIGHER EDUCATION ACT OF 1965*

Catalogs of Institutes Offered	Total Number of Institutes Offered	Institutes Related to Subject	Institutes Possibly Related to Subject
Summer 1973; 1973–1974 and Summer 1974	29	1	4
Summer 1972; 1972–1973	17	1	4
Summer 1971; 1971–1972	38	1	6
Summer 1970; 1970–1971	42	2	4
Summer 1969; 1969–1970	92	3	9
Summer 1968; 1968–1969	39	0	3
Total	257	8	40

Excluded from this inventory were institutes addressed exclusively to media specialists, or to leadership per se, unless interviewing or communication was specifically mentioned in the title.

These publications include names of institute directors and therefore provide a good resource for drawing on interested and experienced personnel. The lists are available from the U.S. Office of Education, Bureau of Libraries and Learning Resources, Washington, D.C.[17-22]

RESOURCES

Responses to the questionnaires, particularly those from public libraries, revealed that libraries have used a variety of sources for providing training in reference interviewing techniques and interpersonal communication skills. Some of these sources, as well as other suggestions, are presented below as possibilities to be considered by those who might want to structure training programs.

It is possible, as reported in the survey, to enroll in formal, separate courses of instruction in communication skills at the following graduate library schools: State University of New York at Buffalo; Graduate School of Library and Information Sciences, Pittsburgh; Simmons College, School of Library Service, Boston; Syracuse University, School of Library Science; University of Kentucky, College of Library Science, Lexington; Wayne State University, Department of Library Science, Detroit; University of Oklahoma, School of Library Science, Norman; University of Denver, Graduate School of Librarianship, Denver; University of Toronto, Faculty of Library Science, Toronto.

Colleges and universities usually provide an array of specialists. Resource persons from departments or schools, such as Psychology, Communications, Speech, Social Work, Adult Education, Sociology, Library School, and Business, have been and can be used to conduct institutes, seminars, and lectures in the area of concern. Many universities have personnel departments that will provide training for their own library staff. Universities will frequently contract to provide training programs for other agencies.

State agencies sponsor programs to improve competency in a variety of skills. These agencies can be approached. Some state and regional library associations have developed annual programs around the "Reference Interview." Others can be encouraged to do so. Libraries in states that financially support WICHE (located in Boulder, Colorado) can take advantage of the programs developed by this agency on the reference interview.

Civil Service Commission personnel representatives can, on occasion, when requested to do so, contract with local educational institutions to tailor their courses specifically to unique agency requirements. A list of their packaged courses is available upon request. Examination of the regional office lists—such as those enumerated in *Personnel Management Training Center, Course Schedule* [23] or the Regional Training Center calendars (for example the *Regional Training Center Calendar, Fiscal Year 1974* issued by the San Francisco region),[24] which offer numerous short courses in management training, management sciences, and communication and office skills, may supply useful suggestions for librarians seeking ways and means of sharpening their interpersonal expertise.

Of particular interest may be the skills taught in order to develop rapport with employees or other persons who have developed behavioral and emotional disorders from drugs, alcohol, or other sources and to provide them with referral to community services. This training course is right in line with one kind of community outreach information service mentioned earlier. Discussion of the structure of an interview—the communication process, barriers to communication, question techniques, evaluation, and common pitfalls in interviewing—all have a number of immediate possible library applications, regardless of whether the interview was conducted for personnel management, medical, religious, or guidance counseling. The subjects differ; the techniques and the emphasis on problem solving are very similar.

Libraries, of course, can also contract with private agencies, business firms, associations, etc. The questionnaires revealed such sources as the NTL Institute for Applied Behavioral Science; the American Management Association; the Northwest Educational Laboratory (Portland, Oregon), and the Manpower Development Associates.

Audiovisual materials are also available for use. The Graduate School of Library and Information Sciences at the University of Pittsburgh has produced in their series: *Tracking the Interviewee,* No. 33; *Interviewing and Analysis,* No. 16; and *Non-Verbal Communication,* No. 25. The complete list of tapes and films is available from the school. Three frequently used motion pictures are *The Interview,* 1960; *Chairy Tale,* 1957; and *That's Me,* 1963. Some other audiovisuals on interviewing are: *The Art of the Interview,* 1968; *Effective Interviewing,* 1971; *Employment Interview,* 1966; *The Right Questions,* 1969; *The Customer and You: Starting the Interview,* 1970, and the filmstrip, *Asking Questions,* 1963. Other media that will aid in developing communication skills are: *Are You Listening?* 1967; *Effective Listening,* 1959; *A Measure of Understanding,* 1970; *Roadblocks to Communication,* 1961, and the filmstrip *Communicating Face-to-Face,* 1971.

LIST (*Library and Information Service Today*) reports a project conducted by Jack B. King at Hamline University on the "Development of Interviewing Techniques for Information Specialists." [25] Geared to the needs of librarians, the proposed programmed learning text or workbook will prove most useful in training staff.

Interviewing skills and the ability to communicate can be improved through instruction. It is rather a matter of librarians perceiving the need and then planning for the instruction than a lack of opportunity.

NOTES

1. John M. Christ, *Concepts and Subject Headings: Their Relation in Information Retrieval and Library Science* (Metuchen, N.J.: Scarecrow Press, 1972). John Phillip Immroth, *Analysis of Vocabulary Control in Library of Congress Classification and Subject Headings* (Littleton, Colo.: Libraries Unlimited, 1971). George M. Sinkankas, *A Study in the Syndetic Structure of* the Library of Congress List of Subject Headings (Pittsburgh: University of Pittsburgh, Graduate School of Library and Information Sciences, 1972). Sinkankas has indicated that the syndetic structure of the Library of Congress subject heading list does not provide a systematic cross referencing system; Immroth points out that discrepancies exist between the terminology of the L. C. classification schedules, their own indexes and the L. C. Subject Headings. S. Berman's work treats numerous examples of semantic lag and discriminatory terminology. In addition, differences between the subject headings used in most library catalogs and the terms of an academic discipline are demonstrated by Christ. These semantic and grammatical problems are compounded by elaborate filing rules, making access to library materials via the card catalog far from the simple exercise some would believe.

2. Helen Gothberg, "Communication Patterns in Library Reference and Information Science," *RQ* (Fall 1973), p. 11. It is worth noting that "professionalism" in the helping professions is, in Carl Rogers' view, undesirable, since it can imply withholding oneself as a person and treating the other as an object. This attitude does not have a high probability of being helpful. "I feel quite strongly that one of the important reasons for the professionalization of every field is that it helps to keep distance . . . in teaching and in administration we develop all kinds of evaluative procedures, so that again the person is perceived as an object."

3. Patrick R. Penland, "Counselor Librarianship," in *Encyclopedia of Library and Information Science,* vol. 6 (New York: Marcel Dekker, 1971), pp. 240–254.

4. Bernard Berensen, *The Library's Public* (New York: Columbia University Press, 1949).

5. Margaret Hutchins, *Introduction to Reference Work* (Chicago: American Library Association, 1944).

6. Gothberg, op. cit., pp. 11–12.

7. Donald Blocker, "Tracking Behavior," in Patrick R. Penland, *Advisory Counseling for Librarians* (Pittsburgh: University of Pittsburgh Bookstore, n.d.), p. 149. Reprinted by permission of the publisher.

8. Patrick R. Penland, *Interviewing for Counselor and Reference Librarians* (Pittsburgh: University of Pittsburgh, c. 1970), pp. 22–23. Reprinted by permission of the publisher.

9. "Scale No. 1: Cognitive Flexibility," in Penland, *Advisory Counseling for Librarians,* pp. 150–153.

10. "Scale No. 2: Consistency of Behavior Between Verbal and Nonverbal Behavior," in Penland, *Advisory Counseling for Librarians,* pp. 154–157.

11. "Scale No. 3: Perceptual Sensitivity," in Penland, *Advisory Counseling for Librarians,* pp. 158–160.

12. "Scale No. 4: Involvement with the Client," in Penland, *Advisory Counseling for Librarians,* pp. 161–163.

13. Geraldine King, "Open and Closed Questions: The Reference Interview," *RQ* (Winter 1972), p. 12.

14. U.S. Office of Education. *Statistics of Public Libraries Serving Areas with at Least 25,000 Inhabitants, 1968* (Washington, GPO, 1970).
15. *American Library Directory*, 1972–1973, 29th ed. (New York: R. R. Bowker Co., 1972), pp. 1113–14.
16. Undated letter received August 1973 from Kathleen R. Myerson, Associate Director, ADP User Education, the ADP Management Training Center, U.S. Civil Service Commissioner, Washington, D.C.
17. U.S. Office of Education, Higher Education Act of 1965, *Title IIB Institutes for Training in Librarianship, Summer 1968 and Academic Year 1968–69,* February 1968.
18. ———, *Title IIB Institutes for Training in Librarianship, Summer 1969 and Academic Year 1969–70,* January 1969.
19. ———, *Title IIB Institutes for Training in Librarianship, Summer 1970 and Academic Year 1970–71,* January 1970.
20. ———, *Title IIB Institutes for Training in Librarianship, Summer 1971 and Academic Year 1971–72.* Rev. July 1971.
21. ———, *Title IIB Institutes for Training in Librarianship, Fiscal Year 1973.* n.d.
22. ———, *Title IIB Institutes for Training in Librarianship, Summer 1973, Academic Year 1973–74, Summer 1974,* June 1973.
23. U.S. Civil Service Commission. Bureau of Training, *Personnel Management Training Center, Course Schedule, Fiscal Year 1974; July–Dec. 1973.* n.d.
24. U.S. Civil Service Commission. San Francisco Region, *Regional Letter Subject: Regional Training Center Calendar for the Fiscal Year 1974,* June 11, 1973.
25. *LIST (Library and Information Science Today)* (1972), p. 331.

APPENDIX 1
INTERPERSONAL COMMUNICATION SKILLS QUESTIONNAIRE

(Sent to 58 accredited library schools in the United States and Canada, July 1973)

1. Do you offer instruction in interviewing techniques or interpersonal communication skills in your curriculum, such as that developed in the helping professions of counseling, educational psychology, social work, personnel administration, etc.? (Methods might include sensitivity training, nonverbal communication, simulation games, role playing, videotaping, etc.)

  Yes ———   No ———

2. If the answer to number 1 is yes:

  a. Is the instruction a *separate course* in the library school curriculum?

  Yes ———   No ———

  Course title(s)

  _____

  _____

b. Is the instruction *a unit* in the teaching of a course in:

Course titles(s)

Administration _____

_____

Communications _____

_____

Information Science _____

_____

Resources _____

_____

Technical Services _____

_____

Other _____

3. Is a separate course, basic to interpersonal communication skills, included in your requirements for a graduate library degree?

Yes _____   No _____

Course title(s)

_____

_____

4. If answer to number 3 is yes:

a. What is the official statement of the requirement?

b. How long has this been a requirement? _____

c. Can this requirement be met by enrollment in a class outside of the Library School in another discipline, such as Social Work, Personnel Administration, Psychology, etc.?

Yes _____   No _____

Options available

_____

_____

_____

5. Comments:

APPENDIX 2
INTERPERSONAL COMMUNICATION SKILLS QUESTIONNAIRE

(Sent to 89 ARL libraries & 145 public libraries representing each state's three largest public libraries per U.S.O.E. listing, August 1973)

1. Is there a formal on-the-job training program required in your library in reference interviewing techniques or interpersonal communication skills, such as those developed in the helping professions of counseling, educational psychology, social work, personnel administration, etc.?

   (Methods might include sensitivity training, nonverbal communication, simulation games, role playing, videotaping, etc.)

   Yes _____   No _____

   a. Is this training available for:

   Professionals only   _____
   Support staff only   _____
   Both   _____

   b. At what intervals is this program offered?

   Once a year   _____
   Twice a year   _____
   Other (specify) _____

2. If the answer to number 1 is yes:

   a. Is this training done by:

   A staff member (specify)   _____
   An outside agency (specify) _____

3. Does the library offer a program such as that described in question 1 which is *not required?*

   Yes _____   No _____

   a. Is this training available for:

   Professionals only   _____
   Support staff only   _____
   Both   _____

4. Does the library support (financially or otherwise) staff participation in continuing education programs in this area (workshops, institutes, seminars, classes, etc.)?

   Yes _____   No _____

   a. Is this support available for:

   Professionals only   _____
   Support staff only   _____
   Both   _____

5. What percentage of your staff has participated in continuing education programs during the last two years?

   Professional _____   Staff _____

6. What personnel has participated in continuing education programs?

Job title of participant   Title of institute, seminar, class, etc.

_____   _____

_____   _____

_____   _____

_____   _____

_____   _____

7. Comments:

APPENDIX 3
INTERPERSONAL COMMUNICATION SKILLS INQUIRY LETTER

(Sent to 50 state library agencies, August 1973)

To: Directors of State Libraries   7 August 1973

Gentlemen:

Mrs. Mildred Nilon, Chief of Reference Services at the University of Colorado, and I would like to ask your help in gathering data for an article we are writing on interviewing techniques, which is to be included in the book *Educating the Library User,* edited by John Lubans, Jr., and scheduled for publication by Bowker in the spring of 1974.

We are interested in determining what courses, if any, in continuing education (workshops, institutes, seminars) have offered instruction in communication and counseling skills such as those employed in the helping professions of guidance, educational psychology, personnel administration, social and welfare work, etc.

Would you be good enough to forward any printed lists of such programs of continuing education offered or available to librarians in your region, perhaps checking any which to your knowledge were particularly intended to develop interpersonal communication techniques during the past two years?

We do realize the many demands made upon your time. However, we would appreciate it very much indeed if you could send us any appropriate materials at your earliest convenience in the enclosed stamped and self-addressed envelope.

Thank you in advance for any help you can give us.

Sincerely,

MARCY MURPHY
Special Assistant to the Director
U.S. Air Force Academy Library
U.S. Air Force Academy, CO 80840

LIBRARY HANDBOOKS AND OTHER PRINTED BIBLIOGRAPHIC AIDS

Mona McCormick

Research Editor, Western Behavioral Sciences Institute; formerly Researcher, NBC-TV News; Reference Librarian, New York Public Library; Reference Librarian, The New York Times

Two factors cloud the value of handbooks in the library education process. The first is that they are called "books"—a term that fails to invite the modern users of the mixed-media learning materials center. The second is that many users, especially student users, can't read. Librarians have commented on the lack of reading skills (Bristow,[1] Haag [2]) as has educator Robert M. Hutchins, who has said that one of the "Rs" in education is "remedial readin'."

Nevertheless, handbooks and printed bibliographic aids do make important and vital contributions to the education of the library user. A handbook is, literally, a book that is small enough to be held in the hand that treats broad subjects in a brief fashion. As used here, the term "handbook" refers to material (including mimeographed sheets, paperbacks, etc.) produced by an individual library and describing that library's rules, collection, etc., or to commercially published works that describe the use of books and libraries. Printed bibliographic aids are separate items, such as a map of the library, a chart of the classification schedules, an explanation of the card catalog or an index.

WHY USE HANDBOOKS AND PRINTED AIDS?

SELF-MOTIVATION AND POINT-OF-NEED

A search of the literature on the subject of user education indicates that the use of every available form (books, films, cassettes, tours, etc.) at every point of need offers the best insurance for reaching the user. There seems to be no one key. Nevertheless, a handbook has many advantages, compared with other library-user-education devices. Users can refer again and again to a handbook without hesitation, which they might feel were it necessary for them either to return again to a librarian for help, or to repeat, as seniors, the library tour they took as first-year students. Private handbooks can be given out and commercially published books can be checked out, for use at any time; whereas it is not always possible for the user to take the tour or see the library instruction film at the time it is offered—gathering people together is usually a problem. A problem, too, is that public libraries often do not have tour services available to users. Handbooks also allow selective reading for specific needs, while a tour or film frequently includes information users are not ready for, or do not think they will ever need. A separate printed aid at the point of use, and at a time when some motivation has brought the user to that point, is obviously helpful.

Always a concern of reference librarians is the problem of the users' perceived and expressed needs. Library users may not be good at articulating their requests and may not know there is more than one way to approach a library search. Browsing through published handbooks that carry information on well-known reference works as well as on the use of the specific library gives users a new awareness of the many possibilities for gathering information.

Teaching is an important function of the library, and today the emphasis in the field of education itself is on self-taught project work and private study. Many of the courses offered cut across the boundaries of traditional study and cover several disciplines.[3] These trends increase dependency on the library, and handbooks are one way of covering many subject areas for users at their point and time of need.

There is also a publicity and public relations value to giving users attractive handbooks that boast of special collections, provide brief histories of the library, and otherwise add to the institution's prestige.

LIBRARY STAFF SUPPLEMENT

Until someone invents a handlibrarian, handbooks are particularly valuable because there is probably no library in the country with a staff large enough to accommodate all the questions that users have or large enough to have a librarian in each of the areas of the library where users may have needs. Sul H. Lee gives the following statistics regarding staff–user ratios for academic libraries:

> In 1968–69 the ratio of professional library staff to students was 1 to 450. But only about a third of the professional staff is actually available at any one time for direct user service, so the ratio averages closer to 1 to 1350.[4]

Observations about staff shortages (apparently due more to budget considerations than to lack of available librarians) apply perhaps more urgently to public libraries, especially if reported student pressure on them is correct.[5]

Lee also writes about the frequently expounded fallacy, that the students who need help will ask for it:

> If every student who needed help in a university library were to ask at reference desks, the queue of waiting lines would look like registration day. But one fails to see such a phenomenon. Why? That question posed to many students in the privacy of conversation has brought predictable answers: "I hate to display my ignorance. I figure I should already know." [6]

Of course, in order to ask a librarian a question the user has first to find the librarian.

Mews has pointed out that library instruction is not always best accomplished by a librarian who has no professional training for the teaching task and who may not be suited to the role.[7] Presumably, a handbook, carefully written by a professional author/teacher, can provide the enthusiasm and teaching ability that might not be communicated by an otherwise capable librarian. And a specific library's handbook can relieve the staff of answering, over and over again, the same basic questions about hours, locations of special collections, who may use the library, and so on.

Not only can handbooks supplement the staff and be of service to the user too embarrassed, for whatever reason, to ask. Good handbooks usually encourage library users to ask a librarian for help when they need it.

THE LIBRARY-PRODUCED HANDBOOK

FORMAT

Though the majority of handbooks are traditional in format, it is in this area that the term "library handbook" may be less appropriate than something like "library poster." In discussing handbook design, Cosette Kies states that today's library user is graphically very sophisticated, so the more original the item the better.[8]

Library Journal pictures and reports on Mercyhurst College's "Library Game," an attractively designed folder in the style of a game board that has little specific information, but conveys the feeling that the library is not a forbidding place.[9] And it at least mentions things like interlibrary loan, so it does carry some teaching. The University of Virginia Alderman Library's "At Last the Whole Alderman Catalog: An Alternative Guide to Alderman Library" folds out from a 10-by-6-inch size to a little over larger than a 24-by-36-inch size, with information on both sides (see Figure 1). Though not exactly easy to read, it has lively drawings and is filled with information, including sample cards from the catalog.

The format must suit the material, the audience, the intended approach (informal or strictly factual), and—most important—the budget. Pleasing color, illustrations, floor plans, drawings, and visual appeal combined with information are the goal, within the permissible cost.

If a handbook is too big and has too much information, it is likely to remain unread. Some libraries put out several small handbooks or printed sheets on various subjects (card catalog, indexes, special collections, etc.) or directed at special audiences (undergraduate, graduate, faculty). If students are the primary target, some libraries put the user information on 8½-by-11-inch sheets that can be clipped in a three-ring notebook and retained and easily referred to at any time.

Format should also be defined by considering whether the handbook is designed as a "throwaway" or for retention and whether it will be economical to revise. Other considerations are discussed by Kies [10] and in the Federal Library Committee's *Guidelines for Library Handbooks,* which also discusses content and writing style.[11]

Where possible, it is good public relations to involve the user in the production

Figure 1. Sample of a library-produced aid for library users. From *At Last the Whole Alderman Catalog: An Alternative Guide to Alderman Library* (Charlottesville: University of Virginia Library, 1972). Reproduced and used by permission of Clinton Sisson and Janet Sisson.

of a handbook—a community artist, an art department student, or a faculty member.

CONTENT

While both types of handbook, library produced and commercially published, cover many of the same items, these specifics should be included in every library-produced handbook: the name and location of the library, days and hours of service, a statement of purpose, services (interlibrary loan, reference, reproduction, compilation of bibliographies), regulations regarding use (including eligibility), descriptions of major holdings and special collections, names of library staff and library phone numbers, brief descriptions of the card catalog and major indexes. It is important to date the material, both for the reader's information and as a reminder to the authors to keep it up-to-date, no matter how much guilt that elicits. A handbook should have a table of contents and, if it is large enough to warrant it, an index.

If space, money, and time allow, the handbook can include a history of the library, architectural features, a list of reference books and of periodicals, floor plans, vertical file, government documents, classification system. Mews urges academic libraries to show the actual subarrangement on the shelves by tier and shelf guides.[12]

Certainly staff members at all levels (clerks, librarians, directors) should be consulted about what they think should be included in a handbook.

Naturally, the content is determined by the library and its users. Occasionally a specific library's handbook is of such high quality that it is used elsewhere, as is Barton and Bell's handbook for the Enoch Pratt Free Library and Aldrich's handbook written for the course in library use for first-year students at Louisiana State University.[13,14]

When use indicates the need, as in a university library, a separate publication or considerable space in an overall handbook should be devoted to the card catalog: samples should be provided, as well as filing rules (especially alphabetical arrangement), information on whether it is a divided catalog, whether periodicals are listed there, tracings explanation, library abbreviations.

Separate publications should always be compiled for areas of importance that do not lend themselves to a general book or that would make an overall handbook too large. Examples are Tulane University's "How to . . ." series (*How to Find a Biography, How to Find Book Reviews,* etc.), the New York Public Library's description of the Schomberg Collection of Negro History and Literature, and the Library of Congress's newly done handbook on the *National Union Catalog: Reference and Related Services.*

The Schomberg Collection is a good example of minority information lending itself to special treatment. Sometimes the community of library users may require handbook information in a bilingual format or as a separate booklet in a language other than English.

Audiovisual materials may be given special attention, especially if films and records may be borrowed. Items available on microfilm can be described, and when something like the *New York Times* is available and frequently used, some indication of the usefulness of its index should be given. For example, the *New York Times Index* can be used as a reference tool by itself without necessarily continuing on to the newspaper story. Major news stories are briefly summarized in the index, important events are easily identified by black, boldface type, and since 1965, the index has included graphs, pictures, maps, etc. The *New York Times Index* can also be used to find a story in a newspaper that may not have an index. Information of this kind can be of great service to the library user.

In any school situation, research paper information should get top billing, because a student is more likely to look for aid on a term paper than to seek aids on how to use the library. School library handbooks often include a section on the parts of a book and have workbook tests at the back so students can evaluate their library competence after completing each chapter. Elementary and high school handbooks seem unable to resist a certain amount of preaching about not getting the books dirty and behaving properly in the library. A review of some of this material leads to the conclusion that a lighter touch is needed, so students may feel that they are warmly welcomed to use the library, or, at least, that they may behave naturally there. Counseling on proper care of library property and on decorum might best be dealt with verbally rather than in cold print. As always, what serves a particular library and the needs of its particular users determines what goes into a handbook.

Again, the recommendation is to involve users in the creation of some bibliographic aids and printed material. Seeking the advice of special groups and especially of faculty members gives them an idea of what is available in the collection, and such knowledge usually prompts the teacher to have students use sources known to be part of the library's holdings.

WRITING STYLE

A concise, clean writing style is essential in library handbooks. Illustrations are an asset, but the writer should not depend on them to clarify the text. The terrible risk of boring the reader can best be avoided by keeping the writing simple and by avoiding excessive use of library jargon or terminology. Whatever terms are used should be explained—there are some people who think a vertical file is a tool used in car repair. Headings and outlines are helpful as breaks from large blocks of text. As mentioned earlier, sometimes a bilingual text is in order.

The greatest danger is giving too much information or too detailed information on a certain subject and so overwhelming the readers that they quit on page 3. Start with basic information and progress in easy stages to more complicated ideas. Judgment and a realistic understanding of the users and their needs are essential to the writer. The author's own enthusiasm for books and libraries will be communicated in the writing and set the tone, so such enthusiasm must be present.

A library contemplating a new (or revised edition) of a handbook should take advantage of the American Library Association's offer to loan (usually in groups of about four at a time) the handbooks of other libraries as examples. ALA has three lists available—on school library guides and staff manuals, college and university library handbooks, and junior college handbooks.[15]

EVALUATION

Money and time dictate the thoroughness of evaluating a library's handbook. Feedback from patrons and students can be gathered informally by the staff. Is the librarian still asked the questions that are answered in the handbook? If so, does that mean the user didn't receive the handbook? (Why not?) Or does it mean that the user did receive the handbook, but didn't read it? (Why not?)

Some gentle questioning on a one-to-one basis might reveal a distribution problem or a format problem or a problem resulting from murky writing. The staff can be alert to things that are still required of them, things that could be included in a manual but haven't been.

If the budget will allow, a brief evaluation questionnaire may be inserted in the handbook and the user asked to mail it (envelope included) or hand carry it back to the library. However, there is always the possibility that the returns would be too small to warrant the cost of such a survey.

If staff is available, polling can be conducted in the first-year English classes, for opinions on the usefulness of guides. Similar polls may also be conducted among the faculty and advanced students, so that effectiveness can be evaluated at various user levels.

COMMERCIALLY PUBLISHED HANDBOOKS

The content of commercially produced handbooks, while similar to library-produced material, generally covers more information on specific reference works (arranged by subject and/or by type of reference book: encyclopedias, dictionaries, almanacs, and so forth). The commercial books are usually larger and meant to be retained for a longer time. The range of this published material is wide, and there seems to be something for everyone. Even if a book's specific purpose is, for example, research papers or reference books, in most cases there will be a chapter on how to use the library.

Elementary school children are given a fair amount of commercial attention. One really splendid book is David C. Whitney's *First Book of Facts and How to Find Them*.[16] The text is lively and interesting, and the work, I suspect, would be informative for an adult as well. Modern and witty illustrations augment the text. Another example of a book for younger children is Pekay Shor's *Libraries and You*, which has a greater emphasis on the library itself.[17]

A high school-level book with material so clearly presented that it is found in many college libraries is *Books, Libraries and You*.[18] The excellent presentation is illustrated with photographs and realistic drawings, so that the reader is able, in a sense, to see the card catalog and various indexes. In my own book, *Who-What-When-Where-How-Why . . . Made Easy: A Practical Guide to the Use of Reference Books*, I tried to give interesting examples from well-known reference books on people or place names, etc., so the reader would be amused and also have a vivid idea of what the book contained.[19] Although aimed primarily at high school seniors and first-year college students, it has been used at more advanced levels. Cook's *The New Library Key*, though intended for college students, can be used by advanced high school students.[20] Included early in this work is information on note taking and on organizing material for a

Figure 2. Sample page from a commercially published library handbook. From *Guide to the Use of Books and Libraries* by Jean Key Gates. Copyright © 1969 by McGraw-Hill Book Company. Used by permission of McGraw-Hill Book Company, publisher.

CHAPTER 9
INDEXES

The word "index" comes from the Latin word *indicare,* which means to point out. Thus an index does not provide the information which is sought; it *indicates* where it can be found.

The index [1] of a book points out the page or pages on which certain information can be found. The card catalog, which is made up of individual catalog cards, is an *index* to the materials in a library. Each catalog card indicates, by means of a call number, the location of a book or other kind of material. The catalog card may give the pages on which certain material can be found in a given book; for example, the card may have the notation, Bibliography: p. 210–212.

In addition to card catalogs and the indexes of books, three other kinds of indexes are needed by the student who seeks material on a particular subject: (1) indexes to literature appearing in periodicals, (2) indexes to materials appearing in newspapers, and (3) indexes to literature appearing in collections or anthologies.

PERIODICALS

Periodicals appeared in the sixteenth century soon after the invention of printing. They began as pamphlets, grew into a series of related pamphlets, and by the seventeenth century had taken on the characteristics of our modern periodicals. Throughout the eighteenth century, the word "periodical" was used chiefly as an adjective, e.g., periodical literature, periodical publication. By the end of that century the term was applied to all regularly issued publications except newspapers.

The word "journal" originally meant a daily newspaper or publication; it has since come to mean any publication which contains news or material of current interest in a particular field.

The historical meaning of the word "magazine," deriving from the

[1] A concordance is a type of index which lists, in alphabetical order and in context, the principal or key words in a book or in the works of an author. It may be a part of the book it indexes, or it may be an independent publication.

research paper, because the author believes that the motivation to use the library comes with an assignment to write a paper.

Adults and college students have, for some time now, learned from a standard, thorough tool by Gates, *Guide to the Use of Books and Libraries* (see Figure 2), which includes a brief history of books and libraries in addition to information on the card catalog, classification, reference books, and research papers.[21] A recently published title based on three years of junior college experience is John Lolley's *Your Library—What's in It for You.*[22] Research is also carefully covered by Downs in *How to Do Library Research*[23] and in *The Research Paper* by Hook and Gaver.[24] Finally, for sheer pleasure as well as information, *The Modern Researcher* by Barzun and Graff is literate and appealing to undergraduate and graduate students and anyone involved or interested in research.[25]

Many handbooks are available, and most of them are quite good. The limitations of space prevent comment here on more than the few examples.

LEARNING AS A CONTINUING PROCESS

Ideally, learning how to use the library should be a continuing process, beginning in elementary school and continuing through life. While most of the handbooks and the literature on the subject of user education are geared for student use, the adult patron of any library may also find these works valuable, for business and/or leisure activities. Certainly, the recreational needs of patrons must be met along with their educational needs: it is as important for some libraries to show in their floor plans the location of mysteries and cookbooks as it is to identify the reference area.

Because the right amount of information at the right time is significant in the education of the user, faculty- and graduate-level assistance must be offered. Handbooks are a good source of this kind of aid, especially handbooks covering one subject area; textbooks usually fail to introduce students to the great literature of the subject. Remember, too, that some works thought to be of particular interest to the librarian—such as various subject-heading guides, Winchell's *Guide to Reference Books,*[26] Shores's *Basic Reference Sources,*[27] and guides to government documents—may be recommended to the searcher.

Never assume that a user knows all the basic library tools, no matter how impressive the user's credentials. In a survey of college seniors who were planning to become teachers in elementary and high schools many did not know what the *Readers' Guide* is and had never used the *Education Index.* In mentioning this study in an article Ralph Perkins tells of one university student who asked a reference librarian if he were the *Readers' Guide* and of another student who asked to check out the card catalog overnight.[28]

There is, indeed, good reason for libraries to have a variety of commercially published books available to cover the many stages of user sophistication. And —the existence of these books should not be kept secret. Perhaps they should be taken from their place on the shelf and put out where people will see and use them. Such materials should be publicized and book-talked so users will know about them. A library-produced manual might plug the commercial ones owned by the library.

The claim here is not that handbooks can carry the load alone, but that they are an important tool in the education of the library user. Some handbooks fascinate, others simply instruct. And handbooks and printed aids are getting better—their planners and writers and designers have learned much in recent years from modern audiovisual and electronic media (which were supposed to replace the printed word years ago, we were told!).

A prime goal of library education is to bring everything in the library to life for the user—for everything in the institution has meaning and purpose, and it can all be discovered and be of service to users. And that should be our goal, even if that ideal state may be wildly unattainable—achieving it, at best, is certainly not an easy task; or to paraphrase a John Steinbeck line: educating the library user makes horse racing seem like a solid, predictable business.

Another goal in teaching the use of the library is to make the users' search or study there a pleasurable experience—our hope being that they will come to truly enjoy the place. Knowledge of libraries should increase the likelihood of enjoyment, or else libraries have or will have some other, more serious problem.

In chapter three of Fitzgerald's *The Great Gatsby,* a character says: "I've been drunk for about a week now, and I thought it might sober me up to sit in a library." Perhaps, with a proper education in the use of the library he would not have expected such a sobering experience.

NOTES

1. Thelma Bristow, "Instruction or Induction: The Human Approach to Student Involvement in Library Materials," Seminar on Human Aspects of Library Instruction, *Proceedings* (Reading, England: University of Reading, December 1969), pp. 3–4.
2. Dietrig E. Haag, "The Teaching Function of the University Library," *South African Libraries* 37 (1970): 272–273.
3. L. C. Pugh, "Library Instruction Programmes for Undergraduates: Historical Development and Current Practice," *Library World* 71 (1970): 267–273.
4. Sul H. Lee, ed., *Library Orientation,* Papers presented at the First Annual Conference on Library Orientation held at Eastern Michigan University, 7 May 1971. Library Orientation Series No. 1, published for the Eastern Michigan University Library, Ypsilanti, Michigan (Ann Arbor, Mich.: Pierian Press), p. 2.
5. Frederic R. Hartz, "High School Library: A Study of Use, Misuse, and Nonuse," *Clearing House* 38 (March 1964): 1904.
6. Lee, op. cit., p. 12.
7. Hazel Mews, "Library Instruction Concerns People," *Library Association Record* 72 (January 1970): 8.
8. Cosette Kies, "The Handbook Designer: Consideration of Design in Planning a Library Handbook," *Mountain-Plains Library Quarterly* 12 (Winter 1968): 17–20.
9. "Promoting the Library," *Library Journal* (1973): 55.
10. Kies, op. cit.

11. Federal Library Committee Task Force on Public Relations, *Guidelines for Library Handbooks,* Federal Library Committee, U.S. Department of Health, Education, and Welfare, Office of Education (Washington: Government Printing Office, 1972 ERIC Document: ED 067 137).

12. Hazel Mews, *Reader Instruction in Colleges and Universities: Teaching the Use of the Library* (Hamden, Conn.: Linnet Books and Clive Bingley, 1972), p. 37.

13. Mary Neill Barton and Marion V. Bell, *Reference Books: A Brief Guide for Students and Other Users of the Library,* 7th ed. (Baltimore: Enoch Pratt Free Library, 1970).

14. Ella V. Aldrich, *Using Books and Libraries,* 5th ed. (Englewood Cliffs, N.J.: Prentice-Hall, 1967).

15. American Library Association, Headquarters Library, *School Library Guides and Staff Manuals* (Chicago: American Library Association, 1972).
    College and University Library Handbooks (Chicago: American Library Association, 1972).
    Junior College Library Handbooks (Chicago: American Library Association, 1973).

16. David C. Whitney, *The First Book of Facts and How To Find Them* (New York: Franklin Watts, 1966).

17. Pekay Shor, *Libraries and You* (Englewood Cliffs, N.J.: Prentice-Hall, 1966).

18. Jessie Boyd et al., *Books, Libraries and You,* 3rd ed. (New York: Scribner's, 1965).

19. Mona McCormick, *Who-What-When-Where-How-Why . . . Made Easy, A Practical Guide to the Use of Reference Books* (Chicago: Quadrangle Books, 1971).

20. Margaret G. Cook, *The New Library Key,* 2nd ed. (New York: Wilson, 1963).

21. Jean Key Gates, *Guide to the Use of Books and Libraries,* 2nd ed. (New York: McGraw-Hill, 1969).

22. John Lolley, *Your Library—What's in It for You* (New York: Wiley, 1974).

23. Robert B. Downs, *How to Do Library Research* (Urbana: University of Illinois Press, 1966).

24. Lucyle Hook and Mary Virginia Gaver, *The Research Paper,* 4th ed. (Englewood Cliffs, N.J.: Prentice-Hall, 1969).

25. Jacques Barzun and Henry F. Graff, *The Modern Researcher* (New York: Harcourt, Brace, 1957).

26. Constance M. Winchell, *Guide to Reference Books,* 8th ed. (Chicago: American Library Association, 1967). Supplements edited by Eugene P. Sheehy, 1968, 1969–70.

27. Louis Shores, *Basic Reference Sources* (Chicago: American Library Association, 1954).

28. Ralph Perkins, "Realistic Library Orientation—A Necessity," *Library-College Journal* 3 (Fall 1970): 21.

MOTION PICTURES IN LIBRARY-USE INSTRUCTION

RONALD G. HÉROUX

Reference Librarian, Technical Information Department, Naval Underwater Systems Center, Newport, Rhode Island; Library AV-Orientation Consultant

Motion pictures have proven their ability to captivate and stimulate people of all ages to a degree unmatched by other media. Yet educators, and librarians in particular, have failed to adequately use this popular form of entertainment and communication. In seeking new and better methods to teach and promote the use of the library, few librarians have ventured beyond the printed word or slide/tape presentation, although some progress is being made in the use of educational television and videotape.

I do not want to appear to condemn nonfilm methods employed in communicating information to the library user. All effective public relations and instructional efforts should be applauded. And, in many circumstances, the motion picture is not the proper medium to use. But when it is, why settle for less?

The retort to this question is usually, "We can't afford to make a film," or "We don't know how, and we have no time." The excuses are many; the attempts are few.

WHY AND WHEN TO USE FILM

Let us examine why and when the film medium is more conducive to learning than other forms. First of all, people are multisensory. Motion pictures, with their sophisticated and psychological techniques, are designed to activate the audiovisual senses to a degree that enhances the brain's potential of perceiving and assimilating new information. Moreover, the motion picture enables the viewer to acquire a more precise and realistic understanding of the subject matter.

With the added dimension of dramatization to simulate a problem-solving situation a library user might face, a film can subtly draw the viewer into the

318

action presented on the screen. The viewer then begins to internalize or experience this action. Although this experience is vicarious, it nevertheless plays a major role in the learning process.

The decision to utilize motion pictures over another medium should basically be determined by the amount and effective use that can be made of the major film elements—motion, sound, and color. Without the proper mixture of these elements, a film will probably fail to realize its potential.

Motion is generally the most vital element in a film. It keeps the eyes alert and challenges them to follow the action. When motion cannot be incorporated into a film to transmit a message or augment the learning process, a less expensive and simpler medium should probably be employed. For instance, explaining the use of indexes and abstracts on film without actors present does not warrant movement or motion (by applying a variety of film techniques, movement could be added, but this movement would not greatly enhance the film). Therefore, consideration should be given to using slide/tape or overhead transparencies in place of the motion picture.

Before switching to another medium because little or no motion is involved in the production, think about where and to whom the presentation will be shown. Would it be more advantageous to have the material available for group or individualized instruction or both? Then consider the flexibility of the medium in relationship to the hardware at hand. With a compact cartridge-motion-picture projector available, the film could be encased in a cartridge for point-of-use instruction or for group presentations. (More on film cartridges will be discussed later.)

Sound is another important element of film. It complements the motion on the screen by: (1) pointing out facts that are not or cannot be visually demonstrated, (2) directing the viewers' attention to the relationship of the action, (3) helping set the pace of the film, and (4) creating a mood or effecting audience response.

When all that is available is a silent movie projector, the sound can always be added to a tape, or the librarian could supplement the film with a running, oral commentary. However, the latter should be well planned so as not to confront the audience with uncoordinated or competing visual and oral communication.

The lack of sound in a film will generally not deter from the learning process when the message or idea can be communicated effectively with motion and, if necessary, with the addition of subtitles. Such films are usually short and oriented to a single concept, e.g., "How to Bind a Book."

Color in a film, many psychologists theorize, neither aids nor hinders the learning process. I question this theory unless the viewers are color blind or see the world in shades of black and white. A film critic recently tried to persuade the senior French film director, Jean Renoir, that black-and-white films intensify the drama in certain movies. Renoir remarked quite candidly that the only reason black-and-white film was used in the early days of motion picture was because color film was commercially unavailable.

Educational filmmaker Lewis Herman believes color strengthens the teaching potential of educational films because color more closely resembles reality than black and white. And realism he notes, "increases student interest and attention."

Herman points out other advantages of color: "Photographically, the addition of color provides the illusion of perspective and depth which are often lacking in black and white films. . . . Color also adds additional frames of reference with which a student's orientation to picture relationships can be assured." [1]

If we film the RED-bound *Library of Congress Subject Headings* or the card catalog standing on the library's ORANGE rug, the colors will often be associated by the viewer with the book or area in question. Vivid colors are more striking than call numbers or signs and furniture blending into one another.

SURVEY OF EDUCATIONAL LIBRARY FILMS

To ascertain the state-of-the-art of library-produced user-instruction films, a letter-questionnaire was mailed to 28 libraries during the first few months of 1973. The names of the institutions were obtained from programs of various library orientation conferences where libraries had exhibited films and from colleagues who knew or had heard of libraries producing their own instructional films. (A historical look at the use of film in college and university library orientation programs can be found in a thesis written by Sara Aull of the University of Houston.) [2]

Seven of the 28 libraries contacted were Canadian. Divided by type, there were 23 academic, four public, and one school library. The predominance of academic libraries making films is no surprise since they often have more money, equipment, and a greater number of users to instruct than most other types of libraries.

The aim of the questionnaire was to determine whether these libraries had in fact produced a library-user-oriented motion picture. Once this was established, the following information was sought: the present status of the film, format employed (16mm or 8mm), user response, and production cost and technique.

Sixteen libraries responded that they had produced a film, five said they never had a film (although two mentioned using videotape), and seven libraries did not answer the letter. Only nine (see list of libraries and film titles in Appendix) of the 16 libraries were still using their film. The remaining seven libraries (University of Alaska, University of Houston, University of Illinois at Urbana-Champaign, Simon Fraser University, Merritt College, Purdue University, and Sir George Williams University) switched to another medium for a variety of reasons. Some of these reasons were the difficulty and expense of updating the film, the inflexibility of film, and the preference of another medium.

Twelve of the 16 libraries that produced films employed the 16mm format, three used Super 8mm, and one had both a 16mm and a Super 8 copy available. Production cost ranged from a low of $100 to a high of $6,500. The average was from $800 to $1,000.

The more important factors related to the cost of the film were: the format chosen, whether or not outside filmmakers had to be hired, and the amount of experience the producers had. Based on the films viewed, the amount of money spent did not necessarily relate to the quality of the film. Some low-budget films were of good quality and contained much educational value, while other, more expensive presentations were quite mediocre and uninteresting. One can only conclude that the quality of a film is determined more by the creativeness of the filmmaker than by the amount of money available. (But if only a library could afford the talents of a Fellini or a Nichols!)

Except for two single-concept films, all the motion pictures concentrate on presenting the viewer with a general orientation of the library. Many delve into specifics, such as how to use the card catalog and sign out books, while others primarily focus on the major services of the library and where these services are located.

One of the main reasons why libraries involved in producing a film have centered on the orientation program is that the orientation-type film can most easily exploit the medium of the motion picture. The major elements of film can be easily incorporated into a well-paced, informative, and entertaining tour of the library. Also, a film makes scheduling of the orientation program flexible and not completely dependent on staff time, although it would be advisable to have a librarian introduce the film and answer any questions the film might bring up.

The following is a selection of comments from various libraries concerning their personal evaluation and use of film:

> The film we produced served to take conducted tours out of the library. . . .
> A librarian met with each class when it was scheduled to see the film. . . . After
> the showing . . . we reviewed the reference sources and gave a short quiz. . . .
> We were not sold on film as the most desirable form of orientation. . . .
> —*University of Houston*

> The film was shown every hour, 8–5, for three days in the fall to all freshmen
> in large group showings of up to 500 students each time. The objectives of the
> film were to show the students the physical layout of the library, how to use
> some of the materials and where to ask for help in using the library.—*Purdue
> University*

> Sans insister sur les aspects administratifs du fonctionnement de la biblio-
> thèque, ce film est plutôt celui qui présente l'image vivante et colorée de celle-ci.
> —*Bibliothèque Nationale du Québec*

> The film was shown as part of orientation. . . . Reaction was generally favor-
> able. . . . Students seem to appreciate particularly the brevity of the film and
> the music. . . . We wanted to suggest the range of services without being spe-
> cific or detailed.—*Suffolk Community College*

> The two young filmmakers hired to do the film shared the [library] commit-
> tee's belief that the film should be adventurous in character and more evocative
> than informative. The message would not be "How to Use the Library" or "Look

at All the Good Books." Instead, they photographed, over a six-month period, the actual events that are part of San Francisco Public Library's regular activities.—*San Francisco Public Library*

The film is available at the request of the classroom instructor in place of the services of the library instructor. The individual student may use the Super 8mm format in the library.—*New York City Community College*

Used for incoming freshmen and transfer students to acquaint them with: (*a*) major sections of the library, (*b*) easy to use on self-help basis, and (*c*) friendly, knowledgeable staff available for help when needed.—*Northern Illinois University*

Using the film on a voluntary basis and on a hit-or-miss type of program is of little value. The answer seems to be some sort of compulsory showing, hopefully in conjunction with a regular academic orientation program of considerable support by the library. . . . [Comment from Student Questionnaire in response to]: "Did you like the film?" In almost every case the answer was yes.—*Hofstra University*

The film was designed to be used for fall orientation by librarians giving library instruction. . . . The instructional value . . . is minimal and it cannot be used as a sole vehicle for the library's teaching objectives.—*Sir George Williams University*

Although general library orientation films should be produced in-house to reflect the procedures and architecture of the library using the film, this is not necessary when dealing with single-concept subjects or items of a general nature about books or other library material. In these instances, commercially produced films will often be superior and less expensive than most in-house productions.

Two up-to-date sources of commercial films on library related instructional topics are the *NICEM Indexes* (National Information Center for Educational Media) [3] and Shirley Hopkinson's annotated bibliography.[4] Another bibliography containing a list of commercial films and other library oriented AV material was published by the University of Illinois School of Library Science.[5]

FILM *VS.* VIDEOTAPE

Since film and videotape relate in many ways, a brief comparison is in order. Although both media use similar techniques in capturing the action, the film is far more flexible and the quality is usually better than videotape.

1. Most institutions with videotape capabilities do not have color equipment because of the high cost incurred. But it is rare when you see a black-and-white film today.

2. When an audience is watching a film in a darkened room, its attention is drawn to the screen where the images can be projected larger than life. Videotape is generally shown on a TV screen that is not amenable to large-group showings and offers the distraction of a lighted room. (Of course, if a film is badly done, the audience can easily fall asleep in a darkened room.) Videotape can be projected on a screen with a videoprojector, but the quality has been poor to date.

3. A film can easily be transferred to videotape with little or no loss of quality. This process can be reversed, transposing videotape to film. This type of film is called a kinescope. The quality of kinescope, unless produced by a major TV studio, is not very good when compared with an original film. However, a new technique for quality videotape-to-film transfer has recently been introduced by Video Tran. It promises to produce a film product from videotape comparable to original film at a price described as only slightly higher than kinescope.

4. Motion picture equipment (camera, projector, etc.) is cheaper and more compact than videotape equipment. But when taking into consideration the software, film is more expensive than videotape. A videotape can be used over and over again. Once a film is exposed there is no turning back, unless you desire the special effects of a double exposure.

5. Film is generally easier to edit than videotape. On the other hand, videotape can be played back immediately to check if a scene has been shot correctly, whereas one has to wait for the film to be processed before seeing the results.

Which medium should be chosen—videotape or film? Although I favor film, consider what is available, how the end product will be used, the cost, the quality, and your familiarity with the medium.

FILM FORMAT

Film formats vary from 70mm (widescreen) to 8mm. Since it is not economical for libraries to shoot in the Hollywood 70mm or 35mm format, the remaining two gauges will be discussed, 16mm and 8mm.

The 16mm size offers the filmmaker many advantages: a professional industry, a variety of films, cameras, optical effects, etc. But you must also pay approximately four times the price of an 8mm film. Since one of the main reasons why some libraries have switched from film to another medium is economic, serious consideration should be given to using 8mm film instead of 16mm.

"The filmmaker who works in 8mm should consider the advantages of his film and use them. . . . 8mm cameras are simple to use, less bulky, more automated and less expensive to use than 16mm cameras. . . . The filmmaker who shoots in 8mm can shoot more film because of lower costs." [6]

There are basically two types of 8mm films—Regular 8 and Super 8. The Regular 8, which was the standard for a long time, is now being replaced by the Super 8. The latter is "still 8mm wide, but because the sprocket hole is in a vertical shape, the picture width on the 8mm strip can be made wider. At the same time the height is increased proportionately, and the resultant area is about 50 percent greater, resulting in better image and color quality, as well as allowing more light to reach the screen for brighter images." [7]

No longer does the Super 8 movie have to be silent or kept in synchronization with a taperecorder. Optical or magnetic sound can now be added to Super 8 film. Magnetic is more popular because the sound can be added in-house and can be erased for updating. Good sound Super 8 projectors, such as the Eumig and the Bolex, are available for around $350.

Super 8 films can be cartridged for easy handling by everyone. If the film is looped in the cartridge, it does not have to be rewound and can be shown at the flick of a switch for point-of-use instruction or in the library lobby. Cartridge film loops are permanently enclosed in plastic cassettes that protect the film from handling and dust. The cartridge can be easily inserted into the projector. Technicolor and Fairchild are two major manufacturers of film-loop cartridges and film-loop projectors.

One of the leading reviewers of photographic hardware and software, L. Andrew Mannheim, wrote in a recent article that Super 8 is holding its own and growing "because Super 8 has been here for the last eight years; it is familiar and the software supply is also expanding. . . . Recent developments cover, in particular, sound film systems, integral still and movie presentations on Super 8, film and tape for video presentation and new marketing approaches to software systems." [8]

With the use of Kodak Super 8 Ektachrome film (a high-speed film), a library orientation program can now be filmed indoors using only available light. No more cumbersome setting up of lights. This allows for good candid shots of students using the library and does not disturb students with floodlights. And the resulting color quality is very good.

When showing a Super 8 film to a large audience, the image cannot be projected on a screen as large as the one in a local theater without noticeable loss of light. However, if the image size is reduced to a point where the person in the last row can adequately see the film, if the room is well darkened and if the projector is fairly close to the screen, contains a good light source (such as the halogen lamp), and has a good zoom lens, you can adequately show the film to an audience of 300. This was done successfully at Hofstra University.

One of the major problems with Super 8 is obtaining good copies from the original film. A good independent processor should be sought for best results, otherwise duplicate copies will often be less sharp and grainier than the original. After experiencing this problem at Hofstra University, we were able to obtain acceptable copies only with constant pleading with the processor and finally by going to another processor.

A 15-minute, sound Super 8 orientation film should cost no more than $350 for material and processing, assuming you have someone on the staff or in the AV Department who can creatively use a Super 8 camera and write a good script. If you have to hire someone, it will naturally cost more.

PRODUCTION SUGGESTIONS

Once a librarian gets the idea to produce a library orientation film, how does he or she successfully accomplish this? Much has been written about the subject of filmmaking, and references to such handbooks and guides are indicated in the bibliography. Concerning the production of a *library*-centered film, Steve

Sherman wrote an excellent chapter on this subject (chapter 7: "Films and Slides—Simpler Than Ever") in his book *ABC's of Library Promotion*.

In order not to duplicate the specifics of Sherman's chapter, this section will be limited to discussing some of the major points that should be considered in the production of a library orientation film. Most of the ideas that follow are based on my experiences at Hofstra University where I produced the film *The Library: A Problem Solver*.

1. Write your script first, keeping in mind the students' point-of-view, their needs, and what holds their attention. Do not attempt to show them how to use the library in one easy lesson, but rather give the students a feeling for the library—its varied resources, its departments, and its architectural layout. Try to shoot all your service areas, and emphasize the availability of librarians or technicians in helping the students to locate information and use the library. Make the staff as visible as possible. Shoot the attractive sections of your library. Show students comfortably using the library and interacting with the librarians so the viewers may associate with their peers.

2. Try to get as much action in the film as possible. Since the card catalog, books, and furniture are static items, shoot them being used by students and faculty.

3. Watch out for the composition of your picture. Do not try to shoot too much at once. Pace the film carefully, and work on scene transitions by the careful use of swishwipes, fade-ins, fade-outs, dissolves, etc. Vary your camera angles, especially in long scenes.

4. Shoot at least twice the amount of film footage you need. Experiment! Experiment! Experiment! It is a simple matter in the editing room to exclude various shots from your film, but it is painstaking and time-consuming to have to reshoot certain scenes because they were not long enough or appeared monotonous and uninformative.

5. When filming, do not stick to your script so faithfully that you avoid including something unique or spontaneous. Bernardo Bertolucci, the director of *Last Tango in Paris*, stated in a recent interview that filmmakers should always be ready to change their scripts. "It is," he said, "boring to shoot every line and scene from the printed page. There are no surprises that way." When going to work at Hofstra University one afternoon I was overwhelmed by the sight of a coed playing with a five-foot-long python on the campus green. The python was her "pet." I asked her if she and her pet would like to be in my film. She agreed. I photographed her in front of the library holding a book called *The Living World*. The scene began with a close-up of the book's title as the narrator commented, "And the books in the Hofstra Library are alive with information." At this point I zoomed away from the book, the python crawled up from between the pages and curled itself around the girl's shoulders. Throughout this scene the student continued reading as if nothing had transpired. Needless to say, this section of the film drew much audience response.

6. Since most students do not normally get turned on by a library film, you must see to it that the film holds their attention. You can do this with entertainment, drama, by making a personal appeal to the audience via the narrator, or by promising some concrete reward. Skillfully weave one or more of these elements around the basic subject matter and you should hold your audience's interest; and this is the first step in presenting any information. Also, a good introduction and ending are necessary. The former should bring the audience into the film, and the latter should leave them on a positive note and with a feeling that their time was not wasted.

7. Watch out for the humor you might interject. Although humor can uplift the film tremendously and spark the viewers, it could also portray a false image of the library or the librarians that the viewer might suspect to be more real than fiction.

8. Except for emphasis, the narrator's remarks should complement the visual. Do not have the narrator say what is obvious to the audience.

9. The music soundtrack is very important. Attempting to produce a film without one would be like baking a cake and forgetting to add the icing. The music plays an important role in carrying the mood of the film; and, if well chosen, it will make your film move smoothly, especially in those sections where the narrator is not talking. Silence in a film, except for a special effect, has a tendency to make the film drag and often causes the viewers to fall asleep or think of other things.

10. If possible, a librarian should be at each performance of the film to reinforce the film's basic message and to answer questions. In addition, the presence of a librarian or two should impress upon the students and faculty that the librarians are concerned about the community's educational and informational needs and are willing to help in any way possible.

11. Get as much help and cooperation as you can from members of the AV Department and library staff, but ensure that only one or two persons be responsible for final production decisions. Too many decision makers only lengthen production time and costs. Also, try to elicit ideas from the faculty so that when you are ready to show the film they will be happy to schedule it for their classes.

Although the library orientation film is not a cure-all for solving the library's user-education problems, it is a good beginning. When such a film is well made, it can make ideas vital, real, and meaningful. In turn, this should encourage and motivate students to use the library. In the final analysis, it is when the students interact with the librarian on a one-to-one basis that their information needs can most effectively be satisfied. If the film acts only as a catalyst in bringing the student, the library, and the librarian together, it has accomplished an important function in the education of the library user.

NOTES

1. Lewis Herman, *Educational Films: Writing, Directing, and Producing for Classroom, Television, and Industry* (New York: Crown Publishers, 1965), p. 104.

2. Sara Aull, "Use of Film and Television in College and University Library Orientation Programs: A Survey, 1950–1965," in *"Your Library" an Orientation Film-Tour of the University of Houston Library* (M.A. Thesis, Univ. of Houston, 1965), chapter II.

3. *NICEM Index to 16mm Educational Films* and *NICEM Index to 8mm Motion Cartridges* (Los Angeles: National Information Center for Educational Media, University of Southern California, 1973).

4. Shirley L. Hopkinson, *Instructional Materials for Teaching the Use of the Library: A Selected, Annotated Bibliography of Films, Books, and Pamphlets, Tests and Other Aids* (San Jose: Claremont House, 1971). A new edition is scheduled in 1974.

5. Irving Lieberman, *A Working Bibliography of Commercially Available Audio-Visual Materials for the Teaching of Library Science* (Urbana: University of Illinois Graduate School of Library Science, 1968), Occasional Papers, no. 94.

6. Edward Pincus, *Guide to Filmmaking* (New York: New American Library, 1969), p. 14.

7. Kirk Smallman, *Creative Film-Making* (New York: Collier Books, 1969), pp. 10–11.

8. L. Andrew Mannheim, "AV: Super 8 Goes On," *Photographic Applications in Science, Technology and Medicine* 8 (May 1973), 29.

APPENDIX
IN-HOUSE PRODUCTIONS OF FILMS ON LIBRARY INSTRUCTION OR ORIENTATION IN USE AS OF JUNE 1973

1. *Chut* . . . . 16mm, color
   Bibliothèque Nationale du Québec, Montréal, Québec
   (Entertaining, general library orientation film.)

2. *How to Beat the System.* 16mm, sound, color
   Northern Illinois University, De Kalb, Illinois
   (Entertaining, general orientation film on the use of the library.)

3. *How to Use Microfilm Equipment.* Super 8 loop film, silent, color
   Prince George Community College, Largo, Maryland
   ("An instruction in the use of periodical literature with emphasis on microfilm equipment.")

4. *Library.* 16mm, sound, color
   San Francisco Public Library, San Francisco, California
   ("Deals with the sights and sounds . . . the human and warm and fun aspects of a library. For use with young adults—basically for non-users.")

5. *The Library: A Problem Solver.* Super 8, sound, color
   Hofstra University, Hempstead, New York
   (Entertaining, general orientation film on the use of the library.)

6. (Library Orientation Film) 16mm, sound
   Suffolk Community College, Selden, New York
   (General orientation film on the use of the library.)

7. *A Place to Learn.* 16mm, sound, color
   College of Du Page, Glen Ellyn, Illinois
   (General orientation film portraying the innovative approach of the college's Learning Resources Center.)
8. Readers' Guide—*How to Use It.* Super 8 cartridge loop film, silent, color
   University of Colorado, Boulder, Colorado
   (Experimental single-concept film on use of *Readers' Guide.*)
9. *Where Do I Go?* 16mm and Super 8, sound
   New York City Community College of the City Univ. of N.Y., Brooklyn, New York
   (General orientation film on the use of the library.)

BIBLIOGRAPHY

Aull, Sara. "'Your Library' an Orientation Film-Tour of the University of Houston Library." M.A. Thesis, University of Houston, 1965.

Brodbeck, Emil. *Handbook of Basic Motion Picture Techniques.* New York, American Photographic, 1969.

Colby, Robert A. "Film Stars—Librarians and Students." *Library Journal,* March 15, 1957, pp. 728–30. Discusses the production of a library orientation film at Queens College.

Gerlach, Vernon S. and Farnbach, Irene. "How to Teach Library Skills Without Really Being There." *Library Journal,* February 15, 1964, pp. 921–922. Describes a program for developing 8mm single concept films.

Guber, Peter. "The Cartridge Revolution." In *The Movie Business: American Film Industry Practice,* ed. by A. W. Bluem and J. E. Squire, New York: Hastings House, 1972, pp. 258–291.

Herman, Lewis. *Educational Films: Writing, Directing, and Producing for Classroom, Television and Industry.* New York: Crown Publishers, 1965.

Jamison, Barbara Berch. "Super 8 and the (Almost) Instant Film Maker." *Today's Film Maker,* February 1973, pp. 23–24.

Kuhns, William and Giardino, Thomas F. *Behind the Camera.* Dayton, Ohio: Pflaum, 1970.

Lindgren, Ernest. *The Art of Film.* New York: Macmillan, 1967.

Mannheim, L. Andrew. "Audio-Visual Automation—Packaging the Motion Picture." *Camera,* September 1971, pp. 44–50.

Mannheim, L. Andrew. "AV: Super 8 Goes On." *Photographic Applications in Science, Technology and Medicine,* May 1973, pp. 29–31.

Mannheim, L. Andrew. "More 'Photokina' Reflections." *Camera,* February 1973, pp. 44–54.

Mannheim, L. Andrew. "Recent Super 8 Cine Trends." *Camera,* March 1971, pp. 46–54.

Mascelli, Joseph. *The Five C's of Cinematography: Motion Picture Technique Simplified.* Hollywood, California: Cine/Graphic, 1965.

Matzkin, Myron. *Better Super 8 Moviemaking.* New York: American Photographic, 1967.

Parker, David L. and Wagner, Robert W. *A Filmography of Films about Movies and Movie-Making*. Rochester, New York: Eastman Kodak, 1971. (Kodak Pamphlet No. T-26)

Petzold, Paul. *All-in-One Movie Book*. New York: American Photographic, 1969.

Pincus, Edward. *Guide to Filmmaking*. New York: New American Library, 1969.

Porteus, Richard. "Make an Animated Film." *Arts and Activities*, September 1966, pp. 17–19.

Sherman, Steve. "Do It Yourself—For Under $100." *Film Library Quarterly*, Spring 1969, pp. 46–48. Explanation on how the University of Alaska produced a library orientation film.

Sherman, Steve. "Films and Slides: Simpler Than Ever." In *ABC's of Library Promotion*, Metuchen, N.J.: Scarecrow Press, 1971.

Smallman, Kirk. *Creative Film-Making*. New York: Collier Books, 1969.

Sullivan, Sister Bede. "Making Movies in High School." *English Journal*, May 1965, pp. 433–35.

Vergis, John P. "You Can Even Make Your Own Loops." *Grade Teacher*, February 1966, pp. 80–81.

A number of paperbacks designed for amateur filmmakers such as *How to Do Tricks for Amateur Films*, *How to Make 8mm Films*, *How to Choose Music for Amateur Films*, etc., are available in the series "Focal Cinebooks" published by Focal Press. *Super 8 Filmmaker* is an excellent periodical to guide both the amateur and professional Super 8 users in producing short and relatively inexpensive films; it is filled with suggestions and buying tips on all aspects of movie-making and movie equipment. Although not solely devoted to film-making as the previous one, two other popular magazines containing articles on film-making or movie equipment aimed at the amateur and semiprofessional are *Modern Photography* and *Popular Photography*, the former containing a regular feature called "Movie-Making." Free film-making booklets can often be obtained from many photographic supply stores as well as from major movie equipment manufacturers such as Kodak, Nikon, Bell & Howell, Fuji, etc.

THE SELF-PACED LIBRARY SKILLS PROGRAM AT UCLA'S COLLEGE LIBRARY

MIRIAM DUDLEY

Assistant College Librarian, University of California, Los Angeles

For a number of years the reference staff of the University of California, Los Angeles, College Library has been involved with the usual programs designed to familiarize students with the library and its resources: bibliographic lectures to classes, upon request; tours at the beginning of each quarter, for interested students; a self-guided audio tour of the library; guides to the use of specific reference tools. Valuable as all these methods are, they do not solve the larger problem of how to provide incoming students and indeed all users with library instruction that goes beyond simple orientation; instruction that is necessary for them if they are to make effective use of the library.

Librarians are painfully aware of how common it is to hear juniors or seniors say that this is the first time they have been in the library. And how many librarians have heard their friends boast that they went all the way through college without ever using the library? While exact statistics are not available, we do know that the percentage of undergraduate (and graduate) students who know how to use a library effectively is depressingly low.

UCLA's College Library has developed a program that is at least potentially able to offer effective instruction in the use of the library to all incoming students (over 3,500 a year), with an investment of only ten to 15 hours of student time.

The program, a self-paced, self-directed course, provides students with a workbook of 20 assignments to complete. Each assignment requires the student to actually use the facilities and resources of the College Library and so become familiar with them. The workbook includes an introduction explaining how the course is structured.

Each assignment consists of a brief, simple description of the sources to be used in working through the assignment and from one to three questions that must be answered by using these sources. The student thus learns to use a periodical index, for example, by finding it on the shelf, taking it down, and examining it to find the answer to a specific question, *not* by listening to a lecture about the index or looking at a picture of it.

The 20 assignments are:

1. Library Tour (Thirty-five numbered pink cards are placed in key locations throughout the library. The student is given a map with numbers indicated on it. He is asked to describe what he finds at each numbered location, *e.g.,* dictionary stand, audio room.)
2. Stacks (The student is required to locate, check out, and return three books, whose call numbers are given, in different locations in the stacks.)
3. The Card Catalog—Author and Title Approach
4. The Card Catalog—Subject Approach
5. Library of Congress Classification
6. Dictionaries
7. Encyclopedias
8. Atlases
9. Almanacs
10. Plot Summaries
11. Periodical Indexes
12. Biographies
13. Book Review Indexes
14. News Indexes
15. UCLA Catalog and Schedule of Classes
16. Pamphlets
17. Audio Room
18. Reserve Book Room
19. Other Libraries on Campus
20. Microform

As examples of the workbook's content, Appendixes 1–3 show sheets for Assignment 11.[1]

One hundred different question-and-answer sheets have been prepared, so that in a class of one hundred or less no two persons will have the same questions. (In a class of one hundred or more, every hundredth student will have the same questions, but the chance of one student finding the other student with the same questions is negligible.) This is vitally important to the success of the program, for experience has shown that if all the students have the same questions, they may learn a good deal about sharing and cooperation, but they will not learn much about the resources of the library.

The program has attracted so much attention nationally (libraries at the University of Michigan, University of Alaska, Arizona State University, Boise State College, Central Washington State College, Southern Colorado State College, Texas A & M, California State University, Hayward, have already established courses based on this program) that the most recent edition of the workbook has been specifically designed to be adapted by other libraries for their use.

Each copy of books that are sold contains question-and-answer sheets for all assignments that would apply to all, or most, libraries using the workbook (i.e., the assignments on Library of Congress classification, dictionaries, encyclopedias, atlases, almanacs, plot summaries, periodical indexes, biographies, book reviews, news indexes). These books also provide instructions for preparing questions for assignments relating to the particular resources of the library adapting the program.

The course has been given to more than 3,300 UCLA students in the past five years. Any department wishing to require it of, or offer it to, its students may arrange for the course. The charge, $5.00 per student, covers the cost of printing, filling in, and correcting the workbook, the replacement, binding, and extra copies of reference tools, and extra help at the reference desk. One great advantage of the course is that any number can play. It has been given to classes of ten students, and individual students may take it at any time. The largest class to take the course in any one quarter at UCLA numbered more than 800; with the present course the staff feels it could handle up to 1,000 without any significant difficulty. Thus all incoming first-year students could be accommodated if classes were distributed throughout the year.

EVALUATION

A great number of students can be served by this program, but how well are they being served? In the fall of 1972 the Library Skills course was given to a group of students as part of a "Dynamics of University Adjustment" program. Eighty-five students in the program completed a 12-page evaluation form that included questions on the Library Skills course, to be answered on a 1 (low) through 5 (high) continuum. The results were as follows:

1. Regarding the extent to which the Library Skills course has been informative: 4.59.
2. Regarding the extent to which it was helpful in other classes: 4.29.

When asked whether the Library Skills course should be continued as part of this program, 94 percent responded that it should.

At the end of the form, students were asked to comment on the program in their own words. Twenty of the respondents characterized the Library Skills course as excellent, 16, as helpful, and 30 volunteered the suggestion that it be required of all entering students. Individual comments on this and later programs included the following:

I think it was one of the most informative things I've done since I've been here.

I now have a better understanding of how to use the library. Before I was always reluctant to go to the library because I never knew how to find anything.

Library Skills was a real pain in the ass, but worth every minute of it.

Felt it was very helpful, don't feel lost and now know how to go about using the library.

I have used libraries for years, without really *using* them. I thought it (the course) was a waste of time—before I completed it.

I have worked in the library since I first attended jr. high school, through high school and also my two years in a city college, but I never had the proper library skills. Thanks.

At first, I was embarrassed and kind of upset about the thought of having library assignments such as this. After completing assignment #1, I was a little less shaken. I suddenly began to realize that I earnestly needed this help. After completing the entire book, I had a feeling of achievement and felt that I had gained knowledge that many students (undergraduates and grads) did not possess. I sincerely feel this study is of the highest significance and should be continued. Many of the students don't realize the value in knowing the library until they have to pass their knowledge on to someone else or until they are faced with the problem of using the library themselves.

It's a hassle but it's well worth it.

The library staff is able to gauge the program's success by other, less formalized means. For example, when the 684 students who were taking the course one year were given an exceedingly difficult and unpopular book to read in another course, the reference staff received approximately 684 requests for the appropriate volume of *Masterplots*. When they were told that this title was not included in *Masterplots*, the staff received approximately 684 requests for the appropriate volume of *Book Review Digest*.

Students who take this course become library users.

This is not a course in bibliography, nor is it meant to substitute for one, but it does provide not only preparation but also incentive for students to take bibliography courses. Having learned what they have from the skills course, most of those who have taken it seem to recognize that there is much more to be learned about the library that will be useful to them, and a large number have asked for further instruction.

There is a real need for students to know how to use the library effectively when they enter college, and the consensus is that they don't. This course is an effective and simple way of bringing all college students up to a minimal level of proficiency in the use of the library.

NOTE

1. Miriam Dudley, *Workbook in Library Skills: A Self-Directed Course in the Use of UCLA's College Library* (Los Angeles: University of California, Los Angeles, College Library, 1973). Assignment 11 reprinted by permission of the publisher.

APPENDIX 1
SAMPLE INTRODUCTION SHEET FOR ASSIGNMENT 11
IN UCLA'S LIBRARY SKILLS COURSE

PERIODICAL INDEXES

Encyclopedias, yearbooks, almanacs, and other reference works give you condensed information on almost every subject. But much additional information, discussion, and opinion on these same subjects can be found in the thousands of periodicals published in this country and elsewhere. Your investigation of a topic is seldom complete until you have searched through periodical literature as well as through books.

Indexes to periodical literature usually will give you a complete reference to periodical articles, including author, title of the article, title of the periodical in which the article may be found, volume number, pages, and date, and additional material.

If you need to find an article in a magazine on the subject of education, look under the subject heading "Education" in any one of the indexes described below. A typical entry might read:

> More time for tomorrow. G. Wendt. il Nat Educ Assn J 46:431-2 0'57. The title of the article is "More time for tomorrow," it is written by G. Wendt, it is illustrated, it appeared in the *National Education Association Journal* in volume 46, pages 431 to 432 in the October, 1957, issue.

APPENDIX 2
SAMPLE SOURCE DESCRIPTION SHEET FOR ASSIGNMENT 11
IN UCLA'S LIBRARY SKILLS COURSE

It is important to read the instructions for use and to note the lists of periodicals indexed and their abbreviations in the front of these reference works.

The three most widely used indexes are:

THE READERS' GUIDE TO PERIODICAL LITERATURE: Indexes more than one hundred different general periodicals. Periodical articles are listed under subject and author.

SOCIAL SCIENCES AND HUMANITIES INDEX: Indexes scholarly periiodicals dealing with the humanities and social sciences (psychology, sociology, philosophy, literature, for example). Periodical articles are listed under subject and author.

PUBLIC AFFAIRS INFORMATION SERVICE (PAIS) BULLETIN: Indexes books, pamphlets, and government documents, as well as some one thousand periodicals in the fields of political science, history, legislation, economics, social studies, and government-related subjects. Periodical articles are listed by subject.

For call numbers and locations of periodical indexes in this library, see Appendix I [in Workbook—Editor].

APPENDIX 3
SAMPLE QUESTION PAGE FOR ASSIGNMENT 11
IN UCLA'S LIBRARY SKILLS COURSE

PERIODICAL INDEXES

You are writing a term paper on divorce for your sociology class. You are told to read an article in a popular magazine, an article in a scholarly journal, a book, a chapter in a book, a pamphlet, and a government document. For starters, you take the volumes of the three periodical indexes mentioned in your workbook which cover *June 1940* * and look under the subject heading "Divorce."
                                    month year

1. Which of the three indexes cites an article on divorce from the periodical *Hygeia?*
   _____

   Answer: _____

2. Which of the three indexes cites an article on divorce from the periodical *Moslem World?*
   _____

   Answer: _____

3. Which of the three indexes cites *an act to modernize divorce in Kentucky?*
   _____

   Answer: _____

4. Which of the three indexes cites an article by *N. T. McDermott?*
   _____

   Answer: _____

5. Which of the three indexes cites an article entitled *"Divorce Laws and Prac-*

   Answer: _____
   tices in Modern Ibo Culture"?
   _____

* The articles you find in the three volumes you are using need not be restricted to the month and year given above. (For example, you may be using the volumes covering April, 1971, and find articles published in June, 1970.)

COMPUTER-ASSISTED LIBRARY INSTRUCTION

ALICE S. CLARK

Head, Undergraduate Libraries, The Ohio State University Libraries

Early in the development of computers, it became obvious that they played more than one role in education. The computer "as an instrument and as an actor" was how Anthony G. Oettinger described it in 1966.[1] Silvern and Silvern identified three roles for the computer in the learning process: CAS, or computer-assisted student, where the computer is used to solve problems or to retrieve information; CAT, or computer-assisted teacher, where the human teacher uses a computer to demonstrate solutions to problems; and CAI, where the stored instructional program follows the same principles as teaching machines or programmed textbooks.[2] As a means for programmed instruction, CAI offers some possibilities for individual instruction in use of the library.

HISTORY OF CAI

As one form of programmed learning, CAI owes much to the concept of machine testing first developed by Pressey at Ohio State University in the 1920s and to the work of Skinner at Harvard in the 1950s. Skinner's method was linear and made each student take identical steps through an exercise. Crowder developed a variation that allowed greater flexibility. The students were offered multiple-choice answers, and their responses decided the routes they would take —either back to repeat the questions, branch to another method of presenting the concept, or receive the correct answer and go on. This method is the one employed by CAI.

Certain principles developed for all programmed instruction apply also to CAI. These include:

1. No human instructor is present.
2. Instruction is presented in small steps.

3. The learner must make a response in a two-way conversation which determines the next step.

4. The learner thus proceeds at his own rate.

5. Feedback in the form of responses lead the student in the correct path and reinforce his learning.

The growth of CAI as a development of teaching-machine instruction came about as computer use became economically feasible. Time-sharing systems were necessary, and hardware, especially terminals, had to be reliable enough for student use before CAI could be widely used. Many of the original programs appeared in elementary and secondary schools, often funded by federal agencies, such as the National Science Foundation, or the Office of Education, or by private foundations. Most of the development has taken place since 1960.[3] A good overview of the subject is given in *Computer-Assisted Instruction: A Book of Readings,* edited by R. C. Atkinson and H. A. Wilson (New York: Academic, 1969).

One of the problems in using CAI in the college and university setting has been the necessity to base the program on sound educational theory. This formalization of structure, which omits the extraneous and insists on evidence of learning proven by pretest and posttest results, tends to make teaching very much a science rather than an art. Since teachers in colleges and universities emphasize subject content, and often have little or no background in the field of education, they may be "turned off" by the emphasis on educational theory and its jargon that appears in the literature of CAI. Another aspect that may work in a negative fashion on instructors in the humanities, which often includes librarians, is the systematic or scientific approach recommended in the CAI literature. Its use by computer-science-oriented people has led to an effective technique of flow charting programs. This is an obvious advantage since it makes the step-by-step and branching capability of CAI easily visible. While this is an effective way to force an efficient structure on the subject matter presented, it is not particularly appealing to the teacher who is using a conventional lecture approach.

Fortunately, there are excellent teaching manuals for CAI coding, which explain the practical approach to both authorship and coding in the programming languages.[4] These are written with terminology that is easily understood by anyone and may be the best way to first approach authorship.

With the increased emphasis now being placed on accountability in education, there may be many advantages to instructors if they are forced to look at their courses in this systematic way that CAI demands. Marina E. Axeen, one of the first persons to use CAI for library instruction in a comparative study at the University of Illinois, experienced this benefit in the lectures to her control group. As she said, "The author came to realize, however, that her lectures had improved also as the result of writing the machine program."[5]

The professional organization for users of CAI is ADCIS, the Association for Development of Computer-based Instructional Systems, and its Newsletter provides information on current developments.

THE COMPUTER TERMINAL IN THE LIBRARY

Librarians have to think of computer terminals primarily as tools rather than as sources of information. As a result, the whole question of where CAI terminals belong hasn't been squarely faced by some librarians. Most of the library literature describes the record-keeping ability of the computer and assumes its use in conventional libraries to be by employees in acquisition or circulation departments. Even many of the information systems using computers as an information-storage device are off-line current-awareness programs that come to the user in the form of printed lists or cards. Terminals are, however, extensively used by students, both in an educational role and as an information source, often the same terminal being used for both purposes by means of a dial-up capability.

With these information functions in mind, the library or learning resources center becomes the logical location for CAI terminals, and experience has shown that those located in libraries do, indeed, have the highest use. The students using the library usually have their minds set on studying or doing research and probably want to complete all of their assignments, including those that are computer based.

One of the obvious advantages of having terminals in the library instead of other campus buildings is the greater hours of availability compared with classroom buildings. While some CAI terminals should be in dormitories, their daytime use is limited unless dormitories are close to academic buildings, a situation not too common on most campuses. Noise is, of course, a factor in the library, but no more serious than the clatter of typewriters, which most academic libraries provide for student use. In fact, the same area with sound-proofing often can be shared by computer terminals and typewriters.

Once the terminals are accepted as another information source in the library, there are obvious advantages in using them as an additional means for instruction in the use of the library.

CAI FOR LIBRARY INSTRUCTION

Pioneer work in using CAI for library instruction was done by Axeen as part of the requirements for her doctorate in library science at the University of Illinois at Urbana.[6] Her study was reported in 1967 in *Teaching the Use of the Library to Undergraduates: An Experimental Comparison of Computer-Based Instruction and the Conventional Lecture Method.*

Axeen took the material comprising her regular lecture course, *Introduction to Library Use,* and rewrote it into 14 units of instruction, each requiring two hours of terminal use. Its format included presentation of information on a screen followed by a dialogue to insure transfer of these concepts to the student. Extensive branching was provided to offer practice and help sequences as needed. The course was offered to one section, while another section took the same course using the conventional lecture method. Axeen's conclusions indicated no statistical difference in the amount of learning on the part of the students, a result that conformed to the results in most programmed instruction experiments.

Two other programs have been used in the training of librarians. While these were not designed for instruction in library use, they may have had some effect in making librarians aware of CAI as an educational tool. In 1970, Slavens reported on his use of CAI in teaching a reference course to graduate students in library science at the University of Michigan.[7] Offered as a whole course or as part of a conventional course, CAI allowed students to practice actual reference interviews with the terminal acting as a patron.

Jahoda and Foos, at Florida State University, used CAI as a method for teaching coordinate indexing, both searching and preparation, with an on-line computer-searched coordinate index on library automation systems studies in libraries and indexing.[8]

Some efforts to use CAI for library orientation and instruction have been made at the University of Denver, Ohio State University, and Dartmouth College. Unlike Axeen's work, which involved a credit course, these programs are in the form of short introductions to certain elements of library use that students need to know. While they offer some real instruction, their purpose is often as orientation, and their results show up in the students' ability to ask "intelligent" questions of the reference librarians.

The program at the University of Denver, originally conceived by Eda Mason, Assistant Director for Public Services, and implemented by Patricia B. Culkin, has 21 segments covering the *Readers' Guide, Social Science and Humanities Index,* and *PAIS;* book review sources; biographical sources; general information sources; and two-card catalog segments. The system uses a Burroughs 5500 computer and a Hazeltine 2000 CRT terminal. The terminal, located in the main reference room, is available from 8 A.M. to midnight. Testing of results, which has been confined mostly to opinion questionnaires and machine tabulated comments, has identified very favorable student reaction to the program. An effort is now being made to expand this service to instruction in greater depth for graduate students.[9]

A sample of the section on book reviews, BCKREVI, that appears on the display screen would be as follows:

COMPUTER: BCKREVI WILL HELP YOU TO FIND BOOK REVIEWS WHICH ARE PUBLISHED IN MAGAZINES. DO YOU KNOW WHAT THE BEST INDEX TO REVIEWS IN MAGAZINES IS?

STUDENT: *NO.*

COMPUTER: IT'S A MONTHLY INDEX CALLED *BOOK REVIEW DIGEST. LET'S LEARN SOMETHING ABOUT IT. BOOK REVIEW DIGEST* LOCATES REVIEWS IN MORE THAN 75 DIFFERENT MAGAZINES. IT COMES OUT MONTHLY AND IS CUMULATED ANNUALLY. THE ISSUES GO BACK TO 1905. OUR COPIES ARE KEPT ON THE FREESTANDING SHELVES BEHIND YOU, ARRANGED IN ALPHABETICAL ORDER. WOULD YOU LIKE TO LEARN HOW TO USE IT?

STUDENT: *YES.*

COMPUTER: TO FIND A REVIEW FOR A BOOK, IT'S IMPORTANT TO KNOW AUTHOR, TITLE, AND THE YEAR THE BOOK WAS FIRST PUBLISHED. FOR EACH BOOK INDEXED IN *BOOK REVIEW DIGEST* YOU WILL FIND A SHORT DESCRIPTION OF THE BOOK, REFERENCES TO THE MAGAZINES CONTAINING REVIEWS, AND QUOTATIONS FROM SOME OF THE REVIEWS. BESIDES AUTHOR AND TITLE, WHAT DO YOU NEED TO KNOW ABOUT A BOOK FOR WHICH YOU NEED A REVIEW? A. ANY COPYRIGHT DATE. B. FIRST COPYRIGHT DATE. C. HOW MANY PAGES IT HAS.

STUDENT: *HOW MANY AGES IT HAS.*

COMPUTER: SORRY. MY UNDERSTANDING IS LIMITED. PLEASE CHECK YOUR SPELLING AND TRY AGAIN.

STUDENT: *HOW MANY PAGES IT HAS.*

COMPUTER: SORRY. THE NUMBER OF PAGES HAS NOTHING TO DO WITH FINDING A REVIEW. LOOK AT THE EXAMPLE AND TRY AGAIN.

STUDENT: *COPYRIGHT DATE.*

The CRT terminal that prints 30 characters per second is very fast, but does not provide a printout, so pamphlets have been prepared to supplement the course and provide reinforcement.

The Ohio State program uses an IBM 370/155 Computer and 2740 typewriter terminals and was developed under my direction with the help of Kathryn Fennessy, reference librarian, and Barbara Saddington, a library assistant. It consists of segments on the content of catalog cards; filing arrangements in the card catalog and use of the subject heading list; using a call number to find a book and the same information presented in slightly altered form to teach the pages to shelve books, and the use of basic indexes. Each segment takes about 20 minutes, and students are branched from one to the other, depending upon their responses to questions about their need or identity.

Terminals used for all CAI courses are available in both of the Columbus Campus Undergraduate Libraries. Preliminary testing on students of the English 100 course indicated a slightly better knowledge from the CAI over the control group, but these results may not be valid since the CAI users were volunteers and may, therefore, be more interested in library instruction than the average student. Their opinions of the courses seem very positive:

I think it helps you better understand the library procedure.

I enjoyed taking this course and I hope to take others.

I think these courses could be very helpful. I would like to see a course given on the use of the bibliography room.

Besides being quick, it really allows you to move along at your own pace.

I didn't know there was as much information on a card catalog as I found out by taking this course.

It was interesting—different, not boring.

The following is a sample section of LIBCAT, the course on the use of the catalog:

COMPUTER: WELCOME, BOB, TO THE OSU LIBRARIES. THIS PROGRAM IS DESIGNED TO TEACH YOU HOW TO USE THE CARD CATALOG IN THE LIBRARY SYSTEM. BEFORE STARTING BE SURE THAT YOU HAVE CHECKED OUT A SET OF SUPPLEMENTARY MATERIALS WHICH ACCOMPANY IT.

DO YOU HAVE THEM? TYPE YES OR NO.

STUDENT: ***YES.

COMPUTER: THIS SET SHOULD INCLUDE: A SAMPLE CARD CATALOG DRAWER OF CARDS. A SUBJECT HEADING LIST. WHEN YOU HAVE THIS SET READY TO USE, PRESS THE RETURN KEY.

STUDENT: ***

COMPUTER: THE CARD CATALOG IS MADE UP OF DRAWERS LIKE THE ONE YOU HAVE AND IS USED AS AN INDEX TO SHOW YOU WHERE IN THE LIBRARY SYSTEM A BOOK IS LOCATED. IT USES CALL NUMBERS TO DO THIS. LOOK AT THE FIRST CARD IN THE DRAWER. THE NUMBER UNDER THE RED (1) IS THE CALL NUMBER FOR THE BOOK DESCRIBED. IT ACTUALLY HAS BOTH LETTERS AND NUMBERS. TYPE THE CALL NUMBER. IT IS O.K. TO TYPE IT STRAIGHT ACROSS ON ONE LINE.

STUDENT. ***Oe1693g31970.

COMPUTER: LOOK AGAIN AT THE *FIRST* CARD. THE CALL NUMBER PE1693 G3 1970. LOOK AT THE NEXT CARD. TYPE ITS CALL NUMBER.

STUDENT: ***qb45a2.

COMPUTER: FINE, NOW YOU HAVE THE IDEA. THIS SAME NUMBER APPEARS ON THE SPINE OF THE BOOK WHICH THE CARD DESCRIBES AND THE BOOKS ARE ARRANGED ON THE SHELF IN THIS ORDER. EXAMINE THE SAMPLE CARD CATALOG DRAWER YOU HAVE BEFORE YOU. NOTICE THAT IN GENERAL THE CARDS ARE ARRANGED IN ALPHABETICAL ORDER LETTER BY LETTER. LOOK UP "PLANT COMMUNITIES." TYPE THE CALL NUMBER YOU FIND ON THIS CARD.

STUDENT: ***qk901o51956.

COMPUTER: YOU HAVE THE RIGHT CARD.

The program at Dartmouth is based on the Denver program with modifications to make it conform to their circumstances. The program is still in the development and testing stage.

DEVELOPMENT ASPECTS OF CAI FOR LIBRARY INSTRUCTION

A fairly common fallacy implies that the author of a CAI program must know something about computer science and programming. While undoubtedly this is helpful, the author actually needs to know only the subject matter of the proposed course. Some educational theory or experience in writing conventional programmed instruction is helpful, too. It is probably true that many CAI authors are fairly knowledgeable about certain software concepts, but this is merely a reflection of interest rather than a necessity.

One of the big advantages in CAI programming is its reliance on natural language. IBM Coursewriter III, the language used both at the University of Denver and at Ohio State University, is easy to learn, using mnemonic codes; e.g., *qu* for question, *rd* for read statements, *ca* for correct answer, *wa* for wrong answers. Obviously the professional librarian, who serves as author of the material presented, should not do the computer coding. ("Coding" is probably a better term here than "programming.") In fact, library administrators should be aware of the tendency authors may have to want to "play with the hardware." A certain amount of testing and correcting on the terminal is necessary, of course, since only in the real terminal-response situation can authors see how their programs are shaping up. However, coding is a skill on the level with typing and should be a nonprofessional task. In fact, it can be a desirable duty assigned to a clerical assistant who may want the stimulation of a new kind of typing and the prestige of working with the computer.

Any good use of CAI by libraries has to assume a good ongoing CAI program at the parent institution. Culkin gave credit to William H. Eidelberger, head of the Computer Center at Denver, and without Ronald Christopher, head of CAI at Ohio State, the program there would have been impossible. The participation of the librarian should be confined to teaching library skills. There is little doubt that writing long courses is time consuming. Strum and Ward, in commenting on the failure of CAI as a means for teaching engineering problems, pointed out one of the main problems as "the immense effort required to prepare course material for the system." [10] The authors' efforts should go toward the preparation of the lesson itself; that is, they should identify their goal, specify just what behavioral objective they seek in their students, develop an outline of their lesson content and instructional strategy, and identify the steps to lead toward their objective. At this point, there is no substitute for just plunging in to write a responsive dialogue leading the students to acquire knowledge of the desired concepts.

Many of the complications of CAI authorship only show up when the program has been entered into the computer. The tendency to expound in long statements shows up quickly on the terminal, and the need for breaking up each concept into smaller bits becomes evident. The students should be made to respond often, even if only with a carriage return action.

One of the real advantages of CAI is the capability to use action responses, rather than just reading or typing options. The catalog course at Ohio State uses an actual drawer of cards and constantly requires that students look up various examples in the drawer. Use of the subject heading list is taught by having the student consult pages from the list and, thus, examine its variations in type and cross-references between related subjects. This can easily be done since the computer is proceeding at the students' individual pace and gives them time to perform the actions. Then, when the student enters a response from his or her investigation of the materials, the program continues on. The course on indexes uses superseded issues in the same way, requiring that students familiarize themselves with the actual form of the index and consult its list of abbreviations and list of journals indexed, in what becomes a simulated experience of actual use. This is similar to the system reported by McCoy when he described the programmed instruction project at Southern Illinois, which was directed by Paul R. Wendt. Their teaching machines for instructing students in the use of the catalog were accompanied by sample catalog drawers and actual books to be arranged, so that students could learn on a practical exercise.[11]

The combination of CAI and various audio and visual presentations offers more variety in teaching certain concepts. Some interesting courses using slides are used to teach diagnosis to medical students. The slides show pictures of actual pathological conditions, while the student carries on a question-and-answer dialogue with the computer in a way he or she would question a patient about symptoms. Ohio State now has, in preparation, a course introducing students to its departmental libraries that will use slides. The course is more orientation than instruction, with the objective of introducing undergraduates to these small, but important collections. A trend away from the localism of using one library occurs now, since the whole collection at Ohio State is approachable through an on-line circulation system from any circulation desk terminal or, remotely, by telephone. As patrons have become used to searching the machine-readable data rather than the card catalog, they often end up charging a book from a department library they have never seen. This has spurred an interest in all available facilities. The CAI course will give directions showing slides of both the exterior and interior of the various libraries as well as some of the subject reference tools.

The common problem for all library orientation and instruction always has seemed to be one of motivation. Culkin said that at Denver, "The CAI terminal acts almost as an advertisement for itself," and the flashing cathode-ray tube seemed to be an attraction.[12] This does not seem to have occurred at Ohio State, where typewriter terminals are used and many terminals are available for all kinds of course work so that students take them for granted. As computers become more widely used for CAI in elementary and secondary schools, any curiosity value will be negligible. Regular inclusion in other parts of the orientation program is the obvious solution. Announcements and perhaps short demonstrations can be made part of the orientation tour. Many students take the courses at the suggestion of library personnel. The courses could be made one of the segments of regular credit courses. For example, a CAI course on library instruction could be assigned as a unit to precede a term paper assignment. In this case, students can be assigned separate registration numbers to provide feedback to the subject teacher, permitting a grading system. Where a credit course in orientation to the university or in how to study is offered, there would be an advantage in making the library CAI course a regular part of the curriculum in these courses.

It is necessary that the students be motivated to take the course at all, but it is even more important that they be motivated to learn when they do take it. The CAI program at the University of Denver, located in the main reference room, serves as a point-of-use instruction for many of the reference tools covered by its courses. Other programs have proven this to be effective, since the students are tempted to use the instruction at the time they are confronted with an index or reference book. The Model Library at M.I.T. uses point-of-use instruction effectively by providing instruction, or audiovisual teaching, immediately adjacent to selected indexes and the card catalog. Presumably, the instruction then takes place not only at point-of-use in location but also in time, so that learning occurs when motivation is at its highest level.

Once students have decided to take the course, we can assume they have some motivation to learn, even if only curiosity is involved. Here the format of CAI may have a great advantage. As Chisholm pointed out about machine teaching: "Students accept greater responsibility for their own learning." [13] She also noted that "machine teaching may force the intellectual focus to a degree greater than is possible in a lecture." [14]

Questionnaires and tests results on students using CAI raise a real question of just what is being learned. There is no doubt that present programs are appealing primarily to students with an interest in operating the computer terminal. As Culkin said at Denver, "Patrons are delighted by its twenty-first-century connotations, and often they just stop to watch while someone else is taking a course." [15] At Ohio State, questionnaires indicate 100 percent of those taking a library-use course want to take another course on CAI. There is some validity to the assumption that the students are learning to use a terminal dialogue, even more than they are learning to use the library. This is not necessarily a bad result and may be legitimate library instruction, if we assume the computer in its information-source role. As the computer becomes more commonly the source of catalog information, the users will often have to do their own bibliographic search. Two experimental programs now allowing the patrons to do this computer search start with an instructional program to show them how to search. Project Intrex at M.I.T. provided a "bibliographic search by which the user identifies the documents relevant to his needs." [16] After identifying himself, the patron was given some instruction on how to use the system as on the following sample:

COMPUTER: WELCOME TO INTREX M. OVERHAGE. IF YOU ALREADY KNOW HOW TO USE INTREX YOU MAY GO AHEAD AND TYPE IN COMMANDS. (REMEMBER, EACH COMMAND ENDS IN A CARRIAGE RETURN.) OTHERWISE, FOR INFORMATION ON HOW TO MAKE SIMPLE SEARCHES OF THE CATALOG TYPE

INFO 2

OR, TO SEE THE TABLE OF CONTENTS (PART 1) OF INTREX GUIDE WHICH WILL DIRECT YOU TO OTHER PARTS OF THE GUIDE EXPLAINING HOW TO MAKE MORE DETAILED SEARCHES, TYPE

INFO 1

READY [The computer types READY when it needs a response.—EDITOR]

USER: *INFO 2*

COMPUTER: NOTICE: FOR MORE COMPLETE INFORMATION SEE HARD-COPY GUIDE. PART 2 OF INTREX GUIDE: SIMPLE SEARCHES.[17]

Something of the same kind of instruction is given to the users of LEADER-MART, the information-retrieval system developed under a National Science Foundation Grant by Donald J. Hillman at Lehigh University.

If the use of CAI fails as a library orientation tool, it will be on the basis that not enough students are motivated to use it to justify its cost. That the cost of CAI may be one of its disadvantages was pointed out by Prostano, who said, "Disadvantages of CAI include its high cost, need for standardization of computerized programs, and its limited format." [18] He went on to say, however, that "CAI, largely funded by the federal government at this time, still is in its experimental infancy and may yet be an important contribution to education in the decade that is just beginning (1970)." [19]

Culkin estimated the monthly cost to the library of one terminal offering CAI as $135.55 for 20–30 users per day.[20] At Ohio State, this cost is not assigned to the library since terminals in the libraries are used for all CAI courses. The CAI center estimates CAI costs as $206 per terminal, including supplies, disc and core storage lines, and computer time. The most relevant figure would be cost per student hour, although this fluctuates as system costs remain fairly static and the number of user hours varies. This would permit a comparison with the cost of personal instruction.

The real cost is in author time. This is not only in the original writing of the course, but in the continual refining and revision. Maximum use of CAI requires an almost infinite capability of number of responses and many possibilities for branching. The usual course may start out very similar to a programmed textbook and grow as a result of the student's responses. As the students answer in unexpected ways, the course expands to take care of their needs.

Some of this cost per use could be spread by standardization and distribution of the programs to other institutions. The adoption of the University of Denver's program by Dartmouth is an example. June Hicks, associate director of Library Services, admitted, however, that this required "writing a translator program to make the system compatible with our computer, and . . . revising the text to conform to our own library's locations and policies." [21] She did say, "We have taken advantage of Denver's research and development and, using the results of their efforts, have been able to save many hours of staff time in formulating our own instructional program." [22]

Institutions using CAI have had to develop policies about the distribution of programs. The rights of the author must be protected since the content of the CAI course is the product of his or her talent, knowledge, and scholarly research. The institution also has proprietary rights since the development took place on its equipment, using its computer center personnel, its CAI experts, and usually, the author's work was done on the institution's time. This has led to the conclusion that in transferring programs, the lending institution may be seeking reimbursement of any cost of transfer, and the author may be expecting enhancement of his or her scholarly prestige.

A transfer policy developed by The Ohio State University Office of Academic Affairs, Computer-Assisted Instruction, requires institutions, which are potential users of Ohio State CAI materials, to agree to the following requirements:

> 1. To give recognition to the author and The Ohio State University as the source of the materials in any use or discussion pertaining thereto.
>
> 2. Not to distribute in whole, or in part, any of the materials received without prior written permission of the Coordinator of CAI, The Ohio State University.
>
> 3. To report usage and data acquired through use of the materials periodically to The Ohio State University (approximately every six months).
>
> 4. To discontinue use, return, and/or destroy all materials received upon 30 days written request by The Ohio State University.
>
> 5. Not to make any changes in the materials without prior written approval of the OSU author of the CAI materials.[23]

This statement also includes a provision for engaging the services of the author as a consultant for $100 per day. The transfer policy of Denver is similar in theory:

> The University does own the copyright to the programs. They are available at a cost of $20 per program, or $250 for the entire package of 21 programs. For this price, you receive card listings of each of the programs, offsets of teletype printouts as examples of user interaction, a copy of the CAI program's instructions, and some unit cost information.[24]

These transfer policies developed to encourage the spread of CAI programs, while protecting the developers, seem to conform to other practices regarding computer software. While computer software is usually shared freely, the costs of consulting personnel and expense of transfer are paid by the institution receiving the material. One of the advantages of sharing CAI programs in library instruction will be some replication of the results of the experiments to show the effectiveness of variations in the programs and test results on different groups of students. As more libraries use this method, some of the problems in motivating students may also be solved. Another advantage may be the general acceptance by librarians that terminals do belong in the library as sources of information, or as tools for academic study.

SUMMARY

Any temptation to look at CAI as some kind of panacea for library instruction should be avoided. While it is one good way to give the individualized instruction that libraries should provide, it should never be seen as a substitute for the person-to-person contact offered by a good reference librarian.

No matter what attempts are made to individualize responses, there are always limitations. Some of the individualization is an illusion. Anthony G. Oettinger said this in *Run, Computer, Run: The Mythology of Educational Innovation:*

> This is the sense in which computer programs greet you with "Good morning, Johnny" by filling in the blank in "Good morning, _____" with the name you had to give to identify yourself to the machine in the first place. This is more genteel than "Do not fold, spindle, or mutilate": "Hey you": or "Good to see you, 367-A-45096," but just as superficial, even when randomly selected variations heighten the effect of spontaneity.[25]

Computer-Assisted Instruction should be just one way in which students learn to use the library, and rank with dial-access audio or video systems, slide/tape presentations, cassette tours, and programmed instruction as a technological means for supplementing the person-to-person instruction and assistance that has traditionally been the high point of library service.

NOTES

1. Anthony G. Oettinger, "The Uses of Computers in Science," *Scientific American,* September 1966, p. 160.
2. Gloria M. Silvern and Leonard C. Silvern, "Programmed Instruction and Computer-Assisted Instruction—An Overview," *Proceedings of the IEEE,* December 1966, p. 1651.
3. Wilbur Schramm, *The Research on Programmed Instruction: An Annotated Bibliography* (Washington: U.S. Department of Health, Education and Welfare, 1964), pp. 17–107.
4. Examples of this are: *I.B.M., Coursewriter III, Version 3, Student Text* (White Plains, N.Y.. I.B.M. Corporation, 1971), and *I.B.M., Coursewriter III, Version 3, Application Description* (White Plains, N.Y.: I.B.M. Corporation, 1971).
5. Marina E. Axeen, *Teaching the Use of the Library to Undergraduates: An Experimental Comparison of Computer-Based Instruction and the Conventional Lecture Method* (Urbana. University of Illinois, 1967), p. 72. AD 657 216.
6. Ibid.
7. See Thomas P. Slavens, *The Development and Testing of Materials for Computer-Assisted Instruction in the Education of Reference Librarians* (Washington: U.S. Office of Education, Bureau of Research, 1970).
8. G. Jahoda and Ferol A. Foos, *The Development of an On-Line Searched Coordinate Index for Use in Teaching and Research.* Tech. Memo. No. 22 (Tallahassee: Florida State University CAI Center, 1970).
9. Patricia B. Culkin, "CAI Experiment," *American Libraries,* June 1972, pp. 643–645.
10. Robert Strum and John Ward, "Some Comments on Computer-Assisted Instruction in Engineering Education," *IEEE Transactions on Education,* March 1967, pp. 1–3. Quoted by Rowena W. Swanson, *Move the Information; a Kind of Missionary Spirit* (Arlington, Virginia: Office of Aerospace Research, U.S. Air Force, 1967), p. 116.

11. Ralph E. McCoy, "Automation in Freshman Library Instruction," *Wilson Library Bulletin,* February 1962, p. 470.
12. Culkin, op. cit., p. 644.
13. Francis E. Chisholm, "Media-Assisted Education and Composition Teaching, a Demonstration," *Proceedings of the Two-Year College Conference on English* (Binghamton: State University of New York, 1972), p. 1.
14. Ibid., p. 2.
15. Culkin, op. cit., p. 644.
16. *Project Intrex Samples of Catalog Interactions* (Cambridge: Massachusetts Institute of Technology, 1971), p. 1.
17. Ibid., p. 6.
18. "Four A-V Wonders Boards Will Buy in the 70's," *American School Board Journal,* November 1970, p. 47.
19. Ibid.
20. Culkin, op. cit., p. 644.
21. Letter from June I. Hicks, February 9, 1973.
22. Ibid.
23. The Ohio State University Office of Academic Affairs, Computer-Assisted Instruction, "Form 1,2" mimeographed (Columbus: The Ohio State University Office of Academic Affairs, October 1972), p. 2. This is a three-page statement used in response to requests for CAI materials.
24. Letter from Patricia B. Culkin, May 7, 1973.
25. Anthony G. Oettinger, *Run, Computer, Run: The Mythology of Educational Innovation* (Cambridge: Harvard University Press, 1969), p. 121.

BIBLIOGRAPHY

Atkinson, R. C., and Wilson, H. A., eds. *Computer-Assisted Instruction: A Book of Readings.* New York: Academic Press, 1969.

Axeen, Marina E. *Teaching the Use of the Library to Undergraduates: An Experimental Comparison of Computer-Based Instruction and the Conventional Lecture Method.* Urbana: University of Illinois, 1967. AD 657 216.

Chisholm, Francis E. "Media-Assisted Education and Composition Teaching, a Demonstration." *Proceedings of the Two-Year College Conference on English.* Binghamton: State University of New York, 1972.

Culkin, Patricia G. "CAI Experiment." *American Libraries,* June 1972, pp. 643–645.

————. Letter, May 7, 1973.

"Four A-V Wonders Boards Will Buy in the 70's." *American School Board Journal,* November 1970, pp. 45–47.

Hicks, June I. Letter, February 9, 1973.

I.B.M. *Coursewriter III, Version 3, Application Description.* White Plains, N.Y.: I.B.M. Corporation, 1971.

I.B.M. *Coursewriter III, Version 3, Student Text.* White Plains, N.Y.: I.B.M. Corporation, 1971.

Jahoda, G. and Foos, Ferol A. *The Development of an On-Line Searched Co-ordinate Index for Use in Teaching and Research.* Tech Memo No. 22. Tallahassee: Florida State University CAI Center, 1970.

McCoy, Ralph E. "Automation in Freshman Library Instruction." *Wilson Library Bulletin,* February 1962, pp. 468–470.

Oettinger, Anthony G. *Run, Computer, Run: The Mythology of Educational Innovation.* Cambridge: Harvard University Press, 1969.

———. "The Uses of Computers in Science." *Scientific American,* September 1966, pp. 160–172.

The Ohio State University Office of Academic Affairs, Computer Assisted Instruction, "Form 1,2" mimeographed. Columbus: The Ohio State University of Academic Affairs, October 1972.

Project INTREX Samples of Catalog Interactions. Cambridge: Massachusetts Institute of Technology, 1971.

Schramm, Wilbur. *The Research on Programmed Instruction: An Annotated Bibliography.* Washington: U.S. Department of Health, Education and Welfare, 1964.

Silvern, Gloria M. and Silvern, Leonard C. "Programmed Instruction and Computer-Assisted Instruction—An Overview." *Proceedings of the IEEE,* December 1966, pp. 1648–1655.

Slavens, Thomas P. *The Development and Testing of Materials for Computer-Assisted Instruction in the Education of Reference Librarians.* Washington: U.S. Office of Education, Bureau of Research, 1970.

Strum, Robert and Ward, John. "Some Comments on Computer-Assisted Instruction in Engineering Education." *IEEE Transactions on Education,* March 1967, pp. 1–3 in Swanson, Rowena W. *Move the Information: a Kind of Missionary Spirit.* Arlington, Virginia: Office of Aerospace Research, U.S. Air Force, 1967.

DEVELOPING AWARENESS: A BEHAVIORAL APPROACH

CHARLOTTE HICKMAN MILLIS

Assistant College Librarian in Public Services of Plymouth State College of the University of New Hampshire; formerly Reference and Public Services Librarian of Wabash College

Under a matching grant from the Council on Library Resources (CLR), a program began at Wabash College in Crawfordsville, Indiana, in the fall of 1970 with the expressed objective of integrating use of the library more fully with the programs of instruction at this small four-year liberal arts college for men. This was an experimental program with a five-year span.

BACKGROUND

As initiated, the chief vehicle for the Wabash plan was to be a program of freshman seminars already approved by the faculty, in which an upperclass student would act as an assistant for the professor teaching the course, helping him to plan it and to guide and evaluate student work. When the grant proposal was accepted, this student was allocated the additional responsibility of a liaison in the seminar between the course and the professor and students, and the library. Concurrent with basic instruction in the use of the library, he was to become an interpreter and facilitator for the library, in behalf of the freshmen enrolled in the seminar. He was to attend all seminar meetings as well as meet with the professor and librarian at other different times. It must be noted here that the seminar program was a matter of instruction for selected upperclassmen and only indirectly for freshmen. For the freshmen, the library experience was to come about through assignments that stimulated library use at a time when another student, especially trained, was there to be of help.

Although offered for credit, the seminars were outside the regular college curriculum and were advertised through a separate catalog. Professors had volunteered to teach the seminars in subject areas of particular interest to them personally—often quite esoteric. Course titles, such as "Ancient Ships and Fleets," "Continental Drift," "Espionage as an Organization Activity," and "Censorship," reflect the intellectual interests of those teaching the seminars.

The upperclass students selected as assistants by the professors were better than average if not superior students in all cases, and as *sine qua non,* were all interested in the challenge and eager to learn.

Freshmen taking the seminars elected to do so; these seminars were not required and usually were the only such options for freshmen.

The meld of upperclass assistant, professor, and freshmen is indicative of a very basic ingredient in a library laboratory with a chance of success—the interest of those involved, their motivation to do the job. The people at Wabash were not captive scholars meshed into an academic lockstep. They had all *chosen* the program. The same was true of the reference librarian, who had come to Wabash primarily because of this program.

It was a consummation devoutly to be wished for, in the language of Shakespeare. "If librarians want to reach the vast majority of undergraduate students, they must work with and through the teaching faculty to ensure that use of the library is a required, essential component in course work"—this point was made most emphatically by the late Patricia Knapp at the Institute on Training for Librarians in Undergraduate Libraries at the University of California in San Diego in 1970.[1]

At the conclusion of the first year of the seminar program, another program was added at the suggestion of an involved faculty member, and with enthusiastic endorsement by seminar students: an in-house program to instruct the many representatives of dormitories and fraternities who had indicated their interest in learning more about the library, in library use, so that they would then help others in their residences with their research problems. A few of these students, but not the majority, were freshmen. Again, the outreach was indirect— the librarian working *through* some students, including freshmen, to reach more students.

The in-house students were also highly motivated. They were not all superior students—a number could be called average—and they were rallying to work in a very amorphous context (residence units composed of a heterogeneous assortment of men in different major fields, with varying levels of intelligence).

The problems in reaching this constituency were expected to be greater, and did prove to be greater, than those confronting the seminar assistants who were definitely working in the applauded, course-related situation. As elsewhere, course-related instruction at Wabash had proved to be meaningful; the challenge in a residential program is to give it meaning out of context, by seeking out opportunities for application, by a certain amount of judicious proselytizing in dorms and fraternities: flyers, bookmarks, announcements—intellectual first aid!

It should be noted here and cannot be emphasized enough that both internal and external public relations are large problems for librarians to solve today. The educational establishment is largely unfamiliar with its own built-in resources and, even when familiarity exists, is not using the resources creatively.

Librarians need more than ever to be communicators—mobile, loquacious, and prepared for debate.

Although one does project where to go and why in an experimental program, it is often vitally necessary to depart from plans to respond to new ideas along the way. Insecurity is rampant since experiments provide the possibility of real and dismal failure. It is extremely important to have a steadying philosophical base from which to respond with insight, rather than to react to ideas for change expediently.

Changes that did occur in the first three years at Wabash were largely in response to student input—their suggestions and their criticism. Listening, filtering, and responding became important functions of the librarian.

If the face of the library is changing, as Robert Taylor says, a very dramatic change needs to be in the ears and ego of both the professor *and* the librarian; what is lost to both in established compartmentalization and time-honored procedures may be gained in users. "It is the user who defines systems" is a Taylor tenet.[2]

THE BASIC PLAN FOR THE FIRST YEARS OF THE PROGRAM

Both the seminar and the in-house library instructional programs followed the same basic plan in the first years. It would have been almost impossible to do otherwise, since the majority of the instructional work fell to the reference (later the public services) librarian, one person who also had all other reference responsibilities in a library with a collection estimated at close at 200,000.

Although the plans were so similar, opportunities for individualization occurred. For seminar assistants, problems in the use of resources varied according to the subject matter of their seminars. For in-house assistants, more general problems were constructed, exposing them through a battery of generic resources to the possibilities of retrieving information in as many ways as possible.[3] Groups were small, usually between five and ten, and allowed for concentration on individual needs. Following the course of instruction, the in-house student hung out his shingle in his residence unit. The seminar assistant, usually a high-ranking senior, had the additional challenge of advising freshmen *concurrently* with his own study of resources (that is why the concentration on indexes and the catalog come early in the course).

In addition to the above-mentioned reference librarian, the chief librarian and a professor were involved in the CLR project, the former as an *ex officio* consultant and arbiter; the latter, for the project's first two years, as coordinator. When the professor returned to full-time teaching in 1972, the chief librarian assumed all administrative details of the program and the reference librarian assumed the instructional planning and implementing, the point-of-contact work with students. Both librarians made every attempt to maintain close communication with each other: the chief librarian was welcome to come to instructional sessions, to suggest or arrange for improvements, to interject observations; the reference librarian was on "drop-in" status at the chief librarian's office, any time. Subjective evaluations by students involved in the programs, and sometimes constructed by the students themselves, kept both librarians apprised of student opinions, criticisms, and suggestions.

THE GUIDELINES

The master plan of instruction for the program's first three years was structured on seven basic tenets of the teaching-learning process—steadfastly adhered to—and two phases of problem solving. From this philosophical base, not overtly expressed, sessions met and attempted to respond to needs for improvement and change. It should be noted here that the approach was *behavioral* more than *technical,* in the belief that with the commitment of the person (student or faculty member) to the concept of "library," interest in "how-to" will follow.

Instruction was usually for about ten weeks, in 90-minute weekly sessions in components of presentation/exploration/discussion. The majority of the time was devoted to exploration (problem solving) in the library. Remember—rather than directly involving groups of freshmen, this was an experience for selected students who subsequently would be working with freshmen.

The seven guiding tenets of the teaching-learning process:

1. student involvement,
2. problem-centered approach,
3. focus through models,
4. on-the-job experience,
5. opportunity for creativity (self-expression),
6. encouragement of conceptual thinking,
7. abolishment of the "mystique."

The two phases of the problem-solving process:

1. first four-fifths of the program (approximately): single-focus problems (factual problems illustrating the use of a single generic resource);
2. last fifth (approximately): multiple-focus problems (conceptual/contextual problems involving many kinds of resources).

Since all this was experimental, and since it was related to the needs of a particular college with a particular clientele, it is felt that any possible value to readers will come more from an explanation of the *logic* of the early program than from any statement of specifics as if they might be *established* rather than *evolving* forms of instruction. It is not known that the approach is *right,* it is only known that it was tried—and that students did express interest in the experiment and satisfactions from their personal involvement—and that the library began to change with the stress on use.

A new need for accountability emerged that affected the total library and indicated the need for a fresh look at the expectations for all personnel. As with the proverbial pebble thrown into a pond, the ripples created by the effort in both seminar and in-house programs to make students more aware of the library and then knowledgeable about how to use it were far-reaching, eventually resulting directly or indirectly in questions about the kind and size of staff needed, the layout of the library, and the location of resources, the development and breadth of the collection, the relationship of the staff to the faculty, the status of the staff, etc.

Experimentation in a way resembles autopsy—causing examination of why things are as they are, in order to make recommendations for the future. Upsetting, but useful.

Early in the program, so that they would know what was expected of them, students in the seminar program were presented a list of objectives in broad terms.

Seminar objectives:

1. development of personal familiarity with generic library resources and certain models;
2. integration of this developing awareness of and familiarity with library resources into the learning experience of freshmen in the seminars at every opportunity, and publication of a joint student-produced bibliography of useful resources to be distributed in seminars and at large;
3. provision of assistance to freshmen in the seminars week by week, and students at large at the reference desk after internship.

In-house objectives varied a little:

1. exploring and learning about a resource through solving a problem involving its use;
2. sharing knowledge of the resource so explored with the others in group, and in the sharing, becoming responsible for understanding the use and usefulness of all the resources explored;
3. sharing the cumulated knowledge at the conclusion of the program with one's peers in-house, after internship, by advising them on the resources helpful to their academic needs and instructing them in their use, toward the end of intellectual freedom.

Although this changed from semester to semester and group to group, the following is a fairly representative agenda for a semester's work, the operational base for philosophy, phases, and objectives. It is felt that the use of nonbook media can be incorporated into the weekly schedules as the opportunity arises. It must be noted that all groups began with carefully worked-out agendas, which by the end of the semester had been pretty much reworked to adjust to new needs, pressures, and situations.

Meetings   *Coverage*

Week one   General orientation to the library and to each other (student to student, students to librarian). *Raison d'être* for the program. Objectives for the semester. Assignment in programmed text for next meeting.[4]

Week two   Use of indexes and abstracts. Problems. Conferences to enhance understanding of goals and objectives. Assignment in programmed text.

Week three   Card catalog, I. Problems. Assignment in the *Dictionary of Subject Headings of the Library of Congress.*

Week four   Card catalog, II. Problems in the application of the DSH, above. Assignment in programmed text.

Week five   Use of the reference collection, I. Problems. Assignment in programmed text.

Week six   Use of the reference collection, II. Search strategy. Problems. Assignment in the reference collection and in the library's guide to government documents.

Week seven   Use of government documents in the collection. Problems. Assignment: review and assimilate all to date. Review worksheet to be returned to librarian to evaluate.

Week eight   Midsemester evaluation and planning session. Assignment: stand by to offer extra assistance to students in seminars (in-house) during midsemester period. Make appointments to give extra help in the library.

Week nine   Minicases. Model minicase. Minicases A and B. Assignment: further review where one feels weak. Conference—discussion of weak areas and feelings about the program.

Week ten   Minicases C and D. Summing up. Project due (usually a bibliography of the most useful resources explored, to be combined with those from others in the group).

Thereafter   Assignment to internship at the Reference Desk. Publication of projects. Optional duty at the Reference Desk (if cleared as "ready" in conference) in addition to seminar and in-house advising.

From these guidelines and operational plans, it was felt that the dialogue (presentation/exploration/discussion) could proceed. There is no script!

TEACHING-LEARNING TENETS

STUDENT INVOLVEMENT

Classes in the program were called "library labs" and usually involved no more than four to ten students who met rather informally once a week with the reference librarian in a seminar room in the library for discussion before going to the collection with research problems to solve.

Lecturing in the labs was kept to a minimum. Today, in the time of the Fourth Revolution,[5] learning is enriched by many media and by a renewed emphasis on personal experience. Students, rather than being passive (bored?)

spectators at an instructor's *tour de force* were kept in motion both by solving research problems in the library and by sharing their discoveries with others.

The reference librarian opened labs by introducing students to whichever generic resource or resources were slated for investigation that day. A specific resource or "model" of each kind served to illustrate the generic resource (i.e., *New York Times Index* to illustrate all indexes, as a type of generic resource). Time was taken to respond to student questions or observations.

With an introductory familiarity, students then took assigned problems involving the use of the resource being explained into the library to seek out possible solutions (not "answers," which may suggest a very vertical and narrow approach). Within a given time period, they returned to the seminar room, each one charged to tell the others about his problem and his personal discovery of helpful resources. "Show and tell" was encouraged actually, as it is on the elementary level; students could bring the involved resources back so that others could make a physical and visual contact with them in addition to the intellectual one. This made it easier to "compute" the resource—students could store an awareness of it in their heads.

As in a science lab, there was action in this library lab. Motion, noise, dialogue. Laughter even. Changes occurred. "I didn't know . . . we had such an index"; ". . . what a concordance was"; ". . . that there were dictionaries for biology only." Education is alive and well when there is this process of change.

Just as certain bibliographic resources are guides to information, the librarian was guide for the lab—suggesting, but not telling the way. Pointing out possibilities, never presuming to say "wrong," but rather proposing the consideration of alternatives. She tied the students' involvement together, and commented or explained as she felt necessary when any doubt or confusion existed.

In such a situation, there can be no script (lecture) but only a "happening." The librarian is the yeast that brings about the action, but the students make the bread—and as creators, begin to feel a commitment. It's a demanding situation for the teacher, who must seize every opportunity to make a point.

When the learning comes thus, from the shared experiences of the students rather than from tight lectures, the grounding to the librarian by a professional philosophy is most important. Students ask more questions, seem to get more at the gist of things. Learning can be reinforced then by a timely "You're right, Art, this is why . . ." or "Yes, Mark, there seems to be a pattern . . ."

To facilitate participation, every effort needs to be made to keep communication open and to keep this focus not only on the students and their individual progress in assimilating and understanding, but also on how clearly they share their progress with their peers (fellow assistants and the students he is helping or preparing to help). In this situation, students learn a little about the art and demands of teaching—by teaching each other. This lab actually becomes a model for them of their future experience helping freshmen and other students.

PROBLEM-CENTERED APPROACH

Learning by rote is a way to pass over exam hurdles, but *knowing how by doing* is an important step toward confidence in oneself, toward the self-esteem necessary for maintaining equilibrium in academic or larger societies.

Problems rather than *prescription* are needed in library labs, adding the ingredient of "the way it seems to me" to the learning experience. Doing a problem successfully results in a product, a result to be proud of. Making errors in judgment should be interpreted not as failure, to be marked with a red X, but as that part of an experiment that says "keep trying, we know there are other possibilities."

The fact that the librarian discoursed little in the Wabash program was in part due to students' suggestions that initially there was too much lecturing and not enough contact with the resources themselves. They wanted confrontation, not dissertation. They asked for more problems and more time to solve problems, *to do* and *to share*. They were ready to accept the 1, 2, 3 of the diving board, but after the basic steps, they wanted to jump in and swim.

Years ago, college president Henry Wriston noted that a student does not learn by being told how to use the library, but by using it.[6] More than a generation later, librarians are beginning to concur on a wide scale. Orientation is being seen more as an organic experience than as a trip.

Problems carefully constructed to illustrate the use of one resource invariably show students their way around the library much more effectively than a library tour or a lecture, because of the problem's relation to the students' needs. Learning how to use the *Essay and General Literature Index* really means first having a need for critical or expository material, knowing how to use the card catalog, and knowing how to locate a book in a particular library. *Hearing* about EGLI will not accomplish as much. To use *Biological Abstracts,* a student has to figure out the CROSS and BASIC indexes in relation to a specific need, not a vague generality.

The problem-solving experience related to the real need, therefore, seems to encourage the kind of exploration that helps students to comprehend the underlying logic of the library. Most people forget or never stopped to think that philosophers were the original classifiers; it has long been an art to integrate material. A student given a classification number to locate in the BFs will not learn as much about how to find things as the student challenged to find worthwhile material for a paper on a specific phase of experimental psychology. The latter will have a lot of questions to ask. *That is the point of the problem: to raise questions rather than to encourage a nonquestioning "learning."*

Exploration can be frustrating and it is time-consuming, but it adds enormously to the learning process. It leaves something for the students to contribute, and recognizes them as persons with the capability of contributing. It also says you respect your students.

FOCUS THROUGH MODELS

In the program it seemed to make more sense for a student to examine one representative resource or "model" of a specific category and for the librarian to illustrate a category through one model (i.e., "index" as explained by reference to *Art Index*) rather than by memorizing details about many or explaining a whole span of indexes. The information explosion boggles the mind. The students learning how to use the *Social Sciences and Humanities Index* can focus on it as a representative of its family.

The important thing is that they learn the existence of the category "index" and what its work is, and that there are many, many kinds available—not only the model. This whittled-down approach makes it more possible for students to cope with the flood of resources without drowning in them.

Here is where the working involvement of many students is important. It is an awareness arouser. In a lab on indexes as a generic resource, the librarian could first explain the work of an index and the variety of them available in the particular library to serve the curricular needs of the college, use one only as a teaching model, and then assign problems that would illustrate as many as there are students to share the problem-solving experience: one to show how the *New York Times Index* was useful for a problem about the Nuremberg trials; another to show how the *Social Sciences and Humanities Index* is helpful for the study of espionage, etc.

In a lab with seven students, then, there would be exposure to the ideas of seven indexes, and a student would be conditioned to think when the need arises later, "Isn't there also an index for political science? for chemistry? of bibliography?"

The use of selected students to learn about the library in order to show others the way is another example of adding focus through the use of models. Seminar assistants became exemplars for the freshmen in the seminars and in-house advisers for the students in their residences. As models they helped others to integrate library use into their course work.

One student helped others in the Nuremberg trial seminars to learn how to use the library to find biographical information about the defendants, how to look up source accounts of the long-drawn-out trial, how to find and use the reports of the Tribunal, how to unearth studies of the moral and psychological impacts of the Nazi ideology, etc. This is making use of students as models, just as professors (or parents) serve as models. They set an example; they help solve problems. They are guides and pathfinders.

It might be noted here that upperclass assistants were programmed into seminars because it was felt that students might go to a fellow student for help before going to the authority figure.

A third way in which there was utilization of a model involves professors themselves. A professor interested in teaching a freshman seminar and utilizing a student assistant as bibliographic adviser was thought to be a model for other professors for the possibilities of more planned use of library resources and personnel.

An unexpected by-product of the Wabash plan was that assistants in some cases proved to be models for professors, by pointing out how assignments could be constructed to make better use of the library and helping them to organize the instruction so that students would *need* to use the library. Since it is really with professors that library use begins, this might be one way to get around the reluctance many teachers have to admit they don't know something they think they ought to know, as well as to encourage more advanced planning to utilize enriching resources. Students see this need for preplanning very clearly when they have all-around library experience. They know selection and acquisitions take time; they know some resources are better than others; they know media vary in effectiveness.

Finally, for the in-house students in particular (who, unlike seminar assistants, often worked away from the physical library, advising fellow boarders in the coffee shop, the dining room, or dorms) logs or research designs were mimeographed to serve as a model for the thought processes involved in research.

The log really asked the questions that need to be asked in a reference interview and provided for the written response: articulating the question (defining the negotiation), ascertaining what had been checked and/or needed to be rechecked, suggesting useful generic resources and following this, specific resources (if *index, which index?*), and suggesting keywords to use as subject headings.

It was decided that these logs or patterns for research be also kept at the reference desk for each reference encounter. Students who were not attached to either program often asked for copies to guide them as they were preparing a paper.

REAL EXPERIENCE

As has been noted, the library labs were for the most part of ten weeks' duration, in 90 minute sessions once a week.

Actual on-the-job experience followed. Students first had an internship at the reference desk, with the reference librarian near at hand, and after this trial period, worked at the desk in her absence or while she was involved in other work in the library. This was optional experience (some students simply didn't have time) and was in addition to the primary responsibility in seminars and residences.

It brought theory into practice even more sharply than the experiential lab problems since the element of responsibility to another human being had been added. Problems coming to the reference desk did not have the controlled situation of the lab or the specific subject orientations of the seminars, but might require the discovery of resources not dreamed of, really testing the adequacy of the pathfinder's preparation via the generic category route. "Do I need an index? the card catalog? a bibliography? some combination?" Here is where the generic approach became meaningful, for if specifics had been forgotten, principles remained.

The student on duty as decisionmaker guiding someone else's research problem really has a final exam on his hands at each reference encounter. And he has the added responsibility of remembering to show how, not tell all, to inspire clients to learn to find out for themselves, rather than dole it all out. The overall objective of any program instructing in the use of the library should be intellectual independence for all, viewing learning about the use of the library as one of the liberal arts.

Heads will shake in the profession. "Students alone at the reference desk? But they can't give *our* kind of service!" Probably not, but has professional service to date swelled the libraries with users? The question administrators are asking today is: "Are our resources being used?"

Good students are perceptive and know when they are over their heads. Assistants were advised it could happen (to them as well as to a librarian). They kept the log of the real (not directional) questions . . . the pathfinder model. When they could not solve a problem, they did what they could to give the client a start, and referred him to the librarian who would read the report of all encounters. Her suggestion and follow-up with the client was always transmitted to the student assistant who had had the trouble. If his need were urgent and the student could not wait, the assistant was able to call on the chief librarian or the library intern for immediate help.

The library profession's fear of involving students at the desk robs them of a most meaningful opportunity to learn. This fear, bred perhaps from the desire to have everything just perfect and under control, is not in keeping with the philosophy of learning through doing.

Wabash students were not totally autonomous at the desk, but they were trusted, and given responsibility. They were given guidelines for their interviews and their work was checked. And their peers came to them. Unfortunately, no statistics were kept to indicate whether students come to peers more or less frequently than to a professional.

OPPORTUNITY FOR CREATIVITY

Students at the reference desk had times when there were no clients looming in. These minutes were utilized in the learning experience and often added creatively to the library as a learning resource.

Shelf-reading the reference collection can be turned from a boring chore to a creative encounter with unknown resources. Reference assistants were taught to shelf read and were assigned so many shelves in the collection to read each time on duty, in rotation, with the instruction to take appealing and/or unknown books back to the desk (where they'd be personally visible to clients) in order to become familiar with them by browsing through them.

Their awareness of the collection was heightened considerably, and they enjoyed this freedom of choice in exploring. It often made a difference in their service; they seemed to remember books better, and to zero-in on them faster when they were needed than they could by the catalog route. They began to develop a feeling for the reference collection.

Students also signed up for a choice of one out of three projects that would have input for the library, as well as being a learning experience for them. Guided by a project design, they could take on a book-selection project (collection development in an area of interest to them), create and construct displays, or develop bibliographies for the vertical file, again in subject areas of interest to them. By this participation, they learned how to evaluate materials, they learned how to attract attention to important resources and how to decide resources were important, and they learned more about how to put the tools of bibliography to good use. In addition, students almost always cooperated in publishing a bibliography of the resources they found most useful in their seminars and/or labs. Several planned and wrote a student library handbook. An artist in the seminar group created an amusing bird's-eye view of the library for its cover. The *students*—not the librarian—created input for the library.

They experienced what a library is all about; it is felt that this affected positively their commitment to "library" and their own expectations of library—their critical faculties.

ENCOURAGEMENT OF CONCEPTUAL THINKING

In part, the preceding tenet gets into this one. It is worthwhile to communicate to students that a library is more than a place where information is gathered into neat learning packages. It is . . . civilization? . . . personal freedom? . . . heritage?

The generic-resources idea is an easily grasped concept that simplifies knowing how to use the library, and reduces thousands of possibilities for learning to the intelligent decisions involved in finding the necessary materials from only ten or 12 possible families of resources.

Another instance of encouraging conceptual thinking in the instructional program comes when students worked out "minicases" in the lab, after being graduated from factual problems. These were generated to show how the library responds to ideas or to a series of questions rather than isolated questions. Minicases usually involved discovery of many kinds of resources toward the development of a thesis.

Students can articulate other concepts in helping librarians to develop better libraries—if they are allowed to. Why shouldn't they give time to the thinking out of problems of accessibility, use of all media, and improving the quality of life in a library (environment)? They are the users. "The user defines the system."

Students in the program at Wabash were invited always to make suggestions for the improvement of the library and to articulate what the concept "library" meant to them. The library, in as many ways as possible, was presented to them as a gestalt for learning, not just as a collection of varied resources. They understood.

ABOLISHMENT OF THE MYSTIQUE

Too often, valuable library resources are considered out of bounds for students or not even considered as resources for students, "belonging" to technical services or available for faculty only. An attempt was made at Wabash to bring the whole library into the eminent domain via the seminar and in-house efforts.

Students learned how to use the shelf list along with the public catalog. They learned the use of *Books in Print,* the *National Union Catalog,* and the *Indiana List of Serials.* Tools previously, or at least too frequently considered part of the librarian's mystique ("I'll look it up for you"), were made accessible to them, even though they may have been physically kept in the office for use by staff. Old walls crumbled; the library became an open center. This possibility filtered through to freshmen in the seminars and to students who made use of in-house assistants, and in a way was a measure of the outreach of the student assistants.

PHASES IN TEACHING-LEARNING

There are stages of sophistication in using the library. Four-fifths of the instructional program really was devoted to learning how to find very specific, narrow information—one-step librarianship—through the use of one particular generic resource. It was intended to make all possibilities familiar ones.

In the week for indexes and abstracts, for example, students made many discoveries. An account of the Gulf of Tonkin incident could be found in the *New York Times Index*. A critique of *Steppenwolf* could be found in the *Essay and General Literature Index*. Studies on personal space were searched in *Psychological Abstracts*. These were all factual, and discovered through the use of one type of resource only, member "index" of the generic family.

But toward the last of the course of study, minicases were introduced that would require the use of more than one kind of reference tool, that were geared to the challenges of writing a paper.

Here is a minicase constructed in April 1973 for the second in-house program by a member of the first group who had volunteered to be a facilitator or coteacher for the second group:

> In the sixties, there was a play called *MacBird!* A student is doing a term paper on the play and wants to gain a critical understanding of it as a play itself, and then relate the production of the play to the First Amendment, discussing the political consequences of the issues involved. How would you "solve" this case? [7]

One such challenge at the reference desk, as one student put it, would "open up a whole can of worms!"

Minicases require a weaving together of resources to collate the necessary information. They are like a lawyer's brief, gathering together the necessary information. In the program, they were the dress rehearsal for helping other students on-the-job.

CONCLUSION

An attempt was made at Wabash to develop a library program to match the needs of a liberal education. It is acknowledged in our discipline that one way of doing this is to develop a sense of sharing in instruction between faculty and librarian so that courses can be enriched by building need for library use into the fabric of the course. This is an area where a vast amount still needs to be done, and time allocated to do it properly. It is an area where faculty are apt to demur: "It can't be done that far ahead," and where librarians (including experimenters) are apt to be too bogged down to insist. This was true at Wabash just as anywhere else; the problem wasn't solved, but it was apparent.

The coordinating effort takes time. It is a scholarly effort that cannot easily be squeezed into an overprogrammed day. It requires a new look at reference work loads. Students are entitled to its benefits.

Supportive of the liberal arts idea in the first years of the Wabash program are the accent on the lateral quality of the library (the breadth of possibilities rather than the narrowness of "answer"); students' freedom to explore and their responsibility for their own learning; rejection of the authoritarian or prescriptive classroom style; acknowledgment, synectics-wise, of the creative possibilities of sharing knowledge with peers; and respect paid to two-way communication between establishment and user.

Rather than being a "freshman program," the Wabash program might better be called "Project Awareness," indirectly affecting freshmen through model students and reaching out in widening circles to other students and faculty.

The infancy of the program certainly illustrated that learning to use the library well is not simply a matter of knowing Winchell.

NOTES

1. Patricia B. Knapp, quoted in "The Library, the Undergraduate, and the Teaching Faculty," a paper presented at the Institute on Training for Service in Undergraduate Libraries at the University Library, University of California, San Diego, August 17–21, 1970, p. 12.

2. Robert S. Taylor, *The Making of a Library: The Academic Library in Transition* (New York: Becker and Hayes, Inc., 1972), p. 6.

3. The term generic refers to the well-known "families" of resources—index, abstract, catalog, encyclopedia, dictionary, bibliography, handbook or companion, gazetteer, atlas, and also review and biographical resources. Such resources are also called gates, help, pathfinders, etc. Endless titles need not be memorized if the concept of generic resources is understood and one has knowledge of how/where to find them.

4. The programmed text utilized was *Library Skills: A Program of Self-Instruction* (New York: McGraw-Hill Book Co., 1970), a very good aid, but it was the hope of the librarian some day to write one specifically for these programs, one with a greater degree of sophistication and relevance to liberal arts undergraduates.

5. Carnegie Commission of Higher Education, *The Fourth Revolution: Instructional Technology in Higher Education; a Report and Recommendation* (New York: McGraw-Hill, 1972).

6. Henry M. Wriston, *The Nature of a Liberal College* (Appleton, Wisconsin: Lawrence College Press, 1937), pp. 64–65.

7. Constructed by Bruce Ong of Elkhart, Indiana, now a student at Oxford.

A LIBRARY PROGRAM FOR OPEN ADMISSIONS

Patricia Senn Breivik
*Assistant Dean, Pratt Institute, Graduate
School of Library and Information Science*

A library enrichment program designed to meet the particular needs of "open admissions" students at Brooklyn College was conducted on a limited basis during the spring and fall semesters of 1972. Sponsored by the Brooklyn College Department of Educational Services and using the facilities of the college library, the program was carefully structured to determine what role, if any, library-based instruction could play in the academic success of disadvantaged college freshmen. Many white students, in addition to the normally anticipated black and Puerto Rican students, were enrolled in these courses.

The library proposed three main behavioral objectives for the students: to perceive informational sources, i.e., libraries, as a means to success; to gain confidence in use of libraries, and to derive pleasure from use of library sources. To accomplish these objectives the areas of library instruction would be based on the students' immediate needs in relation to a remedial writing course they were taking, and the instruction would be directed to assisting them to succeed in that course.

The Department of Educational Services was, of course, primarily interested in the first behavioral objective. To determine academic success, open-topic writing assignments were to be given to students near the beginning and the end of the semester. These students' "gain" in competence would be matched against that of students in another section taught by the same professor, but without the library enrichment. The score for each paper would be the average assigned to it by five professors of English after identifying marks were removed.

The library's share of the program consisted of an hour of instruction each week, and regular contact with the professor assured that each library session was as closely related as possible to the English material being covered. The time was divided between instruction and in-library work by the students, and no homework was assigned. The English professor and the librarian informed students from the outset that the library-based instruction was an integral part of the course, that it would provide them with information important to the successful completion of their papers, and that their library "grade" would be determined on the basis of how many assignments were completed.

The program was extended to a second semester in order to include sections being taught by a second professor, and at that time it was broadened in scope. During the second semester a more traditional form of library instruction was added and given to the professor's sections when they were not involved in the principal experiment. The results of this expanded library enrichment were then compared with the other, first-semester findings. This extra instruction comprised three one-hour library sessions respectively devoted to (1) the basic concept of information and library use, including a tour of the Brooklyn College Library, (2) how to obtain information from books, including the use of the card catalog, and (3) how to obtain information from nonbook materials, including the use of indexes. The professor scheduled each hour of "traditional" library instruction at the point in his curriculum he deemed it would be most advantageous.

In conducting the experiment the biggest problem was what materials to use with the students. Although the course content and professors' teaching styles were studied before the experiment began, materials, for the most part, had to be developed as the first semester progressed, and then reworked and rearranged during the second semester.

Six principles were carefully followed:

1. The material should be approached from the viewpoint of student need and not that of a well-rounded library and research skills program. This meant that much attention was paid to areas not traditionally considered the prerogative of libraries, e.g., how to pick topics for papers and how to determine main ideas in books and articles.

2. No library tool should be taught per se, but only as the means to success in writing a paper and success in the course. Therefore, card catalog analytics including subject tracings were discussed at length for the help they could provide in evaluating the worth of available materials in relation to research needs, but atlases were never mentioned during the term.

3. The material taught should have immediate application through on-hand use and, when possible, be adapted to that week's writing assignment. Thus, a pattern often followed was 25 minutes of instruction and 25 minutes of work in the library.

4. Students should be effectively exposed to the wide variety of materials available in a library. For example, each student looked at a different specialized dictionary and shared something about it with his or her class.

5. Students should be taught to evaluate the usefulness of one type of information over another and one tool over another. Thus, students contrasted the information found in *Collier's Encyclopedia* with the *World Book*, the information available in the pamphlet file with that available in books.

6. Students should be shown methods for effectively handling information. For example, a system for taking notes on 3 x 5 cards was demonstrated.

RESPONSES

Faculty and administration response to the program was encouraging. Both instructors were library oriented before they entered in on the experiment, but one of the professors confessed to the librarian that she was ashamed to admit she was unfamiliar with much of the material presented to her students. Both professors became effective promoters of the library program with their colleagues.

Louis McG. Walker, chairman of the Department of Educational Services, summed up his feeling one day by saying that he had to deal with 5,000 students and couldn't afford to give them what the weekly program provided. He concluded, however, that he could give something more to more of them. With one librarian already employed by his department at the beginning of the library enrichment program, Professor Walker has since added two more librarians to his staff (one for Brooklyn College's downtown campus and one to work with a remedial reading program), and he is planning a series of videotapes to provide basic informational concepts.

But the greatest reward came from the response of the students themselves. The two classes varied considerably (chiefly due to student reactions to two very different professors) in their interclass relationships and their conception of the librarian's relation to the professor and the course. There were a few students, of course, who had almost insurmountable educational difficulties. But with these exceptions the students' general enthusiasm and appreciation for their growing confidence in informational activities was most heartwarming.

The only criticisms elicited from one class were (1) that a week apart was too long a stretch of time for the meetings in the library (the students claimed they tended to forget too much between sessions) and (2) that they needed to have the course (both in writing and information skills) before or concentrated early in the semester, because they needed the input for their other courses that required them to write term papers.

The following dialogue occurred with the other class one day when students were complaining about the lack of instruction in writing and research skills:

Student A: This kind of learning should be exploited in junior high school and in high school.

Librarian: I agree with this. For instance with library things, I think children should start learning in first grade . . .

Student A (*Interrupting*): I didn't even know there existed a *Readers' Guide to Periodical Literature*. I didn't know there were books with quotations. I didn't know there were summaries of books 600 pages long made in two paragraphs. I didn't know this.

Student B: I didn't know there is a book for everything—whatever you want to look for, short stories or quotations.

Student A: I only knew there was one type of dictionary. I didn't know there were psychology dictionaries, sociology dictionaries. "Look in the dictionary—

Websters, Websters." Everything is Websters. But if you are doing a course in history there could be a historical dictionary.

Librarian: There are.

Student A: There is! I didn't know this.

Student B: I thought I didn't know it because I didn't go to high school. I only have eighth grade. But now you went to high school, and then you say you didn't even know it.

Student A: You'd be surprised! You'd be surprised!

IMPLICATIONS

The statistics on the experiment won't be completed for a while. At worst they will be victim to the limited time available for the study; at best they will only confirm what is already known: that library enrichment can be effective. Beyond this, however, the experiment does raise a rather interesting question: If library-based instruction can prove so meaningful in remedial college programs, what could it mean in the educational program of academically prepared students?

This does not mean that the weekly instruction is necessarily the answer to collegiate informational problems, but the background research that went into the development of this program and the results at Brooklyn College point to several inescapable conclusions:

1. We need further research and experimentation into different methods for such instruction, including built-in evaluative procedures.

2. We need a clearing house (perhaps the American Library Association Instruction in the Use of Libraries Committee) for the dissemination of evaluative information.

3. Remedial programs associated with open-admissions policies often offer a particularly favorable climate for establishing such programs.

4. Library-based instructional programs will work best if developed with the cooperation of the teaching faculty.

Librarians do have a significant contribution to make in the educational program of their institutions; and, along with their struggles for academic status, it is to be hoped that they will assume this responsibility.

GRADUATE REFERENCE ASSISTANTS AT BROWN UNIVERSITY

CONNIE F. EVRARD
Assistant Director of Admission; formerly Reference Librarian, Brown University

ELIZABETH S. SCHUMANN
Head, Reference Department, Rockefeller Library, Brown University

JANET M. SWIFT
Reference Librarian, Rockefeller Library, Brown University

Brown University in Providence, Rhode Island, founded in 1764, is the seventh oldest institution of higher learning in the nation. The Graduate School has gained in size and importance in the past few decades, but about four-fifths of the student body is still made up of undergraduates. While policy and planning maintain Brown's student enrollment below the numbers declared by its two close neighbors in the Ivy League, Harvard and Yale, its libraries have grown rapidly over the years and now have a collection of about 2 million items. This collection comprises rich and varied holdings providing a wealth of research materials to all students. Thus, the Brown undergraduates have at their disposal an old and voluminous library, a library with all the idiosyncrasies of a venerable institution. The problem: will undergraduates learn how to use these resources to their best advantage?

Over the years various schemes have been tried—compulsory exercises in library orientation, guided tours, some talks to classes—but no one overall plan seemed to meet the problem. In the meantime, of course, sweeping changes in curriculum, encouragement of independent study, and the continued acceleration of library expansion made the situation more acute. At the same time as the students were being given greater freedom in planning their university education, they were being asked to take more responsibility for developing academic self-reliance within an increasingly complex collection.

In 1964 the new John D. Rockefeller, Jr., Library was opened; 1971 saw the completion and opening of the new Sciences Library. Both buildings are organized on the open-stack plan in order to give users easy access to the bulk of the general collection. Study carrels line the outer walls of many of the stack areas.

This very brief review of the Brown Library situation leads to the conclusion that it will probably be only the exceptional student with a high degree of tenacity or bibliographic sophistication who will be able to make optimal use of the material offered. The present emphasis on independent study can compound the problem by giving the bright students an exaggerated sense of confidence in their own capabilities. They do not realize that native talent is not a substitute for knowledge and experience in research techniques, and they are often too proud to approach a member of the library staff when a problem does arise.

Several years ago, some of the reference librarians thought that it might be possible to augment the services of the reference staff through use of students especially trained in reference work. Not only could these students serve at reference desks during extended hours, but they might be available for special service to other undergraduates during regular hours. It was thought that the undergraduates might be less hesitant to approach one of their peers than to ask for help from an older librarian.

A pilot project prompted by this idea was organized by Peter Dollard, then chief reference librarian, for the academic year 1969–1970. Four undergraduate students were enrolled in the program on a work-study basis. Each was given a thorough orientation of the library in its various departments and functions and a 60-hour crash course in reference sources. The trainees worked the rest of the year at the reference desks; they also compiled basic bibliographies in their major fields for the use of undergraduates.

In his report on the program in June 1970, Mr. Dollard noted that "the purpose of the program was to make a preliminary determination of the feasibility of letting students assume partial responsibility for some of the reference duties normally carried out by professional reference librarians." Reading of the report shows that some aspects of the work-study pilot project were more successful than others. It was remarked that "what the student trainees might have gained in approachability was more than compensated for by the broader library experience of the professional reference librarians." Dollard also noted that "the trainees did not demonstrate that their presumed subject competence enabled them to produce guides that were superior to what could be produced more easily by the regular reference staff."

Actually the greatest benefit of the work-study program was to the four students themselves. They found the library training useful in the pursuit of their own studies. Two of them worked later as regular undergraduate student assistants in the Reference Department and performed very capably.

After the experience with this pilot project, some staff members thought that perhaps graduate student assistants might be good subjects for an experimental program. Many of them would still have the presumed "approachability" of a student, but greater expertise in a chosen subject field. Accordingly a proposal was made to the Council on Library Resources outlining a five-year program involving, altogether, 52 graduate students. In the spring of 1970 a grant was awarded by CRL and the National Endowment for the Humanities, the joint fundings to be matched with university funds. The purpose of the grant is to conduct the proposed five-year program to see whether the use of trained graduate student reference assistants can improve the quality of reference service for the undergraduates.

The director of libraries is principal investigator for the Assistant Program; the training and day-to-day administration are carried out by the chief reference librarian and one of the reference librarians acting together as co-coordinators. An advisory committee of faculty members is appointed by the provost of the university to meet with the director of libraries, the associate director of libraries, and the two coordinators. Together the whole group reviews the operation of the program, offers constructive criticism, and suggests guidelines for future activities.

At this writing the program has been in operation for more than three years. The fourth-year group is about to finish its training sessions and take on the standard assistantship work load for the academic year: a combination of desk duty and department/library liaison work. A description of the details of the program follows.

SELECTION OF ASSISTANTS

Eight assistants were appointed for 1970–1971; ten for 1971–1972 and 1972–1973; 12 for 1973–1974, and 12 more will be named for 1974–1975. Assistants are selected in March of each year from candidates nominated by each department. To be eligible for consideration, an individual must be a graduate student in good academic standing whose fellowship application has been approved by the graduate school. No more than two candidates may be nominated by a department. Faculty members are asked to write letters of support. Because applicants typically outnumber positions by a 3–1 ratio and a rather complex set of qualities is sought in each appointee, the candidates then go through a series of interviews at the library. The coordinators of the program and associate director of libraries meet with each prospective assistant to explain the goals of the program and the duties an assistant is expected to carry out. This meeting is followed by an interview with the director of libraries. Finally, the candidate is interviewed by the member of the Faculty Advisory Committee who is in the field most closely related to that of the graduate student. Each interviewer is provided with a checklist of criteria on which to rate the candidates (Appendix 1).

After all interviews are completed, the coordinators, associate director, director, and Faculty Advisory Committee meet to make selections. The choice is always difficult since the nominees have already been screened by their departments and are all highly qualified. A pool of alternates must also be chosen in case anyone declines the offer of an assistantship.

An attempt is made to represent as many different disciplines as possible and to achieve a balance among the humanities, social sciences, and sciences. Until this year, however, few scientists have been attracted to the program, as research grants for them have been more readily available than in other fields. Each year's class of successful graduate students is notified of their assistantship status in May and informed in early June of the summer training calendar.

TRAINING

New graduate reference assistants report the first week in July and complete their training program the last day of August. The program could be termed a selective, but intensive, orientation to reference sources and, indeed, to the whole pattern of functions within a university library. Each year the first month of training is designed with a tight concentration of work on the resources themselves, the second month is planned for rigorous use of the new knowledge. During August, assistants write bibliographic guides, carry out specific biographic assignments for the *Dictionary of American Biography* (which is edited at Brown University), and begin supervised sessions of desk duty.

In the early weeks of the course, students work in clusters of three or four with each of four instructors for maximal personal attenton. Approximately 140 hours of reference instruction and assignments are offered. Acceleration is such that each of the ten reference units—for example "Sources of Bibliographic Information," "Encyclopedias," "The Card Catalog," must be completed within a day or two. Provided with a detailed syllabus, learners are encouraged to take notes as sources are presented and to review all titles independently. Instructors distribute unit worksheets and lead group discussions of the questions following periods of individual investigation. Three comprehensive tests utilizing books from the entire syllabus give unity to the course and aid recall of earlier material. Comprehensive tests include reference questions drawn from past experience with undergraduates at Rockefeller Library.

Aside from the standard form division units on reference sources, practical, on-the-job summer training is scheduled for trainees in government documents, circulation, cataloging, order, and periodicals. It seems essential that the new assistants clarify their understanding of the interrelationships of departments, realizing that the boundaries of patron service extend beyond the physical limits of the Reference Department.

Substantial summer study alterations seemed desirable after the first year. Candid discussions between instructors and assistants showed the need for study of a deeper and wider range of reference titles, more comprehensive testing, and earlier desk experience, with correspondingly less time for extradepartmental orientation. Assistants have been nearly unanimous in acclaiming the value of the summer course in their own advanced studies, as well as acknowledging its necessity to prepare them for a year of assisting undergraduates.

LIAISON WORK

In addition to nine hours of desk duty a week, the assistants each spend six hours serving as a liaison person between their department and the library. Such work varies and is tailored to the needs of the individual department. All assistants speak to classes about the use of the library and ask faculty members to place their names on course syllabi. Several departments have asked assistance to do some searching and coordination of faculty book orders. Sometimes this has involved checking book catalogs against library holdings. A sociology assistant, for example, checked to see if there were any systematic weaknesses of coverage in particular subareas. A unique project has been the development of a card-file system for use in the Classics Department of approximately 400 classics-related periodicals currently received by the library. The intent of this liaison work is to promote closer cooperation between the library and faculty.

A major activity undertaken by nearly all assistants is the compilation of an introductory bibliography in their subject specialty. These attractively printed booklets serve as guides to the basic reference tools in each field and are designed primarily to aid the undergraduate beginning research in an area rather than to serve the more advanced student. So far, 24 brief guides have been published, and four more are at the editing stage. Outside requests for these publications have been frequent enough to warrant charging 15 cents per guide to cover postage and handling costs.

EVALUATION

Anyone who has attempted to measure the efficacy of reference services will appreciate the problems faced in evaluation during this five-year project. It would be pleasant to draw up statistics emphasizing increased *provision* of service, but such data would say nothing about the user.

How has performance and behavior of the undergraduate patron at Brown University libraries changed during the program? One way to determine effectiveness is the information poll. A simple questionnaire sent to 10 percent of the undergraduate student body has gone out each of the three years just completed. Content of the questionnaire is presented in Appendix 2. Each year data obtained are placed on punched cards for ease in studying relationships of the various components within the poll. Frequency tabulations show acceptable validity and reliability because of high return (83–90 percent) and excellent degree of correspondence of sample to universe.

The term "use of the library" is open to individual interpretation, but Brown students populate their libraries in large numbers. Approximately 30 percent use the facilities nearly every day, while an additional 40–45 percent appear once or more a week. To no one's surprise, students using the services of graduate reference assistants are likely to be those who spend more time in the library and who also seek help from the professional reference librarians. Concentrators in areas of the humanities avail themselves of the service in larger numbers than those specializing in the social sciences or "hard sciences."

Since awareness of the program is integral to its use, this variable is measured each year. Knowledge of the program moved from 58 percent the first year to 73 percent the second, then down to 60 percent for 1972–1973. Each year about a third of the group who had heard of the program sought out the assistants for aid.

Those seeking a steady rise in use as the program matures and becomes publicized through an increasing variety of media have thus far failed to find it. Planners and evaluators of the undertaking must constantly bear in mind that they are dealing with *informal* library instruction, initiated *by the student*. Motivation of the student is critical. In the end, it is the student who must seek out the graduate assistant at an appropriate time. Reference problems differ markedly among disciplines in quantity and quality. Cooperation and involvement of faculty in promoting the program vary.

The dedication and aggressiveness of the individual reference assistant are still other variables. The percentage of people in each group who seem to grasp the basic principles of reference service has grown each year. It is a rare occurrence to find an assistant neglecting assigned duties or sitting at the desk looking disinterested. After the summer training and a few weeks' desk experience most of the assistants are able to handle fairly complex questions. If they can't find the answers, they usually know where to go or whom to ask to find out whether there are any answers.

There is reason to assume that benefits to the undergraduate surpass the degree of usage assessed by the poll. Because of the wide range of department/library endeavors, no attempt is presently being made to measure the value of the liaison work of the assistants. There is now, at the end of three years, an obvious accumulation of positive effects simply through continued availability and steady outflow of the bibliographic guides produced in this time. More than 20,000 copies have come off the university presses.

While these guides have probably been one of the most successful aspects of the program, they have also been one of the most time-consuming. Very few of the assistants have been able to turn in finished products. The reference librarians have spent many hours checking and editing, and the department secretary has spent as many again in typing and layouts. Provision should probably have been made in the original proposal for these added activities.

SUMMING UP

A complete evaluation of the Graduate Reference Assistants Program cannot be made until mid-1975, at the departure of the final group of workers. By that time, two undergraduate classes will have had the opportunity to enjoy the services of the assistants. It will be interesting to see whether the assistants will have become a part of the library picture for these two classes. Even more useful will be some determination of whether the lowerclass students who have taken advantage of the assistants' services will miss them if the program is not continued in some form.

Whatever the future of the program, there have been many positive features for the professional staff who have been so intimately involved in training and supervision. Librarians at Brown find that contact with the inquiring minds and the variety of subjects represented provides much intellectual stimulation. The majority of the assistants are gifted and cooperative students with whom it is a pleasure to work. Many of them have been grateful for the opportunity to acquire bibliographic skills useful to them in their future scholarship. The long-term effects of 52 library-minded young scholars set loose in other academic settings may be considerable.

Not least in the scale of positive effects is the increased understanding that has grown up among faculty, librarians, administrators, and students as all work together to learn about and improve undergraduate library instruction.

APPENDIX 1
BROWN UNIVERSITY GRADUATE REFERENCE ASSISTANTS PROGRAM—CHECKLIST FOR RATING CANDIDATES

CRITERIA FOR LIBRARY PANEL USE

Assign a value of 1 to 4 depending on your judgment of the presence of attribute or condition. A total may give some indication of the comparative standing of candidates.

(1) Department of candidate. (Greater weight may be assigned to departments not previously represented, larger in numbers of faculty or students, or broader in scope.)

1 ___ 2 ___ 3 ___ 4 ___

(2) Interest expressed in goals of project.

1 ___ 2 ___ 3 ___ 4 ___

(3) Ability to work with undergraduates.

1 ___ 2 ___ 3 ___ 4 ___

(4) Interest in bibliography.

1 ___ 2 ___ 3 ___ 4 ___

(5) Previous work experience (library work, teaching assistantship, research assistantship).

1 ___ 2 ___ 3 ___ 4 ___

(6) Intangibles—Panel's judgment of attitude, approachability, enthusiasm, range of intellectual interests, etc.

1 ___ 2 ___ 3 ___ 4 ___

APPENDIX 2
BROWN UNIVERSITY GRADUATE REFERENCE ASSISTANTS PROGRAM EVALUATION—INFORMATION POLL

QUESTIONNAIRE

Please assist the librarians of Brown University in providing better service to you by completing this simple survey now and depositing it in the campus mail:

(1) My field of concentration is

[ ] humanities
[ ] social science

[ ] physical science
[ ] biological science

(2) I use the library

[ ] almost every day
[ ] once or more a week
[ ] once or more a month
[ ] almost never

(3) I have asked the reference librarians for assistance

[ ] three times or more
[ ] once or twice
[ ] never

(4) I have heard of the graduate reference assistant program

[ ] Yes   [ ] No

(5) I have asked one of the ten reference assistants for help

[ ] more than once
[ ] once
[ ] never

(6) After graduation I intend to

[ ] attend graduate school
[ ] enter military service
[ ] begin a job
[ ] other

(7) Year in college

[ ] freshman
[ ] sophomore
[ ] junior
[ ] senior

(8) Sex

[ ] M   [ ] F

NAME _____

[NOTE: Each questionnaire was coded so that even if the respondent was not identified by name on the questionnaire, it was possible to ascertain which poll sheets had been filed and thus carry on follow-up activities.]

VIDEOTAPE: A CASE STUDY

Patricia J. Walsh
Library Learning Center Coordinator,
Junior High School, Glen Ellyn, Illinois

This is a discussion of the use of videotape for educating library users at Glen Ellyn Junior High School, which has an enrollment of 1,000 seventh and eighth graders. The social studies department relies heavily on the Library Learning Center for resource materials for their instructional units. These and other students need to be introduced to the types of available reference tools and the location of these tools in the reference area of the center. Videotape rather than slides was selected as the educational medium because it was desirable to show the character walking around the reference area in order to establish the location of the titles being mentioned. Also needed was a format that would allow for dialogue between students and the librarian.

Each social studies teacher received a list of types of available reference books (atlases, almanacs, biographical dictionaries, *Readers' Guide,* and various titles in our United States history section). The teachers were asked to indicate those tools about which they believed their students should learn and also to note any additional titles they believed should be listed. The return on these lists was 100 percent with no additional titles being suggested.

The teachers who seemed most interested in the project were contacted personally and asked for their assistance in finding students to help with the acting. Student library pages were a good source of help.

A basic script was developed along the lines of a student's experiences meeting the reference books as characters in a dream. The students who tried out for the various parts had many suggestions, and these were incorporated into the final script. Among the things they suggested was that an Alfred Hitchcock format be used, since one of the students did an imitation of Alfred Hitchcock. For that matter any talent for imitation and any television program popular with students could have been employed. The students insisted on having a commercial. They changed their lines in many instances to make the character they were portraying seem more real. Following-up on the ideas suggested by these students was a key factor in making the final product effective with other students.

The student audiovisual crew operated the videotape equipment. In addition, the district art director, Don Storey, who was familiar with the idiosyncrasies of the equipment, worked with us.

One camera, a videotape recorder on a cart, a microphone on a stand, a TV monitor on a cart (the camera was not equipped with a monitor), and many extension cords were used. The students learned how to clean the recording heads and cleaned them regularly during taping.

Staff for operating the equipment included one student for the videotape recorder, one at the camera, and one for the microphone. Students were also needed to operate the phonograph and tape recorder for sound effects. These same students worked on props. Black pin-back letters on light blue background worked well for our title, settings, and commercial. For the credits, black felt-tip markers were used on light blue bulletin board backing paper that was rolled slowly past the camera. Since white caused glare, the students were advised to avoid white in their costumes.

The first rehearsal was for the cast and students handling the sound-effects. The students walked through their parts and learned where to stand, walk, sit, etc. They needed direction in moving slowly, looking at the camera, and speaking distinctly. Arrangements for costumes and props were discussed at this meeting. Students developed their own costumes, with suggestions and offers of assistance from others. Their cooperation and ingenuity gave the costumes and props a special flavor.

The second rehearsal was for the camera and sound crew. Camera and microphone positions were worked out. Our script called for moving equipment, and the floor plan for the equipment was worked out. Close-ups of books presented a problem because with our equipment it was not possible to zoom-in close enough to pick up the print on the book covers. A second camera would have allowed us to cut from the character to the book and back again. Color would have been a big improvement for identifying books over the black-and-white television system.

At the following meetings of the cast and crew, taping began. Numerous scenes had to be taped a second or third time to achieve the desired results. The taping was done after school when the library was quiet. The 13-minute final tape took more than four hours of actual taping time to complete. A copy of the script that we developed is presented in the Appendix.

It is suggested that plenty of lead be left at the beginning of the tape, since this is where damage to the tape is most likely to occur. At the end of each scene when the videorecorder was stopped, the tape was moved back manually one inch before proceeding to prevent distortion.

Our social studies teachers are invited to bring their classes to see our production immediately preceding their first assignment involving the library. The teachers accept our emphasis on having the students use the information as soon as possible after being introduced to it.

In the library classroom, the tape is shown to one class of students at a time. The students are told the objectives of the lesson: to learn the types of reference books available for social studies and to discover the location of these books.

Each student is given a list of titles mentoned in the lesson and instructed to watch for them. The students are divided into teams and each team selects a "captain." After the tape is shown, a relay race takes place. At a signal, members of each team go to the reference area one at a time, locate one of the titles, and return to their team. The first team to complete the requirements is declared the winner. This competitive relay-type exercise in conjunction with the video-tape lesson seems to stimulate interest and enhance learning.

When all teams have finished (the race takes about eight minutes) the titles are called off one by one, and each team holds up the books. The student who found the book then returns it to the proper place in the reference area. The classroom teacher watches the reference area to referee the race and to see that the books are returned properly.

The students enjoy seeing their library and the student actors on the TV screen. Although the production is far from the professional programs they are accustomed to seeing, they seem to enjoy it.

The social studies teachers have reacted favorably to the lesson. Some of them discover titles they were unaware of. The students learn to use the books as they need to use them during the year through individual guidance by the library staff, the classroom teacher, or their fellow students. This is determined by accessibility of the librarians and classroom teachers. By the end of the eighth grade year, there are fewer students needing individual guidance.

The experience of working with students in creating an instructional lesson is a rewarding one. Sharing the finished lesson with other students has been a unique and enjoyable experience.

APPENDIX
VIDEOTAPE SCRIPT DEVELOPED AND USED BY GLEN ELLYN (ILLINOIS) JUNIOR HIGH SCHOOL LIBRARY LEARNING CENTER FOR LIBRARY-USER EDUCATION—1972

Camera on title: REFERENCE BOOKS FOR SOCIAL STUDIES

Music: *Theme from Hitchcock*

Hitchcock enters: HITCHCOCK: (*Facing camera*) Good evening. (*Cut music*) Tonight our story shall be concerned with a certain library. A junior high school library learning center. We have a wonderful cast for our little story. Ahhhhh, but now our time is growing short because our sponsor demands a word of interest.

Dissolve to close-up of newspaper held by student: Music: *Theme from "Mission Impossible"*—10 seconds

STUDENT: (*Closing paper and looking at camera*) Reading is what's happening. I said, reading is what's happening. Hey! What are you doing?

Long shot of students at table reading: STUDENTS: (*To camera*) Reading.

Move to close-up of sign:	*Music up*
	GET IT AT YOUR LIBRARY!
Dissolve to Hitch-cock:	*Keep sound five seconds*
	HITCHCOCK: Well, here I am again to show you the location of our story which begins in a certain bedroom.

Move to close-up of sign:

Music up

GET IT AT YOUR LIBRARY!

Dissolve to Hitch-cock:

Keep sound five seconds

HITCHCOCK: Well, here I am again to show you the location of our story which begins in a certain bedroom.

Opening on full view of bedroom scene, student at desk:

MOTHER: (*Off camera*) Jackie, are you sleeping?

JACKIE: No, Mom, I'm trying to get my report done for social studies.

Mother enters:

MOTHER: It's after ten o'clock. Turn off that light and go to bed.

JACKIE: But I haven't even got my report started yet. It's due Thursday.

MOTHER: Well, you should have worked on it instead of watching television all night. Get to sleep now. I mean it! (*Exits*)

(*Jackie covers her head and groans*)

Blur out to indicate dream

Open to full view of teacher and chalkboard:

SOCIAL STUDIES
    ROOM 107

TEACHER: May I have your attention, class? You have each received a list of topics for research. Jackie, have you selected your topic?

JACKIE: (*Off camera*) Yes, Ms. Young. The Ku Klux Klan.

TEACHER: Use at least five different sources for your information. Remember to tell who, what, when, where, and why. Show why the topic you selected is important. Jackie, you'd better get busy.

Dissolve to entrance to library

Patriotic music

Doors open to full view of U.S. History:

Cut music

U.S. HISTORY: Well, Jackie, it's about time you came to the library. You don't know me, but I represent the United States history books in the reference section here. Come on in and get acquainted.

Camera follows
U.S. History:

U.S. HISTORY: I think there are some things you need to know about this library. We books are here just brimful of help and you've been ignoring us all along. Like, remember when you were studying Illinois history? You probably never knew about all of us books written just about Illinois. We're getting so full of dust (*Picks up a volume and blows flour off*) we're choking. And look at this set of books, *Annals of America*. Primary source material. What people living in our past wrote about at the time. Here's the *Dictionary of American History* in six volumes. And over here, *Messages and Papers of the Presidents, Documents of American History,* and *Album of American History*. All the books here are quick sources of information for you on United States history.

Close-up of titles
mentioned

Move to full view
of biography
section

W. C. Fields
enters:

W. C. FIELDS: (*Strolls into picture*) Good day.
JACKIE: (*Off camera*) Who are you?
FIELDS: May I present my card? (*Holds up card: W. C. Fields 920*)
JACKIE: (*Reading*) W. C. Fields, 920. What kind of book is that?
FIELDS: 920 is biography. I've got files on everybody who ever did anything important. Can you think of anybody important?
JACKIE: George Washington?
FIELDS: What a euphonious appellation. Yes, you'll find George in *The Dictionary of American Biography*. He's been dead a long time. (*Exits whistling*)

Close-up of titles
as mentioned

Betsy Ross enters:

BETSY ROSS: Hi, Jackie. I'm Betsy Ross and I'm in the *Dictionary of American Biography,* too. You'll find my old friend George and lots of other dead Americans there. (*Exits*)

J.F.K. enters:

J.F.K.: Yesh. Ah, fine. On the other hand, ah if you were interested in ah contemporary individualsh, let me ah shay ah this about them. In my ah judgment, the ah following biographical dictionaries could be appropriated for your advantage: *Current Biography, Who's Who in America,* and of course ah *Webster's Biographical Dictionary* and ah others like it in one volume. Now, ah, speaking of current individualsh, could you identify yourself please?

Move to atlas stand and Snoopy sitting on top of atlas stand:

MUSIC: *"Snoopy and the Red Baron"*

JACKIE: Snoopy! What are you doing?
SNOOPY: I'm riding my Sopwith Camel.
JACKIE: Good grief! Even I know that's no airplane. That's where the atlases are stored.
SNOOPY: Correct! I'm flying right over the Mississippi River.
JACKIE: Poor Snoopy. Get down off there now before you hurt yourself. That's no doghouse.
SNOOPY: An atlas house is even better than an old doghouse.

Lucy enters:

LUCY: (*Jumping out from behind atlas stand*) Hi there, Charlie Brown! Oooops. You're not Charlie Brown, but I'm Lucy and I know everything. 'Cause I know where aaaaaaall

Follow Lucy to encyclopedias:

the encyclopedias are in this library. Come on over here. I know how to use these encyclopedias, too. Sometimes you need to use the index to find out all the different places where the Ku Klux Klan is mentioned. Poor old Charlie Brown just looks at these encyclopedias with a pencil in one hand and tries to write down every word. But not me! I read about what I need to know and think about it after I read it and then I write it down. Then I look for information in more books. That's why I'm so smart. Because I think about things I read all the time. And I don't stop there. I go on and on. So just you go on. Get out of here. I've got lots to do. (*Picks up encyclopedia and starts reading fast*)

Move on to almanacs and full view of Faxwell Smart:

FAXWELL SMART: (*Looking at camera through large magnifying glass*) Stop right there! Have you got the facts, girl? 'Course you don't. I've got the facts. Some folks call me Faxwell Smart but I'm better known in literary circles as the almanac. Listen, I've heard you asking the librarian and your friends like, who's the imperial wizard of the KKK in America or what's the address of the Society of American Magicians. Did they know? 'Course not. Now (*picks up almanac*) if you pick up this almanac, you've really got the facts at your fingertips. Now let's see, (*looks into almanac*) would you believe . . .

Jackie enters:

JACKIE: (*Moves into picture and shakes Smart's hand*) Thanks, Fax. Hmmm. I wonder if the Ku Klux Klan has been in the news lately. Guess I'll take a look in the *Readers' Guide* while I'm here.

Follow Jackie to Readers' Guide *area:*   JACKIE: (*Sits down and looks into several volumes. Finds entry*) Here's something. I'll write this down and go get it now. (*Finds paper and pencil and begins to write and read aloud*) Murder in Mississippi by D. Whitehead. *Reader's Digest,* September 1970.
MOTHER: (*Off camera*) Jackie.

Open on bedroom scene and Jackie asleep at desk: MOTHER: (*Off camera*) Jackie!
JACKIE: (*Looking up startled*) Mom?

Mother enters: MOTHER: Jackie, you're really worried about that social studies report, aren't you? It's going to ruin your health.
JACKIE: Well, Mom, I think I'll be able to sleep now. I just remembered I can go to the library tomorrow and I can even check out that magazine and read it tomorrow night. Boy, what a dream I had. Talking books!!

Dissolve to Hitchcock: HITCHCOCK: The library has filmstrips showing how to use the books Jackie met in her dream. Come on in and get acquainted. I hope you enjoyed our little story. Here are the books you met once again. (*Exits*)

Book characters move across camera carrying one of the titles they represent and repeat the title

Camera on credits: Dissolve to silhouette of Hitchcock   MUSIC: *Theme from Hitchcock*

Enter Hitchcock: HITCHCOCK (*Moves into silhouette*)

THE CASE FOR INFORMATION OFFICERS

Maurice B. Line

*Director General, British Library Lending
Division, Boston Spa, United Kingdom*

This paper will stray somewhat outside the strict confines of "Educating the Library User"; partly because I am not sure that education is the only, or necessarily the best, way of learning, partly because it is not only library users who need to learn to handle information. Library users are by definition persons who have had the motivation to arrive at this particular source of information, whether they use it wisely and well or not; and, just as many of those who most need social welfare services do not use them, so, I suspect, there are vast numbers of people who need information who never come near a library. I shall then be concerned with *furthering the process of learning to handle and obtain information,* and with the role of information officers in this process. (After spending 20 years in university libraries, where I was involved in various kinds of instruction in library and information use, as a lecturer, day-to-day dispenser of information, organizer of courses, instigator, and investigator, I am now in a library without users. I hope that what I lack in current involvement may be made up by greater objectivity.)

Let us look first at the needs of people for information. Everyone at various times needs information of one kind or another. Much information is of an everyday kind that could be obtained through the media or from other people. The more demanding and intellectual a job, generally speaking, the more information is needed, both to train for it and to perform it. Some of this information can only, or best, be obtained from or through libraries; but we know that not all people go to libraries for it, and in some professions alternative, often elaborate, systems of supplying information are set up. As modern life increases in complexity, the need for information grows greater; so also does the volume of information available, the variety of media in which it is packaged, and the means of access to it. This applies as much to the social worker as to the research scientist.

The literature explosion has been well documented. Whether or not actual information is increasing at the same rate as the literature hardly affects the magnitude of the problem; even if what we are experiencing is merely a garbage explosion, it is no easier to search for valuable objects in garbage than among other valuable objects, particularly as the garbage is usually very carefully disguised. Traditionally, information has been recorded in print, mainly in books and journals; but this is changing, and sound recording, video recording, and a variety of other media, pure and hybrid, are becoming more common. In a few years, videocassettes are likely to be in most homes, for recreation and instruction. As well as an explosion of literature, therefore, the growth rate of which incidentally does not appear to be affected by the growth of other media, we have an explosion of other forms of recorded information.

To cope with the increasing problem of finding what is wanted among a growing amount of what is not wanted, information systems, too, are exploding. New indexes, abstracts, reviews, and current awareness bulletins appear monthly. More and more references are being stored for retrieval by computer, and more and more information is being recorded in microform. In a few years' time, we shall be lucky to have much information at all in a form that is readable by the naked eye without some mechanistic assistance—it will be stored either in the computer or in microform, or both. Indeed, the literature on how to control literature is growing rather faster than the literature it seeks to control; if trends are extrapolated, one can probably show that in 20 or 30 years 80–90 percent of the literature will be concerned with means of coping with itself.

We know from various studies that people will make only a minimal effort to obtain information. This may be regrettable, but we may have to accept it as a fact, changeable only by increasing people's motivation, or increasing ease of use of information tools. But to increase motivation is very difficult; few categories of people can be more highly motivated to obtain information than researchers, but even they are reluctant to use formal information tools if it can be helped. Nor is it easy to increase ease of use. This would perhaps involve reducing the number of secondary tools, or at least reorganizing them, as a total system and as individual tools; perhaps also new kinds of information tools need to be designed. Research to this end is extremely necessary, but one could not, at best, expect fast results.

It is useful to consider information needs before discussing library use, because the precise role of the library needs to be defined in terms of the information it deals with. Using an old-fashioned conventional library is quite a different matter from using a modern experimental library ranging in its services far beyond the printed word. Because most recorded knowledge has until recently been in book form, and books are kept in libraries, libraries have had an important role to play as a means of communication. However, this situation is changing, partly because other media have been developed, partly because it is now possible to by-pass libraries in various ways—the ordinary user or the undergraduate can buy paperbacks very cheaply; the researcher can subscribe to computer-based retrieval services. Now librarians can take the view either that they have books in their libraries because libraries are a convenient way of storing this particular form of recorded knowledge; or that the only reason they have books is that they contain information, and that a library's more basic function is as a communication medium, concerned with *all* forms of recorded knowledge—or, to go further, with all information, whether recorded or not. I believe that if libraries restrict their scope, they are condemning themselves to a rapidly diminishing role; and in the following discussion I shall assume a broad range of activities.

The traditional answer by libraries to the problem of increasing motivation and ease of use is to try to increase both slightly by helping users to become familiar with information tools, in the hope that familiarity will generate greater ease of use, and perhaps also increase enjoyment and so increase motivation, or at least remove inhibitions to use. This has probably worked up to a certain point, but that point was probably passed some years ago.

The real aim of libraries, I would argue, is to see that users get the information they need; and we can and should often enable them to do so without attempting to educate them. When I want to go somewhere quickly, I call a taxi, and do not expect or want to be taught how to drive. Nevertheless, I may not always be able to call a taxi, there may not be one at hand, or it may cost too much, or I may want to have my movements more under my own control. It is therefore useful to learn how to drive, whatever balance I may eventually strike between driving and being driven.

I have chosen this analogy with care; because library information use is, like driving, a practical skill, not something to be taught like history. It is a skill one picks up and acquires facility in through continued practice. For this reason, occasional users will probably neither wish to learn it nor be able to do so very effectively, as they will not have sufficient practice.

Persons who are in fairly regular need of information will need to learn several different skills:

1. how to use the basic library tools (e.g., the catalog), in order to find references they already have;
2. how to find on the library shelves references they have located in the catalog;
3. how to find information on given subjects;
4. how to find specific miscellaneous pieces of information.

It may be noted that (1) and (2) require that the persons enter the library first. Bringing the users to the library is not easy, at least outside controlled environments like universities and research institutes. For (3) and (4), the persons may or may not need to use libraries. I will deal first with basic library use.

A great deal of time and effort can be devoted to instructing library users in basic library use, by lectures, seminars, audiovisual guides, and other devices of greater or lesser sophistication. This effort would in many cases be better spent on designing catalogs and libraries for ease of use; if the catalog is difficult to use, ways of making it less difficult should be explored; and if the library is one that it is difficult to find anything in, it should be made easier. Some libraries are guilty of designing instructional courses to guide users through complexities of the libraries' own devising. In any case, lectures and seminars are hardly appropriate for this kind of instruction—one good practical session should be adequate, supplemented perhaps by some self-instructional device like a tape/slide that users can refresh their memories with. Even then, all lessons in basic library use will not have been learned, or, once learned, will be forgotten; and friendly and helpful library staff should always be at hand, to help answer the query of the moment and in so doing to try to ensure that the inquirer does better next time.

However, looking up an author in the library catalog and finding the required book on the shelves is only the beginning for anyone seriously in search of information. The next leap, unfortunately, is a large one, involving the use of an elaborate system of indexes and bibliographies, at least. Here, the much more open question is whether the users should have the information found for them or be taught to find it themselves. If they are to be taught, various measures can be used and are considered in detail elsewhere in this volume. How far the instructional measures can actually be used, and to what extent they are effective, would depend largely on the compactness and tameness of the clientele. At one extreme, in a public library the proportion of potential users one could reach with these approaches would be extremely small. At the other extreme, in a school or college, courses in information use can be made a compulsory part of the curriculum. Between these two extremes, for example in social welfare, the use of instructional methods may vary from the restricted to the near impossible. One point to be made, therefore, is that instructional methods are not applicable everywhere; though with careful and widespread instruction in school, one might eventually hope to have a fair proportion of the adult population endowed with a reasonable competence in library use.

All or many of these instructional methods may be useful, though they have yet to be evaluated, both relatively and absolutely. They should, with careful planning, be adequate for most straightforward needs; but however effective they are, they cannot cater to all highly specialized needs or problems, particularly those associated with research work. A second point is, therefore, that instructional methods have at best to be supplemented if the users' needs are to be met.

It is here that the information officer comes in. All libraries are familiar with the reference librarian who is available to answer inquiries. It would be difficult to argue that the information officers are an entirely different animal, but they are certainly at the opposite end of the same continuum. Information officers, in my definition, have the prime function of seeing that users are served with the information they require; they are usually subject-specialized, they reach out to the user in person (in contrast to sitting at a reference desk in a library), they are user-oriented rather than book-oriented. The arguments for the development of information officers may be briefly summarized.[1,2]

First, the increasing complexity of information systems means that all but the most persistent and sophisticated user will at times, and probably increasingly, find difficulty in using them effectively, or at all. For example, a research biochemist has to know first, which of several published indexing and abstracting tools to use; second, whether it would be better to use them or a computer-based retrieval service; third, if the published service is used, how best to use it. Numerous studies have shown that researchers rarely use more than one or two indexing and abstracting tools,[3-5] and other studies have shown that to achieve effective retrieval in almost any field, one needs to use at least four or five.[6,7] Even if the users have acquired all the required knowledge of information systems and the skills for using them, most likely they will not find the time to use them fully. At best, users are almost certain to use the information systems less effectively than a trained information officer. On grounds of sheer efficiency, therefore, it will often be better and cheaper for an information officer rather than the user to do a search, whether currently or retrospectively. In other words, information use may now be so specialized that it demands an efficient division of labor.

This issue is incidentally an extremely important one for the development of information systems. If it is once recognized that the effective use of information systems requires, often or usually, an intermediary, a massive constraint on the development of information systems is removed—they no longer have to be usable by anyone but specialists. If, on the other hand, information systems are to be directly usable by almost anyone, they need radical redesigning, as suggested earlier. At present, information systems fall between the two stools—they are neither easy to use, nor do they take full advantage of modern sophistications, technological or bibliographical.

A second major argument in favor of information officers is that studies have shown that users have a decided preference for informal as against formal systems.[8,9] Given a choice between consulting a set of abstracts and asking somebody, they would ask somebody. Therefore it is more likely that queries would be put to information officers than to formal systems. Information officers can be still more accessible by ranging well outside the library, and mixing with their clientele; obviously this is not possible in all environments, but in universities and some other environments it is. In this way, inquiries are not only more likely to be put, they can often be anticipated.

Third, and related to the previous point, information officers provide a great deal of flexibility. A question put to a formal system has to be put in a particular way, or it will not be answered. The information officer is able to interpret the question and restructure it so that it can be put to the formal system. Question-negotiation is a highly skilled process, and ideally requires a comprehensive knowledge of the users who are being served; for this reason, the information officer, working with a limited number of people, is far better placed than a reference librarian sitting at a desk in a library, seeing a large number of people very occasionally. It is true that with more sophisticated on-line computer systems, the matching of questions with systems may become easier; but this requires that users become familiar with on-line computer searching, which typically demands the learning of a set of detailed rules, and can be more frustrating than the use of published secondary tools.

Fourth, the information officer can reach the nonlibrary user. The horse does not have to be brought to the water: water can be taken to the horse.

Finally, and most relevant to the subject in hand, information services of this kind can be a most effective method of training and instruction. Users exposed to an information service will become aware of their inadequacy in a short time, and it will be a good deal easier to bring them to a seminar than when it is put on in isolation and without prior personal contact. But more important, seminars are likely to become much less necessary, because the users pick up their skills by learning on the job, with the information officer. I envisage that some searches would be done by information officers on their own, but many will certainly have to be done together, in order to ensure that the research is pursuing in the right direction.

An attempt to give an information service in depth was carried out at the University of Bath, England, in the three years 1969 through 1971.[10–13] The service was an experimental one, supported by the Office for Scientific and Technical Information, with the aims of obtaining data on the day-to-day information uses and habits of researchers in the social sciences and of evaluating the concept of personalized information services in the university environment. The main part of the exercise consisted of an individualized current awareness service: an interest profile was constructed for each researcher, and relevant current references were identified and notified at frequent intervals. A certain number of retrospective searches were also carried out, and there were a few "fringe" services in addition.

The service was given to social science staff in Bath and to some in the nearby University of Bristol: in 1971, 39 social scientists at Bath and 14 at Bristol were receiving the service (undergraduates were not included in the service). The subjects covered were sociology, economics, and education (represented at both Bath and Bristol), management (Bath only), and psychology (Bristol only). The service was given initially by one full-time person, later in the project by one and a half. The number of researchers served was a little high; a reasonable number to be served by one information officer would be 30, assuming appropriate clerical assistance.

During the service, feedback on the relevance of each reference was obtained, and at the end of the three years, the service was evaluated by questionnaire. At best, evaluation of this kind is a crude instrument, but the results are nevertheless of interest, since information services, while they have been developed in several university libraries in Britain in the last few years,[14] have not hitherto been carried out to this depth.

Of the 3,000 or so references sent out, 28 percent were judged "essential," 52 percent "useful," and 20 percent "marginal." Of the "essential" references only 29 percent had been seen before (compared with 20 percent of all references). Eight percent of all references sent out came from subjects other than the users'; as would be expected, only a handful of these had been seen before, and 88 percent were judged "essential" or "useful."

At the end of the service, 41 users completed the evaluation questionnaire. Only one of these said the service was of little or no use; 20 rated it "very useful," 18 "useful," and 2 "moderately useful." Most of the references given were followed up, whether they were in the library or not.

At the beginning of the service, few of the recipients could be said to have effective literature searching practices, so that the question that asked how far the service had replaced their practices was a little unreal. However, 11 of the 41 respondents stated that some or all of their previous literature searching practices had been replaced. Sixteen said that the service had affected their use of the library mainly in the direction of making it more purposeful. It seems doubtful (though this question was not asked) whether the clients became any more competent in information use than before—rather, they seem to have grasped the opportunity of being served rather than learning to serve themselves. A service in which more searches were done in cooperation with users might well have a different effect.

One question was of particular interest in the present context. Users were asked to rate the value of five different types of service: (1) a selected dissemination of information on cards, (2) retrospective searches on demand, (3) circulation of current awareness bulletins, (4) dissemination of publishers' handouts and other such material, and (5) individual instruction and/or seminars in the use of information tools. The results are given in the tabulation; it will be noted that instruction in the use of secondary services rated far lower than the first three services named.

	Type of Service (see text)				
	(1)	*(2)*	*(3)*	*(4)*	*(5)*
Total Replying	40	38	40	40	39
Very useful	31	29	26	10	8
Fairly useful	9	9	12	20	27
Not useful	0	0	2	10	4
Score *	1.88	1.76	1.60	1.00	1.10

* Calculated as follows: "Very useful" = 2, "Fairly useful" = 1, "Not useful" = 0; the totals are divided by the number replying.

Asked to say whether they would personally regard a social science information officer as a high priority, bearing in mind the limited resources available for library and information services, more than 75 percent said yes. The reasons given included pressure on their time, wider coverage given of possible information sources, reasonable division of labor, and the increasing volume of material to be covered. It will be noted that these reasons, spontaneously given, are not dissimilar to some of the arguments used earlier in this paper for the development of information services. The answers to this question tie in with the answers to one question asked as part of the earlier Investigation into Information Requirements of the Social Sciences; [15] in this, 88 percent of respondents stated that they would be willing to delegate to an information officer, half of them extensively. The majority of our respondents thought that the library should finance the service, either alone or in cooperation with the departments served.

One final point to note is that more satisfaction was expressed consistently by the Bath clients than by the Bristol clients; and, among the Bath clients, by the two departments in closest physical proximity to the information officers. This argues very strongly for the value of continued personal contact.

Whatever the merits of the systematic evaluation, the best evaluation was a practical one: when the project grant was coming to an end, the two professors in the departments most concerned, realizing that the continuation of the service might be a risk, pleaded that every effort should be made to continue it, offering money from their own meager departmental funds.

The cost of the service per individual averaged out at about the same cost as a profile with a mechanized retrieval service in science. The real value is very hard to measure; a certain amount of users' time was saved, but the main benefit was in giving users references that they would otherwise not have seen, or would have seen much later, and it really is not possible to express these benefits in monetary terms. What may be noted is that, at least in a smallish university, it is possible to give such a service without spending more than comparable university libraries, by relegating routine professional work to lower levels. This may of course result in slightly inferior cataloging and classification; but the difference is probably far less than the saving, and in any case deficiencies of this kind do not matter so greatly if all users have access to an expert information service. If carried through thoroughly, an emphasis on information services rather than on acquisition and processing would produce libraries fundamentally different from most of those in existence today; this is relevant to instruction in library use, since people would need to be trained to use this type of library, and this would require a different type of training. One can envisage a library where the library itself, the information service, and training in library and information use are inseparably welded together: the library service consists mainly of an information service, and the information service is partly a substitute for training, partly a training in itself.

This is however a possibility for the future. Much more experiment and evaluation are needed before any firm conclusions can be reached. For example, it is certainly true that most users tend to use people rather than books when they have a choice, but it is also true that some people prefer less personal services, and these too must be served. Although I have suggested that the objectives of libraries may be in need of revision, there will probably be little dispute over a general ultimate objective, and different ways of reaching this could be compared. Further, showing that an information service is acceptable in one smallish university does not prove that a similar pattern could be transferred to a larger university, or to other types of library. As suggested earlier, the concept is much more viable in some environments than in others.

To summarize: Before methods of training users are discussed, it is profitable to ask whether users should be trained or served direct or both; if, as is probable, both, a proper balance must be sought. Moreover, the sort of service a library gives determines to some extent the type of library people have to use. In some environments at any rate, information officers can provide both a substitute for training and at the same time the kind of training that is the most effective of all, because the users learn as they use. Finally, the nonusers as well as the users must be considered, and information officers may be one means of reaching them.

NOTES

1. Maurice B. Line, "Information Services in University Libraries," *Journal of Librarianship* 1 (October 1969): 211–224.

2. Maurice B. Line, "Information Services in Academic Libraries," *IATUL Proceedings* 5 (May 1970): 28–34; also printed (together with discussion) in International Association of Technological University Libraries. *Educating the Library User: Proceedings of the Fourth Meeting, 1970. Edited by C. M. Lincoln.* (Loughborough, IATUL, 1970): B-1–B-10.

3. Bath University Library, *Investigation into Information Requirements of the Social Sciences. Research Report No. 1: Information Requirements of Researchers in the Social Sciences,* 2 vols. (Bath, England, May 1971).

4. Advisory Council on Scientific Policy, "Survey of Information Needs of Physicists and Chemists," *Journal of Documentation* 21 (June 1965): 83–112.

5. Maurice B. Line, "The Information Uses and Needs of Social Scientists: An Overview of INFROSS," *Aslib Proceedings* 23 (August 1971): 412–434.

6. John Martyn and Margaret Slater, "Tests on Abstracts Journals," *Journal of Documentation* 20 (December 1964): 212–235.

7. John Martyn, "Tests on Abstracts Journals: Coverage, Overlap and Indexing," *Journal of Documentation* 23 (March 1967): 45–70.

8. Peter G. Gerstberger and Thomas J. Allen, "Criteria Used by Research and Development Engineers in the Selection of an Information Source," *Journal of Applied Psychology* 52 (1968): 272–279.

9. Victor Rosenberg, "Factors Affecting the Preferences of Industrial Personnel for Information Gathering Methods," *Information Storage and Retrieval,* 3 (July 1967): 119–127.

10. Susan M. Evans and Maurice B. Line, "A Personalized Information Service to Academic Researchers: The Experimental Information Service in the Social Sciences at the University of Bath," *Journal of Librarianship* 5 (July 1973): 214–232.

11. Bath University of Technology, University Library, *Experimental Information Officer in the Social Sciences, Report on work carried out in 1969* (February 1970).

12. Bath University of Technology, University Library, *Experimental Information Service in the Social Sciences, Report on work carried out in 1970* (January 1971).

13. Bath University Library, *Experimental Information Service in the Social Sciences, 1969–1971, Final report* (January 1972).

14. J. Hall, "Information Services in University Libraries," *Aslib Proceedings* 24 (May 1972): 293–302.

15. See note 3.

AN EXAMPLE OF COOPERATIVE DEVELOPMENT OF LIBRARY-USE INSTRUCTION PROGRAMS

FRANK EARNSHAW
University Librarian, University of Bradford, England

The increasing use of audiovisual teaching aids has been a feature of university education in recent years, prompted partly by a search for improvements in teaching methods and partly by a desire, at least on the part of some academic staff, for a move toward learning rather than teaching, thus freeing student-contact hours for discussion and seminar work.

In an attempt to introduce growing numbers of new students to the library films, videotapes and tape/slide presentations have been prepared by many university libraries to replace or supplement the guided tours that have become increasingly difficult with large groups. These presentations are, of course, individually prepared by each library and can be used only in that library. During 1970, however, various groups of librarians in the United Kingdom discussed the possibility of producing audiovisual aids that could be used to educate any library user in any library. It was proposed that such aids would include guides to the literature of particular subjects, guides to abstracts, reports, and other types of literature, and guides to the technique of using certain major reference works

In July 1970 a meeting was held to explore the possibility of cooperation, since by sharing the work it was thought considerably greater benefits could be derived for only a modest effort by each library. It became clear at this meeting that the time was ripe for such a venture; considerable enthusiasm was expressed and some 23 libraries agreed to take part, including 21 university libraries, plus the National Lending Library and the National Reference Library of Science and Invention.

Initially it was agreed to concentrate on one type of production only, namely the tape/slide presentation, defined as a set of projected still photographs linked by a taped commentary, and it may be interesting to explore the reasons for this. They may be summarized as follows:

1. The cost, in production and equipment, is relatively low compared with film or videotape.

2. The presentation is easy to update by replacing one or two slides or re-recording part of the commentary, whereas an out-of-date film often has to be completely remade.

3. The equipment is easy to operate and robust in terms of normal handling, making it possible for a student to use the equipment with minimal guidance.

The use of color is of course not essential for slides of textual material, which would be principally black and white in any case. But for slides that include people or shots of the library color produces a natural effect that is superior to black and white. This is relevant because if color is deemed to be desirable, videotape is automatically eliminated, since most closed-circuit television in British universities is at present black and white.

One potential disadvantage of the tape/slide medium is the lack of movement, and in certain situations film or videotape would have advantages. This does, however, seem much less important for library and bibliographical subjects (except guided library tours) than for other topics, such as the operation of a machine or a demonstration of surgery, where a sequence of movements must be shown.

It is particularly important to consider very carefully whether a subject is suitable for tape/slide presentation. A complete guide to the literature of a subject hardly seems possible, and would be better produced in printed form as a reference book. On the other hand, literature-searching techniques can be presented very effectively in tape/slide format, using the case-study approach where an element of dramatization adds interest. The use of slides makes it easy to show detailed examples of the items found during the search, using enlargements from the actual pages of abstracts, bibliographies, and other reference works.

In considering how to organize and coordinate the work of production, two important decisions were taken. The first was to establish a small Steering Committee, with five members (four librarians and an educational technologist) to prepare plans, consider proposals from libraries, and arrange for the work of production to be appropriately distributed. The second was that each presentation should be the joint responsibility of a small working party consisting of representatives of two or three libraries. The intention here was to provide a wide range of expertise, with one member of the working party undertaking the actual production work and the other members contributing ideas, commenting on draft scripts, and assisting in criticism and evaluation. It was also envisaged that advice would be obtained in the very early stages from subject experts and educational technologists.

Early in the proceedings, it became clear that if presentations produced in one library were to be used in another library, it would be advantageous to encourage the maximum standardization in equipment, particularly in synchronizing the tape recording with the slides and providing signals on the tape for the automatic changing of slides at appropriate points. Notes on techniques and equipment were prepared by colleagues at the Institute for Educational Technology, University of Surrey, and issued to all participants.

Recommendations were also issued about the contents of each package, which should include: a set of slides; a sound recording in cassette form with the necessary pulses for automatic changing of slides; a copy of the script (to facilitate rerecording of the commentary if the purchaser was not using compatible equipment): a statement of the title and aims of the evaluation questionnaire, and a copy of any handout notes for students.

During 1971, production began on 13 presentations, as shown in Table 1.

Table 1. *THE FIRST ROUND OF COOPERATIVE PRODUCTIONS*
FOR LIBRARY-USE INSTRUCTION

| Title | Working Party | |
	Producer	Members
Introduction to Information Retrieval (using a case study in zoology)	Loughborough University	Nottingham University
		Reading University
Guide to Abstracting and Indexing Services	Surrey University	National Reference Library of Science and Invention
		Salford University
Guide to Report Literature	National Lending Library	Durham University
		Sheffield University
Guide to British Official Publications	Warwick University	Durham University
		London School of Economics
How to Search British Patents	National Reference Library of Science and Invention	City University
Guide to the Literature of Chemistry	Royal Holloway College	National Reference Library of Science and Invention
Guide to the Literature of Electrical Engineering	Bradford University	Aston University
		Loughborough University

Table 1. *THE FIRST ROUND OF COOPERATIVE PRODUCTIONS FOR LIBRARY-USE INSTRUCTION (Cont.)*

	Working Party	
Title	*Producer*	*Members*
Guide to the Literature of Medicine (including MEDLARS)	National Lending Library	Birmingham University
		Sheffield University
Guide to the Literature of Mechanical Engineering	Aston University	City University
		Bradford University
Introduction to the Literature of Sociology	Bath University *	
Guide to the London Bibliography of the Social Sciences	York University *	
Guide to the Use of Beilstein	Salford University *	
Guide to the Use of Chemical Abstracts	Southampton University	Chelsea College
		Surrey University

* Arrangements for the formation of working parties were not successfully concluded, and the producing library went ahead independently.

The work of production proceeded during 1971, and the first five presentations were shown to members of the Standing Conference of National and University Libraries (SCONUL) in September. Some of these presentations were preliminary rather than final versions; the exchange of views and comments at this September meeting was extremely valuable and some presentations were subsequently taken back for revision.

Production continued at a rather uneven rate, since the time available varied considerably from one library to another. It became clear, however, that different approaches and techniques were being used; in a cooperative venture involving 23 libraries it was inevitable that needs, ideas and technical facilities would vary considerably. Overall, however, it became clear that the Steering Committee needed to give serious consideration to evaluation procedures, if uniformly high standards were to be maintained. This became all the more important since the Steering Committee had accepted an invitation to bring the scheme under the auspices of SCONUL, thus to some extent involving the reputation of the new parent body in the quality of the product.

After much discussion it was agreed that a centralized system of review and approval would not be desirable, and instead more detailed guidelines were prepared and issued on production and evaluation techniques. These stressed the importance of assessing the need, assigning a target population, and pre-paring written aims and objectives. Particular importance was attached to the preparation of objectives, since it was only in relation to precise objectives that the effectiveness of the learning process could be measured.

It was deemed important to show the preliminary version of each presentation both to members of the working party and to a sample target population, using appropriate questionnaires that might include questions to measure whether the objectives had been attained, and a diagnostic test to indicate technical faults in the presentation. Following such tests, modifications were then to be made as appropriate, and the process repeated until the presentation was regarded as satisfactory.

The care taken to define the production and evaluation procedures can be seen from the following summary:

1. The members of the working party, preferably in consultation with an edu-cational technologist, define the target population and formulate the aims and objectives.

2. The producer prepares a draft script and a list of slides and circulates these to other members of the working party for comment.

3. The script and list of slides are modified as necessary.

4. Production work is begun and a preliminary version of the presentation completed.

5. A trial showing is arranged for all members of the working party.

6. The presentation is modified as necessary, following comments and dis-cussion at the trial showing.

7. The presentation is shown to a sample target population, using appropriate questionnaires. These might include questions to measure whether the objec-tives have been attained and a diagnostic test to indicate technical faults in the presentation.

8. Further modifications are carried out as necessary.

9. Steps 7 and 8 should be repeated until the presentation is considered to meet its objectives satisfactorily.

Of course, evaluation could continue during actual use of each presentation with groups of students, and producing libraries were encouraged to prepare an evaluation questionnaire for inclusion with each presentation sold to other libraries.

The problems encountered during the first round of productions were fully discussed both formally and informally, and in order to make available gener-ally the experience that had been gained the Steering Committee recommended to SCONUL that a booklet should be published setting out all recommended procedures. This booklet appeared in March 1973 and was available for dele-gates at a conference held that month at which arrangements were made for a further round of some 17 productions, involving 35 national, university, and polytechnic libraries (Table 2). This represented a considerable expansion of the original group and was convincing proof of the growing interest aroused by the scheme. A particular feature of the second round of productions was that from the beginning expert advice on the preparation of objectives and production and evaluation procedures would be available to producers from a team of educational technologists at the University of Surrey.

Table 2. *THE SECOND ROUND OF COOPERATIVE PRODUCTIONS FOR LIBRARY-USE INSTRUCTION*

| Title | Working Party | |
	Producer	Members
Case Study in Literature Searching in:		
Biology	British Museum (Nat. Hist.)	Polytechnic of the South Bank
		Imperial College
Building and Civil Engineering	Bradford University	Sheffield Polytechnic
Education	Chelsea College	Reading University
		Southampton University
Production Engineering	Nottingham University	Loughborough University
		Sheffield Polytechnic
Politics	Hull University	York University
Computer Science	National Reference Library of Science and Invention	City University
Economic Statistics	Lancaster University	Lanchester Polytechnic
		Loughborough School of Librarianship
Introduction to:		
The Use of Periodicals and Their Indexes	Exeter University	Bristol University
		Cardiff University College
The Structure of Literature (describing primary and secondary sources, etc.)	City University	Birmingham Polytechnic

Table 2. *THE SECOND ROUND OF COOPERATIVE PRODUCTIONS FOR LIBRARY-USE INSTRUCTION (Cont.)*

		Working Party	
Title	*Producer*	*Members*
The Literature of Law	Trent Polytechnic	Southampton University
		Birmingham University
		Leicester University
Information Retrieval (using a case study in the social sciences)	Loughborough University	Birmingham University
		Lanchester Polytechnic
The Literature of Biology	Royal Holloway College	National Reference Library of Science and Invention
		Thames Polytechnic
How to Use:		
Biological Abstracts	Surrey University	British Museum (Nat. Hist.)
		Sussex University
Reference Books	North London Polytechnic	
Science Citation Index	Dundee University	Glasgow University
Guide to:		
The Population Census	York University	Exeter University
Official Publications of the European Community	Salford University	

Although, at the time of writing, the scheme is still at a relatively early stage of development, summary of some of the lessons learned and advantages derived from this cooperative venture is possible as follows:

1. The tape/slide guide is a versatile teaching package that can in many cases be used either by an individual student or by a librarian with a group of students. Some further work is needed to determine whether this dual use is valid in all cases.

2. So far as individual students are concerned, the guide can be used when they need to know—at the precise moment when for the first time a student may need to use *Chemical Abstracts* he or she may arrange to view the tape/slide introduction to it. This is a significant improvement on the standard course of lectures, where attendance often dwindles because students have no immediate use for the information imparted to them.

3. The use of slides makes it possible for groups of students to see details of what is being discussed. In traditional lectures much time and effort is devoted to finding examples of publications and transporting them to the lecture room, and even then students can really examine these publications only at the end of the lecture, not during the discussion.

4. Each presentation must be aimed at a specific category of user, with accurate definition of the target population and detailed preparation of objectives, followed by adequate evaluation.

5. The working party of two or three members from different libraries is a valuable concept. Experience shows that there is a useful interchange of ideas and criticism, thus contributing to a continuous improvement of the presentation during the production process.

6. Librarians have shown that they are willing to use teaching materials produced in other institutions. A move in this direction may become necessary generally in the academic world in a situation where (in British universities at least) staff/student ratios are deteriorating and at the same time there is some desire to move partly away from formal lectures toward seminar and tutorial work with smaller groups or individuals.

So much for the lessons of the early stages of the scheme. But what of the future? Some of the presentations are already being used in other countries, and there seems to be no reason why cooperation should not be developed on an international scale. This might apply mostly, but not exclusively to English-speaking countries; a copy of the script is supplied with each package, thus permitting translation and rerecording. The slides are universally valid and some of the reference works that have been included in the scheme are used throughout the world. Of course this would not apply to all presentations.

The future work of the group may be extended into the field of other audio-visual aids, but there seems to be a need for further research into the effectiveness of tape/slide presentations as a teaching method compared with other techniques such as videotape, film, computer-aided instruction, or lectures with handouts. This should include an investigation of the type of teaching that each method is most suitable for.

It is also apparent that the useful life of each presentation will vary considerably, some being usable for a number of years while others will require updating much earlier. It has been recommended that purchasers should be permitted to change any presentation for updating purposes or to meet local requirements, but eventually a complete remake may be required. The production of new editions of earlier presentations may have to be added to the expansion of the scheme and the creation of new titles.

The programs described in this chapter are all available for short-term borrowing for evaluation purposes from the British Library Lending Division, Boston Spa, Yorkshire (overseas libraries may not qualify for borrowing this material). The programs are available for purchase from the individual libraries that produced them.

BIBLIOGRAPHY

Earnshaw, Frank. "Co-operative Production of Tape/Slide Guides to Library Services." *Library Association Record* 73 (1971): 192–193.

Earnshaw, Frank, ed. *Tape/Slide Presentations: Recommended Procedures.* r-diff, Wales: Standing Conference of National and University Libraries, 1973.

Hills, Philip J. "The Production of Tape/Slide Guides to Library Services." *Visual Education,* June 1972, pp. 21–22.

LIBRARY-USE INSTRUCTION NEEDS FROM THE LIBRARY USERS'/NONUSERS' POINT OF VIEW: A SURVEY REPORT

JOHN LUBANS, JR.

Assistant Director for Public Services, University of Colorado

Librarians generally agree that library-user education is necessary for students at all levels. There may be some differences of opinion on what the best approach of instruction may be and what the goals of such instruction should be, but the need for library-use instruction in some form or another is not questioned. Librarians who have developed courses of instruction have usually based the content on the assumption that instruction is necessary and that a variety of library skills need to be taught to and developed by students. A few other assumptions have been made by librarians that are germane to library-use instruction:

First, through experience and observation, librarians know that for the most part library users make ineffective use or misuse of library resources when they work without assistance from librarians. In instructing library users it is usually best, regardless of their level—freshman, doctoral candidate, or faculty member—to start at the basics in library use.

Second, users have a distorted (often superior) view of their knowledge of library skills. The study by Lee and Read [1] points this out. Instructing a user in this situation is a delicate and difficult task, particularly when teaching faculty are involved. It is difficult to teach those who assume they don't need to learn what is being taught.

And third, in their studies, Hurt (1934) and Perkins (1965) have demonstrated that when put to a test (a standard library test, such as Feagley or Peabody) the user fails. [2,3]

The user/nonuser has rarely been given the opportunity to describe his or her needs as related to library use knowledge. This is a report of one study that dealt with the assessment of student needs as related to library orientation and instruction.

Under a Council on Library Resources Fellowship [4] a three-page questionnaire was distributed randomly in the Student Union at the University of Colorado during a *normal* month of the academic year. In hopes of stimulating a good response a 10-cent piece was attached to each questionnaire. The return was 65 percent, with over 370 questionnaires returned out of 576 distributed. The distribution point of the Student Union was chosen so that a more representative group of library users and nonusers could be queried than just users entering a library. The objectives of this study were to find out:

1. information about the respondent;
2. the library user/nonuser's history of library-use instruction;
3. the user/nonuser's attitudes toward libraries and librarians;
4. the respondent's self-appraisal of his or her library skills and knowledge;
5. the respondent's awareness and use of the library;
6. the attitudes of the teaching faculty toward library use and knowledge from the student's point of view.

Of those responding to the survey, 139 were nonusers: that is, they indicated they only used the library a few times per semester or very seldom or never. The remainder considered themselves to be frequent users of the library. (It should be noted that the respondent defined "use" for himself or herself when answering the frequency-of-use question.)

The academic level of the 370 respondents was 11 percent first-year students, 24 percent sophomores, 30 percent juniors, 23 percent seniors, 4 percent master's and 3 percent doctoral candidates.

Table 1 reveals some attitudes students appear to have about librarians. Readers will note that both nonusers and users show little agreement with the first

Table 1. *I THINK LIBRARIANS ARE:*

	% Agree		% Neutral		% Disagree		% Don't Know	
	Non-users	Users	Non-users	Users	Non-users	Users	Non-users	Users
1. Possessive of their books	16	12	36	31	34	41	14	16
2. Reluctant to tell you about library services	24	9	23	18	42	66	10	7
3. Overworked; too busy to help me	37	29	23	19	32	43	8	9
4. Resentful of any intrusion	15	10	29	25	47	57	9	8
5. Really interested in my problems	23	38	32	33	33	22	12	6

statement that librarians are possessive of their books: 16 and 12 percent, respectively, agree. The response shows considerable neutrality (about one-third of each group) and some disagreement with the statement (34 and 41 percent).

Statement 2 (Reluctant . . .) shows some of the differences between the nonuser and user groups. For example, 24 percent of the nonusers and 9 percent of the users agree with the statement and 42 percent of the nonusers versus 66 percent of the users disagree.

Statement 3 (Overworked . . .) has a somewhat nebulous response. It can be taken two ways: that librarians are overworked and too busy to help, or that librarians are not overworked and still do not offer assistance.

Statement 4 (Resentful . . .) carries a response that appears strongly in favor of librarians: 47 percent of nonusers and 57 percent of users disagree with the statement while only 15 percent and 10 percent agree.

The final statement (Really interested . . .) has in it what could be a worrisome amount of disagreement (33 percent and 22 percent). At the same time, the user group, at 38 percent agreement, shows some support for the statement.

Table 1 seems overall to show through the large amount of indecision and neutrality in the responses that both users and nonusers have had little contact with librarians. If this is so, then significant work should be done to build up more student awareness of the librarians' role. An encouraging result is that users appear to exhibit a more *positive* attitude toward librarians than do nonusers. Familiarity apparently does not, in this circumstance, breed contempt.

Table 2 looks at the way library users/nonusers *see* libraries. Undoubtedly,

Table 2. *WHEN I WALK INTO A LIBRARY I FEEL:*

	% Agree		% Neutral		% Disagree		% Don't Know	
	Non-users	Users	Non-users	Users	Non-users	Users	Non-users	Users
1. Relaxed, want to pick up an interesting book and read.	20	34	22	24	54	39	4	3
2. Curious, want to browse through the books.	39	50	15	18	44	29	3	0
3. Purposeful, want to do some serious work.	61	78	12	14	25	8	2	0
4. Frustrated, want to get what I need without being there half a day.	67	50	16	13	15	30	2	6
5. Cooped-up; want to get outside and breathe deeply.	58	45	17	25	20	35	4	4

both conceptual and institutional images are involved in the responses. Statement 1 (Relaxed . . .) shows some agreement, but more disagreement, particularly from the nonusers, at 54 percent, which in a way is odd since nonusers hardly ever come into the library. But then this attitude may be a reason for nonuse.

The response to the second statement (Curious . . .) shows agreement at 50 percent for the user while 44 percent of the nonusers disagree.

The response to the next statement (Purposeful . . .) suggests that both groups have a mission or objective in mind when they enter the library: 61 percent and 78 percent, respectively, are in agreement.

Statement 4 (Frustrated . . .) throws a new light on the matter of using a library. Perhaps the frustration to be found in both groups (67 percent and 50 percent) stems from anticipating problems that will occur in making use of the library.

The fifth statement (Cooped-up . . .) reinforces the one immediately preceding. The agreement at 58 percent for nonusers and 45 percent for users may be the result of local conditions, but may also be indicative of frustration in working under pressure, such as research paper deadlines. There is something here for the architects. Openness and rapid access to materials are necessary features in a library building according to both users and nonusers.

Again, Table 2 demonstrates some difference in attitudes between users and nonusers. Throughout Table 2 the users appear to have a more positive attitude toward the library than do nonusers.

Table 3 reveals what users/nonusers think of certain skills in information use. The first three categories reveal strong support among students for what may be

Table 3. *EACH OF THE FOLLOWING I CONSIDER VALUABLE TO STUDENTS REGARDLESS OF THEIR STUDY AREAS:*

	% Agree		% Neutral		% Disagree		% Don't Know	
	Non-users	Users	Non-users	Users	Non-users	Users	Non-users	Users
1. Knowledge of use of bibliographies, abstracts, and indexes.	77	80	10	9	11	9	3	2
2. Awareness of pertinent literature in fields related to his/her own field.	84	87	8	7	8	5	1	0
3. Knowledge of how to look for specific information.	89	93	3	4	7	3	1	0
4. Knowledge of one or more foreign language.	30	34	30	27	30	35	8	3

Table 4. *KNOWING HOW TO USE THE LIBRARY IS OVERRATED.*
YOU CAN GET ALONG WITHOUT INSTRUCTION
IN LIBRARY USE:

% Agree		% Neutral		% Disagree		% Don't Know	
Nonusers	Users	Nonusers	Users	Nonusers	Users	Nonusers	Users
24	21	17	15	53	60	6	4

considered partial objectives of library-use instruction. On the other hand, this may well be what the respondents recommend for *other* students and not for themselves. Whatever the source for the strong agreement with the first three items, the response seems to suggest we are on firm ground in providing library-use instruction programs that attempt to endow students with these skills. The "knowledge of one or more language" category did not fare too well. Approximately a third each agree, feel neutral, or disagree on the desirability of this skill.

Table 4 lends further support to the cause of library use instruction. Although both groups express some agreement with the statement (24 percent and 21 percent) the two groups' substantial disagreement with the statement—53 percent and 60 percent—appears to indicate positive attitudes among library users and nonusers to library-user education.

One section of the questionnaire dealt with certain library services/facilities that the respondents may have used (e.g., card catalog, reference books, etc.). Table 5 shows the results in percentages for nonusers and users when they were asked why they didn't make use of particular library service/facilities.

The major reason for both the nonuser (31 percent) and the user (44 percent) not making use of library services or facilities is they felt no need to use them. The next major reason is that neither group knew of the existence of these

Table 5. *REGARDING THE LIBRARY SERVICES/FACILITIES YOU*
HAVE NOT USED, WAS IT BECAUSE YOU:

% Nonusers	% Users	The Reasons
25	21	Didn't know they even existed.
7	9	Were aware of them but didn't have time.
12	7	Didn't want to ask about how to use them.
31	44	Felt no need to use them.
10	6	Figured it wasn't worth the time spent using them.
1	1	Thought only librarians were supposed to use them.
15	11	Couldn't locate the service even though I knew it existed.

services/facilities (25 percent and 21 percent, respectively). Also a significant number (15 percent and 11 percent) could not locate the service even though they knew it existed. The three principal reasons given appear to indicate another aspect of the problem the user has when faced with library use: that information-seeking users may not know about the services/facilities, but even if they do, they can't find them some of the time. This could be a frustrating situation, indeed, for the user.

In Table 6 users/nonusers identify what it is they would like to have more information about.

The response to the card catalog—the lowest of all the identified categories with 7 percent for nonusers and 4 percent for users—is somewhat significant because inevitably library-use instruction from the elementary school to university level stresses the basics and complexities of the card catalog. Interpretations of this response could be that all the instruction is having an effect or that the users/nonusers do not view the card catalog as an important library tool or that the users have an inflated view of their ability to use the card catalog. Some of the response is interesting, particularly in revealing relatively high interest in such services/facilities as interlibrary loan, special collections, and audiovisual materials.

The final tabulation, Table 7, deals with three areas of inquiry: (1) how the faculty member and the faculty member's view of library use are seen by users/nonusers; (2) what the user thinks of his or her knowledge of library use; (3) what the library can do about helping users/nonusers make better use of the library's resources.

The influence of the teaching faculty on library use is discovered in the response to statement 1. Fifty-one percent of the nonusers and 32 percent of the users disagree with the statement. The users, however, agree with the statement at a high level (68 percent) that assignments in their courses of study do involve the use of library resources. It would appear that the nonusers' claims to having

Table 6. *DO YOU FEEL THAT YOU WOULD LIKE MORE INFORMATION AND/OR EXPLANATION OF ANY OF THESE SERVICES/FACILITIES?*

% Nonusers	% Users	The Services/Facilities
7	4	Card catalogs
14	13	Periodicals, indexes or abstracts
12	14	Government documents
11	8	Reference books (bibliographies, encyclopedias, etc.)
16	20	Interlibrary loan
16	19	Special collections
18	18	Audiovisual materials
5	4	Other

Table 7

Questions	% Disagree		% Agree	
	Nonusers	Users	Nonusers	Users
1. Do assignments in your courses usually involve using library resources other than just books placed on reserve by professors?	51	32	48	68
2. Do your professors, in general, encourage students to use the library?	54	31*	19	40
3. Is your expertise or lack of it in library use taken into account by your professors when they grade your papers?	51	45	8	10
4. Do instructors assume that you already know enough about using the libraries to do an in-depth term paper?	4	6	81	79
5. Are you at a loss when faced with doing a term paper in the library?	35	53	41	23
6. Whenever you do a research paper in the library do you get a feeling that there are information resources on your topic which you are somehow missing?	4	12	80	76
7. Has your undergraduate training given you all the preparation you need for finding information in the library?	48	49	28	40
8. Do you feel well able to do research in the library?	44	23	34	62
9. Do you think that the library should offer courses, clinics, etc., in how to use libraries and their resources?	30	7	61	64
10. Would you take such courses, clinics, etc., if offered at a convenient time?	25	24	38	43
11. If the library staff included an information specialist in your subject area, would you use that person?	8	9	93	91

* Totals of less than 100% represent a response of "don't know" or "neutral."

assignments not involving library use (51 percent) is more than coincidental and may be a reason for the condition of nonuse.

Fifty-four percent of the nonusers in statement 2 feel that their professors in general do not encourage students to use the library. Forty percent of the users agree with the statement while only 19 percent of the nonusers see this happening.

There appears to be substantial disagreement in statement 3 that library use skills are taken into account by the teaching faculty in the grading process. Fifty-one percent of the nonusers and 45 percent of the users claim this. At the same time there is quite a bit (30 percent) of neutrality or what may be ignorance on the topic.

Statement 4 receives a strong affirmative response (81 percent and 79 percent) that the faculty assumes considerable expertise in library use on the part of the student. It would appear that the faculty's assumption is false, particularly when contrasted with the librarian's on-the-job observation of students floundering about in trying to make use of the library. It is possible that the faculty's expectations are not all that high, particularly when viewed in light of the considerable disagreement to statement 3 about grading and library use.

In response to the statement about what the users/nonusers think of their abilities in information use there are some apparently contradictory findings. Statement 5 receives some agreement (41 percent and 23 percent), but more disagreement (35 percent and 53 percent). The respondents have some confidence in their ability to do term papers. In contrast with this show of confidence (at least on the users' part) the reaction to statement 6 reveals a strong common sentiment (80 percent and 76 percent) that there are information resources the nonusers/users miss when working in the library. A valid question might be whether the respondents feel inadequate or whether they blame the library for not having the needed materials.

The percentages (48 percent and 49 percent) at statement 7 indicate some dissatisfaction with the effectiveness of the users' and nonusers' undergraduate training in library use, which would seem to suggest that improvements could be made in the present instruction or that more instruction is needed.

The answer to whether the users/nonusers feel well able to do research in the library is somewhat interesting in that it shows 62 percent of the users agreeing. The nonusers exhibit a considerable lack of confidence in contrast to the users. The users' positive attitude may be an *ignorance is bliss* condition. Regardless of the source of this attitude, it is something librarians must contend with when offering reference service and user-education programs.

The library's role in the educational process is somewhat clarified in statement 9. The respondents agree (61 percent and 64 percent) that the library should offer courses in how to use libraries. However, taking advantage of these courses (statement 10) is another matter. Thirty-eight percent and 43 percent would avail themselves of such opportunities. This is a drop-off from the support shown in statement 9, but it would still provide a base of students that could fill to capacity any instructional program offered by libraries.

Some direction is provided in the reaction to the final statement, 11, about the willingness of users/nonusers to make use of subject specialist librarians: 93 percent and 91 percent agree with the statement. The unqualified endorsement of this concept seems to indicate potential increased use for existing reference staffs and/or new programs assisting users in information use.

What this study has attempted to do is to provide input from the library users/nonusers into the matter of library instruction. Practically, each of the elements in the above tables could be and should be explored further. In fact, the investigation of each statement's response alone could be the basis of a short study.[5]

NOTES

1. John W. Lee and Raymond L. Read, "The Graduate Business Student and the Library," *College and Research Libraries* 33 (September 1973): 403–407.
2. Peyton Hurt, "The Need of College and University Instruction in the Use of the Library," *Library Quarterly* 4 (1939): 436–448.
3. Ralph Perkins, *The Prospective Teacher's Knowledge of Library Fundamentals: A Study of the Responses Made by 4,170 College Seniors to Tests Designed to Measure Familiarity with Libraries* (New York: Scarecrow Press, 1965).
4. John Lubans, Jr., "Report to the Council on Library Resources on a Fellowship awarded for 1971–72," mimeographed (Boulder: University of Colorado Library, November 28, 1972).
5. The completed questionnaires (the raw data) on which this chapter is based are available to students/researchers for further analysis from the author.

A ROSE BY ANY OTHER NAME—
OR LIBRARY INSTRUCTION AND THE
LIBRARY SCHOOL

Patricia Senn Breivik
Assistant Dean, Pratt Institute, Graduate
School of Library and Information Science

While library instruction is a topic of growing concern and interest throughout the profession, library school catalogs, by and large, make no mention of the topic in their curricula. Columbia University School of Library Service does include library instruction as a topic within its advanced reader services course; however, in commenting on the implications of giving library instruction its proper due, one man lamented:

> The implications for library school professors is that library instruction should at least be discussed, and preferably demonstrated, in any course which considers the teaching function of the academic library or the reference librarian. It is depressing to report that I cannot remember the subject of library instruction even being mentioned in reference courses or in college library administration in courses that I took at Columbia and Drexel.[1]

Why have library schools neglected this topic in their course offerings? Three possible answers suggest themselves. First, there is the habitual fear librarians have of impinging on the territorial prerogatives of other professionals, i.e., a librarian is not a social worker, is not a teacher, etc. Second, our library schools concentrate so much on library materials that there is little time left for considering library clientele. Finally, in the case of New York City, a no-credit methods course was required of all school librarians for years, and, as it was particularly disliked by the schools and students alike, anything vaguely reminiscent of training for teaching library skills is thought best avoided.

Yet library schools should address themselves to the topic of library instruction for two basic reasons. The first is that an obvious need of library users is not being met. Given the present state of the library art, library users must acquire a range of skills in order to be comfortable in libraries and to make effective use of library resources. Yet, despite many gestures made in the general direction of teaching the use of the library, it must be admitted that the library profession has failed to make its essentially esoteric tools seem easy to understand and use. Failed, not because of the difficulty of such teaching, but because of unwillingness to insist on the kind and amount of instruction necessary.[2]

The reality of this situation was demonstrated in an Alumni Day discussion group at Columbia in the spring of 1972. Within the group were representatives from all levels of school and academic libraries plus some public librarians. The elementary librarians explained how they taught basic library skills to their students, but the junior high librarians said that was impossible, for when students reached junior high they were without any library knowledge and had then to be taught basic skills. Needless to say, the story was repeated through to the academic librarians, and the public librarians added that few of their users knew even the most elementary skills. Obviously, from the users' viewpoint better library instruction is a very real need.

Another reason library schools should deal with instruction in library use in their curricula is that, although it is certainly not a new topic, our profession is becoming increasingly concerned with it. Over the years library-user instruction has been the subject of countless articles in the library literature. The articles have usually been of the "how-we-do-it" variety, and although "formidable in quantity, this literature does not impress one with its quality." [3] Recently, however, the more scholarly works of Patricia Knapp and the July–October 1971 issue of the *Drexel Library Quarterly* have provided a richer quality of literature on library-user instruction and have also shown that endeavors in this area are being planned better and evaluated better than they were before.

On the national level other indications of this growing concern are evident. The American Library Association established the Instruction in the Use of Libraries Committee in 1967. At the ALA Convention in Chicago in June 1972, this committee sponsored an exhibit of library instruction materials from all types of libraries across the country. The exhibit filled a two-room suite, was open for one evening and the following morning, and an attendance of about 500 people was anticipated for these two periods. Much to the committee's astonishment, within 15 minutes of the opening of the exhibit more than 1,500 people crowded into the committee's exhibit area, making it almost impossible to view the materials, but suggesting that many librarians were already well-motivated in this area.

One librarian predicted that, as censorship had been our profession's "concern" in the sixties, library instruction will be its "concern" in the seventies. What is certain is that library instruction is gaining respectability in our profession and is here to stay, and that library schools must begin dealing effectively with this topic in their curricula.

HOW SHALL WE TEACH?

Although possible, it is not realistic to expect library schools to study the topic of library instruction and then effectively incorporate it into existing curricula; as has already been noted, it usually doesn't work. It's also easy enough to say what a course on library instruction should not be. It should not be an audiovisual production course; this can be handled elsewhere in the curriculum. It should not be a teaching methods course lifted from a teacher's college, because to be effective such courses must be offered on all age levels and for specialized groups, and no school can support a battery of courses on library instruction.

What does that leave in the way of substance for a course on library instruction? Not too much *if* we are limiting the focus to library instruction per se. I believe, however, that the interest in library instruction is a healthy reflection of a somewhat unfocused concern of many dedicated librarians for the broader need to understand their clientele and potential clientele and to meet these individuals at their points of need. Library instruction should not be considered by itself—for in reality it is part of the broader issue, the process of transforming a nonuser or misuser of a library into an effective user of library resources. For this reason library instruction should not be viewed as an end in itself in a library school curriculum anymore than the actual practice of teaching a library skill to an undergraduate should ever be viewed as an end in itself.

Of course, the concept of devoting a course to the nonuser or novice library user may prove a difficult one for library schools to accept. There is little or no precedent for it; library schools are at best just beginning to branch out from their materials-centered curricula to include in-depth considerations of the political and social aspects of librarianship. To date our schools have given little or no emphasis to the needs of potential and current library users other than allusions to the fact that library collections should meet the needs of their communities, that a card catalog should help readers, etc. In contrast, teachers' colleges offer numerous courses directly concerned with the student—from "Psychology of Learning" and "Psychology of Personality" to "Nature and Needs of the Gifted" and "Nature and Needs of Children with Learning Disabilities" to "Colloquium in Youth Culture" and "The American Student and His College"—plus many offerings relating aspects of education to a particular group (similar to library schools' literature courses for particular age groups).[4] Surely, library schools can devote *one* course to the nonuser or novice library user.

A NEW DESIGN

Pratt Institute Graduate School of Library and Information Science has designed an institute based on the concept of transforming the nonusers of the library into effective users. The institute is designed for professionals from public, academic, and school libraries, but in this instance (though certainly it would not need to be so limited) it will focus on the nonuser in an urban setting. The institute will, in turn, serve as the basis for an ongoing course that is the natural home for consideration of library instruction in a graduate library school curriculum. The following excerpt from Pratt's working outline illustrates the possible content of such a course:

The City
  Current urban issues
  Psychological and social effects of
The Non-User in the Inner-City
  Who he is
  His informational needs
  Where he goes for his information
  Reasons he doesn't go to a library
Communicating
  The process
  Social, psychological and ethnic barriers
Reaching the Non-User
  Going outside the library
  Public relations and publicity for the community
  Approaching groups, individuals
Effective Involvement of the Community
  Internally: Administrative and employment opportunities for community
        members within the library
        Friends of libraries
        Advisory boards
        Community control
  Externally: Cooperative efforts with community groups and local agencies
        With other libraries and informational organizations
        With governmental agencies
        With private agencies
Cultivating the Non-User into a User
  Programs and services for: The very young
                School children
                Young adults
                The aged
                Special-interest groups
Molding Information into Desired Forms
  Determining specific informational needs
  Locating informational sources in urban settings
  Determining most effective format for information (consideration of strengths
  and weaknesses of various mediums)
Teaching the New User to Be a More Effective User
  Alternative methods for organizing materials
  Developing techniques and programs for transference of library skills
  Use paraprofessionals
  Evaluative procedures
In-Service Training (for more effective service)
  The professional staff
  Paraprofessionals
  The clerical staff
  Student aides

THE ROSE

The interesting fact emerging from this outline is that library instruction is directly referred to only once, i.e., under "Teaching the New User to Be a More

Effective User." "Effective Involvement of the Community—Internally," "Cultivating the Non-User into a User," "Molding Information into Desired Forms," and "In-Service Training" are topics under which instructional approaches would also be discussed. We must have a broad enough concept of library instruction to include the educating of the public to the total library as well as to individual tools and the continued education of library staff. And this raises a final question.

Is *library instruction* a viable term for what has been discussed here? Probably not. Hopefully, as interest and work in the area of library instruction expands, a euphemism may be found. Besides, being vague (don't we give library instruction in library schools?) library instruction is certainly not the term that will ever elicit interest from many librarians much less administrators, faculty, or students. Somehow *Individualization of Communication Controls* has something that *Library Instruction* doesn't. And maybe that's the best place to begin.

NOTES

1. James R. Kennedy, Jr., "Question: A Separate Course in Bibliography or Course-Related Library Instruction?" (In First Annual Conference on Library Orientation, 1971, Eastern Michigan University Library, Ann Arbor: Pierian Press, 1972), pp. 18–28.

2. Carl M. White, "Services to Scholars," *Library Trends* 3 (October 1954): 153.

3. William Vernon Jackson, "The Interpretation of Public Services," *Library Trends* 3 (October 1954): 189.

4. Examples taken from Teachers' College Bulletin 1971–1972.

HOW BUILDINGS CAN CONTRIBUTE

Ralph E. Ellsworth

Director of Libraries and Professor of Bibliography, Emeritus, The University of Colorado

There are two somewhat, but not exclusively so, opposing positions one may take on the matter of the instructional role library buildings can play in the academic scene.

The first is to assert that the building is merely an enclosed place where libraries live and that, as such, the building can have, at best, merely an indirect role. For those who spent their undergraduate years in the old buildings at Adelbert College (Western Reserve University Men's College Library), Oberlin, Grinnel, Colorado College, or the old Cornell or University of Pennsylvania library buildings—all dirty, crowded, poorly lighted, badly ventilated, difficult to use, uncomfortable to study in, miserably appointed—it would be hard to deny that these buildings made no positive contribution to their learning experience. But one did spend long hours in these buildings because one had to do so if one were to meet the faculty's requirements. The student union buildings, if any, had a different role, and if one's living quarters were good for late night studying, with the coffeepot at hand, one was lucky. Even so, one put up with the situations, and students in these institutions did manage to educate themselves very well indeed, sometimes.

The second position is not to deny the validity of the first, but rather to assert that for most people a spartan environment isn't necessarily an advantage, and that a library building can provide a study environment and can facilitate services that can have both an indirect and direct influence on the students' attitudes toward studying, and to their success in using the tools of learning in the process of educating themselves.

Evidence to support this position doesn't lie in the claim that highly motivated students in colleges with "good" library buildings educated themselves better than did their predecessors who had to study in "bad" buildings, but rather in the unproven, and probably unprovable, belief that the activities that go on in the "good" library buildings do seem to result in a higher percent of the student body using the library, more use per capita, better documentation in reports and papers, more overt expressions of a friendly feeling for the library than one found in the colleges and universities that had "bad" library buildings.

In supporting the second position one does not lose sight of the fact that bright students from good home and school backgrounds, high-quality faculties, instructional methods that stress independent study, and a college tradition of hard work and high achievement are probably the major factors that cause students to use libraries successfully. Still, it is worth calling attention to those special qualities in "good" buildings that are known to make a contribution to the student's learning process. And that is what this paper will attempt to do.

In general, there is universal testimony to the fact that a new and attractive library building on a campus causes a large (usually a 100 percent) increase in student use. I saw this happen in the spring of 1951 at the University of Iowa and the spring of 1973 at the University of Colorado when, in the first case a new building was opened, and in the second case the College Library in the central building was remodeled, redecorated, relighted, and refurnished. On the other hand, last year the librarian at Gettysburg College told me that a new type of curriculum recently introduced had caused a doubling of library use even though the library building at that college would be considered a "bad" building by modern criteria.

In my extensive tour of new academic library buildings in 1969/70, I talked with many students about their attitude toward studying in their new library buildings, and in almost all cases the reactions were one of approval, appreciation, and often of affection.[1]

The qualities in a "good" library building that seem to contribute to its instructional value would include the following:

Direct access to the book collections with a mixture of various kinds of comfortable and attractive furniture, distributed throughout the collection (so that individuals may choose the type that suits their needs and temperaments) has been the keynote factor in the new buildings that is relevant to the subject of this paper. There are hundreds of good examples of fine reading environments (some of which have been pictured in my *Academic Library Buildings*). Some of the best examples are found at Pacific Lutheran University, the Stanford Undergraduate Library, the University of California, Berkeley Undergraduate Library, the University of California, La Jolla central library, Tulane, University of Chicago, University of Denver (Figures 1 and 2), Tufts University, to mention only a few.

The success of direct access has created its own problems. Failure to provide enough copies of books in demand and of enough staff to keep the books reshelved quickly has led to book hoarding, in various forms, and has caused some libraries to go back to closed access to current issues of periodicals, to books in greatest demand, and to AV tapes.

Access to nonbook-type materials (or media, as they are called), which seem to be quite helpful in enriching the reading assignments, is still at the "separate-but-equal" stage, largely because of the difficulties in identifying and controlling

Figure 1. Womb Chairs in Penrose Library, University of Denver

the tapes, and also because of theft of the hardware. Even so, bringing the new software into the library has made it easier for the faculty to assign their use, and for students to use them than was the case where the software was controlled by the AV departments. The new buildings have mostly been able to provide the cables and the acoustical values involved, and thus be said to make a contribution to instruction, whereas in the older fixed-function buildings this transition has not been easy.

A second contribution has been the ability of the new buildings to provide group study rooms to accommodate not only the traditional seminars, but also students who wish to study together in small groups, sometimes using learning hardware that would cause sound disturbances if used out in a reading area. The University of Texas undergraduate library, the Southern Methodist Law Library, the Eastern Michigan University Library, the University of Minnesota Library and the Tufts University Library are a few examples of buildings that have been generous in providing such rooms. Their use has been heavy, especially when students are working on group projects. One such room at Texas has been set aside for reading to blind students.

Rapid expansion of the use of oral and videotapes in classroom instruction has caused heavy demand for reading carrels in which the sound of the machines would not disturb other readers. Few such carrels exist, and the group study rooms are frequently taken over for this purpose—which is all right if it doesn't crowd out the original purpose of the rooms.

Figure 2. Carrels in Penrose Library, University of Denver

Special-purpose instructional rooms seem to encourage faculty to use the new media because the process is so easy, in comparison with older times when hardware had to be requisitioned and other special arrangements made. Another special type of room that has proven to be helpful is the reference instruction room in the new Northwestern University Library. This room, adjacent to the Reference Center, is a handy place to bring students to instruct them in the use of the reference collections. Similar rooms, located near the Rare Book rooms are helpful to faculty who wish to have their students exposed to rare books that might not be taken from the library.

The point is that the new buildings have made it easy for faculty to adopt new teaching methods that, in the past, would have been a nuisance to adopt.

Although the practice is still pretty much limited to the elementary and secondary schools, and to colleges concentrating on teacher preparation, individual professors in other colleges are beginning to need audiovisual preparation laboratories in the library—rooms in which tapes, both oral and video, can be made from their local classroom experiences. The resulting cassettes are then placed in the library and used just like regular books. One of the most carefully thought out facilities for this purpose is to be found at the Fairmont, West Virginia State College, although many other colleges have such facilities in their AV departments. The presence of such facilities in the library is a great convenience.

Housing for librarians who wish to develop new instructional roles for students and faculty now appears to be important. Librarians who are not content with the "sit and wait for students to come for help" attitude need offices where they can be easily seen by students and in which they can use the new electronic learning hardware to teach students about library materials and research methods. Small projectors for filmstrips, computer consoles, microform projectors and cassette players are in common use for this purpose. Also useful is a work room where materials can be prepared and analyzed near the reference staff offices. One good example is to be found at the Portland Oregon State College Library. Other examples of good reference staff housing for instructional work are to be found in the Penn-Morton Colleges Library, the University of Northern Iowa and the University of Nevada.

Students are frequently bewildered by the complexity of a large university library building, especially if the collections and departments are dispersed in an uneven pattern throughout the building. A carefully thought out and imaginatively executed system of graphics can be extremely helpful in getting the student acquainted with the system of shelf arrangements. Most libraries provide a simple directory at the library's entrance, listing the library's departments and sometimes the location of the book-classification divisions. However, graphics that go beyond the verbal listing can do much to untangle the library's complexities. Three libraries have used abstract, universal symbols, or illuminated signs in interesting ways: Guelph University in Canada, Emory University, and the Northern Texas State University in Denton.

Many libraries have developed automated oral or visual individually operated lectures on the use of the library, and these are helpful; but a system of Graphics that can be seen on the run, so to speak, is even more useful. Figure 3 incorporates many of the principles of good graphics design.[2]

A properly designed library building (except those that are single-purpose libraries, such as a rare book library) should not determine or dictate the manner in which the library services or collections are to be organized. And, in fact, the newer modular libraries came into being 25 years ago because at that time library philosophies and procedures were beginning to change, but were inhibited by the fixed-function buildings that were in common use at that period.

Since there is no one single type of library organization that is best for all libraries at all levels of higher education, and since there has been a renewal of interest in expanding the instructional role of libraries (see the older Stephens College attempts and the more recent ones at Hampshire College),[3] this section of the paper will be limited to those concepts of organization that have concentrated on the instructional, rather than the preservation, or storage role. Not, of course, that the latter roles are not important.

First, the separation of library services by level of student progress, as one means of solving some of the problems that arose from the very large enrollments in state-supported universities, or by the very heavy concentration on research in many universities, especially Chicago and Harvard. There has been a difference of opinion, at least since 1940, on the level the separation should be made at (the lower divisional level as at the University of Colorado *versus* the undergraduate level at Harvard and dozens of other campuses).

Figure 3. Example of Library Graphics from University of Colorado College Library

One university has labeled one of the divisions "assigned reading," and the other "independent study." There has also been a difference of opinion on the proper size for a college library within a university library system. The range varies from 50,000 to 100,000 volumes. It is also true that some university librarians have seen no need for any separation, their assumption being that their students are quite capable of working in a single system.

Librarians who have operated separate college or undergraduate libraries seem convinced that they can concentrate better on services and arrangements that make the undergraduate's library experience more convenient and more extensive than they could in buildings serving all kinds of students with one kind of system. No one has attempted to prove in numerically stated terms that this is true.

As one variant of this problem, university librarians are currently concerned with the identification and location of a so-called core collection of books that might be isolated and organized for greater convenience. Obviously, as university collections become very large, the percent of titles receiving heavy use declines, and the library tends to give more attention to the research, or storage, collection than to the core, or "teaching" collection. This problem received considerable attention about 1940 when the subject divisional library concept was inaugurated in full at Colorado and Brown. There had been many partial systems before this time.

This system attempted to offer for the benefit of students, a type of service somewhere in between the departmental library and the single, inclusive central reference department, usually with a closed stack library.

The subject divisional library concept contained two elements—the collection and the staff. Unfortunately, librarians concentrated their attention too much on the location and identification of the collection aspect, and too little on the staff services. This plan gave us the opportunity to develop a corps of librarians with subject competence in a few related disciplines, who could be knowledgeable in greater depth than could the all-inclusive reference librarian. Few universities could afford a full set of well-educated departmental librarians.

Although there were elements in the plan that gave trouble, there can be no doubt but that the plan gave the instructional role of the library new opportunities and possibilities.

In fact, that is what has resulted from the 1940 concepts. In the new Regenstein Library at the University of Chicago, the book collections are shelved in classification sequence in the stack blocks, but the divisional reference experts are housed on the various floors of the library near the collections that they have their competence in. This plan is also followed in the Indiana University Graduate Library. In other libraries, the reference departments are housed in a central pool, usually on the main floor of the building. Common to all the plans is the concept of competence in a limited subject area. Common also is the attempt to offer a better type of information service to students.

In one sense, this is an administrative rather than a building contribution, but the two seem to have evolved at the same time, along parallel lines and intents.

Although the evidence that this concept has advanced the instructional role of the library is subjective and of a testimonial nature, few librarians would dispute that the contribution has been made. And this has occurred at the same time the research services aspects of the libraries has grown very extensively.

As far as the immediate future of this role is concerned, assuming that the computer, the television, the facsimile transmission, and the ultramicrofiche developments are allowed to live up to their present promises, and aren't stymied by legal complications, the instructional contributions of library buildings will continue to lie in their capacity to meet new space needs, most of which would appear to lie in the ability of the users to get the information they need more comprehensively, accurately, and conveniently than they had been able to in the past.

Although most of my work has been in colleges and universities I have studied developments in the secondary schools closely because I learned long ago that teaching innovations usually begin in the lower schools, and twenty years later are introduced at the college level.

The instructional role of the library in the lower schools has been a subject for experimentation for many years. The early Educational Facilities Laboratories, Inc., publication, *Profiles of Significant Schools,* reported, for example, nine such schools.

In recent years the "schools without walls" movement and the individualized curriculum programs have resulted in hundreds of schools in which there has been a fusion of the library and the school in the physical as well as the procedural sense. To cite only one example, in the Clear Creek County high school in Idaho Springs, Colo., there are no separate classrooms or libraries. Instead, there are several instructional clusters in which the instructors are surrounded by all kinds of study carrels, desks, tables, lounge chairs, AV hardware, TV receivers, computers, etc. Each is a total learning environment. There is a Library Center where reference books, catalogs and some basic books are kept, and from which the school-wide library network operates. The work of the librarians and the subject instructors is highly integrated.

In buildings of this kind, the physical structure and the instructional programs and learning activities are completely interdependent.

As libraries become more concerned with information handling directly, and less with technical procedures, their contributions to instruction will become increasingly obvious. Much of this is unrelated to the house in which the library lives and has its being, but a modest part is vitally related.

NOTES

1. Ralph E. Ellsworth, *Academic Library Buildings* (Boulder: Colorado Associated Universities Press, 1973).
2. Gary Hanlon and Associates, "A Proposal for the Interior Signing Program for the University of Colorado, Main Library" (Boulder: Gary Hanlon and Associates, December 1972). Quoting from this document:

   Our basic objectives will be:

   1. Design a style of signage, attractive in appearance and compatible with the recent architectural attitude undertaken.
   2. Design the system at a level of communication sophistication which is both favorable and necessary.
   3. Develop an efficient and functional system—providing maximum visual control with a minimum of management supervision.
   4. Develop an economical system of basic modular interchangeable units which will allow significant long-range cost savings in the purchase of new, revised, or additional signing units.
   5. Develop a system sufficiently flexible in its basic characteristics so that it may be readily adaptable to future change and additions.
   6. Introduce for consideration the most modern and tested materials and methods of sign application available in the field.

3. Robert S. Taylor, *The Making of a Library: The Academic Library in Transition* (New York: Wiley, 1972).

SELECTED BIBLIOGRAPHY

This bibliography is the result of several years' worth of scanning the current and historic international literature through *Library Literature* and *Library and Information Science Abstracts* as well as published bibliographies and surveys of user studies and library user education. Also several contributors to this volume made suggestions of titles for inclusion.

It is a selective alphabetical listing of materials (journal articles, books, reports, theses, and unpublished documents) that have been reviewed and found to offer an example or overview of ideas and concepts on library-use instruction of concern to all types of libraries and librarians. These items would be well worth reading and discussing by anyone interested in or contemplating starting up instructional programs. (The reader is also referred to the substantive bibliographies of many of the chapters.) This bibliography does not list all the material cited in every chapter's notes or bibliography because some of it is highly specialized or not necessarily relevant to a general bibliography.

Several of the materials cited below are themselves bibliographies or surveys of the literature. In this category are: Ahlers, Hopkinson, Lebovitch, Lieberman, Mirwis, New York Library Association, Schwarz, and Scrivener.—Editor.

Ahlers, Eleanor E. "Elementary and Secondary Schools: Instruction in the Use of the Library." Paper presented at the American Library Association Annual Conference, Detroit, 1971. Mimeographed.

Ahlers, Eleanor E. "Instruction in the Use of the Library." A bibliography prepared for the American Association of School Librarians, Chicago, 1962. Mimeographed.

Akers, Susan Grey. "To What Extent Do the Students of the Liberal Arts Colleges Use the Bibliographic Items Given on the Catalogue Card?" *Library Quarterly* 1 (1931): 394–408.

Alaska University Library, Reader Services Department. "Library Skills: How to Use the College Library—a Self-Directed, Self-Paced Program." Revision of Dudley, Miriam, *Course of Study*. Los Angeles: UCLA College Library, 1970. College, Alaska, prepared 1971–1972. Mimeographed.

Albuquerque, New Mexico, Public Schools, Division of Library Services. "An

Outline of Library Instruction for Elementary School Libraries." 1968. Mimeographed.

Alexander, Malcolm D., *A Measure of the Library Skills of High School Graduates of Washington State as Demonstrated by Freshmen of Central Washington State College.* Ellensburg: Central Washington State College, Graduate School 1972, ERIC ED 081 441.

Allen, Kenneth W. "Student and Faculty Attitudes." *The Library–College Journal* 3 (November 1970): 28–36.

Allen, Kenneth W. *Use of Community College Libraries.* Hamden, Conn.: Linnet Books, 1971.

Alston, Annie May. "The Happy Medium in Library Instruction at the College Level." *College and Research Libraries* 21 (November 1960): 469–70.

American Library Association, Association of College and Research Libraries, Ad Hoc Committee on Bibliographic Instruction. "Academic Library Bibliographic Instruction: Status Report, 1972." 1973. Mimeographed. (Also ED 072 823)

American Library Association, Association of College and Research Libraries, Bibliographic Instruction Task Force, "Academic Bibliographic Instruction: Model Statement of Objectives." *LOEX News* 1 (May, 1974): 3–7.

American Library Association, Association of College Research Libraries, Junior College Library Section, Instruction and Use Committee. "Instruction and Use of Materials in the Junior and Community College Library." Compiled for the Association by Sara M. Crittenden, et al., 1969? Mimeographed.

American Library Association, Committee on Instruction in the Use of Libraries. "Show and Tell: A Clinic on Using Media in Library Instruction." American Library Association Annual Conference, Chicago, June 28–29, 1972.

Axeen, Marina E. *Teaching the Use of the Library to Undergraduates: an Experimental Comparison of Computer-Based Instruction and the Conventional Lecture Method.* Report R-361, August 1967. Urbana, Illinois: University of Illinois, Coordinated Science Laboratory, 1967. AD 657 216.

Baillie, J. "Reader Education: II. Student Instruction in Biomedical Bibliography." *Australian Academic and Research Libraries* 1 (Autumn 1970): 21–27.

Barkey, Patrick Terrence. "Patterns of Student Use of a College Library." *College & Research Libraries* 26 (March 1965): 115–118.

Barkley, Margaret. "Arrows for Freshmen." *Library Journal* 64 (May 15, 1939): 402–404.

Bartlett, Beatrice C. "Stephens College Library Instruction Program." *ALA Bulletin* 58 (April 1, 1964): 311–314.

Barton, Anthony. "The Continuum: How to Analyze Your School Environment —and Loosen It Up." *Library Journal* 95 (December 15, 1970): 4317–4323.

Bates, Marcia J. *User Studies: A Review for Librarians and Information Scientists.* March 1971. ED 047 738.

Bath University Library, England. "Experimental Information Officer in the Social Sciences: Report to OSTI on Work Carried Out in 1969." February 1970. Mimeographed.

Bath University Library, England. "Experimental Information Service in the Social Sciences, 1969–1971: Final Report." Project Head, Maurice B. Line. January 1972. Mimeographed.

Bath University Library, England. "Experimental Information Service in the Social Sciences: Report on Work Carried Out in 1970." Project Head, Maurice B. Line. January 1971. Mimeographed.

Bechtel, Joan M. "A Possible Contribution of the Library–College Idea to Modern Education." *Drexel Library Quarterly* 7 (July & October 1971): 189–201.

Beeler, Richard. "Library Orientation and Instruction at the University of Denver." *Colorado Academic Library* 8 (Spring 1972): 20–24.

Benford, John Q. "The Philadelphia Project: 10,000 Students Tell What's Wrong and What's Right About Their School and Public Libraries." *Library Journal* 96 (June 15, 1971): 2041–2047.

Bialec, Verda, comp. *Guidelines for Introducing Mentally Retarded Persons to the Public Library.* Olympia, Wash.: Washington State Library, Institutional Library Services, 1970. ED 067 131.

"Les Bibliothèques Vues par Nos Lecteurs: Une Enquête." *Association Canadienne des Bibliothecaires de Lange Française, Bulletin* 17 (September 1971): 143–147.

Blake, Fay M. "The Library–College Movement." *Drexel Library Quarterly* 7 (July & October 1971): 175–188.

Bock, Gunter. "Hochschuldidaktische Aspekte des Bibliothekswesens: Überlegungen und Vorschläge zu Einer Reform der Einführung von Studenten in die Bibliotheksbenutzung." *Dokumentation Fachbibliothek Werksbuecherei* 19 (February 1971): 33–40.

Bonn, George S. "Training Laymen in the Use of the Library," In *State of the Library Art*, ed. by Ralph Shaw, vol. 1, pt. 1 (New Brunswick, N.J.: Rutgers University, Graduate School of Library Service, 1960).

Bowers, Dorothy. "Maximizing Learning by Minicourse Instruction." *Learning Today* 6 (Spring 1973): 50–60.

Bowers, Melvyn K. *Library Instruction in the Elementary School.* Metuchen, N.J.: Scarecrow Press, Inc., 1971.

Bradshaw, Charles I., Wiggins, Marvin E., and Hall, Blaine. *Using the Library: The Card Catalog.* Provo, Utah: Brigham Young University Press, n.d.

Branscomb, Harvie. *Teaching With Books: A Study of College Libraries.* Hamden, Conn.: Shoe String Press, Inc., 1964.

Brown, Clayton M. "TV or the Herded Tour." *Library Journal* 90 (May 15, 1965): 2214–2218.

Brown, Helen M. "ALA Activities to Promote Better Instruction in the Use of Academic Libraries." *Drexel Library Quarterly* 7 (July & October 1971): 323–326.

Brown, Jeanne Y., and Carter, Robert R. "Mix Well with Media." *California School Libraries* 41 (January 1970): 92–93, 95.

Bundy, Mary Lee. *Metropolitan Public Library Users: A Report of a Survey of Adult Library Use in the Maryland Baltimore–Washington Metropolitan*

Area. College Park, Md.: University of Maryland, School of Library and Information Services, 1968.

California State College Library, Los Angeles. "The Library Game? (or) The Great Santa Barbara Oil Spill." n.d. Mimeographed.

Canfield, Marie P. "Library Pathfinders." *Drexel Library Quarterly* 8 (July 1972): 287–300.

Carey, R. J. P. "Making Libraries Easy to Use: A Systems Approach." *Library Association Record* 73 (July 1971): 132–135.

Carey, R. J. P. "A Systems Approach to Exploitation." *New Library World* 73 (July 1973): 347–349.

Carnegie Commission on Higher Education. *Reform on Campus: Changing Students, Changing Academic Programs.* New York: McGraw-Hill Book Co., June 1972.

Carpine–Lancre, Jacqueline. "Stages d'Initiation des Jeunes Chercheurs à la Bibliographie." *Bulletin d'Informations de l'Association des Bibliothécaires Français* 61 (Winter 1968): 273–279.

Christie, David. "Tutor–Librarianship—A Personal View." *SLA News* (Scottish Library Association) 94 (November–December 1969): 414–416.

Colorado Council on Library Development, Committee on Instruction in the Use of Libraries. "The Report on the Instruction in the Use of Libraries in Colorado." Compiled for the Council by Margaret Goggin, et al., February 9, 1973. Mimeographed.

Crawford, Carolyn, and Chun, May. *Hawaii School Libraries: A Manual for Organization and Services,* rev. ed. Honolulu: State of Hawaii, Department of Education, 1964.

Crosby, Louise, and Totemeier, Sherril. "Library Skills Instruction at Alameda Senior High School and Its Feeder Schools: Is It Developmental?" Master of Arts in Librarianship, University of Denver, May 1971.

Crossley, Charles. "Education in Literature and Library Use." *Library World* 71 (May 1970): 340–347.

Crossley, Charles, "Tuition in the Use of the Library and of Subject Literature in the University of Bradford." *Journal of Documentation* 24 (June 1968): 91–97.

Culkin, Patricia B. "Computer–Assisted Instruction in Library Use." *Drexel Library Quarterly* 8 (July 1972): 301–311.

Culkin, Patricia B. "Creative Approaches to Library Service: Reports on Five Examples. Casebook: CAI Experiment." *American Libraries* 3 (June 1972): 643–645.

Daiute, Robert J., and Gorman, Kenneth A. *Statistical Samplings of Book Readership at a College Library: Sampling Book Readership Inside the Rider Library.* Final report, project no. 9B094, grant no. OEG-2-9-400094-1055010. Trenton, N.J.: Rider College, January 1970. ED 045 149.

Davidson College Library North Carolina, "A Proposal to the Council on Library Resources, Inc. and the National Endowment for the Humanities." Davidson, N.C., June 1972. Mimeographed.

Davies, Ruth Ann. *The School Library: A Force for Educational Excellence.* New York and London: R. R. Bowker Co., 1969.

Davis, Diana L. "New Approaches to Studying Library Use." *Drexel Library Quarterly* 7 (January 1971): 4–12.

Davis, Elmyra. "The Unchanging Profile—A Review of Literature." *The Library College Journal,* November 1, 1970, pp. 11–19.

"Description of the Proposed United Engineering Information Service." *Scientific Information Notes* 1 (November–December 1969): 253–255.

District of Columbia Public Schools, Department of Libraries. "Proposed Schedule for Teaching the Use of the Library and Books: Kindergarten through Grade Six." n.d. Mimeographed.

Dudley, Miriam. "Teaching Library Skills to College Students." *Advances in Librarianship,* ed. by Melvin Voight, vol. 3. New York: Seminar Press, 1972, pp. 83–105.

Dudley, Miriam. *Workbook in Library Skills: A Self–Directed Course in the Use of UCLA's College Library.* Los Angeles: University of California, College Library, 1973.

Edwards, Margaret A. *The Fair Garden and the Swarm of Beasts: The Library and the Young Adult.* New York: Hawthorn Books, Inc., 1969.

Ellsworth, Ralph E. "The Contribution of the Library to Improving Instruction." *Library Journal* 94 (May 15, 1969): 1955–1957.

Evrard, Connie F., and Waddington, Charles C. "The Undergraduate Survey: Its Role in Changing Patterns of Reference Service." *Drexel Library Quarterly* 7 (July & October 1971): 351–356.

Federal Library Committee, Task Force on Public Relations. *Guidelines for Library Handbooks.* Washington, D.C., 1972. ED 067 137.

Fork, Donald. "The Use of the Card Catalog in Junior High: A School Situation." *California School Libraries* 41 (January 1970): 82–83.

Gardner, Jeffrey J. "Point–of–Use Library Instruction." *Drexel Library Quarterly* 8 (July 1972): 281 285.

Gibbons, Andy. "Freshmen Library Orientation: The Experts Speak." *Mountain Plains Library Quarterly* 18 (1973): 8–9, 14.

Gibson, Colleen. "Introducing the Reader to the Library." *Library Association of Alberta Bulletin* 1 (July 1969): 19–23.

Gokkel, H. R. W., and Makken, T. D. "Onderwijsaan Studenten in het Gevbruik van de Juridische Bibliothek." *Open.* 3 (November 1971): 737–738.

Gothberg, Helen M. "Communication Patterns in Library Reference and Information Service." *RQ* 13 (1973): 7–14.

Greaves, F. Landon, Jr., and Dudley V. Yates. "Library Orientation: Varied Approaches to a Common Problem." *Louisiana Library Association Bulletin* 31 (Summer 1968): 61–64.

Griffin, Lloyd W., and Clarke, Jack A. "Orientation and Instruction of Graduate Students in the Use of the University Library: A Survey." *College & Research Libraries* 33 (November 1972): 467–472.

Guide for Development of Library Skills and Services in the Sulphur Springs Independent School District, Grades K–12. Commerce, Tex.: East Texas State University, Department of Library Science, 1972. ED 066 176.

Guinyard, Allene J. *Where the Books Are: English.* Miami, Fla.: Dade County Public Schools, 1971. ED 061 988.

Haag, Dietrig E. "The Teaching Function of the University Library." *South African Libraries* 37 (April 1970): 272–277+.

Hackman, Martha. "Proposal for a Program of Library Instruction." *Drexel Library Quarterly* 7 (July & October 1971): 299–308.

Hansen, Lois N. "Computer–Assisted Instruction in Library Use: An Evaluation." *Drexel Library Quarterly* 8 (July 1972): 345–355.

Haro, Robert Peter. "College Libraries for Students." *Library Journal* 94 (June 1, 1969): 2207–2208.

Harrelson, Larry E. "Large Libraries and Information Desks." Mimeographed. Norman, Oklahoma: University of Oklahoma Libraries, 1973.

Hartz, Frederic R. "High School Library: A Study in Use, Misuse, and Nonuse." *Clearing House* 38 (March 1964): 423–428.

Henning, Patricia A. "Council on Library Resources Activities." *Drexel Library Quarterly* 7 (July & October 1971): 343–345.

Henning, Patricia A. "Research on Integrated Library Instruction." *Drexel Library Quarterly* 7 (July & October 1971): 339–341.

Hering, Millicent B. "The Library as a Lab." *Sourdough: Newsletter of the Alaska Library Association* 9 (July 1972): 3.

Hinchliff, William E. "Urban Problems and Higher Education: Federal City College." *Wilson Library Bulletin* 43 (February 1969): 527–533.

Hopkinson, Shirley L. *Instructional Materials for Teaching the Use of the Library: A Selected, Annotated Bibliography of Films, Filmstrips, Books and Pamphlets, Tests, and Other Aids*, 4th ed. San Jose, Calif.: Claremont House, 1971.

Horton, Allan. "Early Attempts at Reader Education at the University of New South Wales." *IATUL Proceedings* 5 (December 2, 1970): 54–60.

Howison, Beulah C. "Simulated Literature Searches." *Drexel Library Quarterly* 7 (July & October 1971): 309–320.

Hurt, Peyton. "The Need of College and University Instruction in Use of the Library." *LQ* 4 (1934): 436–448.

Idaho State Department of Education. "Library Resource Center (and) Library Resource Skills: Capabilities and Know–How." Boise, Idaho: Department of Education, 1972. Mimeographed.

Idaho State Department of Education. *Managing Learning Resources in Elementary and Secondary Schools*. Boise: Department of Education, 1969.

Indiana State Department of Public Instruction. *Digest of Courses of Study for Secondary Schools of Indiana*. Indianapolis: State Department of Public Instruction, 1961.

"Instruction in Library Use." *Elementary School Library, Bulletin* 100 (1965): pp. 20–25.

Iowa State Department of Public Instruction. "Library–Instructional Materials Center Skills." Des Moines, Iowa, 1968. Mimeographed. Reprinted from: *The Educational Program . . . A Curriculum Design*. Des Moines, Iowa: Iowa Department of Public Instruction, 1966.

Iowa State University. Library Planning Committee. "The Library as a Teaching Instrument." Iowa City, 1945.

Josey, E. J. "The Role of the College Library Staff in Instruction in the Use of the Library." *College and Research Libraries* 23 (November 1962): 492–498.

Kansas State Department of Public Instruction. "I Want to Buy Books for the School Library, BUT . . . !" rev. ed. 1967. Mimeographed.

Katz, William A., *Introduction to Reference Work (Vol. II), Reference Services and Reference Processes,* 2nd edition, N.Y.: McGraw-Hill, 1974.

Keith, Pauline A. and Karish, Paul J., *How to Teach Library Research Skills in Secondary School Social Studies. How to Do It Series, Number 23.* Washington, D.C., National Council for the Social Studies, 1968. ERIC ED 083 057.

Keller, C. Warren. "Monsanto Information Center's Audio-Visual Orientation Program." *Special Libraries* 57 (November 1966): 648–651.

Kennedy, James. "Integrated Library Instruction." *Library Journal* 95 (April 15, 1970): 1450–1453.

Kennedy, James R., Jr.; Kirk, Thomas G.; and Weaver, Gwendolyn A. "Course–Related Library Instruction: A Case Study of the English and Biology Departments of Earlham College." *Drexel Library Quarterly* 7 (July & October, 1971): 277–297.

Kirk, Thomas G. "A Comparison of Two Methods of Library Instruction for Students in Introductory Biology." *College and Research Libraries* 32 (November 1971): 465–474.

Kirk, Thomas G. "Role of the Library in an Investigative Laboratory," in *The Laboratory; A Place to Investigate,* pp. 144–164. Publication 33. Washington, D.C.: Commission on Undergraduate Education in the Biological Sciences, 1972.

Kirk, Thomas; Lynch, Mary Jo; and the ACRL Ad Hoc Committee on Bibliographic Instruction. "Bibliographic Instruction in Academic Libraries: New Developments." *Drexel Library Quarterly* 8 (July 1972): 357–365.

Knapp, Patricia B. "College Teaching and the Library." *Illinois Libraries* 40 (December 1958): 828–833.

Knapp, Patricia B. *An Experiment in Coordination Between Teaching and Library Staff for Changing Student Use of the University Library Resources.* U.S. Office of Education Cooperative Research Project, no. 874. Detroit: Wayne State University, Monteith College, 1964.

Knapp, Patricia B. "Guidelines for Bucking the System: A Strategy for Moving Toward the Ideal of the Undergraduate Library as a Teaching Instrument." *Drexel Library Quarterly* 7 (July & October 1971): 217–221.

Knapp, Patricia B. *Independent Study and the Academic Library: An Approach to Independent Study.* New Dimensions in Higher Education, no. 12. Washington, D.C.: U.S. Office of Education, 1965.

Knapp, Patricia B. "The Library's Response to Innovation in Higher Education." *California Librarian* 29 (April 1968): 142–149.

Knapp, Patricia B. *The Monteith College Library Experiment.* Metuchen, N.J.: Scarecrow Press, Inc., 1966.

Knapp, Patricia B. "A Suggested Program of College Instruction in the Use of the Library." *Library Quarterly* 26 (July 1966): 224–231.

Koster, Gayl E. "Libraries in the Classroom." *Drexel Library Quarterly* 8 (July 1972): 223–229.

Kuo, Frank A. "A Comparison of Six Versions of Science Library Instruction." *College and Research Libraries* 34 (July 1973): 287–290.

La Brant, Lou, and Richards, Violet. "A Study for the Future at Dillard University: A Summary Report." New Orleans: Dillard University, June 1, 1969.

Lancaster, F. W. "User Education: The Next Major Thrust in Information Science?" *Journal of Education for Librarianship* 11 (Summer 1970): 55–63.

Lancaster, John Herrold. *The Use of the Library by Student Teachers: Some Factors Related to the Use of the Library by Student Teachers in Thirty–One Colleges in the Area of the North Central Association.* New York: Columbia University, Teacher's College, Bureau of Publications, 1941.

Lane, David O. "The City University of New York and Open Enrollment." *Bookmark* 31 (January–February 1972): 73–75.

Larson, Dale M. *Library Instruction in the Community College: Toward Innovative Librarianship.* 1971. ED 054 765.

Larson, Dale M. "A System's Approach to Individualized Library Instruction." Fullerton, California: California State College, 1972.

Lebovitch, J. "College Libraries and Tutor Librarianship: an Annotated Select Bibliography." Occasional Papers #5. Hatfield, England: The Hatfield Polytechnic, 1971. (Also ED 066 204.)

Lee, John W., and Read, Raymond L. "The Graduate Business Student and the Library." *College & Research Libraries* 33 (September 1972): 403–407.

Lee, Sul H., ed. *Library Orientation.* Papers presented at the First Annual Conference on Library Orientation held at Eastern Michigan University, May 7, 1971. Library Orientation Series, no. 1. Published for the Eastern Michigan University Library, Ypsilanti, Mich., by Pierian Press, Ann Arbor, Mich., 1972.

Lieberman, Irving. "A Working Bibliography of Commercially Available Audio–Visual Materials for the Teaching of Library Science." Illinois University, Graduate School of Library Science. Occasional Papers, no. 94, December 1968. Mimeographed.

Lincoln, C. M., ed. *Educating the Library User: Proceedings of the Fourth Triennial Meeting of the International Association of Technological University Libraries, Loughborough, April 1–3, 1970.* Loughborough, England: International Association of Technological University Libraries, Loughborough University of Technology Library, 1970.

Line, Maurice B. "Information Requirements in the Social Sciences: Some Preliminary Considerations." *Journal of Librarianship* 1 (January 1969): 1–19.

"Literature Search Seminar: A Powerful Love Potion (Lab Notes from the NOAA Witches)." *Columbine, Bulletin of the Colorado Chapter, Special Libraries Association* 21 (March–April 1971): 12–14.

Louttit, C. M., and Patrick, James R. "A Study of Students' Knowledge in the Use of the Library." *Journal of Applied Psychology* 16 (1932): 475–484.

Lubans, John, Jr. "Nonuse of an Academic Library." *College and Research Libraries* 32 (September 1971): 362–367.

Lubans, John, Jr. "Non–Users and Library Surveys." *Colorado Academic Library* 7 (Summer 1971): 1–3.

Lubans, John, Jr. "Report to the Council on Library Resources on a Fellowship Awarded for 1971/1972." Boulder, Colo.: University of Colorado Library, November 28, 1972. Mimeographed.

Lubans, John, Jr., et al., *A Study with Computer-Based Circulation Data of the Non-use and Use of a Large Academic Library.* (Final Report. U.S.O.E. National Institute of Education.) Boulder, Colorado: University of Colorado Libraries, 1973. ERIC ED 082 756.

Lyle, Guy R. "Use and Misuse of the College Library." In his *The President, the Professor and the College Library.* New York: H. W. Wilson, 1963, pp. 51–57.

Lynch, Mary Jo. "A New Approach to the Guided Tour." *RQ* 11 (Fall 1971): 46–48.

McCoy, Ralph E. "Automation in Freshman Library Instruction." *Wilson Library Bulletin* 36 (February 1962): 468–470, 472.

Marshall, A. P. "Library Outreach: The Program at Eastern Michigan University." *Drexel Library Quarterly* 7 (July & October 1971): 347–350.

Melum, Verna V. "Library Instruction in a University." *Illinois Libraries* 51 (June 1969): 511–521.

Melum, Verna V. "1971 Survey of Library Orientation and Instruction Programs." *Drexel Library Quarterly* 7 (July & October 1971): 225–253.

Melum, Verna V. "A Survey to Aid Your Fall Planning: Library Orientation in the College and University." *Wilson Library Bulletin* 46 (September 1971): 59–66.

Mews, Hazel. "Library Instruction Concerns People." *Library Association Record* 72 (January 1970): 8–10.

Mews, Hazel. *Reader Instruction in Colleges and Universities: An Introductory Handbook.* London: Clive Bingley, 1972.

Milby, T. H. "A Study of Instructional Programs in the Use of Biological Literature at Selected U.S. Universities." Mimeographed. Report to the Council on Library Resources for a Fellowship, 1971.

Millis, Charlotte Hickman. "The Wabash Project: A Centrifugal Program." *Drexel Library Quarterly* 7 (July & October 1971): 365–374.

Mirwis, Allan. "Academic Library Instruction—A Bibliography, 1960–1970." *Drexel Library Quarterly* 7 (July & October 1971): 327–335.

Molz, Kathleen. "The State of the Art of Public Library Orientation." *Maryland Libraries* 34 (Winter 1968): 10–17.

Motley, Drucilla. "Old Wine, New Bottles: How to Use Transparencies, Slides, Your 8mm Camera, and the Tape Recorder to Teach Library Skills." *Library Journal* (October 15, 1968), pp. 3932–3933.

National Academy of Sciences, Washington, D.C. *Scientific and Technical Communication: A Pressing National Problem and Recommendations for Its Solution.* National Research Council, Publication no. 1707, 1969.

Nevada. Nevada Elementary Course of Study: Library Skills. n.d. Mimeographed.

Newell, Mattias G. "GP in the Academic Library." *Catholic Library World* 43 (April 1972): 453–456.

New Jersey School Library Association. "Library Skills Instructional Program—K–12." Prepared by Marguerite Baechtold, et al., Instructional Skills Committee. Trenton, N.J.: New Jersey State Department of Education, Division of the State Library, Archives and History, Public and School Library Services Bureau, 1964. Mimeographed.

New York Library Association. College and University Libraries Section. *Use, Mis-Use and Non-Use of Academic Libraries: Proceedings* . . . Edited by the Committee on the Requirements of the Academic Library User. Watertown, N.Y.: Jefferson Community College, Spring Conference, May 1-2, 1970. N.Y. The Association, 1970.

"North Dakota State University Is Solving Its Library Orientation Problem." *Mountain Plains Library Quarterly* 17 (Spring 1972): 22–24.

Ochsner, Friedrich. "Biblioteksannonser." *Biblioteksbladet* 55 (1970): 122–123.

O'Connor, Elizabeth C. "College Library Preceptorial Instruction Program." *Bookmark* 31 (January–February 1972): 76–79.

Oklahoma. Curriculum Improvement Commission. Library Resources Division and The State Library Service Committee. "Curriculum Guide for the Teaching of Library Skills: Grades K–12." Oklahoma State Department of Education, 1969.

Oklahoma. State Department of Education. *A Guide for Teachers and Librarians with Suggestions for Teaching Indian Students.* Oklahoma City, Oklahoma, 1973.

Olson, Edwin E. *Survey of User Service Policies in Indiana Libraries and Information Centers.* Indiana Library Studies Reports, no. 10. Bloomington, Ind., 1970.

O'Reilly, Shirley. "Reader Education: I. A Readers' Advisor's Programme." *Australian Academic and Research Libraries* 1 (Autumn 1970): 16–20.

Orgren, Carl F. *Production of Slide-Tape Programs.* Iowa City: University of Iowa, School of Library Science, 1972.

Palmer, Millicent C. "Creating Slide-Tape Library Instruction: The Librarian's Role." *Drexel Library Quarterly* 8 (July 1972): 251–267.

Palmer, Millicent C. "Library Instruction at Southern Illinois University, Edwardsville." *Drexel Library Quarterly* 7 (July & October 1971): 255–276.

Palmer, Millicent C. "Problems in Academic Library Instruction: Our Own Creation?" *Catholic Library World* 43 (April 1972): 447–452.

Peacock, P. G., and Cameron, Kenneth J. "The Open University Summer School at the University of Stirling: A Report on Library Usage." *Library Association Record* 74 (December 1972): 237–238.

Perkins, Ralph. *The Prospective Teacher's Knowledge of Library Fundamentals: A Study of the Responses Made by 4,170 College Seniors to Tests Designed to Measure Familiarity with Libraries.* Metuchen, N.J.: Scarecrow Press, 1965.

Perkins, Ralph. "Realistic Library Orientation—A Necessity." *The Library—College Journal* 3 (Fall 1970): 20–27.

Phipps, Barbara H. "Library Instruction for the Undergraduate." *College & Research Libraries* 29 (September 1968): 411–423.

Pierson, Robert M. "A Jaundiced Approach to the Guided Tour." *RQ* 11 (Fall 1971): 55–58.

Powell, Ronald H. "Library Orientation." *RQ* (Winter 1971): 147–148.

Pugh, L. C. "Library Instruction Programmes for Undergraduates: Historical Development and Current Practice." *Library World* 71 (March 1970): 267–273.

Rader, Hannelore B. "Reaching Out to Freshmen." *Michigan Librarian* 37 (Autumn 1971): 11–13.

Ramey, James W. "Classroom Dynamics: Or, Is There a Teacher in the House?" *Drexel Library Quarterly* 8 (July 1972): 237–244.

Rapoport, Roger, and Kirshbaum, Laurence J. *Is the Library Burning?* New York: Random House, 1969.

Reed, Lulu Ruth. "A Test of Students' Competence to Use the Library." *Library Quarterly* 8 (1938): 236–283.

Revill, D. H. "Teaching Methods in the Library: A Survey from the Educational Point of View." *Library World* (February 1970), pp. 243–249.

Ronkin, R. R. "Self-guided Library Tour for the Biosciences." *College and Research Libraries* 28 (May 1967): 217–18.

Rossoff, Martin. *The Library in High School Training*, 2nd ed. New York: H. W. Wilson Co., 1961.

Sadler, Virginia P. "Role of the Library in Education; The Library Image as Presented in Selected Teacher Training Textbooks in Use in the State of Kentucky." Barbourville, Kentucky: Union College, 1970. Mimeographed. (Also ED 073 789.)

Scherer, Henry. "The Faculty and the Librarian." *The Library–College Journal* 3 (November 1970): 37–43.

Schnucker, R. V. "A Method and an Appraisal: For New Stars Through Learning." *Learning Today* 6 (Fall 1973): 55–64.

Schutte, P. J. "Onderrig of Inligting?" *South African Libraries* 39 (October 1971): 118–121, 123.

Schwarz, Philip J. "Instruction in the Use of Microform Equipment." *Wisconsin Library Bulletin* (September 1971), pp. 341–343.

Schwarz, Philip John. "Use of the New Media in College Library Orientation: An Annotated Bibliography." *Mountain Plains Library Quarterly* 15 (May 1970): 19–28, 30.

Scott, D. B. "Training for Educational Self Reliance." *Australian Library Journal* 19 (October 1970): 329–333.

Scrivener, J. E. "Instruction in Library Use: the Persisting Problem." *Australian Academic and Research Libraries* 3 (June 1972): 87–119.

Seminar on Human Aspects of Library Instruction. *Proceedings*. Reading, England: University of Reading, December 9, 1969.

Shephard, Dorothy D. "We Met the Question and Answer Hangups in a Library Orientation Telecast but Success Requires Teacher-Librarian Cooperation." *Illinois Libraries* 53 (September 1971): 507–512.

Simmons, Beatrice D. "Librarian: Instructional Programmer." *Drexel Library Quarterly* 8 (July 1972): 247–250.

Stewart, Alva W. "Independent Study & Library Use." *American Libraries* 2 (January 1971): 17.

Stillman, Mary E. "A Program for Action." *Drexel Library Quarterly* 7 (July & October 1971): 375–378.

Sullivan, Marjorie, and Moore, Jean. "Media Use by Kansas Teachers and Students." Emporia, Kans.: Kansas State Teachers College, Kansas Association of School Librarians and the Department of Librarianship, 1972. Mimeographed.

Swanson, Mary Ann. "Method, Method, Who's Got the Method?" *Learning Today* 6 (Summer 1973): 34–42.

Taylor, Robert S. "Orienting the Library to the User at Hampshire College." *Drexel Library Quarterly* 7 (July & October 1971): 357–364.

Taylor, Robert S. "Question-Negotiation and Information Seeking in Libraries." *College and Research Libraries* 29 (May 1968): 178–194.

Thomason, Ella Nevada Wallis. "An Investigation of Student Attitudes toward and Utilization of Total Media Facilities in Public Junior College Libraries in Texas." Ed.D. dissertation, University of Colorado, 1972.

Thorne, Oakleigh, III. "The Case for the Silent Film." *Instructor* 80 (February 1971): 121.

Treaster, Joseph P. "Student Zeal at Yale Switches from Politics to Learning." *New York Times,* November 8, 1971: 1.

University of California, Berkeley; University of California, Los Angeles; and State College of California, San Jose. *Instruction in the Use of the College and University Library: Selected Conference Papers [from] July 13–14, 1970 Conference/Workshop.* Berkeley: University of California, School of Librarianship, 1970. ED 045 103.

University of Pittsburgh Graduate School of Library and Information Science. "The Interview in Reference and Guidance." Adapted from Bingham, Walter Van Dyke. *How to Interview.* New York: Harper, 1959. Paper presented at the Institute on Readers Advisory Services, Pittsburgh, July 7–25, 1969. Mimeographed.

University of Pittsburgh Graduate School of Library and Information Science. "Interviewing Techniques." Paper presented at the Institute on Readers Advisory Services, Pittsburgh, July 7–25, 1969. Mimeographed.

Virginia State Department of Education. "School Library Instruction in Use of Materials." Richmond, n.d. Mimeographed. Reprinted from: Virginia. Department of Education. *School Library Guide for Grades One through Twelve.* Richmond, 1961.

Vogel, J. Thomas. "A Critical Overview of the Evaluation of Library Instruction." *Drexel Library Quarterly* 8 (July 1972): 315–323.

Wehmeyer, Lillian. "Library Media Center Skills: Audio-Visual Materials for Teaching Library Skills in Grades K–12." *Booklist* 68 (May 15, 1972): 808–814.

Wendt, Paul. "New Library Materials and Technology for Instruction and Research." *Library Trends* (October 1967), pp. 197–210.

Whildin, Sara Lou. "Plimpton Prepares: How to Win the Library Instruction Game." *Drexel Library Quarterly* 8 (July 1972): 231–235.

Wiggins, Marvin E. "The Development of Library Use Instructional Programs." *College and Research Libraries* 33 (November 1972): 473–479.

Wiggins, Marvin E., and Low, D. Stewart. "Use of an Instructional Psychology Model for Development of Library-Use Instructional Programs." *Drexel Library Quarterly* 8 (July 1972): 269–279.

Williamson, John G. "Swarthmore College's 'Teaching Library' Proposals." *Drexel Library Quarterly* 7 (July & October 1971): 203–215.

Winburne, John N. "Written and Spoken English." East Lansing, Mich.: Michigan State University, n.d.

Wisconsin State Department of Public Instruction, Division for Library Services. *Learning to Use Media.* Bulletin no. 197. Madison, Wisc., 1970.

Woelflin, Leslie. "Instruction in the Undergraduate Library-College." *Learning Today* 5 (Winter 1972): 40–48.

Wood, D. N. "Library Education for Scientists and Engineers." *Bulletin of Mechanical Engineering Education* 8 (1969): 1–9.

Young, Arthur P., Boone, Morell, and Salverson, Carol. "Survey of User Education in New York State Academic Libraries." Paper presented at the New York Library Association Annual Conference in New York City, October 6, 1971. Mimeographed. ED055 621